Practical Entity Framework Core 6

Database Access for Enterprise Applications

Second Edition

Brian L. Gorman

Apress®

Practical Entity Framework Core 6: Database Access for Enterprise Applications

Brian L. Gorman
Jesup, IA, USA

ISBN-13 (pbk): 978-1-4842-7300-5   ISBN-13 (electronic): 978-1-4842-7301-2
https://doi.org/10.1007/978-1-4842-7301-2

Managing Director, Apress Media LLC: Welmoed Spahr
Acquisitions Editor: Jonathan Gennick
Development Editor: Laura Berendson
Coordinating Editor: Jill Balzano

Cover designed by eStudioCalamar

Cover image designed by Freepik (www.freepik.com)

Distributed to the book trade worldwide by Springer Science+Business Media LLC, 1 New York Plaza, Suite 4600, New York, NY 10004. Phone 1-800-SPRINGER, fax (201) 348-4505, e-mail orders-ny@springer-sbm.com, or visit www.springeronline.com. Apress Media, LLC is a California LLC and the sole member (owner) is Springer Science + Business Media Finance Inc (SSBM Finance Inc). SSBM Finance Inc is a **Delaware** corporation.

For information on translations, please e-mail booktranslations@springernature.com; for reprint, paperback, or audio rights, please e-mail bookpermissions@springernature.com.

Apress titles may be purchased in bulk for academic, corporate, or promotional use. eBook versions and licenses are also available for most titles. For more information, reference our Print and eBook Bulk Sales web page at http://www.apress.com/bulk-sales.

Any source code or other supplementary material referenced by the author in this book is available to readers on GitHub via the book's product page, located at www.apress.com/9781484273005. For more detailed information, please visit http://www.apress.com/source-code.

Printed on acid-free paper

*This book is dedicated to my wife Cassie and
my children Kiera, Karson, Kreighton, and baby K who have
all made many sacrifices to give me the space and time to write,
as well as for your daily, unceasing love, grace, patience, and
encouragement.*

*This book is further dedicated to you, dear reader.
Thank you for allowing me to be part of your journey to greatness.*

Table of Contents

About the Author

Brian L. Gorman is a Microsoft Azure MVP, developer, computer science instructor, and trainer and has been working in .Net technologies as long as they have existed. He was originally MCSD certified in .Net 1 and re-certified with MCSA: Web Apps and MCSD: App Builder certifications in 2019. From 2019 to 2022, Brian has earned nine Azure certifications, including Azure and Data Fundamentals, Azure Administrator, Database Administrator, Security Engineer, and Developer Associate certifications, Azure Solutions Architect and DevOps Expert certifications, and an IoT Specialty certification.

Additionally, Brian became an MCT as of April 2019 and is focusing on developing and training developers with full-stack web solutions with .Net Core and Azure, and is also focused on helping small businesses meet certification standards to be able to qualify for Microsoft Partnership. Most recently, Brian was employed as a Senior Training Architect with Opsgility, and is still partnering with Opsgility for a number of training initiatives, including taking on the instructor role for an upcoming MSSA offering in January of 2022. As of October 2021, Brian is now fully self-employed as a trainer and curriculum developer, author, and speaker. Brian's company is called MajorGuidanceSolutions.

In addition to working with .Net technologies, Brian has been an adjunct faculty member in the computer science department for Franklin University for the last 11 years, where his courses have included data structures, algorithms, design patterns, and, more recently, full-stack solutions in the capstone practicum course.

About the Technical Reviewer

 **André van Meulebrouck** has a keen interest in functional programming, especially Haskell and F#.

He also likes data technologies from markup languages to databases and F# type providers.

He lives in Southern California with his wife "Tweety" and is active in athletics: hiking, mountain biking, and gravity/balance sports like freestyle skating (inline and ice), skateboarding, surfing, and sandboarding.

To keep his mind sharp, he does compositional origami, plays classical guitar, and enjoys music notation software.

Acknowledgments

I would not have been able to write this book if it were not for a number of people who have both influenced and helped me throughout my career, as well as the multitudes of grace and support that I have received from my family throughout this process.

I'd like to begin by thanking André van Meulebrouck for his excellent work as a technical reviewer and editor. André's thoughts and comments throughout the process have greatly helped to shape this book over the first and second editions. Also, his incredible patience with working through a couple of bugs with the solution files has been an invaluable resource to help ensure the resources work and the directions are easy to follow. An extra special thanks to André as well for consistently putting up with my misuse of setup vs. set up (you would think I'd be better at this by now).

I'd also like to thank the many friends and acquaintances I've made at various tech conferences in the past few years. I've learned so much from all of you. There are a few that I must mention, however. First, Mike Cole, my peer and friend, thank you for introducing me to AutoMapper projections, and thanks for all your candid conversations around Entity Framework (EF) with me as I wrote this book. Thanks to Mitchel Sellers for your talk on Entity Framework that I got to see at Iowa Code Camp and again at our CVINETA meeting a couple of years ago, which focused on addressing the performance pitfalls that arise from misusing Language Integrated Query (LINQ).

Thank you to Apress and the team who have believed in me and have helped to make this book possible. Thanks to Jonathan Gennick and Jill Balzano for running the project, editing, and overseeing the entire schedule and process.

I would be remiss if I didn't also thank Dustin Behn, the leader of the Inspired Nation, and his life coaching and his Emergence program. Thank you for coaching me these past few years and for helping me get out of my own way to do things like this book.

Last, and most importantly, to my wife Cassie and our kids, to whom the book is also dedicated. Thank you for giving me the time and space to make this book happen and for continually checking on my progress by asking how many chapters I have done and how many I have left.

Introduction

Entity Framework is the object-relational mapper (ORM) of choice for a majority
of enterprise application development teams which are leveraging Microsoft .Net
technologies. Through the years, EF has gone through a number of changes, and the move
into the .Net Core world has seen EF become more performant and more user-friendly.

As this book begins, we'll take a look at the state of things as they are and the state of
things to come. We'll begin the real work by touching on the two different approaches to
working with a database using EFCore: database first and code first. After the first three
chapters, we settle in on the code-first approach with EFCore and approach practical,
real-world scenarios to help you and your team develop robust and rugged data solutions
while learning the fundamental concepts necessary to effectively work with EFCore.

The great news is that no matter what approach to the database or version of EF
you are using, with just a few minor exceptions, things will generally work in a similar
fashion, so all of the information in this book is relevant to anyone working with Entity
Framework.

Who this book is for

Practical Entity Framework is written for anyone that is new to Entity Framework or is
still learning and wants to become much better with Entity Framework.

If you are already an expert or a well-established developer with a few years of EF
under your belt, this book will likely not have a lot of new information for you, but there
may be a couple of concepts that you would still benefit from reviewing.

Overall, the book is designed as a practical approach – which means that there is a
lot of hands-on work to step through the moving pieces that are necessary to understand
and work with EFCore, as well as how to approach architecting SOLID solutions around
EFCore.

The practical nature of each activity will give you many examples and cover a lot of
the basic and advanced topics you will likely encounter in real-world applications.

PART I

Getting Started

CHAPTER 1

Introduction to Entity Framework

In this chapter, we are going to cover the history and origins of Entity Framework and then continue into discussions of where Entity Framework is and where it is headed. We'll conclude with what it takes to get Entity Framework into any .Net project.

One, two, three, four versions? Oh my!

Before we begin doing anything, it's important to note that at the time that I'm writing this book, there are currently three active versions of Entity Framework in play that organizations likely have deployed across various solutions, and by the time you are reading this text, you are likely to encounter at least two of them on a regular basis. The good news is that, for the most part, they all work in a very similar fashion, with just a few slight differences in some of the commands and available functionality.

As this is the second edition of this text, this book is an improvement and update on the original *Practical Entity Framework*, which was released in July 2020. The original version was written with EF6 and EFCore for .Net Core 3.1. If you need information that is more specific to these original versions (and still very valid versions) of Entity Framework, I would encourage you to pick up a copy of the first edition. Again, almost everything in this text would also apply to the original versions of Entity Framework – EF6, EFCore3, and EFCore5 – but there are some improvements that will be highlighted in this text that would not work in previous versions.

Before we dive into the meat of EFCore6, in the next few pages, we'll examine where we came from, how we got to this situation of having multiple, active versions, and where we're going from here. Let's start at the very beginning.

3

© Brian L. Gorman 2022
B. L. Gorman, *Practical Entity Framework Core 6*, https://doi.org/10.1007/978-1-4842-7301-2_1

When it all began

Microsoft SQL databases have been around for quite some time. In fact, they existed before .Net was created.

OLEDb and spaghetti database access

Prior to the .Net Framework, often a database connection was handled through code in an `Object Linking and Embedding Database Object` (OLEDb). Developers would often write SQL queries inline and then connect to the database and perform actions using these tools. Furthermore, queries often lacked any kind of security and organization. Similar or identical calls might be written from multiple pages. As if this approach didn't have enough problems to begin with, SQL queries might have even existed within the html, which is easily viewable from a simple "right-click and view-source" operation. In the most egregious situations, database credentials might have even been easily viewable in this same source. Finally, and yes it gets even worse, often the user credentials that were used in these pages had full access to everything in the database, perhaps even multiple databases.

In addition to the problems of having a spaghetti code approach to database operations, exposing queries and credentials to the world leads to extremely dangerous security breaches. One of the most common security risks when working with data, even to this day, is an attack known as a SQL Injection query.

Imagine that your update statement was fully exposed in the source on your web page. All it would take to compromise the database is a savvy hacker to use their knowledge to "inject" a few statements along with your query, and they could accomplish anything from performing destructive actions like dropping tables or other schema objects to mining operations like exporting your data for their own use. Even if your query wasn't directly exposed, if you had given the user a form text field to work with, then the attacker could easily place SQL code right in that form text and potentially hijack or corrupt your database. Obviously, some better approaches to prevent issues like these were critically needed.

ADO.Net – A better tool for application database interaction

For .Net developers, the next step in working with a database relied on a technology known as *ADO.Net*. Believe it or not, ADO.Net is still in use, and it's even possible to use ADO.Net in your greenfield projects, even today (and there may even be some developers who might even die on the hill of the efficiency of this approach).

ADO.Net was developed to help prevent a few of the problems we've previously discussed. One of the most important aspects of the ADO.Net library was the ability to easily parameterize queries. With parameterized queries, developers no longer had to create inline SQL queries directly in the application code. Rather, the ADO.Net approach allowed (and still allows) developers to create a base connection object, `SQLConnection`, with credentials obscured and the connection string stored in one common, secure location. The connection object is directly referenced by a command object, `SQLCommand`. The command object had settings allowing developers to toggle the command to work as a regular query or to execute a database object such as a stored procedure. Most importantly, the query allows the parameters to be defined and constrained by type, as well as allows for automatically replacing bad characters often used in SQL Injection attacks.

Once the queries were executed from the command, the results could be used to hydrate a result set, such as a `DataReader` or a `DataSet`. These results-oriented objects were then used to transport the relevant data and provide access to the data to render it back to the end user. This approach was the best tool we had as developers before Entity Framework (or other ORMs such as *NHibernate*).

A brief note about ADO.Net

As mentioned previously, it is still possible to program database operations directly with ADO.Net. At this point, however, ADO.Net is rarely used directly in current enterprise-level applications. In modern development, we almost always want to wrap our database operations with a unit of work and also potentially provide access through repositories (e.g., the *unit of work* and *repository patterns*), which is generally provided by most *object-relational mappers (ORMs)*. Entity Framework takes ADO.Net to the next level by abstracting the need to directly interact with ADO.Net. Additionally, as a fully capable ORM, EF utilizes both the unit of work and repository patterns by default.

Entity Framework makes its debut

In 2008, when EF was created, the only version of the .Net Framework in play was just that – the .Net Framework (version 3.5 at the time of the first release of EF). The framework had already been released in version 2.0 and then 3.0, and finally, some additional tools came in the framework version 3.5 release, including the first version of Entity Framework. The final release of the .Net Framework came with version 4.8 in late September of 2019. At that point, the version of EF was EF6 (which means there was an EF5 and an EF6, which is why we now have EFCore5 and EFCore6 even though the "core" moniker is now officially dropped from .Net – there will be more on this later).

With each iteration of the .Net Framework, Microsoft revolutionized the way we program in relation to the database with the introduction of Entity Framework and the query syntax known as *LINQ* (Language Integrated Query).

Entity Framework and LINQ

In tandem, *EF* and *LINQ* made it possible to not only work against our database objects using C# or VB.Net code but also gave us the ability to define database structures directly in code. Using code to create database objects rather than traditional SQL scripts is known as working in a *code-first database approach*.

Being able to define and work with objects in memory that modeled the database object while also directly tracking changes against the database was quite a powerful revolution. Directly tracking the changes in memory also leads to a new level of understanding of concurrency issues for those of us who were used to working with disconnected data. This transition from disconnected to connected data was a very good thing, even if it was a slightly painful transition. Additionally, EF provides the ability to easily work with the data in a disconnected fashion, which is also a valid and valuable option. We will examine working with both disconnected and connected data in this text.

While EF and LINQ were some of the more important database tools that were made available to us with each iteration of the .Net Framework, there was more going on than just these language and paradigm changes. Ultimately, the introduction of a new CEO would start to take Microsoft down an entirely different path.

A new direction and a new visionary leader

In early 2014, Microsoft got a new CEO in Satya Nadella. Mr. Nadella started Microsoft on a transitional course that would somewhat shock the developer community. Almost immediately after starting, he simply announced that the Linux operating system (which at the time would have been seen as a direct competitor to Microsoft Windows) would be embraced. Following that, Microsoft quickly started releasing tools that would be able to be run not just on Windows but also on other platforms like Macs and Linux computers. While these initial steps were a revolutionary change in Microsoft's standard operating procedure, what came next was completely unexpected.

Microsoft goes all in for all developers

In late 2016, Microsoft announced that .Net was going to be open sourced. This meant that going forward, all of the tools and code that developers work with on a daily basis could be directly extended and were made open for suggested extensions to the entire world. Any developer with an idea could create a pull request and ask for their changes to be directly implemented into some of the base libraries of the .Net Framework.

From this point on, Microsoft and the .Net Framework were no longer going to be an opaque operation with all development behind closed doors. From that day on, Microsoft's *modus operandi* has been to be fully and intentionally engaging with the entire community of developers, not just its core of .Net developers.

A new vision requires a new path

Making .Net open source was a very strategic and arguably a very wildly successful decision. However, with great changes, often come great needs for new tools and processes. Moving to be an open source language wasn't going to be enough. It was also apparent that the code itself, like some of the recent tools Microsoft was releasing, must also run on any platform. Perhaps it is even as a result of these changes that you find yourself reading this book.

In order for the code that is written to be able to live on any server on any operating system, or even in a container framework like *Docker*, the .Net Framework had to be independent of any Windows-specific API calls. While it might have been possible to run compiled .Net code on a platform like Mono or Xamarin on a Linux or Mac, developing, compiling, and executing code directly were simply not possible with the

.Net Framework. Therefore, along with the release of the information that Microsoft was going open source, came the release of the "Core" platform. In the original release of .Net Core 1.0, a new class library type called the .Net Standard Library was also introduced.

The initial release of .Net Core was targeted for use by web developers, specifically those using the .Net MVC web development framework. Because of the limitations of what could be done with the framework, as well as with the overall change not being extremely lucrative, initial adoption of the .Net Core platform by .Net developers and organizations was fairly slow.

Adoption of .Net Core started to increase with a major release in the core platform 2.0. However, the final release of .Net Core, version 3.1, opened the doors for more than just web development and accelerated the move to .Net Core across all projects, not just web development projects.

Another side effect of this new path by Microsoft was the effect that these changes had on the direction of Entity Framework. With the rewrite of the .Net Framework into .Net Core, along came a new EF, also called *Entity Framework Core*. Therefore, at the time of this writing, and into the direct future for the next few foreseeable years, there will be a minimum of two active versions of EF in play, *EF6* and *EFCore (with EFCore having multiple versions that are likely still active)*.

What is .Net 5 and why is Entity Framework called EFCore5 instead of EF5, and why are we already on .Net 6 and EFCore6

In November of 2020, .Net 5 was officially released. .Net 5 is the end result of two paths converging. The original .Net Framework and the new .Net Core architecture all brought back under one roof. Rather than call it .Net Core Framework 5, the easy solution is to just rebrand back to .Net 5. Don't get too comfortable, however, because .Net 6 and .Net 7 are on the plan for the next couple of years. All of this is to say that with the most recent release at the time of this writing, .Net Core and the .Net Framework are both now merged into .Net 5 and EFCore5, and the next editions are coming soon – .Net 6 with EFCore6.

As previously noted, original versions of EF were released through EF6. By default, this means there was already an EF5 release, which happened in 2012, and an EF6 release that happened in 2013. Therefore, it might create a lot of confusion to call the new versions of EF by the same name as versions already created, which are still very much in active use at this time. For these reasons, it is my guess that the only choice was to keep core in the name of the new releases. However, with .Net 6 and 7 planned, do not be surprised if at some point in the future the official name goes back to something like EF6.5 or EF7, once the original versions are no longer in conflict with the active version of .Net.

The state of the union

Although EF6 has reached end of life on new features, the support for EF6 will go on, likely through the beginning of 2029. Additionally, .Net Core 3.1 will also have a lifecycle that will continue until likely around 2030. With the majority of applications in the real world at the time of this writing that use entity framework being non-core applications and the majority of applications in the real world being written in the future in the .Net 5 stack, it will be very important to understand and know both of these frameworks (EF6 and EFCore) for the next five to ten years.

The good news is that, for the most part, both frameworks are doing the same thing and accomplishing the same goals with the same architectural concepts. The bad news is that these frameworks are somewhat divergent when it comes to working with commands, how they deal with code-first migrations, and working with legacy objects like EDMX files (which exist only in older versions of EF). Additionally, there are many variances in levels of efficiency when it comes to the two versions, with EFCore often outperforming EF6.

As mentioned previously, this book will be primarily focused on working with EFCore6. Currently, EF6, EFCore3.1, and EFCore5 projects should all work in .Net 5 or .Net 6 projects, but new projects in the .Net 6 release should target EFCore6. Additionally, most of what this book will cover using EFCore6 will also work in previous versions of EF. In cases where code would not work in a previous version, this book will make every effort to call out the fact that the code only works in the latest version of EFCore6.

The future

As .Net continues to release and evolve into the future, it is my hope that everything we cover in this text will remain relevant for years to come. Additionally, as previously noted, most of what we cover in this text does translate back to use in EF6 EFCore3 or EFCore5 projects. Finally, I will do my best to keep any resources associated with this book up to date, as much as it makes sense to do so.

Activity 1-1: Getting started with EFCore6

In order to work with Entity Framework Core 6, you need to understand how to get the project up and running. For this reason, in this first activity, you're going to go through the steps it takes for you to implement Entity Framework into any solution.

As with most things in development, there are multiple approaches that can be taken to get started. Over the next couple of chapters, you will be exposed to a few different starting approaches to working with Entity Framework Core 6 (EFCore6).

By completing this first activity, you will see what it takes to get started from scratch with a brand-new project. The main goal here is to see what libraries and configurations are necessary to start a brand-new project.

Note   It is entirely likely you won't need to do a lot of the things you'll see in the remainder of this chapter as many .Net projects already contain EF as part of the working solution, or your organization will have an architect that puts all of this in place, or you may use a boilerplate project that does it all for you.

In any project, you can easily set up Entity Framework (EF). Before you do this, however, a great question to ask yourself as the developer/architect is if the database operations might need to be used across multiple solutions or projects. If that is the case, to use EF across multiple solutions or projects, the best approach is to create a reusable code library that stores your database code, including your context, configuration, and migrations.

Regardless of using a separate library or just including in a single package, the initial setup will be exactly the same, which is to bring the libraries into your solution or project using NuGet. Since using a separate library is a more robust and reusable approach, in this first activity, you'll walk through how to build a reusable database library that leverages EFCore6. You'll begin by taking a look at a greenfield project, and then you'll proceed to import the Entity Framework libraries.

Task 1: Create a new project and add the EF packages

To get started creating a new project, make sure you have previously installed the *Visual Studio IDE* latest edition. Visual Studio Community is available for free for both academic use and open source project development and can easily be installed on any machine. That being said, there may be some limitations if using a Mac or

Linux box. The Visual Studio Community IDE download can be found here: `https://visualstudio.microsoft.com/downloads/`. If the link is no longer working, simply run a Google search for Visual Studio Community Download.

Additionally, if you previously had Visual Studio, make sure you've updated to the latest version and that you have the .Net 6 Framework SDK installed (this book is written using a preview version; however, the .Net 6 SDK and EFCore6 will be automatic once they are generally available in November 2021). You can update your Visual Studio IDE by going to "`Help ➤ Check for Updates`" in the menu on the Visual Studio IDE. If updates are available, you will be given the option to easily install them, which might require a reboot of your machine when completed. Additionally, Visual Studio 2022 should be in public preview by the time this book is published and may even be generally available by the time you are reading this book. If Visual Studio 2022 is out, there should be no reason for you to not use the latest version as EFCore6 and .Net 6 will work in either version of Visual Studio.

Step 1: Create a new .Net 6 console project

Open the Visual Studio IDE and select `Create a new project` as shown in Figure 1-1.

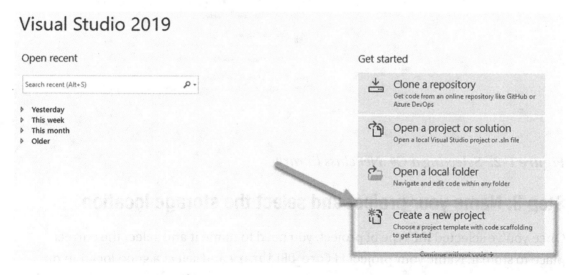

Figure 1-1. *Creating a new project in Visual Studio*

Step 2: Search and select Class Library

For this step, it will be important to select the correct project type. In this activity, you are creating a new *C# .Net* class library. Search for `Class Library` and then select the version of your choice (C# or Visual Basic). This book does everything in C#, but all concepts would be possible in Visual Basic as well. Once you have found the correct library of choice, select Next. You can easily search with the dropdowns as well, limiting language, platform, and template type to *C#*, *Windows*, and *Library*, respectively. Review Figure 1-2 for important details on what to look for when creating your new project.

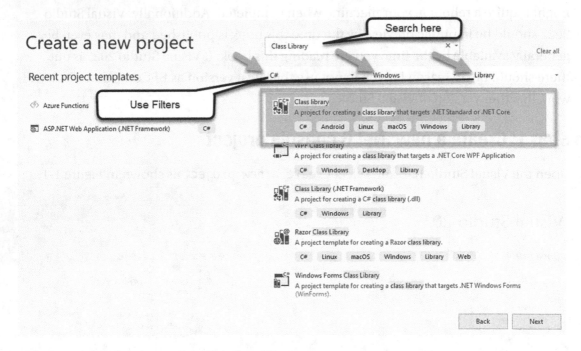

Figure 1-2. *Selecting a C# .Net class library*

Step 3: Name your project and select the storage location

Once you've selected the type of project, you need to name it and select the correct place to store it. Name your project `EFCore_DBLibrary` and select a good location on your computer where you store your projects. For example, I like to store projects under `C:/<Client>/Projects` or `C:/<Client>/Code`. Here I'll place the project in a folder `C:/ApressEntityFramework/Code/`. Figure 1-3 highlights what my creation page looks like, and yours should be similar.

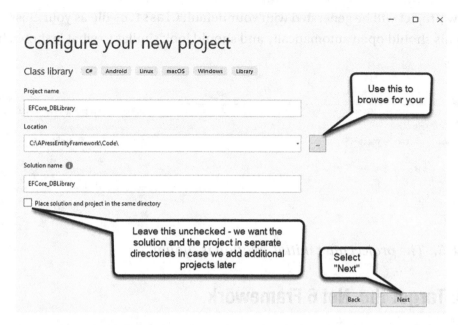

Figure 1-3. *Configuring your new project with name and desired folder for the project selected*

After you have selected Next, you should be prompted to select a `Target Framework`. When prompted, select `.NET 6.0` and then hit `Create` (see Figure 1-4).

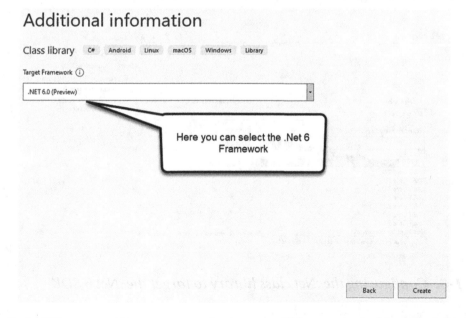

Figure 1-4. *When creating a new project, you will be prompted to select the Target Framework*

A new project will be generated with your default `Class1.cs` file as your class library. This should open automatically and should look similar to what is shown here in Figure 1-5.

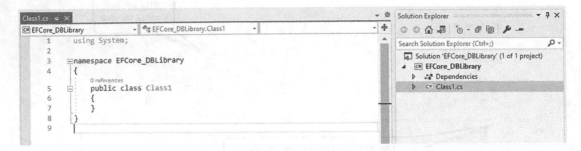

Figure 1-5. *The project after initial creation is shown*

Step 4: Target the .Net 6 Framework

Although you don't need to do this, in case you want to be certain the correct version of .Net is targeted, select the `EFCore_DbLibrary` project in the Solution Explorer, right-click, and select Properties.

Once the menu is open, use the dropdown under the Target Framework to select .NET 6.0 as shown in Figure 1-6.

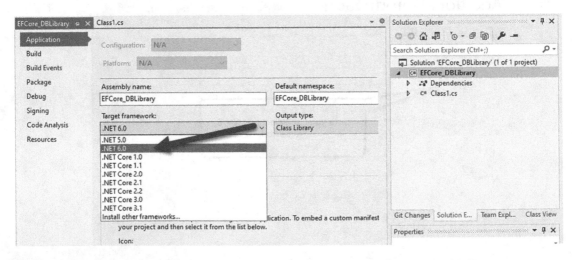

Figure 1-6. *Configuring the .Net class library to target the .Net 6 SDK*

Task 2: Add the EFCore6 packages to your project

Step 1: Determine the latest version of Entity Framework

Now that you have the project created and the Target Framework set to .NET 6.0, you need to install the latest version of Entity Framework.

There are two ways to install NuGet packages into your code in .Net. The first way is the easier way, which is to use the option *Manage NuGet Packages for Solution*, which is found under the menu *Tools* ➤ *NuGet Package Manager*. The second way is to use the Package Manager Console to run a command on the project to import libraries. As a developer, you need to know how to do both. In this activity, you will use the *Package Manager Console*. In future activities in the book for other libraries, you will leverage the *Manage NuGet Packages* option from the *Tools* ➤ *NuGet Package Manager* menu.

To find the latest version, just do a quick Google search for `Entity Framework Core NuGet Package` which should point you to this page: `www.nuget.org/packages/Microsoft.EntityFrameworkCore`.

Once there, you can easily see the latest version and the command to install the package, as shown here in Figure 1-7 (currently preview version 6.0.0-preview.4.21253.1, but will be a newer/official version by the time you are reading this book and working through this activity).

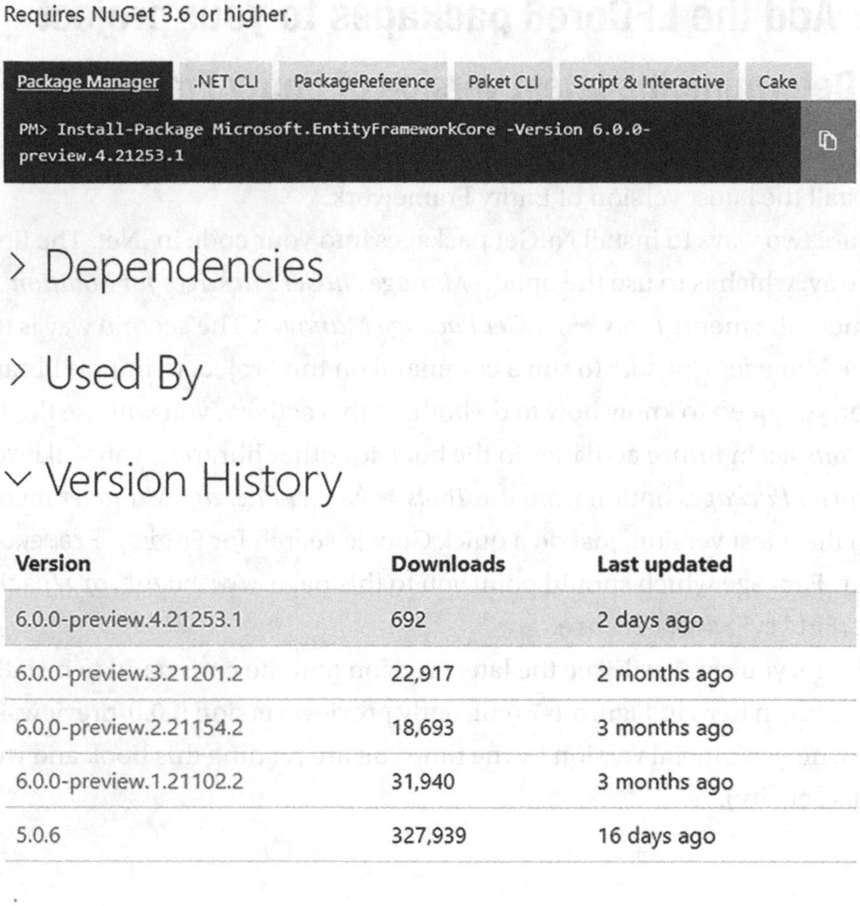

Requires NuGet 3.6 or higher.

Package Manager	.NET CLI	PackageReference	Paket CLI	Script & Interactive	Cake

```
PM> Install-Package Microsoft.EntityFrameworkCore -Version 6.0.0-
preview.4.21253.1
```

> Dependencies

> Used By

∨ Version History

Version	Downloads	Last updated
6.0.0-preview.4.21253.1	692	2 days ago
6.0.0-preview.3.21201.2	22,917	2 months ago
6.0.0-preview.2.21154.2	18,693	3 months ago
6.0.0-preview.1.21102.2	31,940	3 months ago
5.0.6	327,939	16 days ago

Figure 1-7. *Finding the latest version of Entity Framework Core*

Important notes about NuGet packages:

- The command to run is located in the main portion of the page. In this case, it is Install-Package Microsoft.EntityFrameworkCore -Version 6.0.0-preview.4.25253.1. By the time you are working through this text as it is published, the version will be higher and will likely no longer be in preview. You should use the most recent stable version of the library.

- There may be preview versions available. While they are easily installed, they may not yet be stable. When working on application code, I would recommend using the latest stable version. Also note future releases might be marked with an "rc" for release candidate (such as the listing for 5.0.0-rc-2.20475.6). RCs are generally close to stable, but again, not recommended for production use.

- Although the version is specified, if you run the command for install without the version, then generally the latest stable version would automatically be installed for you.

Step 2: Add the Entity Framework libraries to your project

Now that your class library is set up, you can add the Entity Framework libraries using the Package Manager Console. Using the Tools menu at the top of the Visual Studio IDE, select Tools ➤ NuGet Package Manager ➤ Package Manager Console as shown in Figure 1-8 (also note one of the other options is the Manage NuGet Packages for Solution, which you'll use in the future, but not now).

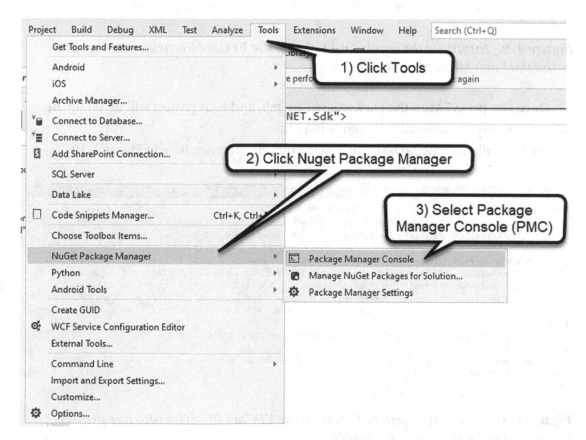

Figure 1-8. *Opening the NuGet Package Manager Console*

This will open the Package Manager Console (PMC) panel into the bottom portion of the Visual Studio IDE.

Once the PMC is open, run the command as found in Step 1 (which will be something like `Install-Package Microsoft.EntityFrameworkCore -Version 6.0.1`, but the version number will be slightly different based on new releases since the time of this writing (see Figure 1-9).

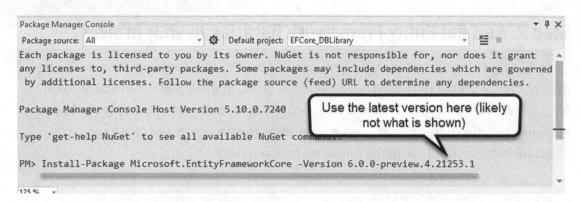

Figure 1-9. *Inputting the command to bring the EFCore libraries into our project in the Package Manager Console*

Once you press `Enter`, the packages will install, and your project will be set up for using the Entity Framework in this code library.

Your installation should be similar to the output as shown here in Figure 1-10.

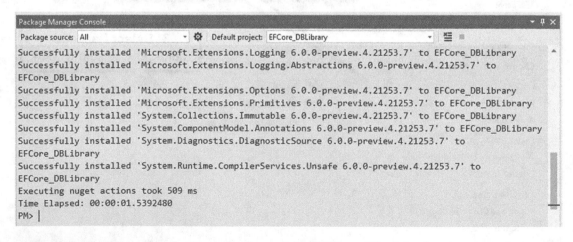

Figure 1-10. *Running the installation of the EFCore libraries into our project using the Package Manager Console*

You have now successfully created a class library that references Entity Framework, but you still have some work to do to get it set up to run against a database.

At this point, you can also validate the packages that are installed, both in the `*.csproj` file and in the `Tools ➤ NuGet Package Manager ➤ Manage Packages for Solution`.

Using the menu to open `Tools ➤ NuGet Package Manager ➤ Manage Packages for Solution`, make sure to select Installed. You should see the *EFCore6* version that you just installed via the *PMC*. This is shown in Figure 1-11.

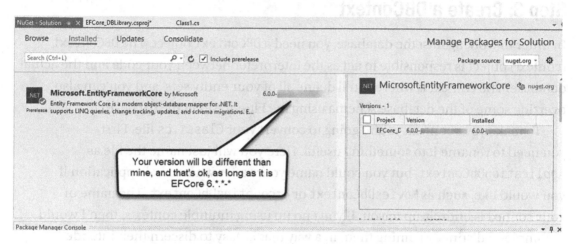

Figure 1-11. *Reviewing the Manage Packages for Solution installed tab reveals that the library is successfully added as part of your project*

Double-click the project name `EFCore_DbLibrary` in the Solution Explorer. This will open the project JSON file, and in the JSON file, you will be able to see the referenced packages for the project, as shown in Figure 1-12. Remember that your version will almost certainly be different than what is shown, and that is OK as long as it is version 6.

Figure 1-12. *The project JSON file reveals the packages that are included in your project, including the Entity Framework Core 6 version that you just installed*

Because the version is still in preview as I'm writing this book, you may note that in future projects the starter and final files will leverage version 6.0.0-*, which brings in the latest release. You can always see the exact libraries imported under the Dependencies of the project.

Step 3: Create a DBContext

In order to work against the database, you need a DBContext object. The DBContext (context) object is responsible to act as the interpreter between your code and the actual database. The context is where you'll define all of your entity sets, and you can also override some of the database schema using the Fluent API in the DBContext.

To make your context, you're going to convert your Class1.cs file. First, you need to rename it to something useful. Here you will just name the file as ApplicationDbContext, but you could name yours after your actual application if you would like, such as MoviesDbContext or AccountingDbContext. The name of your context is entirely up to you. If you end up using multiple contexts, then I would recommend distinctly naming them in a way that is easy to discern their intended purpose, but keep them simple since using multiple contexts requires typing their names a lot.

To rename the file, simply right-click the Class1.cs file in the Solution Explorer in your Visual Studio IDE and select Rename as shown in Figure 1-13.

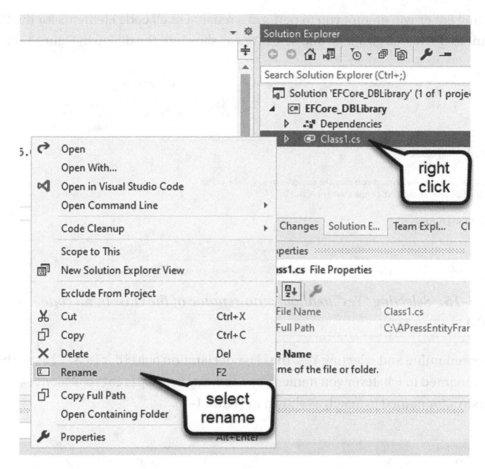

Figure 1-13. *Selecting the Class1.cs file for renaming*

Alternatively, selecting the file in the Solution Explorer and hitting F2 will automatically select the file for renaming.

Once the rename textbox appears with the original name in it, enter your new context name, such as ApplicationDbContext as shown in Figure 1-14.

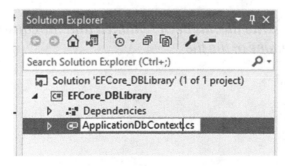

Figure 1-14. *Renaming the Class1.cs file to ApplicationDbContext.cs*

Hitting Enter will prompt you to perform a rename in all code elements for the file. You want to do this, so go ahead and select Yes as shown in the dialog in Figure 1-15.

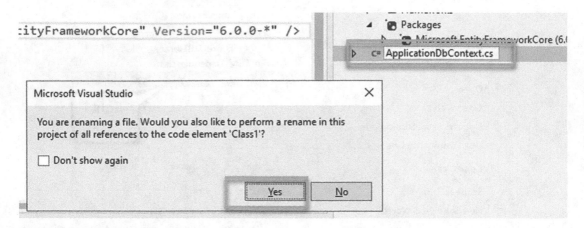

Figure 1-15. *Selecting "Yes" to allow auto-rename of the class in all code elements*

After renaming and selecting Yes, the class declaration public class Class1 should also be renamed to whatever you named your context (i.e., ApplicationDbContext) with the constructor named to match as shown in Figure 1-16.

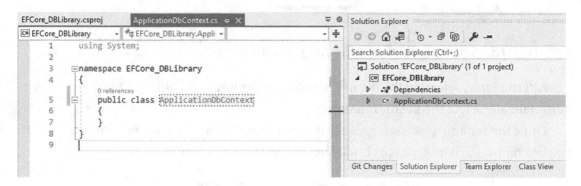

Figure 1-16. *The Class1.cs file has been renamed and the constructor is now named to match the name of the file*

Step 4: Alter your context to implement DbContext correctly

Now that your filename is changed to match your context, you need to alter the context so that it is implemented correctly. To do this, you must accomplish two things:

1. You must inherit and extend `DbContext`.

2. You must have a constructor that allows for injecting the context options.

First, make your `ApplicationDbContext` an actual `DBContext` by extending `DbContext`. Extend `DBContext` and make sure to add the using statement for *Microsoft. EntityFrameworkCore* as shown in Figure 1-17.

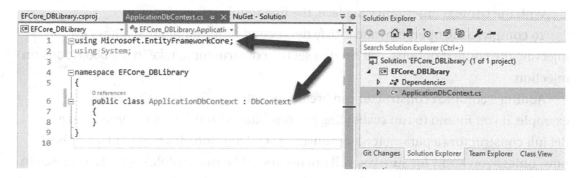

Figure 1-17. *Extending the DBContext class and adding the appropriate using statement*

Note that the using statements that are missing in your code can easily be added by fixing the red squiggly lines that appear under them and selecting the `Show Potential fixes` option to bring up the available fixes, which includes the option to add the using statement. In the previous fix, this would have looked as is shown in Figures 1-18 and 1-19.

First, the selection to Show potential fixes is shown here in Figure 1-18.

Figure 1-18. *The option to Show potential fixes is shown when hovering over or clicking any red squiggly lines in your code*

Once clicked, the missing using statement is added as an option to fix the "problem," as shown in Figure 1-19.

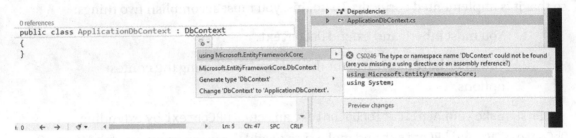

Figure 1-19. *The missing using statement can be easily added*

With the context inheritance in place, the first requirement is met.

To complete the operation and satisfy the second requirement that allows for injecting the context options, you need to set the constructor to take in the DBOptions on injection.

Adding a complex constructor can break some things if you aren't careful. For example, if you intend to run scaffolding options later with this context, you need a default constructor (a parameter-less constructor). Therefore, it's best to just add both now, unless you know for sure you will not use tools like the scaffolding tools available in the Visual Studio IDE.

Place the following code block into your ApplicationDbContext class:

```
//Add a default constructor if scaffolding is needed
public ApplicationDbContext() { }

//Add the complex constructor for allowing Dependency Injection
public ApplicationDbContext(DbContextOptions options)
    :base(options)
{
    //intentionally empty.
}
```

For clarity, review Figure 1-20 to ensure your code is as expected.

```
EFCore_DBLibrary.csproj        ApplicationDbContext.cs  ┼ ✕  NuGet - Solution        EFCore_DBLibrary

⊡ EFCore_DBLibrary                          ▾  ⁑₅ EFCore_DBLibrary.ApplicationDbContext   ▾ ⊙ ApplicationDbContext()
        1       ⊟using Microsoft.EntityFrameworkCore;
        2 ⍰     │using System;
        3
        4       ⊟namespace EFCore_DBLibrary
        5        {
                     2 references
        6     ⊟         public class ApplicationDbContext : DbContext
        7              {
        8                  //Add a default constructor if scaffolding is needed
                         0 references
        9                  public ApplicationDbContext() { }
       10
       11                  //Add the complex constructor for allowing Dependency Injection
                         0 references
       12    ⊟           public ApplicationDbContext(DbContextOptions options)
       13                      : base(options)
       14                  {
       15                      //intentionally empty.
       16                  }
       17
       18              }
       19        }
       20
```

Figure 1-20. *Adding the DBOptions as an injectable object to the constructor and creating the default constructor with no parameters*

Note that in order to accomplish this task, you made a public function with no return type since it's a constructor. The name of the constructor is the exact same as the name of the class, and the new constructor has one injectable parameter of type DbContextOptions. This parameter will include critical information, such as the connection string to your database. Making these options injectable will ensure that the context can be used from any application pointing to any correctly configured database.

Activity summary

In the previous activity, you created a class library and then imported the Entity Framework Core 6 library. After completing that import, you renamed the class file and then set up your DBContext to be ready to be used in any project.

As of right now, you can't necessarily prove that your setup is ready to go, but you can trust that it is either ready or will be very easy to modify once you get an actual application to use the project.

You might ask the question as to why this activity stopped here and did not just make sure that everything is working as expected. To answer that, you need to first decide how you are going to work against your database. Will you use a new database or an existing database? Will you use a *code-first* approach for your database, or are you going to use a reverse-engineering approach? In the next two chapters, you'll take a look at each of these options and get a chance to see how each approach can work. In the real world, your approach will depend on the needs of your application and the requirements based on the existence or non-existence of a database that the application will leverage.

Chapter summary

In this first chapter, you have taken a good look at the history of coding against data and how and why that history has led us to the Entity Framework. You then moved into creating a project in a class library that would be ready to work as a shareable database code library.

Although the first activity didn't create a fully functional library pointing to an actual database, you were able to get a good start and an overview of what it takes at the foundational level to work with Entity Framework. You've also gained an entry-level understanding of the DBContext object and are now familiar with how you might go about setting up the application to leverage Entity Framework.

Important takeaways

After working through this chapter, the things you should be in command of are

- The history of coding against data and the problems that have existed before Entity Framework wrapped the ADO.Net libraries

- How Entity Framework can be implemented into a class library for use in any project (still not entirely useable as is, but the initial setup is in place)

Closing thoughts

In the next chapter, you will examine how to create a project against an existing database using the reverse-engineering approach.

CHAPTER 2

Working with an Existing Database

In this chapter, we are going to look at what it takes to get up and running with Entity Framework when our project already has an existing database. We'll conclude the chapter with an activity to reverse-engineer an existing database in EFCore5 using .Net 6.

Reverse-engineering or database first

When working with an existing database, we have many options, and how we accomplish this task depends on what technology we are using. If we were working in the .Net Framework and using *EF6*, we would need to approach this task with a database-first operation. Since we are working in Entity Framework (*EFCore5*) with .Net 6, we'll need to perform a reverse-engineering operation.

Before diving into the how on this, we should first discuss the why. Additionally, we should take a look at some of the good and bad things about this reverse-engineering approach.

Why would we approach Entity Framework in this manner?

There are going to be times when an application is needed for a database that already exists. In these cases, the database may have many years of history and may be quite involved. Starting from scratch is usually not possible in these cases, because the overall amount of work it would take would overwhelm even the best development teams. However, in these cases, it is also desirable to begin new projects, perhaps to break a monolith into a serverless or hybrid serverless approach or to create a new access layer for a specific application.

© Brian L. Gorman 2022
B. L. Gorman, *Practical Entity Framework Core 6*, https://doi.org/10.1007/978-1-4842-7301-2_2

Rather than spend time trying to work new code into an old system, it is often desirable for both efficiency and security reasons to build new solutions. In these cases, when the database is mature and the desired application is new, a database-first or reverse-engineering approach makes sense.

Another case where this might be highly useful is to start exposing some of the data in a public or private API. Rather than creating a new database and porting data from the old into the new, it is much more efficient and the chance for errors is lessened if the new API just leverages the existing database.

Reverse-engineered solutions

The really good news about this approach is that there are tools in place that allow us to very quickly generate the code we need to work against the database. The bad news is that this code is not very flexible, as we'll see throughout this chapter. To sum it up, essentially a reverse-engineered approach requires regenerating code any time the database is changed where the application needs to interact with the database objects. Need to add a column? You'll need to add it in the database through your official channels, and then you'll need to regenerate your database context. An additional drawback to using the reverse-engineered approach is that your database code is often not stored in the repository. While you will have generated models for the objects you include in your reverse-engineering operation, the scripts that actually created the database objects are often not present. Additionally, there is not a history of objects and their state in the database for versioning. This can make it tricky when trying to restore to a previous patch but needing to have the database schema in the state it was at the time of that release.

Keeping everything in sync

A couple of final thoughts about this approach. In the older version of *EF6*, we often had an *EDMX* file that was a conceptual model of the database. This *EDMX* file was a gigantic *XML* file. If you've ever had to do a code merge in *GIT*, *Subversion*, or *TFS* when a large *XML* file is involved for multiple developers, you don't need me to tell you why that isn't a desirable situation in which to find yourself (massive merge conflicts on every change).

As such, creating the database changes in a database-first *EF6* approach required a great deal of coordination from team members. Additionally, even with a good system for how the team changes the schema, you likely still needed some tool or some other way to make sure you keep track of your database history, changes, scripts, and other important details.

With the EFCore6 reverse-engineered database approach, a few similar issues will arise, but the lack of a massive underlying XML file is an immediate win. Changes in this approach do require model updates that all team members will need to make sure to sync with to avoid future merge conflicts. The team will also need to continue to manage how developers can get their local database copies to map to the production or test database schema.

Interacting with the existing database

Now that we have a decent understanding of why we might want to take a database-first or reverse-engineered approach to the application, let's take some time to work through an activity that will allow us to see how to use the reverse-engineering solution in EFCore5 with .Net 6.

Activity 2-0: Working with a pre-existing database

In this section of the chapter, you're going to work through setting up a pre-existing database. In addition to getting the database up and running, you'll also need to get SQL Server and SSMS installed in order to work with the database locally outside of .Net and Entity Framework code.

To complete this activity, you'll need to have a version of Visual Studio, a working local copy of *SQL Express* or *SQL Server Developer* edition (developer edition is recommended), and *Microsoft SQL Server Management Studio* installed. Additionally, you'll need a backup copy of the existing *AdventureWorks* database.

Task 1: Prerequisites

In this first task, you will ensure that your system is ready to work with Entity Framework by completing two tasks to make sure you have the prerequisites of *SQL Server Developer* edition and *SQL Server Management Studio (SSMS)* installed on your machine.

Task 1-1: Prerequisite – SQL Server Developer edition (or SQL Express)

The activity will use the recommended setup, which leverages the *SQL Server 2019 Developer* edition, available here: `www.microsoft.com/en-us/sql-server/sql-server-downloads`.

For clarity, Figure 2-1 shows the Download button on the page for the *SQL Server Developer* installation. You should use whatever the latest version of SQL Server Developer is at the time you work through this book. Additionally, if you are unsure of what to do during the installation, just use the basic installation options and default settings.

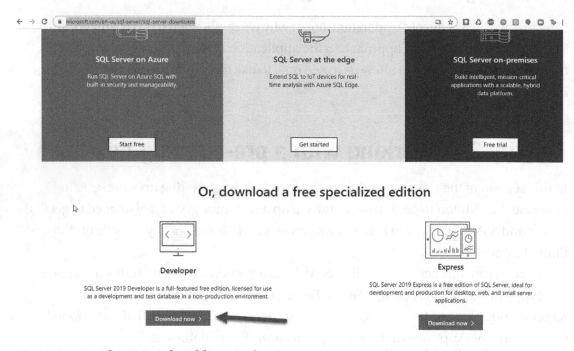

Figure 2-1. *The Download button for SQL Server Developer found online is shown*

If you don't have enough space for the Developer edition or are on a machine with limited power, you may use the Express edition. If you do that, be advised that your connection string will be slightly different than what is shown throughout the rest of the text.

Another note here is that in this book I'm primarily working on a Windows box so I don't have any issues with the default versions of the software. If you are running on Linux or a Mac, you will likely need to take additional steps to install SQL Server, which may also include installing into a container. There are numerous resources available that discuss how to do this online, including the instructions that follow the download highlighted earlier on the same link as earlier. For clarity, these links are shown in Figure 2-2.

Figure 2-2.   *Additional options for installing SQL Server software on non-Windows machines can be found below the original download link, and the images and links are shown in this image*

Task 1-2: Prerequisite – SQL Server Management Studio (SSMS)

To interface with SQL Server 2019 locally, the current version of SSMS at this time is version 18.9.1 and is available here: `https://docs.microsoft.com/en-us/sql/ssms/download-sql-server-management-studio-ssms?view=sql-server-ver15`. Figure 2-3 shows the download page and link.

Download SQL Server Management Studio (SSMS)

04/20/2021 • 6 minutes to read • 👤👤👤👤 📖 +34

Applies to: ✅ SQL Server (all supported versions) ✅ Azure SQL Database ✅ Azure SQL Managed Instance ✅ Azure Synapse Analytics

SQL Server Management Studio (SSMS) is an integrated environment for managing any SQL infrastructure, from SQL Server to Azure SQL Database. SSMS provides tools to configure, monitor, and administer instances of SQL Server and databases. Use SSMS to deploy, monitor, and upgrade the data-tier components used by your applications, and build queries and scripts.

Use SSMS to query, design, and manage your databases and data warehouses, wherever they are - on your local computer, or in the cloud.

Download SSMS

⊕ Download SQL Server Management Studio (SSMS) 18.9.1 ↗

SSMS 18.9.1 is the latest general availability (GA) version of SSMS. If you have a previous GA version of SSMS 18 installed, installing SSMS 18.9.1 upgrades it to 18.9.1.

Figure 2-3. *The SSMS tool is required in order to interface with the database server outside of code. The SSMS download link is shown for clarity in this image*

Task 2: Download and restore the backup file for the latest version of the AdventureWorks database to your machine

Microsoft has made a free database available for use when learning or training on SQL products. The database is called *AdventureWorks* and is available here: `https://docs. microsoft.com/en-us/sql/samples/adventureworks-install-configure?view=sql-server-ver15&tabs=ssms`. Regardless of which version of Entity Framework you want to use for this activity, the two subtasks in this task to get the database downloaded and restored will be the same. After completing the database restoration, you may proceed with Activity 2-1.

Task 2-1: Download the latest version of AdventureWorks DB

Before you begin, it's important to note that I'm running this on a clean machine. If you currently have a version of SQL Server installed and you have restored AdventureWorks in the past, you will need to evaluate the appropriate action(s) to take. To ensure that you have the same version of AdventureWorks (it actually does change from time to time), you may wish to just install the latest version with a new name (i.e., AdventureWorks2019 or AdventureWorks2). While you should be able to have side-by-side instances of SQL Server (such as Developer and Express), your machine may not have space for both. The book uses the Developer edition, but you can easily use SQLExpress. The main difference would be in the connection string. For Developer, the connection string uses the server as `localhost`, whereas SQLExpress generally uses `.\SQLExpress` for the server.

Once you are ready with SQL Server and your plan for where to restore the database, begin by downloading the latest *AdventureWorksXXXX.bak* file to your local machine (i.e., AdventureWorks2019.bak). Figure 2-4 shows the download page on Microsoft's website for clarity.

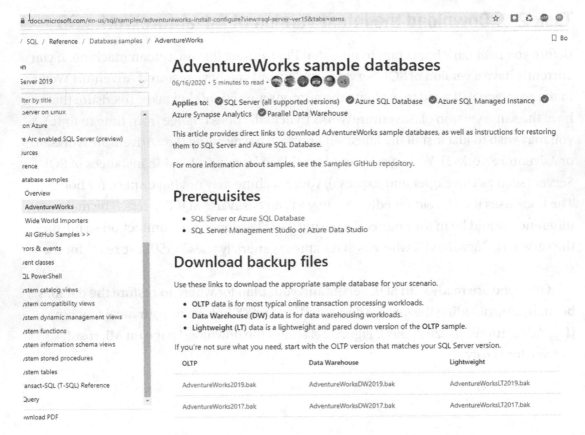

Figure 2-4. *Downloading the latest version of the AdventureWorks database*

For this book, examples will use the OLTP version of AdventureWorks. You would likely be able to complete all the tasks with the lightweight (LT) version as well, but this is untested. If for some reason you need to conserve space, you could try using the LT version of the download but may need to make a few tweaks on your own in future exercises.

Once you've completed the download, you are ready to proceed to the restoration task.

Task 2-2: Restore the AdventureWorks database to your local SQL instance

After downloading the backup file, you need to restore it to your local *SQL Server Developer* or *SQL Express* instance (you should have installed one of those in the previous task).

Connect to your database in SSMS as shown in Figure 2-5. Note that the SQL Server Developer edition references the local database server as localhost. If you are working with *SQLExpress*, you will likely need to reference the server in your connection string as ".\SQLEXPRESS" or something similar, based on how you installed the *SQL Express* edition. Either way, you should use Windows Authentication as your authentication method.

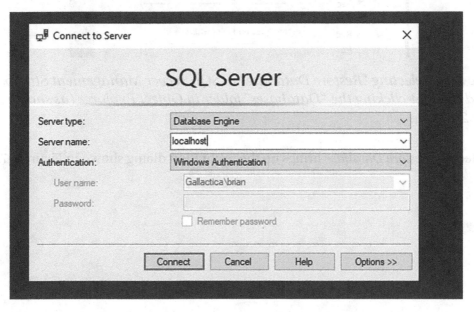

Figure 2-5. *Getting connected to your SQL Server via SSMS*

Once connected, right-click the *Databases* folder under your local server name, and then select *Restore Database*.

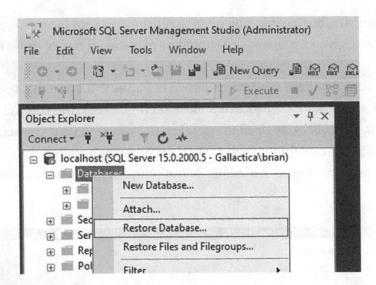

Figure 2-6. *Selecting "Restore Database" in SQL Server Management Studio, located by right-clicking the "Databases" folder in Object Explorer (as shown in Figure 2-6)*

Selecting *Restore Database* brings up the restoration dialog shown in Figure 2-7.

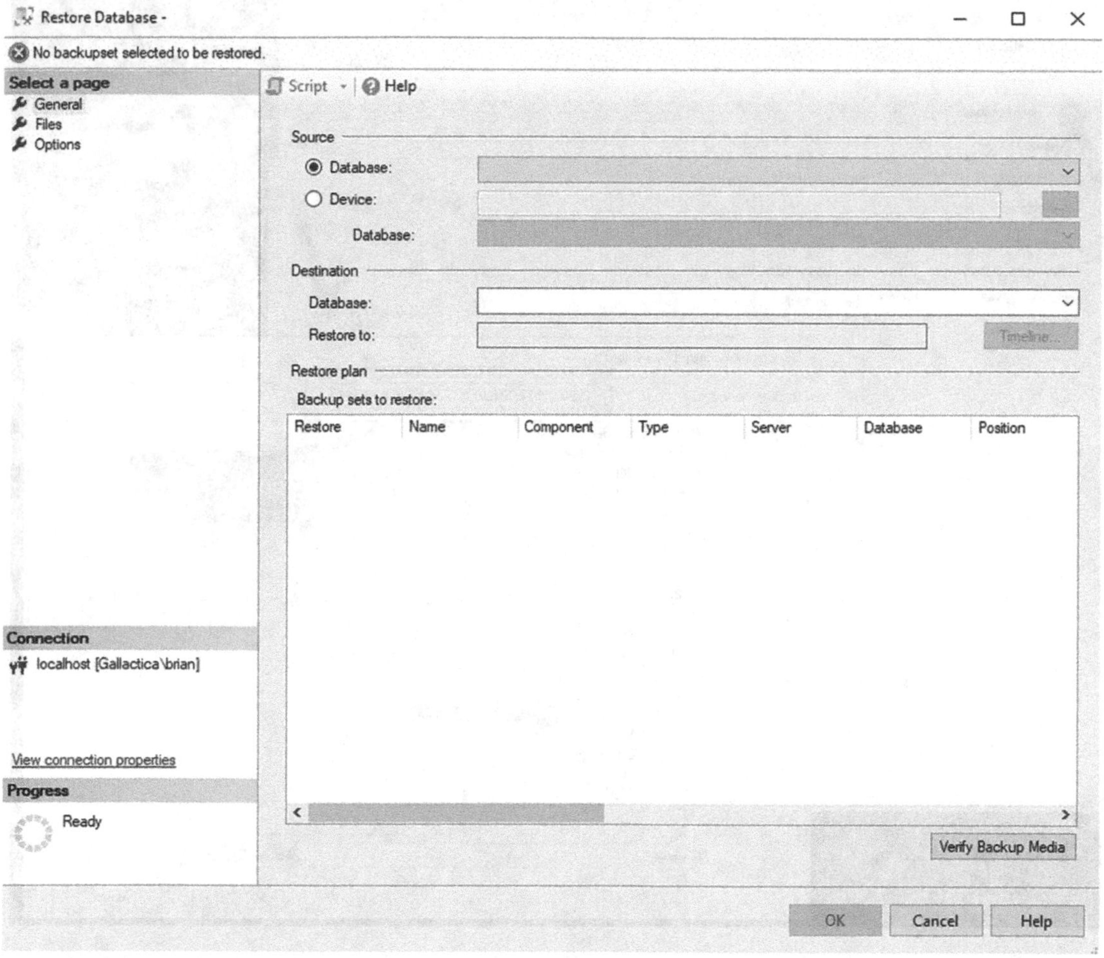

Figure 2-7. *The Restore Database dialog is shown*

With the Restore Database dialog open, select *Device* and then select the button with three periods, which will bring up a dialog entitled *Select backup devices*. In this dialog, select *Add* and then note the default location for backup files as in Figure 2-8. Select the text in the Backup File location and copy it to your clipboard.

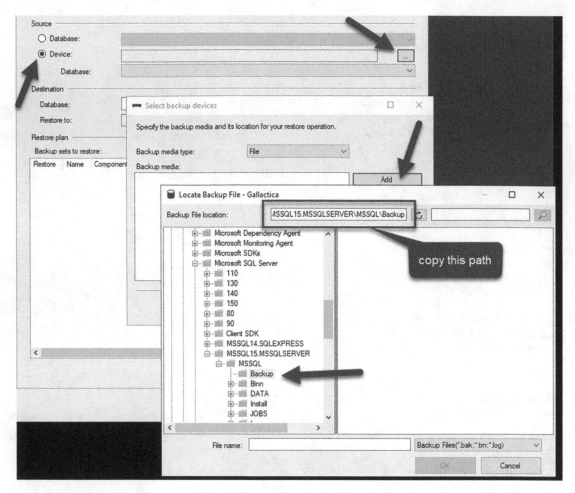

Figure 2-8. *Finding the backup location in the Select backup devices – Add dialog*

Move the backup file from your downloads into the backup location found in the *Locate Backup File* dialog shown in Figure 2-8.

You can copy the location from the dialog directly and open a new File Explorer to that path, or you can make note of the directory location in the directory tree on the left half of the *Locate Backup File* dialog.

Cancel the *Locate Backup File* dialog, copy the backup file to the correct path, and then select *Add* again. You should now see a result like in Figure 2-9. Now that your backup file is in the default location, it should be available in the window for selection as your backup source file.

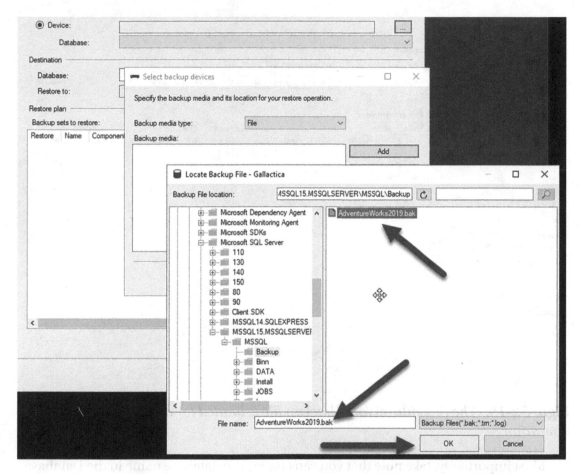

Figure 2-9. *The backup file shows in the dialog once placed in the default backup folder. The file is selected and ready to be restored at the press of a button*

Now that the file is in the correct location, select the file and then press the *OK* button and then select *OK* again on the *Select Backup Devices* dialog. This will fill in information for the backup dialog to the point that you can restore the database.

Before we restore, let's take a quick look and see if there is anything we want to change. Start by looking at Figure 2-10.

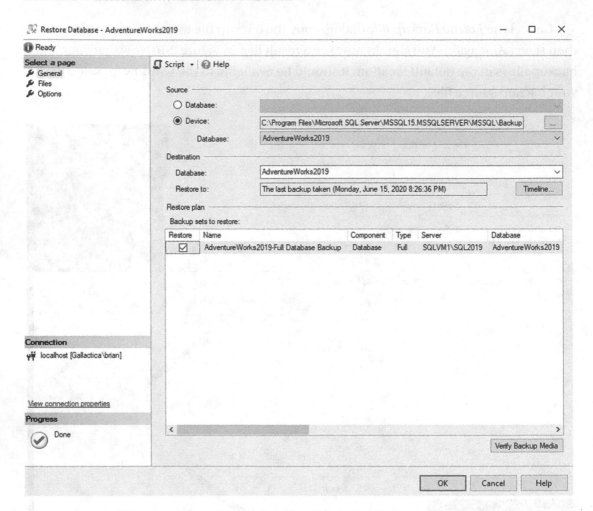

Figure 2-10. *The AdventureWorks backup file is loaded for a potential restore operation*

Most importantly, take note that you can change the database name in the Database dialog (see Figure 2-11). For example, here I am going to remove the year *2019* from the database name. Additionally, you can change the default file location and other options using the *Files* and *Options* tabs on the upper left *Select a page* dialog. I am going to leave both tabs with all the default options as set automatically, so the only thing I'm changing is the year. You may leave the year or change it as you so desire.

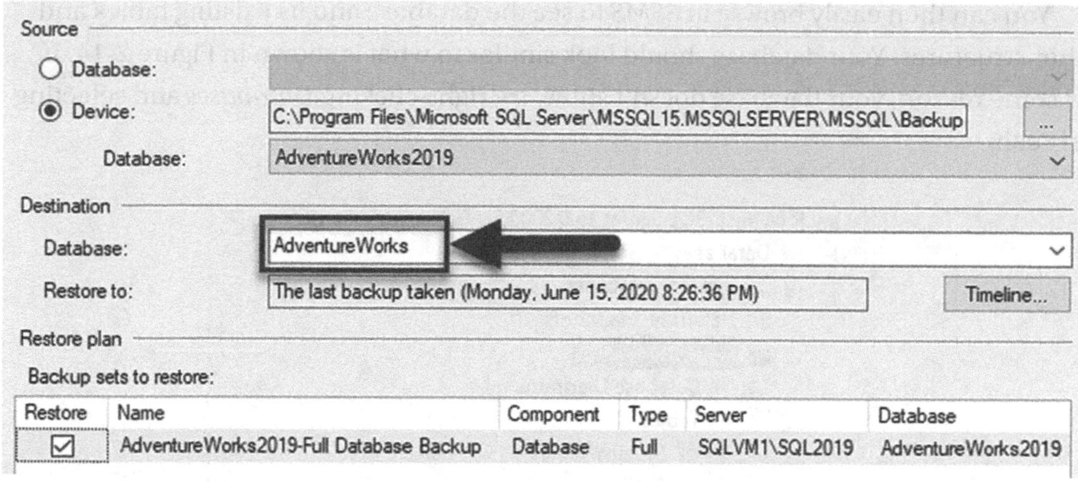

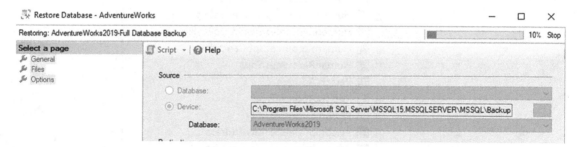

Figure 2-11. *Changing the database name before restoration*

Once all the options you want are selected and the database name is as you want it to be, select *OK* to restore the database. Figure 2-12 shows the restoration progress in action.

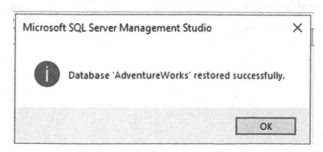

Figure 2-12. *Restoring the AdventureWorks database operation in progress*

Once the restoration is completed, a confirmation dialog (Figure 2-13) will appear.

Figure 2-13. *Restoring the AdventureWorks database operation has completed*

You can then easily browse in *SSMS* to see the database and its existing tables and other structures. Your database should look similar to what is shown in Figure 2-14. If, for some reason, your database doesn't show, try right-clicking *Databases* and selecting Refresh.

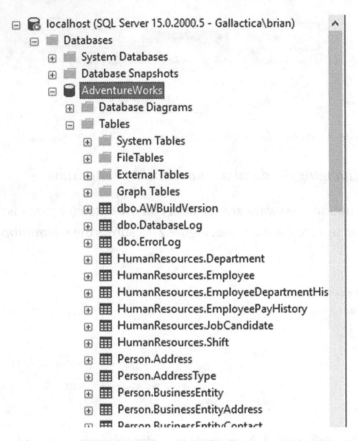

Figure 2-14. *Reviewing the AdventureWorks database in SSMS reveals that there are plenty of tables and assumes they are populated with data correctly*

You have now completed the prerequisite task work for the reverse-engineering database activity that comes next.

Activity 2-1: Reverse-engineering an existing database with EFCore5

In this activity, you will use the AdventureWorks database you previously restored to reverse-engineer an existing database for use in EFCore5.

Task 1: Creating the solution with a new project and referencing the DBLibrary project

In this first task for the activity, you will get started by creating a project and solution and then referencing the library you created in Activity 1-1 in the previous chapter. If you didn't do the activity in the previous chapter, you can choose to go back and do so, or you can download and use the final files for this activity.

Step 1: Create the project and solution

In this first step, to begin the activity, you will start by creating a simple C# console application, which will be your startup project. Open Visual Studio and use the `Create a new project` dialog to create a new C# Console App in .Net Core. Review Figure 2-15 for clarity.

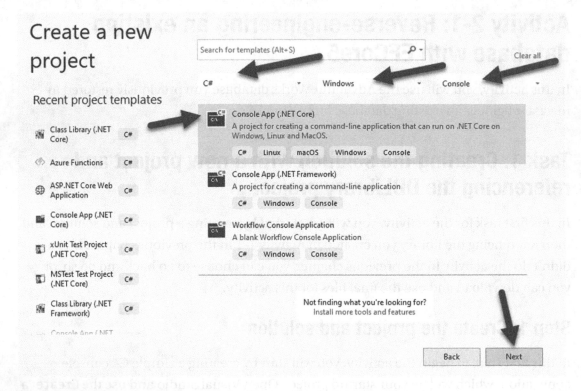

Figure 2-15. *Creating a new console project in .Net Core*

When the Configure your new project dialog comes up, name the project
EFCore_Activity0201. Select a good location for your project, such as C:\<client>\
Projects. In my case, I'm placing all the code in the C:\APressEntityFramework\Code
folder. See Figure 2-16 and use this to guide you to enter the correct information. When
ready, hit the Create button. Make sure that you do not check the button for placing the
solution in the same directory. It is generally good practice to keep your solutions in
their own directory and projects in folders associated with the specific project.

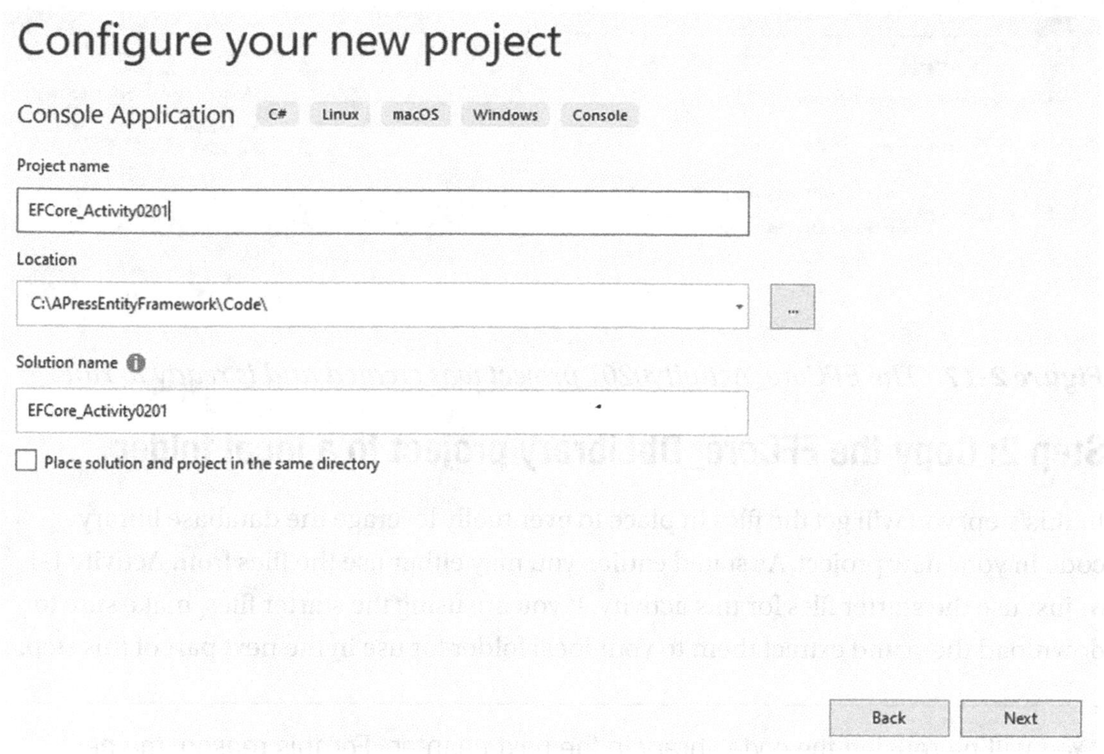

Configure your new project

Console Application C# Linux macOS Windows Console

Project name

EFCore_Activity0201|

Location

C:\APressEntityFramework\Code\

Solution name ⓘ

EFCore_Activity0201

☐ Place solution and project in the same directory

[Back] [Next]

Figure 2-16. *Configuring the new project*

When prompted, select .NET 6.0 as the Target Framework. If not prompted, you can ensure that .NET 6.0 is the version of the framework you are using by setting the properties on the project after creation (see Task 2: Ensure .Net 6...). After selecting .NET 6.0 as the Target Framework, hit the "Create" button.

Hitting "Create" will generate a new console project with a default starter class Program.cs. The project and solution will have the same name, but their respective files will be isolated from each other in separate folders on your hard drive. Figure 2-17 shows the default starter project that was just created.

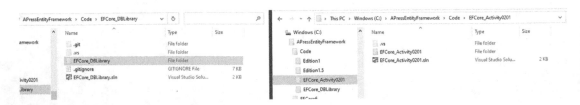

Figure 2-17. *The EFCore_Activity0201 project was created and is ready to run*

Step 2: Copy the EFCore_DbLibrary project to a local folder

In this step, you will get the files in place to eventually leverage the database library code in your new project. As stated earlier, you may either use the files from Activity 1-1 or just use the starter files for this activity. If you are using the starter files, make sure to download them and extract them to your local folder for use in the next part of this step.

You will be reusing the code library in the next chapter. For this reason, the next part of this step will ask you to copy the project folder to a new location.

Locate the folder that contains the project file for the EFCore_DbLibrary (either extracted from the starter files or from your previous work on Activity 1-1). Additionally, open a new File Explorer window to the folder that contains the solution for the Activity 2 project. Open the two windows side by side as shown in Figure 2-18, so that one window has the original EFCore_DbLibrary project and the other is your new project folder with the solution showing (do not worry if you don't see the exact files and folder as shown, as long as you have the EFCore_DbLibrary.csproj file available).

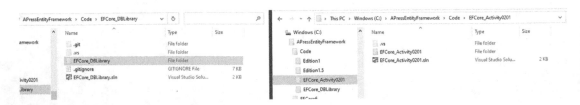

Figure 2-18. *Both folders are open in File Explorer to make it easy to copy the correct project file to the correct location*

In the `EFCore_Activity0201` folder, copy the original project from Activity 1 or make a folder named EFCore5_DbLibrary and add the starter files into that new folder. Figure 2-19 shows the copied folder for clarity.

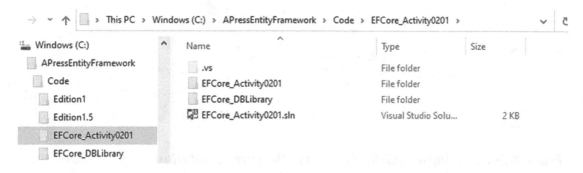

Figure 2-19. *Creating a new folder and copying the original project file into the new folder*

Ordinarily you would not bother to copy the folder and place it in the same solution folder, but rather you would just leave the library on your root code folder and reference it from that location. However, this activity is going to use the library, and then it will be used again in another activity, so making a copy to avoid conflicts here is the logical choice. The normal approach of just referencing an existing library directly will be used in future activities.

Step 3: Reference the code library that will be used to interact with the database

In this final step for Task 1, you will reference the project you just copied in the new console project created in Step 1 of this task.

Return to Visual Studio where the console project `EFCore_Activity0201` is open. Right-click the solution, and select Add ➤ Existing Project as shown in Figure 2-20.

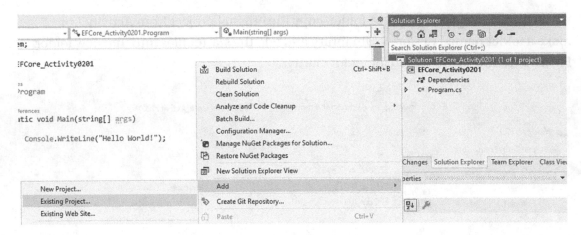

Figure 2-20. *Adding an existing project to the current solution*

Use the Add Existing Project dialog to browse to the EFCore_DBLibrary.csproj project file you just copied into the same solution folder under the folder EFCore_DbLibrary. It is important that you make sure to use the copy that is local to your current solution to avoid conflicts in future activities. Once the project is added, delete the ApplicationDbContext.cs file, as you will not need it for this activity. The result that you get should look as shown in Figure 2-21.

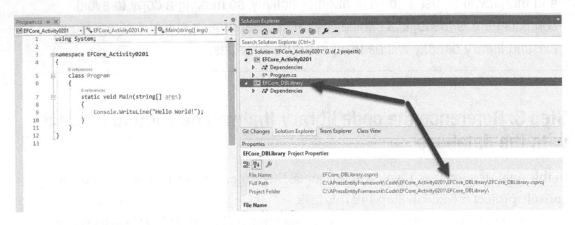

Figure 2-21. *The project is referenced. Notice that selecting the project allows you to validate that the correct project file is referenced in the Properties window*

When you've completed this step, you will see both projects in the solution, and you can validate that the correct DBLibrary project is referenced by clicking it and reviewing the full path in the Properties window. Ensure that the project file for the DBLibrary is located as a subfolder in the EFCore_Activity0201 folder (this is also called out in Figure 2-21).

Task 2: Ensure .Net 6 and update all of the NuGet packages for both projects

In this task, you will ensure that the console project is leveraging .Net 6, and you will proceed to add a few new NuGet packages to the solutions that will be needed to reverse-engineer the existing database.

Step 1: Ensure .Net 6 on the console project

In the Visual Studio IDE (VS), right-click the EFCore_Activity0201 project and select Properties. When the window opens, select .NET 6.0 as the project Target Framework. Figure 2-22 shows the result of this step.

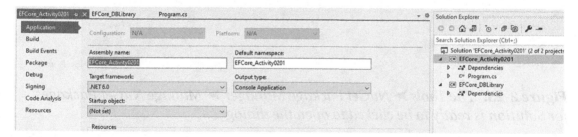

Figure 2-22. *The console project is set to target .Net 5. Save and build the solution to ensure there are currently no errors*

With the projects ready to go, you need to get two packages into the solution for the Entity Framework Tools and the Entity Framework for SQL Server. These packages will be used to reverse-engineer the existing database.

Step 2: Install the Entity Framework Tools (Microsoft. EntityFrameworkCore.Tools) NuGet package

In VS, use the Tools ➤ NuGet Package Manager ➤ Manage NuGet Packages for Solution menu to open the dialog to manage the NuGet packages for all solution projects. See Figure 2-23.

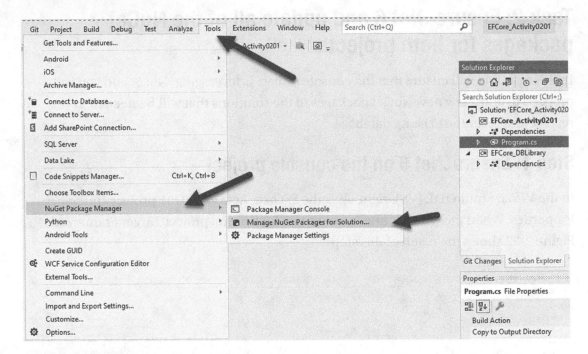

Figure 2-23. *The Tools ➤ NuGet Package Manager ➤ Manage NuGet Packages for Solution is ready to be clicked to open the dialog*

With the dialog opens, select the Browse tab at the top, and type EntityFrameworkCore into the search dialog as shown in Figure 2-24.

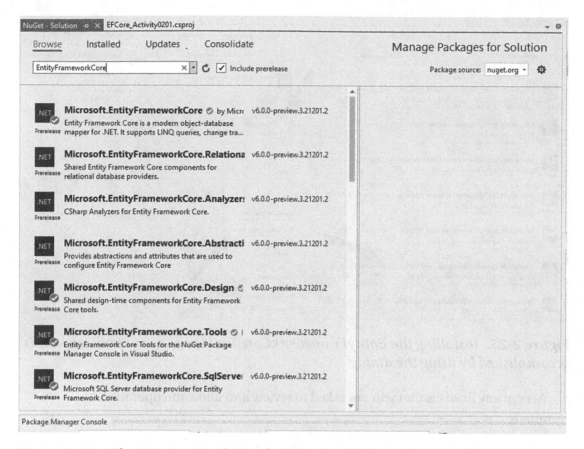

Figure 2-24. *The Manage Packages for Solution dialog is open and the search is entered for EntityFrameworkCore, which lists a number of available packages for selection*

Select the package `Microsoft.EntityFrameworkCore.Tools`, and then check **both** projects and select Install (making sure that the version of the tools matches the version of *EFCore6* that you have installed in the project). Figure 2-25 highlights this operation.

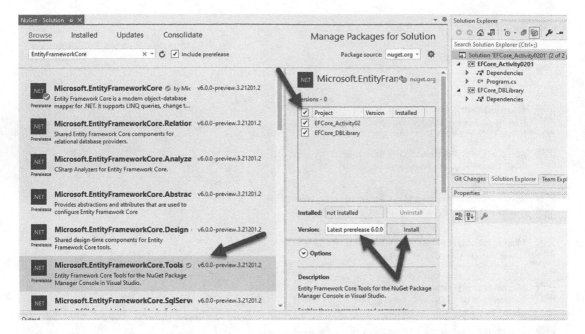

Figure 2-25. *Installing the EntityFrameworkCore.Tools package to both projects is accomplished by using the dialog*

Accept any licenses that you are asked to review and allow the operation to complete.

Step 3: Install the Entity Framework SQL Server (Microsoft. EntityFrameworkCore.SqlServer) NuGet package to both projects in the solution

Repeat the preceding steps or just find the package Microsoft.EntityFrameworkCore. SqlServer in the current list of packages and install to both projects. Figure 2-26 shows the correct package selected for installation to both projects.

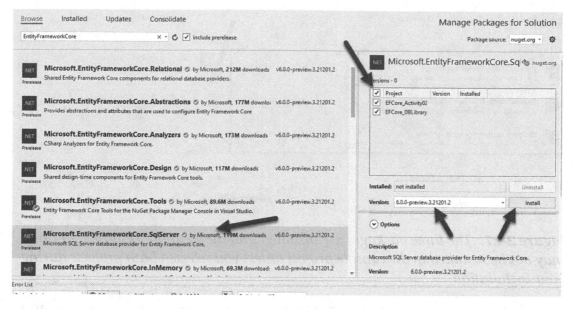

Figure 2-26. *Installing the Microsoft.EntityFrameworkCore.SqlServer package to both projects is accomplished by using the dialog*

Once again, accept any licenses you are asked to accept so the package will install correctly.

Review your installed project packages by selecting the Installed tab in the Manage Packages for Solution dialog. You should see the three expected packages shown in Figure 2-27 (Note: Your version will most likely be different, and that is expected. Additionally, if you have text in the search box, you can hit the "x" to clear it, as the search text may limit you from seeing all of your installed packages).

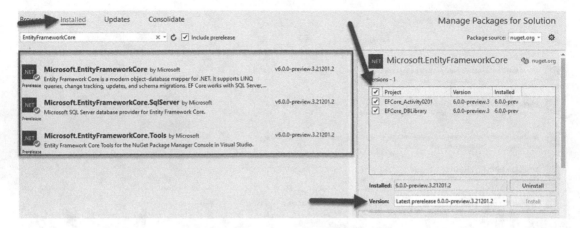

Figure 2-27. *The three packages are installed into the solution. However, EFCore may not be installed in the console project unless you selected both projects during your installation*

One thing to note is that the base `EntityFrameworkCore` library may not be installed in the console library project. To ensure it is installed, select the project as shown in Figure 2-27, then make sure both projects are checked, and hit the `Install` button. This will ensure that you have all the appropriate libraries in both projects. Once again, accept any licenses when prompted. At any point, you can also validate the installed NuGet packages by reviewing the `*.csproj` file, which will list all installed packages.

Step 4: Optionally, create a new GIT repository

If you have not done so, now would be a really great time to create a new GIT repository for your local code in case something goes horribly wrong in the next tasks.

To do this, you must have GIT installed on your machine. If you don't have GIT, go to `https://git-scm.com/downloads`, and download and install it on your machine.

Use GIT commands to create a local repository. You may also wish to create a `.gitignore` file and use the default Visual Studio `.gitignore` text found here: `https://raw.githubusercontent.com/github/gitignore/master/VisualStudio.gitignore`.

Figure 2-28 shows the result of me committing the files in the current state to a new local GIT repository, using a `.gitignore` file to eliminate checking in files that should not go in the repository.

```
brian@Gallactica MINGW64 /c/APressEntityFramework/Code/EFCore_Activity0201 (master)
$ git commit -m "initial commit"
[master (root-commit) d5ac493] initial commit
 5 files changed, 438 insertions(+)
 create mode 100644 .gitignore
 create mode 100644 EFCore_Activity0201.sln
 create mode 100644 EFCore_Activity0201/EFCore_Activity0201.csproj
 create mode 100644 EFCore_Activity0201/Program.cs
 create mode 100644 EFCore_DBLibrary/EFCore_DBLibrary.csproj
```

Figure 2-28. *Creating a new local GIT repository with current state committed*

If you add GIT externally to the project as I did here, you will likely need to restart Visual Studio in order for it to add icons for tracked files. Alternatively, you could have just created the GIT repository using the Visual Studio IDE tools. You should use what makes sense to you and what client you prefer to work with GIT.

Task 3: Scaffold a new database context using the Scaffold-Context command

In this task, you will run a command to scaffold a new context that will create files and a database context that allows you to use *EFCore6* against the existing database. You will need your server information that you used to connect to the database previously in SSMS (either localhost or .\SQLEXPRESS).

Before you scaffold, however, you should be aware that the context will require a full database connection string to be passed in as an option in the options parameter during the command execution. In other words, when you are scaffolding, you will be connecting directly to the existing database to generate the reverse-engineered code. I would not recommend doing this against production for a number of reasons, so hopefully you have the ability to restore a backup or a test server that has a matching schema in the real world. For your activity here, you'll use the *AdventureWorks* database that was previously restored (see Activity 2).

Step 1: Install the Microsoft.EntityFrameworkCore.Design package to the EFCore_Activity0201 project using the PMC

In order to perform the scaffold operation, one more NuGet package will need to be installed – `Microsoft.EntityFrameworkCore.Design`. This will be needed on the main program project only. For this reason, you could install via the dialog as you did earlier, or you can just run a command in the PMC. For simplicity, choose what works easiest for you, but this example will run the command in the PMC. This will also give you a chance to see how to use a specific project to run commands in the PMC.

Open the Package Manager Console in VS and select the `EFCore_Activity0201` project in the dropdown to set the starter project as the target for the operation. Type the command `Install-Package Microsoft.EntityFrameworkCore.Design` and hit Enter (if you get an error, review the following note about specifying a version). This command will install the package to the starter project only. Review Figure 2-29 for clarity.

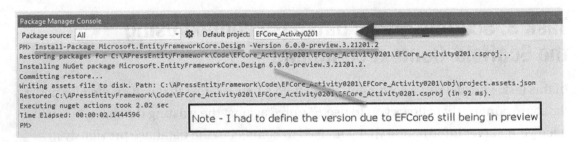

Figure 2-29. *Installing the Microsoft.EntityFrameworkCore.Design package to the EFCore5_Activity0201 project via the PMC*

Note that if you are using a different version of `EntityFrameworkCore` for some reason, you may need to specify the version specifically in the line where you asked to install the package.

Make sure to save, build, and then commit any changes to GIT at this point if you are using a local repository.

Step 2: Determine your connection string

To scaffold, as mentioned, you'll need to use a valid connection string to your database. If you are struggling to get the connection string set correctly, there are tools to help you find the connection string, such as connecting via SSMS or via Server Explorer in VS, as well as sites like `www.connectionstrings.com/`. If you are using the *SQL Server Developer* edition, your source will be `localhost`. If you are using *SQLExpress*, your source will likely be `.\SQLEXPRESS`. You will need to set the Data Source, the Initial Catalog (which needs to match the name of the database as you restored it), and the fact that you want to use a trusted connection (`Trusted_Connection=True`). Your connection string should look something like this:

```
'Data Source=localhost;Initial Catalog=AdventureWorks;Trusted_
Connection=True'
```

The Initial Catalog must match the name of the database, so if you left the year in place (when you named the database during the restore process), adjust appropriately. Additionally, don't forget to adjust the data source appropriately if you are not using *SQL Server Developer* edition.

Step 3: Run the scaffold command

You will run the scaffold command twice to see it in action. The first time you will scaffold the entire database, and the second time you will just scaffold a schema – which is just part of the database. Ordinarily you would only need to do this operation once, but since you are learning about this command, it will be good to see the different ways you can use this command to do all or part of the database in a reverse-engineering operation.

Important   Make sure to select the `EFCore_DBLibrary` project in the PMC for the next step.

To begin the operation, return to or open the PMC, and select the `EFCore_DBLibrary` project.

With the EFCore_DBLibrary project selected, run the following command:

```
Scaffold-DbContext 'Data Source=localhost;Initial
Catalog=AdventureWorks;Trusted_Connection=True' Microsoft.
EntityFrameworkCore.SqlServer
```

Ensure that you've updated the connection string appropriately before running the command. The command is Scaffold-DbContext and the first parameter is your connection string. The third parameter is the provider, which is Microsoft. EntityFrameworkCore.SqlServer in this case (and it's important to note you already added the NuGet package to make this possible earlier).

If everything is set up correctly, you would be able to generate the context and appropriate model files with this simple command. However, there is one error that will need to be corrected. Run the command to see the error, as shown in Figure 2-30.

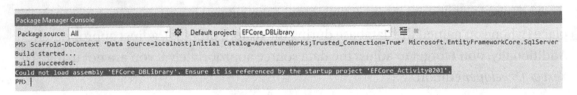

Figure 2-30. *Running the Scaffold-DbContext command at this point generates an error because one critical step was missed*

Earlier, when you were adding the project in, the reference from the startup project to the library was likely not added. If you had previously added the library project, then it's likely everything would work and you won't see the error shown in Figure 2-30. Earlier you did reference the project as you added it into the solution, but in addition to the solution, the other main activity project also needs a project reference to directly reference the project.

Right-click the EFCore_Activity0201 project in the Solution Explorer, and select Add ➤ Project Reference. Adding a project reference is shown in Figure 2-31.

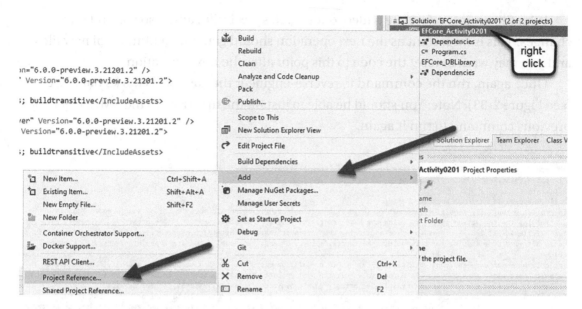

Figure 2-31. *Adding the project reference for the EFCore_DbLibrary project to the EFCore_Activity0201 project*

When the dialog comes up, select the EFCore_DbLibrary project so that the activity startup project references the DBLibrary project as shown in Figure 2-32.

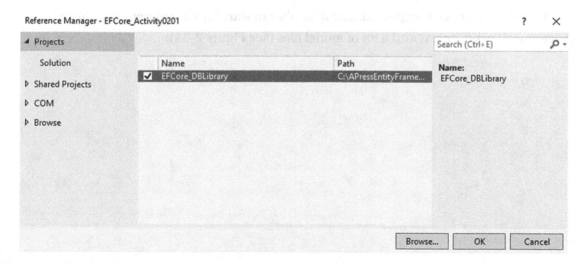

Figure 2-32. *Selecting and adding the project reference*

With the project reference added, once again save, build, and also commit any changes. This is important as the next operation should generate a number of new files, and you may want to reset the code to this point after the next operation.

Once again, run the command to reverse-engineer the `AdventureWorks` database (see Figure 2-33). Note: You should be able to just hit the up arrow in the PMC to get your previous command to run it again.

```
PM> Scaffold-DbContext 'Data Source=localhost;Initial Catalog=AdventureWorks;Trusted_Connection=True'
Microsoft.EntityFrameworkCore.SqlServer
Build started...
Build succeeded.
To protect potentially sensitive information in your connection string, you should move it out of source code. You can avoid
scaffolding the connection string by using the Name= syntax to read it from configuration - see https://go.microsoft.com/
fwlink/?linkid=2131148. For more guidance on storing connection strings, see http://go.microsoft.com/fwlink/?LinkId=723263.
Could not find type mapping for column 'HumanResources.Employee.OrganizationNode' with data type 'hierarchyid'. Skipping
column.
The column 'HumanResources.Employee.SalariedFlag' would normally be mapped to a non-nullable bool property, but it has a
default constraint. Such a column is mapped to a nullable bool property to allow a difference between setting the property to
 false and invoking the default constraint. See https://go.microsoft.com/fwlink/?linkid=851278 for details.
The column 'HumanResources.Employee.CurrentFlag' would normally be mapped to a non-nullable bool property, but it has a
default constraint. Such a column is mapped to a nullable bool property to allow a difference between setting the property to
 false and invoking the default constraint. See https://go.microsoft.com/fwlink/?linkid=851278 for details.
```

Figure 2-33. *Running the Scaffold-DbContext command with the correct connection string generates the code files and DbContext as expected in the EFCore_DBLibrary project*

This time it works as expected, and a number of warnings are generated, but so is the AdventureWorksContext and a lot of model files (see Figure 2-34).

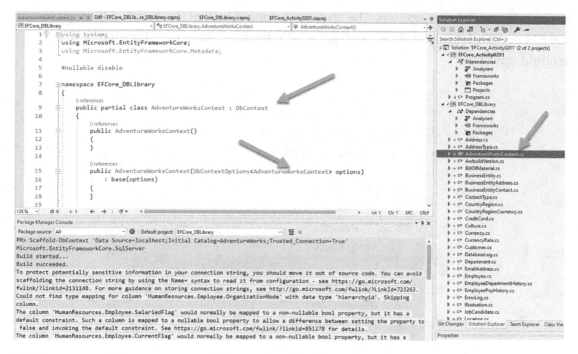

Figure 2-34. *The context and the model files are generated*

Feel free to take a moment to review the files that were generated. At this point, you have successfully reverse-engineered an existing database for use with Entity Framework Core 6 in .Net 6.

At this point, you could start working against the database in your console application, and in fact, this is what you will do later in this activity, after first making a slight tweak that has no effect on the overall project for this activity but is great for the purposes of learning.

Step 4: Repeat the scaffold operation, but change parameters

As an optional learning experiment, wipe out the files you just created with the scaffolding operation (just delete all models and the new context), or you could go to the trouble of creating a new solution and then run the scaffold operation again. To delete all of the models and the new context, find the newly created files in the EFCore_DBLibrary project and simply delete them. If you are using GIT and saved your commit as prompted, you could just run a git reset --hard command to reset to the previous commit and then run a git clean -xfdi command to clean up the files using your choice of deletion options. The end result should be that there are no files left in the EFCore_DbLibrary as shown in Figure 2-35 (back to where you started before the scaffold operation).

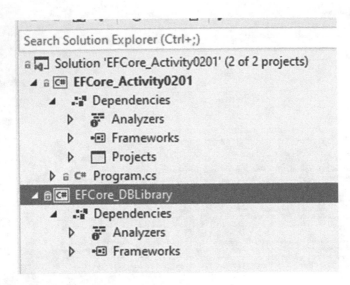

Figure 2-35. *The files generated previously are removed for a second run of the scaffolding operation with a limited scope*

For this run, you will specify only one schema to scaffold (you can go further on your own to specify specific tables if you would like deeper learning). Additionally, instead of using the *Fluent API*, let's specify that we want to use *Data Annotations*. We'll cover what the *Fluent API* and *Data Annotations* are later in this book, but for now just know the difference is in how the models and context work to implement things like required fields, length or size of fields, and overall relationships between the entities. For the scaffold command, this time specify the flag -Schema and then implement only the Person schema. Additionally, use the -DataAnnotations flag to generate data annotations on the models instead of fully relying on the Fluent API. The command to run this time, therefore, is (see Figure 2-36 for clarity)

```
Scaffold-DbContext 'Data Source=localhost;Initial
Catalog=AdventureWorks;Trusted_Connection=True' Microsoft.
EntityFrameworkCore.SqlServer -Schema 'Person' -DataAnnotations
```

Running the command gets the expected results (see Figure 2-36).

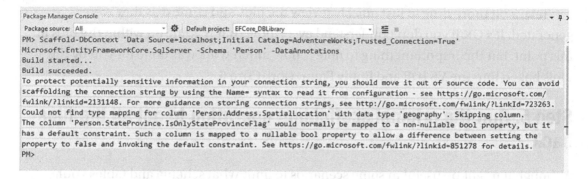

Figure 2-36. *Running the scaffold command but only targeting one schema and using Data Annotations instead of the Fluent API*

This time if you look around, only a few of the files were generated. Additionally, *Data Annotations* were used in the code. See Figure 2-37 for clarity.

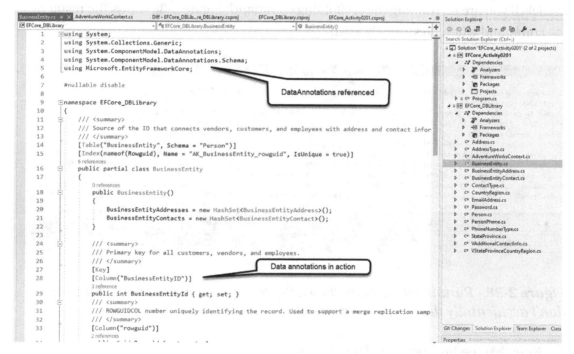

Figure 2-37. *The operation completed and the files generated are only from the Person schema, using Data Annotations*

Take a bit more time to just quickly review the files and context as they were generated. It's OK if you don't understand everything that is going on within the files at this point, but the important thing to note is how much work was done for you by the tools baked into the VS IDE and Entity Framework Core 6.

Step 5: Run the original scaffolding operation to get all the files back

Although it might be useful in some scenarios to limit what schema and tables your EFCore6 library has access to, for your purposes here, you'll want to just get everything back. Re-run the original scaffolding command by just using the arrow up key in the PMC to get back to the original command.

You'll note that running this command gives you an error due to files already existing. This is a good thing – you might not want to destroy previously built data models if you are re-running the scaffolding command. Figure 2-38 shows the result of the command when files already exist.

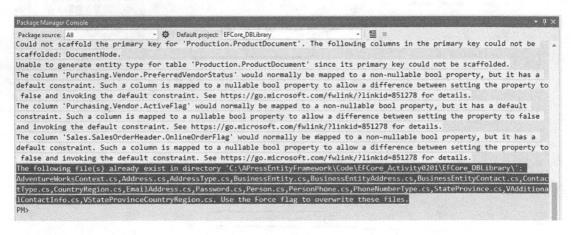

Figure 2-38. *Running the command when files exist gives an error so that you don't accidentally destroy existing models*

Note that the final portion of the text states

"The following file(s) already exist in directory
'C:\APressEntityFramework\Code\EFCore_Activity0201\EFCore_DBLibrary\':
AdventureWorksContext.cs, Address.cs, AddressType.cs, BusinessEntity.cs,
BusinessEntityAddress.cs, BusinessEntityContact.cs, ContactType.cs, CountryRegion.cs,
EmailAddress.cs, Password.cs, Person.cs, PersonPhone.cs, PhoneNumberType.cs,
StateProvince.cs, VAdditionalContactInfo.cs, VStateProvinceCountryRegion.cs. Use the
Force flag to overwrite these files."

Note the fact that there is a -`Force` flag. This is how you can do the operation with destructive consequences. For your learning purposes here, this is fine. In the real world, you would want to be super careful about forcing an overwrite.

Use the up arrow in the PMC to get your original command and add -`Force` to the end of it, and then run the command. The result is that the operation completes as expected. Figure 2-39 shows the command for clarity.

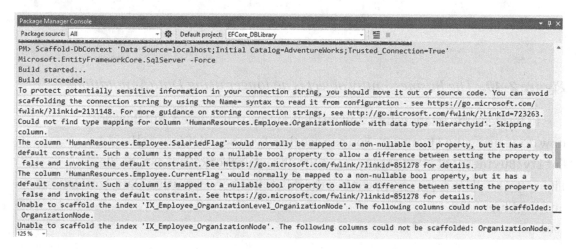

Figure 2-39. *Running the command with the -Force flag will work as expected*

Note that without the -`DataAnnotations` flag, the `BusinessEntity` object shown earlier no longer uses `DataAnnotations` (see Figure 2-40).

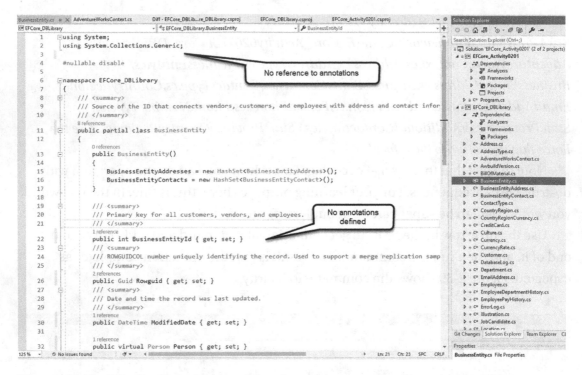

Figure 2-40. *The BusinessEntity object is no longer using DataAnnotations*

To be clear, the relationships and restrictions are still defined, but they are now done using the Fluent API. You can see this if you search for `modelBuilder.Entity<BusinessEntity>(entity =>` in the `AdventureWorksContext.cs` file. Figure 2-41 calls this out so you can see the difference between using Data Annotations and the Fluent API.

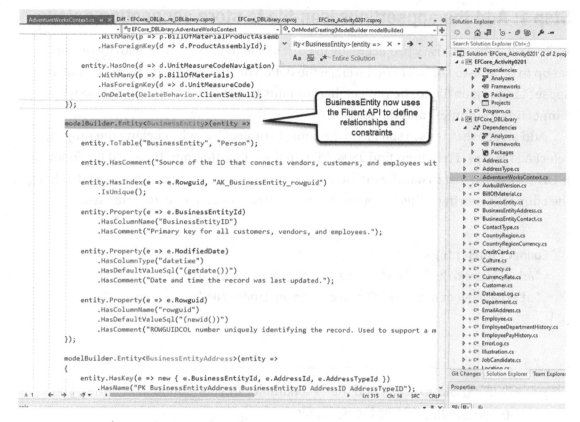

Figure 2-41. *The BusinessEntity object now uses the Fluent API to define relationships and constraints*

Again, the Fluent API and Data Annotations will be covered in more detail throughout this book.

Once again, now would be a good time to save, build, and commit any changes in your local repository.

Task 4: Create a settings file and leverage it from code

In this task, you will create an `appsettings.json` file to store the database connection string. You will then put libraries and code in place to leverage that connection string from the settings file in your activity project and use that to display results to the console from the `AdventureWorks` database.

Step 1: Add the appsettings.json file to store connection details

With the database library project ready to go, it's time to get the main activity project set up to be able to connect and leverage the data. The first step to do this is to add an `appsettings.json` file to the project that contains the connection string for use when connecting the context and database.

Add an `appsettings.json` file to the console project by right-clicking the project, select Add ➤ New Item, then find JSON File in the templates, and then add the following JSON-formatted text to handle the storage of the connection string. Remember to change the connection string if this is not the way you are connecting to your database.

```
{
  "ConnectionStrings": {
    "AdventureWorks": "Data Source=localhost;Initial
    Catalog=AdventureWorks;Trusted_Connection=True"
  }
}
```

If you are using SQLExpress and the "\" character in your connection string, you must use two slashes "\\" in the JSON file.

With the `appsettings.json` file in place, you need to set the file so that it will build and deploy with the project. Click the new `appsettings.json` file in the project, and then use the Properties window to select a build action of Content and the Copy to Output Directory as Copy if newer or Copy always (see Figure 2-42).

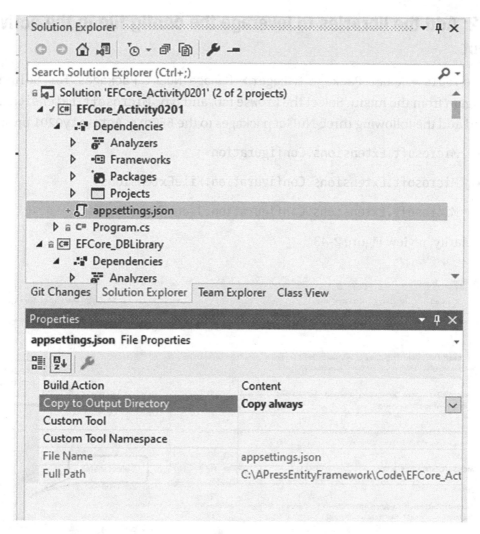

Figure 2-42. *The File needs to be copied to the output directory as content in order to be referenced during runtime*

Additionally, you'll need to add a couple of libraries to the project to be able to access it.

Step 2: Add the libraries to leverage the config file in the activity project

Open the Tools ➤ NuGet Package Manager ➤ Manage NuGet Packages for Solution dialog again from the menu. Select the Browse tab, and type Microsoft.Extensions. Find and add the following three NuGet packages to the EFCore_Activity0201 project:

- Microsoft.Extensions.Configuration
- Microsoft.Extensions.Configuration.FileExtensions
- Microsoft.Extensions.Configuration.Json

For clarity, review Figure 2-43.

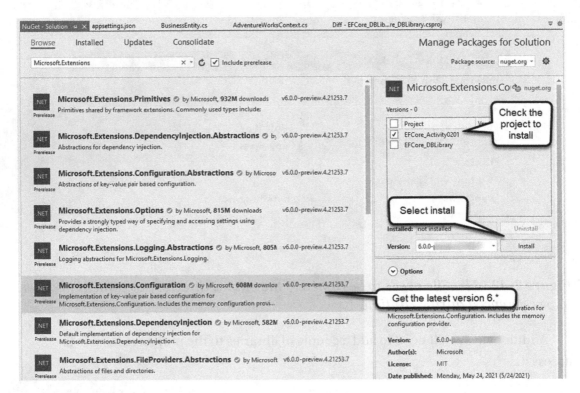

Figure 2-43. *Getting the three additional NuGet packages*

After installing all three, review your installed packages to ensure they are all present. Select the Installed tab, and remember to clear your search or you will likely only see installed packages that match your search terms (see Figure 2-44). Also note that your version will be different than what is shown, so just make sure you are using the latest version.

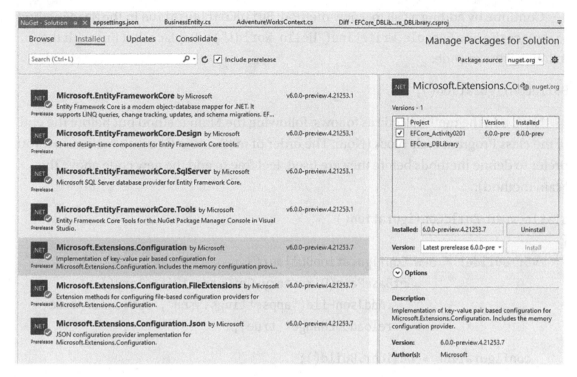

Figure 2-44. *Reviewing the installed NuGet packages shows all the expected packages to this point*

Step 3: Load up the config and leverage the results in the Main method of the Program.cs file in the activity project

Now that you have the file ready to go and all of the NuGet packages that will be necessary for connection, it's time to add code to leverage the connection string from the appsettings.json file.

In the Program.cs class in the EFCore_Activity0201 project, add the following code to the file after the line that states class Program and before the static void Main method declaration:

```
private static IConfigurationRoot _configuration;
```

After adding the code, make sure to hover over the red squiggly line for IConfigurationRoot and select Show potential fixes. When the statements come up, select the statement to add the using statement for Microsoft.Extensions. Configuration.

Continue by adding a call to a new method: BuildConfiguration in the Main method to replace the line Console.WriteLine("Hello World!");. Replace that line with the following line of code:

```
BuildConfiguration();
```

Next, add the method code as follows, following the Main method but before the end of the class Program code block (Note: The order of methods in C# won't matter, so if you prefer to define methods before they are used, feel free to add the new code above the Main method):

```
static void BuildConfiguration()
{
    var builder = new ConfigurationBuilder()
                .SetBasePath(Directory.GetCurrentDirectory())
                    .AddJsonFile("appsettings.json", optional: true,
                    reloadOnChange: true);

    _configuration = builder.Build();
}
```

Remember that any time the Visual Studio IDE shows a red squiggly line, there are errors in your code. For each red squiggly line, attempt to use the suggested fixes. Most of the time, you'll just need to add missing using statements. A quick shortcut is to hit the key chord combination Ctrl+"." – which will bring up the suggestions for you.

Another shortcut you might leverage is the key chord combination of Ctrl+"]", which will help you find matching braces.

Resolve any missing using statements for Directory. For clarity, Figure 2-45 shows the current code as it should look based on the directions earlier.

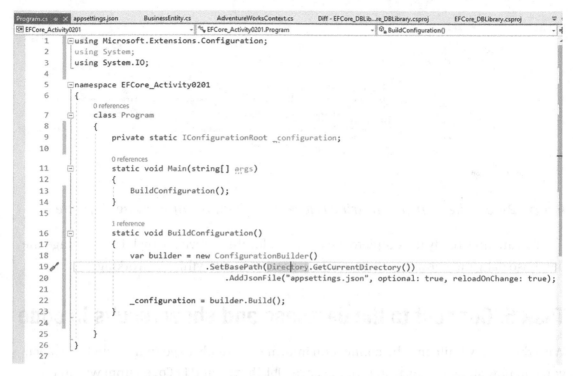

```
Program.cs  -  ×  appsettings.json      BusinessEntity.cs      AdventureWorksContext.cs      Diff - EFCore_DBLib...re_DBLibrary.csproj      EFCore_DBLibrary.csproj
EFCore_Activity0201                              EFCore_Activity0201.Program                              BuildConfiguration()
     1      using Microsoft.Extensions.Configuration;
     2      using System;
     3      using System.IO;
     4
     5      namespace EFCore_Activity0201
     6      {
                0 references
     7          class Program
     8          {
     9              private static IConfigurationRoot _configuration;
    10
                    0 references
    11              static void Main(string[] args)
    12              {
    13                  BuildConfiguration();
    14              }
    15
                    1 reference
    16              static void BuildConfiguration()
    17              {
    18                  var builder = new ConfigurationBuilder()
    19                                  .SetBasePath(Directory.GetCurrentDirectory())
    20                                  .AddJsonFile("appsettings.json", optional: true, reloadOnChange: true);
    21
    22                  _configuration = builder.Build();
    23              }
    24
    25          }
    26      }
    27
```

Figure 2-45. *The code that has been added so far is shown to ensure no mistakes exist at the current time*

This code essentially tells the solution where to find the appsettings.json file and how to load it into the solution for use in getting configuration values.

To ensure that everything is working, you should output the result of the connection string setting from the file to the console. Do this by adding the following line of code directly following the BuildConfiguration() call in the main method:

```
Console.WriteLine($"CNSTR: {_configuration.GetConnectionString(
"AdventureWorks")}");
```

Run the code to see the output and ensure you are able to get the connection string from the appsettings.json configuration file (see Figure 2-46).

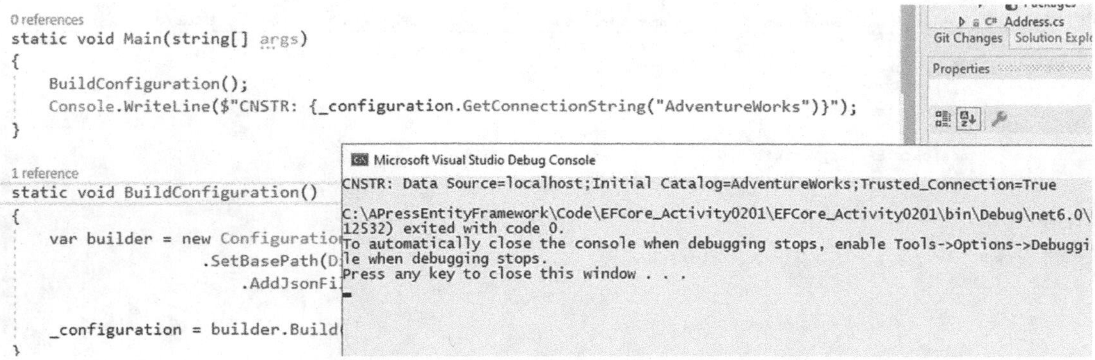

Figure 2-46. *The connection string is leveraged from the appsettings.json file*

You are now ready to complete the final task for this activity, which is to leverage the database data and show it in the console to prove that everything is working.

Task 5: Connect to the database and show results in code

With the library built and the connection information ready to go in the activity project, you can now show results using your EFCore_DbLibrary and EFCore6 from within the console application.

Step 1: Create the ability to connect and use the AdventureWorks DBContext

Add another static variable to store the options builder information. This is a DbContextOptionsBuilder object, which is a generic, with a type argument that contains the type of your generated DbContext. It is likely that this value is AdventureWorksContext. The value needs to match the DBContext value that was generated in the previous task, found in the EFCore_DBLibrary project.

Validate your context name, and then set your static variable is declared as static DbContextOptionsBuilder<AdventureWorksContext> _optionsBuilder;.

Make sure to replace the type in the less than and greater than part of that code if for some reason your context name is different. Review Figure 2-47 for more clarity.

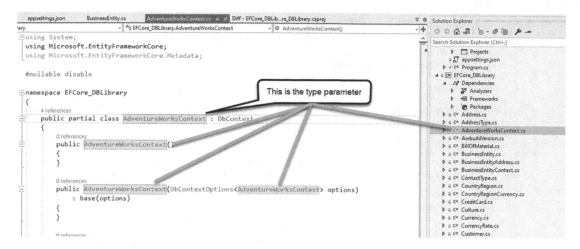

Figure 2-47. *The type parameter for your context was generated in the previous step and is the context class name from the EFCore5_DbLibrary project*

Add the variable into the program class directly under the other static variable for the `IConfigurationRoot` with the following code:

```
private static DbContextOptionsBuilder<AdventureWorksContext>
_optionsBuilder;
```

Next, you will need to add another static method to build the `DbContext` options. Add the following code in the `Program.cs` class, `Main` method after the `BuildConfiguration` method:

```
static void BuildOptions()
{
    _optionsBuilder = new DbContextOptionsBuilder<AdventureWorksContext>();
    _optionsBuilder.UseSqlServer(_configuration.GetConnectionString(
                        "AdventureWorks"));
}
```

This method sets the options builder to a new instance of the options builder on the `DBContext` and then tells the builder to use *SQL* Server with the configuration settings for the connection string as defined in the `appsettings.json` file. Take a minute to resolve any using statements, and then build the project to ensure there are no errors. Currently the code should look similar to what is shown in Figure 2-48.

```
Program.cs* + X   appsettings.json      BusinessEntity.cs      AdventureWorksContext.cs      Diff - EFCore_DBLib...re_DBLibrary.csproj
EFCore_Activity0201                          EFCore_Activity0201.Program                        BuildOptions()
   1    using EFCore_DBLibrary;
   2    using Microsoft.EntityFrameworkCore;
   3    using Microsoft.Extensions.Configuration;
   4    using System;
   5    using System.IO;
   6
   7    namespace EFCore_Activity0201
   8    {
            0 references
   9        class Program
  10        {
  11            private static IConfigurationRoot _configuration;
  12            private static DbContextOptionsBuilder<AdventureWorksContext> _optionsBuilder;
  13
            0 references
  14            static void Main(string[] args)
  15            {
  16                BuildConfiguration();
  17                Console.WriteLine($"CNSTR: {_configuration.GetConnectionString("AdventureWorks")}");
  18            }
  19
            1 reference
  20            static void BuildConfiguration()
  21            {
  22                var builder = new ConfigurationBuilder()
  23                        .SetBasePath(Directory.GetCurrentDirectory())
  24                            .AddJsonFile("appsettings.json", optional: true, reloadOnChange: true
  25
  26                _configuration = builder.Build();
  27            }
  28
            0 references
  29            static void BuildOptions()
  30            {
  31                _optionsBuilder = new DbContextOptionsBuilder<AdventureWorksContext>();
  32                _optionsBuilder.UseSqlServer(_configuration.GetConnectionString("AdventureWorks"));
  33            }
  34        }
  35    }
  36
125 %      No issues found                                                                    Ln: 33   Ch: 10   SPC   CRLF
```

Figure 2-48. *The code as it currently stands is nearly ready to get data*

Step 2: Query the data

In order to get the data, you'll need a query and an output method. Create a method called ListPeople with the code as follows:

```
static void ListPeople()
{
    using (var db = new AdventureWorksContext(_optionsBuilder.Options))
    {
        var people = db.People.OrderByDescending(x => x.LastName).Take(20).
        ToList();

        foreach (var person in people)
```

```
    {
        Console.WriteLine($"{person.FirstName} {person.LastName}");
    }
  }
}
```

The `ListPeople` method should be added in the `Program` class following the `BuildOptions` method. Also remember that any time you are concerned about placement or are having any issues with the code, feel free to review the final version of the files to see how and where I implemented the solution. Finally, don't forget to resolve any missing using statements.

Please note that depending on your reverse-engineering generation settings, you may need to use `Persons` or `People` in the name of the entity set (the entity set is directly defined in the context, if you want to search for it). Review Figure 2-49 if you are having trouble finding the `Person DbSet` property – `DbSet<Person>`. Also note that if you don't see `Person`, you can use another `DbSet`, or you may have set the options incorrectly and need to regenerate the database context in its entirety. The generated `AdventureWorksContext` with the `DbSet<Person> People` entry is shown in Figure 2-49.

Figure 2-49. *The DbSet<Person> People entry in the AdventureWorks DBContext is shown*

Step 3: Print the results to the console

You are now ready to print the results. Add the call to BuildOptions and ListPeople to the Main method right after the call to BuildConfiguration. Also remove the code that writes the connection string out to the console. Your main method should now look as follows:

```
static void Main(string[] args)
{
    BuildConfiguration();
    BuildOptions();
    ListPeople();
}
```

Run the project to see the expected output. The expected result should be similar to what is shown in Figure 2-50.

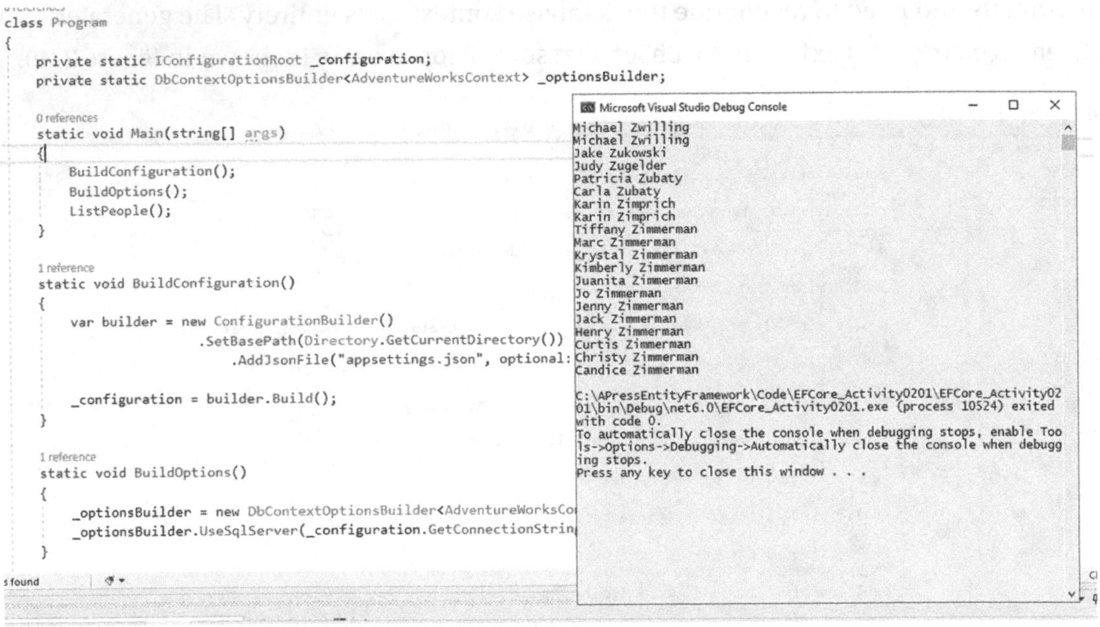

Figure 2-50. *The output of the data is working as expected, and the names of people are shown in the window*

This completes the reverse-engineering database activity with EFCore6 in .Net 6.

Activity summary

In this activity, you walked through getting a backup copy of an existing database restored on your local machine and validating that you could connect to the database using SSMS. You then created a simple console application and leveraged the EFCore6 libraries to reverse-engineer the database, which generated the data context and the model files for each of the tables in the existing database. You finished up the activity by seeing how you might store the database connection string in an `appsettings.json` file and then leveraged that file to connect to the database with the `DBContext` and displayed data from a simple database query.

Chapter summary

In this chapter, you explored the idea of working with an existing database in EFCore6. You learned about the various benefits and a few potential things to be concerned with when working with an existing database in a reverse-engineered solution.

You learned about the commands to run the scaffolding using EFCore6 to generate the database context and model, and you saw how you might be able to do a context against just part of the database, as well as had a brief practical introduction to the difference between using *Data Annotations* and the *Fluent API*.

Important takeaways

After working through this chapter, the things you should be in command of are

- The ability to reverse-engineer an existing database using EFCore6

- A basic understanding of the difference between Data Annotations and the Fluent API

Closing thoughts

Now that you've seen how to create an *EF* code library that interacts with the database for an existing database, it's time to examine how to create an *EF* code library that works in a greenfield project against a brand-new database. In the next chapter, you'll learn about using the *code-first* approach to working with databases in *EFCore6*.

CHAPTER 3

Entity Framework: Code First

In this chapter, we are going to look at what it takes to get up and running with Entity Framework using the code-first approach. As we move through this chapter, we'll learn about the code-first approach to Entity Framework, and we'll take note of some of the advantages that working with a code-first approach brings to our development process. We'll conclude this chapter by working through some activities to create a code-first Entity Framework project in *EFCore6*.

Code first doesn't always mean code first

Even though the name *code first* implies that the database doesn't exist until code is written, it is entirely possible to employ a code-first approach with an existing database, as well as in a new greenfield project. As with any development scenario, there are multiple things to consider when attempting to determine if the code-first approach is correct for your project.

When not to use the code-first approach

Sometimes when trying to determine when something is the right answer, the way to start is to determine when it is not the right answer. That being said, in most production applications that you'll encounter in today's world, there are very few reasons that code first doesn't make a lot of sense.

The primary reason to avoid using the code-first approach would relate to having a legacy system that is not capable of supporting the required tools. For example, a project that was written in any .Net Framework prior to .Net 3.5. In those projects, Entity Framework didn't exist, so using the code-first approach is simply not possible.

© Brian L. Gorman 2022

B. L. Gorman, *Practical Entity Framework Core 6*, https://doi.org/10.1007/978-1-4842-7301-2_3

Another reason that you may be forced to avoid the code-first approach could be organizational restrictions. Perhaps there are greater security concerns at play, making it against the law or highly dangerous for your company to expose so much power over the data structure to any developer through code. Perhaps your company will not allow anyone but that one mysterious *DBA* to touch the database for any reason. In both of the preceding cases, there may be some training or education that can overcome the issues, or it may truly just be impossible to work with code first in your development efforts.

Yet another reason to avoid using the code-first approach with EF could be due to personal preference. Perhaps you don't like the normalization structure required to use an ORM. You might also have another solution that you prefer for database interaction, such as F# type providers (which can be used in parallel with EF as well). Maybe you've been using NHibernate and you don't want to change something that you know already works, although you could also implement a code-first solution with NHibernate.

A final reason to avoid using code-first could simply be that there is a high risk of losing data in a mature database (this is no different than the risk that could exist from running any database script that drops columns or tables; it's not that EF code first is just going to randomly lose data). While it is entirely possible to overcome this issue with additional work (just like if you were running manual scripts), there will always be a chance that forgetting to plan for database migrations that affect data can (and perhaps will) happen. Before leaning on this argument as the reason not to choose code first in your solution, please make sure to remember that you would have to overcome the same data loss issues in traditional database development and that the solution is usually exactly the same (i.e., back up the data to a temp table, run the script, restore the data).

For example, to handle a simple data loss operation, it is entirely possible to create a migration that runs a script that backs up data from a table; then run a migration to modify the table or the database schema as intended, truncating or causing data loss; and then complete the operation with another, final migration to restore the original data. The final operation will likely massage the original data to fit the new table structure. This procedure is almost identical to how you would traditionally have to use scripts to modify the database structure. The added benefit here is everything is documented, guaranteed to run in order, testable, repeatable, and stored in source control. Therefore, as we'll examine next, the advantages of a code-first approach could even make it a better choice in this situation. It's hard to argue with testable and automated processes when the argument is a single person running manual operations including scripts that may or may not be tested.

When to use the code-first approach

If you're wondering when you should use the code-first approach going forward, simply put, the answer should be "every time you can." While there may still be some unique situations as discussed in the previous section that exist where you simply cannot use the code-first approach, any time you can use code first, you should use code first.

With *EFCore*, there is no longer an ability to create a model file like the *EDMX* files you may be used to from earlier versions of *EF*. While we can always generate a reverse-engineered database (as seen in Chapter 2), the fact remains that we will likely have a model-based approach to all development going forward. This is a very good thing for several reasons.

Code first in an existing project

Now that you've completely bought in and are ready to build out a code-first approach with Entity Framework, what do you do when you have an existing and mature project with an existing database? Since the database already exists, you could begin with a reverse-engineering approach with scaffolding to get the code models auto-generated into your solution. This approach also makes sure the *DBContext* is generated and populated for you (as you've seen in Chapter 2).

With the reverse-engineered approach, to make the project operate in a code-first manner, you would then just need to enable migrations and start working with the migrations against the data structures.

After enabling migrations, from then on, the project would be able to continue to build out new models and database objects and apply further migrations as needed using the code-first approach.

If you take this approach, just be cautious, because a great level of care would still be needed in this approach. With a database that is already mature, you need to be protected from accidental changes that might truncate data from tables or break critical performance enhancements (such as a change dropping a view or an index might do). This is especially important if other legacy line-of-business applications are relying on these original data structures for normal operation.

Code first in a new project against a mature database

Another approach that might be taken when working with Entity Framework in a code-first manner might be to develop a new application that leverages an existing database.

In a situation such as this, the development team will also need to use a great deal of caution to avoid breaking legacy functionality that might be a dependency in other existing applications. In addition to protecting schema changes from breaking the existing legacy applications, any changes made in the code-first project would also need to be propagated into any legacy applications, in order to avoid potentially causing outages or other potentially disastrous consequences for other business units in the organization. As with anything, this always comes down to your job as the developer. You must ensure that changes and upgrades that you are making will work in the legacy systems with extensive regression testing.

Code first in a new project with a new database

An entirely greenfield scenario is an obvious choice for working with a code-first approach. Even if you don't want to use migrations for some reason, at some point you will still need data models that define how to work with the various database objects in order to use *Entity Framework* and *LINQ to EF* (LINQ stands for "Language Integrated Query" and is covered in more detail later in the book).

Since a greenfield project is new and has a new database to accompany it, using code first will provide the best flexibility and ease of use from your codebase. In this case, it only makes sense to use the code-first approach.

The benefits of a well-executed code-first development effort

In case there is still any doubt about the level of success your team can achieve by using the code-first approach, I'd like to take a moment to highlight some of the greatest benefits of using the code-first approach.

Ability to get up and running quickly

Since the entire database structure is defined in code via migrations, any developer can open the project, validate that the connection string works, and run a simple command to get a local copy of the database in the exact state that it is in, in any environment where it is currently deployed. Obviously, there would still be work to do with data, as while some data would likely be created by seeding the database, there will likely still be a number of data tables that need human interaction or stubbed in test data. This is no different than the issues any project using a database would encounter, even in a traditional approach.

A complete record of database changes in source control

As mentioned earlier, using the code-first approach allows for every piece of the database to be imperatively defined in code. As the structure and needs of the database were changed, these changes were implemented in code files and a new migration was created and executed to affect the changes on the database.

In the past, you might have tried migrations and found them to be tricky. In fact, migrations before *EFCore* might have even caused you pain when multiple developers created conflicting migrations. In previous versions of EF, even if the migrations created by multiple developers didn't conflict, you were still forced to re-scaffold your migration if another developer pushed their changes first, since the overall model hash code saved in the database would be different and order of migration application mattered. With *EFCore6*, most of these pain points have been eliminated, and, although migration conflicts can still happen, they are mainly the result of conflicting changes to the same database objects and not just because two or more developers are both modifying the database schema.

Since our code is defined directly within the project in this approach, the files and changes are all tracked in source control. There is no longer any need to create a database project with a bunch of generated and non-generated scripts, or worse, manually put your scripts into source control and hope developers keep them up to date.

Having the changes in source control is a very important advantage and should not be taken lightly. If drives and/or backups fail, there is always a potential of losing your database entirely. Even if you don't lose your database, when a database failure happens, you would likely still lose all the transactions that had been run since the previous backup. Although both database and backup failure combined at the same time is rare, and may never happen, if it did, and you still have your project code, migrations could be run to restore the structure and seed initial data from the database. To be practical, this feature is more useful for quickly establishing the application data on your developers' machines. As soon as one developer's changes make it into your developer source branch, other developers can update their own local database by pulling the changes and running a couple of quick commands, such as `update-database`. This is highly advantageous when it comes to avoiding conflicts and bugs.

Agility when needing to revert to a previous state

With the code being in source control, EF migrations also have the added benefit that, when written correctly, can allow for automation to easily roll back a change against the database. Rolling back a change can be a destructive event that loses data, but this is also something that is rarely, if ever, done in production. In fact, there is a camp that exists where some users don't use the migration rollbacks at all. The theory in that camp is that it is better to just add another migration to move the database back by going in a forward direction. Either way, whether you allow rollbacks or essentially do revert migrations, you're still going to need to plan for how the data is affected in either scenario.

With the ability to roll back a migration, however, it is extremely easy to set a local developer database to match the exact state a database was in at any point of development. For example, it is easy to roll back the database to the state in time when a bug was introduced to your codebase or a patch was released. This allows for effectively coding against the database as it was at that time, making it easier and safer to release a common modification across all official releases of your project or to patch a bug fix.

Another advantage of the migrations is the fact that changes can be reverted at will. For example, if a feature is released and then eventually eliminated, migrations allow the feature to continue to exist at a patch level but to be removed from future development by adding further migrations that essentially revert the changes.

Having a complete history of database changes and the ability to easily reset the database to the state it needs to be for development of a patch or testing of a bug is all managed by the code that is generated and/or modified in the specific migrations. Therefore, as a developer, you don't have to spend your time trying to remember which scripts to run and test to make sure your tables and other object structures are correct for the patch, fix, or feature on which you are working.

Shifting from declarative to imperative database programming

Another important concept with the use of code-first database development is that we are making a conscious transition to *imperative* database programming and saying goodbye to *declarative* programming around our database.

Imperative programming is the concept that as developers, we are directly defining what should happen, thereby locking in the details of the implementation, leaving little to interpretation or fluctuation of implementation.

Declarative programming is just getting to an end result, regardless of how you get there. In the declarative paradigm, often the details of the implementation are not as clear and/or not as scrutinized, as long as the desired end result is achieved.

For example, a declarative approach to development around the database might look something like you know there is a table that holds some data that was defined somewhere. You could query that data and perhaps connect to another table or maybe a view to build out a result set, but as long as the data shows up, it is not important how you got it to render. Also, you can sort of count on some fields being in the table for the important information like name, age, date of birth, email, and maybe even a phone number, but it may have changed so you better double-check before counting on that data. If the data isn't there, or has changed, maybe you can ask to store that important information somewhere and someone can build out the database scripts so that you can get it eventually.

An imperative approach is more defined, and code first is most definitely imperative by nature. Every database structure is exactly modeled in code. This means you know exactly what tables exist and what fields exist on those tables. In fact, you can easily create an instance of a model that holds exactly the correct data, with exactly the correct limitations that exist in the database, including type and any other constraints like length or range. Furthermore, relationships are directly defined, so you can be certain that a foreign key exists in each related table and you can easily query and populate related data.

For the most part, Entity Framework has always been somewhat imperative, with well-defined structures in place. However, the code-first approach has solidified the imperative approach with the ability to force the database to conform to specific requirements rather than relying on things to potentially be implemented correctly in the database.

It's time to see code-first database programming in action

Now that you've seen some of the advantages and reasons behind using a code-first approach, it's time to dive in with a couple of activities. These activities will help you to learn more about how the code-first approach works and also see the power that it gives you to work with this approach.

One thing you will not see here is what it would take to put code first into an existing project that is mature (i.e., a legacy application that has ADO.Net or a previous version of EF without a code-first approach). The overall approach in that case would be the same as if using a code-first approach against an existing database (as shown in the first activity). In the legacy system, code would then need to be updated to start working against EF for new and maintenance development, and the original connections and code (such as *ADO. Net* implementation) would also remain in place, creating a sort of hybrid approach.

In the next two activities, you'll look at using a code-first approach in a new greenfield project in *EFCore6*. You'll also use *EFCore6* to create a new implementation against a mature database.

A final thought before diving into the activities

I want to take a final moment before diving into some coding activities to make sure a couple of other things are clear. We're about to learn how to leverage Entity Framework against an existing and a new database in *EFCore6*.

Please note that in order to keep the focus on the actual implementation and use of Entity Framework, I've chosen to make the startup projects work as console applications throughout this book. This simplistic approach is not likely to be how your project will work in the real world. However, learning to do things like making web controllers and displaying data on views, or rendering information to Xamarin forms, or other similar practical activities is outside of the scope of this book. It is my belief that if you are a web developer or a Xamarin developer or a UWP or WPF developer, you already have the skills you need in those arenas (or you will likely have resources available to learn them at your organization). Therefore, the choice to restrict the GUI portion of these activities to a minimal implementation is a conscious choice and is done to allow focus on the EF technology while not muddying the water with the specifics of desktop, device, or web development.

With that choice comes a small price, however, which I feel is important to address. If you are building out solutions in WPF, UWP, Xamarin, and/or ASP.Net MVC, it is highly likely that those project templates have tools in place to scaffold out an implementation directly to Entity Framework for you, so going through the setup and working in a new manner will likely not be necessary in many of these cases. It is far more likely that you will encounter projects where EF is already baked in or it is configured for you by the project templates or your organization's technical architect. Even so, learning how to build out a solution from the ground up will position you to rearchitect your solutions to make a more robust implementation, as well as expose you to the moving pieces that you need to understand in order to have a more solid foundation in EF. By the end of these activities, you'll likely have everything you need to understand how to build out an *EFCore6* code-first solution into any new .Net 6 project, whether you are using an existing or a new database.

Activity 3-1: Creating a new code-first project against an existing database in EFCore6

In this first activity, you're going to go through building out an *EFCore* code-first implementation against an existing database. This will give us the opportunity to see what it might be like to spin up a new project in a mature business environment against a mature database that likely has other line-of-business applications working against it.

Use the starter files or your project from Chapter 2

To begin, you're going to pick up where you left off at the end of Chapter 2, where you had built out a reverse-engineered database project against the *AdventureWorks* database, using Entity Framework Core.

If for some reason you do not have these files or you simply want a fresh start, the code resources for this book include a starter zip file package for this activity called EFCore_Activity03-1_StarterFiles.

Another important thing to note is that this activity assumes you have restored a local copy of the *AdventureWorks* database to your local machine. If you have not done that previously, you should go back to Activity 2-1 at the end of Chapter 2 and ensure that you've completed the steps to get the *AdventureWorks* database restored on your machine.

Always remember, if you use one of the provided sets of files (starter or final), then you should double-check to ensure the connection string is set correctly in the `appsettings.json` file.

I did modify the implementation from the final version at the end of Chapter 2, Activity 2-1, a bit. The change allows the use of a singleton class for the configuration builder. This required a simple change to add a new class for `ConfigurationSingletonBuilder` and using a singleton pattern to get the configuration from the `appsettings.json` file and then just calling to get the configuration from the singleton in the `BuildOptions` method of the `Program` file. If you would like more clarity on this, review the starter files for `EFCore_Activity0301`.

An additional change I made is that I named my project for the chapter as earlier rather than keeping the `Activity0201` project name. Other than those two changes, everything else in the `Activity0301` project is the same as where you landed at the end of Chapter 2, Activity 2-1. Always remember that, at any point, you can use the starter files or you can also review and/or leverage the final files `EFCore_Activity03-1_FinalFiles` as a reference for clarity while working through the activities in this book.

At this point, I'm assuming you are well versed in getting started with Visual Studio and getting a project open or up and running, so you're going to dive right in on the activity.

Moving the builder code to a singleton is not a necessary task; I've simply done this to get the code out of the way of our learning. Once again, if you want to see how to implement, you can review the implementation in the starter files `EFCore_Activity03-1_StarterFiles`.

Task 1: Getting started with the activity

In this first task, you will get set up to work through the activity, including getting the project up and running and setting the project into a mode that will allow it to work as a code-first project that runs migrations. You will also take a quick look at the database to make a note of the state of the database prior to this activity.

Step 1: Getting the project started for the activity

To begin, review the project structure. The base project should look similar to what is shown here in Figure 3-1.

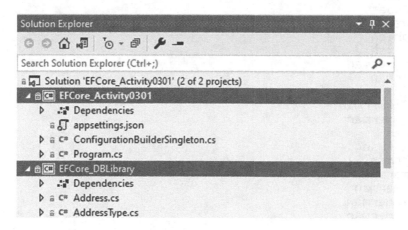

Figure 3-1. *The Activity 3-1 starter project is up and ready to go*

Note that it is expected that the solution would have two projects, EFCore_ Activity0301 (or EFCore_Activity0201 if you are using the code from Activity 2-1) and EFCore_DbLibrary. As stated, this version has additionally moved the configuration builder into a singleton as a purely cosmetic choice and not a functional choice for the purposes of learning.

Once you have opened the project and validated the structure, run the project to confirm that everything is working as expected. The output will be a list of names of people, as was the output at the end of the previous chapter (see Figure 3-2).

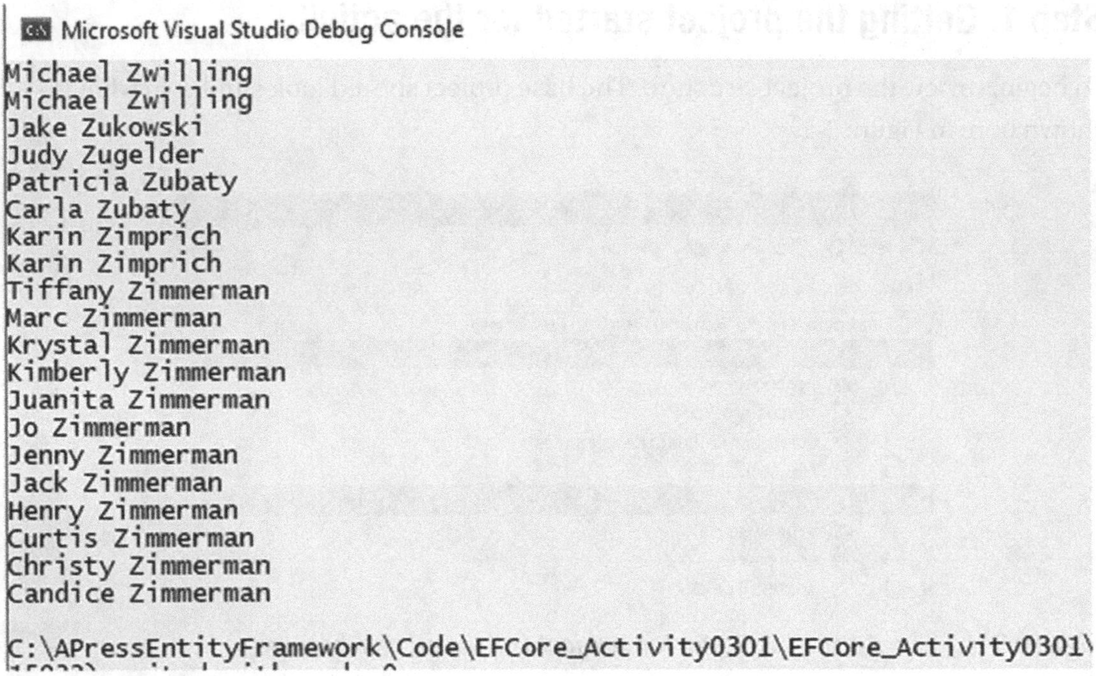

```
[C#] Microsoft Visual Studio Debug Console
Michael Zwilling
Michael Zwilling
Jake Zukowski
Judy Zugelder
Patricia Zubaty
Carla Zubaty
Karin Zimprich
Karin Zimprich
Tiffany Zimmerman
Marc Zimmerman
Krystal Zimmerman
Kimberly Zimmerman
Juanita Zimmerman
Jo Zimmerman
Jenny Zimmerman
Jack Zimmerman
Henry Zimmerman
Curtis Zimmerman
Christy Zimmerman
Candice Zimmerman

C:\APressEntityFramework\Code\EFCore_Activity0301\EFCore_Activity0301\
```

Figure 3-2. *The expected output for the project at the initial run is shown*

Step 2: Ensure that the project is ready to work with EFCore5

In this step, you will make sure that the project is ready to run migrations. With the project up and running, you've already proven that the project can leverage EFCore6 and use the reverse-engineered AdventureWorksContext to interact with the database. The next thing you need to do is ensure that migrations can be used.

To begin, validate that all of the correct NuGet packages are installed. Navigate to Tools ➤ NuGet Package Manager ➤ Manage NuGet Packages for Solution, and then select the Installed tab. Your project should include packages similar to those shown in Figure 3-3 (v6.x.x – using the latest versions).

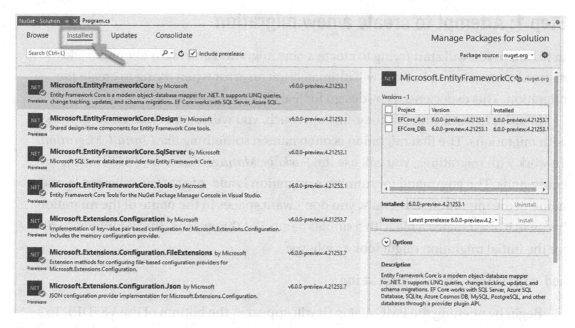

Figure 3-3. *The NuGet packages are listed for the activity project using the Manage NuGet Packages for Solution option*

Validate that at minimum you have all of the following packages on the EFCore_ Activity project:

- `Microsoft.EntityFrameworkCore`

- `Microsoft.EntityFrameworkCore.Design`

- `Microsoft.EntityFrameworkCore.SqlServer`

- `Microsoft.EntityFrameworkCore.Tools`

You will have the extensions as well, but the `EFCore` packages are critical for the remainder of this activity.

Task 2: Creating and reviewing the initial migration

In this task, you will create and review the initial migration. This will help you to learn the command necessary to create a migration and to understand how migrations work in a code-first approach to database development.

Step 1: Attempt to create a new migration

In this step, you will start trying to create a new migration and learn about the add-migration command, but you will ultimately get an error when trying to create the migration. This experience is by design for learning purposes.

In order to work with the code-first approach, you will need to learn how to work with migrations. The first migration is often named something like "*Initial_Migration.*" To work with migrations, you will use the *Package Manager Console (PMC)* to run commands. The command for running a migration is add-migration followed by the name of the migration. Generally, you don't want spaces in the name of the migration because it also creates a file with a similar name. For that reason, the command to run for the initial migration might look as follows:

add-migration Initial_Migration

Begin by opening the PMC dialog (it will appear at the bottom of the VS IDE). To open the PMC, use the menu Tools ➤ NuGet Package Manager ➤ Package Manager Console. It is imperative that you select the project that contains your DBContext to run commands. By default, the EFCore_Activity project is likely selected, so you'll need to select the DBLibrary project. If you don't, running the command to add the migration will create an error. With the EFCore_Activity0301 project selected (the incorrect project), at the prompt in the PMC, type the command as shown: add-migration Initial_Migration. The resulting error is shown in Figure 3-4.

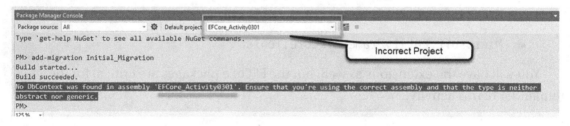

Figure 3-4. *If the wrong project is selected, the PMC will output an error when trying to run code-first migration commands*

The resulting error tells you everything you need to know:

No DbContext was found in assembly 'EFCore_Activity0301.' Ensure that you're using the correct assembly and that the type is neither abstract nor generic.

Step 2: Create the initial migration

In this step, you will create the initial migration using the `add-migration` command in the PMC.

To remedy the error from the previous step, select the correct project in the dropdown list at the top center of the PMC next to `Default project:`, which is the `EFCore_DbLibrary` project in the dropdown. With the correct project selected, run `add-migration` command again (you can easily get the commands you have previously run by hitting the up arrow). The resulting output is shown in Figure 3-5.

```
4    namespace EFCore_DBLibrary.Migrations
5    {
         1 reference
6        public partial class Initial_Migration : Migration
7        {
             0 references
8            protected override void Up(MigrationBuilder migrationBuilder)
9            {
10               migrationBuilder.EnsureSchema(
11                   name: "Person");
12
13               migrationBuilder.EnsureSchema(
14                   name: "Production");
15
16               migrationBuilder.EnsureSchema(
17                   name: "Sales");
18
19               migrationBuilder.EnsureSchema(
20                   name: "HumanResources");
21
22               migrationBuilder.EnsureSchema(
23                   name: "Purchasing");
24
25               migrationBuilder.CreateTable(
```

125 %   ● No issues found   Ln: 1   Ch: 1   SPC   CRLF

Package Manager Console

Package source: All   ⚙ Default project: EFCore_DBLibrary

```
PM> add-migration Initial_Migration
Build started...
Build succeeded.
The property 'SystemInformationId' on entity type 'AwbuildVersion' is of type 'byte', but is set up to use a SQL Server identity column;
this requires that values starting at 255 and counting down will be used for temporary key values. A temporary key value is needed for
every entity inserted in a single call to 'SaveChanges'. Care must be taken that these values do not collide with real key values.
The property 'ShiftId' on entity type 'Shift' is of type 'byte', but is set up to use a SQL Server identity column; this requires that
values starting at 255 and counting down will be used for temporary key values. A temporary key value is needed for every entity inserted
in a single call to 'SaveChanges'. Care must be taken that these values do not collide with real key values.
To undo this action, use Remove-Migration.
PM>
```

125 %

Figure 3-5. *The command succeeds when the correct project is selected*

Now the initial migration is created as expected. Note that in the Solution Explorer a file with the timestamp and datestamp and the name of the migration as you named it was created, shown here in Figure 3-6 (your timestamp/datestamp will obviously be different).

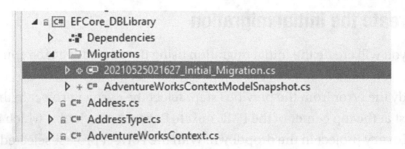

Figure 3-6. *The Initial Migration file YYYYMMDDHHMMSS_migration_name was created when the command was executed successfully*

Task 3: Comment out the initial migration, run the update, and review the database

In this task, you will first comment out the initial migration since your database is actually in place already. You will then learn what it takes to apply a migration and run the command to get your initial migration (which is commented out) applied to the database. You will finish this step with a review of the database to see what has changed.

Step 1: Review the initial migration and then comment out the Up method and delete the code in the Down method

Click the migration file that was generated in the previous task. You will see that there are a number of commands in the migration. This tells you a couple of things right away.

The most important thing to note is that you can do more than one command in a single migration. Additionally, you can do commands that ensure schemas, create tables, alter tables, create and alter indexes, stored procedures, or just run raw scripts. You will get a chance to see all of this in future exercises throughout the book.

The second thing this will point out is that no data is migrated. This migration is only for the database schema, and no data is created in the migration. You can create data in the migration by running a raw script, but there is a better way to seed data, which will also be covered later in the book.

In a closer look at the migration, everything that is needed to create the database schema is scripted out in the first method, which is the Up method. The Up method will always be where the code exists to run the migration in the forward direction.

At the start of the initial migration, in the Up method, commands like

```
migrationBuilder.EnsureSchema(
                name: "Person");
```

use the `migrationBuilder` object (the executor) to run a command that ensures the schema exists for `Person` in this case.

If you scroll down a bit, another command states

```
migrationBuilder.CreateTable(
                name: "AddressType",
                schema: "Person",
                columns: table => new
                {
```

This command clearly creates the `AddressType` table, and more of the command that is not shown here creates the columns, constraints, and other pertinent table information.

Later in the migration, statements begin to create indexes. Use `Ctrl+Shift+F` to find the text "`migrationBuilder.CreateIndex`". Statements to create a new index look like this one:

```
migrationBuilder.CreateIndex(
                name: "AK_Address_rowguid",
                schema: "Person",
                table: "Address",
                column: "rowguid",
                unique: true);
```

Once you get far enough down, you'll see that there is also a `Down` method. In the `Down` method, the commands that are done in the Up method are reverted. The `Down` method is what is executed when you roll a migration back, reverting the objects to their state as they were prior to this migration.

As you can see, in the `Down` method, a number of `Drop` statements exist. This would be obviously bad for an existing database. Because this first migration is being run against an existing database, it is highly unlikely the Down method would ever need to be run, and even more likely that running it would create a major issue if it ran in production. Therefore, the very first thing you should do is delete all the code in the `Down` method. This also lets you know that just because code was generated doesn't always mean you have to keep it in order for things to work. In fact, there are some teams that never run the Down method, and they likely just delete all of this generated code in every migration to avoid any potential issues. While I don't personally recommend this approach, the argument can be made that a roll-forward-for-revert approach might be the correct way to go in your organization.

Take a minute now to delete the code in the Down method and add a comment such as

```
//Down method should likely never be run on an existing database for the
first migration.
```

The expected code is shown in Figure 3-7.

```
2793            migrationBuilder.CreateIndex(
2794                name: "IX_WorkOrderRouting_ProductID",
2795                schema: "Production",
2796                table: "WorkOrderRouting",
2797                column: "ProductID");
2798        }
2799
         0 references
2800        protected override void Down(MigrationBuilder migrationBuilder)
2801        {
2802            //Down method should likely never be run on an existing database for the first migration.
2803        }
2804    }
2805 }
2806
```

Figure 3-7. *The generated code in the Down method for the initial migration is deleted and replaced with a comment*

Now that you have a migration ready to go, you might be tempted to jump right in and run the migration. This would be a very big mistake, as the initial migration scaffolded has a lot of tables that it is planning to create which already exist in your database. In fact, with this current setup, the migration would likely fail if you run it since the tables already exist.

Remember the earlier discussion of the pros and cons of using the code-first approach? This is one of the very small downsides. Right now, you have no migrations applied in the database, so the migrations builder thinks you need to create all the tables. However, your database already has all the tables, so you need to make sure that the migration doesn't try to recreate them.

So, what should you do next? There are a couple of approaches you can take. One approach would be to comment out everything in the Up method and apply the migration with the update-database command.

This approach will work, but it begs the question about what the next developer would do, and the developer after that, especially if they have a fresh start with no copy of the existing database on their machine.

Since your database already exists, there should not be a reason that you need to generate the tables as is. You can likely assume other developers would be able to get a backup to restore to their machine as well. Therefore, go ahead and comment out the code in the *Up* method.

Another potential solution would be to make the call idempotent, and only run the create table and index statements if the table or index doesn't already exist.

An idempotent operation is an operation that can be executed multiple times, and, as long as the same input conditions exist, the output will always be the same.

Making this first migration idempotent would not be trivial, as every object would need to be wrapped in IF NOT EXISTS statements, and the migration would then only run the CREATE statements when the objects do not exist. Not to say that you couldn't do this, and you may actually want to do this in the real world. For this activity, you can just assume that like you did previously, your team members will also be restoring a backup. For that reason, you can safely just comment out the code in the Up method.

Go ahead and comment out the code in the Up method now. The result will be an Up method that is entirely commented out and a Down method with a comment and no code. Essentially the first migration is not doing anything as it stands, and that is what you want in this case.

Step 2: Run the update

Even though the migration is going to do nothing, it is imperative that you run the update to get the system into a state that recognizes that this migration has been applied. Before running the update, use SSMS to take a quick look at your current copy of AdventureWorks and the tables that exist. Figure 3-8 shows the expected current state of the database.

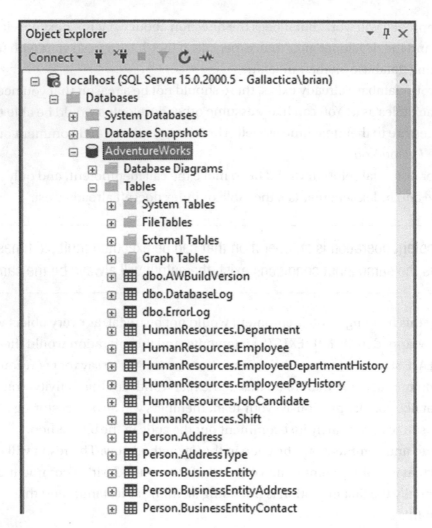

Figure 3-8. *The current local AdventureWorks database is shown. There is currently no table for migrations in the database*

The main thing to note is that there is currently no table that is tracking migrations. This is to be expected.

In SSMS, run the following query:

```
SELECT *
  FROM [AdventureWorks].[dbo].[__EFMigrationsHistory]
```

The result of running this query will be an error that says Invalid object name 'AdventureWorks.dbo.__EFMigrationsHistory'.

Return to the VS IDE and run the command update-database in the PMC. This will trigger the migrations to run. Running of the command and the expected result are shown in Figure 3-9.

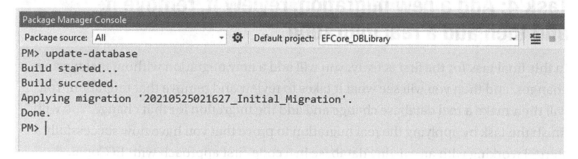

Figure 3-9. *Running the update-database command works as expected, and the database migration is completed successfully*

There is no need to fear the update-database command right now. If this operation goes sideways, you can restore from backup. That being said, please do not run the update-database command against a production database until you are certain the results you want will be achieved.

Return to SSMS and run the query again. This time you should see a result that shows the name of the migration that has been applied. This local table is how your database will know which migrations have been applied and which migrations have not been applied (see Figure 3-10).

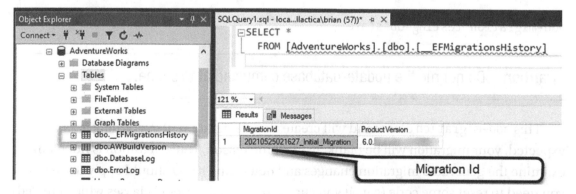

Figure 3-10. *The migration has been applied and the table for migrations now exists*

Note also that the product version is shown for the update. Your version will be newer than what is shown in the image, and that is to be expected.

Task 4: Add a new migration, review it, remove it, and then add a real migration

In this final task for the first activity, you will add a new migration without making any changes, and then you will see what it takes to review and remove that migration. You will then make a real database change and add the migration for that change. You will finish the task by applying the real migration to prove that you have now successfully started working with an existing database in a code-first approach with EFCore6.

Step 1: Add a new migration without making any changes, review it, and remove it

Whenever you have created code-first database schema changes, you will need to migrate the database. However, if no changes are present, creating a new migration will generate a blank migration.

This is exactly how you want it to be. You want to know that your current database is up to date and that there are no pending changes. In fact, if you have pending changes that don't map and try to add a new migration, you will get an error that you first need to resolve the pending changes.

In this step, you are going to create a new migration to ensure that the database is up to date and that there are no pending changes.

Run the command as follows:

```
add-migration testing-db-state
```

Caution   Do not run the update-database command at this time.

This `add-migration` command will create a new migration. If everything is as expected, your migration will be blank. If, for some reason, your migration is not blank, examine the generated migration changes and determine if you should apply them or if you need to reset some code (e.g., if you changed one of the model classes which created a column change or added a class that would trigger a table change).

The expected result is shown in Figure 3-11.

Figure 3-11. *The generated migration is blank since there are no pending changes*

Since there are no pending changes, it is OK to just remove this migration. Notice that there is a statement in the PMC that says *"To undo this action, use Remove-Migration."* That is exactly what you should do. In this case, with no pending changes, just remove the migration.

Please be aware that once a migration is applied using the update-database statement, you cannot simply remove it in EFCore6. If you've applied a migration, you must first change the database by rolling your changes back using the syntax `update-database -migration <migration_id_here>` (see Step 3).

Run the command `remove-migration`, which will remove the migration that you have not applied. Figure 3-12 shows the result of running the remove-migration command, which effectively reverts and removes the migration.

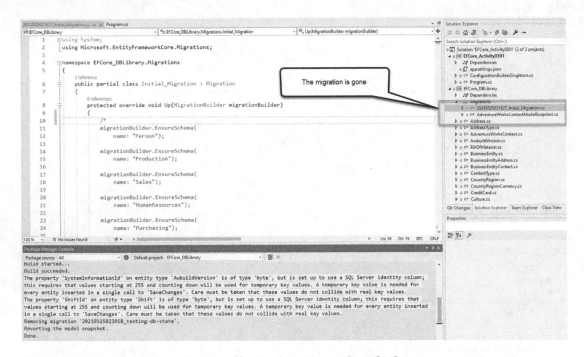

Figure 3-12.   *The migration is effectively removed with the remove-migration command*

Step 2: Make a code change, and then add a new migration and update the database

Next, you will make a simple code change that will trigger the need for a migration, and then you will add and run the migration.

Begin by creating a new object that will serve as a table in the database. In the `EFCore_DbLibrary` project, create a new class called `ImprovementPlan` in a code or class file named `ImprovementPlan.cs`. You won't be using this in the solution, but imagine a scenario where you needed to link an employee with an improvement plan, and the plan would eventually have subclasses that model metrics that could be chosen as part of the improvement plan.

In this case, you will start with a simple class to model the name of the improvement plan and the employee id that the plan will be assigned to, with a start and end date to the plan. To do this, in the new class just added, add the following code:

```
public class ImprovementPlan
{
    [Key]
    [ForeignKey("Employee")]
    public int BusinessEntityId { get; set; }
    public virtual Employee Employee { get; set; }

    [Required]
    public DateTime PlanStart { get; set; }
    public DateTime PlanComplete => PlanStart.AddDays(90);
}
```

For clarity, the complete file is shown in Figure 3-13.

```
ImprovementPlan.cs*  ⊕ ✕  20210525021627_Initial_Migration.cs        Program.cs
C# EFCore_DBLibrary                              ▾  ⚙ EFCore_DBLibrary.ImprovementPlan                ▾

     1       ⊟using System;
     2        │using System.Collections.Generic;
     3        │using System.ComponentModel.DataAnnotations;
     4        │using System.ComponentModel.DataAnnotations.Schema;
     5        │using System.Linq;
     6        │using System.Text;
     7        │using System.Threading.Tasks;
     8
     9       ⊟namespace EFCore_DBLibrary
    10        {
              0 references
    11       ⊟    public class ImprovementPlan
    12            {
    13                [Key]
    14                [ForeignKey("Employee")]
                    0 references
    15                public int BusinessEntityId { get; set; }
                    0 references
    16                public virtual Employee Employee { get; set; }
    17
    18                [Required]
                    1 reference
    19                public DateTime PlanStart { get; set; }
                    0 references
    20                public DateTime PlanComplete => PlanStart.AddDays(90);
    21            }
    22

125 %  ▾    ⊘ No issues found      | ⌀ ▾
```

Figure 3-13. *The ImprovementPlan class is ready to be migrated to the database as a new table*

After adding the code, you need to also add the new model to the DBContext. In the AdventureWorksContext, add the following code before the OnConfiguring method (use search to find "OnConfiguring"):

```
public virtual DbSet<ImprovementPlan> ImprovementPlans {get;set;}
```

With the code in place, return to the PMC and run the command add-migration create_improvement_plans.

Running this command results in a new migration, as shown in Figure 3-14.

```
namespace EFCore_DBLibrary.Migrations
{
    1 reference
    public partial class create_improvement_plans : Migration
    {
        1 reference
        protected override void Up(MigrationBuilder migrationBuilder)
        {
            migrationBuilder.CreateTable(
                name: "ImprovementPlans",
                columns: table => new
                {
                    BusinessEntityId = table.Column<int>(type: "int", nullable: false),
                    PlanStart = table.Column<DateTime>(type: "datetime2", nullable: false)
                },
                constraints: table =>
                {
                    table.PrimaryKey("PK_ImprovementPlans", x => x.BusinessEntityId);
                    table.ForeignKey(
                        name: "FK_ImprovementPlans_Employee_BusinessEntityId",
                        column: x => x.BusinessEntityId,
                        principalSchema: "HumanResources",
                        principalTable: "Employee",
                        principalColumn: "BusinessEntityID",
```

Figure 3-14. *A migration is created for the new ImprovementPlans table to be added to the existing database*

Next, run the `update-database` command to apply the migration. When the command is completed and the migration is applied, examine the database to see the new table (see Figure 3-15). The table will contain the columns and relations as expected. Note that you will likely have to refresh your database in SSMS to see the new table.

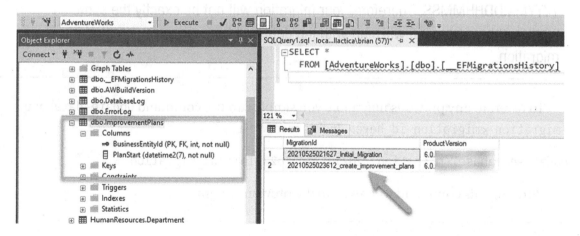

Figure 3-15. *The ImprovementPlans table is created in the database after the migration is applied*

This operation has further proven that you have correctly set the existing database to work in a code-first approach.

Step 3: Roll back the changes and remove the migration, and then remove the code change

To finish up the activity, you will revert the migration that you just ran and then remove the new model file and reset the AdventureWorksContext so that there are no pending changes in the event that future changes and migrations are needed on this database.

Even though you were able to set the new entity and use it, you really don't want this entity in your database, so you need to remove it. This also simulates any situation where you created a change and want to revert it.

Since the change was already applied, you cannot simply run the remove-migration command, as that will not work once a migration is applied in the database. The first thing you need to do is revert to a previous migration. To do this, find the last valid migration you want to keep, which, in this case, should be something like the initial_migration that was applied earlier. You will need the full name of the migration as it is stored in the database. Looking back at Figure 3-15, the migration name of the previous migration is 20210525021627_Initial_Migration.

Note   The migration starts with a date timestamp in the format YYYYMMDDHHMMSS. Therefore, your migration will not be exactly the same as what is shown here but will start with the date and time when you created the migration.

To revert to any previous migration, you simply run the command update-database -migration <migration_id_here>. In this case:

```
update-database -migration  20210525021627_Initial_Migration
```

Running this command will revert to the previous migration.

You can revert more than one migration at a time. This can be useful if you have multiple migrations to revert, which would execute each of the Down methods in sequence. If there are errors, the operation would abort when an error is encountered.

Figure 3-16 shows the command as it was executed.

```
Package Manager Console
Package source:  All                       ▼  ⚙  |  Default project:  EFCore_DBLibrary
Applying migration '20210525023612_create_improvement_plans'.
Done.
PM> update-database -migration 20210525021627_Initial_Migration
Build started...
Build succeeded.
Reverting migration '20210525023612_create_improvement_plans'.
Done.
PM>
```

Figure 3-16. *The update-database -migration <target> command will revert any number of migrations. The revert to the initial migration is shown here*

With the migration now successfully reverted, examine your database to ensure the table is gone and the migration table no longer lists the migration you created earlier. When you are satisfied that the migration is successfully reverted, run the command `remove-migration` to now remove the migration that you created earlier, as shown in Figure 3-17.

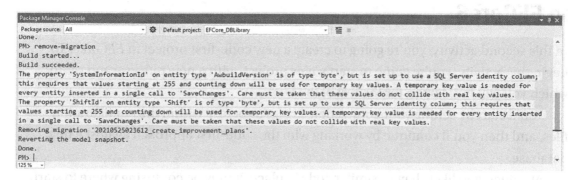

Figure 3-17. *The migration that is no longer applied after being reverted can now be safely removed*

You have now learned how to work with migrations and roll back any changes when there is an issue with the migration or the migration was not actually desired.

To clean up your solution, delete the `ImprovementPlan` class and also remember to remove the line of code `DbSet<ImprovementPlan> ImprovementPlans { get; set; }` from the `AdventureWorksContext`. Clean and build your project to ensure there are no lingering errors. If you want to go the extra mile, add a new migration and ensure no code is generated in the `Up` and/or `Down` methods, and then just remove the migration.

Activity 3-1 summary

In this activity, you learned how to create a new project that uses a legacy (existing) database and then sets the project to use the code-first approach to changes. You completed the first part by creating an initial migration and essentially making it do nothing so that future migrations would not keep trying to create the database tables that already exist and so that running the rollback would never accidentally drop all the tables in the existing database.

You then learned how to create and add a new entity to the DBContext so that it would create a new table in the database using a migration. You then added the migration and applied it, reviewed the database change, and then finally reverted the change and cleaned up the code. In this manner, you've quickly learned how to work with code-first migrations in the forward and backward direction, and you also further proved that you can do this against an existing legacy database.

Activity 3-2: Creating a new code-first project in EFCore6

In this second activity, you're going to create a new code-first project in *EFCore6*. To begin this activity, you're going to start a new project, with a new purpose and setup, which you will build upon for the rest of the book.

You'll start by setting your connection strings as before within the configuration files, and then you'll continue by working with the code-first approach against a new database.

Although you likely have a similar code in place, it may be confusing where to start with this activity. For this reason, I recommend that you simply start with the files from the project EFCore6_Activity03-2_StarterFiles which has been pre-configured with a code library and startup console project.

Feel free to update the *EFCore6* packages to the latest version at the time you are starting this project using the Manage NuGet Packages for Solution dialog, as it is likely that a new version will be released by the time you are working through this activity.

Task 1: Begin a new project for managing inventory

In this activity, you're going to build a simple database that will ultimately grow to manage inventory. You will build upon this project throughout the rest of this book. Inventory items could be any object you have around your house, such as a bunch of movies, books, or board games, and can also include items like computers, cameras, or clothing items.

If you are using the starter files, skip to Task 2 at this point. Task 1 is going to quickly show how to build the Inventory project starter files from the ground up. This will be the last time this will be demonstrated but is a technique you might choose to use in future activities.

Step 1: Set up a new project

To begin from scratch, create a new .Net Core console project and name the project `EFCore_Activity0302`.

Start by opening Visual Studio and selecting `Create a new project`. When the dialog opens, choose a .Net Core console application, name it appropriately, and save in a location that makes it easy for you to find it later. Figure 3-18 shows a similar result as to what your new project configuration dialog should likely show, with the exception of the folder location where you are storing your files.

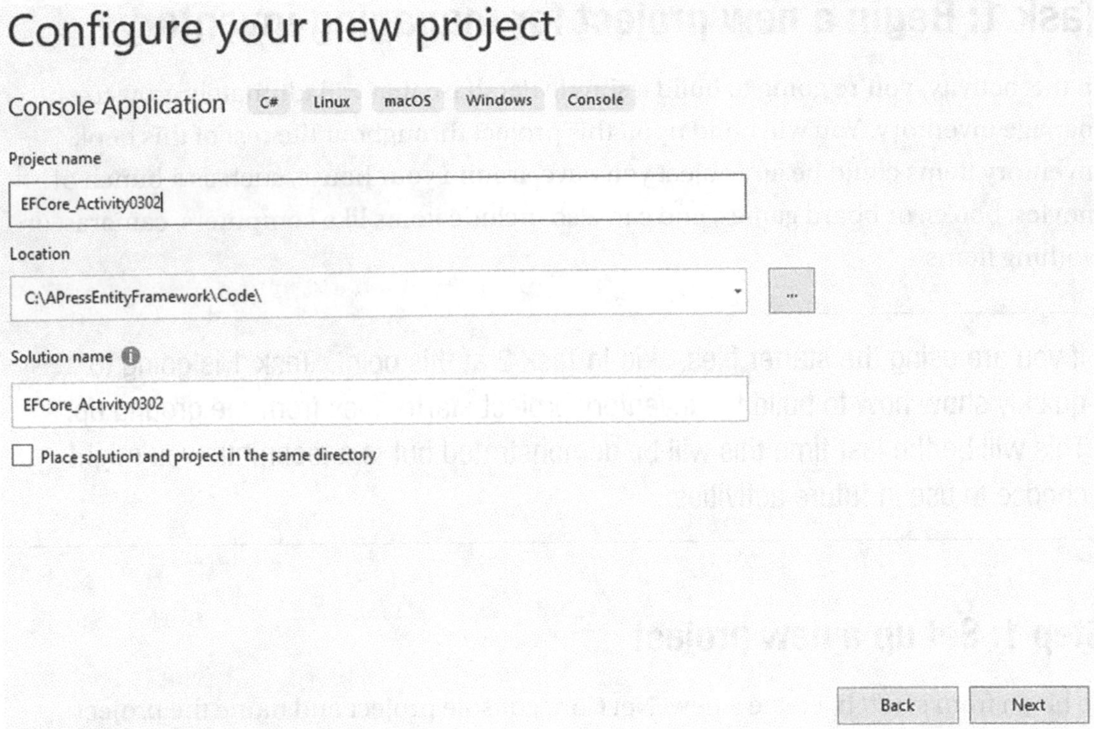

Configure your new project

Console Application   C#   Linux   macOS   Windows   Console

Project name

EFCore_Activity0302|

Location

C:\APressEntityFramework\Code\

Solution name ⓘ

EFCore_Activity0302

☐ Place solution and project in the same directory

| Back | | Next |

Figure 3-18.   *The Configure your new project dialog is shown, as the new .Net Core console project is being created*

After the project is created, open the project properties by right-clicking the project name. When the project properties open, change the Target Framework to .NET 6.0 (or ensure that the target is .NET 6.0 if this is preset for you; see Figure 3-19).

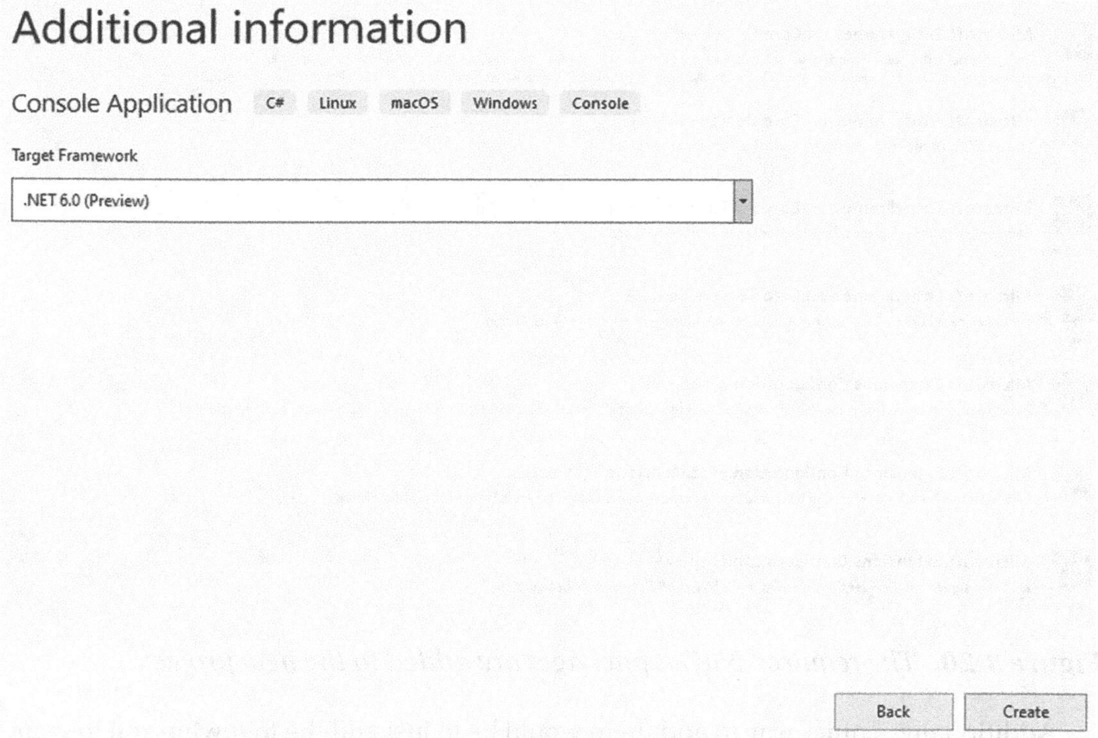

Additional information

Console Application   C#   Linux   macOS   Windows   Console

Target Framework

```
.NET 6.0 (Preview)                                                    ▾
```

Back   Create

Figure 3-19. *The Target Framework is set to .NET 6.0*

After setting the framework to .Net 6, you will need to bring in the following NuGet packages that will be used in the solution:

- Microsoft.Extensions.Configuration

- Microsoft.Extensions.Configuration.FileExtensions

- Microsoft.Extensions.Configuration.Json

- Microsoft.EntityFrameworkCore

- Microsoft.EntityFrameworkCore.Design

- Microsoft.EntityFrameworkCore.SqlServer

- Microsoft.EntityFrameworkCore.Tools

All of these packages can be easily found in the `Manage NuGet Packages for Solution` dialog (review Figure 3-20).

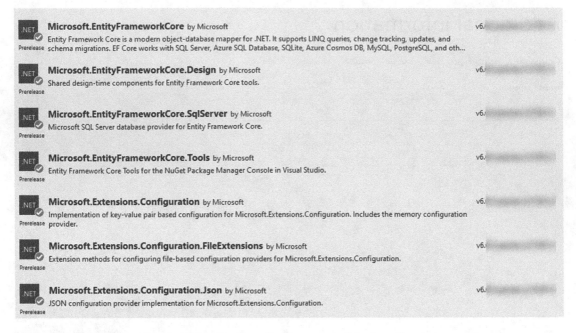

Figure 3-20. *The required NuGet packages are added to the new project*

Additionally, a quick way to add them would be to just add the following xml to your EFCore_Activity0302 project file:

```
<ItemGroup>
  <PackageReference Include="Microsoft.EntityFrameworkCore" Version="6.0.0-
  preview.3.21201.2" />
  <PackageReference Include="Microsoft.EntityFrameworkCore.Design"
  Version="6.0.0-preview.3.21201.2">
    <PrivateAssets>all</PrivateAssets>
    <IncludeAssets>runtime; build; native; contentfiles; analyzers;
    buildtransitive</IncludeAssets>
  </PackageReference>
  <PackageReference Include="Microsoft.EntityFrameworkCore.SqlServer"
  Version="6.0.0-preview.3.21201.2" />
  <PackageReference Include="Microsoft.EntityFrameworkCore.Tools"
  Version="6.0.0-preview.3.21201.2">
    <PrivateAssets>all</PrivateAssets>
    <IncludeAssets>runtime; build; native; contentfiles; analyzers;
    buildtransitive</IncludeAssets>
  </PackageReference>
```

```
<PackageReference Include="Microsoft.Extensions.Configuration"
Version="6.0.0-preview.3.21201.4" />
<PackageReference Include="Microsoft.Extensions.Configuration.
FileExtensions" Version="6.0.0-preview.3.21201.4" />
<PackageReference Include="Microsoft.Extensions.Configuration.Json"
Version="6.0.0-preview.3.21201.4" />
</ItemGroup>
```

If you use this code in your project file, you should use the Update tab in the NuGet Package Manager to update the versions, because newer versions will most likely be in use by the time you are working through this text.

The next few steps are fairly code intensive. If you can't copy/paste the code or if you get off track, always remember that you can just review the code in the starter files and you will be able to compare to see anything that got messed up or didn't get implemented as intended.

Next, create a new class file called ConfigurationBuilderSingleton.cs, and place the following code in the file:

```
private static ConfigurationBuilderSingleton _instance = null;
private static readonly object instanceLock = new object();

private static IConfigurationRoot _configuration;

private ConfigurationBuilderSingleton()
{
    var builder = new ConfigurationBuilder()
                    .SetBasePath(Directory.GetCurrentDirectory())
                    .AddJsonFile("appsettings.json", optional: true,
                    reloadOnChange: true);

    _configuration = builder.Build();
}
```

```
public static ConfigurationBuilderSingleton Instance
{
    get
    {
        lock (instanceLock)
        {
            if (_instance == null)
            {
                _instance = new ConfigurationBuilderSingleton();
            }
            return _instance;
        }
    }
}

public static IConfigurationRoot ConfigurationRoot
{
    get
    {
        if (_configuration == null) { var x = Instance; }
        return _configuration;
    }
}
```

This will create the configuration builder singleton code so that it's easy to load the configuration file. Additionally, change the class to be a `public sealed class` so that it cannot be further modified through inheritance. You will also need to resolve a couple of dependencies for `IConfigurationRoot` and `Directory`. The using statements at the top of the class can be replaced to contain just the following two using statements:

```
using Microsoft.Extensions.Configuration;
using System.IO;
```

At this point, you may wish to take a moment to save and build your project, just to ensure you don't currently have any errors.

This is also a great time to add source control if you would like to ensure you have a way to restore changes to this point should something go wrong in the next steps. Adding a new GIT repository is easy enough to do via the controls in Visual Studio, via the command line, or with your GIT IDE of choice. You will also want to ensure that you add a .gitignore file for Visual Studio projects to avoid checking in files you don't want to have in your repository.

Next, add the configuration file appsettings.json. Place the following JSON-formatted code in the new file:

```
{
    "ConnectionStrings": {
        "InventoryManager": "Data Source=localhost;Initial Catalog=
        InventoryManagerDb;Trusted_Connection=True"
    }
}
```

You might infer this from the connection string here, but you'll soon be creating a new database called InventoryDb.

Make sure to set the appsettings.json file as Content and Copy if newer (or Copy always) as shown in Figure 3-21.

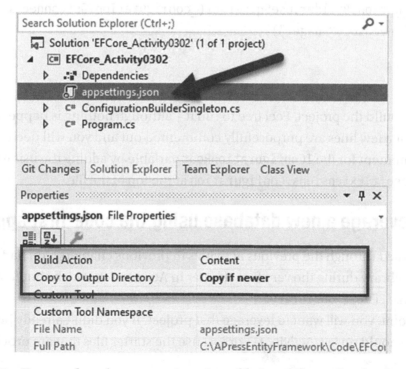

Figure 3-21. *Ensure that the appsettings.json file is configured to be Content and will be copied into the output when the project is built*

Open the `Program.cs` file and replace the existing program class code with the following code:

```
public class Program
{
    private static IConfigurationRoot _configuration;
    //private static DbContextOptionsBuilder<InventoryDbContext>
    _optionsBuilder;

    static void Main(string[] args)
    {
        BuildOptions();
    }

    static void BuildOptions()
    {
        _configuration = ConfigurationBuilderSingleton.ConfigurationRoot;
        //_optionsBuilder = new DbContextOptionsBuilder<InventoryDbContext>();
        //_optionsBuilder.UseSqlServer(_configuration.GetConnectionString(
            "InventoryManager"));
    }
}
```

Save and build the project. Feel free to run it – although nothing is happening yet. Note also that a few lines are purposefully commented out and you will need to resolve the using statement for the `IConfigurationRoot` variable by adding the using statement using `Microsoft.Extensions.Configuration` at the top of the file.

Step 2: Leverage a new database using the code-first approach

If you've worked through the previous activities in previous chapters, you had created a simple code library during the very first chapter in Activity 1-1, which should be named something like `EFCore_DbLibrary`.

At this point, you will want to leverage that project. If you didn't already build that project, you should review Activity 1-1 or just use the starter files that are provided for this activity.

Copy the project that was created in Activity 1-1 and place it in the same folder as the solution for your current Activity 3-2 project. For clarity, you should have two folders and the solution as shown in Figure 3-22.

This PC › Windows (C:) › APressEntityFramework › Code › EFCore_Activity0302 ›			
Name	Type	Size	
.git	File folder		
.vs	File folder		
EFCore_Activity0302	File folder		
EFCore_DBLibrary	File folder		
.gitignore	GITIGNORE File	7 KB	
EFCore_Activity0302.sln	Visual Studio Solu...	2 KB	

Figure 3-22. *The original code library from Activity 1-1 is copied into the folder with the new project for Activity 3-2*

With the project folder copied, add the existing project to the solution and then add a project reference to the main project in your solution to include the EFCore_DBLibrary project you just copied. You can easily do this by right-clicking the solution and selecting Add ➤ Existing Project (see Figure 3-23).

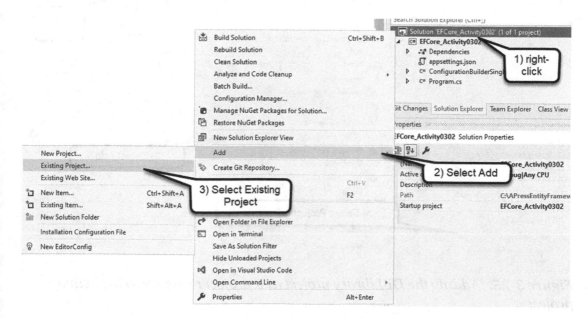

Figure 3-23. *Adding an existing project to the solution*

Next browse to the folder to find the project, and then select the project and open it (see Figure 3-24).

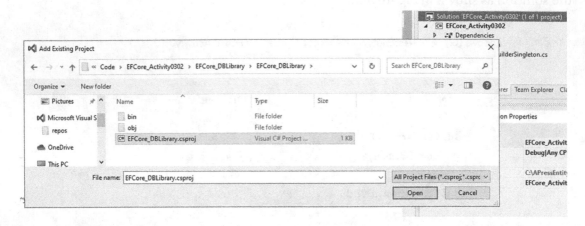

Figure 3-24. *The project is selected to be added to the existing solution*

Once the project is added, you need to add it as a project reference in the EFCore_Activity0302 project. Right-click the activity project and select Add ➤ Project Reference (see Figure 3-25).

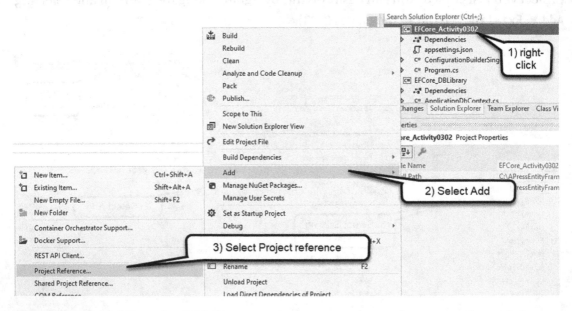

Figure 3-25. *Adding the DBLibrary project as a project reference to the activity project*

Check the EFCore_DBLibrary project, and then press OK to complete the operation (as in Figure 3-26).

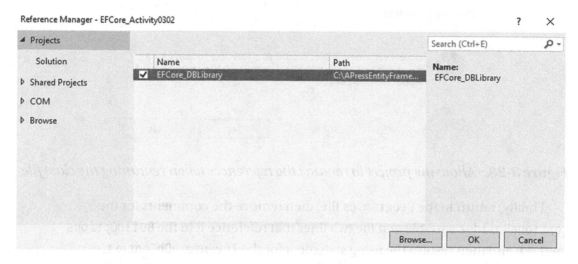

Figure 3-26. *Completing the process to add the DBLibrary project as a project reference to the activity project*

In the DBLibrary project, rename the current file ApplicationDbContext.cs to InventoryDbContext.cs by right-clicking and selecting Rename (see Figure 3-27) or by hitting the "F2" key.

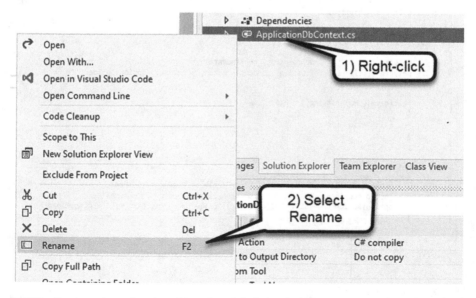

Figure 3-27. *Renaming the ApplicationDbContext*

When prompted, also rename any references by selecting Yes in the dialog that is shown in Figure 3-28.

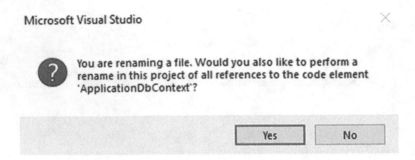

Figure 3-28. *Allow the project to rename the references when renaming the class file*

Finally, return to the `Program.cs` file, then remove the comments for the `_optionsBuilder` variable and the two lines that reference it in the `BuildOptions` method, and then resolve the using statement for the `InventoryDbContext`.

For clarity, the `Program.cs` file is shown in Figure 3-29. Review the code and make sure to save and build the project to ensure there are currently no errors.

```
appsettings.json        ConfigurationBuilderSingleton.cs        EFCore_Activity0302.csproj        NuGet - Solution        Program.cs  ⇥ ✕
EFCore_Activity0302                                                   EFCore_Activity0302.Program
    1     using EFCore_DBLibrary;
    2     using Microsoft.EntityFrameworkCore;
    3     using Microsoft.Extensions.Configuration;
    4     using System;
    5
    6     namespace EFCore_Activity0302
    7     {
              0 references
    8         public class Program
    9         {
   10             private static IConfigurationRoot _configuration;
   11             private static DbContextOptionsBuilder<InventoryDbContext> _optionsBuilder;
   12
              0 references
   13             static void Main(string[] args)
   14             {
   15                 BuildOptions();
   16             }
   17
              1 reference
   18         static void BuildOptions()
   19             {
   20                 _configuration = ConfigurationBuilderSingleton.ConfigurationRoot;
   21                 _optionsBuilder = new DbContextOptionsBuilder<InventoryDbContext>();
   22                 _optionsBuilder.UseSqlServer(_configuration.GetConnectionString("InventoryManager"));
   23             }
   24
   25         }
   26
   27     }
   28
```

Figure 3-29. *The Program.cs file is shown for clarity, and the project is ready to go*

Your project is now set up and ready to start working with code in a code-first approach against a new database. This would be a really great time to establish your project in a GIT repository if you have not already done so.

Task 2: Add a new library for your database models – the "code" of code first

In this task, you will build the code-first Models project, where you will store the code that will ultimately model the database schema. Putting this code in its own project is a best practice, because this will allow you to reuse the code in other projects if you needed to do so.

Step 1: Create a new project library

In this first step for Task 2, you need to create a new reusable code library to house the database models. The models are just classes in C# that define the attributes that will be translated to the database schema.

Begin by right-clicking the solution and selecting Add ➤ New Project (see Figure 3-30).

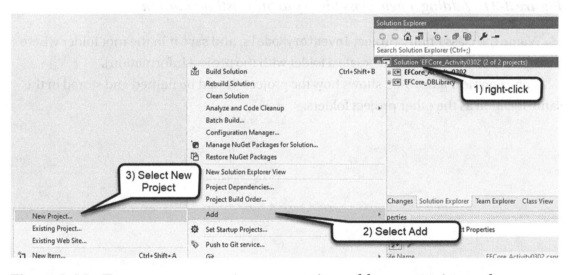

Figure 3-30. *To create a new project, you can just add a new project to the solution, as shown here*

For the project type, select Class library as shown in Figure 3-31, and then hit "Next."

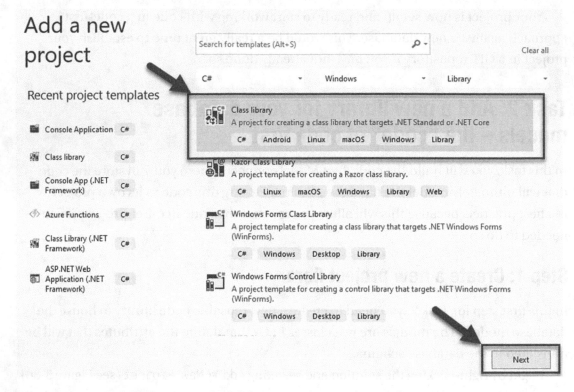

Figure 3-31. *Adding a new class library to the existing solution*

Name the class library project InventoryModels, and save it in the root folder where the solution is saved (this will create a folder with the project information).

For example, Figure 3-32 shows how the project should be named and stored in the same location as the other project folders.

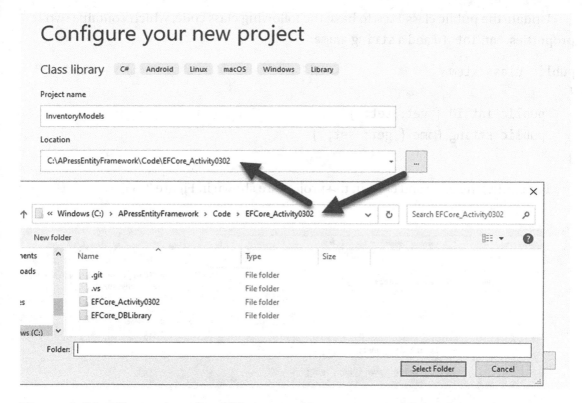

Figure 3-32. *The project should be named InventoryModels and stored in the same location as the other project folders*

When prompted, make sure to select .NET 6.0 for the Target Framework, and hit the Create button.

Step 2: Update the automatically generated Class1 to be an Item object

When the project is created, you will see one class that is named Class1.cs. Right-click (or hit F2 when you are on the class) and rename the class to Item.cs. When prompted, select Yes for updating references.

Update the public class Item to have the following class code, which contains two properties – an int Id and a string Name:

```
public class Item
{
    public int Id { get; set; }
    public string Name { get; set; }
}
```

For clarity, the code and class in the project are shown in Figure 3-33.

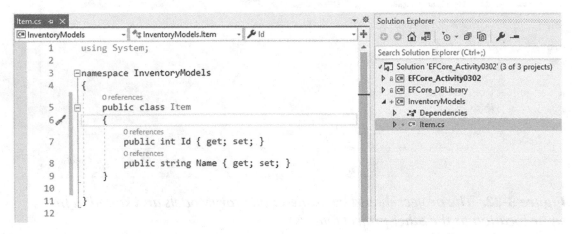

Figure 3-33. *The Item class is created with two properties for Id and Name*

You will create the Item object in a migration and ensure that this new object is able to be used in the database before the activity is over. However, a quick note about this object. As it currently stands, this code is not very good. The reason for this is that it is too basic. The first thing to note is that there are no constraints on any of the fields. For example, the Id is going to be the primary key, so it should always be a positive integer. The Name field is a string, and, as it stands, there are no length limits or requirements on the name (currently it could be null or have a length of 0, which, by the way, are not the same).

Do not worry, you will get a chance to learn how to make these fields better in the next couple of chapters; and you will get a chance to learn about the differences between null and the empty string and why they are not the same thing. For now, just note that this design is simplistic and is not supposed to represent production code but will give you a great start on your Inventory system.

Step 3: Set the project to be (or ensure that it is) a .Net 5 library

To ensure compatibility and the use of the .Net 6 library, right-click your new InventoryModels project, and then select Properties. When the properties come up, ensure that the Target Framework is set to target .NET 6.0. With these changes, the code is ready to be used in your database library.

Task 3: Reference the InventoryModels project and use it to create a migration

In this task, you will reference the new project in the EFCore_DbLibrary project and then add the Item to the InventoryDbContext. Once the code is in place, you will then create a migration and update the database. You will finish this task by reviewing the database to ensure the table was created as expected.

Step 1: Add a project reference to the EFCore_DbLibrary for the InventoryModels

Now that the project is created, you will need to leverage it in the DbLibrary project. To do this, right-click the EFCore_DbLibrary project and select Add ➤ Project Reference, and then check the box next to InventoryModels and select OK. Adding the project reference is highlighted in Figure 3-34.

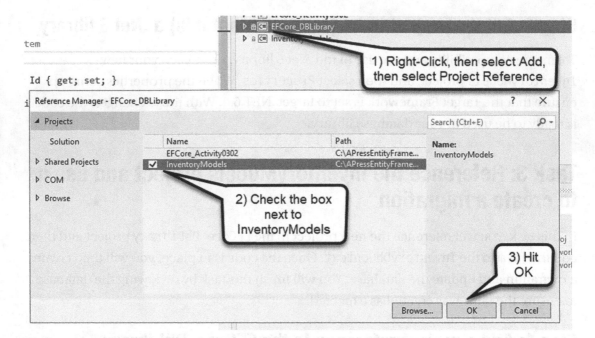

Figure 3-34. *Adding a project reference for the InventoryModels project to the EFCore_DbLibrary project*

Go ahead and build the project to ensure there are no errors. Additionally, if you are working with a repository, you may wish to commit changes at this point as a commit that you could easily use as a rollback or reset target commit.

Step 2: Add the Item class to the InventoryDbContext

For the second step, you need to let the database context know that a new entity is needed to map with the Item class that was created in the previous task. If you don't add new entities as a DBSet<T> in the database context, then your solution will just ignore them. This is a good thing because you may not want a table for every model you create. However, I cannot tell you how many times I've forgotten to add the entity, created a migration, and then had to remove the empty migration and make sure to add the entity to the application's database context.

In the EFCore_DbLibrary project, double-click to open the InventoryDbContext.cs file. In this file, in the InventoryDbContext class, simply add the following code to the top, after the first curly brace and before the comment or declaration of the default empty constructor:

```
public DbSet<Item> Items { get; set; }
```

Adding this code will also force you to need to resolve the reference for the Item class. Resolve the using statements now, so that you will not have any errors. When completed, you will have the following using statements at the top of the InventoryDbContext.cs file:

```
using InventoryModels;
using Microsoft.EntityFrameworkCore;
using System;
```

At present, the using System using statement is not necessary, so you could opt to remove it.

For clarity, the code is shown in Figure 3-35 here.

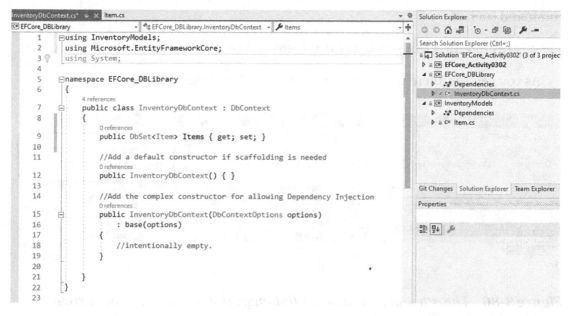

Figure 3-35. *The code for the InventoryDbContext is shown for clarity, including the declaration of the DBSet for Items*

Note that the code you have added is for a DbSet of Item and that you named the property Items. The DbSet uses generics to allow you to inject the type of DbSet to map to any of your models. Additionally, the property name is what is used to create the database table name by convention. Adding this code, therefore, allows you to be able to anticipate a new migration would need to add the Items table and that the migration would contain columns added to the table to map to each of the properties in the Item class.

Step 3: Set the EFCore5_DbLibrary project to use the code-first database approach as a stand-alone library

Currently, the EFCore_DbLibrary project is not ready to be a stand-alone project. The main reason is that it doesn't have any way to determine what database to connect to at this point, and the InventoryDbContext is not set up correctly to work against any database.

To make this happen, you need to do a couple of things on the project before trying to use the code-first approach.

To see the problem, attempt to add a new migration now. Using the *PMC*, making sure that the project selected is the EFCore_DbLibrary project, use the add-migration command to create a new migration. This is the initial migration, so you could use a command such as

```
add-migration initial_setup_create_items_table
```

As you can see, there is an error that is generated (see Figure 3-36).

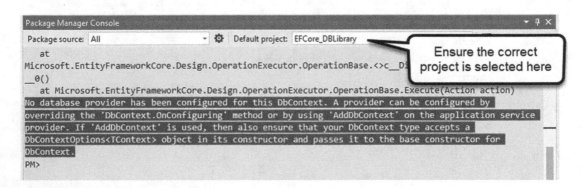

Figure 3-36. *The attempt to add the initial migration has failed. The current solution is not configured correctly, and an error is generated and shown here*

The actual text of the error is

```
No database provider has been configured for this DbContext. A provider
can be configured by overriding the 'DbContext.OnConfiguring' method
or by using 'AddDbContext' on the application service provider. If
'AddDbContext' is used, then also ensure that your DbContext type accepts a
DbContextOptions<TContext> object in its constructor and passes it to the
base constructor for DbContext.
```

OK, that seems like a lot, but it's actually not that bad. So how do you fix this issue?

As it turns out, you just need to do what it says in the error. The easiest solution to solve this issue is simply to override the OnConfiguring method. In fact, if you go back to Activity 3-1 from earlier in this chapter and take a look at the context that was generated, you'll see exactly the code that you need. Review Figure 3-37 to see the code from the OnConfiguring method from the AdventureWorksContext that was generated in Activity0301.

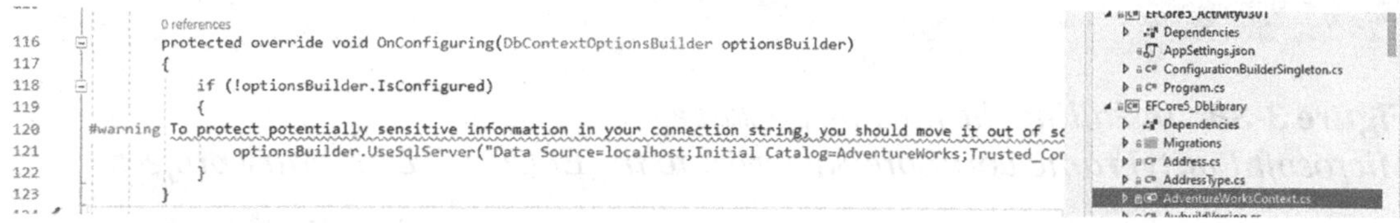

Figure 3-37. *The OnConfiguring method was successfully overridden in the AdventureWorksContext in the previous activity and is shown here*

Add the following code into the InventoryDbContext toward the bottom, after the constructors:

```
protected override void OnConfiguring(DbContextOptionsBuilder
optionsBuilder)
{
    if (!optionsBuilder.IsConfigured)
    {
        optionsBuilder.UseSqlServer("Data Source=localhost;Initial Catalog=
        InventoryManagerDb;Trusted_Connection=True");
    }
}
```

Adding this code will also force you to resolve an error for the call to UseSqlServer. This is due to a missing NuGet package. Open the Tools ➤ NuGet Package Manager ➤ Manage NuGet Packages for Solution and bring up the dialog, and then select the Installed packages tab. On the tab, select the package for Microsoft. EntityFrameworkCore.SqlServer. With that package installed, check the EFCore_DbLibrary project and install it. For clarity, this is shown in Figure 3-38.

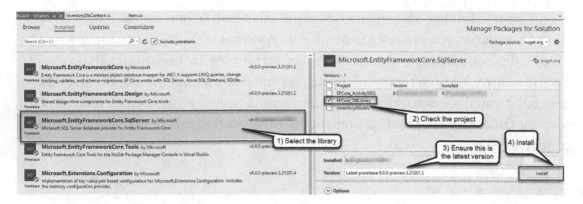

Figure 3-38. *Installing the missing package for the Microsoft.EntityFrameworkCore.SqlServer to the EFCore5_DbLibrary project*

Accept any licenses. Importing this library should fix the issue with the call to UseSqlServer in the InventoryDbContext. Ensure the project builds in the current state, and check in any changes if you are using source control.

Step 4: Move the connection string out of the EFCore5_DbLibrary project

While you could proceed at this point, it is a good idea to get the connection string out of the code and into a configuration file. In fact, even the VS IDE has given a warning in the previous activity (review Figure 3-37) that stated

#warning To protect potentially sensitive information in your connection string, you should move it out of source code. You can avoid scaffolding the connection string by using the Name= syntax to read it from configuration - see https://go.microsoft.com/fwlink/?linkid=2131148. For more guidance on storing connection strings, see http://go.microsoft.com/fwlink/?LinkId=723263.

To fix this, you just need to do a couple of quick things.

First, you should already have the Manage NuGet Packages for Solution dialog open, but if you don't, just reopen it. You'll need to add references for the three *Microsoft.Extensions.Configuration* packages to the EFCore5_DbLibrary project. Select each of the following and install them into the EFCore_DBLibrary project:

- Microsoft.Extensions.Configuration

- Microsoft.Extensions.Configuration.FileExtensions

- Microsoft.Extensions.Configuration.Json

Next, you need a class-level variable for the configuration. Add the following to the top of the InventoryDbContext class, right before the declaration of the Items property that you added previously:

```
private static IConfigurationRoot _configuration;
```

To use the file, update the code in the OnConfiguring method in the InventoryDbContext to the following:

```
protected override void OnConfiguring(DbContextOptionsBuilder optionsBuilder)
{
    if (!optionsBuilder.IsConfigured)
    {
        var builder = new ConfigurationBuilder()
                    .SetBasePath(Directory.GetCurrentDirectory())
                    .AddJsonFile("appsettings.json", optional: true,
                    reloadOnChange: true);

        _configuration = builder.Build();
        var cnstr = _configuration.GetConnectionString("InventoryManager");
        optionsBuilder.UseSqlServer(cnstr);
    }
}
```

This will require adding a couple of using statements. The current using statements that are required are shown in Figure 3-39, along with the rest of the code for clarity. They are

```
using InventoryModels;
using Microsoft.EntityFrameworkCore;
using Microsoft.Extensions.Configuration;
using System.IO;
```

```
using InventoryModels;
using Microsoft.EntityFrameworkCore;
using Microsoft.Extensions.Configuration;
using System.IO;
using System;

namespace EFCore_DBLibrary
{
    4 references
    public class InventoryDbContext : DbContext
    {
        private static IConfigurationRoot _configuration;

        0 references
        public DbSet<Item> Items { get; set; }

        //Add a default constructor if scaffolding is needed
        0 references
        public InventoryDbContext() { }

        //Add the complex constructor for allowing Dependency Injection
        0 references
        public InventoryDbContext(DbContextOptions options)...

        0 references
        protected override void OnConfiguring(DbContextOptionsBuilder optionsBuilder)
        {
            if (!optionsBuilder.IsConfigured)
            {
                var builder = new ConfigurationBuilder()
                                .SetBasePath(Directory.GetCurrentDirectory())
                                .AddJsonFile("appsettings.json", optional: true, reloadOnChange: true);

                _configuration = builder.Build();
                var cnstr = _configuration.GetConnectionString("InventoryManager");
                optionsBuilder.UseSqlServer(cnstr);
            }
        }
    }
}
```

> This is collapsed for brevity

Figure 3-39. *The InventoryDbContext class is set up to be a stand-alone class now, with a configuration file to allow for connecting to the database and the overridden OnConfiguring method completed*

Step 5: Create a new migration for the Inventory system

In this step, you will add the migration for the InventoryManager system. Since there are currently no migrations, this will be the first one created for this solution.

Run the command that was used in the previous step once again. The command should be accessible with a simple press of the up arrow in the PMC, and for clarity, it should be

```
add-migration initial_setup_create_items_table
```

Running the command this time will generate the migration as expected, now that a connection can be established. Figure 3-40 shows the expected output, including the successfully generated migration that contains the code to add the Items table.

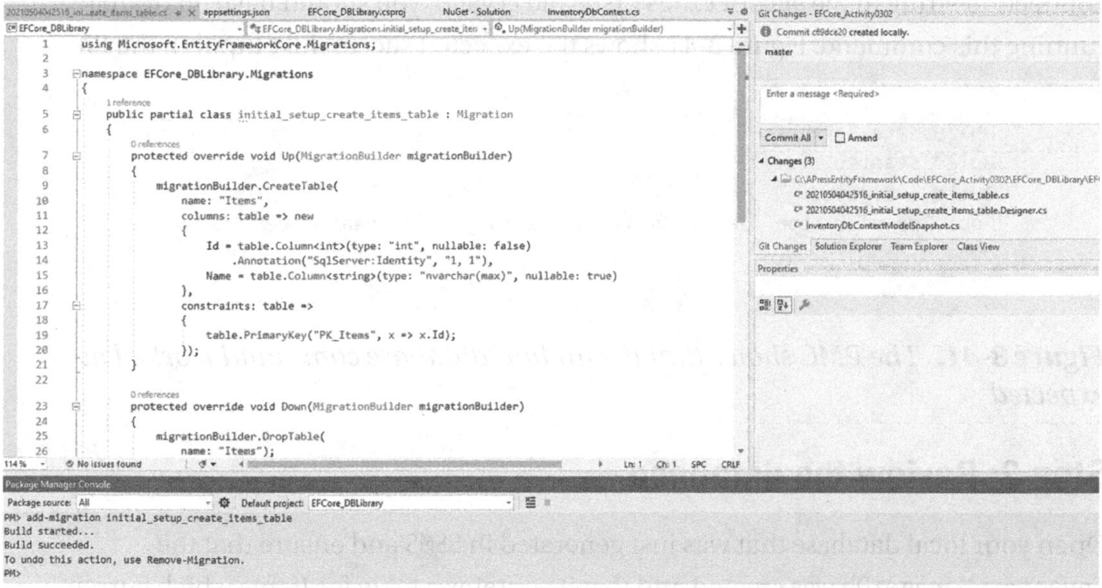

Figure 3-40. *The migration is created, and running the update command to apply this migration will create the database (since this is the first migration) and the Items table*

Reminder   The filename is going to be entirely different for you, depending on the date and time when the migration was generated in combination with how you named your migration.

Task 4: Update and review the database

In this task, you will apply the generated migration and review the database to ensure that the project is now set up and ready to be used with a new database as a code-first Entity Framework Core 6 project.

Step 1: Update the database

First, you need to apply the migration generated in the previous step. In the PMC, run the update-database command. Provided everything is set up correctly and the connection string in the appsettings.json file is valid, you should have no trouble running this command. Figure 3-41 shows the expected successful output in the PMC.

```
PM> update-database
Build started...
Build succeeded.
Applying migration '20210504042516_initial_setup_create_items_table'.
Done.
PM>
```

Figure 3-41. *The PMC shows that the update-database command worked as expected*

Step 2: Review the database

Open your local database that was just generated in SSMS and ensure that the InventoryManagerDb was created and that it contains a table for Items which currently contains no records. If you already had SSMS open, you may need to right-click the Databases folder and select Refresh. Review Figure 3-42 to see the expected solution.

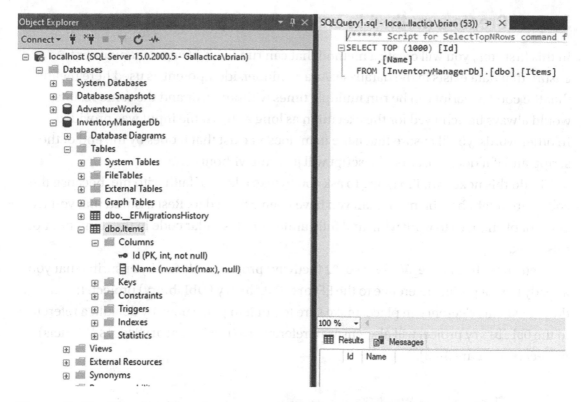

Figure 3-42. *The database is generated and has a table for Items ready to be utilized*

Now the project is working as expected and the entity models are fully integrated. The final step to prove this solution is working is to utilize the library and interact with the database.

At this point, if you are working with your code in a local repository, this would be a great place to commit your changes before moving to the next task.

Task 5: Add code to insert and query a list of items

In this final task, you will create a method to ensure the existence of a few inventory items. You will also create a method that will read the items from the Items table, and then you will output those items to the screen.

Step 1: Create a method to ensure the existence of some Items

In this first step, you will create a method that can run in an *idempotent* manner to ensure that data exists in the database. As a reminder, idempotent as used here means that the code or script can be run multiple times without error and the same results would always be achieved for the execution as long as the same input was provided. In other words, you'll ensure that if the item doesn't exist that it does by the end of the script, and if it does exist that the script will just run without error.

To do this next part, I'm going to ask you to take a leap of faith with me, because the code here might be a bit more than you have been exposed to. Rest assured that you will get a lot of chances to work with, and fully understand, similar code in the remainder of this book.

Return to the EFCore_Activity0302 (activity) project, and start by ensuring that you already have a project reference to the EFCore_DbLibrary (DbLibrary) project. If you don't have this reference in place, make sure to put it in place now. By default, a reference to the DbLibrary project will also ensure a reference to the InventoryModels (Models) project (see Figure 3-43).

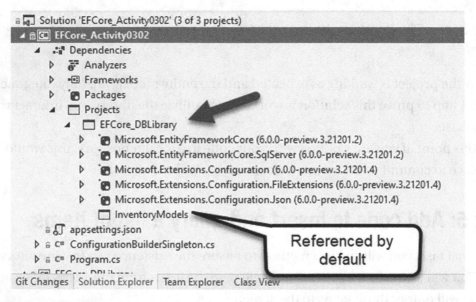

Figure 3-43. *The project reference to the DbLibrary is shown, which has the cascading dependency to the Models project*

With the project reference in place, add a call in the Main method of the Program.cs file following the BuildOptions method for a new method called *EnsureItems* using the code EnsureItems(). This method will call a small helper to generate an item if it doesn't already exist in the database for five simple items.

Add the following method to the class following the completion of the BuildOptions method code and before the end of the class:

```
static void EnsureItems()
{
    EnsureItem("Batman Begins");
    EnsureItem("Inception");
    EnsureItem("Remember the Titans");
    EnsureItem("Star Wars: The Empire Strikes Back");
    EnsureItem("Top Gun");
}

private static void EnsureItem(string name)
{
    using (var db = new InventoryDbContext(_optionsBuilder.Options))
    {
        //determine if item exists:
        var existingItem = db.Items.FirstOrDefault(x => x.Name.ToLower()
                                                     == name.ToLower());

        if (existingItem == null)
        {
            //doesn't exist, add it.
            var item = new Item() { Name = name };
            db.Items.Add(item);
            db.SaveChanges();
        }
    }
}
```

This code will first check for each of the five movies to see if they exist, and if they don't exist, the code will add the movies that are not present. The end result is that no matter how many times this is run, there will only be five items and they will all be in the database. This code is therefore idempotent.

Do not forget to bring in all the missing using statements to ensure that the code builds. For example, you may need to add the statement using System.Linq manually to resolve the database call to FirstOrDefault. You will likely also need to add a statement for using InventoryModels to leverage the Item class.

Also note that the context is wrapped in a using statement and the variable db is used to work against the database. You will learn more about all of this in the next few chapters. For now, just know that the using statement allows the proper connection and disposal of the context, and the LINQ queries used allow for you to get the data and add items to the context and save the changes.

For clarity, your code should look like the code shown in Figure 3-44.

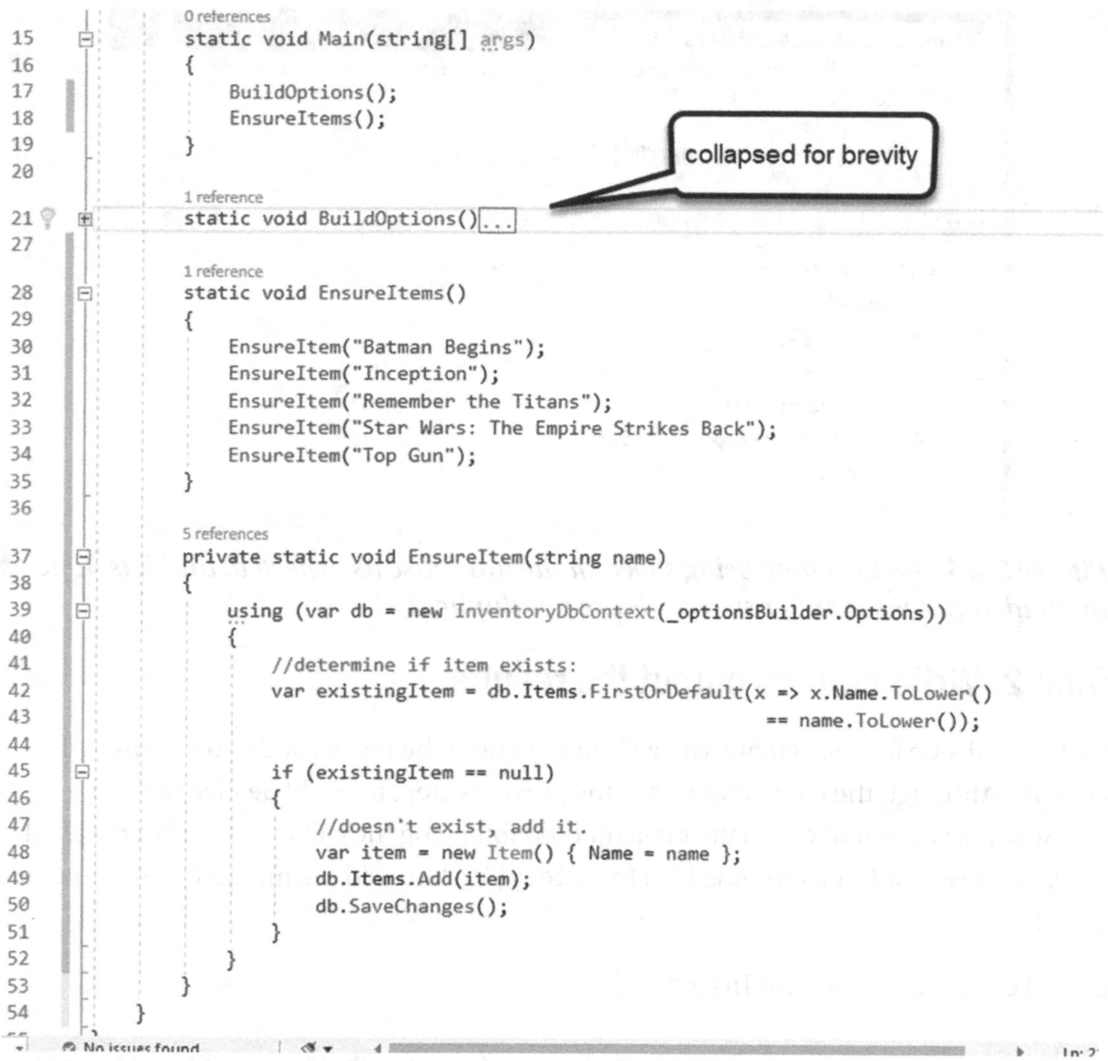

```
     0 references
15       static void Main(string[] args)
16       {
17           BuildOptions();
18           EnsureItems();
19       }
20

     1 reference
21       static void BuildOptions()...
27

     1 reference
28       static void EnsureItems()
29       {
30           EnsureItem("Batman Begins");
31           EnsureItem("Inception");
32           EnsureItem("Remember the Titans");
33           EnsureItem("Star Wars: The Empire Strikes Back");
34           EnsureItem("Top Gun");
35       }
36

     5 references
37       private static void EnsureItem(string name)
38       {
39           using (var db = new InventoryDbContext(_optionsBuilder.Options))
40           {
41               //determine if item exists:
42               var existingItem = db.Items.FirstOrDefault(x => x.Name.ToLower()
43                                                          == name.ToLower());
44
45               if (existingItem == null)
46               {
47                   //doesn't exist, add it.
48                   var item = new Item() { Name = name };
49                   db.Items.Add(item);
50                   db.SaveChanges();
51               }
52           }
53       }
54   }
```

collapsed for brevity

No issues found

Figure 3-44. *The EnsureItems and EnsureItem methods as implemented are shown*

Build and run the code now to see that the solution works as expected. In fact, run it a couple of times. While there is currently no output in the console, after running the program performing a quick review of the database in SSMS should show that results are now being entered into the table (see Figure 3-45).

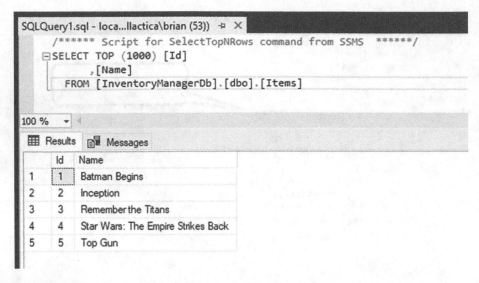

Figure 3-45. *Data is now being saved in the database as expected, and it is done in an idempotent manner so records are not duplicated*

Step 2: Write code to output the results

In this final step for the activity, you will simply query the results and show them in the console. Although the data is verified in the previous step, it would be nice to see it.

Add a new method call in the Main method following the call to EnsureItems called *ListInventory* by adding the code ListInventory(). Then add the method with the code as follows:

```
private static void ListInventory()
{
    using (var db = new InventoryDbContext(_optionsBuilder.Options))
    {
        var items = db.Items.OrderBy(x => x.Name).ToList();
        items.ForEach(x => Console.WriteLine($"New Item: {x.Name}"));
    }
}
```

Build and run the solution. You should now see all of the items in the console as shown in Figure 3-46.

```
56    private static void ListInventory()
57    {
58        using (var db = new InventoryDbContext(_optionsBuilder.Options))
59        {
60            var items = db.Items.OrderBy(x => x.Name).ToList();
61            items.ForEach(x => Console.WriteLine($"New Item: {x.Name}"));
62        }
63    }
64
65    }
66    }
67
```

```
Microsoft Visual Studio Debug Console
New Item: Batman Begins
New Item: Inception
New Item: Remember the Titans
New Item: Star Wars: The Empire Strikes Back
New Item: Top Gun

C:\APressEntityFramework\Code\EFCore_Activity0302\EFCore_Activity0302\bin\Debug
To automatically close the console when debugging stops, enable Tools->Options-:
Press any key to close this window . . .
```

Figure 3-46. *The expected output is shown with the inventory printed to the console*

Running the program over and over again will yield the same result. You've now successfully created a new solution that leverages the database via EFCore6, and you've even gotten a sneak peek into using the context to add and retrieve data.

Activity 3-2 summary

In this final activity for Chapter 3, you went through setting up a new .Net 6 project and were able to integrate a new EFCore6 library to create the database. You learned how to make the project work as a stand-alone project with the connection string in the configuration file, and you learned how to leverage the code-first approach to create a new table.

To create the new table, you first added a new code library to separate the concerns. This is a nice approach because the code library is positioned well to be reused in other projects as necessary. Additionally, the EFCore6_DbLibrary project is also ready to be reused in other projects as necessary.

Chapter summary

In this chapter, you learned the basics of getting started with a code-first approach. The chapter began with a quick look at when you can implement a code-first solution and how a code-first solution doesn't always have to start with a brand-new database.

You then worked through a couple of activities where you got to implement a new project in a code-first approach against an existing database, and you also got to work through a project that was completely greenfield and had no code or database to start.

Through the activities, you also got further exposure to working with the commands in the Package Manager Console to create migrations, update the database, revert migrations, and remove migrations.

At the end of the second activity, you also saw code that wrote to the database and saved changes after writing the data, and then you saw how to read from the database using EFCore6.

Important takeaways

After working through this chapter, the things you should be in command of are

- Working in a code-first approach against an existing database

- A good understanding of the Up and Down methods in a migration and how and when each is applied

- An understanding of what it takes to revert a migration once it has been applied

- How to remove a migration

- An ability to understand where to check in the database to see if a migration has been applied

- The ability to leverage a code library with models that can be used as entities for the database schema

- How to add new entities to the database using the DBContext

- A basic understanding of the override of OnConfiguration

- How Entity Framework can be implemented into a class library for use in any project

Closing thoughts

In the next chapter, you will start diving deeper into building out a robust data solution using EFCore6 by learning more about working with models, contexts, and migrations.

PART II

Building the Data Solution

CHAPTER 4

Models and the Data Context

In this chapter, you are going to examine the data context and the creation of models, as well as look in a bit more detail about how these objects work in concert for code-first database programming with Entity Framework.

By the end of the chapter, you will have reviewed and become even more familiar with some of the inner workings of the database context (DBContext). Through practical examples, you'll also become very familiar with using models to build out your database tables.

Eventually, you will learn more about structuring schema and relationships in your databases with models and migrations, but this chapter will concentrate on the basic setup of your database tables and how to use the DBContext to identify objects for inclusion in migrations. You will build on this knowledge in future chapters.

What is the database context and why do we need it?

Before diving into the DBContext and why it is important, it is also critical to identify that you may have never worked with a DBContext before. If you are reading this and you are used to working with an older version of EF (versions prior to EF4.1) or if you have been working in a non-code-first approach in previous database work, you've perhaps never seen or used the DBContext. In such use cases, you might be familiar with an object called the ObjectContext. The ObjectContext contains all of the methods necessary to work against the database, such as CreateDatabase, SaveChanges, and more [see https://docs.microsoft.com/en-us/dotnet/api/system.data.entity.core.objects.objectcontext?view=entity-framework-6.2.0 for more information].

© Brian L. Gorman 2022
B. L. Gorman, *Practical Entity Framework Core 6*, https://doi.org/10.1007/978-1-4842-7301-2_4

Please know that going forward you will no longer be using the ObjectContext, but instead you will be using the DBContext object.

DBContext vs. ObjectContext

In the previous versions of EF, the DbContext could, in some instances, act like a decorator on the ObjectContext, as it is possible for the DBContext to be created by wrapping an ObjectContext. It was also possible to gain access to the underlying ObjectContext from the DBContext when necessary. You will no longer be able to take this sort of approach in EFCore6, nor would you want to. In most cases, you'll now be leveraging the DBContextOptionsBuilder.

In *EF6*, both DBContext and ObjectContext are implementations of the same interface, the IObjectContextAdapter. By having this common definition, and the ability for a DBContext to work like a decorator, it was possible to make the transition from the older style *EF* with the *.edmx* files from existing databases to the code-first approach with no *.edmx* files while still being able to support the original *.edmx* implementations.

In both *EF6* (the previous version of *EF* before *EFCore*) and *EFCore*, the DbContext object is a critical component for code-first implementations. The DBContext contains all of the critical methods necessary to work against the database. With *EF* using a DBContext, a lot of the underlying patterns are implemented by default and don't require manual intervention from developers.

We will focus on working with the DBContext for the remainder of this book. Additionally, we will be homing in on *EFCore6* for our examination of the DBContext and will not be implementing any legacy code around the DBContext. Along the way, however, we will still take time when appropriate to discuss how things were different in *EF6*, just in case you're working with *EF6* in legacy code or in the case where you are upgrading to EFCore6 from other legacy versions and need to know about the differences between the two implementations.

What is the DBContext?

To begin looking at the DBContext, let's get the official statement from the Microsoft documents about what the DbContext class is. The official documentation from https://docs.microsoft.com/en-us/dotnet/api/microsoft.entityframeworkcore. dbcontext?view=efcore-6.0 states the following about the DbContext Class:

> *A DbContext instance represents a session with the database and can be used to query and save instances of your entities. DbContext is a combination of the unit of work and repository patterns.*

Using the DbContext, therefore, we get orchestration around two significant patterns in database development, the *unit of work (UoW)* pattern, and the *repository* design pattern. This means that by using the DBContext, we don't have to explicitly manage simple transactions when working with the DBContext, as they will be handled by the context implementing the *UoW* pattern.

Another way to think about this is to understand that when you are working with the code and objects from the DBContext, everything that has been set to be modified is managed in the same implicit transaction. Therefore, all operations are pending and not applied until an explicit call is made to SaveChanges. If something fails during that final call to SaveChanges, the entire modified set is rolled back, which can be both a blessing and a curse for developers.

To be more prepared and to gain a better understanding of how all of this works, we will take a deeper look at the *UoW* and *repository* patterns in more detail later in the book. At that time, we will also discuss working with explicit transactions and when it might be appropriate for developers to use explicit transactions. Until then, we'll just leverage the built-in *UoW* and *repository* patterns.

Although most of the interaction we will have with the DBContext in many applications will be limited to adding DBSets and a few other small code modifications, it is a good use of our time to learn more about how the DBContext works. It is also a good idea to learn about how the DBContext is constructed while gaining knowledge of some of the options available to us through the DBContext. We can examine this in more detail by diving into the inner workings of the DBContext, which we'll do next.

Constructing a new DBContext

In *EFCore6*, there are only two constructors for the DBContext. We've already seen both constructors in use in our activities from the previous chapter. If you didn't already work the activities in the previous chapter, you may wish to do so now. Alternatively, you could just review the final files from Activity 3-2.

In most cases, when creating the DBContext, we'll use the complex constructor, which takes a DbContextOptions object, but there are specific instances when the default constructor with no parameters will be used. Primarily, the default constructor is used when running migrations or scaffolding controllers for a context.

The DBContext class gives us the ability to inject options for use during normal operation of the database interactions with EF via the DBContextOptions class. When working with the DBContextOptions class, we generally will use a DBContextOptionsBuilder object, as the DBContextOptions class is usually composed and/or injected, not directly created. As previously mentioned, if you worked through the activities in Chapter 3, you've already seen this in action.

The DBContextOptionsBuilder gives us a couple of critical operations that we'll leverage. In the last chapter, we set the type of database we wanted to use and injected the connection string for the DBContext through the DBContextOptionsBuilder and the DBContextOptions as follows:

```
protected override void OnConfiguring(DbContextOptionsBuilder optionsBuilder)
{
    if (!optionsBuilder.IsConfigured)
    {
        var builder = new ConfigurationBuilder()
                        .SetBasePath(Directory.GetCurrentDirectory())
                        .AddJsonFile("appsettings.json", optional: true,
                         reloadOnChange: true);

        _configuration = builder.Build();
        var cnstr = _configuration.GetConnectionString("InventoryManager");
        optionsBuilder.UseSqlServer(cnstr);
    }
}
```

Most importantly, in this implementation, we did not have a startup class or method in place that leveraged dependency injection via services at runtime. Therefore, no DBContextOptions were injected into the DBContext. To remedy this, we configured the options by overriding the OnConfiguring method as shown earlier. As a result of overriding the OnConfiguring method and building the options builder as we did in this example, we could also further configure the DBOptionsBuilder if we needed to implement any other custom functionality, such as adding interceptors or enabling logging.

We should also note through this examination that any creation of the DBContext will use the OnConfiguring method, so we can continue to modify the options for our DBContext, even if the system is leveraging dependency injection.

As an alternative to overriding the OnConfiguring method, we can build the options inline and inject them into the constructor of the DBContextOptions directly as is shown in the following code block (which is easily generated by creating a new *ASP.Net MVC* project):

```
public void ConfigureServices(IServiceCollection services)
{
    services.AddDbContext<ApplicationDbContext>(options =>
        options.UseSqlServer(
            Configuration.GetConnectionString("DefaultConnection")));
    services.AddDatabaseDeveloperPageExceptionFilter();

    services.AddDefaultIdentity<IdentityUser>(options =>
    options.SignIn.RequireConfirmedAccount = true)
        .AddEntityFrameworkStores<ApplicationDbContext>();
    services.AddControllersWithViews();
}
```

What's important to note here is the fact that in the *ASP.Net MVC* project, the project template sets the DBContextOptions to use *SQL Server* and leverages a configuration entry by name to get the connection string.

In both preceding cases, we've set the database to use *SQL Server*. There are many other database options available if your organization or project cannot leverage *SQL Server*.

Critical properties and methods available when working with the DBContext

In the next couple of sections, we'll take a look at a couple of the properties and methods that exist for our use when building up and working with a DBContext. This reference is not an exhaustive list of all properties and methods available but should cover many of the common properties and methods that we're likely to use.

For your reference, the full list of detailed specifications for each object available for use in *EFCore6* is available in the documentation at Microsoft, which can be found here: https://docs.microsoft.com/en-us/dotnet/api/microsoft.entityframeworkcore?view=efcore-6.0.

Important properties on the DbContextOptionsBuilder object

Each of our objects used in the composition of the DBContext for normal operations contains a couple of noteworthy properties. At the time of this writing, there are two properties of the DbContextOptionsBuilder class, which are IsConfigured and Options, and they are shown in Table 4-1.

Table 4-1. *Properties of the DbContextOptionsBuilder class*

Property	Purpose
IsConfigured	Gets a value indicating whether any options have been configured.
Options	Gets the options being configured by giving direct access to the DBContextOptions object.

We've already seen these properties in action in the last chapter, although the call for Options to get the connection string was implicit in the DBContext, whereas we directly coded against the IsConfigured property to ensure that options were configured.

Important properties on the DBContextOptions object

Even though we don't directly create a DBContextOptions object, we may still wish to code against a couple of the properties. There are three properties available to us in the DBContextOptions class, which are ContextType, Extensions, and IsFrozen as described in Table 4-2.

Table 4-2. *Properties of the DbContextOptions class.*

Property	Purpose
ContextType	Gets the type for the context; if no type is defined, then DBContext will be returned.
Extensions	Gets a list of extensions as configured, such as the type of database being leveraged.
IsFrozen	Used to determine if the DBContext is open for further configuration. If true, the system cannot further override the context options in the OnConfiguring method.

In most cases, we won't have a need to leverage these properties directly, but it's good to know they are available should we need to provide an implementation that is more defined than a default implementation would be. I can definitely see a use case where locking the options from further configuring could be a nice security feature, potentially preventing logging or even injecting a new database connection string.

Important properties on the DBContext object

The DbContext itself also has four properties which we can leverage. As with the other objects, we don't have to do anything with these properties if we don't need to, but there are some cases where it might make sense to work with the properties. The four properties of the DBContext are ChangeTracker, ContextId, Database, and Model, as listed in Table 4-3.

Table 4-3. *Properties of the DbContext class*

Property	Purpose
ChangeTracker	Allows us to get direct information about the interactions with entities in our context. Can be used to determine if Lazy Loading is enabled, if the context entities have changes, and is leveraged for major operations like accepting changes and cascading deletes.
ContextId	Every context has a unique id. This can be useful information for logging what context was being leveraged to perform an operation when there are multiple contexts or multiple instances of a context.
Database	This property implements a façade on the database and is primarily used for determining and working with critical database operations like connections, commands, and transactions.
Model	Gets the metadata for the underlying entities and relationships as mapped in the database.

Although it is not always necessary to work with any of these properties, there may be times when you'll want to get direct access to the underlying database to perform operations. A particularly common use to accommodate this need of direct access to the database would be to execute a command that runs a stored procedure, which we'll examine in more detail later in the book.

In addition to the properties on each of these objects, there are some methods that we'll be leveraging for the remainder of our work in this book. Let's start with the DBContext, which contains the majority of the methods we'll be using.

Methods available on the DBContext

When working with the DBContext, we'll first note that most methods have both a traditional synchronous method and also an asynchronous implementation. The main reason for using an asynchronous method is to try to avoid blocking your main thread when making calls to the database. In general, you should try to do this whenever possible for a better user experience. That being said, it's important to note that the DBContext is **not** a thread-safe object, so you may run into concurrency issues and other painful situations if you are building out a multithreaded application.

The methods shown in Table 4-4 are not an exhaustive list of the methods available in the DBContext but are some of the more critical methods you'll encounter both in the real world and while working through this book. To get the full list, you can always reference the full documentation at Microsoft. Table 4-4 shows some of the more common methods we'll use to give us a general idea of what the DBContext can do.

Table 4-4. *Methods of the DbContext class*

Method	Purpose
Add/AddAsync	Allows insertion of the entity into the database; begins tracking the entity. Added objects will be tracked and will be added once the SaveChanges method is called. Note that you can add in a number of ways, including an AddRange method, which allows adding more than one entity at a time.
Find/FindAsync	Find a specific entity by the entity's primary key value (generally an Id).
OnConfiguring	Allows for us to override the options and other information about the database.
OnModelCreating	Allows us to use the FluentAPI to further define our entities and their relationships by configuring the models, their properties, and any relationships.
Remove	Delete an entity from the database. This option also has a RemoveRange ability.
SaveChanges/Save ChangesAsync	Apply the tracked changes in a single transaction.
Update	Used to perform an update to the tracked entity. There is also an ability to update a range of tracked entities with UpdateRange.

What we can see is that the DBContext itself has all the methods necessary for performing *CRUD* operations against the database entities, as well as the critical method for saving changes to apply all of the tracked changes. Even though these methods exist, as we'll see in upcoming examples, we'll actually leverage methods and extensions on the specific DBSet<TEntity> objects to do the majority of our *CRUD* operations. This will become clearer as you gain experience and work through the various activities throughout this book.

Methods and extensions on the DBSet<TEntity> object

The DBSet<TEntity> object has a couple of critical methods and extensions that we will leverage in code, specifically for *CRUD* operations. Table 4-5 shows some of the more important methods and extensions we will rely on when working with DBSet<TEntity> objects.

Table 4-5. *Methods and extensions of the DBSet<TEntity> object*

Name	Method or Extension	Purpose
Add/AddAsync	Method	Adds the entity to the context for insert, begins tracking the entity, and the entity is added on the call to SaveChanges. Also has an AddRange option to do multiple entities at once.
AsNoTracking	Method	Gets an entity that is not tracked so that any modifications do not cause concurrency issues. Calling SaveChanges will not persist any changes or modifications on the entity state.
Find/FindAsync	Method	Locates an entity by primary key (generally Id) and attaches to the current context. Returns null if no match is found.
Include	Method	Used to fetch related entities. Using Include and ThenInclude will be critical to ensure that full data objects are attached to the context.
Remove	Method	Sets the entity as deleted in the context. Changes are persisted only on the call to SaveChanges. Also has a RemoveRange option for multiple entities at once.
SqlQuery	Method	Allows execution of a raw *SQL Query*.
Update	Method	Sets the entity state to modified for the tracked entity; changes are persisted on call to SaveChanges. Also has an UpdateRange option to do multiples at once.
FirstOrDefaultAsync	Extension	Returns the first element that matches a provided condition, or null if no matches.
SingleOrDefaultAsync	Extension	Returns the only possible match to a specified condition. If multiple matches exist, throws an exception. If no matches exist, returns null.

While the majority of the methods we work with will be from the DBSet<T> or DBContext objects, there may be a few instances where methods from the DBContextOptions and/or DBContextOptionsBuilder could be leveraged. For the DBContextOptions, the most common method that would likely be leveraged would be the Freeze method, which prevents the builder options from being further configured in the OnConfiguring method.

Working with models

Assuming you've worked through the previous chapters in this book, you've already had a chance to create a class called Item. You then were able to use the Item class as a model to define the structure of a table in the database by adding a property for DbSet<Item> in the InventoryDbContext and then creating and applying a code-first migration (for more information, review EFCore_Activity03-2_FinalFiles). In that activity, however, we only touched the surface of working with models in the code-first approach.

Two immediate benefits of code-first models

The real power of writing the database objects as code is twofold. The first benefit is that we have an immediate object which we can directly use in code throughout our system.

The second benefit is that we get to define every critical piece of the database in a common language every developer understands while also having that code tracked in our source control repository.

Building a database entity model

In a closer examination, a model is nothing more than another *C# .Net* class that is coded by the developer. This means we can implement models with all of the same tools and techniques we would expect for any object-oriented system.

For example, we can define properties, which then become fields in the database. We can also set constraints on the models, as well as track relationships. Since everything is defined in code, building the models correctly will be critical. The power of an object-oriented approach becomes even more clear when a number of models share basic properties, such as fields for auditing, setting the entity as active, or using a soft delete approach to entities with something like an IsDeleted field.

A final thought about models

To this point in the book, we have not done a lot with models. Don't worry, we'll be getting into working with models more substantially as we progress through the remainder of the text, including seeing how to leverage inheritance to enhance our database solution in the activities for this chapter. We'll also take time to cover what it takes to add constraints and build out relationships in the database. We will cover this in more detail in the next chapter.

For now, we simply need to be aware of the fact that we can model a table directly in a code-first implementation. This is accomplished by taking the following steps:

1. Create the model as a *C# .Net* class to generate a table.

2. Add public properties to the model with a data type and a name for fields.

3. Add the entity to the DBContext (if not already there) as DBSet<TEntity> where TEntity is the type of your model. If the model is already in the DBContext, skip this and proceed to Step 4.

4. Generate a new code-first migration to apply the modeled changes using the add-migration command.

5. Update the database using the update-database command.

In general, these five steps also directly translate to actions you would take in any previous version of EF, including EFCore3, EFCore5, and even EF6.

Activity 4-1: Modifying the Item model

In this activity, you will modify the Item class you created in the last chapter by adding a couple of additional properties. You will then add a new database migration and update the database to get the new fields into the database table.

After you have completed that operation for the critical fields on the Item class, you'll build out an auditing hierarchy to finish up the activity. The auditing hierarchy will leverage inheritance and will allow you to easily configure all of your entities with basic common properties that are useful for auditing and tracking data changes such as who created or was the last person to modify a record.

Practical application for your daily routine

Going forward, as you build out your systems, you will be using a similar flow in most of your daily work. This activity is an exercise to give you another chance to practice building model properties and using them to generate a database migration and then perform the update.

While everything you will do in this activity can be done in one set of operations with just one migration, if you would like even more practice, take the time to add only one property at a time and create a new migration each time, and then update the database each time. No matter how you approach the solution, this activity will give you more practice with generating migrations and updating the database, such as you would do in your day-to-day development routine.

Starter files

From this point on, with the exception of a couple of activities, you will use the same project for the remainder of the book. As you go through each chapter, feel free to just use the same project you have created. However, if you would like to start fresh, each activity for each chapter will have a set of files that are labeled as the starter files. These files will be in the correct state for you to work with them throughout the activity. Additionally, final files will be provided with the solution to the activity in place. Feel free to use the final files to compare your work or see the full final solution in place.

Please review Appendix A for more information on how to work with starter files for each activity.

Task 1: Creating the base project

The easiest way to get started for this activity is to use the starter files located in the zip file labeled `EFCore_Activity04-1_StarterFiles.zip`. Alternatively, if you've worked through all of the activities in Chapter 3, you could just continue working with the solution you had previously used in Activity 3-2.

When working with starter files, make sure to set or validate the connection string to map to your database in the `appsettings.json` files, and then run an initial `update-database` command to get the database up to speed at the start of the project. Also, be aware of migration conflicts that could arise due to my migrations being run with a different timestamp than yours. For more information on using starter files, please review Appendix A.

Step 1: Ensure the code is set up for the activity

As just mentioned, the first thing you need to do is ensure that your project structure looks as follows (names of the projects, especially the activity project, may be different). As long as the functionality is similar, the name is not that important. Review Figure 4-1 to see the starter project structure.

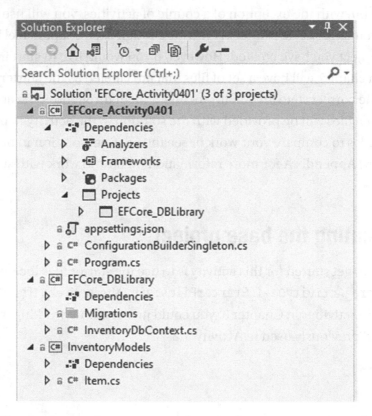

Figure 4-1. *The starter project consists of a simple activity project, the DbLibrary project, and the InventoryModels project in a solution*

Next, run an `update-database` command to ensure that the database is up to date and any pending migrations are applied (don't forget to select the `EFCore_DBLibrary` project in the default project dropdown for the PMC). Additionally, this ensures that your connection string is set correctly. The expected output is shown in Figure 4-2.

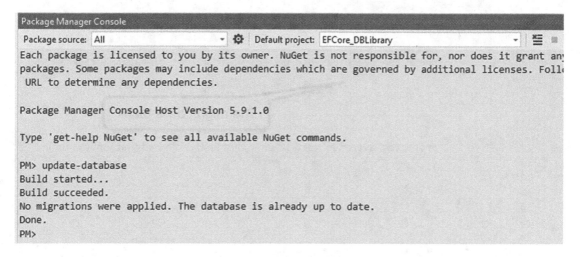

Figure 4-2. *Running an update-database command ensures the database is up to date*

After the `update-database` command, run the following command:

`add-migration test_blank_migration`

When this command completes, you should see a blank migration. If any changes show up, determine if they are necessary (e.g., if the Item table was never added, you should keep this migration and apply it). Assuming there are no pending changes, simply run the `remove-migration` command to delete the generated blank migration. Review Figure 4-3 for clarity.

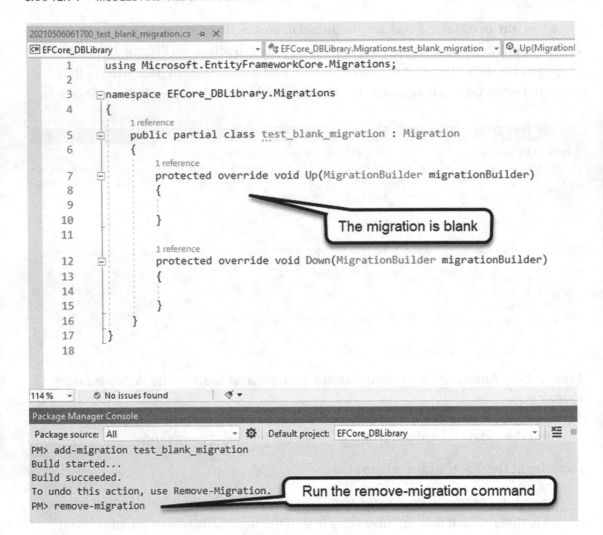

Figure 4-3.   *The remove-migration command is run and generates a blank migration. This is followed by a remove-migration command to clean up the unnecessary migration*

Finally, run the program to ensure the output is as expected for the original five items, as shown in Figure 4-4.

```
New Item: Batman Begins
New Item: Inception
New Item: Remember the Titans
New Item: Star Wars: The Empire Strikes Back
New Item: Top Gun

C:\APressEntityFramework\Code\EFCore_Activity0401\EFCore_Activity0401\
15020) exited with code 0.
To automatically close the console when debugging stops, enable Tools-
le when debugging stops.
Press any key to close this window . . .
```

Figure 4-4. *The expected output of the activity at inception is shown*

Once you are confident your code is in the correct state, you are ready to begin the activity.

This is the only time we'll see these steps in action to ensure the starting state, but you should take this approach before starting any of the activities in the future.

Another final note here is that this would be a really great time to establish a GIT repository on your code if you have not already done so.

Step 2: Move the Configuration Builder Singleton class to a new project

As a purely cosmetic move, the first thing you will do is just move the ConfigurationBuilderSingleton.cs file into a new project. This will serve two purposes, which are to get it out of the way and to make the project easier to reuse in future projects.

Right-click the solution and select Add ➤ New Project, and then select a new Class Library project. Name the project InventoryHelpers, and save it in the same place as the solution file for this activity. Open the project properties and ensure that the new project is set to be configured for .Net 6. For clarity, review Figure 4-5, which shows the newly added project with the properties open and configured to .Net 6.

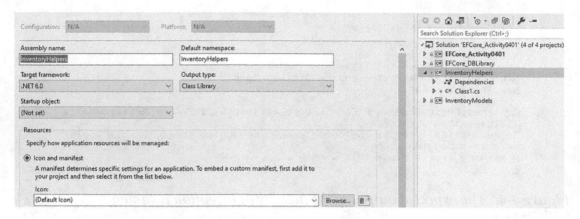

Figure 4-5. *Creating a new helpers project that will allow the singleton to be reused easily in future projects. Additional helper methods can also be added to this project going forward*

Next, delete the Class1.cs class from the new InventoryHelpers project.

After deleting Class1.cs, click the ConfigurationBuilderSingleton.cs class in the activity project and drag it to the new InventoryHelpers project, which will copy the code to the new project. Open the new ConfigurationBuilderSingleton.cs class file in the InventoryHelpers project and change the namespace to InventoryHelpers. Review Figure 4-6 to see the current expected state of the changes made to this point.

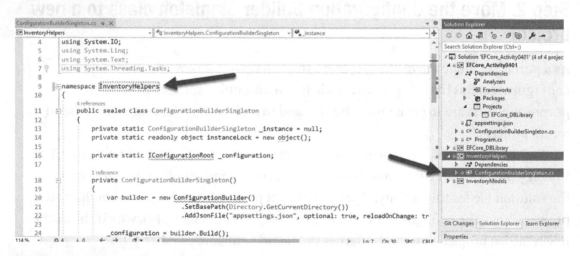

Figure 4-6. *The current changes have placed a copy of the ConfigurationBuilderSingleton.cs in the new project and the namespace is changed to match the new project name*

You'll notice that some red squiggly lines have appeared. You need some NuGet packages. The easiest way to get them is to copy them from the other projects that have them. To save you time, just double-click the new `InventoryHelpers` project to open the `.csproj` file in the VS IDE. With the project open, add the following xml to the `.csproj` file below the `PropertyGroup` and before the closing project tag:

```
<ItemGroup>
  <PackageReference Include="Microsoft.Extensions.Configuration"
  Version="6.0.0-preview.3.21201.4" />
  <PackageReference Include="Microsoft.Extensions.Configuration.
  FileExtensions" Version="6.0.0-preview.3.21201.4" />
  <PackageReference Include="Microsoft.Extensions.Configuration.Json"
  Version="6.0.0-preview.3.21201.4" />
</ItemGroup>
```

Save the file, and this will automatically import the missing NuGet packages (see Figure 4-7).

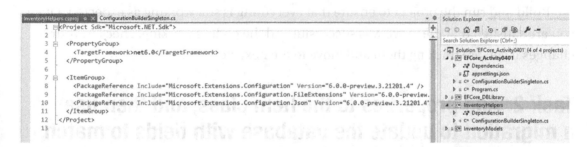

Figure 4-7. *The missing NuGet packages are easily imported by adding them as a reference in the .csproj ItemGroup section*

After saving and importing the project files, build the solution to see if you have any remaining errors. At this point, you should not. You may also wish to open the NuGet Package Manager for the solution and update any packages to the latest versions (if any have updates).

Next, add a project reference in the activity project to include the new `InventoryHelpers` project using Add ➤ `Project Reference`, and check the `InventoryHelpers` project.

With the new helpers project referenced, delete the original
`ConfigurationBuilderSingleton.cs` file from the activity project, and then set all
references to the new project's `ConfigurationBuilderSingleton` as seen in Figure 4-8.

Figure 4-8. *The ConfigurationBuilderSingleton class is now successfully moved to a helpers project and the references are updated, cleaning up the activity project and making this code reusable for future projects*

Build and run the project to ensure that everything is still working as expected. Once
you are satisfied that the move was successful and the code is working, check in your
changes if you are tracking them and move to the next step.

Task 2: Add properties to the Item class, and then use a migration to update the database with fields to match the properties

As you continue to work with the data, you will often need to modify objects in the
database. For this next part of the activity, you will add a few new properties to the Items
class and then use a migration to make the matching fields in the Items table.

Step 1: Add properties to the Item class

For this example, you'll start by adding an `integer` to track *Quantity*, strings for
Description and *Notes*, and a `boolean` property for tracking if the item is on sale.
Additionally, you'll use *nullable objects* to optionally track two `DateTime` fields and two
`decimal` fields. These fields will be named `PurchasedDate`, `SoldDate`, `PurchasePrice`,
and `CurrentOrFinalPrice`.

As you build this out, you'll be placing properties with non-nullable fields at the top and nullable properties at the bottom of the class. This structure is not a requirement – the properties could be in any order that you desire. For example, if you wanted, you could enforce that properties are listed alphabetically. No matter what order you put the properties in for the code in your class, you'll eventually see that the generated migration doesn't care how you order the properties, they will be generated first by alphabetical organization, and then each consecutive change will be done following the original fields, also in alphabetical order for each generated migration.

One last thought before you modify some code. If you are experienced with database development, you might already be thinking about auditing the rows with properties such as *CreatedDate, CreatedBy, ModifiedDate, ModifiedBy, IsActive, IsDeleted*, and any other auditing information you might find useful. You'll get to that before the end of the activity, so please be patient and do not add these fields until prompted to do so.

Begin by opening the `Item.cs` file from the `InventoryModels` class, and then start the task by adding the `integer` for quantity with a property named *Quantity*:

```
public int Quantity { get; set; }
```

Follow that by adding `string` fields for *Notes* and *Description*:

```
public string Description { get; set; }
public string Notes { get; set; }
```

Continue by adding a `boolean` property for tracking if the item is listed for sale:

```
public bool IsOnSale { get; set; }
```

Next, add the `DateTime` fields with properties for *PurchasedDate* and *SoldDate* using the "?" to make sure both fields are nullable in case we haven't yet sold the item or in case we simply don't remember or want to track the date of purchase for an item:

```
public DateTime? PurchasedDate { get; set; }
public DateTime? SoldDate { get; set; }
```

Complete the initial `Item` object rework by adding the nullable `decimal` fields for purchased price and current or final value:

```
public decimal? PurchasePrice { get; set; }
public decimal? CurrentOrFinalPrice { get; set; }
```

The final Item class at this point should look similar to what is shown in Figure 4-9.

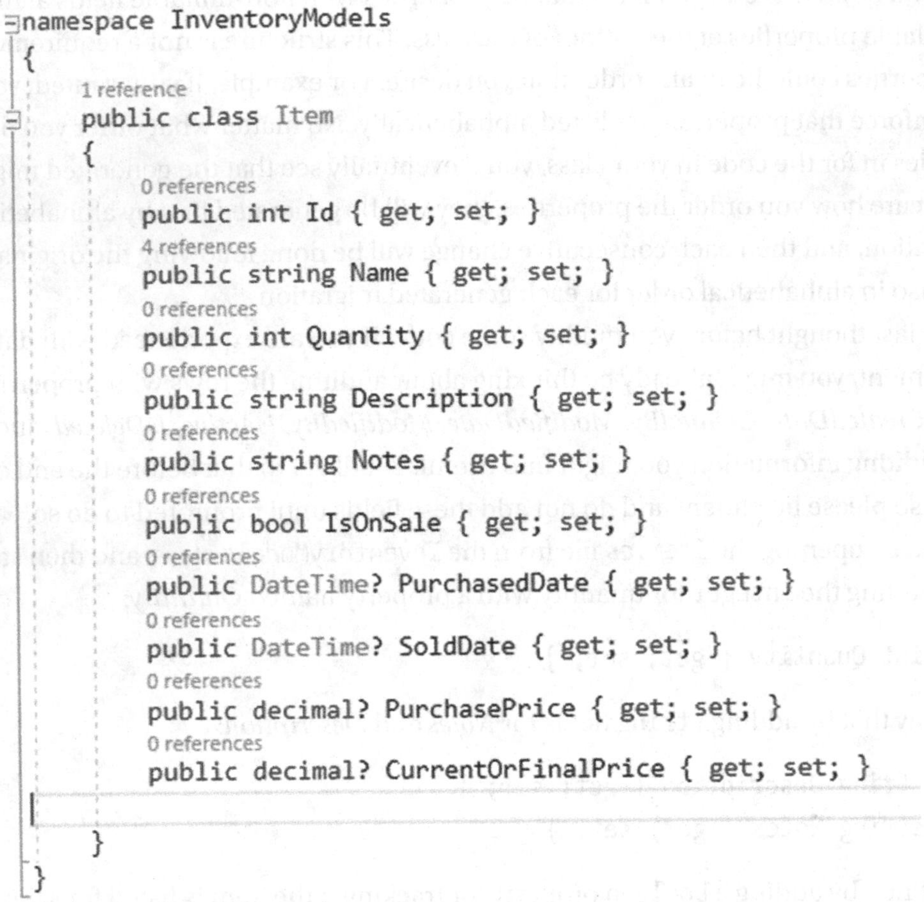

```
namespace InventoryModels
{
    1 reference
    public class Item
    {
        0 references
        public int Id { get; set; }
        4 references
        public string Name { get; set; }
        0 references
        public int Quantity { get; set; }
        0 references
        public string Description { get; set; }
        0 references
        public string Notes { get; set; }
        0 references
        public bool IsOnSale { get; set; }
        0 references
        public DateTime? PurchasedDate { get; set; }
        0 references
        public DateTime? SoldDate { get; set; }
        0 references
        public decimal? PurchasePrice { get; set; }
        0 references
        public decimal? CurrentOrFinalPrice { get; set; }
    }
}
```

Figure 4-9. *The current Item.cs class has the new properties added as defined*

Step 2: Add a new migration to get the properties into the database as fields on the Items table

With your Item model changed, the next thing you need to do is add a new migration to make the changes propagate into the database.

Begin by making sure you save all your changes, and then run a build to ensure there are no errors. Generally, you'd hit the chord *Ctrl+S* and then *Ctrl+Shift+B* to save and then build. That being said, building the solution should save changes, so the step to save may be extraneous.

To be clear, it is also not necessary to build the project. Building the project will happen before the add-migration command is applied. However, by building the project first, we ensure that we can clean up any errors before trying to create the migration. If we simply run the add-migration command and the project won't build, we'll get an error notification and the migration will not be generated.

Build the project, and then run the command

```
add-migration updated_items_table
```

Figure 4-10 shows the successful generation of the migration.

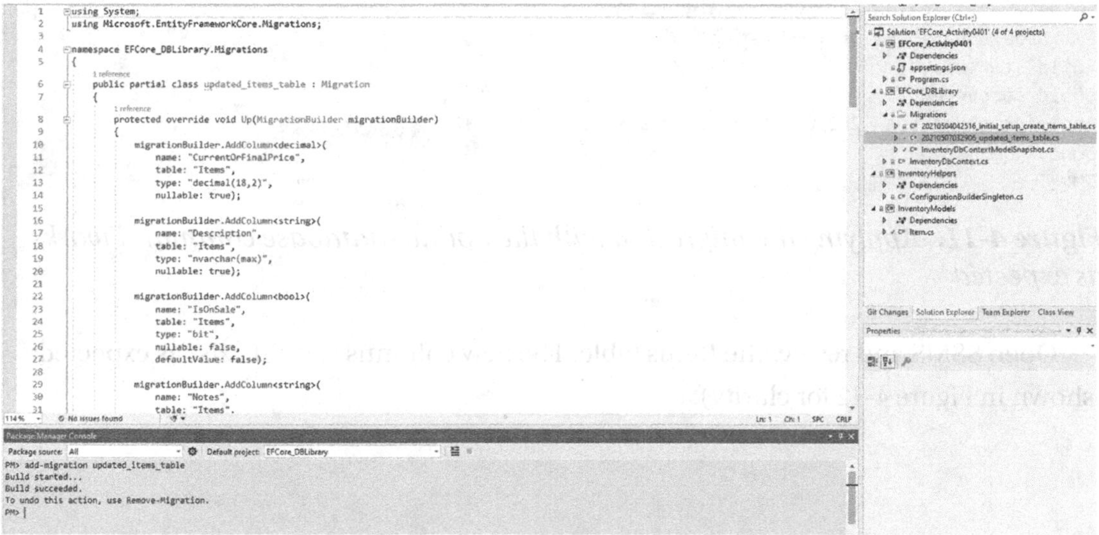

Figure 4-10. *The project builds as expected and a migration is added*

You should take a moment to review the code generated in the migration. You should see each of the new fields added as a column in the Up method and then also dropped in the Down method. You can also check the type and the ability for a field to be null, as per the generated migration.

You might then notice that every field generated is nullable. This is OK for now, but probably not the desired solution overall. The reason they are null by default here is twofold. The first reason is because you never stated that any fields were required. The second reason is because data may already exist in the table, and, if so, adding a required field would also require that the field has a default value. Without a default value, adding a new required field to the table requires a truncation of data, and the migration would fail to apply due to the potential loss of data. You will learn more about these issues as you work through future activities with constraints in the next chapter.

Step 3: Apply the migration and review the database structure

To complete this task, run the update-database command to apply the migration generated in the previous step (see Figure 4-11).

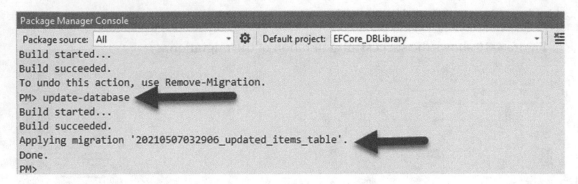

Figure 4-11. *Applying the migration with the update-database command works as expected*

Open SSMS and review the Items table. The new columns should exist as expected (shown in Figure 4-12 for clarity).

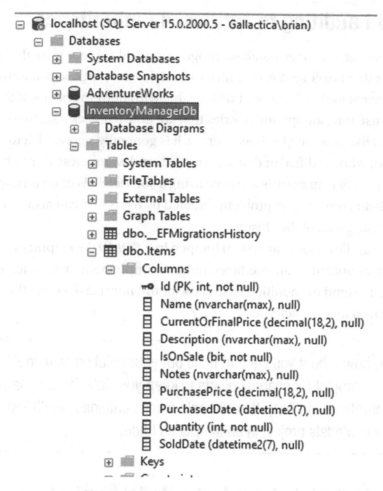

Figure 4-12. *The Items table is updated after the migration is applied*

In Figure 4-12, while reviewing your database table, you can see a couple of important notes. First, the fields that were just applied were in alphabetical order regardless of how you coded them in the model. If we had examined the migration, you would have seen them also laid out in this manner. Additionally, you see that the original fields are still at the top of the column list. This tells us that fields are generally created in alphabetical order, but their positions are kept in sequence with the migrations. The same thing would happen if more fields were added in a new migration, as they would be generated alphabetically and would follow the SoldDate column.

Task 3: Add auditing to entities via inheritance

As mentioned earlier, seasoned database programmers likely recognize that there are a couple of things that are generally very nice to track for the purpose of auditing the data changes. As a caveat to this, however, I will say that with newer versions of *SQL Server*, it is possible to use timestamps and queries that are able to check data to see what the database looked like at a specific time. Even so, it is generally a good idea to track who created a record, who modified or deleted a record, and when these things happened. Additionally, tracking if an entry is active or using a soft delete is often an approach that is favorable to help recover from problems created by users and can also be used to filter items without losing a lot of data history.

To make the auditing for your system happen in a *SOLID* development approach, you will create a couple of small interfaces and then implement them in an auditing base class. You'll then extend the auditing base class for the *Item* class, create the resulting migration, and update the database.

Depending on how robust you want to build out your solution, you could choose to create a new project for shared objects to keep your interfaces separate from your implementations. To keep this example more contained, you'll just put the interfaces in the Models project in an Interfaces folder.

Step 1: Create the interfaces in the Models project

To begin this activity, create a new folder in the Models project and name the folder Interfaces. Once the folder is created, right-click and select Add ➤ New Item, then choose Code ➤ Interface, and name the file IIdentityModel.cs. In the file, make sure that the code is for a new interface and contains the following code:

```
public interface IIdentityModel
{
    public int Id { get; set; }
}
```

For clarity, the new interface code in the new file is shown in Figure 4-13.

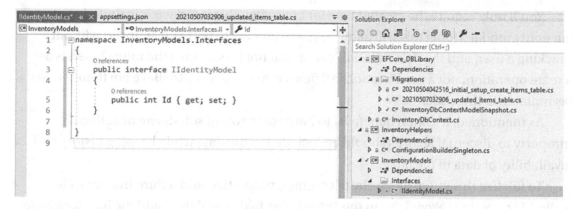

Figure 4-13. *A new Interfaces folder is created, and a new file IIdentityModel.cs is created in the folder, with the code for the IIdentityModel interface*

Remember that if any part of the activity becomes confusing or you are encountering strange errors, you may always refer to my final solution for the activity to see how I intended for you to implement the code.

Depending on how you are tracking your users by Id, we'll need to respond accordingly with the type for the user id. When working with built-in *ASP.Net MVC* users, likely this will be a `string` to map to a `guid`. For other systems, you might be using an `int` or `long` type. We don't have users in this system, so for now we'll use `strings`, for the simple reason that any data can be used as a string, and we could update this later as the need arises. If you wanted to use int or long, you can do so, just make sure that they are nullable (`int?` or `long?`) for now, since you haven't yet learned about constraints or how to deal with required fields on existing tables.

Next, you will need to create another file for `IAuditedModel.cs` in the `Interfaces` folder, then write the code to create an interface called `IAuditedModel`, and add properties for tracking who created or modified the data row using the following code:

```
public interface IAuditedModel
{
    public string CreatedByUserId { get; set; }
    public DateTime CreatedDate { get; set; }
    public string LastModifiedUserId { get; set; }
    public DateTime? LastModifiedDate { get; set; }
}
```

You'll only require the created date for now when this interface is included on an entity model. Doing this will allow a system process to perform an insert without tracking a user, and the default modification will not be set since the initial insert is a create operation, not a modification. All fields other than CreatedDate are therefore set as nullable in this code.

As mentioned, it's often beneficial to have some sort of soft delete or activatable property to discern if records should be included in the data while keeping history and availability of data in the table.

To finalize this initial hierarchy of common properties, add a third interface file called IActivatableModel.cs in the Interfaces folder, and then add the interface code as follows in the file:

```
public interface IActivatableModel
{
    public bool IsActive { get; set; }
}
```

Now that all the interfaces are in place, you could create multiple base classes to make various entity implementations. Since C# .Net doesn't allow for multiple inheritance, you'll just create one base class to rule them all: FullAuditModel.cs.

At the top level of the InventoryModels project, create a new class file called FullAuditModel.cs, then make the class abstract, and implement all three of the new interfaces. Also remember, you will never want to add this class to your DBContext as a DBSet. Keeping the base class as an abstract class should also prevent future confusion on this point.

```
public abstract class FullAuditModel : IIdentityModel, IAuditedModel,
IActivatableModel
{
    public int Id { get; set; }
    public string CreatedByUserId { get; set; }
    public DateTime CreatedDate { get; set; }
    public string LastModifiedUserId { get; set; }
    public DateTime? LastModifiedDate { get; set; }
    public bool IsActive { get; set; }
}
```

You will also need to bring in the using statement for the interfaces once you implement them on this abstract class. Figure 4-14 shows the base class and the expected placement in the project hierarchy for clarity.

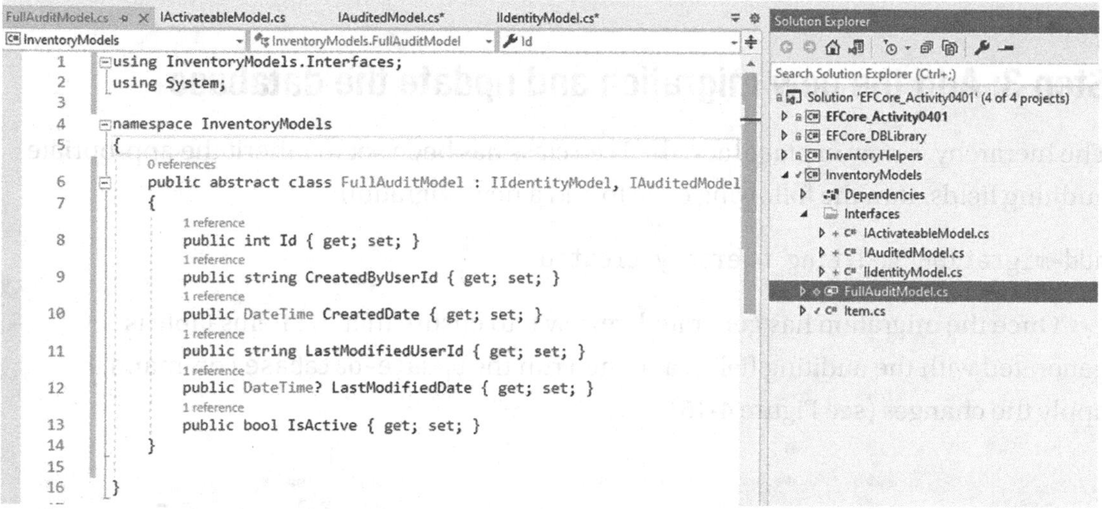

Figure 4-14. *The FullAuditModel class is at the top level of the InventoryModels project and implements all of the auditing interfaces. This base class will allow entities to easily be configured with common auditing properties*

Step 2: Extend the `FullAuditModel` on the Item class to add auditing properties

To complete the auditing hierarchy work, you'll need to inherit the `FullAuditModel` on the `Item` class. Open the `Item` class and modify it to use the code as follows – extending the abstract base `FullAuditModel` and removing the `Id` property since it will be included via inheritance:

```
public class Item : FullAuditModel
{
    public string Name { get; set; }
    public int Quantity { get; set; }
    public string Description { get; set; }
    public string Notes { get; set; }
    public bool IsOnSale { get; set; }
    public DateTime? PurchasedDate { get; set; }
```

```
    public DateTime? SoldDate { get; set; }
    public decimal? PurchasePrice { get; set; }
    public decimal? CurrentOrFinalPrice { get; set; }
}
```

Step 3: Add the new migration and update the database

The hierarchy is now in place, and the Item class has been set to inherit the appropriate auditing fields. Run the following code to add a new migration:

```
add-migration Auditing_hierachy_created
```

Once the migration has generated, review it to ensure that the Items table is generated with the auditing fields, and then run the update-database command to apply the changes (see Figure 4-15).

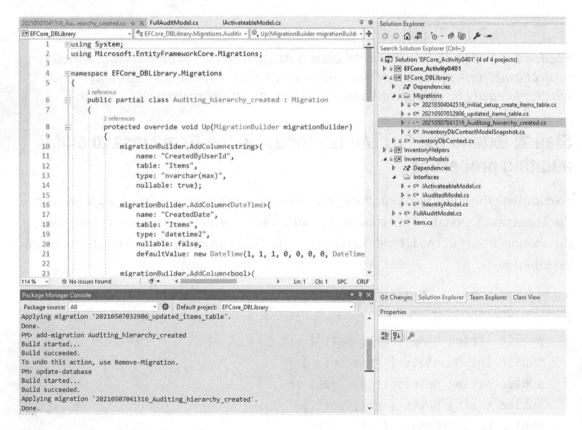

Figure 4-15. *The auditing hierarchy is completed, and the migration is generated and applied to modify the Items table with the appropriate fields*

Step 4: Review the database

Once again, return to SSMS and review the Items table. The new auditing fields should appear as expected and as shown in Figure 4-16.

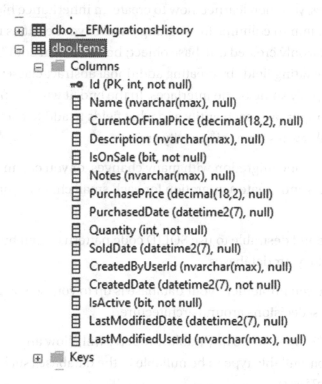

Figure 4-16. *The auditing fields are successfully added to the Items table in the database via the migration*

At this point, we have completed the activity and are prepared to move on to the next activity. If you are tracking your code in source control, now would be a good time to commit your changes as an excellent restore point.

Please also note that if you tried to run the code from the console and you needed to add a new item, it will not really work in its current state since you are not handling the additional required fields (i.e., CreatedDate). You will be looking at this in more detail in the next activity.

Activity 4-1 summary

In this activity, you learned how to work with the database to create changes on an existing table. You first modified the Item class to add properties to the database table. After the initial changes, you then learned how to create an inheritance hierarchy to allow easily creating common columns for auditing on all of your entities in the future.

In this example, you only created one base object; however, you could easily have done only part of the auditing fields by creating additional abstract classes or just directly implementing only some of the interfaces. In the end, it will be up to you as the developer as to how to approach each entity and what fields to add to each table.

Some of the key takeaways from this activity are

- You can create one migration with many changes, or you can make small changes and create a migration for each small change along the way.

- It is possible and desirable to use SOLID code patterns when building the models for your databases.

- The way that you implement your database is up to you, so you must make the best decisions around architecture.

- Adding the "?" operator to any public property will allow any normally non-nullable type to be nullable in the database (such as int? or DateTime?).

- Strings and other nullable types are defaulted as nullable in the database.

- Using the add-migration and update-database commands will be a common operation for any developer in a code-first approach.

- It does not matter what order you create properties in the model class. Each migration will alphabetize the properties for creation.

- Additional properties in a consecutive migration are applied after original columns (appended) – the entire table is not restructured to alphabetize the order of columns.

Activity 4-2: Using the ChangeTracker to inject some automated auditing

In the previous activity, you learned how to set up a hierarchy to track auditing information about entities in the database. You then applied that hierarchy and created the appropriate migrations so that the Items will be auditable going forward. Adding these common fields is a great way to track all this information, but you will also want to be able to create a way to automate this auditing so that you don't have to write the same kinds of auditing code around each entity in a repetitive fashion.

In this activity, you will learn how to use the ChangeTracker from EF in order to inject some automated auditing information at the time that database changes are applied.

Remember how you already set up the DBContext

You've already seen a few examples in this book and seen scenarios where you've covered setting up the context to work against existing or new databases. The main takeaways from what you've already learned about EF and the DBContext include

- The DBContext needs to be able to connect to the database via a connection string. This is accomplished in the pre-configured DbContextOptions in *EFCore6*.

- *EFCore6* gives us a method that allows us to check if the context options are configured. When they are not, we can perform custom code to ensure the configuration is built as needed.

- You can work with a new or existing database, and either approach can allow for working in the code-first approach to development.

- All EF operations are applied with the UoW pattern baked in, meaning that transactions are handled without you having to do any additional work.

- In the code-first approach, C# classes can be used to define the schema as entity models, and when the model is added to the context with the DbSet<TEntity>, migrations can be applied that allow the model to dictate the structure of the database table.

Common critical underlying objects

In addition to the things you've already seen, a couple of critical notes about the DBContext include the fact that in *EFCore6*, and previous versions of EF as well (including *EFCore3*, *EFCore5*, and even *EF6*), the underlying Database is able to be exposed and used as an object. Additionally, the DBContext relies heavily on an object to track changes, which can be leveraged through the DBContext property ChangeTracker.

You'll take a deeper look at accessing the underlying database later in the book when we cover database objects like stored procedures. For this activity, however, you're going to work solely with the ChangeTracker.

The ChangeTracker is the lifeblood of our interaction with the Entity Framework

In a typical workflow, some items are fetched and displayed to the user. After the user has time to review the objects, they may perform updates on one or more of the objects, may insert new objects, or may delete objects.

As the user performs actions, *EF* is working behind the scenes to orchestrate the changes while having the ability to undo the changes if something goes wrong (remember that the UoW pattern is applied by default in EF without any interaction from the developer). The changes are generally only in memory, until a point when an explicit call is made to update the database via the DBContext – SaveChanges method.

At the time that the SaveChanges method is called, the changes that are stored in the ChangeTracker are applied to the database through the underlying connection to the database from *EF*.

Task 1: Getting started

In this task, you will ensure that you are set up for success on the activity. To do this, you can either continue with the code that was generated by working through the previous activity (Activity 4-1), or you may simply get the starter files: EFCore_Activity04-2_ StarterFiles.

Remember that no matter which path you take, it is always a good idea to ensure you have all pending migrations applied and that adding a migration generates a blank migration. More information on how to do those initial checks was provided at the start of Activity 4-1. Additional information about working with starter files can be found in Appendix A.

Step 1: Clean up the data, and then run the program

As it currently stands, the database is now expecting auditing data, as well as additional fields in regard to the items. Since the data was originally created with a fairly limited model (just the Id and Name), it's a good time for you to just wipe the table.

Open the database in SSMS and run the following query to delete the data:

```
TRUNCATE TABLE dbo.Items
SELECT * FROM dbo.Items
```

It will just delete the items and will also reset the auto-generated identity to start over at 1. If you have relationships defined, you can't truncate without first removing constraints. At this point, you should not have any of those constraints in place, however. In the end, the data should be blank as shown in the result from the query in your SSMS window.

Next, try to run the program. At this point, you won't see an error, but the CreatedDate is non-nullable, so it will be inserted with a really bad date of 0001-01-01 00:00:00.0000000 (see Figure 4-17).

	Id	Name	CurrentOrFinalPrice	Description	IsOnSale	Notes	PurchasePrice	PurchasedDate	Quantity	SoldDate	CreatedByUserId	CreatedDate	IsActive	LastModifiedDate	LastModifiedUserId
1	1	Batman Begins	NULL	NULL	0	NULL	NULL	NULL	0	NULL	NULL	0001-01-01 00:00:00.0000000	0	NULL	NULL
2	2	Inception	NULL	NULL	0	NULL	NULL	NULL	0	NULL	NULL	0001-01-01 00:00:00.0000000	0	NULL	NULL
3	3	Remember the Titans	NULL	NULL	0	NULL	NULL	NULL	0	NULL	NULL	0001-01-01 00:00:00.0000000	0	NULL	NULL
4	4	Star Wars: The Empire Strikes Back	NULL	NULL	0	NULL	NULL	NULL	0	NULL	NULL	0001-01-01 00:00:00.0000000	0	NULL	NULL
5	5	Top Gun	NULL	NULL	0	NULL	NULL	NULL	0	NULL	NULL	0001-01-01 00:00:00.0000000	0	NULL	NULL

Figure 4-17. *The program works, but new Items are generated with bad data as currently written. This is expected*

Also note that other default values are entered, such as 0 for IsOnSale and Quantity and IsActive. These are all things that will need to be addressed at some point (and they will be, in time).

181

Step 2: Add a method to delete all Items at the start of the program

In the future, we may wish to persist data past each run. For now, this is a good chance to see how easy it is to use EF to delete records.

Add a new method call in the Main method of the Program.cs file before the call to EnsureItems, with the call as DeleteAllItems(). Then add the new method in the Program class:

```
private static void DeleteAllItems()
{
    using (var db = new InventoryDbContext(_optionsBuilder.Options))
    {
        var items = db.Items.ToList();
        db.Items.RemoveRange(items);
        db.SaveChanges();
    }
}
```

Note that deleting the items is different from truncating the table. When you truncate, you reset the identity. When you delete, you just remove the data but the identity increment will not be reset. Additionally, you can always delete as long as the cascading delete options are configured for referential integrity, whereas you cannot truncate if there are relationships in place as previously mentioned.

After adding the method, run the code a few times, and then select from the Items table to see that the identity counter has continued to increment, even though you only have five records. Figure 4-18 shows a possible result, along with a view of the DeleteAllItems method for clarity.

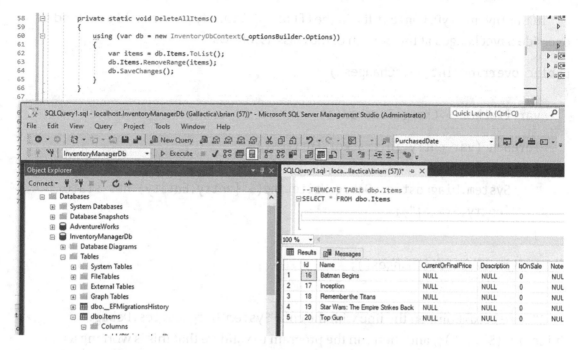

```
58          private static void DeleteAllItems()
59          {
60              using (var db = new InventoryDbContext(_optionsBuilder.Options))
61              {
62                  var items = db.Items.ToList();
63                  db.Items.RemoveRange(items);
64                  db.SaveChanges();
65              }
66          }
67
```

Figure 4-18. *The DeleteAllItems method is run at the start of each run and deletes the records but does not reset the identity counter*

At this point, you are ready to start using the ChangeTracker to add some automated auditing to your solution.

Task 2: Use the change tracker to inject auditing information on calls to save changes

In this task, you will leverage the fact that the change tracker and the UoW are implemented in EF to intercept the call to SaveChanges() and add some code to inject auditing information.

Step 1: Override the SaveChanges() method

In every instance where you are making changes to the database, the final step that you take is to call to the SaveChanges method to apply the tracked changes. As of right now, you are letting the default operation take place. In this step, you will change that by overriding the SaveChanges method.

In the InventoryDBContext file in the EFCore_DbLibrary project, add a method to override SaveChanges at the bottom of the class as follows:

```
public override int SaveChanges()
{
    var tracker = ChangeTracker;

    foreach (var entry in tracker.Entries())
    {
        System.Diagnostics.Debug.WriteLine($"{entry.Entity} has state
        {entry.State}");
    }

    return base.SaveChanges();
}
```

Place a breakpoint on the line with the code System.Diagnostics.Debug. WriteLine($"...");, and then run the program to validate that this is working as expected. Once you have seen enough iterations to get a grasp on the ChangeTracker, feel free to remove the breakpoint and run to completion. Make sure to also hover over or add a watch on the entry.Entity and entry.State when the debugger is paused on the breakpoint to see the values. Figure 4-19 shows the execution of this code, with the expected output values in the Output window.

Figure 4-19. *The change tracker has a reference to every object that has been added or deleted in our example*

Taking a closer look at the valid states of an entity in the ChangeTracker, you can leverage any of these states in code. Additionally, your "logging" was fairly vanilla in this case, as you could also have grabbed the entity Id and other properties from the entry.Entity if you would have need to do so (you do have to check type and make sure to cast to the correct type to get to the inner properties like Id and Name).

Diving into the documentation at https://docs.microsoft.com/en-us/dotnet/ api/microsoft.entityframeworkcore.entitystate?view=efcore-6.0, you can see the valid entity states which you can write code against. The valid states are Added, Deleted, Detached, Modified, and Unchanged.

In our code, with the CreatedDate, we'll care about the Added state; and with the LastModifiedDate, we'll care about Deleted and Modified state.

Step 2: Respond to the entity state in the change tracker

In this step, you will write the code that allows you to override the SaveChanges method and inject values for each entity's auditing trail based on the user and date information and the state of the entity.

Before you build your automated logging however, you need to address an elephant in the room. As of right now, the system is not tracking users. Therefore, at this time, you don't have a way to correctly set a valid user id. If you were working in *ASP.Net MVC* with default identities, you could easily grab the logged in user id from session and just pass it in with the model. Depending on where you are performing the save, you might even have direct access to that session information.

Additionally, if you want to ensure a user id, you might need to also block the default method from executing and create an *overload* that contains the user id as a parameter and then proceed to set the values accordingly and call to the base.SaveChanges method from the overloaded method.

For this example, just start by going back to the program and setting a default user Id to add for the operations on the Item directly. This will simulate what you could do in your code provided you had some way to get the user id of the logged in user.

Add the following code to the Program class in the Program.cs file, after the creation of the configuration and optionsBuilder variables:

```
private const string _systemUserId = "2fd28110-93d0-427d-9207-d55dbca680fa";
private const string _loggedInUserId = "e2eb8989-a81a-4151-8e86-
eb95a7961da2";
```

Next, in the `EnsureItem` method, change the code for creating new items to have some valid values:

```
private static void EnsureItem(string name)
{
    Random r = new Random();
    using (var db = new InventoryDbContext(_optionsBuilder.Options))
    {
        //determine if item exists:
        var existingItem = db.Items.FirstOrDefault(x => x.Name.ToLower()
                                              == name.ToLower());

        if (existingItem == null)
        {
            //doesn't exist, add it.
            var item = new Item() { Name = name,
                                    CreatedByUserId = _loggedInUserId,
                                    IsActive = true,
                                    Quantity = r.Next()};
            db.Items.Add(item);
            db.SaveChanges();
        }
    }
}
```

Return to the `InventoryDbContext`, and add the following code right after the creation of the configuration variable:

```
private const string _systemUserId = "2fd28110-93d0-427d-9207-d55dbca680fa";
```

One important thing that you still need to do is modify the entity's `CreatedDate` or `LastModifiedDate` property, along with setting the user id if it is not provided. This is a bit tricky, because you'll need to do some type checking first to make sure the type has the correct field, and then you'll set the value when it does. Even though you've set a pretty solid example and the `Item` has the fields for auditing, as of right now, there could still be a rogue entity that another developer has created without the auditing fields on that entity.

After validating that this is an entity type that has auditing, you can then create a switch to handle the various entity states and update your entry with a local reference according to what operation is happening and what information you do or do not have available.

Implement the following code to check entry entity type and use a switch when you are set to modify the entry:

```
public override int SaveChanges()
{
    var tracker = ChangeTracker;

    foreach (var entry in tracker.Entries())
    {
        if (entry.Entity is FullAuditModel)
        {
            var referenceEntity = entry.Entity as FullAuditModel;
            switch (entry.State)
            {
                case EntityState.Added:
                    referenceEntity.CreatedDate = DateTime.Now;
                    if (string.IsNullOrWhiteSpace(referenceEntity.
                    CreatedByUserId))
                    {
                        referenceEntity.CreatedByUserId = _systemUserId;
                    }
                    break;
                case EntityState.Deleted:
                case EntityState.Modified:
                    referenceEntity.LastModifiedDate = DateTime.Now;
                    if (string.IsNullOrWhiteSpace(referenceEntity.
                    LastModifiedUserId))
                    {
                        referenceEntity.LastModifiedUserId = _systemUserId;
                    }
                    break;
```

```
            default:
                break;
        }
    }
}

    return base.SaveChanges();
}
```

Note that this code ensures that user ids will always be set and the correct date is updated by default based on the state of the entity. When implemented correctly, the code should look as is shown for clarity in Figure 4-20.

```csharp
public override int SaveChanges()
{
    var tracker = ChangeTracker;

    foreach (var entry in tracker.Entries())
    {
        if (entry.Entity is FullAuditModel)
        {
            var referenceEntity = entry.Entity as FullAuditModel;
            switch (entry.State)
            {
                case EntityState.Added:
                    referenceEntity.CreatedDate = DateTime.Now;
                    if (string.IsNullOrWhiteSpace(referenceEntity.CreatedByUserId))
                    {
                        referenceEntity.CreatedByUserId = _systemUserId;
                    }
                    break;
                case EntityState.Deleted:
                case EntityState.Modified:
                    referenceEntity.LastModifiedDate = DateTime.Now;
                    if (string.IsNullOrWhiteSpace(referenceEntity.LastModifiedUserId))
                    {
                        referenceEntity.LastModifiedUserId = _systemUserId;
                    }
                    break;
                default:
                    break;
            }
        }
    }

    return base.SaveChanges();
}
```

Figure 4-20. *The SaveChanges method is overridden, and the auditing information is added to each eligible entity on save so that developers will not have to implement this logic on every entity directly*

Run the application again, and then check the table for results. At this point, you should have the default five records, but now they should all have a valid created date and user id. Figure 4-21 shows a sample of what the data should look like after a new run with the latest version of the code by executing the query

```
SELECT Id, Name, Quantity, CreatedByUserId, CreatedDate, IsActive
FROM dbo.Items
```

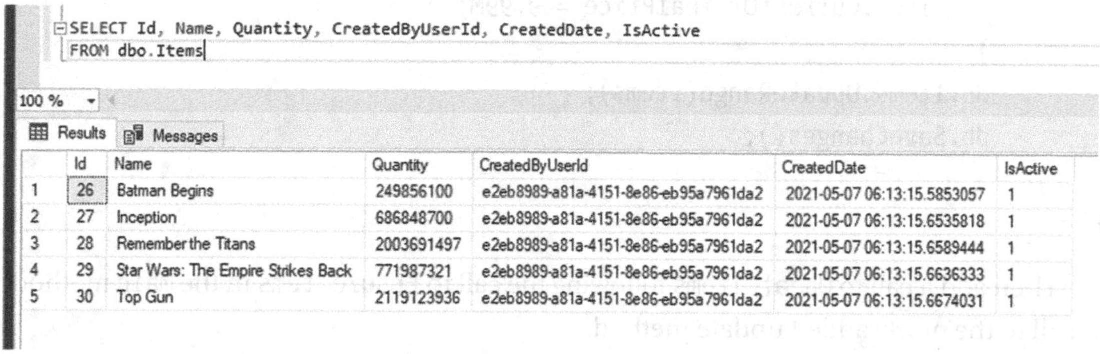

Figure 4-21. *The results are working as expected with a valid CreatedDate and CreatedByUserId*

Although the automated auditing is working, currently all of the data is wiped out so there is no proof that the system id is being used on modification or delete.

Task 3: Add an update method to validate last modified auditing is working as expected

In this next task, you will add a method to update a record so that you can be certain the last modified information is audited as expected, simulating another user with the default system user id and last modified date.

Step 1: Add the update method

In the Program class in the Program.cs file, add the following code to the end of the file for the Update method:

```
private static void UpdateItems()
{
    using (var db = new InventoryDbContext(_optionsBuilder.Options))
    {
        var items = db.Items.ToList();
        foreach (var item in items)
        {
            item.CurrentOrFinalPrice = 9.99M;
        }
        db.Items.UpdateRange(items);
        db.SaveChanges();
    }
}
```

Then add a call to `UpdateItems` following the call to `EnsureItems` in the `Main` method to call to the newly added update method.

This is a contrived update that simply updates all the items with a current or final price, but it is enough to trigger the last modified information on the entities.

Run the program, and then examine the results. You should now see updated items with a current or final price set and both the created and last modified auditing fields set. Note that the user id for the update was allowed to be set to the system id to prove that the id can be injected at any part of the process. You could just as easily have passed a user id from the `Main` method. Figure 4-22 shows the updated result (remember that the items are deleted so the create and update dates will likely be only milliseconds different from one another – if you don't like that, wait about five minutes and comment out the delete call). Use the following query to view the data:

```
SELECT Id, Name, CurrentOrFinalPrice, Quantity, CreatedByUserId,
CreatedDate, IsActive, LastModifiedDate, LastModifiedUserId
FROM dbo.Items
```

```
SELECT Id, Name, CurrentOrFinalPrice, Quantity, CreatedByUserId, CreatedDate, IsActive, LastModifiedDate, LastModifiedUserId
FROM dbo.Items
```

	Id	Name	Current...	Quantity	CreatedByUserId	CreatedDate	IsActive	LastModifiedDate	LastModifiedUserId
1	31	Batman Begins	9.99	2099283818	e2eb8989-a81a-4151-8e86-eb95a7961da2	2021-05-07 06:...	1	2021-05-07 06:...	2fd28110-93d0-427d-9207-d55dbca680fa
2	32	Inception	9.99	1293400000	e2eb8989-a81a-4151-8e86-eb95a7961da2	2021-05-07 06:...	1	2021-05-07 06:...	2fd28110-93d0-427d-9207-d55dbca680fa
3	33	Remember the ...	9.99	771478800	e2eb8989-a81a-4151-8e86-eb95a7961da2	2021-05-07 06:...	1	2021-05-07 06:...	2fd28110-93d0-427d-9207-d55dbca680fa
4	34	Star Wars: The ...	9.99	2144376104	e2eb8989-a81a-4151-8e86-eb95a7961da2	2021-05-07 06:...	1	2021-05-07 06:...	2fd28110-93d0-427d-9207-d55dbca680fa
5	35	Top Gun	9.99	641692682	e2eb8989-a81a-4151-8e86-eb95a7961da2	2021-05-07 06:...	1	2021-05-07 06:...	2fd28110-93d0-427d-9207-d55dbca680fa

Figure 4-22. *The last modified auditing information is now proven as being appropriately tracked*

Step 2: Update the Insert method to add a couple of Notes and Description information to the Items

To complete this activity, you'll finish up by making the initial items just a bit more robust.

Update the EnsureItem method to take a string for Description and Notes, and then pass the information by updating the code for EnsureItems and EnsureItem to the following code:

```
static void EnsureItems()
{
    EnsureItem("Batman Begins", "You either die the hero or live long
    enough to see yourself become the villain", "Christian Bale, Katie
    Holmes");
    EnsureItem("Inception", "You mustn't be afraid to dream a little bigger,
    darling", "Leonardo DiCaprio, Tom Hardy, Joseph Gordon-Levitt" );
    EnsureItem("Remember the Titans", "Left Side, Strong Side", "Denzell
    Washington, Will Patton" );
    EnsureItem("Star Wars: The Empire Strikes Back", "He will join us or
    die, master", "Harrison Ford, Carrie Fisher, Mark Hamill");
    EnsureItem("Top Gun", "I feel the need, the need for speed!", "Tom
    Cruise, Anthony Edwards, Val Kilmer");
}
```

```
private static void EnsureItem(string name, string description,
string notes)
{
    Random r = new Random();
    using (var db = new InventoryDbContext(_optionsBuilder.Options))
    {
        //determine if item exists:
        var existingItem = db.Items.FirstOrDefault(x => x.Name.ToLower()
                                                == name.ToLower());

        if (existingItem == null)
        {
            //doesn't exist, add it.
            var item = new Item() { Name = name,
                                    CreatedByUserId = _loggedInUserId,
                                    IsActive = true,
                                    Quantity = r.Next(),
                                    Description = description,
                                    Notes = notes };
            db.Items.Add(item);
            db.SaveChanges();
        }
    }
}
```

Run the program and review the output and the database data to ensure that everything is as expected. Figure 4-23 shows the expected output in the database using the query

```
SELECT Id, Name, [Description], Notes, CurrentOrFinalPrice,
LastModifiedDate, LastModifiedUserId
FROM dbo.Items
```

```
SELECT Id, Name, [Description], Notes, CurrentOrFinalPrice, LastModifiedDate, LastModifiedUserId
FROM dbo.Items
```

	Id	Name	Description	Notes	CurrentOrFinalPrice	LastModifiedDate
1	36	Batman Begins	You either die the hero or live long enough to s...	Christian Bale, Katie Holmes	9.99	2021-05-07 06:23:00.79124(
2	37	Inception	You mustn't be afraid to dream a little bigger, da...	Leonardo DiCaprio, Tom Hardy, Joseph Gordon-Levitt	9.99	2021-05-07 06:23:00.79135(
3	38	Remember the Titans	Left Side, Strong Side	Denzell Washington, Will Patton	9.99	2021-05-07 06:23:00.79136
4	39	Star Wars: The Empire Strikes Back	He will join us or die, master	Harrison Ford, Carrie Fisher, Mark Hamill	9.99	2021-05-07 06:23:00.79136
5	40	Top Gun	I feel the need, the need for speed!	Tom Cruise, Anthony Edwards, Val Kilmer	9.99	2021-05-07 06:23:00.79136

Figure 4-23. *The data is now more robust, and the auditing is in place and working as expected*

At this point, you should go ahead and comment out the call to the DeleteAllItems method, as it is no longer needed, and the code should still be idempotent for ensuring items. Additional runs after commenting out the code should provide more separation in the created and modified dates.

Activity 4-2 summary

In this final activity for Chapter 4, you learned about how you can use the fact that all of the data is saved via a call to SaveChanges on the database context. Although you have not yet learned about the UoW pattern directly, you have seen it in action and leveraged the fact that it is built into the EF context.

By overriding the SaveChanges method, you were able to inject some automated auditing into each entity that is appropriately constructed via the auditing interfaces that were established in Activity 4-1.

Putting this all together, you've now seen how to get started with the database and use the context and models to generate tables in the database, as well as how to leverage properties of the tables for CRUD operations through the context. Further, you have seen how to override the SaveChanges method to allow for final data manipulation before saving to the database.

Chapter summary

In this chapter, you learned how to leverage the DBContext when creating models to define the database schema. You got to see some of this in action by running a few migrations as you made changes to the Item class. You also learned how to set up an object hierarchy using inheritance and SOLID principles so that you could build a robust automated auditing solution in your EF database operations.

Important takeaways

After working through this chapter, the things you should be in command of are

- Adding migrations

- Updating the database via migrations

- Creating an entity hierarchy via interfaces and abstract classes

- Leveraging an override to the SaveChanges method to inject data changes for saving the data to the database

- General understanding of the basic underlying pieces in any code-first database solution

Closing thoughts

Although you learned a great deal and have set up a SOLID start to building a robust data solution, the examples to this point have been fairly basic and the data has been able to be used without much concern for valid values and ranges, or whether or not values can be null or empty or have a default value set. As such, there really isn't much integrity in the current solution as it stands at the end of this chapter. In the next chapter, you will learn about constraining your data so that your database integrity can be enforced.

CHAPTER 5

Constraints, Keys, and Relationships

In this chapter, you are going to learn about how you can use Data Annotations to further constrain your database structures from code. In addition, you'll look at how you can easily build out some relationships in your models that translate directly into relationships in the database.

When you've finished with this chapter, you'll have the ability to correctly create entities that not only specify type but have further constraints like primary and secondary keys and limiting the length on strings. Additionally, you'll learn to enforce required fields and default values and how you can build one-to-many and one-to-one relationships modeled in code and enforced in *EF*.

As another reminder, at this point, this book is focused in on the *EFCore6* version of Entity Framework; however, everything you do at this level can also be done in the same or a very similar manner in *EFCore3*, *EFCore5*, and even *EF6* if you happen to be supporting a legacy codebase.

Constraining your data to enhance your solutions

To this point in the book, you've simply created properties on your only model – the Item. You were able to work with the Item class without any problem; however, as you might expect, working with everything in the default mode is usually not going to be considered the preferred mode. As such, you need to learn more about structuring your models so that you can build solutions in a preferred manner.

© Brian L. Gorman 2022
B. L. Gorman, *Practical Entity Framework Core 6*, https://doi.org/10.1007/978-1-4842-7301-2_5

One issue with leaving the properties of Item in a default state is that nothing is constrained. When working with databases, constraining the data means that you need to lock it down so that only the appropriate operations can take place. Some examples of constraints you'll examine throughout this chapter in more detail are

- Size limitations – for example, minimum and maximum string length

- Value constraints – that is, min, max, and range of acceptable values on numeric fields

- Default values – such as making sure a bit is always true or false by default

As you approach each of these constraints, you'll need to evaluate your systems to make sure that what you are applying to the database constraints makes sense. It is also highly likely that as you maintain an existing project, you'll need to rely on a few of these constraints to keep from having to do further manipulation to protect existing data.

Size limitations

In the activity at the end of the chapter, you'll look at putting a size limitation on string properties. This is incredibly important, even though you've not applied the constraint in your earlier activities.

One thing you might have noted to this point is that in your original database, all your string fields have NVARCHAR(MAX) values. While this is definitely a functional solution, having an unlimited size is both unnecessary and considered bad practice.

In most cases, your string field will not need to exceed 250, 500, or 1000 characters. In other instances, you might want 4000 or 8000 characters in a field for a longer input like a Notes or a Comments field. However, there are very few, if any, reasons to have 2GB available allocation on the size of a single column.

Doing the math on this, you know there are one billion bytes in a GB, so this is *two billion available bytes*. Using NVARCHAR allows for unicode characters, which is useful if you need to store complex characters such as diacritical marks, Cyrillic, Arabic, Mandarin, or other similar characters. As an aside, the data type VARCHAR only stores non-unicode characters. No matter what data type you are storing, it is highly unlikely you need enough room to store the text of an entire novel in a single field, let alone also needing multiple fields of unlimited length on the same table.

Going even one step deeper, `unicode` characters require two bytes per character, and `non-unicode` characters would require only one byte of storage. Assuming you use `NVARCHAR`, this means you can store `one billion characters` in that single field when allocated as `NVARCHAR(MAX)`. Fortunately, most instances of the database will grow to match size needs and not just use the full allocation of 2GB from the initial creation of the column. Even so, do you really want every row to have one or more fields that can expand to use up to 2GB of storage space? The entire size allotment of the *SQLExpress* database and also on the least expensive plan at Azure is only 2GB, so it would be really unfortunate to use the entirety of that size capacity on one string column.

Imagine you have the most powerful supercomputer available to mankind, and it comes with unlimited storage, which therefore takes size constraints off the table as a reasonable reason to constrain a text field. Would it really be a problem to use `NVARCHAR(MAX)` in this case? The answer, of course, is still an invariable "Yes."

As a database developer, you must consider what happens not just when you store data but also when you fetch or parse the data in queries. Assuming you have just a few of these unlimited length columns and also assuming many of them have grown to very large lengths (i.e., each one is storing the entire text of a novel for some reason), what happens when you run a query that is looking for a partial match such as "`WHERE field like '%contains_text%'`"?

You can reasonably assume that queries such as the earlier will quickly become useless in a system where the data is not properly constrained. With potentially unlimited text to search over multiple rows, the execution time would quickly grow exponentially out of a reasonable response time (imagine how long it would take and the number of results you would get when searching for the word "jedi" in a database that stores the entire text of each of the *Star Wars* books ever written in plain text fields).

To limit the length of a string field, you simply add a data annotation called `StringLength`, which is applied as an attribute by placing the following code above any string property in your model:

```
[StringLength(<size, int>)]
```

In addition, most annotations provide the ability to add an error message that is the default error message sent to the UI client when the validation fails, for example:

```
[StringLength(50, ErrorMessage = "The value of this field is limited to 50 characters")]
```

Value constraints

In addition to size constraints, another important type of constraint is a limitation on the expected value of a column. This value could be anything from a limitation on the numeric value to be in a range, such as minimum and maximum values. This could also be as simple as making sure that a field is not able to be set to *null* as its value.

Required fields are created with a simple attribute [Required] to reference the required *data annotation*, placed on top of any existing property. This attribute should be used anytime the database field needs to store a value other than *null* in the table, for example, a *primary* or *foreign* key.

The data annotations for setting minimum and maximum constraints on the properties in code is the *Range* attribute. For example, a range of 0 to max int could be [Range(0, int.MaxValue)]. In any range annotation, the first number is the minimum value and the second number is the max value.

Default values

A final consideration in constraining your data is the default value of an unset column. This is an extremely important aspect in a mature system, because null or inaccurate values on a row could cause a lot of problems for your existing codebase and users.

As you add a field to any new or existing table, you can set a constraint on the field to enforce a default value. There are many situations where this approach can save you a lot of trouble.

One critical use of this functionality would be adding a new field with a required value to an existing table with data. The field could be an easily managed field such as an IsActive boolean flag, or it could be more complex, such as a number to store the id of a user preference from a pre-defined list of options that references the available options stored in another table.

In the first case, you can just set the default for every row to active. The second case will never be as simple, as there are ramifications of every choice around existing data. What if you default to some simple value? What if you add an "unset" element to the options? How will this work in your current system?

Adding a default value is also accomplished with a data annotation and looks as follows:

```
[DefaultValue(<the_value>)]
```

Other data annotations

In addition to data annotations already discussed, there are a couple of other data annotations to be aware of. In every case, these annotations exist to apply further constraints on what can be used to store in the database. The main difference with a few of these is that while the constraint still applies, in some cases, the constraint is accomplished at the code level rather than the database level.

The `StringLength`, `Range`, and `DefaultValue` attributes each contributed a specific result to the underlying database structure. But what if you want to only allow an email address, zip code, phone number, or other special type of data into the field? In these cases, you can use another annotation, but just remember that these don't apply at the database level. For example, limiting to an email address is easily accomplished with the attribute

```
[EmailAddress(ErrorMessage = "Invalid Email Address")]
```

In this case, your code will prevent inserting and updating if the input does not conform to a pre-defined email address format. However, the database is still just storing an `NVARCHAR` or `VARCHAR` and does not have any other information about the format of the string.

Some other annotations/attributes to be aware of are

- `RegularExpression` – Format must match your expression for the model state to be valid.

- `Display` – Sets the text to replace the display text for the field in the UI. This is useful if you have a field like `FirstName` and you want to display "First Name."

- `Table` – It is possible to name the table differently than the name of the model if so desired (affects database structure).

- `Index` – Applies an index to the column (affects database structure) (shown in the next section).

- `NotMapped` – Allows a field to exist that is not tracked in the database.

- `Compare` – Allows making sure one field is the same as another (i.e., password creation for a user taking a second input to validate) (does not affect database structure).

Further annotations can be found by looking at the DataType enumeration: https://docs.microsoft.com/en-us/dotnet/api/system. componentmodel.dataannotations.datatype?view=netcore-6.0.

Attributes can be found by looking at the DataAnnotations documentation here: https://docs.microsoft.com/en-us/dotnet/api/system. componentmodel.dataannotations?view=net-6.0.

Using keys in database tables for unique and relational results

If you've completed the activities in previous chapters, you've already seen how using an Id field has generated a primary key on your Items table. However, there will be times when you need to do more than just define the primary key.

By default, the field Id is going to implicitly be the primary key. In addition to the implicit generation, you can explicitly define keys. This is accomplished with the [Key] annotation as an attribute.

Suppose, however, that you have a join table and we want to create a composite key on the two ids. In *EF6*, this could be accomplished a couple of ways using data annotations. The first way was to use the [Key] attribute with a column order [Column(Order=n)] (the order groups the keys). The problem with this is you cannot use this approach if you already had a primary key defined. The second approach was to use an index annotation as an attribute. This is a great way to create a composite key in *EF6* but, unfortunately, at the time of this writing, is not possible in any version of *EFCore*. To accomplish the creation of a composite key in the final activity later in this chapter, you'll have to use the *Fluent API*.

Indexes allow us to tell the database what fields are most important on the table, so that the database can precompile some statistics using those fields. This allows, among other things, more efficient queries where those fields are critical in searching for results. Additionally, indexes can be used to make sure column combinations are unique.

Applying an index for any field by itself is as simple as adding the [Index] annotation attribute to the field. When creating a *composite key* or *non-clustered* index, you can use the [Index] annotation with the order, just like the key with column order earlier, and you can also set a third property to make the combination unique with a unique constraint. For example, consider a system where you have items that have a group of unique objects (like movies with actors), and you create a table called "ItemObjects" that stores various actor/actress names and other common properties you care about across various objects. In this case, you need a many-to-many relationship to store objects and items together, and you don't want to create duplicates of the same relationship. To make this happen, you could use the following setup in a join table called ItemObjects:

```
[Index("IX_ItemObjectUnique", 1, IsClustered = false, IsUnique = true)]
public int ItemId {get;set;}
[Index("IX_ItemObjectUnique", 2, IsClustered = false, IsUnique = true)]
public int ActorId {get;set;}
```

By creating the index and ensuring that it is unique, you make sure that records cannot have duplicate index keys. Now that you have a good understanding of constraints and keys, you can examine what it takes to set up relationships between tables in the database.

Working with relational data

Most of the systems you will build for line-of-business applications require some sort of relational data. Orders need items with quantity. Addresses require states and/or regions and countries. User preferences require selections. SaaS systems often have things like editions, features, and multi-tenancy. While it is possible to implement solutions without an RDBMS (think NoSQL here), if you're using Entity Framework, you're also going to be working with relational data.

First, second, and third normal form

A quick dive into relational database theory would help you to understand normalization and the difference between first normal form (1NF), second normal form (2NF), and third normal form (3NF). There are also other normalization schemas in fourth normal form (4NF) and Boyce-Codd normal form (BCNF).

In most business applications, the deepest level of normalization that is practical and performant would be 3NF. As such, this book will not touch on 4NF or BCNF in this text, but you may want to study them further if normalization is important and/or interesting to you. It is also important to note that ORMs violate BCNF and 4NF by default to allow for efficiency gains and practical usage scenarios, which is another reason why this book will not dive deeper into them.

First normal form (1NF)

1NF is the simplest form of normalization. For a database to be considered 1NF, the table rows must each have a unique key and the rest of the fields in any combination must not be the same as any other row.

Looking at the AdventureWorks database, there is a table Production.Location which has a few fields. The fields include LocationID, Name, CostRate, Availability, and ModifiedDate. The LocationID field is a unique key, and it can be assumed that although there may be duplicates in CostRate, Availability, and/or ModifiedDate, it is likely the case that the Name will not be duplicated. Even if the Name field were duplicated, if the CostRate and Availability are different, then the table would still be 1NF. Therefore, this table is a great example of 1NF. Make note, however, that fields like CostRate and Availability may have the same value across many rows (i.e., 0.00, 120.00, 12.25). Figure 5-1 shows the Production.Location table.

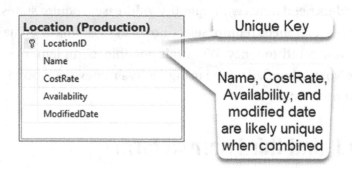

Figure 5-1. *The Production.Location table from AdventureWorks as an example of first normal form (1NF)*

Second normal form (2NF)

2NF requires that the table is in 1NF and also prevents duplicated data that can be directly related to another column in the table. For example, in AdventureWorks the table Person.Address has a field StateProvinceId. Suppose you also had tracked the name of the state or province as a field, in addition to tracking the StateProvinceId. If the StateProvinceId ever changed, then the state or province name field would also have to change.

Another example of a violation of 2NF might be a field called FullAddress that is just a combination of the two fields from the table: AddressLine1 and AddressLine2. In that case, if either address line changes, FullAddress would also have to change.

The following query shows what the Person.Address table might look like in violation of 2NF, by also containing the StateProvinceName:

```
SELECT pa.AddressID, pa.AddressLine1, pa.AddressLine2, pa.AddressLine1 + '
' + COALESCE(pa.AddressLine2, '') as FullAddress
            , pa.City, pa.StateProvinceID, psp.[Name] as StateProvinceName
            , pa.PostalCode, pa.SpatialLocation, pa.rowguid, pa.ModifiedDate
FROM Person.Address pa
LEFT JOIN Person.StateProvince psp on pa.StateProvinceID =
psp.StateProvinceId
```

Figure 5-2 shows the results of executing the query.

```
SELECT pa.AddressID, pa.AddressLine1, pa.AddressLine2, pa.AddressLine1 + ' ' + COALESCE(pa.AddressLine2, '') as FullAddress
     , pa.City, pa.StateProvinceID, psp.[Name] as StateProvinceName
     , pa.PostalCode, pa.SpatialLocation, pa.rowguid, pa.ModifiedDate
FROM Person.Address pa
LEFT JOIN Person.StateProvince psp on pa.StateProvinceID = psp.StateProvinceId
```

100 %

Results   Spatial results   Messages

	AddressID	AddressLine1	AddressLine2	FullAddress	City	StateProvinceID	StateProvinceName	PostalCode	SpatialLocation
76	76	2598 La Vista Circle	NULL	2598 La Vista Circle	Duvall	79	Washington	98019	0xE6100000010CB
77	77	9693 Mellowood Str...	NULL	9693 Mellowood Street	Duvall	79	Washington	98019	0xE6100000010C2
78	78	1825 Corte Del Prado	NULL	1825 Corte Del Prado	Duvall	79	Washington	98019	0xE6100000010C1
79	79	5086 Nottingham Pl...	NULL	5086 Nottingham Place	Duvall	79	Washington	98019	0xE6100000010C3
80	80	3977 Central Avenue	NULL	3977 Central Avenue	Duvall	79	Washington	98019	0xE6100000010C0
81	81	8209 Green View C...	NULL	8209 Green View Court	Duvall	79	Washington	98019	0xE6100000010C8
82	82	8463 Vista Avenue	NULL	8463 Vista Avenue	Duvall	79	Washington	98019	0xE6100000010CA
83	83	5379 Treasure Islan...	# 14	5379 Treasure Island Way # 14	Duvall	79	Washington	98019	0xE6100000010C2
84	84	3421 Bouncing Road	NULL	3421 Bouncing Road	Duvall	79	Washington	98019	0xE6100000010CA
85	85	991 Vista Verde	NULL	991 Vista Verde	Duvall	79	Washington	98019	0xE6100000010CE
86	86	390 Ridgewood Ct.	NULL	390 Ridgewood Ct.	Cam...	79	Washington	98014	0xE6100000010C8
87	87	1411 Ranch Drive	NULL	1411 Ranch Drive	Cam...	79	Washington	98014	0xE6100000010C8
88	88	9666 Northridge Ct.	NULL	9666 Northridge Ct.	Cam...	79	Washington	98014	0xE6100000010CB
89	89	3074 Arbor Drive	NULL	3074 Arbor Drive	Cam...	79	Washington	98014	0xE6100000010C8
90	90	9752 Jeanne Circle	NULL	9752 Jeanne Circle	Cam...	79	Washington	98014	0xE6100000010C8
91	91	7166 Brock Lane	NULL	7166 Brock Lane	Seattle	79	Washington	98104	0xE6100000010C8
92	92	7126 Ending Ct.	NULL	7126 Ending Ct.	Seattle	79	Washington	98104	0xE6100000010C9
93	93	4598 Manila Avenue	NULL	4598 Manila Avenue	Seattle	79	Washington	98104	0xE6100000010C7

Figure 5-2. *What the Person.Address table might look like if it violated second normal form (2NF) in a couple of different ways*

There is another example in AdventureWorks where violation of 2NF is prevented. This is more common in our day-to-day work and very much like what we'll build in our examples.

The table Person.StateProvince is set up well to be in 2NF. For example, the table has the primary key of StateProvinceID, and then, instead of repeating data like the name of the Country or the name of the Territory, those pieces of information are brought in through foreign key relationships to the tables Person.CountryRegion and Sales.SalesTerritory, respectively.

By following this normalization, the names of the Country and Territory can be derived, but they are not going to require extra fields being changed in the StateProvince table if for some reason the country name changes or the territory name changes. Figure 5-3 highlights an example of 2NF.

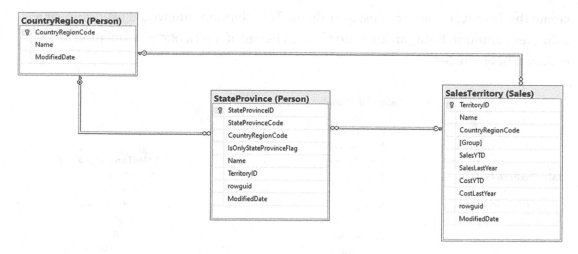

Figure 5-3. *The Person.StateProvince table follows 2NF*

Third normal form (3NF)

3NF attempts to further break down 2NF into a unique group of columns (i.e., there are no transitive dependencies in the database) so that there is not any issue with compositional data becoming corrupted or incomputable due to changes in related data. For me, this can be a bit confusing, so it might help if you think in terms of auditing the database.

For example, in `AdventureWorks`, the `Sales.SalesOrderHeader` table has a column `SubTotal` and a column `TaxAmt` and then `Freight` and then `TotalDue`. Knowing that `TotalDue` is calculated from `SubTotal`, `TaxAmt`, and `Freight`, we have a couple of potential normalization problems, where either this table is in violation of 2NF (`TotalDue` changes if `SubTotal`, `Tax`, and/or `Freight` change for some reason) or we are in violation of 3NF. Since the `TotalDue` field is computed, the 2NF issues are mostly eliminated as the value automatically updates.

However, since that `TaxAmt` field is likely equal to the `SubTotal` multiplied by the `TaxRate` of the shipping address of the `StateProvince` where the customer lives and is likely calculated at the time of the order processing, then the problem becomes an auditing issue without 3NF.

Looking at the `Sales.SalesTaxRate` table, there is a column `TaxRate` and a foreign key to `StateProvinceId`. What happens if legislation changes in the `StateProvince` that raises the `TaxRate` for that region? In that case, the new `TaxRate` would be used on future orders, but the old one would have been used during the original calculation to create the `TaxAmt`. Because of this, the original `TotalDue` amount would likely appear as a different amount during an audit due to the change of the `TaxRate`. A violation of 3NF is shown in Figure 5-4.

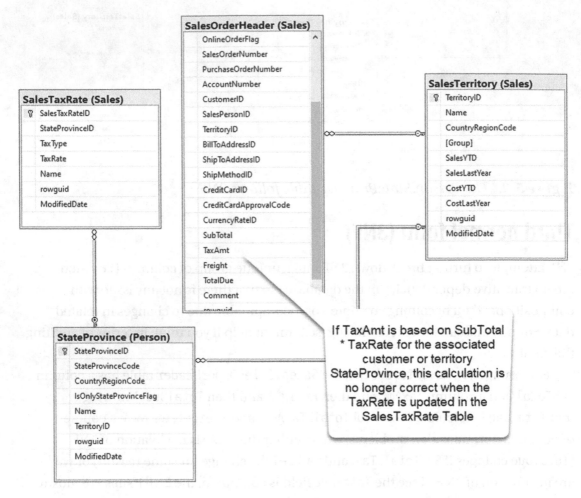

Figure 5-4. *A violation of 3NF happens when a field in one table is dependent on the value of another table, and that other table has a dependency on a third table. When that third table changes and results in changes to the related table, then the resulting dependency is also affected*

If the `Sales.SalesOrderHeader` table was in proper 3NF, the tax rate would have been stored at the time of the placement of the order so that the total due column could be correctly calculated using the subtotal multiplied by the tax rate at the time of the order.

To be clear, consider the following values for a sale.

Assume that SubTotal is 99.99, and TaxRate at the time of the original sale is 7%. Ignoring the Freight for this example, the TotalDue would be $99.99 + ($99.99*.07), or roughly $106.98. Now assume legislation passes and taxes are raised to 8% and appropriately updated in the TaxRate column. Now an auditor comes and sees a SubTotal of $99.99 and a TaxRate of 8%. The expected SubTotal based on those numbers would be approximately $107.98. The value changed based on a dependency. Without an audit trail, this could cause some serious issues for the company.

While understanding the differences between 1NF, 2NF, and 3NF goes well beyond the depth covered in this book, it is important to be aware of them when creating your entities. With this awareness, you can now start to create proper, normalized relationships.

Types of relationships

When working with relational data, you have three types of relationships that you can leverage. They are

- One-to-one

- One-to-many

- Many-to-many

All three of the relationships have distinct purposes and are easily built out in code-first implementations. The way they are built is directly related to how the code is referenced from one model to another. What's more, in the many-to-many relationship, you can either define the join table explicitly, or you can rely on the implicit creation of the table. In most cases, you'll use a one-to-many or a many-to-many relationship, even if you have a one-to-one correlation as the result. However, you should also know how a one-to-one relationship would work in case we ever need to set one up.

Additionally, as of EFCore5, another feature has been added around these relationships that makes it a bit easier to work with them. With EFCore5, you can now create a many-to-many relationship without having to explicitly map the join table. For example, prior to EFCore5, if you wanted to have a many-to-many relationship, you would create three entities – the left table, the right table, and the join table that mapped the left and the right to each other. With EFCore5, and therefore EFCore6, you simply reference the other table in each model as an ICollection<T>, and EFCore6 implicitly creates the join table via the functionality added as of EFCore5. If necessary, you could still further define fields on the join table should the need arise.

One-to-one relationships

One-to-one relationships are useful when there are two tables that are directly linked to each other, but there is only one row in each table that is joined. The relationship is built with a primary key in one table and the foreign key in the other table and to be truly one-to-one should go in both directions (both tables are modified with a foreign key to relate to the only matching row in the other table).

One-to-one relationships generally provide additional attributes that are created to further define an object, which, when coupled, create a more detailed implementation of the object.

An example of a one-to-one relationship from `AdventureWorks` happens between the tables `Person.BusinessEntity` and `Person.Person` and another from `Person.Person` to `HumanResources.Employee` and finally another one from `HumanResources.Employee` to `Sales.SalesPerson`. In this setup, each `Person.BusinessEntity` is given an ID, and that ID is used to relate directly to an individual with more details in the `Person.Person` table, more details in the `HumanResources.EmployeeTable`, and finally, if they are a sales person, more details in the `Sales.SalesPerson` table. This allows for a `BusinessEntity` to have the properties of a `Person` (`Title`, `FirstName`, `LastName`) and `Employee` details like `HireDate` and `VacationHours`. Finally, if the employee happens to be a sales person, they can have further associated information for their `TerritoryID` and `CommissionPct`. Figure 5-5 shows how these tables each form a one-to-one relationship with each other defining more details about the person at each level.

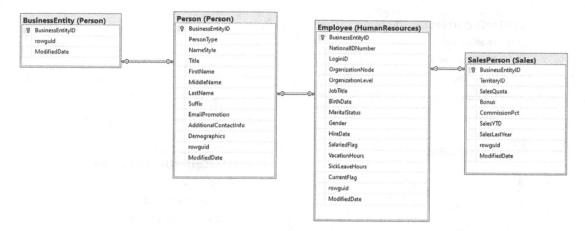

Figure 5-5. *The Person.BusinessEntity is related in a one-to-one relationship with Person.Person, which is also in a one-to-one relationship with HumanResources. Employee, which has a one-to-one potential relationship with Sales.SalesPerson. Each table further defines the original entity with more details about the entity*

One-to-many relationships

A one-to-many relationship is likely the most common relationship you'll encounter when working with relational data. Generally, one-to-many relationships rely on a key object that is then configured or further defined with options. One-to-many relationships are easily set up to serve as things like dropdown lists or option lists when building out objects for making selections in the UI. For example, in AdventureWorks, `Sales.SalesOrderHeader` has a one-to-many relationship to `Sales.SalesOrderDetail`. For every sales order header, you can have as many related details as you need to fulfill the order. A simpler example was already shown in Figure 5-3, where you had the `Person.CountryRegion` table having a one-to-many relationship with `Person.StateProvince` and the `Sales.SalesTerritory` table also had a one-to-many relationship with `Person.StateProvince`. Figure 5-6 illustrates how `SalesOrderHeader` to `SalesOrderDetail` is a one-to-many relationship.

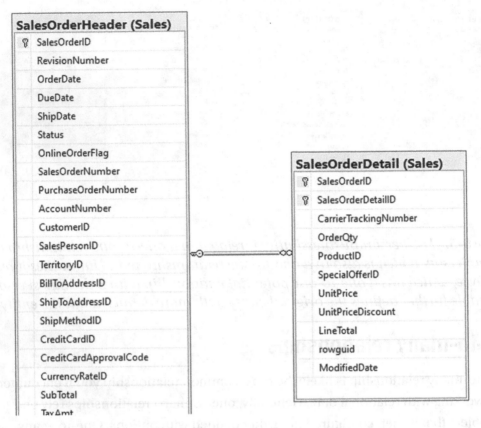

Figure 5-6. *An example of a one-to-many relationship in the AdventureWorks database is the Sales.SalesOrderHeader to the Sales.SalesOrderDetail table, where one SalesOrderHeader entry might be related to many SalesOrderDetail entries*

Many-to-many relationships

Many-to-many relationships are a bit more complex than the other two relationship types. In any many-to-many relationship, a join table exists to relate two separate entities to each other, with each side of the relationship being a one-to-many relationship from the entity table to the join table.

This join table allows for a two-way relationship between the two entities. The first table can join and get all elements from the second table that match via the grouping in the join table, and the second table can do the same thing in reverse.

In a straightforward example, we might use many-to-many relationships for things like user preferences. We could look for any users that have set a single preference value, or we can look for all the preferences of a single user. This is very useful for correctly mapping data.

An example from AdventureWorks exists where the HumanResources.Employee table is in a many-to-many relationship with the HumanResources.Department table. This means that an employee could have history as having worked in one or more departments, or a single department can easily be mapped to all the current and past employees. You can perform queries in either direction, and you can expect to get valid results from your query, as long as the data is correctly joined together via the HumanResources.EmployeeDepartmentHistory table. Figure 5-7 displays the many-to-many relationship between Department and Employee via the EmployeeDepartmentHistory join table.

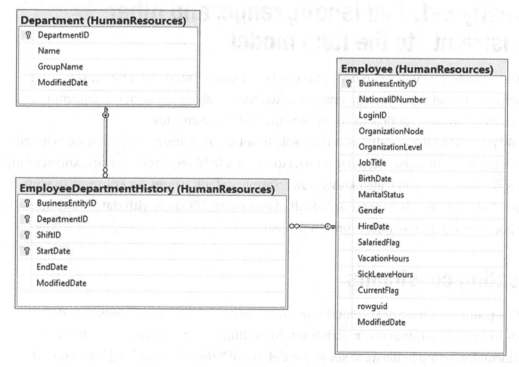

Figure 5-7. The Employee to Department relationship is a many-to-many relationship with the EmployeeDepartmentHistory table acting as the join table for the relationship. In this way, one employee may have history with many departments, or one department can easily be mapped to current and/or past employees

Some final thoughts about relationships and normalization

When working with any *RDBMS*, forming the correct relationships will be critical in order to effectively work with the data. By knowing the different types of normalization and relationships available to you, you will be able to make sure to build out the best solutions as needed.

With the many different forms of normalization, you also will need to find the balance between what works and what works with a desired level of efficiency. As the database developer, it will be your job to understand the trade-offs that will happen if you want to design a database all the way to 3NF, BCNF, or 4NF vs. the problems that might happen if you only use a 1NF normalization strategy.

Activity 5-1: Add length, range, and other constraints to the Item model

In this activity, you will again dive into the Item class to build out a better database structure. This will give you the chance to see how to apply some of the common data annotations in your models to constrain your database entities.

By the end of the activity, you'll be able to set the minimum and maximum length of a string field, understand what it takes to make a field required or a key, and set range limits on data, and you'll also know how to apply default values for columns in your tables. You will be able to accomplish all of this using EFCore6 with data annotations in any code-first database development project.

Creating constraints

To this point, you have not created any constraints, and that has allowed the data fields to be built without any restrictions, including required values or null values. Additionally, string fields were set to the default of NVARCHAR(MAX), which is not ideal – as you've already read about in the preceding text.

In this activity, you will see how to create constraints that will allow restrictions on your data that make your applications more robust. In the end, having data integrity is going to be one of the key elements to producing a system that works well and doesn't require a lot of additional support due to bugs or invalid scenarios that users will likely enter on forms. For example, you wouldn't want a person with a negative age or a product you are selling to have a negative price. You also likely want every product to have a name, and you want to set limits on the length of that name to prevent overflow issues in your UI from extremely long strings of text.

Prerequisite: Get set up for this activity

To get started with this activity, you could use the code you have been building along with the text that has all of the implementations from activities through the first four chapters, or you could grab the EFCore_Activity05-1_StarterFiles which positions you to start exactly in the place the code needs to be to do this activity. Remember to check Appendix A for more information about using the starter files.

Task 1: Setting length constraints on columns

In this first task, you will work through setting constraints on the Item model class to ensure that string columns are no longer set to be NVARCHAR(MAX) but will have a maximum length.

Step 1: Identify the fields that need constraints and create constants for the values

To start this activity, take a look at the Items table as it stands in the database. Right now, the fields Name, Description, and Notes are all NVARCHAR(MAX) length. Additionally, CreatedByUserId and LastModifiedUserId are also NVARCHAR(MAX) as shown in Figure 5-8.

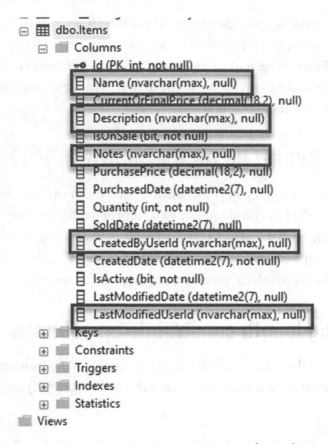

Figure 5-8. *All string fields are currently NVARCHAR(MAX) length*

In the real world, if you already have data in the tables, changing the length is likely to be a problem, because this could cause a loss of data in the case where you decrease the length of the field. One way to prevent issues could be to quickly select the data from the table into a backup table using a query, and then once the operation is completed, restore by selecting the data back into the table from the backup table. A great way to ensure you don't have mistakes in such a scenario would be to script this process and ensure it works as expected. You could even do the entire operation as a series of migrations to ensure the operation will run in any environment.

In this case, you are not concerned with lost data, so you can proceed as such.

Before you add the constraints, a good practice for reusability, testability, and general organization of your code is to simply set some static constants in place. In this manner, you don't have to use magic numbers in your code (a magic number is any number that is hard-coded that could cause issues if someone changes it unexpectedly, especially if the value is set in more than one location). In the InventoryModels project, create a file called InventoryModelConstants.cs and add the following code to the file:

```
public class InventoryModelsConstants
{
    public const int MAX_DESCRIPTION_LENGTH = 250;
    public const int MAX_NAME_LENGTH = 100;
    public const int MAX_NOTES_LENGTH = 2000;
    public const int MAX_USERID_LENGTH = 50;
}
```

Here, you could choose different values if you want to. The description should likely be fairly short and the name should likely be even shorter, with the notes being the largest field. Additionally, it is likely that 32 would be long enough for the MAX_USERID_ LENGTH, assuming that it is a GUID, which has a length of 32. If more characters are needed, you could easily expand this now or do it in the future. In order to make sure there is enough room, just set the length to 50. If you want to be extra cautious, you could even set this length to 64.

You might also ask something like "Why aren't the class or the variables static?" In case you weren't aware of this, a const value in C# is static by default.

Step 2: Add constraints to appropriate properties in the Item and FullAuditModel classes

With the constants in place, open the Item.cs file for the Item model and add the following code above the Name property:

```
[StringLength(InventoryModelsConstants.MAX_NAME_LENGTH)]
```

Adding the StringLength annotation attribute will require adding the using statement using System.ComponentModel.DataAnnotations to the top of the file, so make sure to go ahead and add the appropriate using statement.

Repeat the operation to add the following line of code above Description:

```
[StringLength(InventoryModelsConstants.MAX_DESCRIPTION_LENGTH)]
```

And this line of code above Notes:

```
[StringLength(InventoryModelsConstants.MAX_NOTES_LENGTH, MinimumLength = 10)]
```

In this example, the minimum length is set to simply show that it can be done and how it works when you do it. In the real world, the minimum length may be left blank or may be set, depending on the needs of your solution.

Make a note that while the maximum length is enforced at the database level in schema, a minimum length will be enforceable only by the model state. Even after creating this, someone could come along and do a manual insert to the table with a Notes entry having a length less than 10. As an aside, since the minimum length on the Notes field here is for demonstration purposes only, you did not create a constant to map the minimum length of 10. If you wanted, you could map that minimum length to a constant, just as you did to the other fields.

Figure 5-9 shows the reworked Item model with constraints applied.

```
public class Item : FullAuditModel
{
    [StringLength(InventoryModelsConstants.MAX_NAME_LENGTH)]
    4 references
    public string Name { get; set; }
    1 reference
    public int Quantity { get; set; }
    [StringLength(InventoryModelsConstants.MAX_DESCRIPTION_LENGTH)]
    1 reference
    public string Description { get; set; }
    [StringLength(InventoryModelsConstants.MAX_NOTES_LENGTH, MinimumLength = 10)]
    1 reference
    public string Notes { get; set; }
    0 references
    public bool IsOnSale { get; set; }
    0 references
    public DateTime? PurchasedDate { get; set; }
```

Figure 5-9. *The Item class is configured to enforce maximum length on the string properties that are part of the Item class*

The UserId properties are part of the FullAuditModel. As such, open the FullAuditModel and update both the CreatedByUserId and the LastModifiedUserId with the following data annotation:

```
[StringLength(InventoryModelsConstants.MAX_USERID_LENGTH)]
```

Make sure to save and build the project.

Step 3: Create the migration

With the string properties now all configured to have a maximum length, open the *PMC* and make sure you have your EFCore_DbLibrary project selected, and then run the command add-migration updateItem_enforceStringMaxLength.

You should not have any errors, but you should receive a warning that states "*An operation was scaffolded that may result in the loss of data. Please review the migration for accuracy*". This is because you are shortening the length of fields, and if there is currently data that is longer than the new constraint, those fields would see a truncation of data. Take a minute to review the migration. Figure 5-10 shows part of the migration and highlights how the migration will now set the fields in the database to enforce a maximum length.

```
protected override void Up(MigrationBuilder migrationBuilder)
{
    migrationBuilder.AlterColumn<string>(
        name: "Notes",
        table: "Items",
        type: "nvarchar(2000)",
        maxLength: 2000,
        nullable: true,
        oldClrType: typeof(string),
        oldType: "nvarchar(max)",
        oldNullable: true);

    migrationBuilder.AlterColumn<string>(
        name: "Name",
        table: "Items",
        type: "nvarchar(100)",
        maxLength: 100,
        nullable: true,
        oldClrType: typeof(string),
        oldType: "nvarchar(max)",
        oldNullable: true);

    migrationBuilder.AlterColumn<string>(
        name: "LastModifiedUserId",
        table: "Items",
        type: "nvarchar(50)",
        maxLength: 50,
        nullable: true,
        oldClrType: typeof(string),
        oldType: "nvarchar(max)",
        oldNullable: true);
```

Figure 5-10. *The new migration adds a length constraint on a number of fields*

Step 4: Update the database

Once you are satisfied that the length constraints are set as expected, go ahead and run the update-database command to apply the changes to your database. Execute the command now. It is likely you won't have an error and could proceed to the next step. However, if you currently have data in the table that would be truncated, you would see an error, shown here in Figure 5-11.

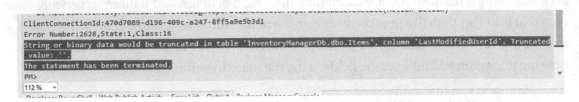

Figure 5-11. *The migration will not work if you currently have data in your database*

While this may seem annoying at first, this error is actually a very good thing that EF is doing. You see, the PMC update-database command just prevented you from accidentally wiping out portions of data.

If you wanted to see this error, before adding the migration, you could have set the length of the user ids to something like 30. The data would then be truncated. If this happens, you have a few choices at this point. The first thing you could do is just go manually wipe the data (which is reasonable for this test scenario, but not so good for a production scenario). The second option is you could write scripts that manually back up the table and wipe the data (which again is not a real great choice if you have a production scenario with constraints on the data). A third option is to add scripts into this migration that back up the string fields and then wipe the data directly from those columns and then restore it. This is again not likely to work well in the long run. A fourth option would be to write scripts that delete all relationships, back up the data, run the migration, then restore the data, and finally restore the relationships. That final option is likely what you would need to do in a real-world, production scenario.Here, you would have nothing to lose by doing any of the options, since there is only one table, and the data is volatile and easily restored by running the program which will ensure your default records. To simulate what you might do in the real world, you could add the following code to the top of the migration (do not do this unless you are getting an error, and if you are getting an error, make sure to increase field lengths appropriately to avoid truncating data):

```
migrationBuilder.Sql("SELECT * INTO ItemsBackup FROM Items");
migrationBuilder.Sql("DELETE FROM Items");
```

You could also run a quick script to make sure that you remove any relationships.

At the end of the migration, you would then add the revert statements (these statements are untested as they are for illustration only and may contain a small error):

```
migrationBuilder.Sql("SET IDENTITY_INSERT Items ON");
migrationBuilder.Sql("INSERT INTO Items (Id, Name, CurrentOrFinalPrice, Description," +
    "IsOnSale, Notes, PurchasePrice, PurchasedDate, Quantity, SoldDate" +
    "CreatedByUserId, CreatedDate, IsActive, LastModifiedDate,
    LastModifiedUserId)" +
    "SELECT * FROM ItemsBackup");
migrationBuilder.Sql("SET IDENTITY_INSERT Items OFF");
migrationBuilder.Sql("DROP TABLE ItemsBackup");
```

You could avoid dropping the table if you get nervous about that, and just do it manually later. You could also add a statement to restore any relationships at this point. Once you had that code in place, you could proceed with the update, and it should work, as long as you are no longer truncating any data on the re-insert of data from the backup.

In any scenario, by now, you should have the new constraints in place and the migration applied. Figure 5-12 shows the new constraints are in place on the database table in SSMS.

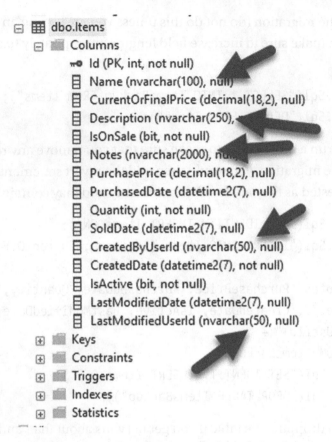

Figure 5-12. *The migration applied as expected and the database fields are now set to have appropriate maximum lengths for string values*

As with other activities, the end of a task in an activity is a great place to check changes into source control to create a safe restore point in case things go wrong during future tasks.

Task 2: Creating a range on numeric fields

When working with the database, you'll often have fields that should be further constrained to limit what values make sense. For example, you should never have a negative quantity, and you likely want to lock down the price on an item so that it is also not negative.

Step 1: Add range values to the quantity and price fields

Once again, you don't want to use magic numbers, so for this step, you will start by adding some constants for minimum and maximum quantity and price in the InventoryModelsConstants file. Add the following code to the constants class after the MAX_USERID_LENGTH:

```
public const int MINIMUM_QUANTITY = 0;
public const int MAXIMUM_QUANTITY = 1000;
public const double MINIMUM_PRICE = 0.0;
public const double MAXIMUM_PRICE = 25000.0;
```

Next, add the constraints to the appropriate fields in the Item class.

Above the Quantity field, add the constraint as follows: [Range(InventoryModelsConstants.MINIMUM_QUANTITY, InventoryModelsConstants.MAXIMUM_QUANTITY)]

Above the PurchasePrice and CurrentOrFinalPrice, add the following code:

```
[Range(InventoryModelsConstants.MINIMUM_PRICE, InventoryModelsConstants.
MAXIMUM_PRICE)]
```

Once again, you'll see that these range values are not going to generate constraints on the table, but only constraints that your code would have to respect in the model state, which you can check to ensure that no bad data is saved to your database. Figure 5-13 shows the current Item class for clarity.

```
1 reference
public class Item : FullAuditModel
{
    [StringLength(InventoryModelsConstants.MAX_NAME_LENGTH)]
    4 references
    public string Name { get; set; }
    [Range(InventoryModelsConstants.MINIMUM_QUANTITY, InventoryModelsConstants.MAXIMUM_QUANTITY)]
    1 reference
    public int Quantity { get; set; }
    [StringLength(InventoryModelsConstants.MAX_DESCRIPTION_LENGTH)]
    1 reference
    public string Description { get; set; }
    [StringLength(InventoryModelsConstants.MAX_NOTES_LENGTH, MinimumLength = 10)]
    1 reference
    public string Notes { get; set; }
    0 references
    public bool IsOnSale { get; set; }
    0 references
    public DateTime? PurchasedDate { get; set; }
    0 references
    public DateTime? SoldDate { get; set; }
    [Range(InventoryModelsConstants.MINIMUM_PRICE, InventoryModelsConstants.MAXIMUM_PRICE)]
    0 references
    public decimal? PurchasePrice { get; set; }
    [Range(InventoryModelsConstants.MINIMUM_PRICE, InventoryModelsConstants.MAXIMUM_PRICE)]
    1 reference
    public decimal? CurrentOrFinalPrice { get; set; }
}
```

Figure 5-13. *The current code for the Item class is shown for clarity*

Step 2: Create the migration

Make sure to save and build, and then add the migration with the command add-migration updateItems_setMinMaxValuesOnQuantityAndPrice.

Generating the migration backs up what we expected – that the constraint from these data annotations is only on the model state and not enforced in the database. As such, the generated migration is blank. You might be tempted to just run the remove-migration command and let it be, but this is a great chance to run a script to also enforce these constraints on the fields in the database. However, the following text is only going to update quantity. For this reason, run the remove-migration command, and then run the command add-migration updateItems_setMinMaxValuesOnQuantity to generate a new blank migration.

In the empty Up method of the blank migration, add the following code:

```
migrationBuilder.Sql("UPDATE Items SET Quantity = 0 WHERE Quantity < 0");
migrationBuilder.Sql("UPDATE Items SET Quantity = 1000 WHERE Quantity > 1000");
migrationBuilder.Sql(@"IF NOT EXISTS(SELECT *
```

```
FROM INFORMATION_SCHEMA.TABLE_CONSTRAINTS
WHERE CONSTRAINT_NAME='CK_Items_Quantity_Minimum')
BEGIN
    ALTER TABLE [dbo].[Items] ADD CONSTRAINT CK_Items_Quantity_Minimum
    CHECK (Quantity >= 0)
END

IF NOT EXISTS(SELECT *
    FROM INFORMATION_SCHEMA.TABLE_CONSTRAINTS
    WHERE CONSTRAINT_NAME='CK_Items_Quantity_Maximum')
BEGIN
    ALTER TABLE [dbo].[Items] ADD CONSTRAINT CK_Items_Quantity_Maximum
    CHECK (Quantity <= 1000)
END");
```

Notice that the first two statements are run to ensure no data exists in the table that is outside of the required constraint values. If data violates a constraint, you can't add the constraint, so the first two statements ensure the data is compliant.

Remember to also include a "rollback" statement to drop the constraint if it exists. Additionally, note that it is a good practice to ensure that your Down statements and Up statements are idempotent. In this manner, the migration can be run without error regardless as to whether the objects do or don't exist. Add the following code to your Down method:

```
migrationBuilder.Sql(@"IF EXISTS(SELECT *
    FROM INFORMATION_SCHEMA.TABLE_CONSTRAINTS
    WHERE CONSTRAINT_NAME='CK_Items_Quantity_Minimum')
BEGIN
    ALTER TABLE [dbo].[Items] DROP CONSTRAINT CK_Items_Quantity_Minimum
END");

migrationBuilder.Sql(@"IF NOT EXISTS(SELECT *
    FROM INFORMATION_SCHEMA.TABLE_CONSTRAINTS
    WHERE CONSTRAINT_NAME='CK_Items_Quantity_Maximum')
BEGIN
    ALTER TABLE [dbo].[Items] DROP CONSTRAINT CK_Items_Quantity_Maximum
END");
```

Although it is not shown here or added to the database code, you could repeat these statements for the price columns to add the check constraints on price values. In that case, you would again start by ensuring all data is conformant to the expected constraints.

After saving and building the project, run the command update-database. Once the command has completed, right-click and script the Items table for create in *SSMS* to view the constraints and field information.

Figure 5-14 shows the current table, refreshed and with the Constraints expanded.

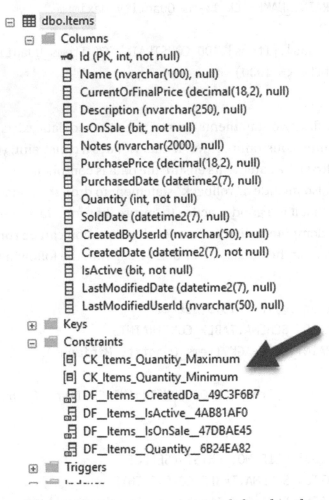

Figure 5-14. *The table has the two constraints as defined in the migration*

Task 3: Ensuring a field is a key, making fields required, and setting default values on a column

As you've seen, a property called Id on the model acts implicitly as the primary key on the table. It is possible, however, to explicitly name a database field as a key. In fact, it is possible to have multiple fields as keys.

Step 1: Ensure the Id field is a key

While it is not necessary to do this, you can explicitly define the Id field as a key on the database. Using data annotations, you can mark any field as a key. To see this in action, open the FullAuditModel class and add the data annotation [Key] on top of the Id field. Figure 5-15 shows the updated code for clarity.

```
3 references
public abstract class FullAuditModel : IIdentityModel, IAuditedModel, IActivatableModel
{
    [Key]
    1 reference
    public int Id { get; set; }
    [StringLength(InventoryModelsConstants.MAX_USERID_LENGTH)]
    4 references
    public string CreatedByUserId { get; set; }
    2 references
    public DateTime CreatedDate { get; set; }
```

Figure 5-15. *The data annotation [Key] is added to the Id field to explicitly define the Id as a key on the models*

Step 2: Making some fields required (not able to be set to null – must have value)

In most cases, the ability to make a field required in the database is determined by the data type. If you want the field to be non-nullable, you use a non-nullable type. If you want it to be nullable, you use the question mark to indicate a nullable type. Take a look at the FullAuditModel and note how CreatedDate is not nullable, but LastModifiedDate can be null due to having the DateTime? data type. Additionally, in the Item class, note that the Quantity and the IsActive fields cannot be null because they are set to int and bool, which are not nullable.

However, some fields can be ambiguous, like strings. To ensure that a field always has a value when you are working with your data, even if it is a nullable type, you can use the [Required] data annotation. The required annotation will enforce the field to be required in the database as well as invalidate the model state if the field is left null (Note: Null and the empty string are not the same thing, so even with this in place, an empty string could be stored!).

Since every item should have a name, add the [Required] annotation attribute to the Name field in the Item.cs file as shown in Figure 5-16.

```
1 reference
public class Item : FullAuditModel
{
    [StringLength(InventoryModelsConstants.MAX_NAME_LENGTH)]
    [Required]  ⬅
    4 references
    public string Name { get; set; }
    [Range(InventoryModelsConstants.MINIMUM_QUANTITY, InventoryModelsConstants.MAXIMUM_QUANTITY)]
    1 reference
    public int Quantity { get; set; }
```

Figure 5-16. *Use the [Required] data annotation to ensure that a field always has value*

Feel free to make other fields required as you see fit. Additionally, feel free to add a new migration and run the update-database command at any point to apply changes. The final task in this activity will be to generate a new migration, which will include all of the changes. In a real project, you may not want to combine so many changes into one migration, so it is up to you to determine how you would like to proceed.

It is also possible that you may wish to keep the number of migrations to a minimum to avoid having hundreds of migrations. For that reason, waiting until you are ready is a great idea. There are a couple of things to note about this. At any point, you can remove and recreate an unapplied migration. Therefore, if you want to see the migration, go ahead and generate it with an add-migration command. Then if you want to redo the migration with more changes later, just remove it and then run the exact same command to regenerate the unapplied migration.

One final note is based on an upcoming new feature of EFCore6 that I'm pretty excited about. This feature is the ability to squash your migrations. This feature will allow you to combine multiple migrations into one migration, similar to squashing GIT commits into one commit. I hope this will be implemented in time to cover later in the book. If not, I'll make sure to blog about it when it is available so that you can read more about it in one way or another.

Step 3: Adding a default value to a field

In a previous activity, you likely read that there is a way to do a soft delete by adding an IsDeleted boolean value to the table. Once your table has data in it, however, you can only add fields as nullable, unless you enforce a default value.

Assuming that you now want to make items able to be deleted without losing data, you can do this in the object hierarchy. First, you would create another interface in the InventoryModels project called ISoftDeletable, adding the property IsDeleted as a boolean.

```
public interface ISoftDeletable
{
    bool IsDeleted { get; set; }
}
```

You would then want to set the value to false and make the field required to avoid any confusion (e.g., is *null* signifying that the record is deleted or not deleted? You don't want any ambiguity on this matter).

Implement the interface on the FullAuditModel, and add the following data annotations:

```
[Required]
[DefaultValue(false)]
```

The DefaultValue requires bringing in the using statement using System. ComponentModel; so make sure to do that to avoid a build error.

The updated FullAuditModel is shown in Figure 5-17.

```
3 references
public abstract class FullAuditModel : IIdentityModel, IAuditedModel, IActivatableModel, ISoftDeletable
{
    [Key]
    1 reference
    public int Id { get; set; }
    [StringLength(InventoryModelsConstants.MAX_USERID_LENGTH)]
    4 references
    public string CreatedByUserId { get; set; }
    2 references
    public DateTime CreatedDate { get; set; }
    [StringLength(InventoryModelsConstants.MAX_USERID_LENGTH)]
    3 references
    public string LastModifiedUserId { get; set; }
    2 references
    public DateTime? LastModifiedDate { get; set; }
    2 references
    public bool IsActive { get; set; }
    [Required]
    [DefaultValue(false)]      ⬅
    1 reference
    public bool IsDeleted { get; set; }
}
```

Figure 5-17. *The default value and required attributes are added to the IsDeleted property*

Note that adding the DefaultValue constraint requires the using statement using System.ComponentModel.

Task 4: Add a new migration and apply these changes to the database

As previously mentioned, it would likely have been better to do a couple of migrations for practice in the previous task, but there is no hard and fast rule that says you must do small migrations. However, by waiting until now to create the migration, you are taking a calculated risk. The risk is that there is a possibility that you may have quite a few errors by now that would prevent the migration from working.

Step 1: Create the new migration

With all of the data formatting in place, go ahead and create a new migration to lock down the database and create the changes you've implemented in the last three tasks. Run the command add-migration updateItems_ addSoftDeleteIdKeyAndRequiredName. The migration generated should look similar to what is shown in Figure 5-18.

```
5 references
protected override void Up(MigrationBuilder migrationBuilder)
{
    migrationBuilder.AlterColumn<string>(
        name: "Name",
        table: "Items",
        type: "nvarchar(100)",
        maxLength: 100,
        nullable: false,
        defaultValue: "",
        oldClrType: typeof(string),
        oldType: "nvarchar(100)",
        oldMaxLength: 100,
        oldNullable: true);

    migrationBuilder.AddColumn<bool>(
        name: "IsDeleted",
        table: "Items",
        type: "bit",
        nullable: false,
        defaultValue: false);
}
```

Figure 5-18. *The migration generated by the additional constraints for required fields and default values is ready to be applied to the database*

Once again, you will see the warning that an operation was scaffolded that may result in the loss of data. In this small system, there is no concern about losing data, but when/ if you see this in a real-world scenario, remember to evaluate your backup options to ensure you do not lose critical data.

Step 2: Update the database

Now that the migration is in place, run the update-database command to apply the changes.

This should run without any issues. You can review your database to ensure that you have a new field for IsDeleted which is false for all rows. Additionally, ensure the name field is no longer nullable. See Figure 5-19.

Figure 5-19. *The database is updated as expected with the new required fields and non-nullable field constraints*

Step 3: Run the program

To complete this activity, you should make sure the code works as expected. Unfortunately, the code is currently not quite correct. Running the program as is could reveal a potential violation due to the new maximum quantity check constraint (see Figure 5-20).

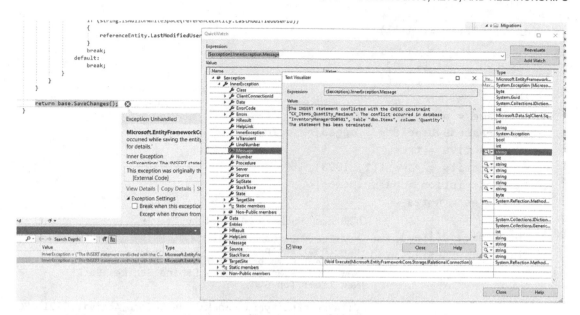

Figure 5-20. *The maximum quantity check constraint blocks inserting new items if the quantity is greater than 1000*

To fix this issue, find the line of code Quantity = r.Next(), which is located in the EnsureItem method in the Program class of the EFCore_Activity0501 project.

Change the code to use a minimum and maximum range for the quantity as follows: Quantity = r.Next(1, 1000).

With the new constraints in place and the range for the quantity set to generate from 1 to 1000, run the program again. This time the program should run as expected. You may wish to run the program a few times to ensure that it was not a fluke that it executed successfully this one time.

For clarity, a final view of the output and the updated line of code is shown in Figure 5-21.

```
if (existingItem == null)
{
    //doesn't exist, add it.
    var item = new Item()
    {
        Name = name,
        CreatedByUserId = _loggedInUserId,
        IsActive = true,
        Quantity = r.Next(1, 1000),
        Description = description,
        Notes = notes
    };
    db.Items.Add(item);
    db.SaveChanges();
}
```

```
Select Microsoft Visual Studio Debug Console
New Item: Batman Begins
New Item: Inception
New Item: Remember the Titans
New Item: Star Wars: The Empire Strikes Back
New Item: Top Gun

C:\APressEntityFramework\Code\EFCore_Activity0501\EFC
```

Figure 5-21. The code executes as expected and the range for the random number generated for the quantity is shown

Activity 5-1 summary

This activity gave you a good look at how you can use annotations and migrations to modify your database schema. Some of the things you learned were

- You can set the key fields for the table with the [Key] annotation.

- Making fields required is possible with the [Required] annotation.

- Use [StringLength] to set the maximum and minimum length of a string.

- Use [DefaultValue(<value>)] to set the default value of a field.

- Some of the annotations (attributes) only apply to the model state. In these cases, we can create a script to run *T-SQL* statements. This was highlighted with the Range attribute on the Quantity and Price properties.

- Use [Range] to set the minimum and maximum values of a field in the model state.

This concludes Activity 5-1.

Activity 5-2: Working with relationships

In this activity, you will create a one-to-one relationship, a one-to-many relationship, and a many-to-many relationship. You'll build out the relationships and the data structures in code, but you will not yet be implementing them in the UI (you will finish the implementations in the coming chapter on *CRUD* operations).

By the end of the activity, you'll be able to define a one-to-one, a one-to-many, and a many-to-many relationship in code. You'll also understand the difference between the two types of relationships and when it will be appropriate to use either.

Creating a one-to-many relationship

One of the most common relationships you'll encounter is the one-to-many relationship. In this system, to model a one-to-many relationship, you'll create a table to store *Categories*, and then you'll create a one-to-many relationship so that you can create a few categories and then have many items in each category. In this scenario, items will only be able to have one category assigned (otherwise, this would be a many-to-many relationship). Truly, having only one category per item might prove to be a bit limiting. Soon you'll also be creating a many-to-many relationship, so here you can think of the category as broad strokes (movies, books, games, etc.), whereas the many-to-many relationship later will be more specific (genres like fantasy, horror, and Sci-Fi).

Task 0: Getting started

As with every activity, you'll need a good launching point to start from. Here, you need to use the files you were working with at the end of the previous activity, or you can once again just leverage the starter files `EFCore_Activity05-2_StarterFiles`. Remember to check Appendix A for more information about using the starter files. Also remember that the final files for each activity are available if something about the activity instructions is unclear.

Task 1: Create the Categories in a one-to-many relationship with Items

In some ways, I'd like to just give you a simple spec and tell you to go build out the database for the model (not the relationship yet). If you want to try to work a bit as a challenge, what you are going to build is a new entity called Category that is a FullAuditModel, and for now, it will only have one simple additional property for Name, which should have a length and required attribute applied to it. A good challenge would be to try to go make this happen on your own and then come back here for help or validation and to complete the effort by building the correct relationship with the Items table.

Step 1: Create the Category entity model

To begin the walk-through, open the InventoryModels project, and add a new entity entitled Category in a file named Category.cs. For the Category, you'll use a FullAuditedModel and set an additional field for the Name of the category.

```
public class Category : FullAuditModel
{
    [StringLength(InventoryModelsConstants.MAX_NAME_LENGTH)]
    public string Name { get; set; }
}
```

Having this category entity in place, open the InventoryDbContext file from the EFCore_DbLibrary project, and add the DBSet<Category> to the InventoryDbContext in the InventoryDatabaseCore file:

```
public DbSet<Category> Categories { get; set; }
```

This code should be placed directly below the line that contains DbSet<Item> Items { get; set; }.

With the context reference in place and the entity set up, you could create the migration. At this point, however, you have yet to create the one-to-many relation, so you should do that first before adding the migration.

Step 2: Create the one-to-many relationship

To create a relationship in your code-first implementation, you need to reference the types that are related to the models involved in the relationship on both sides of the equation.

For this example, each of your Item objects should have one Category. Each of your categories can have many items. By saying this out loud, you can determine which types to place in each entity. For example, you could say the following phrase out loud to express the relationship: "One category has many items while each item has only one category."

Since the Item only has one Category, you need to create a virtual reference to the single category. In the InventoryModels project, in the Item.cs file at the bottom of the file after the CurrentOrFinalPrice property, add the lines

```
public int? CategoryId { get; set; }
public virtual Category Category { get; set; }
```

The placement of this code in the Item class doesn't really matter – these lines could go anywhere in the file. However, I personally find it is nice to have the relational entities defined after the regular properties of the entity model.

You need to make the CategoryId nullable because the database may already have data at this point. With that data, you won't be able to set the category id to map until you have some categories to map to. Therefore, for now you'll allow null in this relationship to prevent the migration from failing.

If you must make the Category for each item required, you'll need to back up your data, delete from the table, run the migration with a non-nullable CategoryId property, and then re-insert the data while also selecting valid category ids for each row, which will also require at least one Category to select from the Categories table. Again, the best way to do backup operations such as this would be to use a script that you write to ensure you don't lose any data and to run the entire process via one or more migrations so that every environment receives the same process for update of the data schema and consistency of existing data.

Note that it is also imperative that your Id field name matches exactly to the name of the virtual item. If these names are not the same, by convention, an extra Id field would automatically be added to line up to your virtual Category field, unless you add a specific notation to map the foreign key relationship.

If for some reason your Items table has a field that is already named CategoryId, you can explicitly set the name of the Id field by using the data annotation [ForeignKey("CategoryId")] as an attribute to any nullable int property you want to map as the foreign category id. Another option would be to rename the Category property to something like ItemCategory and use a field ItemCategoryId.

Additionally, you want to use the virtual keyword on any of your relationships so that *EF* can override and/or extend the properties to support lazy loading of the relational data. This will become incredibly important when you want to use LINQ later to select data and include relationship data in the model state.

Next, on the Category object, you need to create a list of items to map the relationship in the other direction. Remember, any category can have many items – which indicates an ICollection<Item> should be available, preferably IQueryable and/or IEnumerable. For that reason, it is very common to just use a List object to model the relationship. By default, a List is an IEnumerable object. If the List needs to be queried, you'll need to do a cast or use the LINQ expression .AsQueryable(). To complete the relationship, go to the Category entity model and add the following code after the Name property:

```
public virtual List<Item> Items { get; set; } = new List<Item>();
```

You will need to add the using statement using Systems.Collections.Generic to the top of your Category code file.

Make sure to set the List to a new list by default to avoid null reference exceptions on the list in the cases where the related items are not loaded into scope. This is one of the biggest gotchas in EF and LINQ programming. This simple addition of the new list will save you a number of headaches, keeping you from having to always create a new list with each entity or trying to reference Items from the Category when none are present or the Items were never included in the original query.

For clarity, the current code of the Category class is shown in Figure 5-22.

```
using System.Collections.Generic;
using System.ComponentModel.DataAnnotations;

namespace InventoryModels
{
    2 references
    public class Category : FullAuditModel
    {
        [StringLength(InventoryModelsConstants.MAX_NAME_LENGTH)]
        0 references
        public string Name { get; set; }

        0 references
        public virtual List<Item> Items { get; set; } = new List<Item>();
    }
}
```

Figure 5-22. *The new Category entity code is shown for clarity. Ensure you've added the inheritance for the FullAuditModel and that you've created the two properties as shown*

Step 3: Create the migration

Provided everything is set up correctly, the migration will generate the new Categories table and will correctly set a new CategoryId in the Items table.

Ensure your *PMC* is pointed at the EFCore_DBLibrary project and then run the command add-migration createCategoriesTable_withItemsRelationship. This should generate a migration similar to what is shown in Figure 5-23.

```
protected override void Up(MigrationBuilder migrationBuilder)
{
    migrationBuilder.AddColumn<int>(
        name: "CategoryId",
        table: "Items",
        type: "int",
        nullable: true);

    migrationBuilder.CreateTable(
        name: "Categories",
        columns: table => new
        {
            Id = table.Column<int>(type: "int", nullable: false)
                .Annotation("SqlServer:Identity", "1, 1"),
            Name = table.Column<string>(type: "nvarchar(100)", maxLength: 100, nullable: true),
            CreatedByUserId = table.Column<string>(type: "nvarchar(50)", maxLength: 50, nullable: true),
            CreatedDate = table.Column<DateTime>(type: "datetime2", nullable: false),
            LastModifiedUserId = table.Column<string>(type: "nvarchar(50)", maxLength: 50, nullable: true),
            LastModifiedDate = table.Column<DateTime>(type: "datetime2", nullable: true),
            IsActive = table.Column<bool>(type: "bit", nullable: false),
            IsDeleted = table.Column<bool>(type: "bit", nullable: false)
        },
        constraints: table =>
        {
            table.PrimaryKey("PK_Categories", x => x.Id);
        });

    migrationBuilder.CreateIndex(
        name: "IX_Items_CategoryId",
        table: "Items",
        column: "CategoryId");

    migrationBuilder.AddForeignKey(
        name: "FK_Items_Categories_CategoryId",
        table: "Items",
        column: "CategoryId",
        principalTable: "Categories",
        principalColumn: "Id",
        onDelete: ReferentialAction.Restrict);
}
```

Ensure that you have this entry to create the appropriate foreign key

Figure 5-23. *The Foreign Key is shown, as is a table for Categories and the CategoryId column that will be used to map an Item to a Category*

Once you've reviewed the migration and it looks like it is set to correctly create the new schema changes, go ahead and run the update-database command to apply the changes.

Step 4: Review the database

With the changes applied, open SSMS and review the tables to ensure that they are there and that the appropriate association is created for the Categories table to the Items table. For clarity, the data relationship is shown in a diagram in Figure 5-24.

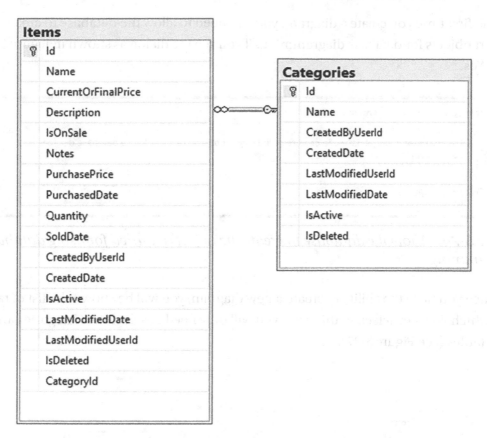

Figure 5-24. *The new Categories table exists, and the data is correctly related in a one-to-many relationship with the Items table*

As an aside, if you would like to create your own database diagram, use SSMS and right-click `Database Diagrams`, and then select `New Database Diagram` (see Figure 5-25).

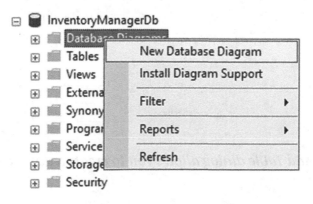

Figure 5-25. *The process to create a new database diagram starts by right-clicking and selecting New Database Diagram as shown here*

The first time you create a diagram, you will need to allow the database to create support objects for database diagramming. If you see the dialog as shown in Figure 5-26, select Yes.

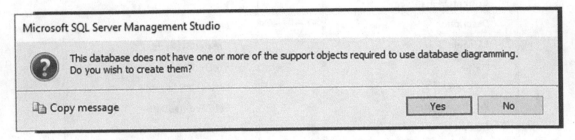

Figure 5-26. *Allow the database to create the objects required for using database diagramming*

Once you have the ability to create a new diagram, you will be shown the list of tables from which you can select. In this case, you will only need to select the Categories and Items tables (see Figure 5-27).

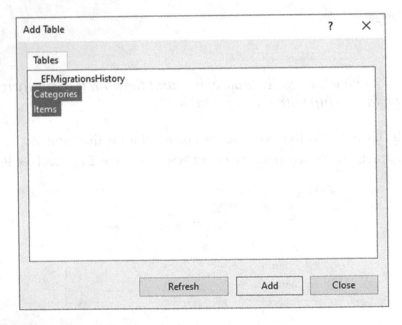

Figure 5-27. *The Add Table dialog allows you to create a database diagram*

Once you've selected both tables, hit the Add button to create the diagram. After the Add button is pressed, you will need to press Close, and then you will see the diagram in a similar fashion to what was shown in Figure 5-24. You can drag and resize the tables as necessary for your needs.

For further clarity, reviewing the data structure is shown in Figure 5-28, where the index is now existing in the Items table.

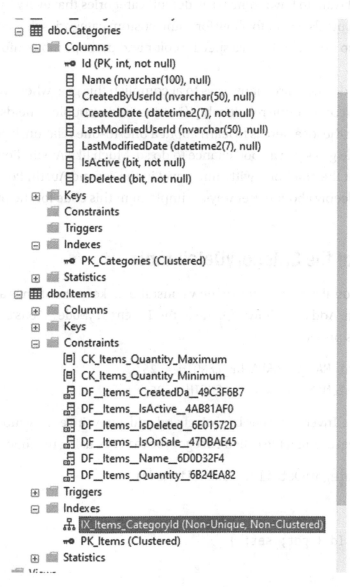

Figure 5-28. *The Index exists on the Items table that shows a foreign key relationship from the CategoryId to the Categories table*

Task 2: Create a one-to-one relationship from Category to CategoryDetail

If you remember reading earlier about the setup in the *AdventureWorks* database, you saw how a business entity object was further decorated as needed by using one-to-one relationships. Assume that, in your system here, you might have multiple users and that the system would want to have some basic default categories that everyone can see; however, maybe you also want to allow for some custom categories that could be used as categories but also associated with a specific color and perhaps more information like a description.

As a quick aside, there are many ways to accomplish this goal where you wouldn't necessarily need a one-to-one relationship (i.e., just add a couple of fields to the Categories table); the idea here is to learn about a one-to-one relationship, and this contrived example gives you a good chance to do so. Much like Austin Powers tells you not to think about the plot holes with time travel in the second Austin Powers movie, try not to think too deeply about better ways to implement this code for the purposes of this activity.

Step 1: Create the CategoryDetail table

To start this off, you'll need a couple of new constants to keep the strings at a reasonable length. Add the following code to the InventoryModelsConstants file in the InventoryModels project:

```
public const int MAX_COLORVALUE_LENGTH = 25;
public const int MAX_COLORNAME_LENGTH = 25;
```

Next, go to the InventoryModels project and add a new inventory model that is called CategoryDetail in a file called CategoryDetail.cs using the following code:

```
public class CategoryDetail : IIdentityModel
{
    [Required]
    public int Id { get; set; }

    [Required]
    [StringLength(InventoryModelsConstants.MAX_COLORVALUE_LENGTH)]
    public string ColorValue { get; set; }
```

```
[Required]
[StringLength(InventoryModelsConstants.MAX_COLORNAME_LENGTH)]
public string ColorName { get; set; }
}
```

Ensure that you have resolved the missing using statements for using InventoryModels.Interfaces and using System.ComponentModel.DataAnnotations.

One other thing to do, to make sure this is not forgotten, is to go into the EFCore_DbLibrary project and add the following code after the line that contains public DbSet<Category> Categories ...:

```
public DbSet<CategoryDetail> CategoryDetails { get; set; }
```

If you forget to do this, the migration will not work as expected later in the activity. See Figure 5-29.

```
12 references
public class InventoryDbContext : DbContext
{
    private static IConfigurationRoot _configuration;
    private const string _systemUserId = "2fd28110-93d0-427d-9207-d55dbca680fa";

    7 references
    public DbSet<Item> Items { get; set; }
    0 references
    public DbSet<Category> Categories { get; set; }
    0 references
    public DbSet<CategoryDetail> CategoryDetails { get; set; }

    //Add a default constructor if scaffolding is needed
    0 references
    public InventoryDbContext() { }

    //Add the complex constructor for allowing Dependency Injection
    4 references
```

Figure 5-29. *The InventoryDbContext contains the new table as a DbSet*

This code sets you up well to have both tables in place but has yet to build the one-to-one relationship.

Step 2: Create the one-to-one relationship for the Category to the CategoryDetail table

As with the one-to-many relationship, you still need to create the relationship in code before creating the migration. Here, you'll just need add the direct one-to-one relationship by giving the color object one category and the category object one color. The problem is that this creates a somewhat weird scenario as to which is the primary and which is the foreign key. You'll solve this by identifying the foreign key directly in the entity code.

In the CategoryDetail entity, add the following code:

```
public virtual Category Category { get; set; }
```

Then set the Key field to also be a foreign key to the Category (setting this makes it so that the table is related but does not store the CategoryId as an additional field in the table). You'll do this on the Id field of the CategoryDetail object to essentially direct this table to use the same Id as the Category table for the record as a direct one-to-one relationship:

```
[Key, ForeignKey("Category")]
[Required]
public int Id { get; set; }
```

You will need to bring in the using statement for using System.ComponentModel. DataAnnotations.Schema, so don't forget to do that.

For clarity, review Figure 5-30 to see what the CategoryDetail entity model should look like at this point.

```
1 reference
public class CategoryDetail : IIdentityModel
{
    [Key, ForeignKey("Category")]
    [Required]
    2 references
    public int Id { get; set; }

    [Required]
    [StringLength(InventoryModelsConstants.MAX_COLORVALUE_LENGTH)]
    0 references
    public string ColorValue { get; set; }
    [Required]
    [StringLength(InventoryModelsConstants.MAX_COLORNAME_LENGTH)]
    0 references
    public string ColorName { get; set; }

    0 references
    public virtual Category Category { get; set; }
}
```

Figure 5-30. *The CategoryDetail entity with reference to the Category entity for creation of a one-to-one relationship*

Do not miss the `ForeignKey` constraint on the `Id` field. If you miss adding this, then the one-to-one relationship will not map and your solution will not work as expected.

Once the CategoryDetail entity is in place, add the relationship to the `Category` class as you would expect to add a direct relationship (just like adding one `Category` to the `Item` in the previous task). The main difference this time is you will **not** add the foreign key id to map, since the mapping is literally the same key as the primary key in the Category table.

```
public virtual CategoryDetail CategoryDetail { get; set; }
```

For further clarity, review Figure 5-31.

```
namespace InventoryModels
{
    3 references
    public class Category : FullAuditModel
    {
        [StringLength(InventoryModelsConstants.MAX_NAME_LENGTH)]
        0 references
        public string Name { get; set; }

        0 references
        public virtual List<Item> Items { get; set; } = new List<Item>();

        0 references
        public virtual CategoryDetail CategoryDetail { get; set; }
    }
}
```

Figure 5-31. *The Category entity with reference to the CategoryDetail for a one-to-one relationship*

The reason you want the virtual mapping is for the ability to use the navigation properties that it will generate. You don't want the Id from the other table as you would usually reference in a relationship, however, because that just creates a giant mess with the same Id as the key for the Category table and it doesn't update or get set correctly by default, since EF is expecting you to use the same id in both tables to directly map the one-to-one relationship.

Step 3: Create the migration and update the database

Now that the entities are in the context and the relationships are modeled to build a one-to-one relationship, add the migration with the command add-migration createCategoryDetail_withCategoriesRelationship.

For this migration, you should expect to see the new table created. To see more detail, you'll need to dive into the FluentAPI.

Once the migration is completed, it should be similar to what is shown in Figure 5-32.

```
7 references
protected override void Up(MigrationBuilder migrationBuilder)
{
    migrationBuilder.CreateTable(
        name: "CategoryDetails",
        columns: table => new
        {
            Id = table.Column<int>(type: "int", nullable: false),
            ColorValue = table.Column<string>(type: "nvarchar(25)", maxLength: 25, nullable: false),
            ColorName = table.Column<string>(type: "nvarchar(25)", maxLength: 25, nullable: false)
        },
        constraints: table =>
        {
            table.PrimaryKey("PK_CategoryDetails", x => x.Id);
            table.ForeignKey(
                name: "FK_CategoryDetails_Categories_Id",
                column: x => x.Id,
                principalTable: "Categories",
                principalColumn: "Id",
                onDelete: ReferentialAction.Cascade);
        });
}
```

Figure 5-32. *The generated migration for building the Category to CategoryDetail one-to-one relationship*

Note that the table is created, but it is not clear how the entities are related other than the foreign key mapping in the constraints listing. Also note that the onDelete action is set to ReferentialAction.Cascade. This means that if a Category is deleted, so is the CategoryDetail. If you think about it, this makes sense because the CategoryDetail doesn't make any sense without a Category.

Step 4: Review the ModelBuilder FluentAPI code in the migration

To this point, you've not used the FluentAPI much, if at all. That's OK – for now, but you will want to grow in this area as you continue working through this book and with EFCore6 in general.

Behind the scenes, some FluentAPI code has been generated for you all along. In EFCore6, the FluentAPI uses the model builder to quickly model and relate the entities from the code.

Open the file that is nested under your migration, which has the same name but also has the extension Designer in the name. See Figure 5-33 for clarity.

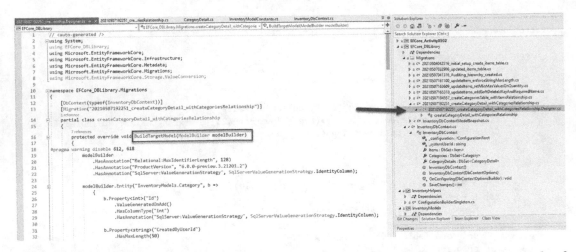

Figure 5-33. *The Designer file contains FluentAPI code that is directly the result of your entire database state and the current migration that you have just generated*

Of particular interest is how the relationship is defined in the *FluentAPI*. Search for the text "modelBuilder.Entity("InventoryModels.CategoryDetail", b =>", and then find the second instance of this text, which should be located near the end of the file. The code to examine should be similar to the following:

```
modelBuilder.Entity("InventoryModels.CategoryDetail", b =>
    {
        b.HasOne("InventoryModels.Category", "Category")
            .WithOne("CategoryDetail")
            .HasForeignKey("InventoryModels.CategoryDetail", "Id")
            .OnDelete(DeleteBehavior.Cascade)
            .IsRequired();

        b.Navigation("Category");
    });
```

Note how the CategoryDetail has one (.HasOne) Category that has one (.WithOne) CategoryDetail, mapped by the CategoryDetail Id field. This is how the relationship is created. Take a minute to look through some of the other Fluent API code that is in the file. Toward the very end, you will also see the navigation properties for the InventoryModels.Category as defined in the following code:

```
modelBuilder.Entity("InventoryModels.Category", b =>
    {
        b.Navigation("CategoryDetail");

        b.Navigation("Items");
    });
```

You don't need to modify any of the code in the Designer file, but it is good to review it to start seeing more about the plumbing that is going on behind the scenes.

Step 5: Update the database

With the migration reviewed, save and build, and then run the update-database command to execute the changes. Once the database migration has completed, open the tables in *SSMS* to review. Figure 5-34 shows the two tables with the established relationship from a database diagram.

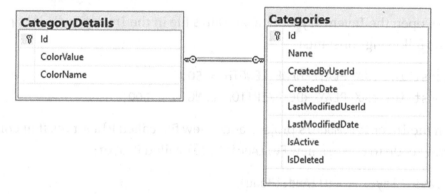

Figure 5-34. *The Categories and CategoryDetails one-to-one relationship after database migrations are applied*

Task 3: Create a many-to-many relationship

In this third task, you will be learning about a new feature that is now available since EFCore5 that has not been available in previous versions of EFCore. This feature was available in EF6, so if you are used to using it there, you will like that it is again available in EFCore5 and EFCore6. In this task, you will use code to create a many-to-many relationship without explicitly building a join table. EFCore will provide the join table for you by convention.

Step 1: Create a new Player entity

Earlier, you read about the different forms of normalization. One thing that was mentioned was how 2NF requires unique data in each row. Another thing that was not directly discussed is that there should be no composite data. One problem is that the current setup uses the Notes field to hold the names of the actors and actresses in the movies. To give the ability to easily do this in a 2NF approach, you need to allow each entity to be unique and directly linked to the Item.

Eventually, you'll likely want to store more than movies, so you might add other things like authors for books or production company for games. For the purposes of this learning, you'll create a table called Players that stores the name of a person or company (a Player object) and allows for easy expansion to track other details later if you so desire. The Players table will join to the Items table in a many-to-many relationship. For example, Tom Cruise might be in many movies, and *Top Gun* has many other actors like Val Kilmer and Tom Skerritt, so the many-to-many relationship makes sense.

To start, open the InventoryModelsConstants file in the InventoryModels project and add the following constants:

```
public const int MAX_PLAYERNAME_LENGTH = 50;
public const int MAX_PLAYERDESCRIPTION_LENGTH = 500;
```

Also in the InventoryModels project, add a new file called Player.cs that contains the following code to create a new FullAuditModel called Player:

```
public class Player : FullAuditModel
{
    [Required]
    [StringLength(InventoryModelsConstants.MAX_PLAYERNAME_LENGTH)]
    public string Name { get; set; }

    [StringLength(InventoryModelsConstants.MAX_PLAYERDESCRIPTION_LENGTH)]
    public string Description { get; set; }

    public virtual List<Item> Items { get; set; } = new List<Item>();
}
```

Notice the properties for the Name and Description but also the virtual List of Items that will serve as part of the many-to-many relationship. Additionally, you'll need to bring in the using statements for System.Collections.Generic and System.ComponentModel.DataAnnotations.

Figure 5-35 shows the new class code for clarity.

```csharp
public class Player : FullAuditModel
{
    [Required]
    [StringLength(InventoryModelsConstants.MAX_PLAYERNAME_LENGTH)]
    0 references
    public string Name { get; set; }

    [StringLength(InventoryModelsConstants.MAX_PLAYERDESCRIPTION_LENGTH)]
    0 references
    public string Description { get; set; }

    0 references
    public virtual List<Item> Items { get; set; } = new List<Item>();
}
```

Figure 5-35. *The new Player class has a name, a description, and a reference to the List of Items*

Next, open the Item.cs file and add the following code at the bottom of the Item class (don't forget to bring in any missing using statements):

```csharp
public virtual List<Player> Players { get; set; } = new List<Player>();
```

This list of Player will represent the other side of the many-to-many relationship. In the past, you would have needed to manually create and define an entity to represent the join table for the ItemPlayers. With EFCore6, this will be done by convention.

Step 2: Create the new migration

With everything in place to create the many-to-many relationship, make sure the project builds, and then run the command add-migration createPlayers_withItemsRelationship. When you create the migration, you'll see that it will create the new Players table, as well as the ItemPlayer table that will act as the join table.

One thing to note here is that with the ItemPlayer table being auto-generated, you don't have a lot of control over the object from the code-first perspective. In the future, if you want to add more information to this table, you may need to directly add a new model entity or you could use scripts to change the schema.

Review the migration to ensure both tables are there with the appropriate fields and relationships. Also note the indexes that will be created.

The migration should look like what is shown in Figure 5-36.

```
migrationBuilder.CreateTable(
    name: "Player",
    columns: table => new
    {
        Id = table.Column<int>(type: "int", nullable: false)
            .Annotation("SqlServer:Identity", "1, 1"),
        Name = table.Column<string>(type: "nvarchar(50)", maxLength: 50, nullable: false),
        Description = table.Column<string>(type: "nvarchar(500)", maxLength: 500, nullable: true),
        CreatedByUserId = table.Column<string>(type: "nvarchar(50)", maxLength: 50, nullable: true),
        CreatedDate = table.Column<DateTime>(type: "datetime2", nullable: false),
        LastModifiedUserId = table.Column<string>(type: "nvarchar(50)", maxLength: 50, nullable: true),
        LastModifiedDate = table.Column<DateTime>(type: "datetime2", nullable: true),
        IsActive = table.Column<bool>(type: "bit", nullable: false),
        IsDeleted = table.Column<bool>(type: "bit", nullable: false)
    },
    constraints: table =>
    {
        table.PrimaryKey("PK_Player", x => x.Id);
    });

migrationBuilder.CreateTable(
    name: "ItemPlayer",
    columns: table => new
    {
        ItemsId = table.Column<int>(type: "int", nullable: false),
        PlayersId = table.Column<int>(type: "int", nullable: false)
    },
    constraints: table =>
    {
        table.PrimaryKey("PK_ItemPlayer", x => new { x.ItemsId, x.PlayersId });
        table.ForeignKey(
            name: "FK_ItemPlayer_Items_ItemsId",
            column: x => x.ItemsId,
            principalTable: "Items",
            principalColumn: "Id",
            onDelete: ReferentialAction.Cascade);
        table.ForeignKey(
            name: "FK_ItemPlayer_Player_PlayersId",
            column: x => x.PlayersId,
            principalTable: "Player",
            principalColumn: "Id",
            onDelete: ReferentialAction.Cascade);
    });
```

Figure 5-36. *The migration is generated to create the Player and ItemPlayer tables to create the many-to-many relationship between Players and Items*

One thing you might note here is that the names of the fields in the join table are not ideal, nor is the name of the join table. For example, you likely don't want to have a singular `ItemId` referenced as `ItemsId`, and the same goes for `PlayerId` referenced as `PlayersId`.

Additionally, you likely want the table to be pluralized, such as ItemPlayers instead of ItemPlayer.

To accomplish this task, you could manually modify the migration. However, there is a better way to do this to ensure you don't have any pending migrations.

Since you are going to recreate the migration, just run the remove-migration command to get rid of the pending migration.

Step 3: Update the FluentAPI to name the fields as expected

Instead of proceeding with the migration update, add the following code into the InventoryDbContext.cs file between the OnConfiguring and SaveChanges methods:

```
protected override void OnModelCreating(ModelBuilder modelBuilder)
{
    modelBuilder.Entity<Item>()
                .HasMany(x => x.Players)
                .WithMany(p => p.Items)
                .UsingEntity<Dictionary<string, object>>(
                    "ItemPlayers",
                    ip => ip.HasOne<Player>()
                            .WithMany()
                            .HasForeignKey("PlayerId")
                            .HasConstraintName("FK_ItemPlayer_Players_
                            PlayerId")
                            .OnDelete(DeleteBehavior.Cascade),
                    ip => ip.HasOne<Item>()
                            .WithMany()
                            .HasForeignKey("ItemId")
                            .HasConstraintName("FK_PlayerItem_Items_
                            ItemId")
                            .OnDelete(DeleteBehavior.ClientCascade)
                );
}
```

This code will override the OnModelCreating method and use the ModelBuilder to run FluentAPI commands to further define relationships and constraints and will even be used for some simple database seeding in future chapters.

For this specific instance, note that the modelBuilder object will define the relationship further for Items and Players and will set the value of the fields to PlayerId and ItemId, respectively. Additionally, the entity will be defined as ItemPlayers. Use the up arrow in the PMC to get your add-migration command back and run it again. For reference, the command was add-migration createPlayers_withItemsRelationship. This time the migration generates with field names as you would likely expect, thanks to the pre-defined model relationships in the FluentAPI (see Figure 5-37).

```
migrationBuilder.CreateTable(
    name: "Player",
    columns: table => new
    {
        Id = table.Column<int>(type: "int", nullable: false)
            .Annotation("SqlServer:Identity", "1, 1"),
        Name = table.Column<string>(type: "nvarchar(50)", maxLength: 50, nullable: false),
        Description = table.Column<string>(type: "nvarchar(500)", maxLength: 500, nullable: true),
        CreatedByUserId = table.Column<string>(type: "nvarchar(50)", maxLength: 50, nullable: true),
        CreatedDate = table.Column<DateTime>(type: "datetime2", nullable: false),
        LastModifiedUserId = table.Column<string>(type: "nvarchar(50)", maxLength: 50, nullable: true),
        LastModifiedDate = table.Column<DateTime>(type: "datetime2", nullable: true),
        IsActive = table.Column<bool>(type: "bit", nullable: false),
        IsDeleted = table.Column<bool>(type: "bit", nullable: false)
    },
    constraints: table =>
    {
        table.PrimaryKey("PK_Player", x => x.Id);
    });
```

```
migrationBuilder.CreateTable(
    name: "ItemPlayers",
    columns: table => new
    {
        ItemId = table.Column<int>(type: "int", nullable: false),
        PlayerId = table.Column<int>(type: "int", nullable: false)
    },
    constraints: table =>
    {
        table.PrimaryKey("PK_ItemPlayers", x => new { x.ItemId, x.PlayerId });
        table.ForeignKey(
            name: "FK_ItemPlayer_Players_PlayerId",
            column: x => x.PlayerId,
            principalTable: "Player",
            principalColumn: "Id",
            onDelete: ReferentialAction.Cascade);
        table.ForeignKey(
            name: "FK_PlayerItem_Items_ItemId",
```

Figure 5-37. *The migration is generated, and the table name and field names for the join table are aligned with what would likely be expected in traditional development standards for a join table*

Step 4: Update the database

Now that the migration is in place to create the many-to-many relationship between Players and Items via a table called ItemPlayers, run the update-database command to apply the changes to the database.

Step 4: Review the database

Finally, take a minute to review the database to ensure that the tables and relationships have been created as expected. Figure 5-38 shows a database diagram that contains the many-to-many relationship that was just created.

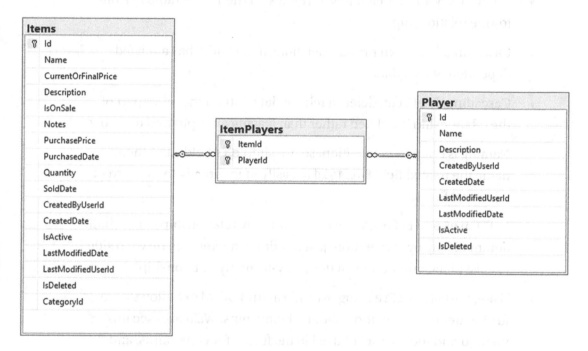

Figure 5-38. *The relationship for Items to Players via the ItemPlayers table is shown in this database diagram*

Step 5: Ensure the code executes

Run the program to ensure that the program executes as expected. The final output has not changed, so it is the same as you would see in Figure 5-21.

Activity 5-2 summary

In this activity, we learned how to build out a one-to-many relationship, a one-to-one relationship, and also a one-to-many relationship. Important things to remember are

- Build out the entities, and then build the relations in the entities using virtual objects.

- If using a one-to-many, create a `List` of the related objects in the "one" table and a direct reference to the "one" object in the "many" object entity.

- Set both Key and Foreign Key attributes on the `Id` of a table in a one-to-one relationship.

- Cascading delete can prevent deletions if the entity has a related dependency with data.

- Cascading delete can delete a related data entry if the other part of the relationship is deleted rather than leaving an orphaned data row.

- Naming is done by convention, so use simple `Id` fields and then name the related field `EntityId` to easily map directly to the correct relational fields.

- In `EFCore5` and `EFCore6`, the many-to-many relationship can be built automatically by convention, just by adding a reference on each side to a list of the other entity in the many-to-many relationship.

- Using the `OnModelCreating` override in the `DbContext` allows us to further define information about relationships. We'll also see this method and the FluentAPI used in the future for constraints, and we'll also use this method with the FluentAPI to create simple seed data.

Activity 5-3: Using a non-clustered, unique index

This final activity for Chapter 5 will serve a dual purpose. First, you will examine what it takes to build out a many-to-many relationship in the traditional manner (prior to `EFCore5`'s new many-to-many relationship convention). After setting up that relationship, you'll also see what it takes to create a non-clustered index that is unique on the many-to-many relationship. The unique constraint is critical to make sure that you don't have duplicate records in the database.

Soft delete or hard delete, either way, just make sure it works

A good thing to remember about this setup is that if you are using a soft delete approach, you'll need to make sure that any relationships are still intact if you delete and then restore an object. This could be accomplished by soft deleting the join entry or just leaving it alone while making sure the data is handled correctly in both directions.

If you use a hard delete approach, then deleting one of the sides of the relationship should also delete the entry in the join table via a cascading delete operation.

By the end of the activity, you'll be able to define a many-to-many relationship in code explicitly. You'll also understand what it means to set up a unique constraint as a non-clustered index on your database using the code-first approach.

Task 0: Getting started

Once again, you can continue to use the code that you've been working on through the chapter, or you can grab the EFCore_Activity05-3_StarterFiles and use those to complete this activity. Remember to check Appendix A for information about using starter files.

Task 1: Create the Genre

As you're tracking items, you likely have some inventory categories like movies and books, games, or other types of media. One common grouping that might exist across categories would be Genre. For example, you can have books and movies that are considered to be "Western" or "Sci-Fi."

Step 1: Add the Genre entity model

To get started, add a new constant in the InventoryModelConstants file in the InventoryModels project as follows:

```
public const int MAX_GENRENAME_LENGTH = 50;
```

Next, create a new entity in the InventoryModels project for Genre as a FullAuditModel. Add a string Name property to describe the Genre, and constrain the Name field using constraints that already exist. Make sure to add any missing using statements so the code will compile. You'll keep the Genre model pretty simple for purposes of demonstration and brevity.

```
public class Genre : FullAuditModel
{
    [Required]
    [StringLength(InventoryModelsConstants.MAX_NAME_LENGTH)]
    public string Name { get; set; }
}
```

As always, in order to add the entity, you'll need to put the Genre into the DBContext. Open the InventoryDbContext file in the EFCore_DbLibrary and add the following code after the line of code that contains public DbSet<CategoryDetail> CategoryDetails...:

```
public DbSet<Genre> Genres { get; set; }
```

For clarity, part of the InventoryDbContext is shown in Figure 5-39.

```
private static IConfigurationRoot _configuration;
private const string _systemUserId = "2fd28110-93d0-427d-9207-d55dbca680fa";

7 references
public DbSet<Item> Items { get; set; }
0 references
public DbSet<Category> Categories { get; set; }
0 references
public DbSet<CategoryDetail> CategoryDetails { get; set; }
0 references
public DbSet<Genre> Genres { get; set; }

//Add a default constructor if scaffolding is needed
0 references
public InventoryDbContext() { }
```

Figure 5-39. *The InventoryDbContext is shown to illustrate the code changes*

Step 2: Add the migration and update the database

Instead of trying to do everything in one migration, this time you'll separate the different actions into their own migrations. This will allow for both migrations to be managed more easily.

Make sure that you've pointed your PMC at the EFCore_DbLibrary, and then run the command add-migration createGenreTable.

Once you've added the migration, validate that the migration is set to create the Genres table as expected.

With the migration in place and validated, run the update-database command to add the Genres table to the database.

Task 2: Create the ItemGenre and the many-to-many relationship

Now that the Genre table is in place, you'll create a new entity to model the join table called ItemGenre. You will then add the associations to join both the Items and the Genres tables in a many-to-many relationship.

Step 1: Create the ItemGenre entity model

In the InventoryModels project, add a new file called ItemGenre.cs to create a new class ItemGenre.

In the new class, add the following code:

```
public class ItemGenre : IIdentityModel
{
    public int Id { get; set; }

    public virtual int ItemId { get; set; }
    public virtual Item Item { get; set; }

    public virtual int GenreId { get; set; }
    public virtual Genre Genre { get; set; }
}
```

Step 2: Add references to the Item and the Genre classes to fully create the relationship

Open the Item class and add a new property as follows to associate the Items to Genres via the ItemGenres table:

```
public virtual List<ItemGenre> ItemGenres { get; set; } = new
List<ItemGenre>();
```

Next, open the Genre class and add a new property as follows to associate the Genres to Items via the ItemGenres table:

```
public virtual List<ItemGenre> GenreItems { get; set; } = new
List<ItemGenre>();
```

Step 3: Create a new migration

With both of the sides of the equation in place, that is enough to generate the table and relationships via a migration, even without adding the ItemGenre entity as a DbSet in the InventoryDbContext. If you would like to directly query the ItemGenre table, you could add it to the context. However, you will likely only query this relationship from the Item or the Genre and won't need a direct query against the ItemGenre table.

Run the command add-migration createItemGenreJoinTableAndRelationships. Once the migration is generated, review it to ensure that the table to join Items and Genres is created as expected. The migration should look like what is shown in Figure 5-40.

```
protected override void Up(MigrationBuilder migrationBuilder)
{
    migrationBuilder.CreateTable(
        name: "ItemGenre",
        columns: table => new
        {
            Id = table.Column<int>(type: "int", nullable: false)
                .Annotation("SqlServer:Identity", "1, 1"),
            ItemId = table.Column<int>(type: "int", nullable: false),
            GenreId = table.Column<int>(type: "int", nullable: false)
        },
        constraints: table =>
        {
            table.PrimaryKey("PK_ItemGenre", x => x.Id);
            table.ForeignKey(
                name: "FK_ItemGenre_Genres_GenreId",
                column: x => x.GenreId,
                principalTable: "Genres",
                principalColumn: "Id",
                onDelete: ReferentialAction.Cascade);
            table.ForeignKey(
                name: "FK_ItemGenre_Items_ItemId",
                column: x => x.ItemId,
                principalTable: "Items",
                principalColumn: "Id",
                onDelete: ReferentialAction.Cascade);
        });

    migrationBuilder.CreateIndex(
        name: "IX_ItemGenre_GenreId",
        table: "ItemGenre",
        column: "GenreId");

    migrationBuilder.CreateIndex(
        name: "IX_ItemGenre_ItemId",
        table: "ItemGenre",
        column: "ItemId");
}
```

Figure 5-40. *The migration to create the ItemGenre table includes the constraints and the indexes necessary to link the Items to the Genres in a many-to-many relationship*

Once again, note that the table name here is not pluralized. There are a couple of ways to fix this. As before, you could define it in the FluentAPI. However, this time you will do it via Data Annotations.

Run the `remove-migration` command to delete the recently generated migration. Once the migration is removed, return to the ItemGenre.cs class and add the following Data Annotation to the top of the class:

```
[Table("ItemGenres")]
```

This will require adding the using statement `using System.ComponentModel.DataAnnotations.Schema` to the top of the class. Review Figure 5-41 for clarity.

```
ItemGenre.cs  ⊞ ✕  20210507204438_createGenreTable.cs      InventoryDbContext.cs
lodels                        ▼  ⚙ InventoryModels.ItemGenre          ▼  🔧 Id
 ⊟using InventoryModels.Interfaces;
  using System.ComponentModel.DataAnnotations.Schema;

 ⊟namespace InventoryModels
  {
       [Table("ItemGenres")]
       4 references
 ⊟     public class ItemGenre : IIdentityModel
       {
            3 references
            public int Id { get; set; }

            0 references
            public virtual int ItemId { get; set; }
            0 references
            public virtual Item Item { get; set; }
```

Figure 5-41. *The ItemGenre class code is shown to highlight the use of the Table data annotation*

With the annotation in place, recreate the migration with the command `add-migration createItemGenreJoinTableAndRelationships`.

Review the migration to see the table name is updated as expected.

If you want to look even closer, open the `Designer` file to once again review how the `modelBuilder` is generating the relationships. Once you've reviewed the migration, run the `update-database` command to apply the changes.

Step 4: Review the database to ensure the structure is as expected

After the changes are applied, review the tables to ensure that all of the tables you expect are in place, and relationships and indexes exist as expected.

Figure 5-42 shows the many-to-many relationship in a database diagram.

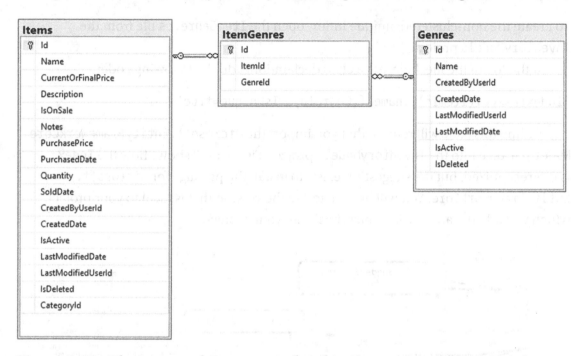

Figure 5-42. *The Items and Genres are related in a many-to-many relationship via the ItemGenres join table*

The main benefit of this approach is you now have full control of the join table, should you have a desire or need to do so.

Task 3: Use the Index attribute to create a unique, non-clustered index

To keep from having multiple rows in the database that map the same two Item and Genre entities into a relationship, you need to create a new index that makes that combination unique. This is important so that you can make sure that when you create a new record, update a row, or perform a soft delete or restore from delete, you don't create duplicate rows that are essentially mapping the same two entities.

In EF6, this task was easily accomplished using an Index attribute. In EFCore versions prior to EFCore5, you had to do this via the Fluent API. In EFCore5 and EFCore6, the Index attribute has returned, so creating a unique, non-clustered index is accomplished by adding an attribute to the class.

Step 1: Add the Index to the ItemGenre class

To create the non-clustered, unique index, open the ItemGenre.cs file from the InventoryModels project.

At the top of the file, before the class declaration, add the following code:

```
[Index(nameof(ItemId), nameof(GenreId), IsUnique=true)]
```

Adding this code will require that you import the Microsoft.EntityFrameworkCore NuGet package into the InventoryModels project. Figure 5-43 shows how the Index is not recognized, but the suggestion exists to install the package for Microsoft. EntityFrameworkCore. You will be able to use the version that is local to your project, which will add the appropriate references into your project.

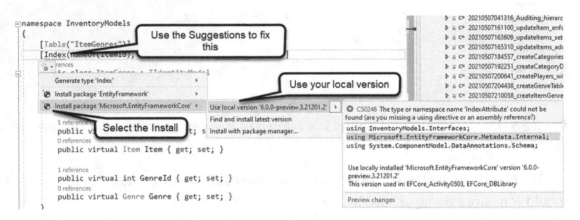

Figure 5-43. *Using the Index attribute will require a reference to Microsoft. EntityFrameworkCore in the InventoryModels project*

Once the package is imported, make sure that you've added the using statements using Microsoft.EntityFrameworkCore and using Microsoft.EntityFrameworkCore. Metadata.Internal at the top of the class. The suggestion might ask you to use Metadata.Internal, but you will need to remove that statement if it is added to your using statements.

Step 2: Add the migration

With the Index attribute in place, you can add a new migration to see the changes that will be applied to the database. Run the command add-migration createUniqueNonClusteredIndex_ItemGenres. The resulting migration should look similar to what is shown in Figure 5-44.

```
11 references
protected override void Up(MigrationBuilder migrationBuilder)
{
    migrationBuilder.DropIndex(
        name: "IX_ItemGenres_ItemId",
        table: "ItemGenres");

    migrationBuilder.CreateIndex(
        name: "IX_ItemGenres_ItemId_GenreId",
        table: "ItemGenres",
        columns: new[] { "ItemId", "GenreId" },
        unique: true);
}
```

Figure 5-44. *The migration drops an existing index and builds a new unique, non-clustered index on the two columns ItemId and GenreId*

After you've reviewed the migration, go ahead and run the update-database command.

Step 3: Review the database

Once the database changes are applied, you can review the ItemGenre table to see that the index is in place to ensure that the ItemId and GenreId are grouped in a unique, non-clustered index (see Figure 5-45).

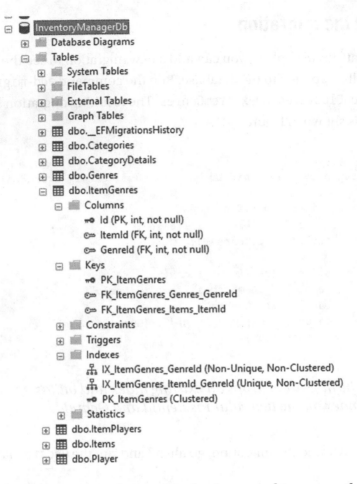

Figure 5-45. *The unique, non-clustered index is created to ensure that the combination of the two Ids must be unique in the table*

Step 4: Ensure the code executes

As always, run the program to ensure that the program executes as expected. The final output has not changed, so it is the same as you would see in Figure 5-21.

Activity 5-3 summary

In this third activity, you created a many-to-many relationship for tracking Genres and associating them to Items. In this scenario, you can have a Genre that is associated with many items, and you can have an Item that has one or more Genres associated with it.

In the previous activity, you saw how EFCore6 created a join table by convention, and in this activity, you learned how to explicitly create the join table.

You also had a chance to see how to add a unique, non-clustered index to the table by using the Index attribute. The Index attribute was around in EF6 but then wasn't available in EFCore in versions prior to EFCore5. Now, since EFCore5, the Index attribute is able to be used once again.

One thing you didn't get to see was working directly with the Fluent API on a table to define the clustered index, which is also possible, and is how you may have approached this issue in EFCore prior to EFCore5.

Indeed, using the FluentAPI may be preferable to some, as the command is quite simple. Had you desired or needed to use the FluentAPI in the OnModelCreating method of the DbContext file to define the relationship, you could do that with code similar to the following:

```
modelBuilder.Entity<ItemGenre>()
        .HasIndex(ig => new { ig.ItemId, ig.GenreId })
        .IsUnique()
        .IsClustered(false);
```

As you can see, the FluentAPI code is straightforward and easy to use for creating indexes. You do not need to add that code to your solution, unless you wish to try it out for yourself.

Chapter summary

In this chapter, you've learned how to build out a better database schema in a code-first database approach.

At this point, you are in a really good place to start generating some solid database architectures and implementations. As the developer, it will be your job to know how to work with constraints and relationships, as well as how to work with them correctly to achieve the best overall results with your databases.

Important takeaways

After working through this chapter, the things you should be in command of are

- Limiting the length of fields

- Setting constraints on the values of the fields

- Setting default values on fields

- Creating one-to-one, one-to-many, and many-to-many relationships

- Redefining table names and relationships in the FluentAPI and through the use of Data Annotations

- Adding unique indexes to a table

Closing thoughts

In the next chapter, you'll take a deeper dive into working with real data in this system we're building, so that you'll not only have the tools to architect a solid solution but the skills to develop against the data using common Create, Read, Update, and Delete (CRUD) actions.

CHAPTER 6

Data Access (Create, Read, Update, Delete)

In this chapter, you are going to learn about the basic tenets of data access using Entity Framework. By the end of the chapter, you'll have a good understanding of how to interact successfully with the data in your database.

CRUD

The common actions that most applications need are lovingly referred to as CRUD, which stands for Create, Read, Update, and Delete. Working with EF to perform CRUD operations is generally easy and efficient but also requires at least a basic understanding of the Language Integrated Query (LINQ) syntax.

LINQ

You may already have some understanding of LINQ. You may even be an expert with LINQ. Perhaps you consider yourself fairly new to LINQ or you have always felt that it is confusing. Luckily, there are tools all developers can use to generate some of the basic LINQ you would need when just getting started. Additionally, you will learn more about LINQ later in this book.

Basic interactions

In order to work against the database, you need to understand a few of the common commands that you'll rely upon to perform common operations.

© Brian L. Gorman 2022
B. L. Gorman, *Practical Entity Framework Core 6*, https://doi.org/10.1007/978-1-4842-7301-2_6

Leverage the DbSet<T> objects

As you've built out your database library (EFCore_DbLibrary) in previous activities through the first five chapters, you added properties on a few of your entities to the InventoryDbContext (context) using code, such as `public DbSet<Item> Items { get; set; }`. By adding these properties, you can now leverage the power of EF and work against these entity sets directly.

For example, if you want to add a new Item, you can build a new Item object in code and then use the inventory context to add the item with code similar to this block of code:

```
var existingItem = db.Items.FirstOrDefault(x => x.Name.ToLower()
                                               == name.ToLower());


if (existingItem == null)
{
    //doesn't exist, add it.
    var item = new Item()
    {
        Name = name,
        CreatedByUserId = _loggedInUserId,
        IsActive = true,
        Quantity = r.Next(),
        Description = description,
        Notes = notes
    };
    db.Items.Add(item);
    db.SaveChanges();
}
```

This code is directly from the Progam.cs file in the EnsureItem method that you've used in previous activities. In the code, you leveraged the context and made sure an item didn't already exist, and if not, you specified the new Item details and used the extension Add to add a new item on the context Items, and then you saved the changes. Other examples in the sample code from previous activities leverage the commands RemoveRange (Remove) and UpdateRange (Update) as well. As such, you've already been exposed to basic create, update, and delete methods, and you've easily leveraged read operations to get the results to the console.

Common commands

When getting started with EF, you will want to have a few commands in your toolbox. As you continue to learn and as you build on your skills through this text, you'll cover more than just some of these commands. For now, there are a few common commands you need to know.

A comprehensive list of commands will always be available on the official documentation site, which can be found here: `https://docs.microsoft.com/en-us/dotnet/api/microsoft.entityframeworkcore.dbset-1?view=efcore-6.0`.

An additional consideration is that there are some *asynchronous* methods available. For most of the code in this book, you'll leverage the synchronous calls as you are learning. Later in the book, there is a chapter where you'll move all the calls to an asynchronous pattern. The operations are pretty much identical, and for simplicity in these activities, it's just more convenient to use synchronous calls. In most real-world applications, especially disconnected scenarios like the Web and APIs, you will most definitely be using asynchronous calls.

For your immediate understanding, Table 6-1 examines a few of the common commands. When looking at the code in Table 6-1, all commands would be run as the preceding one, with a variable that references the `DbContext`, and then the specific property on that context variable to leverage the entity, followed by the command text. For example, entities referenced from your previous work include entities like `Items`, `Genres`, `Players`, and `Categories`.

Table 6-1. *Common commands for CRUD operations against the datastore*

Command Text	Example	Use
Add	db.Items.Add(item)	Add a new Item (or other entity) to the database table.
AddAsync	await db.Items. AddAsync(item)	Add a new Item (or other entity) to the database table.
AddRange	db.Items. AddRangeAsync(items)	Sets an IEnumerable<Item> to be tracked and ready to insert each item in the IEnumerable.
AddRangeAsync	await db.AddRangeAsync(items)	Sets an IEnumerable<Item> to be tracked and ready to insert each item in the IEnumerable.
Find	db.Genres.Find(2)	Find a Genre (or other entity) by the Id [when the Id is a key].
FindAsync	await db.Genres.Find(7)	Find a Genre (or other entity) by the Id [when the Id is a key].
Remove	db.Categories. Remove(aCategory)	Remove a Category (or other entity) by passing a tracked entity.
RemoveRange	db.Items. RemoveRange(items)	Remove all of the IEnumerable<T> from the database.
Update	db.Items.Update(item)	Update a tracked Item (or other entity) by passing a tracked entity with modified values.
UpdateRange	db.Items. UpdateRange(items)	Update all of the IEnumerable<T> objects.

Please note that most of the operations in the preceding list also require an additional call to SaveChanges or SaveChangesAsync in order to persist the changes in the database (up to that point they are simply tracked for save, in what you can call a transaction – if you don't make the call to SaveChanges, it is like you rolled the transaction back). Note also that SaveChanges is called on the context variable itself, not on one of the entities within the context. In this manner, all pending changes across all entity sets are saved with one call to SaveChanges.

As previously mentioned, there are other methods available to you, as well as more preferred ways to work with LINQ to get query results. You will see some of this in action in the activity that concludes this chapter.

A final thought before diving into the activities

To this point, you've been working with a database library and have mostly focused on the schema for the database and how to work with the code-first approach to affect the schema.

In this project, you will just spin up a new database and leverage your previously built models in the project to quickly see how easily you can port your code.

It is entirely possible that you could bring your EFCore_DBLibrary project into the solution as well, but if you do this, you would need to understand how to work with multiple contexts in your solution. The concept of multiple contexts will be covered later in the book, if you are interested in how to do this. For now, you'll just use the default context that is brought into the project.

Activity 6-1: Quick CRUD with scaffolded controllers

To this point in the book, there hasn't been any focus on picking a UI implementation. As such, for all the activities, you have only worked with console applications. This is purposeful, and with a couple exceptions, all activities will be using the console as it would be easy for any developer to port the UI work to their UI of choice, be it WPF, ASP. Net MVC, Blazor, Razor Pages, or even just to expose the data via a REST API.

However, for this activity, to get started with learning practical CRUD activities, you will be creating a simple web application to let the system do the scaffolding work for you. For this reason, you're going to leverage a very simple *ASP.Net* MVC implementation with scaffolded views and controllers. If you want to try other frameworks, such as Blazor, that is fine as well, but this book will only be supporting the MVC framework for this activity, so I'd suggest you use that first and then try again with Blazor or another UI framework.

The main learning here will be the code that is generated in the controllers, but you'll also get to see how quickly you can spin up a basic web application in ASP.Net MVC.

Task 0: Getting started

For this activity, I would encourage you to just start with a brand-new project and follow the tasks and steps in the activity to complete the work.

However, for reasons of simplicity and clarity, a starter file set is also available if you wish to skip the setup and creation of a new web project. If you are using the starter files, locate the EFCore_Activity06-1_StarterFiles, extract the files, build the project, update the database, and run the project (it will spin up a website locally). If you run into an issue with the database, make sure the connection string points to your local database implementation. If you continue to have issues, consider using a different database name than you've been using in the previous chapters.

Once you've ensured that the project is ready, using the starter files, you can skip Task 1 and go directly to Task 2.

Task 1: Creating the new MVC project

In this first task, you will create a new MVC project from the ground up, and you will associate the EFCore_DbLibrary project and the InventoryModels project with the new web project.

Step 1: Setup

As mentioned, for this activity, you are going to start from scratch and import the database code you've already written.

To begin, open the VS IDE and select Create a new project. In the Create a new project dialog, select the C# ASP.Net Core Web Application (Model-View-Controller) template (see Figure 6-1).

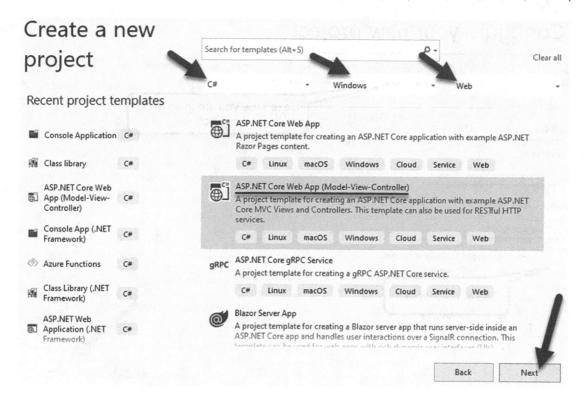

Figure 6-1. *Use the Create a new project dialog to select a new ASP.Net Core Web App (Model-View-Controller)*

On the Configure your new project dialog, choose an appropriate folder (e.g., C:\APressEntityFramework\Code) to save the project. Name the project EFCore_ Activity0601 (refer to Figure 6-2 for clarity).

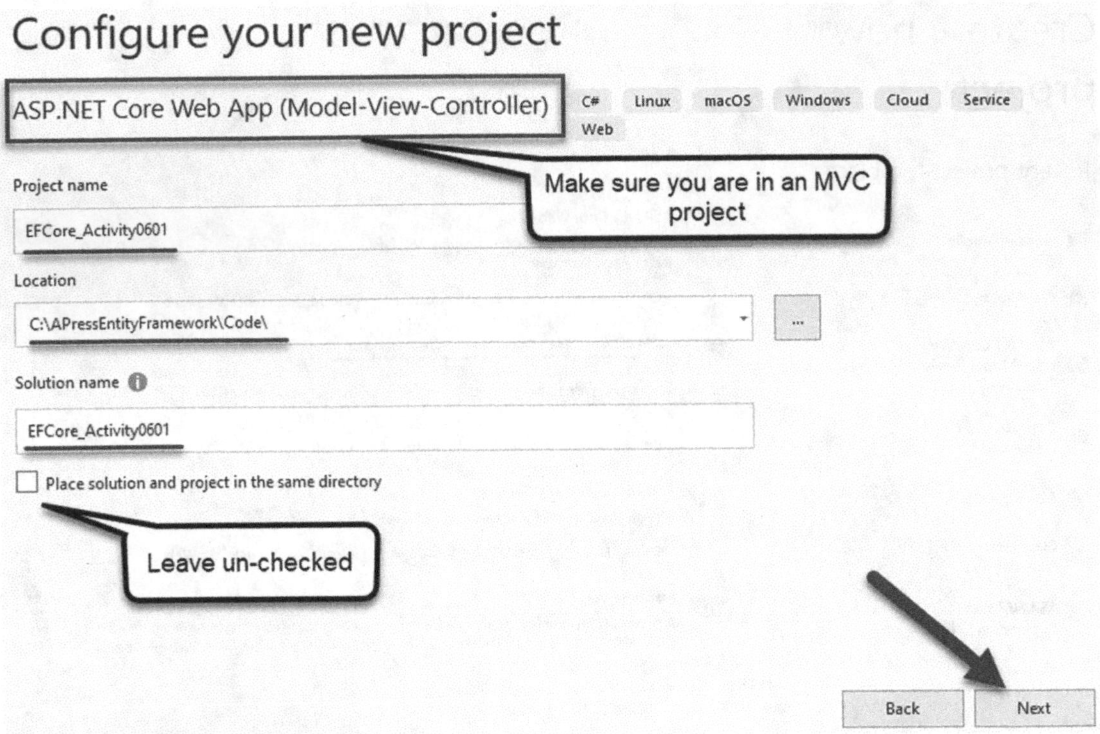

Configure your new project

Figure 6-2. *Use the Configure your new project to name the project and select the location on your hard drive to store the solution*

In the Additional information dialog, select the `Target Framework` as `.NET 6.0`, and then use individual accounts for the authentication type. Leave `Configure for HTTPS` checked; if you are on a Windows box, do not check Enable Docker but make sure to check `Enable Razor runtime compilation` (at the time of this writing, failing to check the compilation results in an error on load for not being able to find Home/Index).

If you are on a Linux box or a Mac, you may need to use Docker (or desire to use docker). In the end, if you do use containers, you will need to be able to connect to a local database from the web application. Note that the use of containers is not covered in this book.

Figure 6-3 shows the Additional information dialog in more detail.

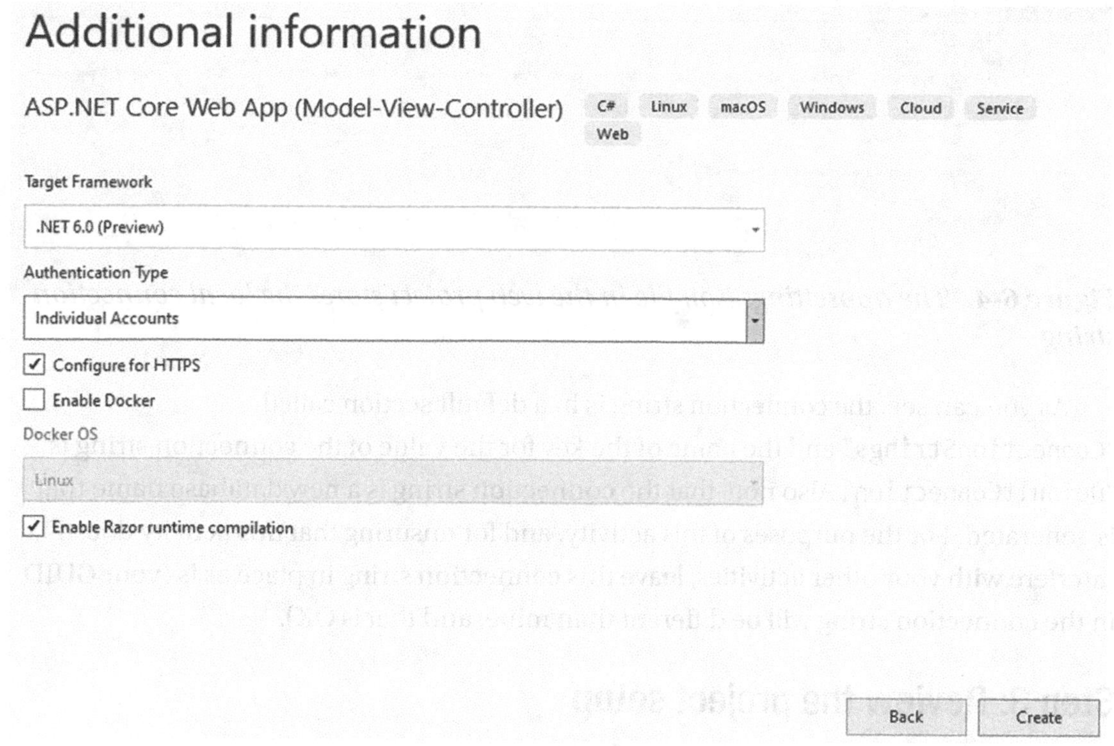

Additional information

ASP.NET Core Web App (Model-View-Controller)   C#   Linux   macOS   Windows   Cloud   Service
                                                 Web

Target Framework

.NET 6.0 (Preview)   ▾

Authentication Type

Individual Accounts   ▾

☑ Configure for HTTPS

☐ Enable Docker

Docker OS

Linux   ▾

☑ Enable Razor runtime compilation

Back   Create

Figure 6-3. *Use the Additional information dialog to set the Target Framework to .NET 6.0, the Authentication Type to Individual Accounts, and Configure for HTTPS*

If you fail to change the Authentication Type to Individual Accounts, you can still bring in the EFCore6 libraries and work with a database, but you would have to set that up manually and it's a lot easier to just let this template do it all for you.

Additionally, by using the Individual User Accounts setting, your solution will have a fully built authentication schema working for you immediately.

Step 2: Review the connection string

In ASP.Net MVC Core web projects, the database connection string is stored in the appsettings.json file by default. Open the appsettings.json file now to review the current connection string information (see Figure 6-4).

```
appsettings.json  ⊅  ×  HomeController.cs
Schema: https://json.schemastore.org/appsettings.json
    1   ⊟{
    2   ⊟    "ConnectionStrings": {
    3           "DefaultConnection": "Server=(localdb)\\mssqllocaldb;Database=aspnet-EFCore_Activity0601-0DB378D9-3598-4100-A415-1EA7643AA4CB;Trusted_Connection=T
    4       },
    5   ⊟    "Logging": {
    6   ⊟       "LogLevel": {
    7              "Default": "Information",
    8              "Microsoft": "Warning",
    9              "Microsoft.Hosting.Lifetime": "Information"
   10          }
   11      },
   12      "AllowedHosts": "*"
   13  }
   14
```

Figure 6-4. *The appsettings.json file in the web project stores the local connection string*

As you can see, the connection string is in a default section called "ConnectionStrings" and the name of the key for the value of the connection string is "DefaultConnection". Also note that the connection string is a new database name that is generated. For the purposes of this activity, and for ensuring that this activity doesn't interfere with your other activities, leave this connection string in place as is (your GUID in the connection string will be different than mine, and that is OK).

Step 3: Review the project setup

Note in the default project that there are folders for Views, Models, Data, and Controllers. The Data will have all the data migrations and the context (ApplicationDbContext in this case). Also note that the Data folder has an initial migration to run that will set the identity into place for managing users.

The ApplicationDbContext is where the project will interact with the database in the same manner that the InventoryDbContext has done in previous projects to this point.

The Models folder holds entities, just like the InventoryModels project you've used in previous activities. The Views folder holds the UI layout and page views for the various routes that are implemented in the project. Finally, the Controllers folder is where the logic happens to drive the project by responding to routes. For example, the HomeController responds to the route https://yourapplication/home/.... And the "..." in this case can be blank, which directs the route to Index, or you can create other routes manually. Each route should have a matching view in the Views folder under the appropriate controller. ASP.Net MVC uses convention over configuration – so as long as everything is named correctly, the solution will just work for you.

Step 4: Review the Startup.cs file

The Startup.cs file is the lifeblood for the application at startup and handles the configuration and initialization for the project. Most importantly, the context is initialized for use in the rest of the project via dependency injection.

Open the Startup.cs file and review the ConfigureServices method. Here, you will see the code to add the DbContext, as well as other initialization calls. Note that the name of the connection string here directly matches the name of the connection string in the appsettings.json file. See Figure 6-5 for more clarity.

```
// This method gets called by the runtime. Use this method to add services to the container.
0 references
public void ConfigureServices(IServiceCollection services)
{
    services.AddDbContext<ApplicationDbContext>(options =>
        options.UseSqlServer(
            Configuration.GetConnectionString("DefaultConnection")));
    services.AddDatabaseDeveloperPageExceptionFilter();

    services.AddDefaultIdentity<IdentityUser>(options => options.SignIn.RequireConfirmedAccount = true)
        .AddEntityFrameworkStores<ApplicationDbContext>();
    services.AddControllersWithViews();
}
```

Figure 6-5. *The Startup.cs file ensures the ApplicationDbContext is loaded and available for reference in the project*

If you continue examining the Startup.cs file, you will also see the default routing and other initializations for authentication and authorization.

Step 5: Get your Models project into the solution but do not reference them yet

In order to complete this activity, you'll need your model files from previous activities. For now, you'll just put them in place in the project, but you won't use them yet.

Locate the folder on your hard drive that contains the files previous activity (your files as they were at the end of Activity 5-3). In that folder, you should have project folders for the activity, the DbLibrary, the InventoryHelpers, and the InventoryModels (see Figure 6-6).

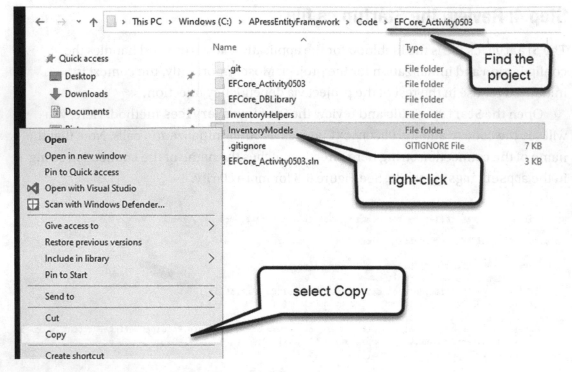

Figure 6-6. *Locate the project folder for the InventoryModels from EFCore_Activity0503 and copy them to the clipboard*

Copy the InventoryModels project folder and paste it in the folder that contains your Activity 6 solution.

If you don't have the files or didn't do the previous activities, you could get the final version of the files from Activity 5-3 and use the project folder from that solution.

After you paste the files in the solution folder, your current physical folder should look like what is shown in Figure 6-7.

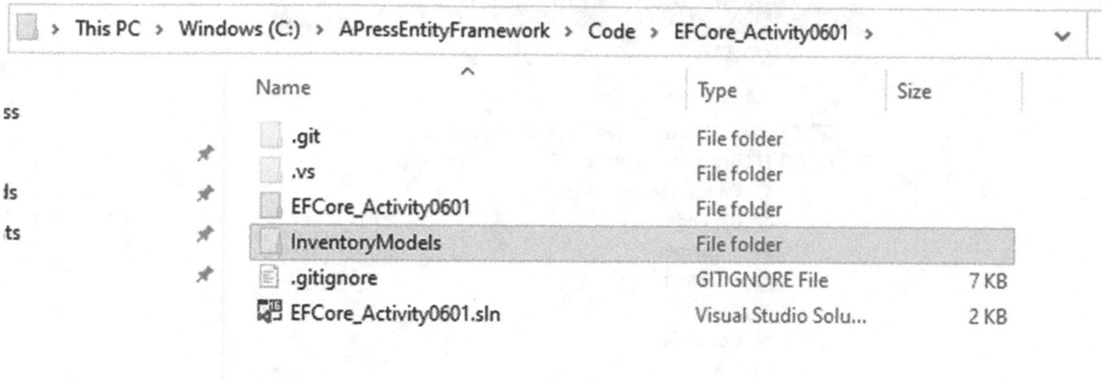

Name	Type	Size
.git	File folder	
.vs	File folder	
EFCore_Activity0601	File folder	
InventoryModels	File folder	
.gitignore	GITIGNORE File	7 KB
EFCore_Activity0601.sln	Visual Studio Solu...	2 KB

This PC > Windows (C:) > APressEntityFramework > Code > EFCore_Activity0601 >

Figure 6-7. *The InventoryModels project has been copied to the solution folder for Activity0601*

As a final step, add the project into the web solution by right-clicking the EFCore_Activity0601 solution (not the project) and selecting Add ➤ Existing project, and then import the InventoryModels project. When the operation is completed, your solution should look like what is shown in Figure 6-8.

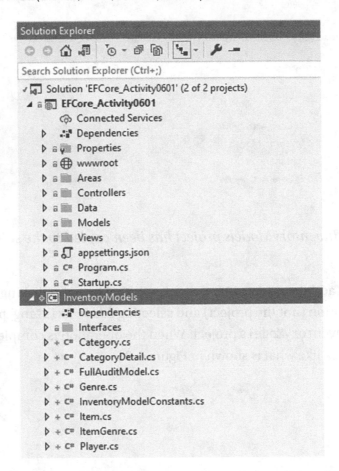

Figure 6-8. *The InventoryModels project has been imported to the solution but is not yet referenced in the web project*

You are now ready to start working in the project to build out simple scaffolded CRUD operations for your entities. Additionally, the code should now be in the exact same state that it would be if you were to have grabbed the starter files for the activity, with the exception that the starter files have been cleaned of generated code like what you would find in bin and obj folders.

Task 2: Start working with the ASP.Net MVC project

In this next task, you will ensure that the initial migration is run and that you can easily register users and run the basic web project.

Step 1: Update the database

Make sure that you have the project open, and then browse to the `appsettings.json` file. In this file is the connection string for the database. Do not point this at the implementation you have been using in previous activities, but instead just leave the default connection set as is.

Open the PMC and make sure it is pointed at the `EFCore_Activity0601` project. There is no separate database library in this solution. Run the `update-database` command to create the initial migration.

If you receive an error due to an inability to connect to the database, then go ahead and change the connection string to point to your `localhost` or `SQLExpress` instance that you generally use. In that case, ensure that you are not using the same database name as your other activities have used. It will be important to keep this activity in its own database.

After the command succeeds, use SSMS to review the new database (see Figure 6-9). Note that you will need to connect to the `(localdb)\mssqllocaldb` in this case, not your original localhost or SQLExpress (use the connection string to guide you on the connection). One other note – the `appsettings.json` file uses an escape slash in the original connection string [`(localdb)\\mssqllocaldb`]. You will need to remove the extra slash to connect in SSMS [`(localdb)\mssqllocaldb`].

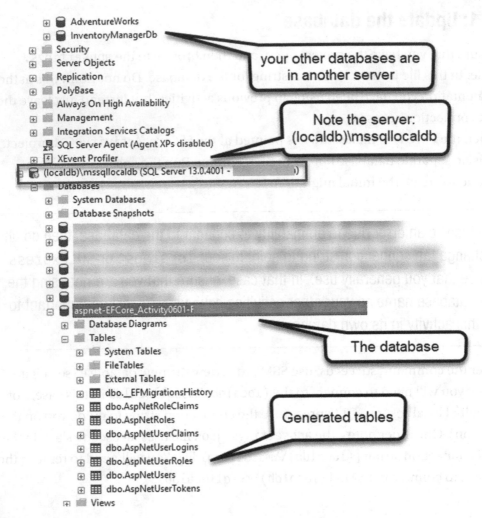

Figure 6-9. *The database is created successfully, and all of the identity tables are in place as expected*

Step 2: Run the project and register a couple of users

After you've validated that the connection is working, run the project by hitting "F5" or the green play button, which will open up your browser to the localhost:<some_port_number>\home\index route (which will likely just show localhost:<some_port_number> in your browser).

Use the `Register` link at the top right to add a new user, and then give the user an email such as bob@bob.com and a password that has at least eight characters, an uppercase character, and a special character like any of the shifted numbers (!@#$%^&*). Make sure you can remember the password. Figure 6-10 is shown for clarity.

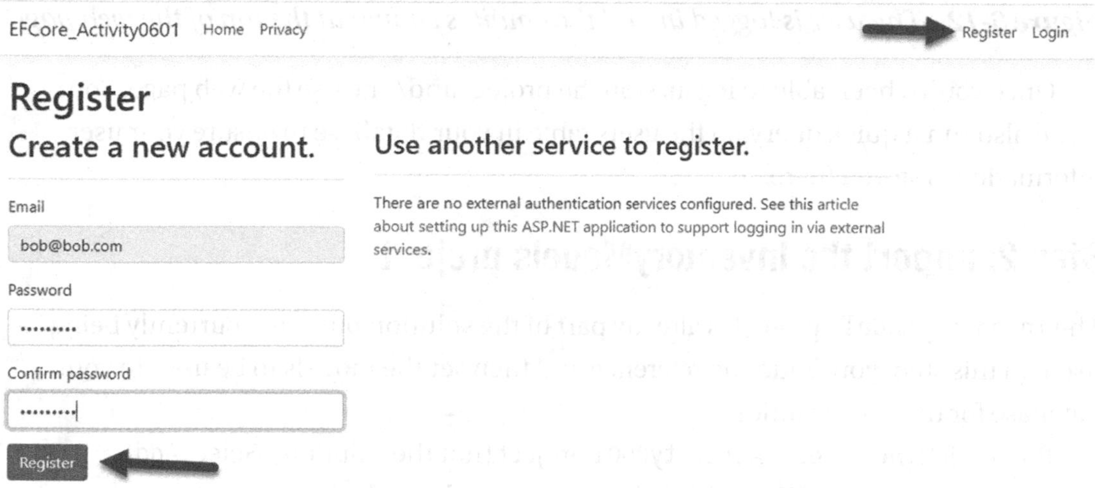

Figure 6-10. *The registration is in process for bob@bob.com*

Important! After registering your user, ensure that you click the link that says Click here to confirm your account (see Figure 6-11). If you fail to do this, you will need to manually update the user record in the database to set the value for `EmailConfirmed` to 1 in order to log in successfully.

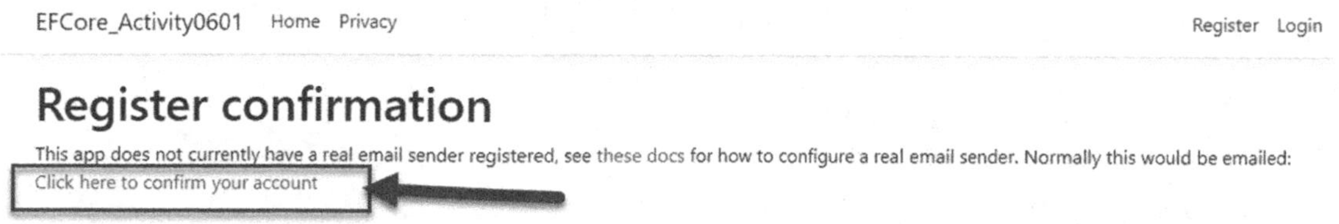

Figure 6-11. *It is important that you click the link to confirm the account; otherwise, the user won't be able to log in*

After confirming the account, use the `Login` button at the top right to log the user in. When logged in, the user email should be shown at the top right as in Figure 6-12.

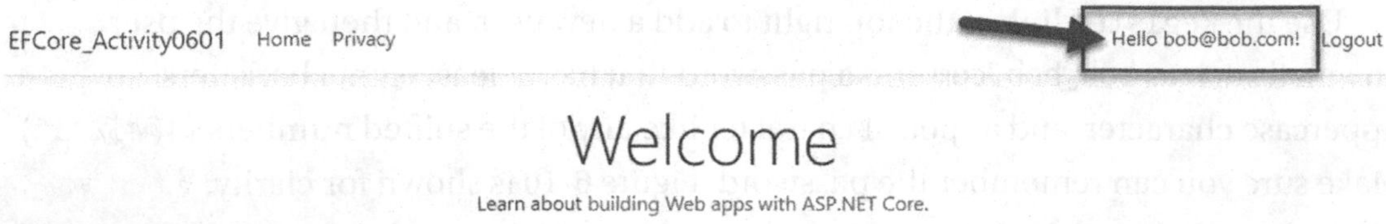

EFCore_Activity0601   Home   Privacy    Hello bob@bob.com! Logout

Welcome

Learn about building Web apps with ASP.NET Core.

Figure 6-12. *The user is logged in and the email is shown at the top of the web page*

Once you've been able to log in, stop the project and/or close the web page. You could also run a quick query on the users table in your database to ensure your user information is stored there.

Step 2: Import the InventoryModels project

The InventoryModels project is already part of the solution but is not currently being used. In this step, you'll add the reference and then set the models to be used in your database for this web solution.

Right-click the EFCore_Activity0601 project (not the solution). Select Add ➤ Project Reference. When the dialog comes up, check the box next to the InventoryModels project. When completed, you should see the reference listed in the Solution Explorer as highlighted in Figure 6-13.

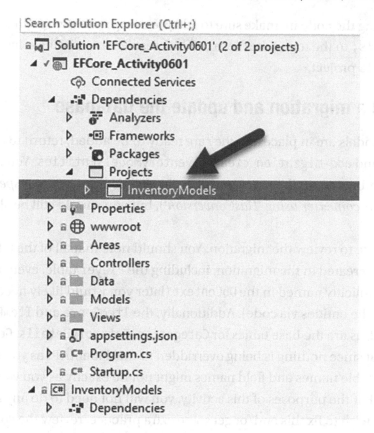

Figure 6-13. *The InventoryModels project is now referenced in the base activity project*

Before you will be able to add the models to the database, you will need to reference them in the ApplicationDbContext via the DbSet<TEntity> pattern you've seen in previous activities.

Open the ApplicationDbContext.cs file, located in the Data folder of the main EFCore_Activity0601 project. Add the following code to the file after the class declaration and before the public constructor (if you've done the previous activities, this code should look very familiar):

```
public DbSet<Item> Items { get; set; }
public DbSet<Category> Categories { get; set; }
public DbSet<CategoryDetail> CategoryDetails { get; set; }
public DbSet<Genre> Genres { get; set; }
```

After bringing the code in, make sure to add the using statement `using` `InventoryModels;` to the top of the file in order to resolve the missing reference to the `InventoryModels` project.

Step 3: Add a migration and update the database

Now that the models are in place and they are ready to be added, return to the PMC and run the command `add-migration createInventoryModelsEntities`. You may receive a couple of warnings about the precision on decimals (*No store type was specified....or configure a value converter using 'HasConversion'*), but you should still be able to create the migration.

Take a minute to review the migration. You should note that all of the tables are scheduled to be created in the migration, including the `Player` table, even though that table was not explicitly named in the `DbContext` (later you would likely need to add it to get access to the entities via code). Additionally, the `ItemGenre` and `ItemPlayer` join tables are listed, as are the base tables for `Categories`, `CategoryDetails`, `Genres`, and `Items`. Note that since nothing is being overridden in this FluentAPI as you've done in prior chapters, table names and field names might not be exactly as you would desire in the real world. For the purposes of this activity, you will not need to do any additional changes. If you wish to fix this and/or get some extra practice, review the code from the end of Activity 5-3. You could potentially override the `OnModelCreating` method in the `ApplicationDbContext` and rework the migration to match what you did in the last chapter.

With the migration in place, run the `update-database` command to apply the migration. Note that the warnings about precision will be repeated but will not block the migration from being applied.

Step 4: Review the database

Once the migration has been applied, open the database in SSMS and refresh, and then validate that the expected tables are in place. Figure 6-14 shows the expected database structure after applying the migration.

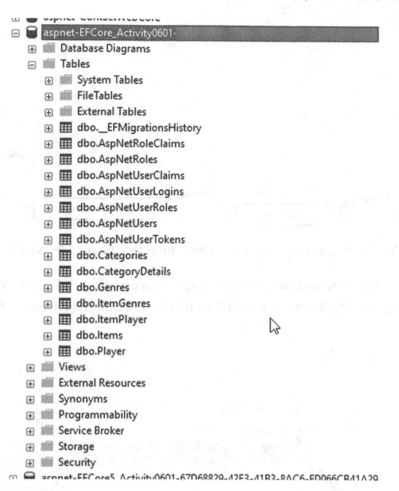

Figure 6-14. *The database is now set with users and all of the expected tables from the InventoryModels project*

Task 3: Create CRUD for the items

In this task, you will use the built-in tools within the ASP.Net MVC framework to quickly generate a number of CRUD operations to work with your database.

Step 1: Scaffold the Items controller and views

To begin, it's time to see if you can leverage the database in the web project. Start by right-clicking the Controllers folder and selecting Add ➤ Controller (shown in Figure 6-15).

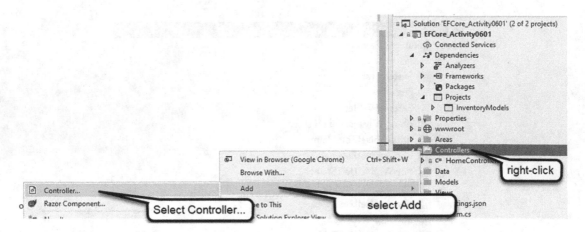

Figure 6-15. *Adding a new controller starts by selecting Add ➤ New Controller*

When the Add New Scaffolded item dialog comes up, select MVC Controller with views, using Entity Framework, and then hit the Add button (see Figure 6-16).

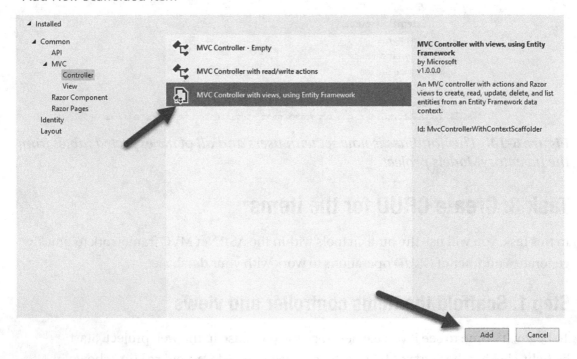

Figure 6-16. *Selecting the scaffolding options*

On the `Add MVC Controller with views, using Entity Framework` dialog, select the `Item (InventoryModels)` for `Model class` and the `ApplicationDbContext` for `Data context class`. Leave all other options as they are by default. Note that the new controller will be named `ItemsController`. Hit the Add button. Review Figure 6-17 for clarity.

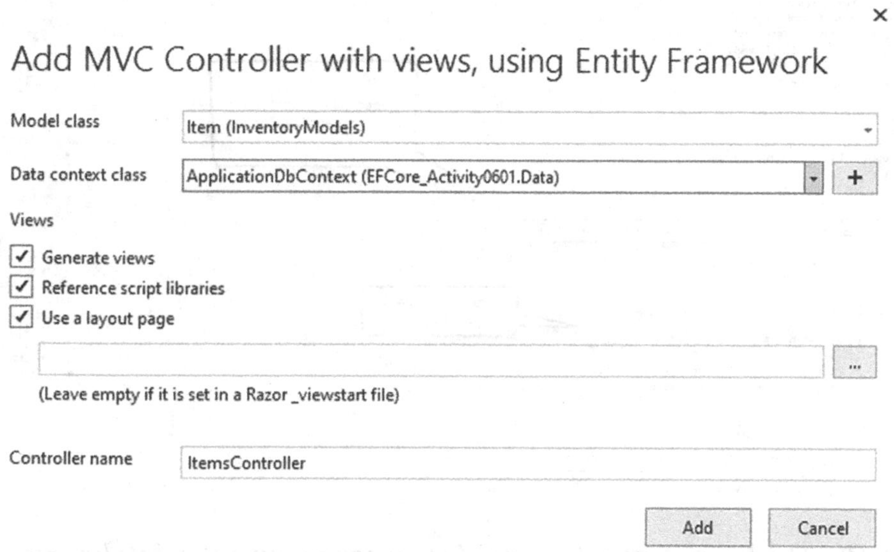

Figure 6-17. *The Model class and Data context class are set, and the new controller will be named ItemsController*

This process will take a minute or two to complete, but when it is done, you will have a fully functional UI for CRUD operations on Items. It will not be completely user-friendly, however.

Step 2: Review the Items controller that was generated

Open the `ItemsController.cs` file in the `Controllers` folder of the main activity project. Note that the controller has an `ApplicationDbContext` that is injected for use against the data.

Notice that both the `Index` and the `Details` methods leverage the context to get items (read). Also note that operations are asynchronous by default in this web solution.

Notice the `Post` methods for `Create` and `Edit` and how the context is leveraged to update data that is passed in from the UI.

Also notice there is a `Delete` method that is ready to remove items once confirmed by the user.

Figure 6-18 shows part of the generated code with a few callouts.

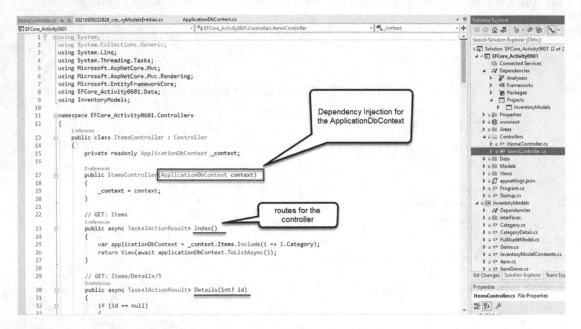

Figure 6-18. *The Items controller is ready to work against the database for CRUD operations on the Item entity*

Step 3: Run the project to see the CRUD operations in action

Once the scaffolding is completed and you have reviewed the controller, go ahead and run the project.

Once the project comes up, navigate to the route: `localhost:<some_port_number>/Items` to execute the `Items/Index` route (see Figure 6-19).

Figure 6-19. *The Items default view is shown, with no items listed since none currently exist*

Click the Create New link and you'll notice you don't have any Categories to choose from, since none exist in the database. Another problem is going to be the required CreatedByUserId. If you want to save a record, just put any string in that field for now (it's not referential as it should be). Figure 6-20 shows a record I created by setting my own name in the field. Obviously, in a real-world solution, you would want to use the id of the logged in user, and you wouldn't even present these fields to the user for editing or viewing.

EFCore_Activity0601   Home   Privacy   Hello bob@bob.com!   Logout

Index
Create New

Name	Quantity	Description	Notes	IsOnSale	PurchasedDate	SoldDate	PurchasePrice	CurrentOrFinalPrice	Category	CreatedByUserId	CreatedDate
An Item	20	Any Description	This is a test	☐	12/25/2015 10:47:00 PM		2345.67			brian	5/9/2021 10:47:00 PM

Figure 6-20. *A record can be created as long as all required fields are satisfied. Currently, the user is not wired up as would be expected in a real-world scenario*

Go ahead and try creating a couple items, and then scroll over to the far right and try editing and deleting items. You should be able to easily see that the data can easily be worked with.

If you want to see even more CRUD in action, scaffold the Categories by repeating the preceding steps for the Category and Genres entities, and then navigate to each of those controller routes and add a couple of each type to the solution. Figure 6-21 shows a quick look at what it might look like to add some categories in your solution (note that the final files have these controllers scaffolded).

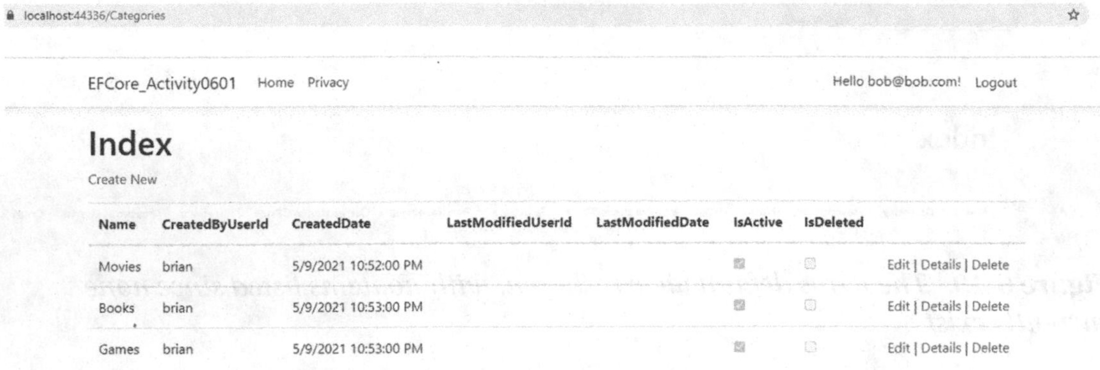

localhost:44336/Categories

EFCore_Activity0601   Home Privacy

Hello bob@bob.com! Logout

Index

Create New

Name	CreatedByUserId	CreatedDate	LastModifiedUserId	LastModifiedDate	IsActive	IsDeleted	
Movies	brian	5/9/2021 10:52:00 PM			☑	☐	Edit | Details | Delete
Books	brian	5/9/2021 10:53:00 PM			☑	☐	Edit | Details | Delete
Games	brian	5/9/2021 10:53:00 PM			☑	☐	Edit | Details | Delete

Figure 6-21. *With Categories scaffolded, you could easily add some categories to the database*

With `Categories` in place, go back to the `Items` view, select `Create New`, and you should see available categories to choose from when adding items. Figure 6-22 shows what this might look like if you go through with this effort (also note that the final version of the files has all of this in place if you just wanted to look there).

Notes

Categories are sort of working

☐ IsOnSale

PurchasedDate

mm/dd/yyyy --:-- --   🗓

SoldDate

mm/dd/yyyy --:-- --   🗓

PurchasePrice

CurrentOrFinalPrice

CategoryId

2	⌄
1	
2	
3	

CreatedDate

Figure 6-22. The Items create and edit will now have the ability to select one of the existing categories. The current view is set to show the Id. You could adjust this to show the name easily enough by manipulating the Item's Create.cshtml file to show the category name

Please note that this is not a production-ready solution. There are too many reasons to list here, but a couple critical ones are that there are a number of security issues, the code is not set to handle the logged in user or be unique to the user, and sensitive fields are shown directly to the user for manipulation. The code also doesn't work without magic knowledge (i.e., enter a string for created user id), and the Categories list is showing the id and not the name. For this reason, please do not take this solution and utilize it in production.

The activity is completed, but spend some time looking at the generated CRUD code in each of the controllers and review how LINQ is used to interact with the database. You will get plenty of opportunities in the rest of this book to use similar code, but seeing it here should help you to get started learning more about the expected ways to interact with the context using LINQ.

Activity 6-1 summary

In this activity, you took the InventoryModels project that you had worked with in the past and included it into a new web solution. You were able to use code-first migrations to update the new database, and with just a few more clicks, you were able to use built-in tools in the MVC framework to generate fully operational CRUD web pages.

Even though these pages aren't production ready, you were able to see that separating your models out into their own file is extremely nice for reusability. Additionally, you were able to use the scaffolded controllers to be able to easily see how to perform some of the CRUD operations you will need to know without having to struggle to write any of the code.

Chapter summary

In this chapter, you learned a little bit about CRUD and using LINQ with the database context. You were then able to quickly spin up a new web solution and use the built-in tools to generate a starter project for working against your inventory.

Important takeaways

After working through this chapter, the things you should be in command of are

- Leveraging existing model projects in a new project

- Creating a new web solution and importing projects

- Basic knowledge of adding built-in authorization and authentication to an ASP.Net web project

- How to scaffold controllers in ASP.Net MVC

- What it looks like to use LINQ and the database context for CRUD operations on data

Closing thoughts

This chapter gave you a good overview and really served as a checkpoint to how far you've come in the first six chapters. By now, you are really starting to take command of working with code-first solutions to design and implement robust solutions.

In the next chapter, you will take a look at how you can continue to build out your data solution to use database objects like stored procedures, functions, and views.

CHAPTER 7

Stored Procedures, Views, and Functions

In this chapter, you are going to look into ways to leverage the built-in programmable features of SQL Server that allow for maximum performance and efficiency.

You've already seen that you can easily create tables in a code-first approach with Entity Framework. However, in real-world applications, you are going to need to start building out more robust database solutions. By the end of this chapter, you will have a working understanding of what it takes to leverage database objects like stored procedures, views, and functions. You'll also know how to set up your code and migrations to create and manage versions of these objects. Along the way, you'll also learn more about the *Fluent API* and how you can leverage it to further define entities and data in your solutions.

Understanding stored procedures, views, and functions

Before you dive into working with stored procedures, views, and functions, you should make sure that you are fully aware of what they are and why you would use them. Additionally, with these schema objects, you'll be working with datasets that don't necessarily map to a tracked database object. For that reason, you need to learn a couple of new techniques when working with your database context and the model builder.

In the course of the activities at the end of the chapter, you'll see what it takes to add a query set into the database context so that you can get the results you are expecting when working with stored procedures, functions, and views. With all that, it's time to take a brief moment to discuss stored procedures, functions, and views, so that you will be ready to leverage them in your database solutions.

B. L. Gorman, *Practical Entity Framework Core 6*, https://doi.org/10.1007/978-1-4842-7301-2_7

Stored procedures

As developers, we can easily write code in *C#* or *VB.Net* that does repetitive operations like looping, making calculations, or mutating data. However, you are likely aware that it is also possible to write code in Microsoft SQL using the *T-SQL* syntax. If you weren't aware of this, you will be very aware of it by the end of this chapter.

Advantages of stored procedures

Writing some code on the server has a number of advantages, with the main advantage being efficiency. When you create a stored procedure, you are essentially writing a functional unit of code that can take parameters and perform queries and data manipulation on the server. By using the server to run this prepared code, the server itself can create and store execution plans, thereby speeding up the operation for each subsequent call to the code. An additional benefit of this approach is that using the stored procedure allows for returning the manipulated data directly rather than returning a large set of data and then still needing to use *C#* or *VB.Net* code with LINQ to further process the data in memory.

Creating a stored procedure

You can easily create a new procedure with the syntax `CREATE OR ALTER PROCEDURE <name>`. The easiest way to get a procedure script started is to right-click `Stored Procedures` under `Programmability` in SSMS and select `Stored Procedure`, which generates a script.

Great examples and use cases for stored procedures generally fall around operations, such as getting large result sets and performing calculations as part of the results.

Functions

Scalar and table-valued functions are extremely versatile and can help you to easily set up a routine that can manipulate your data, even when the view selection is part of a larger query.

Advantages of functions

Like stored procedures, functions can take parameters and can be optimized by query execution plans stored on the server.

The two types of functions have distinctly different uses. For situations where a single-value result is needed, you can create a scalar function. In other situations, you might need a result set, which can be returned as an in-memory table as a table-valued function.

Examples of functions

A good example of a scalar-valued function would be a function that manipulates data from an array into a comma-separated list as a single string. An example of a good table-valued function might be to get the items that were added to a table in the last two weeks and then further use that data to join against another table or to potentially get a limited set of data based on those results compared to some metric in the fields from that result set.

Views

Another scenario that happens frequently in the real world is one where you need to get some conglomerated data, which generally requires joining one or more tables. You then need to be able to perform some sort of sorting or filtering against that data, such as getting the top ten results or results where a field contains some key value.

Advantages of views

Anytime you run into a situation where you need to denormalize your data to present a segment of data for user review or reporting and then filter that result, a view can be a very handy asset.

Where a stored procedure takes parameters and manipulates data using prepared statements, you can think of a view as a prebuilt query that gets the results as designed and allows further filtering against that data.

Another way to think of this is that a view can be envisioned as an in-memory table with denormalized data based on pre-specified table joins.

The benefit of using a view is that you've abstracted the denormalization so that the filtering can happen simply without having to also redefine the join statements.

Once a view is in place, you can make calls against the view data with a simple SELECT ... WHERE query statement against the view, or you can use the view to join to other tables for even more specific results.

Examples of using views

A very typical use of a view would be to generate data for a report, such as all items with an included category name. You could then further limit that view to only return those rows that have a category name of movie.

When building out your solutions, you will rarely be needing data from just one table. You could create a call that joins data and returns it to the calling code for further manipulation with LINQ, which would work well in most scenarios. However, if you have a common query that you need for a specific view that the user can easily interact with, consider building a view to increase the performance of your system.

Setting up the database to run scripts efficiently

In the past, out of the box, EFCore hasn't had a super nice way to handle non-table database structures. In older versions of the .Net Framework, you would have been able to write files and then use those files to generate a SQL database script. In code-first entity framework solutions, you can add a migration and then put a script in the migration directly for execution. Even though this is possible, having random scripts in your migrations is not the most ideal solution and can lead to a couple of problems, which you'll examine in the following.

Therefore, in order to work with non-table database objects in EFCore code first, we generally need to implement a quick solution. One caveat to this approach is that EFCore5 implemented some new functionality around some of these items, including the ability to do a ToFunction or ToView call in the Fluent API to map queries to table-valued functions and views, which you can leverage in EFCore6.

The problem

To make the issues with directly scripting a stored procedure in a migration clearer, let's examine a potential migration and then an update to that procedure in a second migration.

First, here is a script that would easily generate a stored procedure to get items with genre and category information:

```
CREATE OR ALTER PROCEDURE dbo.GetItemsForListing
     @minDate DATETIME = null,
     @maxDate DATETIME = null
AS
BEGIN
     SET NOCOUNT ON;

    SELECT item.Name, item.Description, item.Notes
     , item.IsActive, item.IsDeleted, g.Name as Genre, cat.Name as
     Category
     FROM dbo.Items item
     LEFT JOIN dbo.ItemGenres ig on item.Id = ig.ItemId
     LEFT JOIN dbo.Genres g on ig.GenreId = g.Id
     LEFT JOIN dbo.Categories cat on item.CategoryId = cat.Id
     WHERE (@minDate IS NULL OR item.CreatedDate >= @minDate)
     AND (@maxDate IS NULL OR item.CreatedDate <= @maxDate)
END
GO
```

This is a straightforward query, but if you put this query into a migration directly, it would look like what is shown in Figure 7-1.

```
namespace EFCore_DBLibrary.Migrations
{
    1 reference
    public partial class createProc_GetItemsForListing : Migration
    {
        12 references
        protected override void Up(MigrationBuilder migrationBuilder)
        {
            migrationBuilder.Sql(@"CREATE OR ALTER PROCEDURE dbo.GetItemsForListing
@minDate DATETIME = null,
@maxDate DATETIME = null
AS
BEGIN
    SET NOCOUNT ON;

    SELECT item.Name, item.Description, item.Notes
    , item.IsActive, item.IsDeleted, g.Name as Genre, cat.Name as Category
    FROM dbo.Items item
    LEFT JOIN dbo.ItemGenres ig on item.Id = ig.ItemId
    LEFT JOIN dbo.Genres g on ig.GenreId = g.Id
    LEFT JOIN dbo.Categories cat on item.CategoryId = cat.Id
    WHERE (@minDate IS NULL OR item.CreatedDate >= @minDate)
    AND (@maxDate IS NULL OR item.CreatedDate <= @maxDate)
END
GO ");
        }

        12 references
        protected override void Down(MigrationBuilder migrationBuilder)
        {
            migrationBuilder.Sql(@"DROP PROCEDURE IF EXISTS dbo.GetItemsForListing");
        }
    }
}
```

Figure 7-1. *The migration to create a stored procedure is possible by just using inline SQL in the migration itself, but this can get messy very quickly*

As you might imagine, putting the code inline inside the migration makes it somewhat tricky to do a code review on the script. Additionally, putting in the second and consecutive migrations leads to large scripts in both the Up and Down methods. In this scenario, the first query joined Items to both Genres and Categories. Consider what would happen if the next update is requiring that the join to Genres and ItemGenres be removed. For an example of how verbose the migrations could become in a scenario such as this, review the following code, which updates the original query to remove the association to Genres:

```
    protected override void Up(MigrationBuilder migrationBuilder)
    {
            migrationBuilder.Sql(@"CREATE OR ALTER PROCEDURE
            dbo.GetItemsForListing
@minDate DATETIME = null,
@maxDate DATETIME = null
AS
BEGIN
    SET NOCOUNT ON;

  SELECT item.Name, item.Description, item.Notes
  , item.IsActive, item.IsDeleted, cat.Name
  FROM dbo.Items item
  LEFT JOIN dbo.Categories cat on item.CategoryId = cat.Id
  WHERE (@minDate IS NULL OR item.CreatedDate >= @minDate)
  AND (@maxDate IS NULL OR item.CreatedDate <= @maxDate)
END
GO");
    }

    protected override void Down(MigrationBuilder migrationBuilder)
    {
        migrationBuilder.Sql(@"CREATE OR ALTER
        PROCEDURE dbo.GetItemsForListing
@minDate DATETIME = null,
@maxDate DATETIME = null
AS
BEGIN
    SET NOCOUNT ON;

  SELECT item.Name, item.Description, item.Notes
  , item.IsActive, item.IsDeleted, g.Name, cat.Name
  FROM dbo.Items item
  LEFT JOIN dbo.ItemGenre ig on item.Id = ig.ItemId
  LEFT JOIN dbo.Genres g on ig.GenreId = g.Id
  LEFT JOIN dbo.Categories cat on item.CategoryId = cat.Id
```

```
        WHERE (@minDate IS NULL OR item.CreatedDate >= @minDate)
        AND (@maxDate IS NULL OR item.CreatedDate <= @maxDate)
END
GO");
        }
    }
```

The complexity to perform a code review also increases, as the available choices are to compare the code in the Down method to the code in the Up method for changes, or to find the previous migration for this procedure and compare the scripts as hard-coded in each migration's Up method.

As if that isn't bad enough, although you have history via this code, you don't have a well-organized history that is easy to review or even find the version for which you are looking. Once you get to version 6, for example, you would have to sort through all of your migrations to find the six migrations to compare to figure out where in the history of the code the issue you might be looking for exists or was created.

Therefore, you and your team need a better solution, a solution that is a nice and easy way to keep your migrations to a minimal footprint while also giving your fellow developers an easy way to review your changes and ultimately making it easier to track code versions in a historical fashion.

The solution

As you've seen earlier, you can run a script in the migration using the migrationBuilder calling the Sql method. As with other objects in .Net, migrationBuilder can be extended. To make a solution to the migration with hard-coded scripts, you'll be writing a simple extension that will get the script by reading a text file to a string.

After creating the extension method, all you need to do is add the text files into your project as embedded resources, and you no longer have to write your Sql scripts inline. You then reference the file directly in the migration.

In addition to removing the code from the migration file, this solution gives you and your team the ability to easily keep and track all versions of the scripted database objects. You'll take a look at this solution in more detail as you work through the first activity for this chapter.

Fluent API

To this point in the book, you haven't really spent a lot of time taking a look at the *Fluent API* and how you can use it in your code. When you worked with models in Chapter 4 and relationships in Chapter 5, you saw *Data Annotations*, and you used the data annotations to build things like required fields, string length, keys, and the various relationships between entities. However, you did get a chance to take a quick look at working with the FluentAPI to directly define the field names and table names for the many-to-many relationship join tables for `Players` to `Items`.

What can you do with the Fluent API

The *Fluent API* can do everything you can do with data annotations, but it also allows for more specific configurations that you can configure directly. In the activities for this chapter, you'll leverage the *Fluent API* to make sure that an entity you are creating does not generate a new table in the database or insert itself into every migration while still being available to be used for querying objects. Additionally, as mentioned previously, EFCore5 introduced a new feature for doing flexible entity mapping in the *Fluent API* to make calls, such as `ToFunction` or `ToView`, so you will be able to take advantage of flexible entity mapping in this EFCore6 implementation as well.

How do you work with the Fluent API

In order to work with the *Fluent API*, you'll need to override another method in your database context. The method that you will override is called `OnModelCreating` which has a parameter of type `ModelBuilder`. If you worked through the Chapter 5 activities, you've already done this. If not, the code already exists in the starter files and you will get to work with the OnModelCreating method in this chapter as well.

The *Fluent API* is leveraged from this model builder with references, such as

```
modelBuilder.Entity<Item>().Property(x => x.Name).IsRequired()
```

and

```
modelBuilder.Entity<Item>().HasOne(x => x.Category).WithMany(y => y.Items)
```

Even now, there are already references to the `Fluent API` in place in the projects you have been building without you even knowing about them. If you have a project open, take a quick look at the auto-generated file `InventoryDbContextModelSnapshot.cs` in the `InventoryDatabaseCore` project to see more *Fluent API* calls in action. Additionally, look at the subdirectory for every migration. Each one has some Fluent API code in it. Figure 7-2 shows part of the current `InventoryDbContextModelSnapshot` as of the end of Activity 5-3 and the start of Activity 7-1.

```
                    O references
                    protected override void BuildModel(ModelBuilder modelBuilder)
                    {
#pragma warning disable 612, 618
                        modelBuilder
                            .HasAnnotation("Relational:MaxIdentifierLength", 128)
                            .HasAnnotation("ProductVersion", "6.0.0-preview.3.21201.2")
                            .HasAnnotation("SqlServer:ValueGenerationStrategy", SqlServerValueGenerationStrategy.IdentityColumn);

                        modelBuilder.Entity("InventoryModels.Category", b =>
                            {
                                b.Property<int>("Id")
                                    .ValueGeneratedOnAdd()
                                    .HasColumnType("int")
                                    .HasAnnotation("SqlServer:ValueGenerationStrategy", SqlServerValueGenerationStrategy.IdentityColumn);

                                b.Property<string>("CreatedByUserId")
                                    .HasMaxLength(50)
                                    .HasColumnType("nvarchar(50)");

                                b.Property<DateTime>("CreatedDate")
                                    .HasColumnType("datetime2");

                                b.Property<bool>("IsActive")
                                    .HasColumnType("bit");

                                b.Property<bool>("IsDeleted")
                                    .HasColumnType("bit");

                                b.Property<DateTime?>("LastModifiedDate")
                                    .HasColumnType("datetime2");

                                b.Property<string>("LastModifiedUserId")
                                    .HasMaxLength(50)
                                    .HasColumnType("nvarchar(50)");
```

Figure 7-2. *The InventoryDbContextModelSnapshot has been using the Fluent API all along, and part of it is shown here*

For the activities in this chapter, you'll be building out the override for `OnModelCreating` to set entities to not have a key and to act like a read-only view. You'll see this in full detail in the activities, but a sample of what you'll see looks like this:

```
modelBuilder.Entity<GetItemsForListingDto>(x =>
{
    x.HasNoKey();
    x.ToView("ItemsForListing");
});
```

Here you can see how the GetItemsForListingDto entity object will be set to an object with no key – that is no Id field – and then will be set to act as a view called ItemsForListing.

Working with the database objects

In the final part of this chapter, you will again dive into three new examples where you can learn about building out your scripting solution and working with non-table database objects.

While these activities focus on stored procedures, views, and functions, please remember that with this scripting solution using files, you will be able to run any database script to create or modify any database objects. For example, you could easily create scripts for other objects like indexes or triggers, if desired, or you could run scripts from files to modify data, if that made sense for your solution.

A final thought before diving into the activities

The concept of working with stored procedures, functions, and views is an important part of any developer's toolbox and should be an area that you spend a bit of time making sure that you are good at this type of development.

There will always be a trade-off – everything you do in a view can likely be done via LINQ in memory in the UI, and that type of development generally moves a bit more quickly than investing the time into creating the database objects. However, the payoff for using the database objects is nearly always worth it when you have a system under load and want your users to have the best user experience possible.

In the next three activities, you will touch on the concepts that you need as a database developer and should leave this chapter with a very solid understanding of how to move some of your logic into the database to build high-performant systems.

Activity 7-1: Working with stored procedures

In this first activity, you are going to learn how to work with stored procedures in your solution. For the first part of the solution, you will utilize the inline scripting method to create a stored procedure. While this works, you should be able to quickly see the pain points this would cause for your development team.

You will then write the extension method to leverage the stored procedures (and any other custom database scripts) from files stored in the solution. You will then conclude the activity by utilizing the scripting files approach.

Through this practical approach, you should hopefully be able to see how scripting in files will generally be much better for you and your development teams. Additionally, you should be in command of writing and using stored procedures in your code-first database solutions after working through this activity.

Task 0: Getting started

The first activity will pick up where you left off at the end of Chapter 5, with the code in place as it was at the end of Activity 5-3. As such, you can continue to work with your solution from that point (Chapter 6 was a web solution that was divergent from this path, and you can leave that code behind for now).

As an alternative, feel free to leverage the starter files EFCore_Activity07-1_ StarterFiles. If you start with the starter files, as always, review Appendix A for information on working with starter files. Always remember a final version of the files is available for you to review as well, in the event something from the activity instructions is not clear.

Task 1: Create a new stored procedure using inline code in your migration

In this first task, you will design a new stored procedure and test it locally in the database. When you are comfortable with the code and ready to set it into a migration, you will then create the new migration and use inline SQL to manually create the stored procedure with the migration.

Step 1: Design the stored procedure

To begin this task, open SSMS and connect to your local InventoryManagerDb database. Once you've connected, right-click the database and select New Query to open a new query editor window (see Figure 7-3).

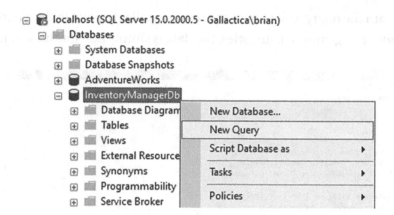

Figure 7-3. *Getting a new query editor window open*

For this stored procedure, you are going to do a simple query to get the items for listing, much like you would want to do if you were building a page that needed this data for display to a customer.

To simplify the request, you are going to get all of the important Item data, along with making joins to get Genre and Category information. Additionally, you will want to be able to set a minimum and maximum date for the items based on the date of item creation. If you wanted, you could even go further to filter on data for IsActive and IsDeleted (but that is not part of this activity).

In SSMS, enter the following code into your editor. Feel free to tweak this if you would like to try more code:

```
DECLARE @minDate DateTime
DECLARE @maxDate DateTime

SET @minDate = '2020.01.01'
SET @maxDate = '2022.12.31'

SELECT item.[Name], item.[Description]
    , item.Notes, item.isActive, item.isDeleted
    , genre.[Name] GenreName, cat.[Name] CategoryName
FROM dbo.Items item
LEFT JOIN dbo.ItemGenres ig on item.Id = ig.ItemId
LEFT JOIN dbo.Genres genre on ig.GenreId = genre.Id
LEFT JOIN dbo.Categories cat on item.CategoryId = cat.Id
WHERE (@minDate IS NULL OR item.CreatedDate >= @minDate)
AND (@maxDate IS NULL OR item.CreatedDate <= @maxDate)
```

When you run the query, you should see results similar to what is shown in Figure 7-4. Note that without any genres or categories, the data is simply null for those values.

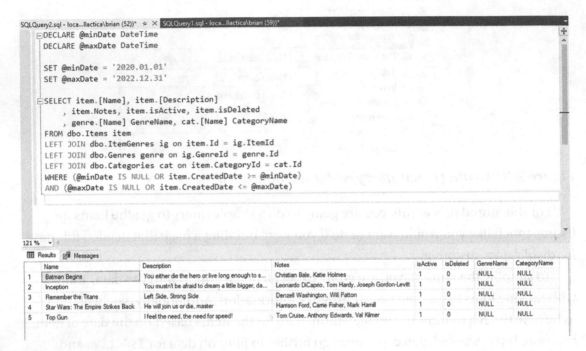

Figure 7-4. *The result of running the query when there are no categories and/or genres present*

If you want to add categories and genres and link them to items, feel free to do so, but you will officially do that soon.

Step 2: Create the migration for adding the GetItemsForListing stored procedure

Now that you have the code you want to use in the stored procedure, it's time to add it in a migration. Ensure you are pointed at the EFCore_DbLibrary project and run the command add-migration createProc_GetItemsForListing. This should generate a new blank migration.

If for some reason your migration is not clean, you had some pending changes that needed to be applied to your local database. As long as the changes look good/relevant, you should just apply them via the update-database command and then make a new blank migration to continue with this activity. If the changes are bad, examine your current models and ensure nothing is out of line.

In the Up method for the migration, add the following code (but do not update the database yet):

```
migrationBuilder.Sql(@"CREATE OR ALTER PROCEDURE dbo.
GetItemsForListing
@minDate DATETIME = '1970.01.01',
@maxDate DATETIME = '2050.12.31'
AS
BEGIN
    SET NOCOUNT ON;

   SELECT item.[Name], item.[Description]
            , item.Notes, item.isActive, item.isDeleted
            , genre.[Name] GenreName, cat.[Name] CategoryName
        FROM dbo.Items item
        LEFT JOIN dbo.ItemGenres ig on item.Id = ig.ItemId
        LEFT JOIN dbo.Genres genre on ig.GenreId = genre.Id
        LEFT JOIN dbo.Categories cat on item.CategoryId = cat.Id
        WHERE (@minDate IS NULL OR item.CreatedDate >= @minDate)
        AND (@maxDate IS NULL OR item.CreatedDate <= @maxDate)
END
GO");
```

This code will create the new stored procedure. Note also that this code is idempotent, using the CREATE OR ALTER PROCEDURE statement so that even if the procedure exists, it will just be altered to match this code and the migration will always succeed when running forward (the Up method).

Next, place the following code in the Down method:

```
migrationBuilder.Sql(@"DROP PROCEDURE IF EXISTS dbo.GetItemsForListing");
```

This code will also execute idempotently and will always remove the procedure if it is there when running the rollback of the database via these migrations.

For clarity, Figure 7-5 shows the full migration in place ready to be run.

```
namespace EFCore_DBLibrary.Migrations
{
    1 reference
    public partial class createProc_GetItemsForListing : Migration
    {
        12 references
        protected override void Up(MigrationBuilder migrationBuilder)
        {
            migrationBuilder.Sql(@"CREATE OR ALTER PROCEDURE dbo.GetItemsForListing
@minDate DATETIME = '1970.01.01',
@maxDate DATETIME = '2050.12.31'
AS
BEGIN
    SET NOCOUNT ON;

    SELECT item.[Name], item.[Description]
        , item.Notes, item.isActive, item.isDeleted
        , genre.[Name] GenreName, cat.[Name] CategoryName
    FROM dbo.Items item
    LEFT JOIN dbo.ItemGenres ig on item.Id = ig.ItemId
    LEFT JOIN dbo.Genres genre on ig.GenreId = genre.Id
    LEFT JOIN dbo.Categories cat on item.CategoryId = cat.Id
    WHERE (@minDate IS NULL OR item.CreatedDate >= @minDate)
    AND (@maxDate IS NULL OR item.CreatedDate <= @maxDate)
END
GO");
        }

        12 references
        protected override void Down(MigrationBuilder migrationBuilder)
        {
            migrationBuilder.Sql(@"DROP PROCEDURE IF EXISTS dbo.GetItemsForListing");
        }
    }
}
```

Figure 7-5. *The migration to create the GetItemsForListing procedure is ready to go*

Now that both the Up and Down methods are in place, go ahead and run the update-database command to apply the new migration.

Step 3: Validate that the migration was applied

To ensure that the migration worked as expected, run the statement `execute dbo.GetItemsForListing` in an SSMS query window. You should see results based on the stored procedure. You can also check under the database in `Programmability` ➤ `Stored Procedures` to see the procedure (you may need to refresh). Figure 7-6 shows the results of executing the procedure.

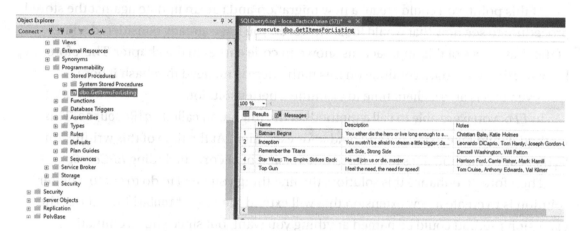

Figure 7-6. *The procedure exists on the database and running the query works as expected*

Run the query passing in some dates that will limit results to validate the date filtering is working. Then run another query using a valid created date range, and ensure results are returned, for example:

```
execute dbo.GetItemsForListing '2001.09.11', '2021.01.01'
execute dbo.GetItemsForListing '2022.01.01', '2025.01.01'
execute dbo.GetItemsForListing '2021.01.01', '2021.12.31'
```

One thing to note is that you have gotten the procedure in place, and everything should work as expected. However, you should also note that any code review on this migration would have to look at the text in the file to ensure it is good.

Noting that the next procedure would require comparing the code in the `Up` method to the `Down` method just to see the changes, you should be able to start seeing that this is not a very scalable approach for your team when it comes time to review changes, or to find when changes were applied in the distant future, when you need to see what version changed the procedure to do some functionality.

Task 2: Create the extension method to use local files for scripting

In this task, you will create an extension and then leverage the extension from this point on when creating, updating, or deleting database objects, such as stored procedures, views, and functions. Additionally, these scripts will be usable for any database scripting operation.

At this point, you could create a new migration and run an update against the stored procedure to see how that would look. However, you have already considered some of the drawbacks of this approach, as shown in code earlier in the chapter. Therefore, knowing that you could continue on this path, there is no need to rehash it here. However, this is an excellent time to examine a better solution.

In *EF6*, you were able to call a method on the migration called SqlResource. This method would take in the file and read it for execution. At the time of this writing, this SqlResource method does not exist in any version of EFCore, including *EFCore6*.

Therefore, to enhance this solution, the first thing you need to do to get to a better solution is to create a new extension that will extend the MigrationBuilder class. The extension method could be named anything you want, but since you're emulating behavior from *EF6*, you will just call the extension by the same name: SqlResource.

Once the method is created, you'll leverage the fact that the script is nothing more than text that needs to be run in the migration builder. You can therefore just put your code into a flat *.sql* file and then add that file to your project as an embedded resource. Finally, you use the new extension method to read the file as a stream for execution in the migration.

Step 1: Create the folder to store your script files

First, add a new folder under the Migrations folder entitled Scripts (this is shown in Figure 7-7 with the rest of the initial changes).

The location of this folder is going to be important, but the location of the extension inside this folder will be critical so that you don't have to worry about the path to your script files.

Step 2: Create the extension

In the new Scripts folder, create a new class file called MigrationBuilderSqlResource.cs. You'll write your extension in this class.

In the Scripts folder, you'll create a subdirectory for each object type, and then within each object type folder, you'll create subfolders for each object by name for better organization and maintenance.

Therefore, also in the `Scripts` folder, create a new subfolder called `Procedures`. Within the `Procedures` folder, create a new subfolder called `GetItemsForListing` and then create two new code files in the `GetItemsForListing` folder named `GetItemsForListing.v0.sql` and `GetItemsForListing.v1.sql`. For clarity, the overall look of the project structure as described earlier is shown in Figure 7-7.

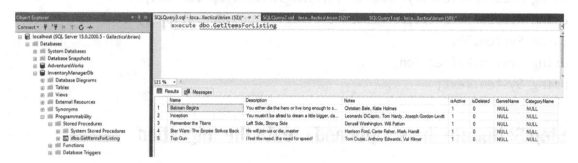

Figure 7-7. *The new Scripts folder is nested in the Migrations folder for easy access from migrations on the relative path in the future. A Procedures folder will hold each of the procedure scripts, which will also be held in their own folder*

Modify the `MigrationBuilderSqlResource.cs` file with the following code, making sure to bring in any missing using statements so the code will compile

```
public static class MigrationBuilderSqlResource
{
    public static OperationBuilder<SqlOperation> SqlResource(this
    MigrationBuilder mb, string relativeFileName)
    {
        using (var stream = Assembly.GetAssembly(typeof(MigrationBuilder
        SqlResource)).GetManifestResourceStream(relativeFileName))
        {
            using (var ms = new MemoryStream())
            {
                stream.CopyTo(ms);
                var data = ms.ToArray();
                var text = Encoding.UTF8.GetString(data, 3, data.Length - 3);
```

317

```
                return mb.Sql(text);
            }
        }
    }
}
```

For clarity, the using statements you will need to add will be as follows:

```
using Microsoft.EntityFrameworkCore.Migrations;
using Microsoft.EntityFrameworkCore.Migrations.Operations;
using Microsoft.EntityFrameworkCore.Migrations.Operations.Builders;
using System.IO;
using System.Reflection;
using System.Text;
```

Step 3: Update the scripts and create the migration

Because v0 was never originally created, you are going to put that code into the v0 file. In this manner, you have the original stored procedure code recorded in a place that is easy to use for comparing the procedure changes in a code review. Place the following code (the same code as your last migration) in the v0 file:

```
CREATE OR ALTER PROCEDURE dbo.GetItemsForListing
    @minDate DATETIME = '1970.01.01',
    @maxDate DATETIME = '2050.12.31'
AS
BEGIN
    SET NOCOUNT ON;

    SELECT item.[Name], item.[Description]
        , item.Notes, item.isActive, item.isDeleted
        , genre.[Name] GenreName, cat.[Name] CategoryName
    FROM dbo.Items item
    LEFT JOIN dbo.ItemGenres ig on item.Id = ig.ItemId
    LEFT JOIN dbo.Genres genre on ig.GenreId = genre.Id
    LEFT JOIN dbo.Categories cat on item.CategoryId = cat.Id
```

```
    WHERE (@minDate IS NULL OR item.CreatedDate >= @minDate)
    AND (@maxDate IS NULL OR item.CreatedDate <= @maxDate)
END
GO
```

Next, you will modify the v1 version to remove all the references to the Genres table, including the select query and the left joins for the join table and the join. Add the following code into the v1 version of the file:

```
CREATE OR ALTER PROCEDURE dbo.GetItemsForListing
    @minDate DATETIME = '1970.01.01',
    @maxDate DATETIME = '2050.12.31'
AS
BEGIN
    SET NOCOUNT ON;

    SELECT item.[Name], item.[Description]
            , item.Notes, item.isActive, item.isDeleted
            , cat.[Name] CategoryName
    FROM dbo.Items item
    LEFT JOIN dbo.Categories cat on item.CategoryId = cat.Id
    WHERE (@minDate IS NULL OR item.CreatedDate >= @minDate)
    AND (@maxDate IS NULL OR item.CreatedDate <= @maxDate)
END
GO
```

To be clear, the v0 file text is just the exact text from the Up method for creating the stored procedure as in the first migration, without the wrapping migrationBuilder.Sql(@"... code. This v0 file is your rollback option, so you want to get back to where you were at the end of the previous migration if you roll back the migration you are about to create using this file.

Before setting up a migration, it's a good idea to double-check that the code you will be creating is going to execute as expected. If you want, you could take the select statement from the v1 file and execute it in SSMS to validate that the results no longer contain any references to the Genres table, have no duplicated entries, and work to return results as expected. You could even execute the whole script and then make a call to the stored procedure. Since the code is CREATE OR ALTER, even running the migration would just restore the same procedure code to the intended state.

With both files containing the code as expected, rebuild and then add a new migration using the command add-migration updateProc_GetItemsForListing_ RemoveGenres. It might surprise you, but the migration will be empty.

Step 4: Leverage the extension in a new migration

Now that the files are in place and you have a blank migration, you need to tell the migration what to do in the Up and Down methods.

In the Up method, simply reference the new extension with the path to the v1 file as follows (use the namespace from the extension, followed by the path from that location to the file):

```
migrationBuilder.SqlResource("EFCore_DBLibrary.Migrations.Scripts.
Procedures.GetItemsForListing.GetItemsForListing.v1.sql");
```

Add the v0 version to the Down method:

```
migrationBuilder.SqlResource("EFCore_DBLibrary.Migrations.Scripts.
Procedures.GetItemsForListing.GetItemsForListing.v0.sql");
```

To make these work without error, you will need to add the using statement using EFCore_DbLibrary.Migrations.Scripts; to the top of the file to incorporate the extension.

For clarity, the migration is shown in Figure 7-8.

```
using EFCore_DBLibrary.Migrations.Scripts;
using Microsoft.EntityFrameworkCore.Migrations;

namespace EFCore_DBLibrary.Migrations
{
    1 reference
    public partial class updateProc_GetItemsForListing_RemoveGenres : Migration
    {
        13 references
        protected override void Up(MigrationBuilder migrationBuilder)
        {
            migrationBuilder.SqlResource("EFCore_DBLibrary.Migrations.Scripts.Procedures.GetItemsForListing.GetItemsForListing.v1.sql");
        }

        13 references
        protected override void Down(MigrationBuilder migrationBuilder)
        {
            migrationBuilder.SqlResource("EFCore_DBLibrary.Migrations.Scripts.Procedures.GetItemsForListing.GetItemsForListing.v0.sql");
        }
    }
}
```

Figure 7-8. *The new migration that leverages the scripts is much cleaner than the migration would be without the scripts and extension*

You should be able to easily see how much cleaner this approach will be, both in the migration files themselves and in the organization of the overall project. Additionally, you should now be able to envision the ease with which you and your team will be able to review the script files in a simple comparison between versions going forward.

Task 3: Apply the migration

In this task, you will apply the migration. This might seem straightforward at this point, but there is one thing left to do.

To this point, one error has been purposefully made so that you will see it and be able to easily identify when this happens to you in the future.

In this task, you will see the error, correct it, and then complete the database update.

Step 1: Run the update database command to see the error

As mentioned, there is a purposeful error still in play at the moment in the current state of the code. To see this error, run the command update-database, and then review Figure 7-9 to see the error Object reference not set to an instance of an object as it is expected to appear.

```
PM> update-database
Build started...
Build succeeded.
Applying migration '20210511052357_updateProc_GetItemsForListing_RemoveGenres'.
System.NullReferenceException: Object reference not set to an instance of an object.
   at EFCore_DBLibrary.Migrations.Scripts.MigrationBuilderSqlResource.SqlResource(MigrationBuilder mb, String relativeFileName) in C:\APressEntityFramework\Code\EFCore_Activity0701
\EFCore_DBLibrary\Migrations\Scripts\MigrationBuilderSqlResource.cs:line 18
   at EFCore_DBLibrary.Migrations.updateProc_GetItemsForListing_RemoveGenres.Up(MigrationBuilder migrationBuilder) in C:\APressEntityFramework\Code\EFCore_Activity0701\EFCore_DBLibrary
\Migrations\20210511052357_updateProc_GetItemsForListing_RemoveGenres.cs:line 18
   at Microsoft.EntityFrameworkCore.Migrations.Migration.BuildOperations(Action`1 buildAction)
   at Microsoft.EntityFrameworkCore.Migrations.Migration.get_UpOperations()
   at Microsoft.EntityFrameworkCore.Migrations.Internal.Migrator.GenerateUpSql(Migration migration, MigrationsSqlGenerationOptions options)
   at Microsoft.EntityFrameworkCore.Migrations.Internal.Migrator.<>c__DisplayClass16_2.<GetMigrationCommandLists>b__2()
   at Microsoft.EntityFrameworkCore.Migrations.Internal.Migrator.Migrate(String targetMigration)
   at Microsoft.EntityFrameworkCore.Design.Internal.MigrationsOperations.UpdateDatabase(String targetMigration, String connectionString, String contextType)
   at Microsoft.EntityFrameworkCore.Design.OperationExecutor.UpdateDatabaseImpl(String targetMigration, String connectionString, String contextType)
   at Microsoft.EntityFrameworkCore.Design.OperationExecutor.UpdateDatabase.<>c__DisplayClass0_0.<.ctor>b__0()
   at Microsoft.EntityFrameworkCore.Design.OperationExecutor.OperationBase.Execute(Action action)
Object reference not set to an instance of an object.
PM>
```

Figure 7-9. *The database update fails with an error stating Object reference not set to an instance of an object*

Anyone who has developed in C# or VB.Net is probably very aware of this error. If you've used Java, you've seen this error as a "Null Reference Exception."

Either way, the issue is simple, but almost impossible to identify. Look closely to see that in the muck of the error there is also a statement about the SqlResource. This is your indication that something is wrong with the file. You might spend hours trying to solve the issue with questions like "Is it the path?" or "Is it the name?" or simply "What ... is going on???"

In the end, the issue is simply that you didn't include the file as an Embedded resource. Yes, that is abundantly clear from the error, right? This is why you needed to see this error now, so you would understand where to look first in the future when you encounter a similar error.

Step 2: Fix the error

To fix the error, click the v0 file and then use the properties to select Embedded resource for the Build Action (see Figure 7-10). Repeat this operation for the v1 file as well. You will need to remember to do this for each of your script files in the future to avoid the Object reference error.

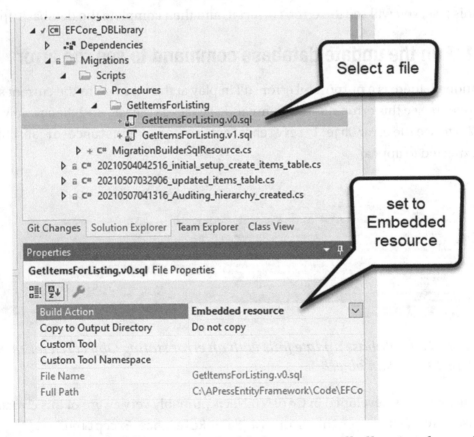

Figure 7-10. *Setting the file to an Embedded resource will allow it to be used in the migration. Failure to do this results in the error seen earlier*

Step 3: Run the update database command to apply the migration

Now that both files are set to be of the type Embedded resource, run the update-database command again. This time, it should run to completion with no issues (provided the code in your scripts is valid, and your files are nested in the correct place).

If you continue to get the Object reference not set to an instance of an object error, ensure that both files are Embedded resource, and then double-check that you have the exact case and spelling for the file path references in the migration (i.e., EFCore_DBLibrary, not EFCore_DbLibrary).   The full path should be the path to your file from project name through all the folders (including the GetItemsForListing twice, such as ProjectName.Migrations.Scripts.Procedures.SpecificProcedure. SpecificProcedure.v#.sql.

Step 4: Review your database to ensure changes happened as expected

As a final step, right-click the stored procedure in your database hierarchy in SSMS and Script Stored Procedure as ➤ CREATE To ➤ New Query Editor Window (see Figure 7-11).

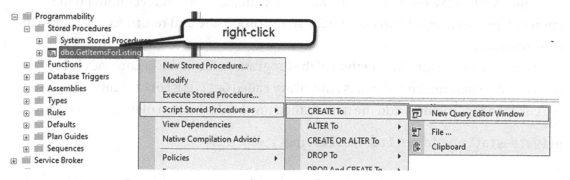

Figure 7-11. *Scripting the stored procedure as create in SSMS*

Review the script to ensure it is in the correct state.

If you want, run a revert by running an `update-database -target <your previous migration>` and see the down script working as well. Make sure to re-apply the migration by running `update-database` again if you do this.

Finally, as another test, you could execute the stored procedure to ensure that values are returned as expected.

Task 4: Leverage the stored procedure in code

In this task, you will leverage the recently created stored procedure to see how this process works, including mapping out a result with the Fluent API. Additionally, you will learn about using parameters with your queries to avoid the risk of opening yourself to a SQL Injection attack.

Step 1: Execute and use the results from the stored procedure

There are a number of ways to get your code to execute a stored procedure. You could write code against a regular ADO.Net `SqlCommand` object, passing in the parameters and working with the data by getting a `DataReader` and reading it into a list of objects. This approach is how you would have worked through executing stored procedures (or other commands) in the past, and, since it is using ADO.Net, this approach doesn't leverage Entity Framework. Even so, using ADO.Net is still a very viable solution, and for reasons of performance and/or using legacy code, you may continue to leverage stored procedures in this manner.

However, this is a book on Entity Framework and, as such, will recommend the approach that leverages EF to execute the stored procedure and return results for use in your solutions.

To get started, in the `Main` method of the `Program.cs` file in the `EFCore_Activity0701` project, add a new method after `ListInventory` called `GetItemsForListing`. After adding the call for a new method, add the new method toward the bottom of the class as follows:

```
private static void GetItemsForListing()
{
    using (var db = new InventoryDbContext(_optionsBuilder.Options))
    {
        var results = db.Items.FromSqlRaw("EXECUTE dbo.
        GetItemsForListing").ToList();
```

```
        foreach (var item in results)
        {
            Console.WriteLine($"ITEM {item.Id}] {item.Name}");
        }
    }
}
```

With the new changes in place, go ahead and run the program. You will see that this generates an unexpected error: The required column 'Id' was not present in the results of a 'FromSql' operation. Basically, at this point, the original procedure didn't return anything that could be used as a key in the result – it's just a flat set of data with no real organization (see Figure 7-12).

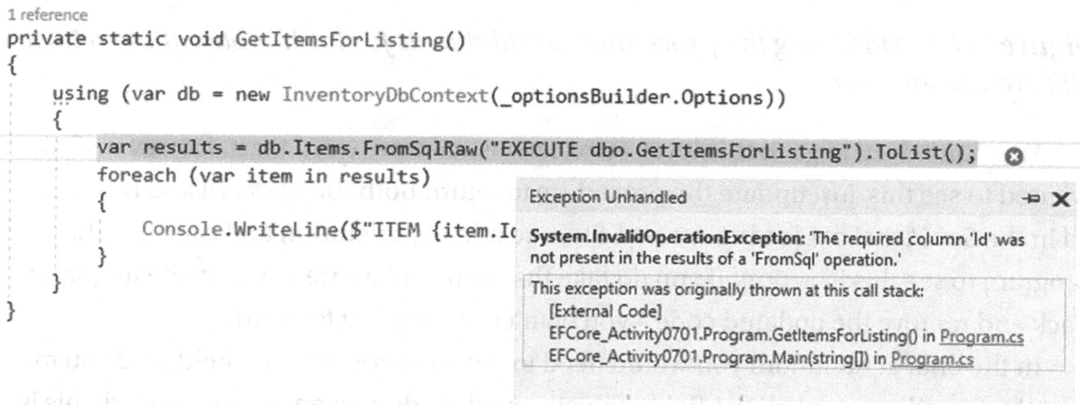

Figure 7-12. *The current procedure returns data, but the solution gives an error when trying to leverage the data for no tracked Id*

If you were to go add the Id for the Item and the Id for the Category just to be safe and then create the migration and apply it, the result would be another error: The required column 'CreateByUserId' was not present in the results of a 'FromSql'. To prove this out, I modified my local procedure and applied an update on the database and then ran the program to get the error (see Figure 7-13).

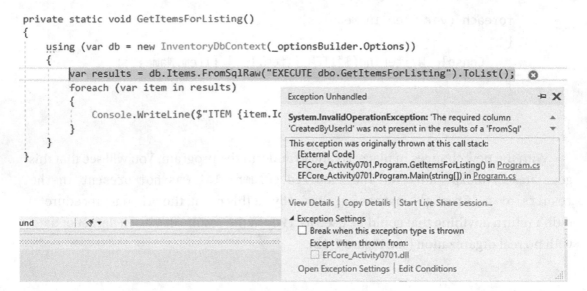

```
private static void GetItemsForListing()
{
    using (var db = new InventoryDbContext(_optionsBuilder.Options))
    {
        var results = db.Items.FromSqlRaw("EXECUTE dbo.GetItemsForListing").ToList();
        foreach (var item in results)
        {
            Console.WriteLine($"ITEM {item.I
        }
    }
}
```

Figure 7-13. Modifying the procedure to add the Ids for both tables in the return still creates an error

You don't need to go to this level – you can just take my word for it. However, if you wanted to see this, just update the procedure to return both the item.Id and the cat. Id in the GetItemsForListing.v2.sql file, and add the migration and then run the program to see this in action. If you do take that step, make sure to revert the migration back and remove the updated code – you won't want it going forward.

In the end, at minimum you would need to return every required field, and you may even be forced to return all the fields, which you likely don't want to do. After all, this is supposed to be a simple procedure to get information specific for a simple view of the data, not every column from every matching row.

Step 2: Use the Fluent API to map out a result set entity for the stored procedure

Before starting this step, if you went to the next level and added a v2 version of the procedure to see the additional error from Figure 7-13, make sure to revert that migration and get your database back to the v1 version of the procedure, and then remove any pending migration for a v2 update of the GetItemsForListing stored procedure. To be clear, the last migration applied at this point should be the updateProc_GetItemsForListing_RemoveGenres migration.

In order to use the Fluent API to modify this solution and use the procedure as is, you will need to do three things. First, you need a *Data Transfer Object (DTO)* to map the result to an object. Second, you will need to add code in the override for the `OnModelCreating` method in the `InventoryDbContext`. Finally, you'll need to modify the call in the original code to leverage the new DTO object.

Begin by creating a new folder in the `InventoryModels` project named `DTOs` to store your DTOs going forward. In the new `DTOs` folder, create a new file named `GetItemsForListingDTO.cs`. Add the following code to the new file for the `GetItemsForListingDTO` object:

```
public class GetItemsForListingDto
{
    public string Name { get; set; } = "";
    public string Description { get; set; } = "";
    public string Notes { get; set; } = "";
    public bool IsActive { get; set; } = true;
    public bool IsDeleted { get; set; } = true;
    public string CategoryName { get; set; } = "";
}
```

For clarity of the code and location of this file, review Figure 7-14.

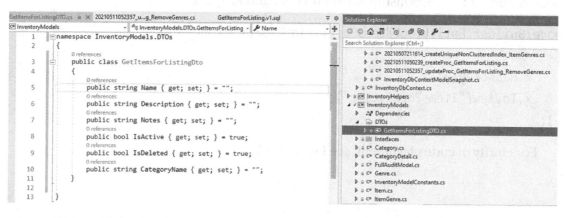

Figure 7-14. *The new GetItemsForListingDto class is shown, nested in the DTOs folder in the InventoryModels project*

This DTO will be used to map the results of the stored procedure so that you will no longer get the error for the missing required fields. Note that if you are going to try to write data with these results, it would be a good practice to still add the Id back to the result set, even though doing so wouldn't fix the error. For the current solution, you are just returning results and you won't use them to do any updating, at least for now.

Now that the DTO is in place, you need to map the result using the Fluent API. Open the InventoryDbContext.cs file from the EFCore_DbLibrary project. In the past, you may have used an object set such as DbQuery<T> to map this result. As of *EFCore3*, the DbQuery object is obsolete, so you need a new solution for this problem (all entity sets in EFCore6 should use DbSet<T>).

Begin by adding the following line to the InventoryDBContext after the DbSet<Genres> property:

```
public DbSet<GetItemsForListingDto> ItemsForListing { get; set; }
```

With this change, you will also need to bring in the using statement using InventoryModels.DTOs since the GetItemsForListingDto object is in the nested DTO folder.

Next, you need to override the OnModelBuilding method in order to leverage the model builder to do some Fluent API manual overrides in your code. To do this, add the following code in the override for OnConfiguring in your InventoryDbContext, after the declaration for the relationship between Items and Players:

```
modelBuilder.Entity<GetItemsForListingDto>(x =>
{
    x.HasNoKey();
    x.ToView("ItemsForListing");
});
```

For clarity of code placement, see Figure 7-15.

```
                    0 references
32  ⊞               protected override void OnConfiguring(DbContextOptionsBuilder optionsBuilder)[...]
45

                    0 references
46  ⊟               protected override void OnModelCreating(ModelBuilder modelBuilder)
47                  {
48                      modelBuilder.Entity<Item>()
49                                  .HasMany(x => x.Players)
50                                  .WithMany(p => p.Items)
51                                  .UsingEntity<Dictionary<string, object>>(
52                                      "ItemPlayers",
53                                      ip => ip.HasOne<Player>()
54                                          .WithMany()
55                                          .HasForeignKey("PlayerId")
56                                          .HasConstraintName("FK_ItemPlayer_Players_PlayerId")
57                                          .OnDelete(DeleteBehavior.Cascade),
58                                      ip => ip.HasOne<Item>()
59                                          .WithMany()
60                                          .HasForeignKey("ItemId")
61                                          .HasConstraintName("FK_PlayerItem_Items_ItemId")
62                                          .OnDelete(DeleteBehavior.ClientCascade)
63                                  );
64
65  ⊟                   modelBuilder.Entity<GetItemsForListingDto>(x =>
66                      {
67                          x.HasNoKey();
68                          x.ToView("ItemsForListing");
69                      });
70
71                  }
72

                    3 references
73  ⊞               public override int SaveChanges()[...]
107                 }
108  }
109
```

Figure 7-15. *The override for OnModelCreating is added to the InventoryDbContext to allow further injection of schema details using the Fluent API (note that for brevity and display, my OnConfiguring and SaveChanges methods are collapsed in this image)*

Note that this code does two things. First, it overrides the default method to allow you to inject additional changes to the context and schema. Second, the internal part of the code sets the entity for the GetItemsForListingDto to map with no key as a view called ItemsForListing. This is pretty cool, because now you can just use the results of the query and you won't have to worry about the mapping error you saw earlier for required fields that are missing.

With the DTO in place and the `OnModelCreating` method overridden, the final task here is to leverage the new DTO in the original query. Return to the `Program.cs` file in the activity project. Modify the original code by replacing it with the following:

```
private static void GetItemsForListing()
{
    using (var db = new InventoryDbContext(_optionsBuilder.Options))
    {
        var results = db.ItemsForListing.FromSqlRaw("EXECUTE dbo.
        GetItemsForListing").ToList();
        foreach (var item in results)
        {
            var output = $"ITEM {item.Name}] {item.Description}";
            if (!string.IsNullOrWhiteSpace(item.CategoryName))
            {
                output = $"{output} has category: {item.CategoryName}";
            }
            Console.WriteLine(output);
        }
    }
}
```

In this query, you modified the original query by first replacing the `db.Items.FromSqlRaw` with `db.ItemsForListing.FromSqlRaw`. Additionally, you changed the output to leverage the data from the stored procedure.

Finally, run the program to see the query being leveraged as expected in the program output. Note that if you added and mapped categories to items you may have a different look than this. You may also wish to do that to see it in action, but you will be seeding data for the categories in the next activity, so if you do it, go ahead and delete them after reviewing the output.

Figure 7-16 shows the expected final output for this activity.

```
G Microsoft Visual Studio Debug Console
New Item: Batman Begins
New Item: Inception
New Item: Remember the Titans
New Item: Star Wars: The Empire Strikes Back
New Item: Top Gun
ITEM Batman Begins] You either die the hero or live long enough to see yourself become the villain
ITEM Inception] You mustn't be afraid to dream a little bigger, darling
ITEM Remember the Titans] Left Side, Strong Side
ITEM Star Wars: The Empire Strikes Back] He will join us or die, master
ITEM Top Gun] I feel the need, the need for speed!

C:\APressEntityFramework\Code\EFCore_Activity0701\EFCore_Activity0701\bin\Debug\net6.0\EFCore_Activit
12172) exited with code 0.
To automatically close the console when debugging stops, enable Tools->Options->Debugging->Automatica
le when debugging stops.
Press any key to close this window . . .
```

Figure 7-16.   The final output correctly leverages the stored procedure as expected

Activity 7-1 summary

In this activity, you learned how to work with stored procedures using inline SQL in migrations. You then assessed this and realized it is not a very useful solution when scaling your efforts across your team.

To remedy the issue, you created an extension that allowed you to run a script as an embedded resource that points directly to a flat file in your solution. In this way, you can easily compare versions and history for all of your database objects.

You also took the time to see an error that may happen if you forget to mark a flat file as an embedded resource. This is highly useful to see the error in case you encounter it in the future.

After getting everything set up correctly, you then were able to update the database to get it to the expected state.

With the database in the expected state, you then modified the UI layer to return the results. To make this happen, you needed to map the result set from the stored procedure to a DTO object that was then treated as a view with results from the query.

Activity 7-2: Working with functions, the FluentAPI, and seed data

In this activity, you will learn how to create and work with both scalar-valued and table-valued functions. In addition to working with functions, you will get a chance to see how to seed some data in your database using the Fluent API.

Task 0: Getting started

To work through this activity, you will either need to continue with your project that you were using from the previous activity, or you can just grab a copy of the starter files, EFCore_Activity07-2_StarterFiles. As always, review Appendix A for information on working with the starter files.

It is critical that you have worked through Activity 7-1 prior to this activity, so that you will understand the nature of scripting your database changes in flat files, as this concept will be used for the remaining activities in this chapter and throughout the rest of the book.

Task 1: Script out a new scalar-valued function

The first type of function you will build is a scalar-valued function. These functions are used to get a single value, generally as the result of a calculation or other manipulation of data. Scalar-valued functions are highly useful for one-off executions but can also be dangerous if you include them as a join in a query (essentially executing the function one time for every use in each row, which can quickly cause performance issues on your data queries).

A good example of a scalar-valued function would be to get a calculation that would be difficult to achieve without multiple built-in SQL commands being executed to return a single result. Another example could be to do something like get a list of the unique values of a field, alphabetized, as a comma-separated value string. However, instead of a comma, consider using a pipe, just in case a field value already has a comma in it.

In this task, you will script out a function to create a new pipe-delimited string that combines the names of all of the items in the Items table. Additionally, the query can allow for including or excluding items based on active status.

Step 0: Eliminate the call to DeleteAllItems

Before starting this activity, one other important thing needs to take place. Make sure to go to the `Program` class in the `Program.cs` file for the `EFCore_Activity0702` project and comment out the line of code that deletes items on every run (`DeleteAllItems();` ➤ `// DeleteAllItems()`). If you don't do this, errors will happen later in the activity.

Step 1: Explore scalar-valued functions

The easiest way to see what the script should be is to open SSMS and then right-click the Functions folder under Programmability and select New ➤ Scalar-valued Function, which will generate the script (see Figure 7-17).

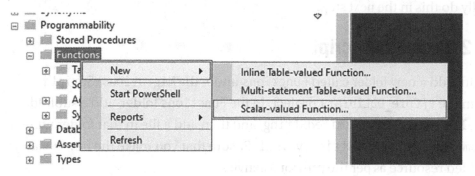

Figure 7-17. *Creating a new scalar-valued function*

Once generated, the function has a lot of overhead in the form of comments that can be removed, and then you should note that the first part of the function requires a name and any parameters that you would want to include. The next statement in the function is the return declaration, and then the function concludes with the function body. The cleaned up, initial function script is shown in Figure 7-18 for clarity.

```
CREATE FUNCTION <Scalar_Function_Name, sysname, FunctionName>
(
    -- Add the parameters for the function here
    <@Param1, sysname, @p1> <Data_Type_For_Param1, , int>
)
RETURNS <Function_Data_Type, ,int>
AS
BEGIN
    -- Declare the return variable here
    DECLARE <@ResultVar, sysname, @Result> <Function_Data_Type, ,int>

    -- Add the T-SQL statements to compute the return value here
    SELECT <@ResultVar, sysname, @Result> = <@Param1, sysname, @p1>

    -- Return the result of the function
    RETURN <@ResultVar, sysname, @Result>

END
GO
```

Figure 7-18. *The initial function script after some cleanup still needs some work*

To make this script suit your needs to get the names of all of the items in the table in a pipe-delimited string, you would start by modifying the function to take the IsActive BIT as a parameter, and then you would likely set the return type to VARCHAR(2500). After making those changes, you would then write the body to get a pipe-delimited list of the names of all active items in alphabetical order where the IsActive flag is matched. You'll officially do this in the next step.

Step 2: Create the script

To begin, add a new folder called Functions under the Migrations\Scripts folder in the EFCore_DbLibrary project. In the Functions folder, add a subfolder named ItemNamesPipeDelimitedString, and then add a file in that folder named ItemNamesPipeDelimitedString.v0.sql. Ensure that you make the new file an embedded resource as per the previous activity.

For clarity, review Figure 7-19.

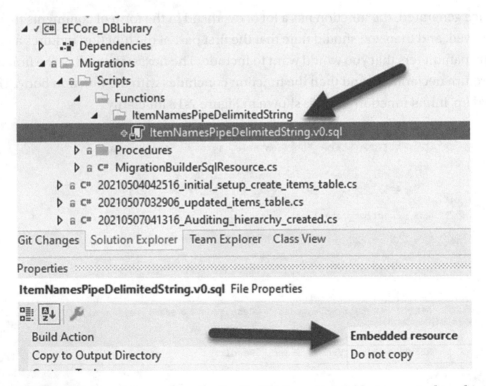

Figure 7-19.   *The ItemNamesPipeDelimitedString.v0.sql file is created and is set as an Embedded resource*

Do not forget to set the new ItemNamesPipeDelimitedString.v0.sql file as an Embedded resource.

In the newly created file, add the following code for the function:

```
CREATE OR ALTER FUNCTION [dbo].[ItemNamesPipeDelimitedString]
(@IsActive BIT)
RETURNS VARCHAR (2500)
AS
BEGIN
    RETURN (SELECT STRING_AGG (Name, '|')
                FROM Items
                WHERE IsActive = @IsActive)
END
```

Step 3: Add a new migration and update the database

With the file in place containing the code and being referenced as an embedded resource, ensure you have selected the EFCore_DbLibrary project in the PMC and then add a new migration with the command add-migration createFunction_ItemNamesPipeDelimitedString. This should generate a blank migration. If for some reason your migration is not blank, ensure that you have previously applied all updates and that you didn't have any pending changes that shouldn't have been created.

In the new migration, add a call to use the new file in the Up method, and add an inline SQL statement to drop the function in the Down method. Using the file will require you to bring in the appropriate using statement to leverage the extension.

Add this code to the Up method: migrationBuilder.SqlResource("EFCore_DBLibrary.Migrations.Scripts.Functions.ItemNamesPipeDelimitedString.ItemNamesPipeDelimitedString.v0.sql");

Then add this code to the Down method:

migrationBuilder.Sql(@"DROP FUNCTION IF EXISTS dbo.ItemNamesPipeDelimitedString");

Once the code is in place, run the update-database command.

Step 4: Validate that the function was added as expected

To ensure the function is in place, open SSMS and refresh the database, and then expand the Functions ➤ Scalar-valued Functions folder. You should see the function in your database.

Right-click the function and select Script Function as ➤ SELECT To ➤ New Query Editor Window. Figure 7-20 shows the menu for selecting as well as the result as it should appear after scripting.

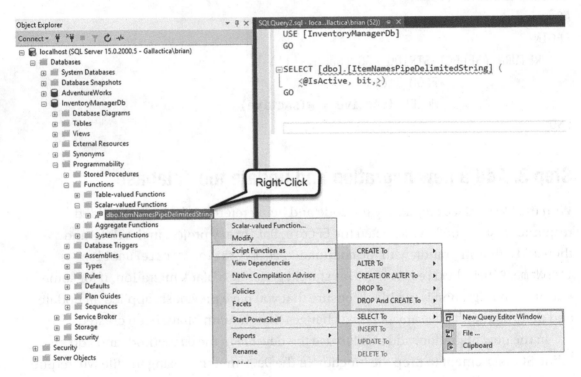

Figure 7-20. *The scalar-valued function is shown with the script option to script to a new query editor window ready to be selected. Additionally, the scripted select is also shown in the query editor window*

Modify the query to replace <@IsActive, bit,> with the single number 1, and then run the query. You should get the result that is a pipe-delimited string listing the names of all of the items in your Items table (see Figure 7-21).

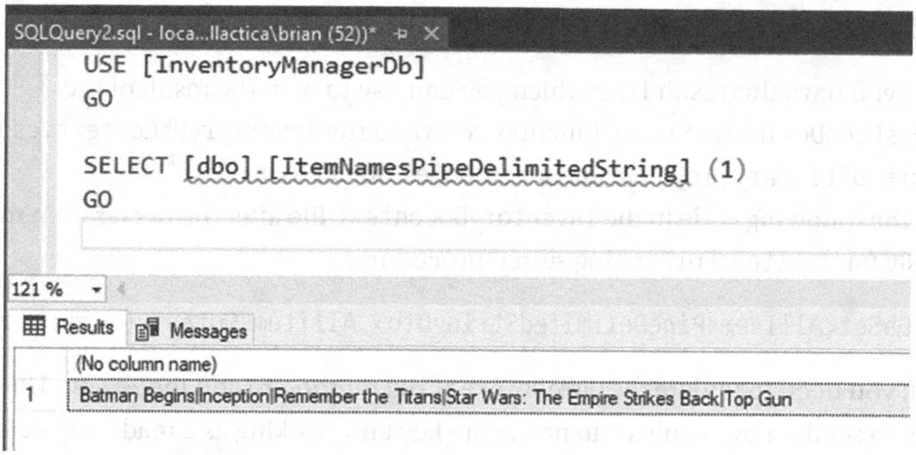

Figure 7-21. The scalar-valued function is executed and the results are as expected

Task 2: Leverage the new function from code

In the real world, you would likely use this function in concert with something else like a stored procedure or another result set, just making it part of the select query. For illustrative purposes, you're just going to call the function directly to validate that it works and that you can leverage it from code.

Before you can run this function to see it in action, just like with the stored procedure, you need to set a result that you can return that isn't tracked in the database.

Step 1: Add a new DTO to map the result of the function

To make sure you can easily work with this result set, you need to create an entity in your Models project that simply has the string return type that you'll be getting from the ItemNamesPipeDelimitedString function.

In the Models project under the Dtos folder, add a new class file AllItemsPipeDelimitedStringDTO.cs with one public string property called AllItems:

```
public class AllItemsPipeDelimitedStringDto
{
    public string AllItems { get; set; } = string.Empty;
}
```

Step 2: Add the DTO as a DbSet in the InventoryDbContext

Now that you have this result DTO which you can use to map the result of the
ItemNamesPipeDelimitedString function, return to the InventoryDbContext.cs file in
the EFCore_DBLibrary project to add a new DbSet object to it.

Add the following code in the InventoryDbContext file after the declaration made
previously for the ItemsForListing stored procedure:

```
public DbSet<AllItemsPipeDelimitedStringDto> AllItemsOutput { get; set; }
```

Next, you need to update the OnModelCreating method to add the *Fluent API*
mapping to set the new result set to having no key and working as a read-only database
object. Add the following code into the OnModelCreating method, following the code
added in the previous activity for the stored procedure mapping:

```
modelBuilder.Entity<AllItemsPipeDelimitedStringDto>(x => {
    x.HasNoKey();
    x.ToView("AllItemsOutput");
});
```

Step 3: Add a call in the Program file to get the results to the UI

Return to the Program.cs file in the main activity project, and add the following call to
the end of the Main method, following the call to GetItemsForListing:

```
GetAllActiveItemsAsPipeDelimitedString();
```

Then add the following method code to the end of the file:

```
private static void GetAllActiveItemsAsPipeDelimitedString()
{
    using (var db = new InventoryDbContext(_optionsBuilder.Options))
    {
        var isActiveParm = new SqlParameter("IsActive", 1);

        var result = db.AllItemsOutput
                    .FromSqlRaw("SELECT [dbo].
                    [ItemNamesPipeDelimitedString] (@IsActive)
                    AllItems", isActiveParm)
```

```
        .FirstOrDefault();

    Console.WriteLine($"All active Items: {result.AllItems}");
  }
}
```

Note that using the `SqlParameter` is a best practice to avoid allowing risky data into your inline SQL statements. Even though you technically have direct control here, you may update this in the future and you should just make it a habit to always parameterize your queries.

Additionally, using `SqlParameter` will require you to bring in the using statement using `Microsoft.Sql.Client`.

Run the program to see the results. The output should be similar to what is shown in Figure 7-22.

```
Microsoft Visual Studio Debug Console
New Item: Batman Begins
New Item: Inception
New Item: Remember the Titans
New Item: Star Wars: The Empire Strikes Back
New Item: Top Gun
ITEM Batman Begins] You either die the hero or live long enough to see yourself become the villain
ITEM Inception] You mustn't be afraid to dream a little bigger, darling
ITEM Remember the Titans] Left Side, Strong Side
ITEM Star Wars: The Empire Strikes Back] He will join us or die, master
ITEM Top Gun] I feel the need, the need for speed!
All active Items: Batman Begins|Inception|Remember the Titans|Star Wars: The Empire Strikes Back|Top Gun

C:\APressEntityFramework\Code\EFCore_Activity0702\EFCore_Activity0702\bin\Debug\net6.0\EFCore_Activity0702.e
10436) exited with code 0.
To automatically close the console when debugging stops, enable Tools->Options->Debugging->Automatically clo
le when debugging stops.
Press any key to close this window . . .
```

Figure 7-22. *The function is leveraged from code as expected*

Task 3: Create a new table-valued function

In this task, you will create a new table-valued function. While this will be another contrived example, it is a good exercise to get your feet wet, and you can learn the concepts so you will be able to use them in your real-world solutions.

As you've already done, a good way to start when creating a new function or procedure is to begin by scripting it out in SSMS and then applying the appropriate changes to implement via a new migration in your project.

For this table-valued function (TVF), you will get a list of items with Name, Quantity, Price, and Total Value [calculated], once again leveraging a filter on the IsActive field. This will be an inline table-valued function. As a reminder, the steps to complete the overall process are

- Script out a new table-valued function and modify it to get the appropriate data (see script).

- Add the folder for the function, include a file in the folder named the same as the function with a version, and ensure that it is set to be an embedded resource.

- Create the migration using the SqlResource approach to leverage the new file.

- Create and map a result set DTO for the result set as returned by the function.

- Add a method call from the UI layer that calls a new method which executes the new function, gets the data into the appropriate result set, and returns the data to be output to the console by the UI.

Step 1: Create the new function

To get started, ordinarily you would open SSMS and right-click Programmability ➤ Functions and then select either a New Inline Table-valued Function or a New Multi-statement Table-valued function. The main difference between the two is how the data is composed and used. In the inline TVF, this is similar to a traditional query with parameters, returned as a table that you can then use just like a view or another query-based result set. In a multi-statement TVF, you are doing a very similar operation, but generally you are also then going to join to your results or perform some further operations within the query. As such, the multi-statement table-valued function will have a bit more overhead as it works with your original query internally and does further operations rather than just returning a single query.

For this task, you will be creating an inline TVF, and you will use the code that follows to do this. Rather than spend the time testing it in SSMS (you can do that if you chose), you will just run the process as if you have already proven out the code.

Begin by adding a new migration with the command `add-migration`
`createFunction_GetItemsTotalValue`. With the migration created, add the following
code in the `Up` method:

```
migrationBuilder.SqlResource("EFCore_DBLibrary.Migrations.Scripts.
Functions.GetItemsTotalValue.GetItemsTotalValue.v0.sql");
```

Next, add the following code in the `Down` method:

```
migrationBuilder.Sql("DROP FUNCTION IF EXISTS dbo.GetItemsTotalValue");
```

You will also need to add the using statement using `EFCore_DBLibrary.Migration.`
`Scripts` to prevent a build error when leveraging the `SqlResource` extension.

After adding the code, navigate to the `EFCore_DBLibrary` projects, find
the `Migrations` ➤ `Scripts` ➤ `Functions` folder, and add a new folder named
`GetItemsTotalValue`. In the new `GetItemsTotalValue` folder, add the v0 script
`GetItemsTotalValue.v0.sql`. Do not forget to then ensure the file is an embedded
resource. For clarity, review Figure 7-23.

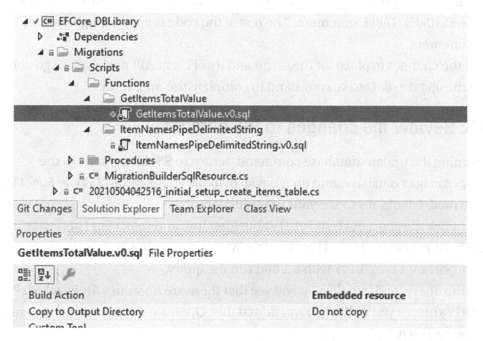

Figure 7-23. *The new file for the GetItemsTotalValue.v0.sql is shown in its proper
location as an embedded resource*

As you can mostly infer from Figure 7-23, the next step is to add the following code into the new file:

```
CREATE OR ALTER FUNCTION dbo.GetItemsTotalValue (
    @IsActive BIT = true
)
RETURNS TABLE
AS
RETURN
(
    SELECT Id, [Name], [Description], Quantity, PurchasePrice, Quantity *
    PurchasePrice as TotalValue
    From Items
    Where IsActive = @IsActive
)
```

Again, this is a simple example, but it gives you an idea of the concept. Note the input parameter of IsActive to toggle showing active Items or inactive Items. Next, note the use of the RETURNS TABLE statement. The rest of the code is just a straightforward T-SQL SELECT statement.

With the changes in place for the script and this Fluent API declaration, go ahead and run the update-database command to complete the migration.

Step 3: Review the changes to the database

After running the update-database command, return to SSMS and refresh the InventoryManager database, and then navigate to the Programmability ➤ Functions ➤ Table-valued Functions to see your new function.

Right-click the dbo.GetItemsTotalValue function, and select Script Function as ➤ SELECT To ➤ New Query Editor Window. When the window comes up, replace the parameter <@IsActive, bit> with a 1 and run the query.

Run the query, and initially you will see that there are no values for PurchasePrice and TotalValue, as you've likely never added this. Open a new query window and run the following T-SQL code:

```
UPDATE Items
SET PurchasePrice = CAST (RAND(25235) * 10 as DECIMAL(18,2))
WHERE Name = 'Batman Begins'

UPDATE Items
SET PurchasePrice = CAST (RAND(3112) * 10 as DECIMAL(18,2))
WHERE Name = 'Inception'

UPDATE Items
SET PurchasePrice = CAST (RAND(62252) * 10 as DECIMAL(18,2))
WHERE Name = 'Remember The Titans'

UPDATE Items
SET PurchasePrice = CAST (RAND(22353) * 10 as DECIMAL(18,2))
WHERE Name = 'Star Wars: The Empire Strikes Back'

UPDATE Items
SET PurchasePrice = CAST (RAND(92359) * 10 as DECIMAL(18,2))
WHERE Name = 'Top Gun'

SELECT Name, PurchasePrice from Items
```

For fun, run it a couple of times to see how the random number is not random. Have even more fun by using the same seed on each RAND statement.

With values in place, execute the function again. This time you should see results, which should be similar in functionality to what is shown in Figure 7-24.

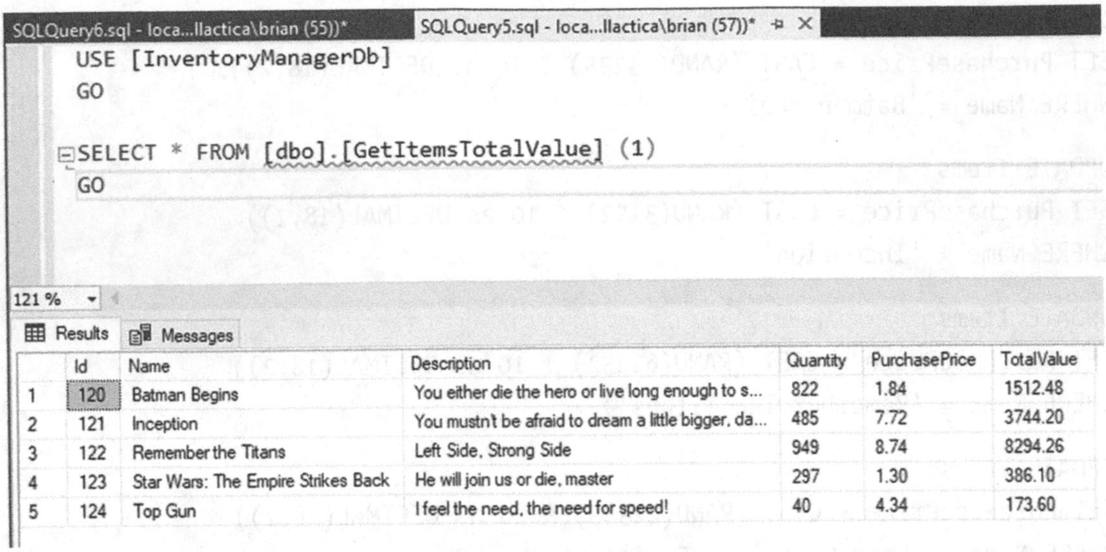

Figure 7-24. *The function returns results when data exists for the appropriate fields in the calculation*

Step 3: Create the DTO for mapping function results

Now that you're certain the function is going to work, it's time to leverage it from the UI layer. To do this, you'll need a DTO for the result set.

Go to the InventoryModels project, and add a new file called GetItemsTotalValueDTO.cs in the DTOs folder. Replace the generated empty class with the following code for the DTO:

```
public class GetItemsTotalValueDto
{
    public int Id { get; set; }
    public string Name { get; set; } = "";
    public string Description { get; set; } = "";
    public int Quantity { get; set; }
    public decimal? PurchasePrice { get; set; }
    public decimal? TotalValue { get; set; }
}
```

Return to the InventoryDbContext in the EFCore_DBLibrary project and add the following code to create a DbSet for the GetItemsTotalValueDto following the DbSet for AllItemsOutput:

```
public DbSet<GetItemsTotalValueDto> GetItemsTotalValues { get; set; }
```

Additionally, configure the *Fluent API* to ensure no table is created for the new *DTO*. Add the following code to the OnModelCreating method in the InventoryDbContext, following the code you created earlier for the AllItemsPipeDelimitedStringDto:

```
modelBuilder.Entity<GetItemsTotalValueDto>(x =>
{
    x.HasNoKey();
    x.ToView("GetItemsTotalValues");
});
```

Step 4: Use the new function and show results in the UI layer

Return to the Program.cs file in the EFCore_Activity0702 project, and add a call in the Main method to a new method called GetItemsTotalValues. Then add the new method as follows at the bottom of the Main method:

```
private static void GetItemsTotalValues()
{
    using (var db = new InventoryDbContext(_optionsBuilder.Options))
    {
        var isActiveParm = new SqlParameter("IsActive", 1);

        var result = db.GetItemsTotalValues
                    .FromSqlRaw("SELECT * from [dbo].
                    [GetItemsTotalValue] (@IsActive)", isActiveParm)
                    .ToList();

        foreach (var item in result)
        {
            Console.WriteLine($"New Item] {item.Id,-10}" +
                            $"|{item.Name,-50}" +
                            $"|{item.Quantity,-4}" +
```

```
                            $"|{item.TotalValue,-5}");
        }
    }
}
```

Run the code, and you should see output similar to what is shown in Figure 7-25.

```
New Item: Batman Begins
New Item: Inception
New Item: Remember the Titans
New Item: Star Wars: The Empire Strikes Back
New Item: Top Gun
ITEM Batman Begins] You either die the hero or live long enough to see yourself become the villain
ITEM Inception] You mustn't be afraid to dream a little bigger, darling
ITEM Remember the Titans] Left Side, Strong Side
ITEM Star Wars: The Empire Strikes Back] He will join us or die, master
ITEM Top Gun] I feel the need, the need for speed!
All active Items: Batman Begins|Inception|Remember the Titans|Star Wars: The Empire Strikes Back|Top Gun
New Item] 120       |Batman Begins                             |822 |1512.48
New Item] 121       |Inception                                 |485 |3744.20
New Item] 122       |Remember the Titans                       |949 |8294.26
New Item] 123       |Star Wars: The Empire Strikes Back        |297 |386.10
New Item] 124       |Top Gun                                   |40  |173.60

C:\APressEntityFramework\Code\EFCore_Activity0702\EFCore_Activity0702\bin\Debug\net6.0\EFCore_Activity0702.ex
3956) exited with code 0.
To automatically close the console when debugging stops, enable Tools->Options->Debugging->Automatically clos
le when debugging stops.
Press any key to close this window . . .
```

Figure 7-25. *The output shows how the program can easily reference the new function in code*

If you are not getting values for the calculation for each of the items, you will not see values following the quantity and pipe. If this is the case, ensure that you have eliminated or commented out the call to DeleteAllItems in the Main method. If you were getting blank numbers, after commenting out that call, return to SSMS and reset the values for the PurchasePrice with the script run earlier.

Task 4: Seed data with the Fluent API

Now that you can render some of the data for Categories, it's time to put some default data into the database. You'll also do some default data for Genres as well as fix up the creation of items to make your data more apparent.

When you want to have some default values that should always exist, the best place to put these is into a seed method. You can use a seed method to make sure that certain data is placed into the tables if it doesn't already exist. The seed will run automatically after every call to update-database in the *PMC* locally. When the solution is released to production, you'll want to make sure the migrations are triggered to ensure your migrations and seed methods are applied.

There are a couple of approaches to working with seed data. The first way you can do this is in the *Fluent API*. Other than using the *Fluent API*, you can create seed methods that can be triggered from the OnModelCreating method where you can execute some custom code.

Step 1: Seed data using the Fluent API

To seed data to the Genres table, add the following code at the bottom of the OnModelCreating() method in the InventoryDbContext file, following the code you recently added for the GetItemsTotalValues function:

```
var genreCreateDate = new DateTime(2021,01,01);
modelBuilder.Entity<Genre>(x =>
{
    x.HasData(
        new Genre() { Id = 1, CreatedDate = genreCreateDate, IsActive =
        true, IsDeleted = false, Name = "Fantasy" },
        new Genre() { Id = 2, CreatedDate = genreCreateDate, IsActive =
        true, IsDeleted = false, Name = "Sci/Fi" },
        new Genre() { Id = 3, CreatedDate = genreCreateDate, IsActive =
        true, IsDeleted = false, Name = "Horror" },
        new Genre() { Id = 4, CreatedDate = genreCreateDate, IsActive =
        true, IsDeleted = false, Name = "Comedy" },
        new Genre() { Id = 5, CreatedDate = genreCreateDate, IsActive =
        true, IsDeleted = false, Name = "Drama" }
    );
});
```

Ensure that your values do not change frequently (don't use a random or volatile value for any field, including CreatedDate).

It is imperative that you do not use a random or volatile value for `CreatedDate` here. If you do, each time you run a migration, the genre data would be recreated due to the ModelBuilder finding "new" values for the records. Therefore, when using this method to seed data, ensure you are not going to change the values of any of the columns regularly, and if you do change a value, ensure you also update the value in the seed to match to avoid recreating or adding new records.

If for some reason you are prompted to bring in a using statement to resolve any red squiggly lines, make sure to do so that program will build.

Right now, if you wanted to add that data, you would need to create a migration, which would script out the insertion of this data into the database. For now, hold off on that so that you can also get some categories and category details into the database.

Task 5: Seed data with a custom solution

In this task, you will build your own database migrator project and ensure the database migrations are run when the project is executed, and then you will have the ability to create and execute one or more custom seed generators.

Step 1: Roll your own custom migrator

To roll your own migration with seed data, as a best practice, you need a new project. You *could* stub this into the main method of the `Program` file, but doing that would be a bad practice in the real world (as is putting in the `Items`, by the way). The reason this is a bad idea is that having the custom migration in the main method of the executing program is only safe for one instance at a time. Likely, your real-world application will have more than one concurrent user.

Another benefit of creating this custom project is that you can include the execution of this project in your build pipeline, thereby making sure to run migrations on the database at the end of your deploy process before starting up the application.

Yet another benefit of the project is the ability to run it from any environment and point at any environment to quickly apply database changes in the event something is not correct in one of your deployment environments.

Right-click the solution and use the menus to create a new console project called `InventoryDataMigrator`. Reference the `InventoryDatabaseCore` and `InventoryHelpers` projects in the new `InventoryDataMigrator` project (see Figure 7-26), and then bring in the NuGet packages for all the *Entity Framework* and configuration files that you've been using (these can easily be found in the `EFCore_Activity0702.csproj` file). Note that `InventoryModels` will be available by the fact that it is referenced in the `EFCore_InventoryDB` project.

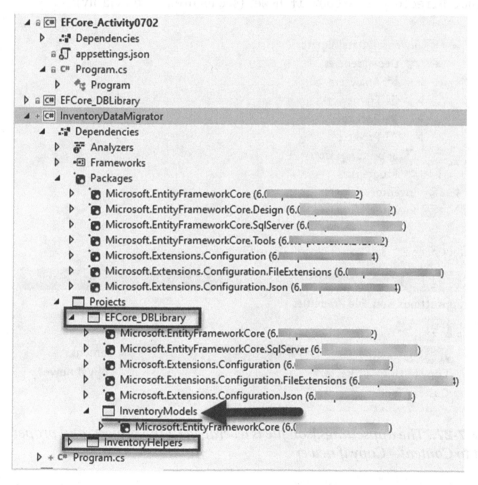

Figure 7-26. *The new project is created with direct references to EFCore_DBLibrary and InventoryHelpers and an indirect reference to InventoryModels through the EFCore_DBLibrary project*

An easy way to bring in all the NuGet packages is to first open the EFCore_Activity0702 project file and select the ItemGroup that contains all the package references and copy that section. Next, open the InventoryDataMigrator.csproj file and paste the ItemGroup entries that exist in the activity console project into the new project file.

Ensure that the project builds before proceeding.

Next, copy and paste the appsettings.json file from the activity project, and then include the file in the project, making sure to also set the project as Content, with Copy to Output Directory set to Copy if newer (see Figure 7-27 for clarity).

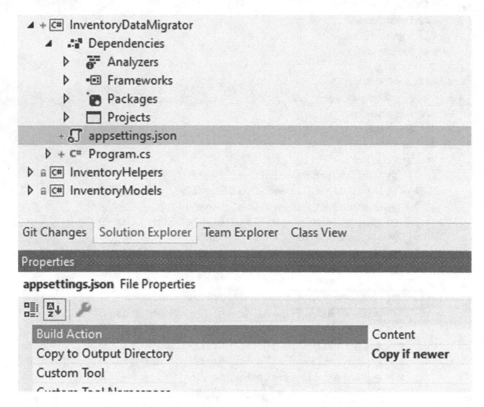

Figure 7-27. *The appsettings.json file is leveraged in the project, and properties are set to Content – Copy if newer*

Leverage the setup that is in the Program.cs file of the activity project to get direct access to the database context in the migrator project. Make sure that you add all required using statements so the code will compile. At this point, your code in the InventoryDataMigrator project's Program.cs file should contain the following lines of code:

```
using EFCore_DBLibrary;
using InventoryHelpers;
using Microsoft.EntityFrameworkCore;
using Microsoft.Extensions.Configuration;
using System;

namespace InventoryDataMigrator
{
    class Program
    {
        static IConfigurationRoot _configuration;
        static DbContextOptionsBuilder<InventoryDbContext> _optionsBuilder;

        static void BuildOptions()
        {
            _configuration = ConfigurationBuilderSingleton.
            ConfigurationRoot;
            _optionsBuilder = new DbContextOptionsBuilder<InventoryDbContext>();
            _optionsBuilder.UseSqlServer(_configuration.GetConnectionString
            ("InventoryManager"));
        }

        static void Main(string[] args)
        {
            BuildOptions();
        }
    }
}
```

Step 2: Run migrations and execute custom seed builders

In the Main method of your migrator project, make a call to a new method named
ApplyMigrations following the call to BuildOptions. Add the method to the bottom of
the program class. To create the method, add the following code:

```
private static void ApplyMigrations()
```

```
{
    using (var db = new InventoryDbContext(_optionsBuilder.Options))
    {
        db.Database.Migrate();
    }
}
```

Having this code would be sufficient to kick off migrations automatically, but you ultimately want to add custom seed data into your pipeline in addition to running migrations. To do this, add a new method call in the Main method called ExecuteCustomSeedData following the call to ApplyMigrations. Then write the method with code as follows:

```
private static void ExecuteCustomSeedData()
{
    using (var context = new InventoryDbContext(_optionsBuilder.Options))
    {
        var categories = new BuildCategories(context);
        categories.ExecuteSeed();
    }
}
```

Next, you need to add the BuildCategories custom seed class.

Step 3: Create the BuildCategories custom seed class

Continue by adding a new class file into the migrator project called BuildCategories. cs. In the BuildCategories class, add a method called ExecuteSeed and a constructor that has a parameter for the InventoryDbContext. Make sure to add any missing using statements. The following code will get you started:

```
private readonly InventoryDbContext _context;
private const string SEED_USER_ID = "31412031-7859-429c-ab21-c2e3e8d98042";

public BuildCategories(InventoryDbContext context)
{
    _context = context;
}
```

```
public void ExecuteSeed()
{
    //seed categories here...
}
```

Additionally, the preceding code adds a private readonly InventoryDbContext
_context; and a private const string SEED_USER_ID = "<GUIDString>"; statement
to create a variable to hold the value of the injected InventoryDbContext and a
simulated user id.

Now replace the line //seed categories here... by pasting the following code into the
ExecuteSeed method of the BuildCategories class:

```
if (_context.Categories.Count() == 0)
{
    _context.Categories.AddRange(
        new Category()
        {
            CreatedDate = DateTime.Now,
            IsActive = true,
            IsDeleted = false,
            Name = "Movies",
            CategoryDetail = new CategoryDetail() { ColorValue = "#0000FF",
            ColorName = "Blue" }
        },
        new Category()
        {
            CreatedDate = DateTime.Now,
            IsActive = true,
            IsDeleted = false,
            Name = "Books",
            CategoryDetail = new CategoryDetail() { ColorValue = "#FF0000",
            ColorName = "Red" }
        },
```

```
    new Category()
    {
        CreatedDate = DateTime.Now,
        IsActive = true,
        IsDeleted = false,
        Name = "Games",
        CategoryDetail = new CategoryDetail() { ColorValue = "#008000",
        ColorName = "Green" }
    }
);
_context.SaveChanges();
}
```

Once again, ensure you've referenced any missing using statements and that the project builds before proceeding.

Now, when you run the project, you will run migrations and run the seed builder(s), applying the changes to your database. Note that the seed here is coded to only execute if there are currently no Categories in the database, which is by design to protect from concurrent runs creating duplicates, but means that adding additional categories would require refactoring this code.

Step 4: Create a migration to apply changes and seed Genre data

In the package manager, ensure you've selected the EFCore_DBLibrary project, and add a new migration with the command add-migration dataUpdate_ SeedGenresMigrationCategoriesInInventoryMigrator. This will generate a new migration as shown in Figure 7-28.

```
16 references
protected override void Up(MigrationBuilder migrationBuilder)
{
    migrationBuilder.InsertData(
        table: "Genres",
        columns: new[] { "Id", "CreatedByUserId", "CreatedDate", "IsActive", "IsDeleted", "LastModifiedDate", "LastModifiedUserId", "Name" },
        values: new object[,]
        {
            { 1, null, new DateTime(2021, 1, 1, 0, 0, 0, 0, DateTimeKind.Unspecified), true, false, null, null, "Fantasy" },
            { 2, null, new DateTime(2021, 1, 1, 0, 0, 0, 0, DateTimeKind.Unspecified), true, false, null, null, "Sci/Fi" },
            { 3, null, new DateTime(2021, 1, 1, 0, 0, 0, 0, DateTimeKind.Unspecified), true, false, null, null, "Horror" },
            { 4, null, new DateTime(2021, 1, 1, 0, 0, 0, 0, DateTimeKind.Unspecified), true, false, null, null, "Comedy" },
            { 5, null, new DateTime(2021, 1, 1, 0, 0, 0, 0, DateTimeKind.Unspecified), true, false, null, null, "Drama" }
        });
}

16 references
protected override void Down(MigrationBuilder migrationBuilder)
{
    migrationBuilder.DeleteData(
        table: "Genres",
        keyColumn: "Id",
        keyValue: 1);

    migrationBuilder.DeleteData(
        table: "Genres",
        keyColumn: "Id",
        keyValue: 2);

    migrationBuilder.DeleteData(
        table: "Genres",
        keyColumn: "Id",
        keyValue: 3);
```

Figure 7-28. *The new migration uses the code from the Fluent API to seed Genre data. No other data is seeded via the migration*

Don't run update-database. Instead, run the migrator project you created to both execute the migration and also seed the Categories and CategoryDetails.

Right-click the InventoryDataMigrator project and select Debug ➤ Start New Instance (see Figure 7-29).

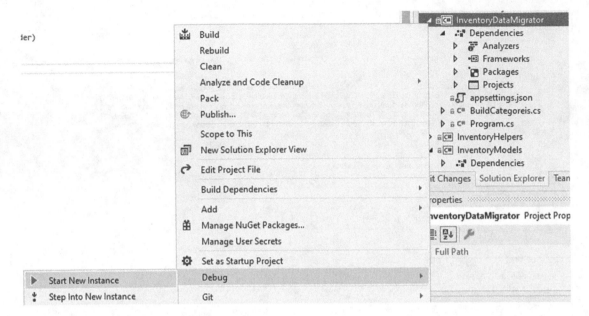

Figure 7-29. *Use the Start New Instance under the Debug menu to easily run the InventoryDataMigrator project*

This is expected to run to completion, and there is no output, so you can just close the window once the program notifies you to press any key to close.

To be certain that the migrations are applied and that genres will not regenerate with each migration, run the command `add-migration test-expected-blank` command in the PMC. You should see a blank migration. If you don't, something is wrong with your seed (ensure your values for Genre are not volatile). You won't be able to just comment code out if generated in a new migration, because if you do that, the Genre values will get dropped in the next migration. If you've applied a migration and need to roll back to the previous migration, use the `update-database -migration <your previous migration name here>` pattern, such as `update-database dataUpdate_SeedGenresMigrationCategoriesInInventoryMigrator`. After the rollback is completed, you can use the `remove-migration` command. Since your `test-expected-blank` migration was never applied, just run the `remove-migration` command now to get rid of the blank migration.

Step 5: Review the database to ensure changes are applied and data exists as expected

Open SSMS and ensure that you have data in the Genres, Categories, and Category Details tables using the following query:

```
SELECT * from dbo.Genres
SELECT * from dbo.Categories
SELECT * from dbo.CategoryDetails
SELECT * FROM __EFMigrationsHistory ORDER BY MigrationId DESC
```

These statements should generate data as shown in Figure 7-30.

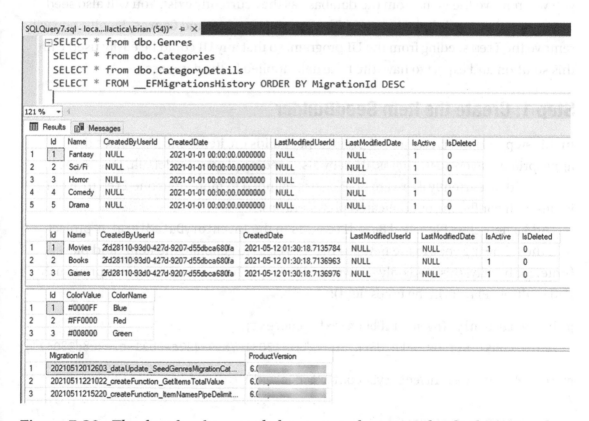

Figure 7-30. *The data has been seeded as expected, proving that both approaches work to seed data, and the migrations can be run using the data migrator project*

If for some reason you don't see categories and details, ensure you included
the lines of code var categories = new BuildCategories(context);
and categories.ExecuteSeed() in the ExecuteCustomSeed method in the
Program.cs of the InventoryDataMigrator.

Task 6: Seed the Players and Items data

Now that the data is in place for the categories and genres, it's time to rework the items.
In this task, you will build another seed builder class to generate the items. Additionally,
you will remove the items from the database as they currently exist. You will also seed
Players and correctly link Items and Players, Categories, and Genres. Finally, you will
remove the Item seeding from the UI program, so that any UI could be easily used with
this solution and expect to have the base data applied in the database.

Step 1: Create the Item SeedBuilder

In this step, you will create a seed builder that builds the items and associates the
appropriate Players to the Items, thereby also seeding players by default. Due to the
nature of this, currently there are no Players mapped to more than one Item to avoid
issues with conflicting or duplicated player entries.

Add a new class file called BuildItems.cs in the InventoryDataMigrator project.
Add the following code to the new BuildItems class to generate the items and players
(note, for brevity, this seed only shows one Player per Item, even though we previously
had multiple Players in the notes field):

```
private readonly InventoryDbContext _context;
private const string SEED_USER_ID = "31412031-7859-429c-ab21-c2e3e8d98042";

public BuildItems(InventoryDbContext context)
{
    _context = context;
}

public void ExecuteSeed()
{
    if (_context.Items.Count() == 0)
```

```csharp
{
    _context.Items.AddRange(
        new Item() { Name = "Batman Begins", CurrentOrFinalPrice =
        9.99m, Description = "You either die the hero or live long
        enough to see yourself become the villain",
                    IsOnSale = false, Notes = "", PurchasePrice =
                    23.99m, PurchasedDate = null, Quantity = 1000,
                    SoldDate = null, CreatedByUserId = SEED_USER_ID,
                    CreatedDate = DateTime.Now,
                    IsDeleted = false, IsActive = true, Players = new
                    List<Player>() {
                        new Player() { CreatedDate = DateTime.
                        Now,IsActive = true,IsDeleted =
                        false,CreatedByUserId = SEED_USER_ID,
                                        Description = "https://www.
                                        imdb.com/name/nm0000288/",Name
                                        = "Christian Bale"}
                    }
        },
        new Item() { Name = "Inception", CurrentOrFinalPrice = 7.99m,
        Description = "You mustn't be afraid to dream a little bigger,
        darling",
                    IsOnSale = false, Notes = "", PurchasePrice =
                    4.99m, PurchasedDate = null, Quantity = 1000,
                    SoldDate = null, CreatedByUserId = SEED_USER_ID,
                    CreatedDate = DateTime.Now,
                    IsDeleted = false, IsActive = true, Players = new
                    List<Player>() {
                        new Player() { CreatedDate = DateTime.
                        Now,IsActive = true,IsDeleted =
                        false,CreatedByUserId = SEED_USER_ID,
                                        Description = "https://www.
                                        imdb.com/name/nm0000138/",Name
                                        = "Leonardo DiCaprio"}
                    }
        },
```

```
    new Item() { Name = "Remember the Titans", CurrentOrFinalPrice
    = 3.99m, Description = "Left Side, Strong Side",
            IsOnSale = false, Notes = "", PurchasePrice =
            7.99m, PurchasedDate = null, Quantity = 1000,
            SoldDate = null, CreatedByUserId = SEED_USER_ID,
            CreatedDate = DateTime.Now,
            IsDeleted = false, IsActive = true, Players = new
            List<Player>() {
                new Player() { CreatedDate = DateTime.
                Now,IsActive = true,IsDeleted =
                false,CreatedByUserId = SEED_USER_ID,
                            Description = "https://www.
                            imdb.com/name/nm0000243/",Name
                            = "Denzel Washington"}
            }
    },
    new Item() { Name = "Star Wars: The Empire Strikes Back",
    CurrentOrFinalPrice = 19.99m, Description = "He will join us or
    die, master",
            IsOnSale = false, Notes = "", PurchasePrice =
            35.99m, PurchasedDate = null, Quantity = 1000,
            SoldDate = null, CreatedByUserId = SEED_USER_ID,
            CreatedDate = DateTime.Now,
            IsDeleted = false, IsActive = true, Players = new
            List<Player>() {
                new Player() { CreatedDate = DateTime.
                Now,IsActive = true,IsDeleted =
                false,CreatedByUserId = SEED_USER_ID,
                            Description = "https://www.
                            imdb.com/name/nm0000434/",Name
                            = "Mark Hamill"}
            }
    },
```

```
        new Item() { Name = "Top Gun", CurrentOrFinalPrice = 6.99m,
        Description = "I feel the need, the need for speed!",
                    IsOnSale = false, Notes = "", PurchasePrice =
                    8.99m, PurchasedDate = null, Quantity = 1000,
                    SoldDate = null, CreatedByUserId = SEED_USER_ID,
                    CreatedDate = DateTime.Now,
                    IsDeleted = false, IsActive = true, Players = new
                    List<Player>() {
                        new Player() { CreatedDate = DateTime.
                        Now,IsActive = true,IsDeleted =
                        false,CreatedByUserId = SEED_USER_ID,
                                    Description = "https://www.
                                    imdb.com/name/nm0000129/",Name
                                    = "Tom Cruise"}

                    }
                }
            );

        _context.SaveChanges();
    }
}
```

Step 2: Seed the Items and Players

In this step, you will seed the Items and Players. To do this, add a line of code to the
ExecuteCustomSeedData method in the Program.cs file of the InventoryDataMigrator
project as follows:

```
var items = new BuildItems(context);
items.ExecuteSeed();
```

Before you can run this code, you need to clean a couple of things up. First, you need
to delete all the existing items from the table. Use the following T-SQL code in a new
query window in SSMS to wipe the Items and ItemPlayers tables clean:

```
DELETE FROM ItemPlayers; DELETE FROM Items;
```

Review the database to ensure your items are clear. Also note that the Players table was never defined in the DbContext or directly defined in the FluentAPI, so it is likely called Player in your database. Make sure you currently have no players listed in that table as well. Use the T-SQL statement DELETE FROM Player to wipe out any entries in the table.

With the lines of code in place, use the Start New Instance in the Debug menu for the InventoryDataMigrator as described earlier to run the additional seed. This should build and run with no issues or output, so just close the window when it completes.

Run the following T-SQL commands to ensure your data is seeded as expected:

```
SELECT * FROM Items
SELECT * FROM ItemPlayers
SELECT * FROM Player
```

Your results should be similar to Figure 7-31.

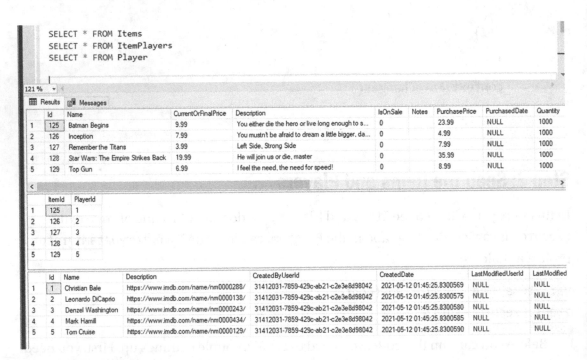

Figure 7-31. *The data is seeded as expected for Items and Players*

Step 3: Remove the calls to EnsureItems, UpdateItems, and DeleteAllItems methods from the Main method code in the EFCore_Activity0702 project

Now that you have seeded Items and Players, as well as Genres, Categories, and CategoryDetails, you need to make sure running the program will not try to create more items.

Return to Program.cs in the main activity project and remove the calls for EnsureItems, UpdateItems, and DeleteAllItems from the Main method, and then comment out their respective methods as well (or remove them). You will not need them and/or you will be building a better solution to manage this through the rest of the book. What remains should be a number of Get and/or List methods.

Run the program to ensure there are no errors and that you still see data. For now, you are not going to modify these methods any further. You will take care of that as you learn about LINQ in the next couple of chapters. Output from your solution should be similar to what is shown in Figure 7-32.

```
Microsoft Visual Studio Debug Console
New Item: Batman Begins
New Item: Inception
New Item: Remember the Titans
New Item: Star Wars: The Empire Strikes Back
New Item: Top Gun
ITEM Batman Begins] You either die the hero or live long enough to see yourself become the villain
ITEM Inception] You mustn't be afraid to dream a little bigger, darling
ITEM Remember the Titans] Left Side, Strong Side
ITEM Star Wars: The Empire Strikes Back] He will join us or die, master
ITEM Top Gun] I feel the need, the need for speed!
All active Items: Batman Begins|Inception|Remember the Titans|Star Wars: The Empire Strikes Back|Top Gun
New Item] 125      |Batman Begins                          |1000|23990.00
New Item] 126      |Inception                              |1000|4990.00
New Item] 127      |Remember the Titans                    |1000|7990.00
New Item] 128      |Star Wars: The Empire Strikes Back     |1000|35990.00
New Item] 129      |Top Gun                                |1000|8990.00

C:\APressEntityFramework\Code\EFCore_Activity0702\EFCore_Activity0702\bin\Debug\net6.0\EFCore_Activity0702.
12012) exited with code 0.
To automatically close the console when debugging stops, enable Tools->Options->Debugging->Automatically cl
le when debugging stops.
Press any key to close this window . . .
```

Figure 7-32. *The program runs as expected, and the data that was seeded via the FluentAPI and the InventoryDataMigrator project is available*

Activity 7-2 summary

In this activity, you learned how to roll your own database migrator project that allowed you to build custom seeds for your data solutions. You also learned how to build both table-valued and inline functions and use migrations to get them into the database, as well as code to execute the functions directly. Finally, you learned about seeding data via the Fluent API, and you also learned how to use the Fluent API to map an entity as a function without a key value so that it would not be migrated as a table into the database when using a DTO to gather the data results from execution of the function.

Activity 7-3: Working with views

In this final activity for the chapter, you will be creating and using a view. Utilizing similar methods as earlier, you will migrate the view as a new script and then use the Fluent API to map a DTO object for results from the view for use in your code.

Task 0: Getting started

As with most activities at this point, to get started with this activity, either continue using the code you have built to this point or grab a copy of the starter files EFCore_ Activity07-3_StarterFiles and use them. If you use the starter files, as usual, refer to Appendix A for more information on working with starter files.

Additionally, if you are using the starter files for this project, you will also want to run the InventoryDataMigrator project before proceeding to ensure seed data is in place that was created in Activity 7-2.

Task 1: Create the view

In this task, you will create the view. This view will give full information about Item, including any category, genre, and player information that is associated to the item.

Before getting started, also note that I've removed all commented code from the previous activity to clean up the Main method in the EFCore_Activity0703 project.

Step 1: Write the script

Ordinarily, you would take the time to write the script and test it in SSMS (you may still do this). For brevity, you will simply add the script into the project and then migrate it for this activity. Feel free to test the script on your own in SSMS before applying the changes if you desire.

To start, add a new folder under the `Migrations/Scripts` folder in the `EFCore_` `DBLibrary` project called `Views`. In the Views folder, create a new folder for the view called `FullItemDetails`. Once you have the new folder, add a file `FullItemDetails.` `v0.sql` and then ensure that you have added the file as an embedded resource. Review Figure 7-33 for clarity.

Figure 7-33. *The new view is scripted and nested in folders as an embedded resource as expected*

Once you have the file in place, add the following code to script the new view (also shown in Figure 7-33):

```
CREATE OR ALTER VIEW [dbo].[vwFullItemDetails]
AS
SELECT item.Id, item.[Name] ItemName, item.[Description] ItemDescription
        , item.IsActive, item.IsDeleted, item.Notes, item.
        CurrentOrFinalPrice
        , item.IsOnSale, item.PurchasedDate, item.PurchasePrice, item.
        Quantity
        , item.SoldDate, cat.[Name] Category, cat.IsActive
        CategoryIsActive
        , cat.IsDeleted CategoryIsDeleted, catDetail.ColorName,
        catDetail.ColorValue
        , player.[Name] PlayerName, player.[Description]
        PlayerDescription
```

```
    , player.IsActive PlayerIsActive, player.IsDeleted
    PlayerIsDeleted
    , genre.[Name] GenreName, genre.[IsActive] GenreIsActive,
    genre.IsDeleted GenreIsDeleted
FROM Items item
LEFT JOIN Categories cat on item.CategoryId = cat.id
LEFT JOIN CategoryDetails catDetail on cat.Id = catDetail.Id
LEFT JOIN ItemPlayers ip on item.Id = ip.ItemId
LEFT JOIN Player player on ip.PlayerId = player.Id
LEFT JOIN ItemGenres ig on item.id = ig.ItemId
LEFT JOIN Genres genre on ig.GenreId = genre.Id
```

Step 2: Add the new migration and update the database

Now that the script is in place, add a new migration by ensuring you have the EFCore_
DBLibrary project selected in the PMC and then running the command add-migration
createView_FullItemDetails. In the Up method, place the following code (don't
forget to bring in the using EFCore_DBLibrary.Migrations.Scripts statement so the
SqlResource extension will work):

```
migrationBuilder.SqlResource("EFCore_DBLibrary.Migrations.Scripts.Views.
FullItemDetails.FullItemDetails.v0.sql");
```

Then place the following code in the Down method:

```
migrationBuilder.Sql("DROP VIEW IF EXISTS [dbo].vwFullItemDetails");
```

And once you have the code in place, update the database by running the update-
database command.

Step 3: Validate the view was created and works

After the update-database command has completed, open SSMS and refresh the
database, and then review the Views folder to see your new view that was created. Once
you've validated that the view is there, run a simple T-SQL statement to prove the data
works and that you can easily order it as follows:

```
SELECT * FROM [dbo].[vwFullItemDetails]
ORDER BY ItemName, GenreName, Category, PlayerName
```

The result of running this query should look similar to what is shown here in Figure 7-34.

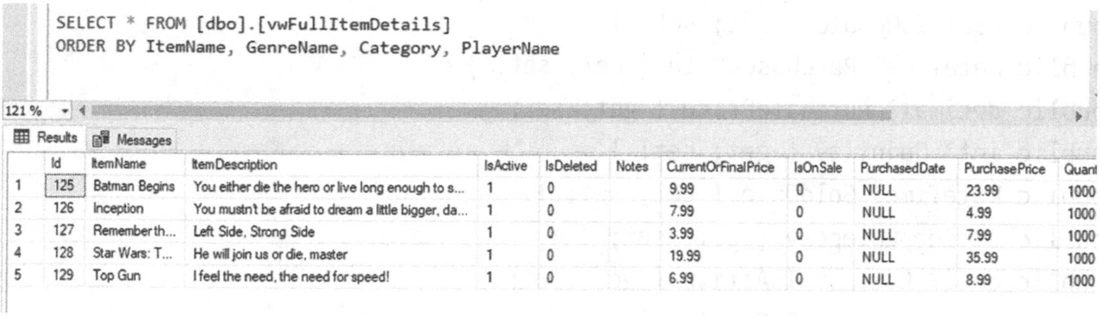

```
SELECT * FROM [dbo].[vwFullItemDetails]
ORDER BY ItemName, GenreName, Category, PlayerName
```

	Id	ItemName	ItemDescription	IsActive	IsDeleted	Notes	CurrentOrFinalPrice	IsOnSale	PurchasedDate	PurchasePrice	Quant
1	125	Batman Begins	You either die the hero or live long enough to s...	1	0		9.99	0	NULL	23.99	1000
2	126	Inception	You mustn't be afraid to dream a little bigger, da...	1	0		7.99	0	NULL	4.99	1000
3	127	Remember th...	Left Side, Strong Side	1	0		3.99	0	NULL	7.99	1000
4	128	Star Wars: T...	He will join us or die, master	1	0		19.99	0	NULL	35.99	1000
5	129	Top Gun	I feel the need, the need for speed!	1	0		6.99	0	NULL	8.99	1000

Figure 7-34. *The view data is easily returned and ordered*

Do not be alarmed if your Ids are different – that is just fine. Additionally, if you scroll right in the results, you will likely see that there are a lot of null columns for Categories and Genres. This is because you have never associated categories and genres to the Items, even though data exists and it could be done at this point. You will build these data relationships when you learn more about working with LINQ in the next chapter.

Task 2: Expose the view data from the UI layer

The final piece of the puzzle is to expose the view data from the UI layer. By now, you should be very familiar with this process, but it's good to practice it one more time.

As with functions, the first thing you will need to do is model the view data into an object for use as an entity. You will then need to add that entity to the DBContext. Finally, you'll use the Fluent API in the OnModelCreating method to ensure the view is treated as a view and not as a table in the database.

Step 1: Create a DTO object to model the view data

In the InventoryModels project, under the DTOs folder, add a new file called FullItemDetailDTO.cs. In the file, add the following code:

```
public int Id { get; set; }
public string ItemName { get; set; }
public string ItemDescription { get; set; }
public bool IsActive { get; set; }
```

```
public bool IsDeleted { get; set; }
public string Notes { get; set; }
public decimal? CurrentOrFinalPrice { get; set; }
public bool IsOnSale { get; set; }
public DateTime? PurchasedDate { get; set; }
public decimal? PurchasePrice { get; set; }
public int? Quantity { get; set; }
public DateTime? SoldDate { get; set; }
public string Category { get; set; }
public bool? CategoryIsActive { get; set; }
public bool? CategoryIsDeleted { get; set; }
public string ColorName { get; set; }
public string ColorValue { get; set; }
public string PlayerName { get; set; }
public string PlayerDescription { get; set; }
public bool? PlayerIsActive { get; set; }
public bool? PlayerIsDeleted { get; set; }
public string GenreName { get; set; }
public bool? GenreIsActive { get; set; }
public bool? GenreIsDeleted { get; set; }
```

Additionally, to follow the standards from other DTO classes, change the class declaration in the file (not the file itself) to public class FullItemDetailDto.

Step 2: Add the DbSet<FullItemDetailDto> to the InventoryDbContext, and update the OnModelCreating method

Return to the InventoryDbContext.cs file in the EFCore_InventoryDB project. Add the following code to create the DbSet following the line of code to create the DbSet for GetItemsTotalValuesDto:

```
public DbSet<FullItemDetailDto> FullItemDetailDtos { get; set;  }
```

With the DbSet in place, scroll down to find the OnModelCreating method, and add the following code to ensure the entity is treated as a view:

```
modelBuilder.Entity<FullItemDetailDto>(x =>
{
    x.HasNoKey();
    x.ToView("FullItemDetailDtos");
});
```

Build the project and run it to ensure there are no errors.

Step 3: Leverage the data from the UI

The final step to prove this is working is to leverage the view from the UI layer.

In the Program.cs file for the activity project, add a new call in the Main method to a new method named GetFullItemDetails. Then add the following code to create the GetFullItemDetails method at the end of the Program class:

```
private static void GetFullItemDetails()
{
    using (var db = new InventoryDbContext(_optionsBuilder.Options))
    {
        var result = db.FullItemDetailDtos
                    .FromSqlRaw("SELECT * FROM [dbo].
                    [vwFullItemDetails] " +
                            "ORDER BY ItemName, GenreName,
                            Category, PlayerName ")
                    .ToList();
        foreach (var item in result)
        {
            Console.WriteLine($"New Item] {item.Id,-10}" +
                            $"|{item.ItemName,-50}" +
                            $"|{item.ItemDescription,-4}" +
                            $"|{item.PlayerName,-5}" +
                            $"|{item.Category,-5}" +
                            $"|{item.GenreName,-5}");
        }
    }
}
```

Once you have the code in place, run the program to see the expected output (review Figure 7-35).

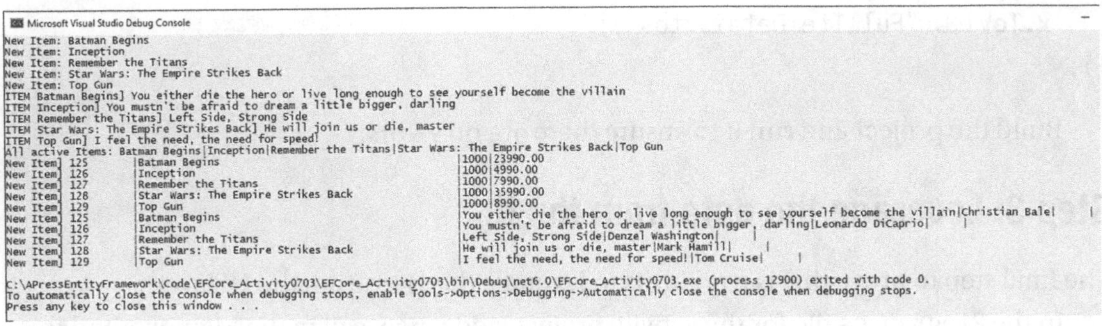

Figure 7-35. *The output for the program includes the results of the view as expected*

Activity 7-3 summary

In this final activity for Chapter 7, you were able to leverage the skills you've learned in the previous two activities to complete the chapter by adding a new view that gets full item details.

As with functions and procedures, you were able to easily add scripts in place to generate the new database object, and then you were able to leverage the new database objects by creating a DTO to map the object result output and add the object to the inventory database context. You then used the Fluent API in the OnModelCreating method to ensure the view was not added to the database as a table. Finally, you were able to add a quick method into the main program to make a call to the view and get results as expected to the UI layer.

Chapter summary

In this chapter, you learned about working with database objects like functions, views, and stored procedures. By using the migrations and applying the scripting paradigm shown in this chapter, you will be able to set yourself and your team up for great success at managing your database in a code-first approach.

The use of the script file makes your life (and your team's life) a lot easier when it comes time to do code reviews or to look through the history of an object to see where code problems or features were introduced.

You also took a deeper look into the Fluent API and how you can use the override of the OnModelCreating method to further define structures in your database. Having data annotations is still a good idea for your models, because it will enforce the client and the server to both ensure relationships are in place and data integrity is maintained. However, using the Fluent API will be something you also want to get familiar with because you will have the ability to do more fine-grained tuning on your objects using the Fluent API.

The chapter concluded with three activities that gave you a practical example of each of these concepts.

Important takeaways

After working through this chapter, the things you should be in command of are

- Using migrations for creating and updating stored procedures

- Using migrations for creating and updating functions

- Using migrations for creating and updating views

- Leveraging an override to the OnModelCreating method to enhance your database with the FluentAPI

- Working with DTO objects to model result output data

- An approach to creating some seed data from the Fluent API

- An approach to enforce migrations and run custom seed methods from a new custom project

Closing thoughts

In this chapter, you have spent a lot of time learning about how to work with database objects. You've covered how to work with functions, views, and stored procedures. You also dove into creating seed data and handling migrations from the *Fluent API* and from your own custom solution.

In the next chapter, you'll take your first look into working with LINQ to do some sorting, filtering, and paging of results from your database.

CHAPTER 8

Sorting, Filtering, and Paging

In this chapter, you're going to build on what you've learned in the previous seven chapters. Up to this point, you have created a database using the code-first approach, and now you are ready to start working with the data in a more robust fashion. In other words, since the database structure is in place, now it's time to learn how to leverage it for enterprise applications.

It's time to learn LINQ

Now that the inventory manager data is modeled and you have the `InventoryDBContext` in place to get the data, it's time to start learning and working with *LINQ* in your solutions. To be clear, LINQ exists outside of *Entity Framework*, with options like *LINQ to Objects*, *LINQ to XML*, and even *LINQ to ADO.Net*, so don't make the mistake of thinking that *LINQ* is just for working with the *Entity Framework*. For the work in this book, you're going to focus on *LINQ to Entities*, which allows you to work against *EF* with *LINQ*. Before you move on, however, you must first address the elephant in the room. Perhaps you've heard in the past that LINQ is not performant. The first thing to understand is that this is simply not true.

LINQ is generally not the problem

One of the most prevalent misconceptions about working with LINQ and EF is that using LINQ is slow and bulky. Additionally, many developers have struggled with some of the concepts around making LINQ performant. To answer the question, yes, absolutely, LINQ is highly performant. The real problem is not LINQ per se. The real problem exists with the way LINQ is implemented by the developer. As with any programming language, if the developer doesn't set things up correctly, the language cannot do its best work.

© Brian L. Gorman 2022
B. L. Gorman, *Practical Entity Framework Core 6*, https://doi.org/10.1007/978-1-4842-7301-2_8

Use a profiler or another tool

There are some instances where you can instantly find and fix issues with your queries. In other cases, you might be receiving complaints from users about pages taking too long to load, but you didn't even know there was a performance issue because you never tested a particular feature under load or with a database that potentially has millions of records to search. To make sure that your code is not causing problems, it's critical to have some sort of tool that helps you trace through execution and identify bottlenecks as they happen.

There are many tools available for this specific reason, with the most popular tool being the *Entity Framework Profiler*. The *Entity Framework Profiler* is a solid tool for determining execution bottlenecks and other issues with your code, but using it requires purchasing a license.

When working with web solutions, there is another alternative that I highly recommend called *Stackify Prefix*. Using the free version of prefix does require installing a program on your machine, and at the time of this writing, the free version of *Prefix* only works for web solutions. In order to use *Prefix* to work against non-web solutions, you would need to upgrade to the paid version of the program.

Another tool that any developer can use is the *SQL Server Profiler*, which you can easily turn on in SSMS to monitor calls as they happen against your database. The profiler tool is also great for seeing what is going on with our database calls. The main drawback with this tool is that the *SQL Server Profiler* can be a bit chatty without configuration. Additionally, to get the filters set correctly so that the tool can be used well takes a decent amount of practice. For learning purposes, you'll be using this tool in the activities for this book, but I highly encourage you to check out the other available tools as well as you have time.

Issues and solutions

In order to make sure you don't fall into some of the more common incorrect implementations, you'll first examine a few statements and then examine the problems they have, as well as the way to correctly implement the code.

Issue #1: Pre-fetching results and then iterating in code to filter the results

There are a number of things that *Entity Framework* does well. One of the things that *EF* handles well is *lazy loading* results as needed. Lazy loading is essentially the art of getting the data just in time, without pulling all the data until needed.

A great example of where this takes place is when you build out queries to get data into a list. The data from the query is only pulled when the query is executed. This is why when you are debugging an application, you might have seen statements like *"Expanding the results view will enumerate the IEnumerable"* when debugging database calls. The expansion forces the execution because the loading hasn't happened since it previously was not needed.

Because of this implementation and the misconceptions around it, one of the most prevalent issues when working with *Entity Framework* is causing these executions to take place and then doing more work against the data that should have been done before the execution took place.

You can think of it like this. If you are going to paint a room, you know you are going to need paint brushes and paint. You have three choices as to how you approach the task. The first is just to get a bunch of stuff, even if you won't need it. The second is to do lazy loading and third is eager loading.

First, you could go to the store and buy a whole bunch of supplies, brushes, and many gallons of paint and primer; bring them all home; and start the project. In the end, you likely have a lot of waste, because you bought a ton of materials without thinking about what you really needed. This is the opposite of lazy loading and is generally expensive, because with all of the materials, you have to put them somewhere and sort through them to get what you really need.

The second way you could do this is make a trip to the store and get a couple gallons of paint and primer and a couple of brushes and then come home and start working. When you are ready, you make another trip to the store to get some paint and maybe some extra brushes and tape because you realized you needed to block off a window and your current brushes were too big to do the fine details you needed. This approach is similar to lazy loading.

A final way you could approach the problem is to first measure the room, then make a list of all of the materials you need, then go to the store, and bring home only what you need. In this approach, you don't get as much waste, because you only bought and brought home what you needed. You also might anticipate a bit of what you will need along with the predicted materials, so you might also bring that along. When you get home, you have less to sort through and generally only have the materials you need. This approach is similar to a concept that is called eager loading.

As it applies to database programming, consider the following statement:

```
var query = db.Person.ToList().OrderByDescending(x => x.LastName);
```

as compared to

```
var query = db.Person.OrderByDescending(x => x.LastName);
```

Then, use either query in code to get the first ten:

```
var result = query.Take(10);
foreach (var person in result)
```

In the first example, the call to get the result `ToList` will first bring back all the results in the table and then iterate those results to sort on all of the table rows in memory on the application side. Whereas in the second query, the deferred execution allows for the query to apply the transformations prior to the execution, thereby only needing to work with the limited results. As would be expected, the second query can perform much better in most situations, since the database performs the sorting and the result set is limited to ten records vs. the entire list.

Issue #2: Not disconnecting your data

If you've worked through the activities in the preceding chapters, you've already seen a few queries in your work to this point that fetched data for display. In those queries, you did something like `<DBContext>.<Entity>.ToList()`, where you got a list of the objects in the database. What you maybe didn't know at the time is that each one of these entities in the result set has change tracking enabled. Change tracking allows the `DBContext` to track the changes that have happened, so that you can perform any updates and save changes back to the database.

If the only thing you are going to do with your data is render it for review, there is no need to track the changes. Additionally, if you are working in a stateless environment like the Web, when you are going to perform an update, you likely will retrieve the data to be updated again before massaging that data with the appropriate updates. Consider the following code again, as it could be used to get a list of Person objects and display those people on a grid for review:

```
var query = db.Person.OrderByDescending(x => x.LastName);
var result = query.Take(10);

foreach (var person in result)
```

The user would likely then select one of the Person objects to modify and then make their changes and post that data back to the controller, where the controller would then retrieve the Person by Id, update the fields, and then save the changes.

In this and similar scenarios, the first call could have been done in a disconnected fashion, as is shown here:

```
var query = db.Person.AsNoTracking().OrderByDescending(x => x.LastName);
var result = query.Take(10);

foreach (var person in result)
```

It is even possible to set your *Entity Framework* DBContext so that all of your requests are set to operate without change tracking by default. This can be accomplished by adding the following statement to the DBContext constructor:

```
ChangeTracker.QueryTrackingBehavior = QueryTrackingBehavior.NoTracking;
```

The main advantage of working with a disconnected result set is that it will be more performant with less overhead since the application is no longer tracking changes against that result set.

A final thought about tracking and disconnected results is that any query that uses a projection to a DTO or an anonymous class will also not be tracking an entity, since no entity exists for that DTO or anonymous class. You'll be taking a deeper look at using DTOs and anonymous classes when you look into the concept of LINQ with projections in the next chapter.

Issue #3: IEnumerable vs. IQueryable

Which object type should you use when creating our queries and why? There are many to choose from. In most queries, the end result is a collection of objects, which are often rendered as a List<T>. As you already saw in Issue #1, it's not always ideal to get the results into a `List<T>`. This issue is really the same as getting items into a list too early in the process, but by understanding the differences here, you can gain a very good understanding of how to write the best code when working with EF.

To go deeply into the difference between `IEnumerable` and `IQueryable`, the main differences come down to when and where the code is executed. Is query execution on the server side or in memory? What about filtering, sorting, limiting, and/or transforming that data? These questions are the most critical concerns you should have when determining performance of your query. Table 8-1 shows how each of these object types handles queries and filtering.

Table 8-1. *IEnumerable vs. IQueryable and how they each handle queries and filtering*

	IEnumerable	IQueryable
Initial query	Server side	Server side
Filtering	Client side	Server side

Looking at the table and based on everything discussed to this point in the chapter, it should be clear by now that lazy loading with deferred execution can generally allow for your queries to be more performant, as well as limit your results to only include the objects that you need in scope.

The fact that the `IEnumerable` object requires pulling data at the onset means that lazy loading is off the table when using an `IEnumerable` object, such as a `List<T>`. The `IQueryable` object, however, allows for building out your entire query, with filters, and then, on execution, you end up only pulling the exact data that is needed into memory.

Practical application

In the next part of the chapter, you're going to be working with LINQ to build out some real-world queries that require filtering, paging, and sorting. As you do this, you'll take a look at ways that work that aren't as efficient as possible, and then you'll fix the queries so that you have a full command of how to write the most efficient queries you need to accomplish the task at hand.

Activity 8-1: Sorting, paging, and filtering

In this activity, you're going to use LINQ to build out robust and efficient queries for use in your applications.

In most applications, there is some requirement to display a grid or list of objects that contains the data for each of the objects. Additionally, the application generally provides the user an ability to sort the items and enter a text-based search for items that match and provides the ability to page through results.

As you've read earlier, the options are that you can either get all the results at once and then filter them in memory or pull only the data you need to display at the current time and perhaps rely on lazy loading to get additional data as needed. Depending on what you are trying to accomplish, there are advantages and disadvantages in each approach to consider. As always, as the developer, it will be up to you to make the correct choice.

For the Chapter 8 activity, you could take some time and build out your entire Items database with lots of records. Please feel free to do that if you'd rather continue working with your Items database. However, in the interest of time and to help illuminate the ramifications of non-performant queries, the Chapter 8 activity will point to your previously installed instance of the AdventureWorks database, which is loaded with many records and can help to further illustrate the efficiency of different approaches to getting data with LINQ.

If for some reason you don't have AdventureWorks installed, for more information, you could refer back to the Chapter 2 activity, which walked through restoring a backup of the AdventureWorks database.

Task 0: Getting started

For this activity, it would be easiest to just grab a copy of the starter files, EFCore_ Activity08-1_StarterFiles, especially if you didn't work through the activity at the end of Chapter 3. If you did work through Activity 3-1, you may also feel free to use the files from the end of that solution. For this activity, the code is working against the *AdventureWorks* database. As such, you will not be doing any migrations, but you should ensure that your connection string is correct and that the files run before you get started with the tasks for this activity. For more information on working with the starter files, refer to Appendix A.

If, for some reason, you'd rather just create the starter pack yourself, you can easily do so. There isn't much to it. Simply implement the following instructions:

1. Create a new .Net Core console project for .Net 6 called something like `Activity0801`.

2. Find the `EFCore_DbLibrary` project folder from the end of Chapter 3, Activity 1 (you could use the final files version if you don't have your own), copy it to your local solution directory, and add a reference to the project in your new activity project.

3. Find the `InventoryHelpers` project folder from any of the Chapter 7 projects, copy it to your local solution directory, and add a project reference to it in the activity project.

4. Add the `appsettings.json` file from the Activity 3-1 project into the main activity project to contain the `AdventureWorks` database connection string, and then edit the connection string to connect to your local version of `AdventureWorks` as needed. Don't forget to mark the file as content with the action "Copy if newer."

5. Install each of the NuGet packages individually using the Manage NuGet Packages for Solution dialog:

    a. `Microsoft.EntityFrameworkCore`

    b. `Microsoft.EntityFrameworkCore.Design`

    c. `Microsoft.EntityFrameworkCore.SqlServer`

    d. `Microsoft.Extensions.Configuration.FileExtensions`

    e. `Microsoft.Extensions.Configuration`

    f. `Microsoft.Extensions.Configuration.FileExtensions`

    g. `Microsoft.Extensions.Configuration.Json`

Note   Make sure your versions match across all projects. For example, if some time has passed since you worked on Chapter 3, you may need to update `EFCore_DBLibrary` packages to a newer version.

---

6. Add the code that follows into the `Program.cs` class in the main activity project, add any missing using statements, and then run the project to validate you have no errors:

```
private static IConfigurationRoot _configuration;
private static DbContextOptionsBuilder<AdventureWorksContext> _optionsBuilder;

static void Main(string[] args)
{
    BuildOptions();
}

static void BuildOptions()
{
    _configuration = ConfigurationBuilderSingleton.ConfigurationRoot;
    _optionsBuilder = new DbContextOptionsBuilder<AdventureWorksContext>();
    _optionsBuilder.UseSqlServer(_configuration.GetConnectionString("
    AdventureWorks"));
}
```

Task 1: Compare the execution efficiency of two queries

To begin this activity, start by looking at the execution of two queries that will garner the exact same results. This will give you a chance to see the difference in how queries are applied during execution.

Step 1: Create two new methods to house the different queries

In this step, you will create two new methods in the `Program.cs` file for the activity project. The first method will be called `ListPeopleThenOrderAndTake`. The second method will be called `QueryPeopleOrderedToListAndTake`.

Add the following code to the Main method to call the two new methods:

```
Console.WriteLine("List People Then Order and Take");
ListPeopleThenOrderAndTake();
Console.WriteLine("Query People, order, then list and take");
QueryPeopleOrderedToListAndTake();
```

With the new code in place, add the following code to implement the two new methods:

```
private static void ListPeopleThenOrderAndTake()
{
    using (var db = new AdventureWorksContext(_optionsBuilder.Options))
    {
        var people = db.People.ToList().OrderByDescending(x => x.LastName);
        foreach (var person in people.Take(10))
        {
            Console.WriteLine($"{person.FirstName} {person.LastName}");
        }
    }
}

private static void QueryPeopleOrderedToListAndTake()
{
    using (var db = new AdventureWorksContext(_optionsBuilder.Options))
    {
        var query = db.People.OrderByDescending(x => x.LastName);
        var result = query.Take(10);

        foreach (var person in result)
        {
            Console.WriteLine($"{person.FirstName} {person.LastName}");
        }
    }
}
```

Don't forget to bring in any using statements to ensure the code will build as expected, if any using statements are missing from your solution.

Run the program to see the results. They should look similar to what is shown in Figure 8-1.

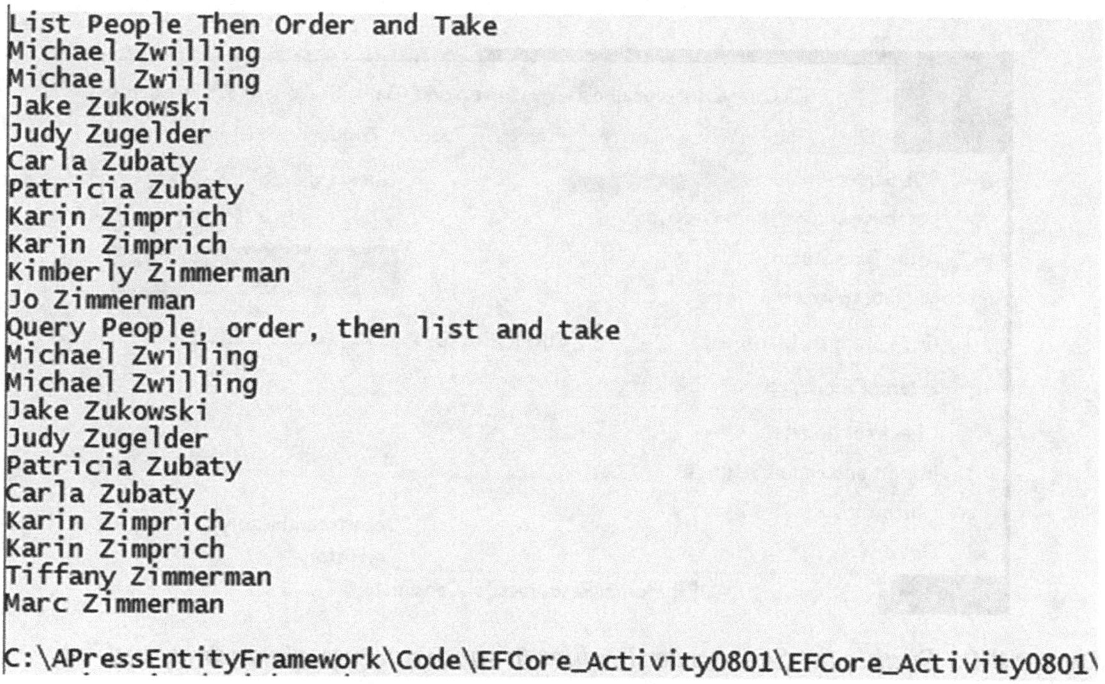

```
List People Then Order and Take
Michael Zwilling
Michael Zwilling
Jake Zukowski
Judy Zugelder
Carla Zubaty
Patricia Zubaty
Karin Zimprich
Karin Zimprich
Kimberly Zimmerman
Jo Zimmerman
Query People, order, then list and take
Michael Zwilling
Michael Zwilling
Jake Zukowski
Judy Zugelder
Patricia Zubaty
Carla Zubaty
Karin Zimprich
Karin Zimprich
Tiffany Zimmerman
Marc Zimmerman
C:\APressEntityFramework\Code\EFCore_Activity0801\EFCore_Activity0801\
```

Figure 8-1. *Both methods execute and get the same results*

As you can see, both methods execute and get results. You may also have noticed a long start and then a quick ending, likely due to the performance of the first query.

Step 2: Analyze the two queries with the SQL Query Analyzer

As you've just seen, both queries perform fairly well in these examples, and both return the exact same results. Therefore, you must ask, "Are these two queries equally effective and efficient when it comes to the implementations?"

To find out, you need to perform an analysis. In SSMS, turn on the tool to profile your server calls by going to Tools ➤ SQL Server Profiler. Enabling SQL Server Profiler is highlighted in Figure 8-2 for clarity.

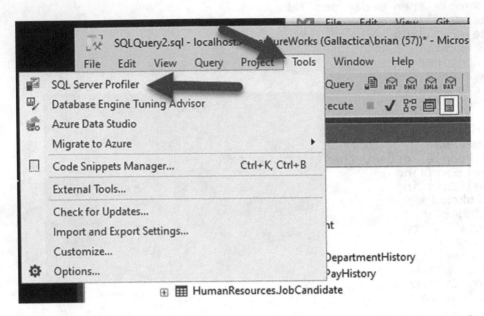

Figure 8-2. *Enable the SQL Server Profiler to show query performance and analysis*

After bringing up the profiler, connect to the database server with whatever database connection you are using for the *AdventureWorks* database. Connecting to a SQLExpress database is shown in Figure 8-3. Make sure to use the correct server based on your implementation.

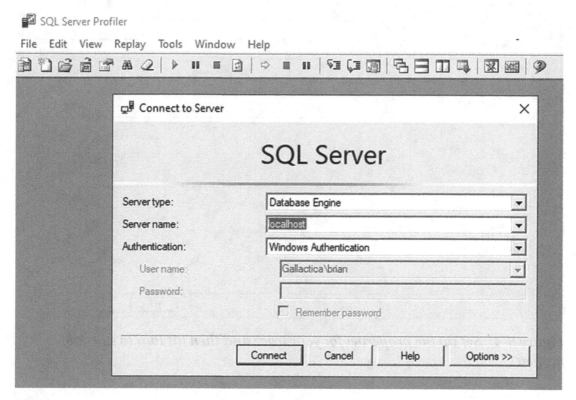

Figure 8-3. *Connect to the database server that hosts the AdventureWorks database*

After connecting, you could name your Trace, or just hit Run. Either way, hit Run to start the trace (see Figure 8-4).

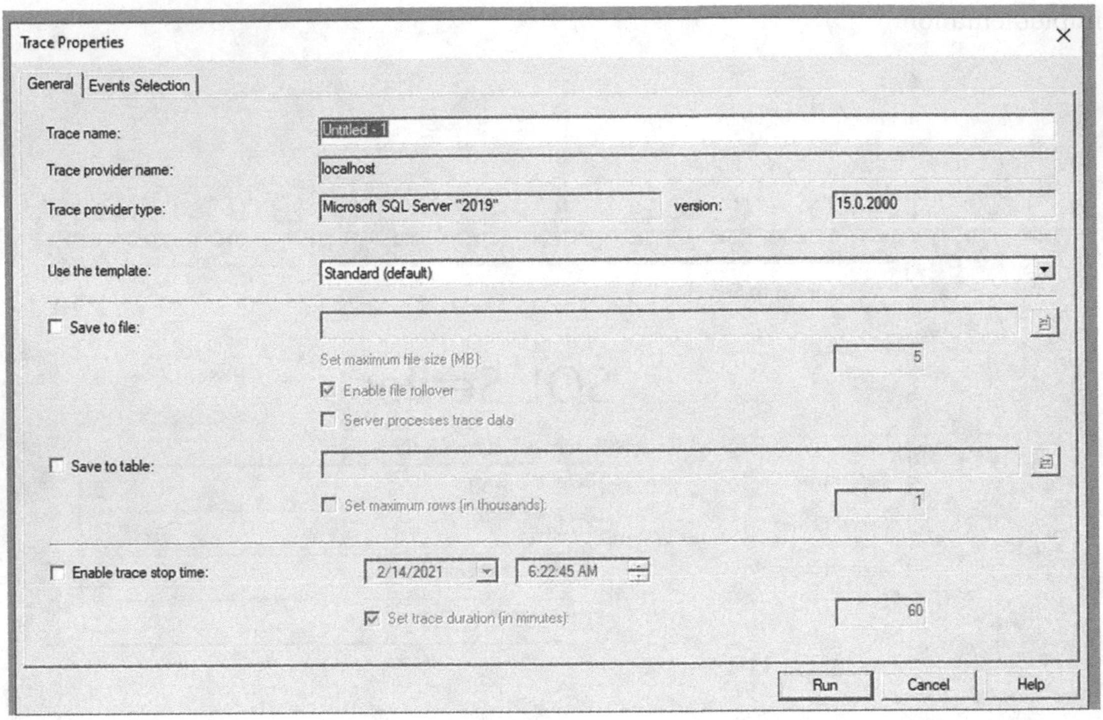

Figure 8-4. *Set up the properties for your trace and then hit Run to start the profiler*

Once the trace is running, you'll see anything that hits your database for operations against the datastore (review Figure 8-5). Note that your results will likely not be exactly as shown.

EventClass	TextData	ApplicationName	NTUserName	LoginName	CPU	Reads	Writ
ExistingConnection	-- network protocol: LPC set quoted...	Microsoft SQ...	brian	Gallac...			
ExistingConnection	-- network protocol: LPC set quoted...	Microsoft SQ...	brian	Gallac...			
ExistingConnection	-- network protocol: LPC set quoted...	Microsoft SQ...	brian	Gallac...			
Audit Logout		SQLServerCEIP	SQLTELE...	NT SER...	0	20	
Audit Login	-- network protocol: LPC set quoted...	SQLServerCEIP	SQLTELE...	NT SER...			
SQL:BatchStarting	SET DEADLOCK_PRIORITY -10	SQLServerCEIP	SQLTELE...	NT SER...			
SQL:BatchCompleted	SET DEADLOCK_PRIORITY -10	SQLServerCEIP	SQLTELE...	NT SER...	0	0	
SQL:BatchStarting	SELECT target_data FROM sy...	SQLServerCEIP	SQLTELE...	NT SER...			
SQL:BatchCompleted	SELECT target_data FROM sy...	SQLServerCEIP	SQLTELE...	NT SER...	31	0	
Audit Logout		SQLServerCEIP	SQLTELE...	NT SER...	31	0	
RPC:Completed	exec sp_reset_connection	SQLServerCEIP	SQLTELE...	NT SER...	0	0	
Audit Login	-- network protocol: LPC set quoted...	SQLServerCEIP	SQLTELE...	NT SER...			
SQL:BatchStarting	SET DEADLOCK_PRIORITY -10	SQLServerCEIP	SQLTELE...	NT SER...			
SQL:BatchCompleted	SET DEADLOCK_PRIORITY -10	SQLServerCEIP	SQLTELE...	NT SER...	0	0	
SQL:BatchStarting	if not exists (select * from sys.dm_...	SQLServerCEIP	SQLTELE...	NT SER...			
SQL:BatchCompleted	if not exists (select * from sys.dm_...	SQLServerCEIP	SQLTELE...	NT SER...	0	20	

```
if not exists (select * from sys.dm_xe_sessions where name = 'telemetry_xevents')
    alter event session telemetry_xevents on server state=start
```

Figure 8-5. *The trace is running, and all telemetry from the database is shown*

At any point, you can clear the trace window by hitting the eraser button on the toolbar, shown in Figure 8-6.

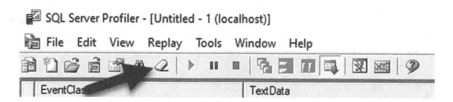

Figure 8-6. *Use the eraser button to clear the trace*

Once you have cleared out your window, go back to the code and place breakpoints on the start of each method and the end of each method. This will help you to easily track the code that is executed in each statement (see Figure 8-7).

Because SQL Server is running, you may get notifications about Locks and Audits periodically in the window. While these can be filtered out, you can always just clear the window before running your code.

```
31        private static void ListPeopleThenOrderAndTake()
32        {
33            using (var db = new AdventureWorksContext(_optionsBuilder.Options))
34            {
35                var people = db.People.ToList().OrderByDescending(x => x.LastName);
36                foreach (var person in people.Take(10))
37                {
38                    Console.WriteLine($"{person.FirstName} {person.LastName}");
39                }
40            }
41        }
42

        1 reference
43        private static void QueryPeopleOrderedToListAndTake()
44        {
45            using (var db = new AdventureWorksContext(_optionsBuilder.Options))
46            {
47                var query = db.People.OrderByDescending(x => x.LastName);
48                var result = query.Take(10);
49
50                foreach (var person in result)
51                {
52                    Console.WriteLine($"{person.FirstName} {person.LastName}");
53                }
54            }
55        }
56
57    }
```

Figure 8-7. *The code with breakpoints, ready for profiling*

Run the code, and make sure to clear the profiler before running the queries. Make sure to review the SQL Server Profiler often to see the queries as you build out this activity. A sample of the output is shown in Figure 8-8.

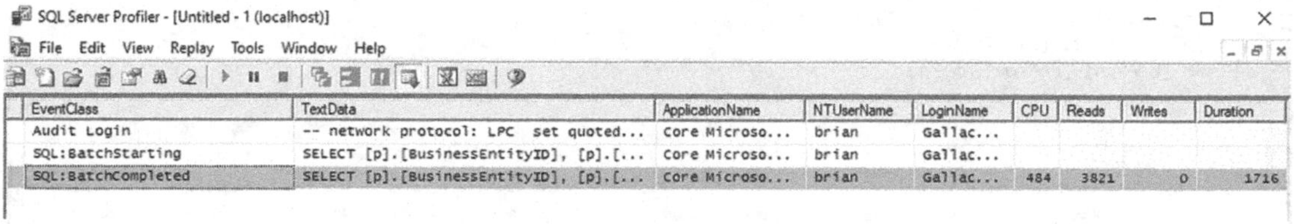

Figure 8-8. *The first query profiled in the SQL Server Profiler*

Here you see the first query as sent to SQL Server for getting results. If you click the query, you can see the direct query in the window below the log. Also note that it looks like the query executed twice. It did not. What you're seeing is the start and end of the batch request. The `BatchCompleted` entry (highlighted earlier) contains the execution time, reads, and other information about the query. Drilling into the entry to get the query text is shown in Figure 8-9.

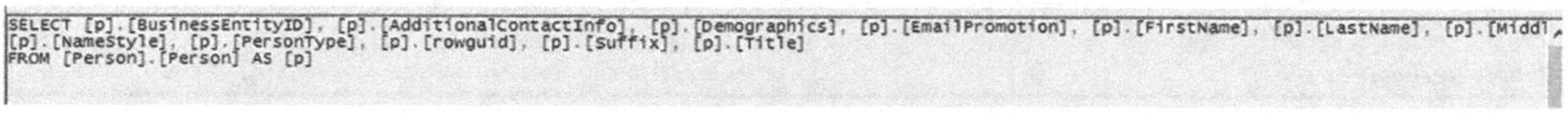

Figure 8-9. *The first query as executed according to the profiler*

While your numbers may be different than mine (i.e., 3821 reads and execution duration of 1716 is unique to my run), your resulting query text should be exactly the same as mine.

Next, execute that query text in our SQL Server with a new query to the database directly to see the results from SSMS.

Right-click your `AdventureWorks` database entry in SSMS and select `New Query` to open a new query window. Copy and paste the query from the profiler into the window. The query should be as follows:

```
SELECT [p].[BusinessEntityID], [p].[AdditionalContactInfo],
[p].[Demographics], [p].[EmailPromotion], [p].[FirstName], [p].[LastName],
[p].[MiddleName], [p].[ModifiedDate], [p].[NameStyle], [p].[PersonType],
[p].[rowguid], [p].[Suffix], [p].[Title]
FROM [Person].[Person] AS [p]
```

Run the query to see the results (as is shown in Figure 8-10).

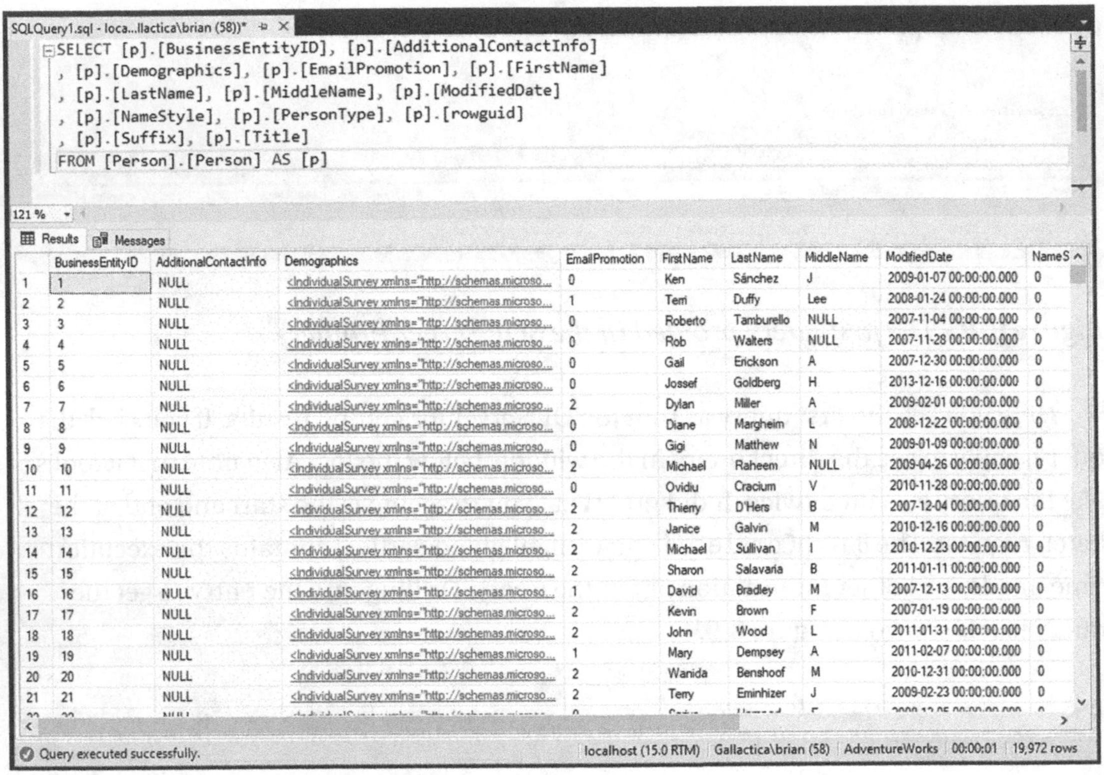

Figure 8-10. *The results of the query are shown in SSMS*

Important notes here, for my query, the execution took about a second and returned nearly 20,000 rows. That's pretty much to be expected when pulling all people into a list.

Another thing that you should do is run your query with the execution plan displayed. By doing this, you will be able to notice any bottlenecks or potential issues with your query.

In SSMS, turn on the profiler using the icon highlighted in Figure 8-11 or by pressing "Ctrl+M" with your focus on an SSMS query.

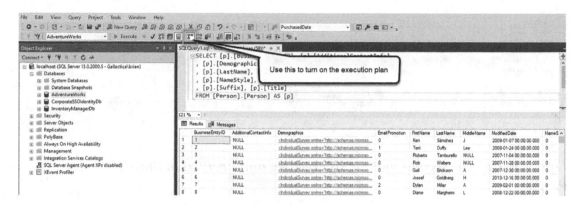

Figure 8-11. *Using the Include Actual Execution Plan in SSMS can help you trace through queries*

Run the same query again, and then review the execution plan (shown in Figure 8-12).

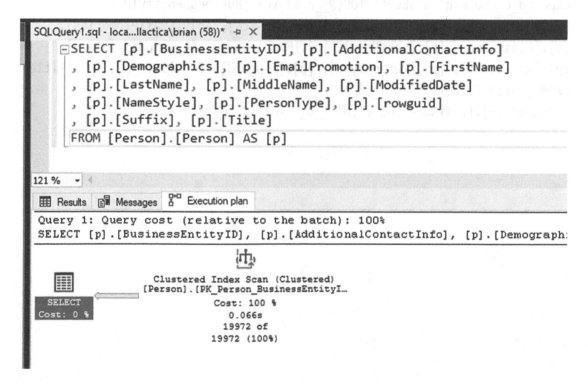

Figure 8-12. *The execution plan shows that only one query is run and it is the entire cost of the overall result*

Clear out the profiler again and continue executing the program code through the second query (review Figure 8-13).

EventClass	TextData	ApplicationName	NTUserName	LoginName	CPU	Reads	Writes	Duration
Audit Logout		Core Microso...	brian	Gallac...	609	3821	0	116443
RPC:Completed	exec sp_reset_connection	Core Microso...	brian	Gallac...	0	0	0	0
Audit Login	-- network protocol: LPC set quoted...	Core Microso...	brian	Gallac...				
RPC:Completed	exec sp_executesql N'SELECT TOP(@__p...	Core Microso...	brian	Gallac...	0	62	0	0
Audit Logout		Core Microso...	brian	Gallac...	0	3883	0	87

```
exec sp_executesql N'SELECT TOP(@__p_0) [p].[BusinessEntityID], [p].[AdditionalContactInfo], [p].[Demographics], [p].[EmailPromotion],
[p].[FirstName], [p].[LastName], [p].[MiddleName], [p].[ModifiedDate], [p].[NameStyle], [p].[PersonType], [p].[rowguid], [p].[Suffix],
[p].[Title]
FROM [Person].[Person] AS [p]
ORDER BY [p].[LastName] DESC',N'@__p_0 int',@__p_0=10
```

Figure 8-13. *The second method as executed and profiled in the SQL Server Profiler*

Running through the second query provides the following in the SQL Server Profiler showing that a stored procedure was executed, and here you have only 62 reads with a duration of 0. Again, your execution times may vary, but your query should be

```
exec sp_executesql N'SELECT TOP(@__p_0) [p].[BusinessEntityID],
[p].[AdditionalContactInfo], [p].[Demographics], [p].[EmailPromotion],
[p].[FirstName], [p].[LastName], [p].[MiddleName], [p].[ModifiedDate],
[p].[NameStyle], [p].[PersonType], [p].[rowguid], [p].[Suffix], [p].[Title]
FROM [Person].[Person] AS [p]
ORDER BY [p].[LastName] DESC',N'@__p_0 int',@__p_0=10
```

Take that code and run it in the SSMS query window to see it perform there as well (as shown in Figure 8-14).

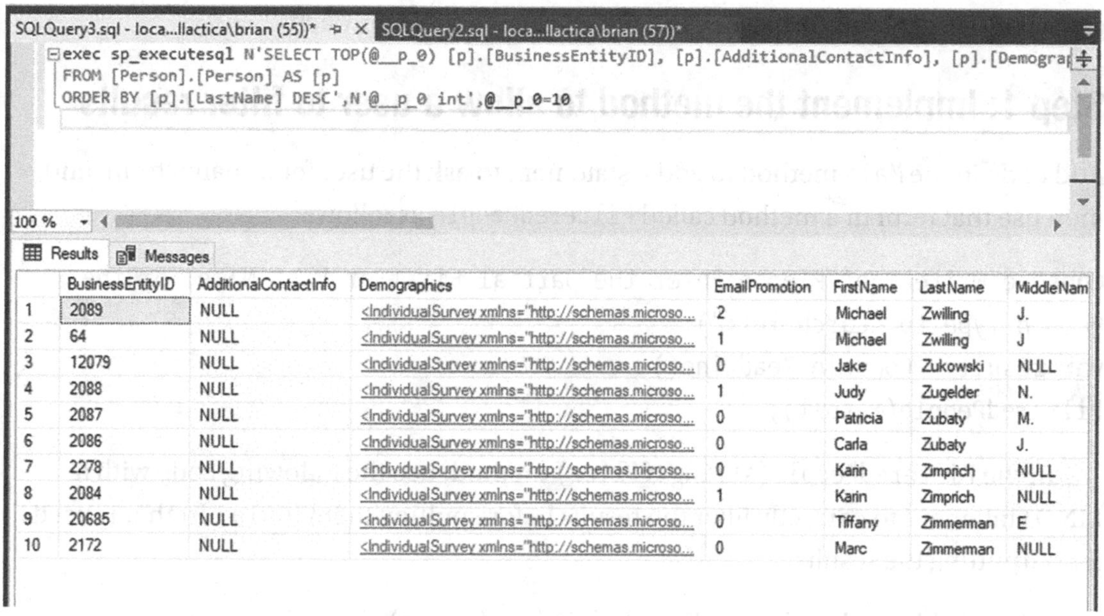

Figure 8-14. *The second query as profiled shows a much better performance, as well as only the results we wanted*

Here you can easily see that only returning the ten results you wanted is much more efficient and will make your front end that much more efficient as well. In addition to the efficiency of the query, the ordering was done for the result set on the server, not in memory, providing the exact results in the order as expected.

Clearly, how you write your queries matters when working with EF. Just getting the results you want does not always mean you are using EF correctly, and just because the first result set was not returned very quickly does not mean that EF is slow. In fact, here you see that some of the stigma about EF being slow may in fact be your own fault and not the fault of EF.

Task 2: Filtering our results

By now, you should know that pulling code into a list before doing sorting and filtering is a bad thing. For that reason, you won't be pulling data into a list until the end of the query in order to make your queries as efficient as possible. If you want to prove it out, however, feel free to repeat a similar test run to what you have done to evaluate the efficiency of the queries in the last task.

As with most things, it will be up to you as the developer to find the correct approach to what your system needs. For this next part, you'll be filtering by partial name or by the Person Type. In your real-world applications, you will likely need to allow the user to give you input to filter results in a manner similar to this approach.

Step 1: Implement the method to allow a user to filter results

Add code in the Main method to add a statement to ask the user for a search term, and then use that term in a method called FilteredPeople as follows:

```
Console.WriteLine("Please Enter the partial First or Last Name, or the
Person Type to search for:");
var result = Console.ReadLine();
FilteredPeople(result);
```

In the FilteredPeople(string filter) method, use the following code with a LINQ statement to correctly filter the results before pulling them into a List that is used for outputting the results:

```
private static void FilteredPeople(string filter)
{
    using (var db = new AdventureWorksContext(_optionsBuilder.Options))
    {
        var searchTerm = filter.ToLower();
        var query = db.People.Where(x => x.LastName.ToLower().
        Contains(searchTerm)

                                    || x.FirstName.ToLower().
                                    Contains(searchTerm)
                                    || x.PersonType.ToLower().
                                    Equals(searchTerm));

        foreach (var person in query)
        {
            Console.WriteLine($"{person.FirstName} {person.LastName},
            {person.PersonType}");
        }
    }
}
```

Now run the code to ensure it works, entering some text to filter, such as 'Gonza' or 'Mich' or 'VC' (review Figure 8-15 to see sample results).

```
Victoria Gonzales, IN
Raymond Gonzalez, IN
Brett Gonzalez, IN
Monica Gonzalez, IN
Emma Gonzales, IN
Cassandra Gonzalez, IN
Gloria Gonzalez, IN
Patricia Gonzalez, IN
Cynthia Gonzalez, IN
Rachel Gonzales, IN
Jasmine Gonzales, IN
Nicole Gonzales, IN
Donald Gonzalez, IN
Joel Gonzalez, IN
Ronald Gonzalez, IN
Phillip Gonzalez, IN
Alyssa Gonzalez, IN
George Gonzalez, IN
Chloe Gonzales, IN
Julia Gonzales, IN
Jennifer Gonzales, IN
Kaitlyn Gonzales, IN
Morgan Gonzales, IN

C:\APressEntityFramework\Code\EFCore_Activity0801\EFCore_Activity0801\
```

Figure 8-15. *Searching for anyone with a partial name match to 'Gonza' produces results as expected*

Step 2: Analyze the query

Grabbing the query from SQL Server Profiler yields the following query that was executed on the server:

```
exec sp_executesql N'SELECT [p].[BusinessEntityID],
[p].[AdditionalContactInfo], [p].[Demographics], [p].[EmailPromotion],
[p].[FirstName], [p].[LastName], [p].[MiddleName], [p].[ModifiedDate],
[p].[NameStyle], [p].[PersonType], [p].[rowguid], [p].[Suffix], [p].[Title]
FROM [Person].[Person] AS [p]
```

```
WHERE (((@__searchTerm_0 LIKE N'''') OR (CHARINDEX(@__searchTerm_0,
LOWER([p].[LastName])) > 0)) OR ((@__searchTerm_0 LIKE N'''') OR
(CHARINDEX(@__searchTerm_0, LOWER([p].[FirstName])) > 0))) OR (LOWER([p].
[PersonType]) = @__searchTerm_0)',N'@__searchTerm_0 nvarchar(50)',
@__searchTerm_0=N'gonza'
```

Further scrutinization of the executed query shows that the query was filtered by lower case letters based on the search term you sent in from the previous query. Running the code shows some 288 results. Figure 8-16 shows the query with results.

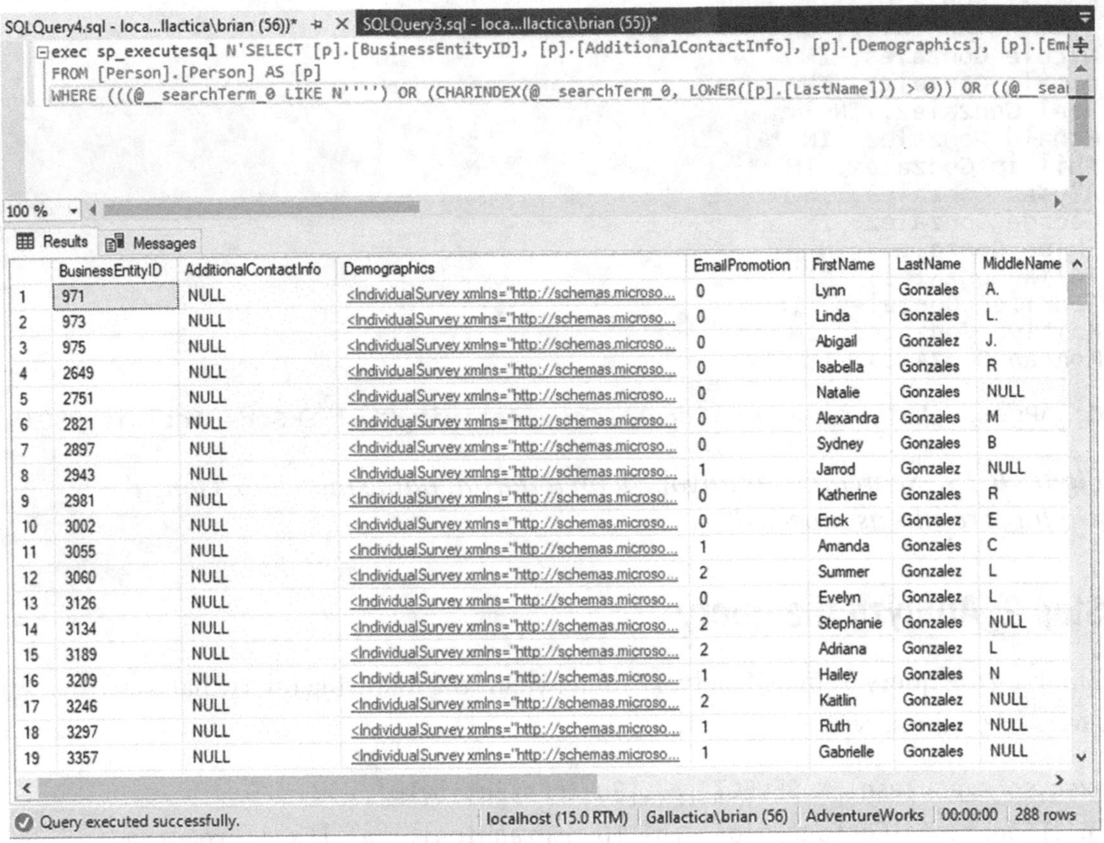

	BusinessEntityID	AdditionalContactInfo	Demographics	EmailPromotion	FirstName	LastName	MiddleName
1	971	NULL	<IndividualSurvey xmlns="http://schemas.microso...	0	Lynn	Gonzales	A.
2	973	NULL	<IndividualSurvey xmlns="http://schemas.microso...	0	Linda	Gonzales	L.
3	975	NULL	<IndividualSurvey xmlns="http://schemas.microso...	0	Abigail	Gonzalez	J.
4	2649	NULL	<IndividualSurvey xmlns="http://schemas.microso...	0	Isabella	Gonzales	R
5	2751	NULL	<IndividualSurvey xmlns="http://schemas.microso...	0	Natalie	Gonzales	NULL
6	2821	NULL	<IndividualSurvey xmlns="http://schemas.microso...	0	Alexandra	Gonzales	M
7	2897	NULL	<IndividualSurvey xmlns="http://schemas.microso...	0	Sydney	Gonzales	B
8	2943	NULL	<IndividualSurvey xmlns="http://schemas.microso...	1	Jarrod	Gonzalez	NULL
9	2981	NULL	<IndividualSurvey xmlns="http://schemas.microso...	0	Katherine	Gonzales	R
10	3002	NULL	<IndividualSurvey xmlns="http://schemas.microso...	0	Erick	Gonzalez	E
11	3055	NULL	<IndividualSurvey xmlns="http://schemas.microso...	1	Amanda	Gonzales	C
12	3060	NULL	<IndividualSurvey xmlns="http://schemas.microso...	2	Summer	Gonzalez	L
13	3126	NULL	<IndividualSurvey xmlns="http://schemas.microso...	0	Evelyn	Gonzalez	L
14	3134	NULL	<IndividualSurvey xmlns="http://schemas.microso...	2	Stephanie	Gonzales	NULL
15	3189	NULL	<IndividualSurvey xmlns="http://schemas.microso...	2	Adriana	Gonzalez	L
16	3209	NULL	<IndividualSurvey xmlns="http://schemas.microso...	1	Hailey	Gonzales	N
17	3246	NULL	<IndividualSurvey xmlns="http://schemas.microso...	2	Kaitlin	Gonzalez	NULL
18	3297	NULL	<IndividualSurvey xmlns="http://schemas.microso...	1	Ruth	Gonzalez	NULL
19	3357	NULL	<IndividualSurvey xmlns="http://schemas.microso...	1	Gabrielle	Gonzales	NULL

Figure 8-16. *The results of the filtered query*

Run a couple more search filter queries to see the results you would expect and validate that the query is working.

Now you might be asking about *SQL Injection* at this point. What happens if I search for O'Brien, for example, or try to run some other malicious code in my search term? Figure 8-17 gives a look at an attempt at SQL Injection.

```
Please Enter the partial First or Last Name, or the Person Type to search for:
O'Bri
Tim O'Brien, VC

C:\APressEntityFramework\Code\EFCore5_Activity0801\EFCore5_Activity0801\bin\Debu
ss 1560) exited with code 0.
To automatically close the console when debugging stops, enable Tools->Options->
le when debugging stops.
Press any key to close this window . . .
```

Figure 8-17. *Testing to see if the LINQ query used for filtering is vulnerable to SQL Injection attacks*

Executing the program as shown renders the following query in the SQL Profiler:

```
exec sp_executesql N'SELECT [p].[BusinessEntityID],
[p].[AdditionalContactInfo], [p].[Demographics], [p].[EmailPromotion],
[p].[FirstName], [p].[LastName], [p].[MiddleName], [p].[ModifiedDate],
[p].[NameStyle], [p].[PersonType], [p].[rowguid], [p].[Suffix], [p].[Title]
FROM [Person].[Person] AS [p]
WHERE (((@__searchTerm_0 LIKE N'''') OR (CHARINDEX(@__searchTerm_0,
LOWER([p].[LastName])) > 0)) OR ((@__searchTerm_0 LIKE N'''') OR
(CHARINDEX(@__searchTerm_0, LOWER([p].[FirstName])) > 0))) OR (LOWER([p].
[PersonType]) = @__searchTerm_0)',N'@__searchTerm_0 nvarchar(50)',
@__searchTerm_0=N'o''bri'
```

And you can see that the search term is indeed protected from the single quote, suggesting that your LINQ query is parameterized. Even so, it's still your responsibility to make sure that any code you write is secure.

As an additional test, you could try the typical injection attack string – passing the text " ' or 1=1 --" into the search filter to see if your query returns filter results or all the results in the database. When the query does not return all the results, you can have some assurance that your query is working as expected without being open to SQL Injection.

Task 3: Paging the filtered results

Even with filtering in place, you saw that your preceding results contained some 288 results in the previous query. While there may be some instances where you would be fine with returning all of these results (your UI control handles paging well and won't freeze up with large result sets), it is often ideal to just page the results and get only the records being rendered to the user at the time of the request. To do this easily, you can further modify your LINQ query from the previous task.

Step 1: Create the method to filter and page the results

To get started, add a new method that uses the same search term for simplicity. Call the method FilteredAndPagedResult([filter], [pageNumber], [pageSize]). Note that the method has three parameters. Write the method to take the string filter as before, this time also returning a number of records equal to page size and the results from the expected page. Also give the method the ability to select a subset of the records based on an offset and a subset length for how many records to show on a page.

To prove this out, just do a for loop around the call in the Main method to simulate paging. Add a breakpoint to the database call to see each page in action. Use a page size of 5, 10, 15, 20, or 25. For even more fun, make sure to order the results by Last Name so that they are not just filtered but also sorted and paged.

Add the following code to the Main method:

```
int pageSize = 10;
for (int pageNumber = 0; pageNumber < 10; pageNumber++)
{
    Console.WriteLine($"Page {pageNumber + 1}");
    FilteredAndPagedResult(result, pageNumber, pageSize);
}
```

When making the call, we can see paged results as expected. Please note that if you do a more extensive search, the code as written will print out page numbers with no results. If you don't like that functionality, you could move the printout of the page to the method and only show the page number if there are results to print.

```
private static void FilteredAndPagedResult(string filter, int pageNumber,
int pageSize)
{
    using (var db = new AdventureWorksContext(_optionsBuilder.Options))
    {
        var searchTerm = filter.ToLower();
        var query = db.People.Where(x => x.LastName.ToLower().
        Contains(searchTerm)
                                    || x.FirstName.ToLower().
                                    Contains(searchTerm)
                                    || x.PersonType.ToLower().
                                    Equals(searchTerm))
                            .OrderBy(x => x.LastName)
                            .Skip(pageNumber * pageSize)
                            .Take(pageSize);

        foreach (var person in query)
        {
            Console.WriteLine($"{person.FirstName} {person.LastName},
            {person.PersonType}");
        }
    }
}
```

And the result as rendered when searching for 'Gonz' is shown in Figure 8-18.

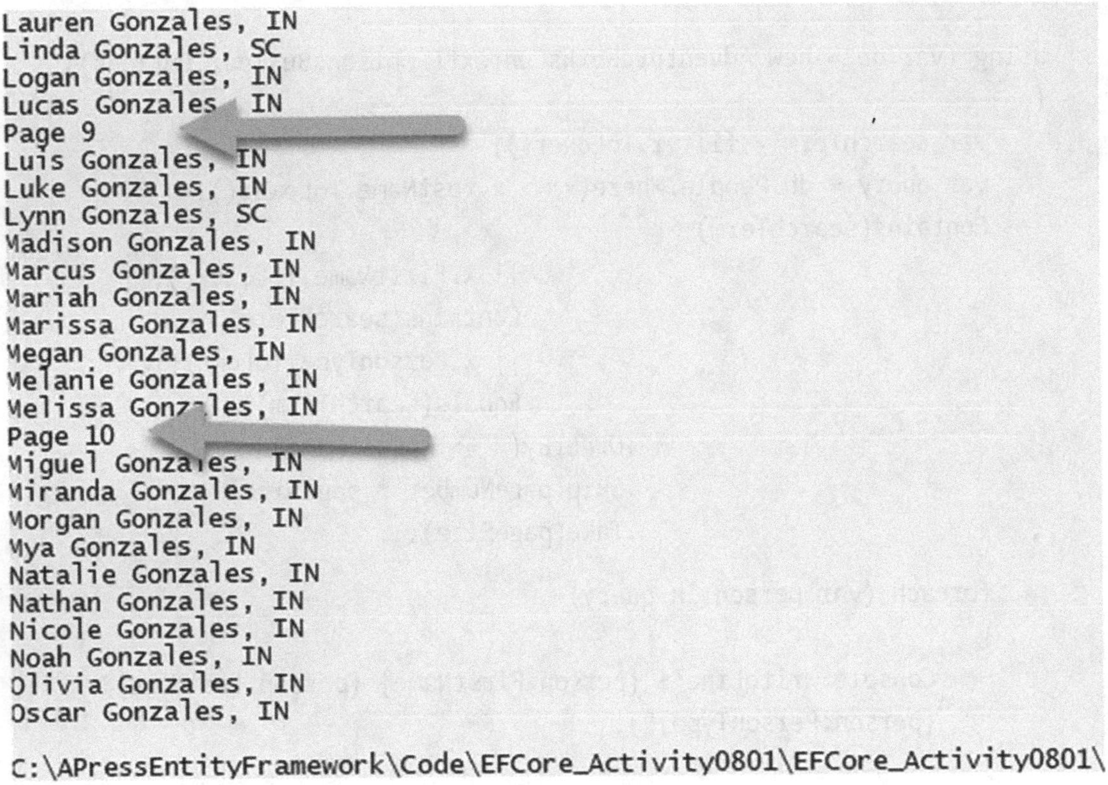

```
Lauren Gonzales, IN
Linda Gonzales, SC
Logan Gonzales, IN
Lucas Gonzales, IN
Page 9
Luis Gonzales, IN
Luke Gonzales, IN
Lynn Gonzales, SC
Madison Gonzales, IN
Marcus Gonzales, IN
Mariah Gonzales, IN
Marissa Gonzales, IN
Megan Gonzales, IN
Melanie Gonzales, IN
Melissa Gonzales, IN
Page 10
Miguel Gonzales, IN
Miranda Gonzales, IN
Morgan Gonzales, IN
Mya Gonzales, IN
Natalie Gonzales, IN
Nathan Gonzales, IN
Nicole Gonzales, IN
Noah Gonzales, IN
Olivia Gonzales, IN
Oscar Gonzales, IN
```

C:\APressEntityFramework\Code\EFCore_Activity0801\EFCore_Activity0801\

Figure 8-18. *The results are paged as expected, and each page is printed as the results are executed and written to the console*

Step 2: Analyze the query results

Again, it is critical to inspect your queries in the profiler to make certain they are performing as expected. The paging method makes multiple calls, as we would anticipate, each one limited to the correct set of results. The final query should be similar to the code that follows:

```
exec sp_executesql N'SELECT [p].[BusinessEntityID], [p].
[AdditionalContactInfo], [p].[Demographics], [p].[EmailPromotion], [p].
[FirstName], [p].[LastName], [p].[MiddleName], [p].[ModifiedDate], [p].
[NameStyle], [p].[PersonType], [p].[rowguid], [p].[Suffix], [p].[Title]
FROM [Person].[Person] AS [p]
```

```
WHERE (((@__searchTerm_0 LIKE N'''') OR (CHARINDEX(@__searchTerm_0,
LOWER([p].[LastName])) > 0)) OR ((@__searchTerm_0 LIKE N'''') OR
(CHARINDEX(@__searchTerm_0, LOWER([p].[FirstName])) > 0))) OR (LOWER([p].
[PersonType]) = @__searchTerm_0)
ORDER BY [p].[LastName]
OFFSET @__p_1 ROWS FETCH NEXT @__p_2 ROWS ONLY',N'@__searchTerm_0
nvarchar(50),@__p_1 int,@__p_2 int',@__searchTerm_0=N'gonz',@__p_1=90,
@__p_2=10
```

By validating this approach, you can see that EF is highly performant against large database tables as long as your queries are written correctly. To see how much worse the performance could have been, you could try that last method by pulling to a list first and then doing the filtering, ordering, and paging on the results.

Just imagine the performance hit you would have if you made the call for every page in this code, pulling back all nearly 20,000 records. Then, only after getting all 20,000 records on each iteration, perform another operation in memory to further filter down to just the ten records you need for every page of results displayed to the *UI*.

Task 4: Disconnecting the result sets

In this final task for the activity, you will learn how to easily disconnect any recordset from the database. This can greatly improve your overall performance.

Step 1: Set the code to use queries AsNoTracking

For the next part of this activity, you'll learn about one other performance enhancement discussed in this chapter – disconnecting the data. For every single result you pulled back in this application, you don't always need to keep tracking in place.

To make your queries as lightweight as possible, therefore, you can simply add the .AsNoTracking() statement to each query right after the db.People statement. Go ahead and do that now. Search for db.People in your code, and replace with db.People. AsNoTracking. A sample of what this might look like is

```
var query = db.People.AsNoTracking().OrderByDescending(x => x.LastName);
```

Run the code again to validate that all of the queries still work. If you continue to profile the code, you may see some performance increases in the duration column, but they are likely not extremely noticeable on the IQueryable methods.

Step 2: Discuss setting the entire context to disable tracking of entities by default

Another thing you could do is disable the tracking completely on the entire context. Locate the AdventureWorksContext in the EFCore_DbLibrary project, and add the following to the public constructors:

```
ChangeTracker.QueryTrackingBehavior = QueryTrackingBehavior.NoTracking;
```

Setting the entire context to avoid tracking behaviors is shown in Figure 8-19.

```
namespace EFCore_DBLibrary
{
    11 references
    public partial class AdventureWorksContext : DbContext
    {
        0 references
        public AdventureWorksContext()
        {
            ChangeTracker.QueryTrackingBehavior = QueryTrackingBehavior.NoTracking;
        }

        4 references
        public AdventureWorksContext(DbContextOptions<AdventureWorksContext> options)
            : base(options)
        {
            ChangeTracker.QueryTrackingBehavior = QueryTrackingBehavior.NoTracking;
        }
    }
```

Figure 8-19. *Setting the entire context to default to disconnected data on all queries*

While you don't really want to do this for this project, knowing that it is possible could be highly advantageous to your overall performance on libraries designed to be read-only, such as a reporting library.

Activity 8-1 summary

In this activity, you've seen how to use sorting, filtering, and paging to refine your results. By making certain to optimize your query formation, you've set up your EF instance to optimize for both performance and functionality when working against a large dataset.

Chapter summary

In this chapter, you learned about a few of the common issues that arise when working with LINQ and your data. You learned that you should not just blindly pull everything into a List and then iterate on the list. Rather, you should filter your query as much as possible to ensure that only the results you need are contained in the result set.

Important takeaways

This chapter gave us our first deep dive into working with LINQ and specifically working with LINQ to Entities. We still have a lot to learn when it comes to LINQ, but with the knowledge we gained in this chapter, we now understand the impact that a few differences in how things are coded can work. The main takeaways from this chapter are

- Make sure to perform the execution of the queries at the latest possible opportunity in the codebase.

- Remember to disable change tracking when entities do not need to stay connected for tracking in the DBContext.

- When working with LINQ to Entities and the Entity Framework in general, make sure to use some sort of profiler to help examine the actual queries you are executing on the database.

In the next chapter, we'll continue looking at how we can use LINQ to get results from our database into disconnected DTO objects using projections and anonymous classes.

Closing thoughts

In the next chapter, you will continue looking at how you can use LINQ to get results from your database into disconnected DTO objects by using projections and anonymous classes.

PART III

Enhancing the Data Solution

CHAPTER 9

LINQ for Queries and Projections

Data in the real world

In this chapter, you are going to learn how to use queries in complex scenarios to get the data you want. To this point, you've worked with the database in a fairly superficial manner. As this is a book on practical application of the concepts, you really need to experience working with data in real-world scenarios.

Often, when working with data, there will be a need to perform join operations across multiple tables and then use that data in some manner. There are a couple of approaches that you can employ in these scenarios.

LINQ vs. stored procedures

In the past, you would simply create views and stored procedures to make all the joins and then rely on the database server to optimize the execution plans for these scenarios. This is similar to the approach that was taken in Chapter 7.

With LINQ, you are also able to command the server to perform the joins and get the data just as easily as if you had written a stored procedure. The benefits of using LINQ include the fact that you can write more flexible code with the ability to simply change a few things here and there to get a more advanced result set as needed. By using LINQ, you also avoid having to rewrite or modify an entire stored procedure. Additionally, not having to rework server objects avoids the necessity of going through the governance channels that are generally involved in pushing changes to the production database.

© Brian L. Gorman 2022

B. L. Gorman, *Practical Entity Framework Core 6*, https://doi.org/10.1007/978-1-4842-7301-2_9

There are a couple of drawbacks to this approach, however. The major thing to consider is what was discussed earlier – execution plans. With stored procedures, the server itself will store a cached execution plan. This means that while you still have the pain of the first execution runtime, the second and consecutive executions of that stored procedure should be run with greater efficiency. Using LINQ does not allow the server to store up an execution plan, so each query must be treated like a new execution on the server. Even with optimized queries, the loss of the execution plan might be enough to consider using a stored procedure in some instances. It will be your job as the developer to determine the best approach.

Complex data and the code-first approach

After getting your data from these complex join queries, either via a stored procedure or through LINQ queries, you need to be able to pass the data to your controller or view layers or, at minimum, to some other layer where the data will be utilized.

When you built out the models for the inventory manager system, you were able to quickly create the exact structures that you wanted to exist in the database. With data being returned from the database from a complex query, you're likely not going to want to have a table or other structure that is directly modeled in the code-first approach, but rather you would prefer to just leverage a dynamic solution.

A couple of options exist for you, which would allow you to use that data efficiently. As with any system, you, as the developer, should consider the best approach for your system. Additionally, you'll want to make sure any architecture decisions you make are based on the standards of your organization.

The first approach you could easily take is to just keep adding models to your InventoryModels project. Another approach you could take is to modify some of the existing models to hold transformed data. Always remember that unless you create direct dependencies and/or add the model to the DBContext, in the code-first approach, a model can exist without needing to be migrated into the database. Furthermore, on existing models that you have, simply adding the Data Annotation [NotMapped] to any field will allow you to add fields that do not get placed into the database, even if the model is part of the database schema.

While this approach works well and may even be the desired approach in your current system, I would advise against using this strategy. There are two downfalls to this approach that I simply prefer to avoid. They both relate to confusion and maintainability in the future.

In my opinion, the first issue with adding fields that are NotMapped in your models is that this action just clutters them up with more fields while also making it so the model and the database itself are not in a one-to-one synchronized relationship. Again, it's not necessary to map fields one-to-one in the model to what's in the table, but it becomes more confusing for other developers in the long run, especially over time and as the models continue to change. In this scenario, you also end up sending more information to the UI layer in many cases than the UI layer actually needs, which could present other issues like security concerns around exposed data.

The second issue with continued use of the existing models approach is that your Models project can start to experience class explosion; and, as with the first problem, now you'll have entire classes that don't map to the database. Having this class explosion with mismatched data schema structures can add yet another layer of confusion.

DTOs, view models, or domain models

Before I get hate mail (or @'s on Twitter), let's clear a few things up. *DTOs*, *view models*, and *domain models* are not the same thing and generally should not be used in an interchangeable manner. Clearly, each has a specific purpose. For example, you can have view models that don't map to any database objects at all, with a primary purpose of just mapping information for user interaction on a screen. You might also see domain models that could be the result of data from multiple models interacting with each other for some specific behavior. DTOs, on the other hand, could just be a simple way to map fields from one data type to another. So yes, I concede to you that these three objects are not even close to the same thing. That being said, when I'm talking about DTOs for the rest of this chapter, a DTO could be substituted in your system with a view model or a domain model, if that's what makes sense for your system.

Decoupling your business or view logic from the database

In my opinion, one of the better approaches to work with composed data is to create DTO objects that map the data needed for the next layer of the system to a class specifically molded to meet the needs of the business or view logic. In this approach, you generally would place these DTOs in some sort of stand-alone project or at least at some layer of the architecture that is separate from the database Models project.

This approach should ultimately keep both layers cleaner, more testable, and easier to maintain in the long run.

By placing the data into specific DTOs in a separate project, you can be much more granular about the structure and application of these objects. This solves the problems created earlier with having too many classes and fields in the Models project and classes, respectively. In the end, your business logic or view layer logic is then decoupled from your database logic, which is a very good thing.

Sometimes, a pre-defined object is overkill

In some cases, going to the trouble of creating a DTO object is not practical and can lead to excessive overhead in your projects. When it's your data and we want it now, but you don't want to build out yet another class to hold that modeled data, you can perform an operation known as projecting the data into an anonymous class (or anonymous type).

Anonymous classes were introduced in C# 2.0, so they've been around for some time now. Likely you've seen some sort of application where an anonymous class was defined for quick use within a method or class body. A simple anonymous class that holds information about an Item might look like this:

```
var item = new { Name = "ROG Zephyrus M15", Brand = "Asus", Price = 1629.00 };
```

In that declaration, a new anonymous class was created and assigned to the item variable. If you wanted, you could then use that object just like any other class while it remained in scope. For example, you could write out the details of the item with calls to item.Name and item.Brand, just as if they were full public properties in a well-defined class.

Putting that knowledge to use, you can easily see how it would be easy to use LINQ to get some data and then combine that with the ability to create a new anonymous type to model that data.

For example, a simple query against the Person.Person table in the AdventureWorks joined to the HumanResources.Employee table, then joined to the Sales.SalesPerson table, further joined to Sales.OrderHeaders, then Sales.OrderDetails, and all the way through to Product could yield some great results which we might want to map to just have access to the fields Product.Name, SalesPerson.FirstName, OrderHeader. OrderDate, and others. That kind of interaction can easily be accomplished using LINQ and anonymous types in a query similar to this one:

```
var salesReportDetails = db.SalesPeople.Select(sp => new
{
    beid = sp.BusinessEntityId,
    sp.BusinessEntity.BusinessEntity.FirstName,
    sp.BusinessEntity.BusinessEntity.LastName,
    sp.SalesYtd,
    Territories = sp.SalesTerritoryHistories.Select(y => y.Territory.Name),
    OrderCount = sp.SalesOrderHeaders.Count(),
    TotalProductsSold = sp.SalesOrderHeaders.SelectMany(y =>
    y.SalesOrderDetails).Sum(z => z.OrderQty)
}).Where(srds => srds.SalesYtd > 1000000).AsQueryable()
.OrderByDescending(srds => srds.LastName).ThenBy(srds => srds.FirstName).
ThenByDescending(srds => srds.SalesYtd)
.Take(20).ToList();
```

One tool to rule them all

Anytime you have fully modeled your DTO objects and perform a bunch of queries, you'd run into the same problem. At some point, you'd be manually creating an instance of some DTO object and then mapping each field, one by one to the DTO object from either a model or an anonymous type.

While this approach works, like many others, it is not the best solution. For one thing, writing line after line of code to map one object to another object that is often nearly identical in structure is tedious. This approach also can lead to errors where the programmer accidentally copies and pastes the field mappings and forgets to update one or two so that one or more fields have incorrect or no data in them. This is where *AutoMapper* comes in like Mighty Mouse, singing "Here I come to save the day!"

AutoMapper

The most successful tool available today that correctly translates objects from one type to another is AutoMapper, which is available here: www.nuget.org/packages/automapper/.

In addition to the ability to correctly map one type to another, AutoMapper has an even niftier ability to project data from LINQ queries directly into their types, thereby even skipping the step of getting the data into one type and then calling AutoMapper's Map<T> function. Don't worry if this is unclear right now. As you work through the following activities, you'll learn more about how this works.

While it is unmistakably the best tool for the job, highly performant, and simple to use for mappings and projections, the main issue I've run into with AutoMapper is the complexity of getting set up to use the tool correctly in a project. Once you get past the initial setup (correctly) and then learn a couple of quick tricks about how the tool syntax works to automatically map identically named fields while providing ways to code for the exceptions to the rule (i.e., mapping fields that don't have the same name), the value of AutoMapper easily becomes worth the initial price point, which is free, with the tiniest ounce of pain (initial setup and a few things to learn about mappings). By the time you complete this chapter, I imagine you will think of AutoMapper as one of the most important libraries you must add to your robust solutions.

Chapter 9 activities: Using LINQ, decoupled DTO classes, projections, anonymous types, and AutoMapper

In the activities for this chapter, you'll start by building out a solution to use LINQ to perform some more complex queries against the *AdventureWorks* database. You'll then see the differences between different approaches to working with LINQ using projections to anonymous types to evaluate the performance implications of each implementation decision you make.

After getting through the more advanced interactions with LINQ, you'll move back to your Inventory project, where you'll first set up AutoMapper.

You'll then finish up with a look at using AutoMapper to project your data from one type to another, making sure to spend some time working with directly and indirectly mapped fields to get a solid grasp on working with AutoMapper.

Activity 9-1: Working with LINQ in complex queries

For the first activity for Chapter 9, you're going to dive a lot deeper into working with LINQ in your projects. To this point, you've seen some of the really great features of LINQ with the ability to quickly select `IEnumerable` or `IQueryable` result sets, and you've learned how to chain commands to filter, sort, and apply other transformations. However, you've not spent a lot of time working across table joins.

As you start joining tables, you'll be bringing more data into the result sets than you'll likely need to send back for use by the calling program. As you then start working with this data, not only will we need to combine the results of different tables, but we'll want to pare them down to contain only specific pieces of information.

There are a couple of ways we can pare things down, with the first being that you can just select everything and then manually transform that data in memory into some sort of DTO object for transmission. The other option is you can limit your queries to get just the right amount of information for your results and then send that information in some sort of DTO object. As you've seen before, the more you can refine your queries, the better you can expect query (and application) performance to be.

Task 0: Getting started

This first activity for the chapter will use the same solution that you were using at the end of Chapter 8 (the Activity08-1 files, which were originally the Chapter 3 files). If you worked through that activity, you may continue to use your own solution. If, however, you either did not do that solution or you would just like to start fresh, grab a copy of the `Activity09-1_StarterFiles` and just use them. Review Appendix A for more information on working with the starter files.

Running the program as is should reveal results from the database similar to what is shown in Figure 9-1.

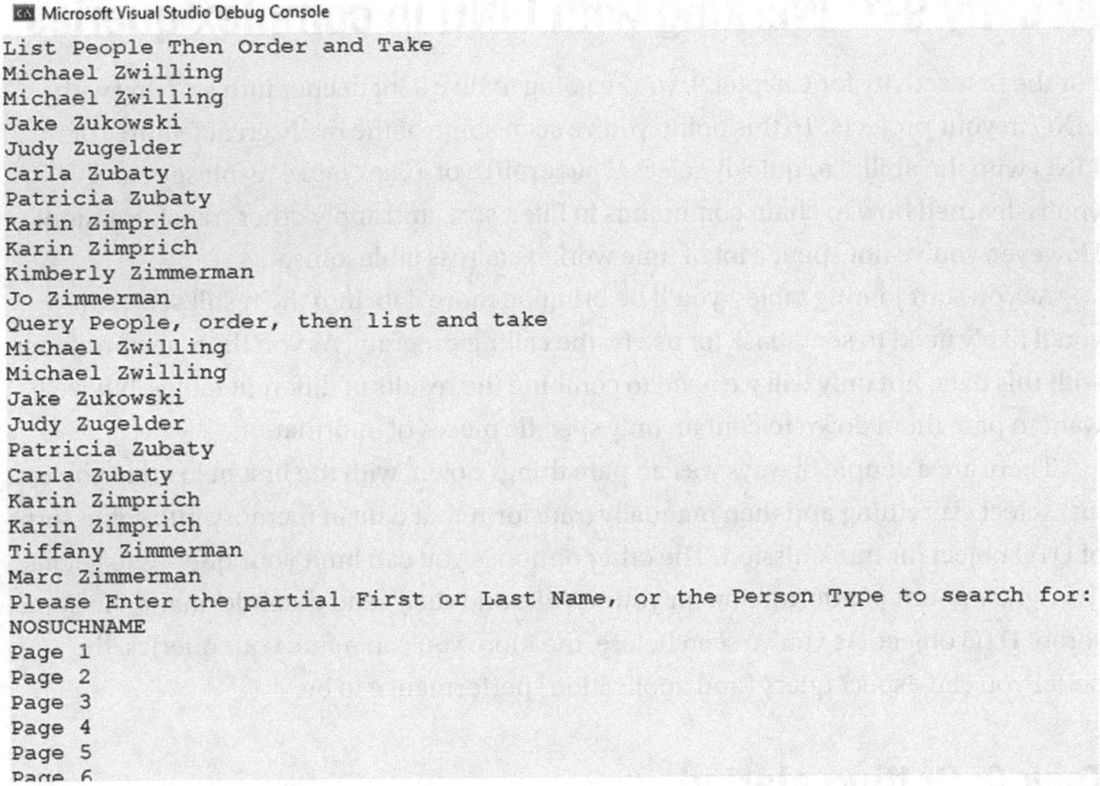

Microsoft Visual Studio Debug Console

```
List People Then Order and Take
Michael Zwilling
Michael Zwilling
Jake Zukowski
Judy Zugelder
Carla Zubaty
Patricia Zubaty
Karin Zimprich
Karin Zimprich
Kimberly Zimmerman
Jo Zimmerman
Query People, order, then list and take
Michael Zwilling
Michael Zwilling
Jake Zukowski
Judy Zugelder
Patricia Zubaty
Carla Zubaty
Karin Zimprich
Karin Zimprich
Tiffany Zimmerman
Marc Zimmerman
Please Enter the partial First or Last Name, or the Person Type to search for:
NOSUCHNAME
Page 1
Page 2
Page 3
Page 4
Page 5
Page 6
```

Figure 9-1. *The program should return results with no modifications*

Task 1: Get all the salespeople

In this task, you will take the solution as it stands and get a list of all salespeople with details about their sales numbers as they are reported for the year.

Step 1: Quickly comment out other method calls to get them out of the way

To begin, just comment out the calls to the other methods in the `Main` method in the `Program.cs` class of the `Activity0901` project (`Activity0801` or `Activity0301` if you are using your own files from the previous chapter or from Chapter 3). The only method that should not be commented out is the `BuildOptions` method. Running the program would output nothing at this point (see Figure 9-2).

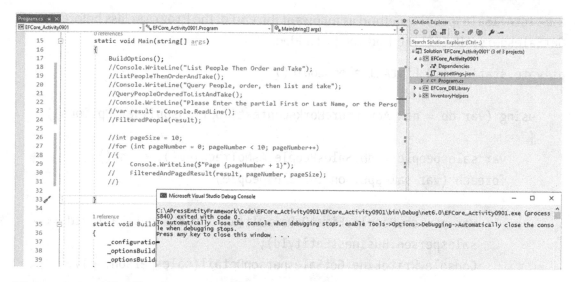

Figure 9-2. *All calls are commented so no results show when the program is run*

Step 2: List out the salespeople and their important metrics

In this step, you will write a query to get the salespeople and their important numbers for the year.

To begin, add a method to give a friendly print out of a SalesPerson with Person information as follows to the end of the Program class in the Program.cs file:

```
private static string GetSalespersonDetail(SalesPerson sp, Person p)
{
    return $"ID: {sp.BusinessEntityId}\t|TID: {sp.TerritoryId}\t|Quota:
    {sp.SalesQuota}\t" +
            $"|Bonus: {sp.Bonus}\t|YTDSales: {sp.SalesYtd}\t|Name: \t" +
            $"{p?.FirstName ?? ""}, {p?.LastName ?? ""}";
}
```

Next, add a method call to highlight a way to get the salespeople. Although this will work, it is not going to be the best solution. In the Program.cs file at the end of the Main method after the commented code, add a method call to ListAllSalespeople. Then add the `ListAllSalespeople` method as follows at the end of the `Program` class before the `GetSalespersonDetail` method you just added:

```
private static void ListAllSalespeople()
{
    using (var db = new AdventureWorksContext(_optionsBuilder.Options))
    {
        var salespeople = db.SalesPeople.AsNoTracking().ToList();
        foreach (var salesperson in salespeople)
        {
            var p = db.People.FirstOrDefault(x => x.BusinessEntityId ==
            salesperson.BusinessEntityId);
            Console.WriteLine(GetSalespersonDetail(salesperson, p));
        }
    }
}
```

Running the code gives output as shown in Figure 9-3.

```
ID: 274 |TID:   |Quota:            |Bonus: 0.0000  |YTDSales: 559697.5639 |Name: Stephen, Jiang
ID: 275 |TID: 2 |Quota: 300000.0000 |Bonus: 4100.0000 |YTDSales: 3763178.1787 |Name: Michael, Blythe
ID: 276 |TID: 4 |Quota: 250000.0000 |Bonus: 2000.0000 |YTDSales: 4251368.5497 |Name: Linda, Mitchell
ID: 277 |TID: 3 |Quota: 250000.0000 |Bonus: 2500.0000 |YTDSales: 3189418.3662 |Name: Jillian, Carson
ID: 278 |TID: 6 |Quota: 250000.0000 |Bonus: 500.0000  |YTDSales: 1453719.4653 |Name: Garrett, Vargas
ID: 279 |TID: 5 |Quota: 300000.0000 |Bonus: 6700.0000 |YTDSales: 2315185.6110 |Name: Tsvi, Reiter
ID: 280 |TID: 1 |Quota: 250000.0000 |Bonus: 5000.0000 |YTDSales: 1352577.1325 |Name: Pamela, Ansman-Wolfe
ID: 281 |TID: 4 |Quota: 250000.0000 |Bonus: 3550.0000 |YTDSales: 2458535.6169 |Name: Shu, Ito
ID: 282 |TID: 6 |Quota: 250000.0000 |Bonus: 5000.0000 |YTDSales: 2604540.7172 |Name: José, Saraiva
ID: 283 |TID: 1 |Quota: 250000.0000 |Bonus: 3500.0000 |YTDSales: 1573012.9383 |Name: David, Campbell
ID: 284 |TID: 1 |Quota: 300000.0000 |Bonus: 3900.0000 |YTDSales: 1576562.1966 |Name: Tete, Mensa-Annan
ID: 285 |TID:   |Quota:            |Bonus: 0.0000  |YTDSales: 172524.4512 |Name: Syed, Abbas
ID: 286 |TID: 9 |Quota: 250000.0000 |Bonus: 5650.0000 |YTDSales: 1421810.9242 |Name: Lynn, Tsoflias
ID: 287 |TID:   |Quota:            |Bonus: 0.0000  |YTDSales: 519905.9320 |Name: Amy, Alberts
ID: 288 |TID: 8 |Quota: 250000.0000 |Bonus: 75.0000 |YTDSales: 1827066.7118 |Name: Rachel, Valdez
ID: 289 |TID: 10 |Quota: 250000.0000 |Bonus: 5150.0000 |YTDSales: 4116871.2277 |Name: Jae, Pak
ID: 290 |TID: 7 |Quota: 250000.0000 |Bonus: 985.0000 |YTDSales: 3121616.3202 |Name: Ranjit, Varkey Chudukatil

C:\APressEntityFramework\Code\EFCore_Activity0901\EFCore_Activity0901\bin\Debug\net6.0\EFCore_Activity0901.exe (process 9336)
```

Figure 9-3. *The salespeople details are listed, but extra database calls will hinder performance*

Luckily, there aren't that many salespeople in the database. Do you see the problem with the working solution? If not, recall our use of the SQL Server Profiler in Chapter 8. Go ahead and turn on the profiler and watch your queries run for the preceding code to see the issue with this solution (review Chapter 8 for information on working with the *SQL Server Profiler* in *SSMS*). Figure 9-4 shows the output from this query to help illuminate the problem.

EventClass	TextData	Application Name	NTUserName	LoginName	CPU	Reads	Writes	Duration
Audit Login	-- network protocol: LPC set quoted...	Core Microso...	brian	Gallac...				
SQL:BatchStarting	SELECT [s].[BusinessEntityID], [s].[...	Core Microso...	brian	Gallac...				
SQL:BatchCompleted	SELECT [s].[BusinessEntityID], [s].[...	Core Microso...	brian	Gallac...	0	2	0	
Audit Logout		Core Microso...	brian	Gallac...	0	2	0	240
RPC:Completed	exec sp_reset_connection	Core Microso...	brian	Gallac...	0	0	0	0
Audit Login	-- network protocol: LPC set quoted...	Core Microso...	brian	Gallac...				
RPC:Completed	exec sp_executesql N'SELECT TOP(1) [...	Core Microso...	brian	Gallac...	0	3	0	
Audit Logout		Core Microso...	brian	Gallac...	0	5	0	30
RPC:Completed	exec sp_reset_connection	Core Microso...	brian	Gallac...	0	0	0	0
Audit Login	-- network protocol: LPC set quoted...	Core Microso...	brian	Gallac...				
RPC:Completed	exec sp_executesql N'SELECT TOP(1) [...	Core Microso...	brian	Gallac...	0	3	0	
Audit Logout		Core Microso...	brian	Gallac...	0	8	0	
RPC:Completed	exec sp_reset_connection	Core Microso...	brian	Gallac...	0	0	0	
Audit Login	-- network protocol: LPC set quoted...	Core Microso...	brian	Gallac...				
RPC:Completed	exec sp_executesql N'SELECT TOP(1) [...	Core Microso...	brian	Gallac...	0	3	0	
Audit Logout		Core Microso...	brian	Gallac...	0	11	0	
RPC:Completed	exec sp_reset_connection	Core Microso...	brian	Gallac...	0	0	0	0
Audit Login	-- network protocol: LPC set quoted...	Core Microso...	brian	Gallac...				
RPC:Completed	exec sp_executesql N'SELECT TOP(1) [...	Core Microso...	brian	Gallac...	0	3	0	
Audit Logout		Core Microso...	brian	Gallac...	0	14	0	
RPC:Completed	exec sp_reset_connection	Core Microso...	brian	Gallac...	0	0	0	
Audit Login	-- network protocol: LPC set quoted...	Core Microso...	brian	Gallac...				
RPC:Completed	exec sp_executesql N'SELECT TOP(1) [...	Core Microso...	brian	Gallac...	0	3	0	
Audit Logout		Core Microso...	brian	Gallac...	0	17	0	
RPC:Completed	exec sp_reset_connection	Core Microso...	brian	Gallac...	0	0	0	
Audit Login	-- network protocol: LPC set quoted...	Core Microso...	brian	Gallac...				

```
[p].[FirstName], [p].[LastName], [p].[MiddleName], [p].[ModifiedDate], [p].[NameStyle], [p].[PersonType], [p].[rowguid], [p].[Suffix],
[p].[Title]
FROM [Person].[Person] AS [p]
WHERE [p].[BusinessEntityID] = @__salesperson_BusinessEntityId_0',N'@__salesperson_BusinessEntityId_0 int',@__salesperson_BusinessEntityId_0=275
go
exec sp_executesql N'SELECT TOP(1) [p].[BusinessEntityID], [p].[AdditionalContactInfo], [p].[Demographics], [p].[EmailPromotion],
[p].[FirstName], [p].[LastName], [p].[MiddleName], [p].[ModifiedDate], [p].[NameStyle], [p].[PersonType], [p].[rowguid], [p].[Suffix],
[p].[Title]
FROM [Person].[Person] AS [p]
WHERE [p].[BusinessEntityID] = @__salesperson_BusinessEntityId_0',N'@__salesperson_BusinessEntityId_0 int',@__salesperson_BusinessEntityId_0=276
exec sp_executesql N'SELECT TOP(1) [p].[BusinessEntityID], [p].[AdditionalContactInfo], [p].[Demographics], [p].[EmailPromotion],
[p].[FirstName], [p].[LastName], [p].[MiddleName], [p].[ModifiedDate], [p].[NameStyle], [p].[PersonType], [p].[rowguid], [p].[Suffix],
[p].[Title]
FROM [Person].[Person] AS [p]
WHERE [p].[BusinessEntityID] = @__salesperson_BusinessEntityId_0',N'@__salesperson_BusinessEntityId_0 int',@__salesperson_BusinessEntityId_0=277
go
exec sp_executesql N'SELECT TOP(1) [p].[BusinessEntityID], [p].[AdditionalContactInfo], [p].[Demographics], [p].[EmailPromotion],
[p].[FirstName], [p].[LastName], [p].[MiddleName], [p].[ModifiedDate], [p].[NameStyle], [p].[PersonType], [p].[rowguid], [p].[Suffix],
[p].[Title]
FROM [Person].[Person] AS [p]
WHERE [p].[BusinessEntityID] = @__salesperson_BusinessEntityId_0',N'@__salesperson_BusinessEntityId_0 int',@__salesperson_BusinessEntityId_0=278
```

Figure 9-4. *The current query is making one call to get the results plus one call per result to get further result details. Only some of the calls are shown in this image*

The query that was just written is called an *n + 1 query*. This is a mistake that many beginning developers make (and experienced ones do too). Essentially, for every record, the solution has to make another query to get more details (n iterations) with the original query being the plus one (+ 1) for (n + 1 queries total). Wouldn't it be better if you could just do one query and get all of the results? Think about how a query like this would perform in the situation where you have thousands of results (with one new query per result). Indeed, many a web page grid has waited needlessly due to poorly written queries such as this one.

Step 3: Use navigation properties to get the data

To get the data correctly using the code-first approach, you will want to use navigation properties to include the other entities to allow for easily grouping this data together into one query. To solve this issue, you should get the first and last name of the `SalesPerson` using navigation properties rather than making a separate call per row to get it from the database directly. Because *AdventureWorks* has a lot of stuff going on across multiple schemas, you need to be sure to double-check relations to use navigations correctly. The `SalesPerson` navigation for `BusinessEntity` will map to `HumanResources.Employee`, which also has a navigation for `BusinessEntity` to `Person`, where the first and last name of the person can be found. Therefore, we go from `SalesPerson` to `Employee` to `Person` using the `BusinessEntity` property of each object. Because of this, our code will look repetitive. What might make it more confusing is that you can directly join them in the database. For example, running the following query in SSMS produces valid results as shown in Figure 9-5:

```
SELECT sp.*, p.FirstName, p.LastName FROM Sales.SalesPerson sp
LEFT JOIN Person.Person p on sp.BusinessEntityID = p.BusinessEntityID
```

This is simply because of the ID maps, not because it is the correct direct relationship. If you follow the keys, you would see that `SalesPerson` is indeed mapped to `HumanResources.Employee` (also shown in Figure 9-5).

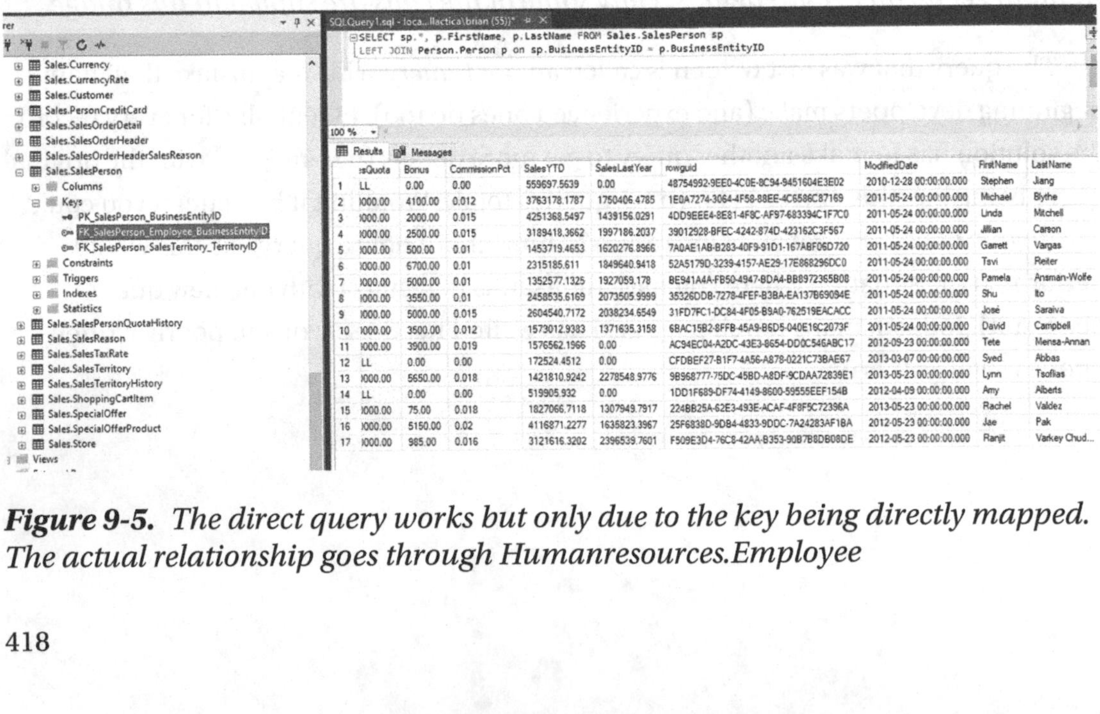

Figure 9-5. *The direct query works but only due to the key being directly mapped. The actual relationship goes through Humanresources.Employee*

Review the database diagram shown in Figure 9-6 to further understand the relationship.

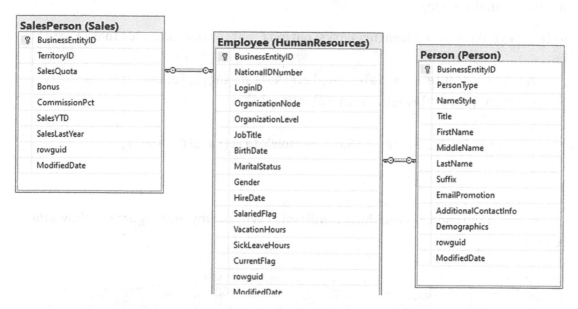

Figure 9-6. *The relationship is modeled for clarity in a database diagram from Sales.SalesPerson to HumanResources.Employee to Person.Person*

Armed with this knowledge, you can see that even though the code will look repetitive, you need to go through the `BusinessEntity` of `Employee` to its `BusinessEntity` mapping to `Person` to get the first and last name of the `SalesPerson`.

To affect these changes in code, first modify the helper function that gets the salesperson details to a friendly string by using the following code:

```
private static string GetSalespersonDetail(SalesPerson sp)
{
    return $"ID: {sp.BusinessEntityId}\t|TID: {sp.TerritoryId}\t|Quota:
    {sp.SalesQuota}\t" +
            $"|Bonus: {sp.Bonus}\t|YTDSales: {sp.SalesYtd}\t|Name: \t" +
            $"{sp.BusinessEntity?.BusinessEntity?.FirstName ?? ""}, " +
            $"{sp.BusinessEntity?.BusinessEntity?.LastName ?? ""}";
}
```

Next, remove the extra database call in the foreach loop so that only one database call is made before the loop iterates (replace the code in the ListAllSalespeople method with this code):

```
using (var db = new AdventureWorksContext(_optionsBuilder.Options))
{
    var salespeople = db.SalesPeople.AsNoTracking().ToList();
    foreach (var salesperson in salespeople)
    {
        Console.WriteLine(GetSalespersonDetail(salesperson));
    }
}
```

Now run the code. Do you think it will work? Why or why not? Figure 9-7 shows the results.

```
ID: 274 |TID:    |Quota:             |Bonus: 0.0000    |YTDSales: 559697.5639  |Name:   ,
ID: 275 |TID: 2 |Quota: 300000.0000  |Bonus: 4100.0000  |YTDSales: 3763178.1787 |Name:   ,
ID: 276 |TID: 4 |Quota: 250000.0000  |Bonus: 2000.0000  |YTDSales: 4251368.5497 |Name:   ,
ID: 277 |TID: 3 |Quota: 250000.0000  |Bonus: 2500.0000  |YTDSales: 3189418.3662 |Name:   ,
ID: 278 |TID: 6 |Quota: 250000.0000  |Bonus: 500.0000   |YTDSales: 1453719.4653 |Name:   ,
ID: 279 |TID: 5 |Quota: 300000.0000  |Bonus: 6700.0000  |YTDSales: 2315185.6110 |Name:   ,
ID: 280 |TID: 1 |Quota: 250000.0000  |Bonus: 5000.0000  |YTDSales: 1352577.1325 |Name:   ,
ID: 281 |TID: 4 |Quota: 250000.0000  |Bonus: 3550.0000  |YTDSales: 2458535.6169 |Name:   ,
ID: 282 |TID: 6 |Quota: 250000.0000  |Bonus: 5000.0000  |YTDSales: 2604540.7172 |Name:   ,
ID: 283 |TID: 1 |Quota: 250000.0000  |Bonus: 3500.0000  |YTDSales: 1573012.9383 |Name:   ,
ID: 284 |TID: 1 |Quota: 300000.0000  |Bonus: 3900.0000  |YTDSales: 1576562.1966 |Name:   ,
ID: 285 |TID:    |Quota:             |Bonus: 0.0000    |YTDSales: 172524.4512  |Name:   ,
ID: 286 |TID: 9 |Quota: 250000.0000  |Bonus: 5650.0000  |YTDSales: 1421810.9242 |Name:   ,
ID: 287 |TID:    |Quota:             |Bonus: 0.0000    |YTDSales: 519905.9320  |Name:   ,
ID: 288 |TID: 8 |Quota: 250000.0000  |Bonus: 75.0000  |YTDSales: 1827066.7118 |Name:   ,
ID: 289 |TID: 10 |Quota: 250000.0000  |Bonus: 5150.0000  |YTDSales: 4116871.2277 |Name:   ,
ID: 290 |TID: 7 |Quota: 250000.0000  |Bonus: 985.0000  |YTDSales: 3121616.3202 |Name:   ,
C:\APressEntityFramework\Code\EFCore_Activity0901\EFCore_Activity0901\bin\Debug\net6.0\EFCore_Activity0901.
```

Figure 9-7. *The results come back, but the data has no first and last name*

Technically, the code will work, but you don't get any names and just get a blank and a comma and another blank. This is because the navigation properties were never filled in the original query, and they are currently null. This is a very good thing. EF does not get data unless you tell it to (lazy loading, and/or just not fetching unnecessary data). As such, you only get the top-level results here. In order to fill the navigation properties, you have to explicitly ask EF to do this for you. Modify the query in the ListAllSalespeople method as follows:

```
var salespeople = db.SalesPeople
                    .Include(x => x.BusinessEntity)
                    .ThenInclude(y => y.BusinessEntity)
                    .AsNoTracking().ToList();
```

Note that this query makes a call to `Include` and to `ThenInclude`. Here you can see that you are explicitly defining the navigations to bring into the query.

With this new code, run the query. This time you should see results as shown in Figure 9-8.

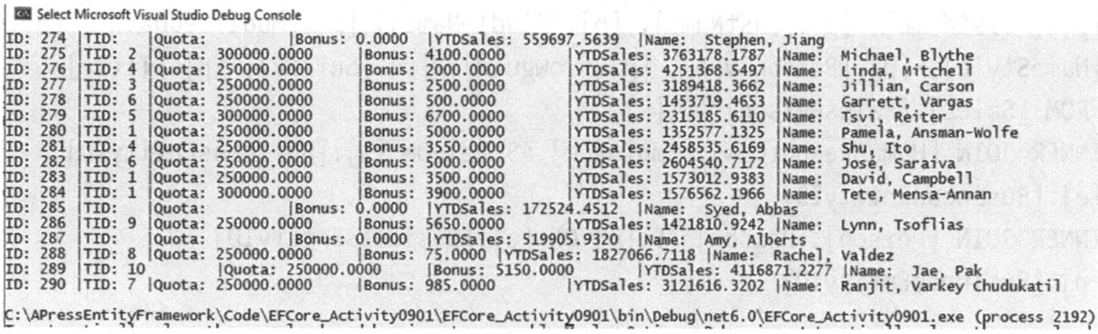

Figure 9-8. *The use of Include and ThenInclude has correctly asked EF to fill the navigation properties, and data is returned*

Furthermore, a simple look at the SQL Server Profiler shows how much better your query strategy is now that you are using the include statements (see Figure 9-9).

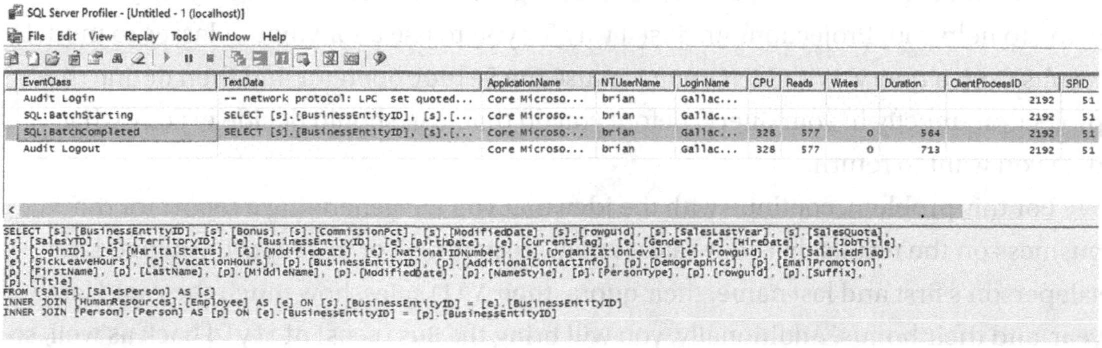

Figure 9-9. *The query is now correctly making only one call to the database and leveraging the inner joins that hydrate the data for your navigation properties*

Indeed, the query generated by EF in this scenario is

```
SELECT [s].[BusinessEntityID], [s].[Bonus], [s].[CommissionPct],
[s].[ModifiedDate], [s].[rowguid], [s].[SalesLastYear], [s].[SalesQuota],
[s].[SalesYTD], [s].[TerritoryID], [e].[BusinessEntityID], [e].[BirthDate],
[e].[CurrentFlag], [e].[Gender], [e].[HireDate], [e].[JobTitle],
[e].[LoginID], [e].[MaritalStatus], [e].[ModifiedDate], [e].[NationalIDNumber],
[e].[OrganizationLevel], [e].[rowguid], [e].[SalariedFlag],
[e].[SickLeaveHours], [e].[VacationHours], [p].[BusinessEntityID],
[p].[AdditionalContactInfo], [p].[Demographics], [p].[EmailPromotion],
[p].[FirstName], [p].[LastName], [p].[MiddleName], [p].[ModifiedDate], [p].
[NameStyle], [p].[PersonType], [p].[rowguid], [p].[Suffix], [p].[Title]
FROM [Sales].[SalesPerson] AS [s]
INNER JOIN [HumanResources].[Employee] AS [e] ON [s].[BusinessEntityID] =
[e].[BusinessEntityID]
INNER JOIN [Person].[Person] AS [p] ON [e].[BusinessEntityID] =
[p].[BusinessEntityID]
```

You could run the query directly if you wanted to prove out the results. In the end, you have a much better solution by using the Include and ThenInclude navigations to bring in the data.

Task 2: Use projections to get more efficient queries

To start with the idea of projections, consider again what they are and why they are going to help you. Projections are just a way for you to use anonymous classes to model results from a query. With LINQ, you can use the Select operator and then define the projection directly in your query. Before you do that, you should decide exactly what data you want to return.

For this problem, continue with the idea that you are generating a report for the business on the results that your salespeople are getting. For this report, you need the saleperson's first and last name, their quota, their YTD sales, how much they sold last year, and their bonus. Additionally, you will bring the BusinessEntityId back as well, so that you could use these results further if necessary.

Step 1: Add the new method

Begin by adding a call to a new method named ShowAllSalespeopleUsingProjection in the Main method of the Program class in the Program.cs file after the call to ListAllSalesPeople, and then add the method as follows after the GetSalespersonDetail method and before the end of the class:

```
private static void ShowAllSalespeopleUsingProjection()
{
    using (var db = new AdventureWorksContext(_optionsBuilder.Options))
    {
        //query here...

        //foreach loop here...
    }
}
```

Next, replace the comment //query here... with the following code to get the data as an anonymous class using a projection:

```
var salespeople = db.SalesPeople
    .Include(x => x.BusinessEntity)
    .ThenInclude(y => y.BusinessEntity)
    .AsNoTracking()
    .Select(x => new
    {
        x.BusinessEntityId,
        x.BusinessEntity.BusinessEntity.FirstName,
        x.BusinessEntity.BusinessEntity.LastName,
        x.SalesQuota,
        x.SalesYtd,
        x.SalesLastYear
    }).ToList();
```

Then replace the comment //foreach loop here... with the following code:

```
foreach (var sp in salespeople)
{
    Console.WriteLine($"BID: {sp.BusinessEntityId} | Name: {sp.LastName}" +
            $", {sp.FirstName} | Quota: {sp.SalesQuota} | " +
            $"YTD Sales: {sp.SalesYtd} | SalesLastYear
            {sp.SalesLastYear}");
}
```

For clarity, the entire code is shown in Figure 9-10.

```
private static void ShowAllSalespeopleUsingProjection()
{
    using (var db = new AdventureWorksContext(_optionsBuilder.Options))
    {
        var salespeople = db.SalesPeople
                            .Include(x => x.BusinessEntity)
                            .ThenInclude(y => y.BusinessEntity)
                            .AsNoTracking()
                            .Select(x => new
                            {
                                x.BusinessEntityId,
                                x.BusinessEntity.BusinessEntity.FirstName,
                                x.BusinessEntity.BusinessEntity.LastName,
                                x.SalesQuota,
                                x.SalesYtd,
                                x.SalesLastYear
                            }).ToList();


        foreach (var sp in salespeople)
        {
            Console.WriteLine($"BID: {sp.BusinessEntityId} | Name: {sp.LastName}" +
                    $", {sp.FirstName} | Quota: {sp.SalesQuota} | " +
                    $"YTD Sales: {sp.SalesYtd} | SalesLastYear {sp.SalesLastYear}");
        }
    }
}
```

Figure 9-10. *The code is shown in its entirety for clarity*

Now run the program to see the results (expected output is shown in Figure 9-11).

```
ID: 279 |TID: 5 |Quota: 300000.0000    |Bonus: 6700.0000    |YTDSales: 2315185.6110 |Name: Tsvi, Reiter
ID: 280 |TID: 1 |Quota: 250000.0000    |Bonus: 5000.0000    |YTDSales: 1352577.1325 |Name: Pamela, Ansman-Wolfe
ID: 281 |TID: 4 |Quota: 250000.0000    |Bonus: 3550.0000    |YTDSales: 2458535.6169 |Name: Shu, Ito
ID: 282 |TID: 6 |Quota: 250000.0000    |Bonus: 5000.0000    |YTDSales: 2604540.7172 |Name: José, Saraiva
ID: 283 |TID: 1 |Quota: 250000.0000    |Bonus: 3500.0000    |YTDSales: 1573012.9383 |Name: David, Campbell
ID: 284 |TID: 1 |Quota: 300000.0000    |Bonus: 3900.0000    |YTDSales: 1576562.1966 |Name: Tete, Mensa-Annan
ID: 285 |TID:   |Quota:           |Bonus: 0.0000   |YTDSales: 172524.4512 |Name: Syed, Abbas
ID: 286 |TID: 9 |Quota: 250000.0000    |Bonus: 5650.0000    |YTDSales: 1421810.9242 |Name: Lynn, Tsoflias
ID: 287 |TID:   |Quota:           |Bonus: 0.0000   |YTDSales: 519905.9320 |Name: Amy, Alberts
ID: 288 |TID: 8 |Quota: 250000.0000    |Bonus: 75.0000 |YTDSales: 1827066.7118 |Name: Rachel, Valdez
ID: 289 |TID: 10 |Quota: 250000.0000    |Bonus: 5150.0000    |YTDSales: 4116871.2277 |Name: Jae, Pak
ID: 290 |TID: 7 |Quota: 250000.0000    |Bonus: 985.0000  |YTDSales: 3121616.3202 |Name: Ranjit, Varkey Chudukatil
BID: 274 | Name: Jiang, Stephen | Quota:      | YTD Sales: 559697.5639 | SalesLastYear 0.0000
BID: 275 | Name: Blythe, Michael | Quota: 300000.0000 | YTD Sales: 3763178.1787 | SalesLastYear 1750406.4785
BID: 276 | Name: Mitchell, Linda | Quota: 250000.0000 | YTD Sales: 4251368.5497 | SalesLastYear 1439156.0291
BID: 277 | Name: Carson, Jillian | Quota: 250000.0000 | YTD Sales: 3189418.3662 | SalesLastYear 1997186.2037
BID: 278 | Name: Vargas, Garrett | Quota: 250000.0000 | YTD Sales: 1453719.4653 | SalesLastYear 1620276.8966
BID: 279 | Name: Reiter, Tsvi | Quota: 300000.0000 | YTD Sales: 2315185.6110 | SalesLastYear 1849640.9418
BID: 280 | Name: Ansman-Wolfe, Pamela | Quota: 250000.0000 | YTD Sales: 1352577.1325 | SalesLastYear 1927059.1780
BID: 281 | Name: Ito, Shu | Quota: 250000.0000 | YTD Sales: 2458535.6169 | SalesLastYear 2073505.9999
BID: 282 | Name: Saraiva, José | Quota: 250000.0000 | YTD Sales: 2604540.7172 | SalesLastYear 2038234.6549
BID: 283 | Name: Campbell, David | Quota: 250000.0000 | YTD Sales: 1573012.9383 | SalesLastYear 1371635.3158
BID: 284 | Name: Mensa-Annan, Tete | Quota: 300000.0000 | YTD Sales: 1576562.1966 | SalesLastYear 0.0000
BID: 285 | Name: Abbas, Syed | Quota:      | YTD Sales: 172524.4512 | SalesLastYear 0.0000
BID: 286 | Name: Tsoflias, Lynn | Quota: 250000.0000 | YTD Sales: 1421810.9242 | SalesLastYear 2278548.9776
BID: 287 | Name: Alberts, Amy | Quota:      | YTD Sales: 519905.9320 | SalesLastYear 0.0000
BID: 288 | Name: Valdez, Rachel | Quota: 250000.0000 | YTD Sales: 1827066.7118 | SalesLastYear 1307949.7917
BID: 289 | Name: Pak, Jae | Quota: 250000.0000 | YTD Sales: 4116871.2277 | SalesLastYear 1635823.3967
BID: 290 | Name: Varkey Chudukatil, Ranjit | Quota: 250000.0000 | YTD Sales: 3121616.3202 | SalesLastYear 2396539.7601

C:\APressEntityFramework\Code\EFCore_Activity0901\EFCore_Activity0901\bin\Debug\net6.0\EFCore_Activity0901.exe (process 5628)
```

Figure 9-11. *The projected results work as expected, and data is easily shown for the salespeople*

As always, you should review the output in the SQL Server Profiler to ensure you are running a good query that is efficient. Reviewing the results shows the query is generated as follows:

```
SELECT [s].[BusinessEntityID] AS [BusinessEntityId], [p].[FirstName],
[p].[LastName], [s].[SalesQuota], [s].[SalesYTD] AS [SalesYtd],
[s].[SalesLastYear]
FROM [Sales].[SalesPerson] AS [s]
INNER JOIN [HumanResources].[Employee] AS [e] ON [s].[BusinessEntityID] =
[e].[BusinessEntityID]
INNER JOIN [Person].[Person] AS [p] ON [e].[BusinessEntityID] =
[p].[BusinessEntityID]
```

Additionally, the output is shown in Figure 9-12 for you to review.

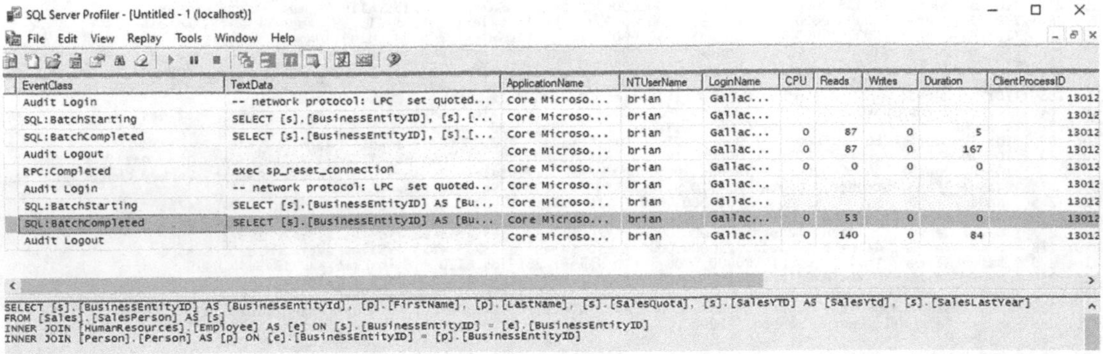

Figure 9-12. *The SQL Server Profiler confirms the query is effective and efficient*

This is an incredible finding! Do you see how much more efficient your query is using projections? Look at the overall results. The number of reads is lower, and the duration is almost 50% lower. Why do you think that is? Review both queries to see the difference. In the first query, your request pulled all of the columns from every table across all of the joins. Using the projection, EF was able to interpret exactly what you needed and only queried for those results. This proves that EF is every bit as efficient as you need it to be – or rather – as you tell it to be. If you aren't convinced now that using projections is an extremely powerful tool to maximize the efficiency of your queries using EF and that EF is every bit as efficient as you can be with direct queries, then I think you should rework this activity to further realize the power of using projections and the effect of well-defined queries in EF with LINQ.

As any good salesperson (see what I did there?) would do, I have a "but wait, there's more" moment for you to ensure you take me up on this deal.

Go back to the query you just added and remove the two statements that do the `Include` and the `ThenInclude` to hydrate the navigation properties. Trust me, just do it. Then run the program. Do you think it will work (the current state of the code is shown in Figure 9-13 for clarity)?

```
using (var db = new AdventureWorksContext(_optionsBuilder.Options))
{
    var salespeople = db.SalesPeople
                        .AsNoTracking()
                        .Select(x => new
                        {
                            x.BusinessEntityId,
                            x.BusinessEntity.BusinessEntity.FirstName,
                            x.BusinessEntity.BusinessEntity.LastName,
                            x.SalesQuota,
                            x.SalesYtd,
                            x.SalesLastYear
                        }).ToList();

    foreach (var sp in salespeople)
    {
        Console.WriteLine($"BID: {sp.BusinessEntityId} | Name: {sp.LastName}" +
            $", {sp.FirstName} | Quota: {sp.SalesQuota} | " +
            $"YTD Sales: {sp.SalesYtd} | SalesLastYear {sp.SalesLastYear}");
    }
}
```

Figure 9-13. *The Include and ThenInclude navigation properties are removed from the query when using a projection*

Running the program should yield the same results you've seen before, even though the Include and ThenInclude statements are removed from your code.

As you can see, EF automatically fills in the gaps for the missing data when you use a projection. You really can write extremely efficient queries against your database and write less code using EF with LINQ and projections.

Now we have a solid foundation for using LINQ with projections, and we understand when to perform the various transformations. Armed with this understanding, we are ready to go just a bit deeper, as you likely will have to do in a real-world solution.

Step 2: Filter and sort the data

Imagine your solution needs to get data for a manager that reports the information for your salespeople (as earlier) but also includes things like the territories that the salesperson is in, the number of orders, and a count of products that the salesperson has sold. The manager also needs to sort this data by last name and then first name and needs to be able to filter the list to only those who have hit a certain sales dollar amount, which they will input as a filter.

This is some heavy lifting for sure and might be worthy of views and stored procedures, depending on how much data and manipulation you truly need, and you might also use JavaScript or another tool to further filter results in something like a web application that shows results in a grid. However, you can do this all efficiently in the query itself, which you will do next. To do this well, you'll have to leverage everything you've learned to this point regarding LINQ, EF, and projections.

There are things you should learn along the way, so rather than building this all at once, you'll build it from the top down to see a few things in action as you go.

Start with the basics of the data request as discussed earlier. You need to get a lot of the same information you've already seen, but you also need a list of the territories, a count of total orders, and a count of total products. Total products will be tricky because there is a quantity in each order detail. Review Figure 9-14 to see the overall structure of the database that you need to be aware of for your results to work as expected, which includes the tables SalesTerritoryHistory, SalesTerritory, SalesOrderHeader, SalesOrderDetail, SpecialOfferProduct, SalesPerson, Employee, Person, SpecialOffer, and Product.

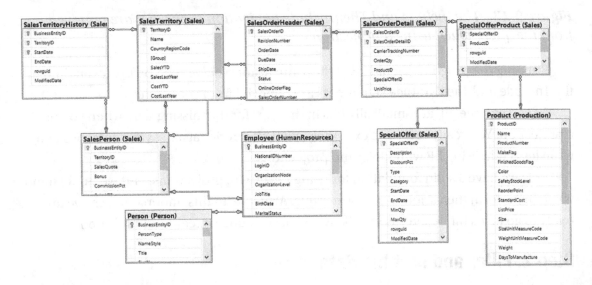

Figure 9-14. *The database diagram that shows all entities in play for this query includes the tables as identified earlier*

To make this work, start by adding a bit of code to the main method that makes an appropriate call to a new method named GenerateSalesReportData. Comment out the other two method calls in the Main method so that only this new method will run.

Then add the following code for the new method:

```
private static void GenerateSalesReportData()
{
    using (var db = new AdventureWorksContext(_optionsBuilder.Options))
    {
        var salesReportData = db.SalesPeople.Select(sp => new
        {
            beid = sp.BusinessEntityId,
            sp.BusinessEntity.BusinessEntity.FirstName,
            sp.BusinessEntity.BusinessEntity.LastName,
            sp.SalesYtd,
            Territories = sp.SalesTerritoryHistories
                        .Select(y => y.Territory.Name)
        }).OrderBy(srds => srds.LastName)
            .ThenBy(srds => srds.FirstName)
            .ThenByDescending(srds => srds.SalesYtd)
            .ToList();

        foreach (var srd in salesReportData)
        {
            Console.WriteLine($"{srd.beid}| {srd.LastName}, {srd.FirstName}
            |" +
                $"YTD Sales: {srd.SalesYtd} |" +
                $"{string.Join(',', srd.Territories)}");
        }
    }
}
```

This code will start you off with a projection to get the data for the salespeople with their names and sales YTD, as well as information about their territories.

Note that it is further ordered by last name, then first name, and then the number of sales. Feel free to change this ordering if you want to see a different order, such as by the highest amount of YTD sales to lowest.

In the previous code insertion, you added the following foreach loop code to print the data following the query to get sales report data:

```
foreach (var srd in salesReportData)
{
    Console.WriteLine($"{srd.beid}| {srd.LastName}, {srd.FirstName} |" +
        $"YTD Sales: {srd.SalesYtd} |" +
        $"{string.Join(',', srd.Territories)}");
}
```

Running the query gives the results shown in Figure 9-15.

```
│ID: 290 | Name: Varkey Chudukatil, Ranjit | Quota: 250000.0000 | YTD Sale:
285| Abbas, Syed |YTD Sales: 172524.4512 |
287| Alberts, Amy |YTD Sales: 519905.9320 |
280| Ansman-Wolfe, Pamela |YTD Sales: 1352577.1325 |Northwest
275| Blythe, Michael |YTD Sales: 3763178.1787 |Northeast,Central
283| Campbell, David |YTD Sales: 1573012.9383 |Northwest
277| Carson, Jillian |YTD Sales: 3189418.3662 |Central,Northeast
281| Ito, Shu |YTD Sales: 2458535.6169 |Southwest
274| Jiang, Stephen |YTD Sales: 559697.5639 |
284| Mensa-Annan, Tete |YTD Sales: 1576562.1966 |Northwest
276| Mitchell, Linda |YTD Sales: 4251368.5497 |Southwest
289| Pak, Jae |YTD Sales: 4116871.2277 |Canada
279| Reiter, Tsvi |YTD Sales: 2315185.6110 |Southeast
282| Saraiva, José |YTD Sales: 2604540.7172 |Canada,United Kingdom
286| Tsoflias, Lynn |YTD Sales: 1421810.9242 |Australia
288| Valdez, Rachel |YTD Sales: 1827066.7118 |Germany
278| Vargas, Garrett |YTD Sales: 1453719.4653 |Canada
290| Varkey Chudukatil, Ranjit |YTD Sales: 3121616.3202 |France

C:\APressEntityFramework\Code\EFCore_Activity0901\EFCore_Activity0901\bin\│
```

Figure 9-15. *The results are shown with the start of the sales report data*

Next, you need to get information about order counts. To do this, you're going to need to get all the sales orders and use those results, which you'll do with the line of code OrderCount = sp.SalesOrderHeaders.Count() added to the query after the declaration of Territories in the projection. The new query should be as follows:

```
var salesReportData = db.SalesPeople.Select(sp => new
{
    beid = sp.BusinessEntityId,
    sp.BusinessEntity.BusinessEntity.FirstName,
    sp.BusinessEntity.BusinessEntity.LastName,
```

```
    sp.SalesYtd,
    Territories = sp.SalesTerritoryHistories
                    .Select(y => y.Territory.Name),
    OrderCount = sp.SalesOrderHeaders.Count()
}).OrderBy(srds => srds.LastName)
    .ThenBy(srds => srds.FirstName)
    .ThenByDescending(srds => srds.SalesYtd)
    .ToList();
```

Replace the output in the foreach loop to show the count of orders as follows:

```
Console.WriteLine($"{srd.beid}| {srd.LastName}, {srd.FirstName} |" +
    $"YTD Sales: {srd.SalesYtd} |" +
    $"{string.Join(',', srd.Territories)} |" +
    $"Order Count: {srd.OrderCount}");
```

Run the program to see the additional results. Ensure they look as you would expect.

Next, you need to get the total number of products sold. This is going to be more difficult because of the setup of the tables and the fact that an order detail might have multiple products in it based on quantity. To get this right, you need to get all of the order details for each order header and then sum up the quantity of products sold across all of those order details.

To make this happen, you'll leverage the power of SelectMany. The SelectMany operator will allow you to instantly grab all the order details and use them as a result set in your query. Add the following line of code to the projection in the query after the call to get the OrderCount (don't forget to add a comma after the sp.SalesHeader.Count() statement):

```
TotalProductsSold = sp.SalesOrderHeaders
                        .SelectMany(y => y.SalesOrderDetails)
                        .Sum(z => z.OrderQty)
```

Note the select many that gets all the order details and then sums their quantity.

Replace the output statement in the foreach loop with the following code:

```
Console.WriteLine($"{srd.beid}| {srd.LastName}, {srd.FirstName} |" +
    $"YTD Sales: {srd.SalesYtd} |" +
    $"{string.Join(',', srd.Territories)} |" +
    $"Order Count: {srd.OrderCount} |" +
    $"Products Sold: {srd.TotalProductsSold}");
```

Now run the program and ensure you have the results to include order count and product sold count. Your results should be similar to what is shown in Figure 9-16.

```
285| Abbas, Syed |YTD Sales: 172524.4512 |  |Order Count: 16 |Products Sold: 825
287| Alberts, Amy |YTD Sales: 519905.9320 |  |Order Count: 39 |Products Sold: 2012
280| Ansman-Wolfe, Pamela |YTD Sales: 1352577.1325 |Northwest |Order Count: 95 |Products Sold: 7360
275| Blythe, Michael |YTD Sales: 3763178.1787 |Northeast,Central |Order Count: 450 |Products Sold: 23058
283| Campbell, David |YTD Sales: 1573012.9383 |Northwest |Order Count: 189 |Products Sold: 8172
277| Carson, Jillian |YTD Sales: 3189418.3662 |Central,Northeast |Order Count: 473 |Products Sold: 27051
281| Ito, Shu |YTD Sales: 2458535.6169 |Southwest |Order Count: 242 |Products Sold: 15397
274| Jiang, Stephen |YTD Sales: 559697.5639 |  |Order Count: 48 |Products Sold: 3095
284| Mensa-Annan, Tete |YTD Sales: 1576562.1966 |Northwest |Order Count: 140 |Products Sold: 5650
276| Mitchell, Linda |YTD Sales: 4251368.5497 |Southwest |Order Count: 418 |Products Sold: 27229
289| Pak, Jae |YTD Sales: 4116871.2277 |Canada |Order Count: 348 |Products Sold: 26231
279| Reiter, Tsvi |YTD Sales: 2315185.6110 |Southeast |Order Count: 429 |Products Sold: 16431
282| Saraiva, José |YTD Sales: 2604540.7172 |Canada,United Kingdom |Order Count: 271 |Products Sold: 15220
286| Tsoflias, Lynn |YTD Sales: 1421810.9242 |Australia |Order Count: 109 |Products Sold: 4123
288| Valdez, Rachel |YTD Sales: 1827066.7118 |Germany |Order Count: 130 |Products Sold: 7033
278| Vargas, Garrett |YTD Sales: 1453719.4653 |Canada |Order Count: 234 |Products Sold: 11544
290| Varkey Chudukatil, Ranjit |YTD Sales: 3121616.3202 |France |Order Count: 175 |Products Sold: 14085

C:\APressEntityFramework\Code\EFCore_Activity0901\EFCore_Activity0901\bin\Debug\net6.0\EFCore_Activity0901.e
```

Figure 9-16. *The results are shown to use as validation that all of the data is showing as expected*

Next, you need to add a filter for the employee sales YTD minimum as requested. At the start of the method, prompt the user to enter a minimum dollar amount for SalesYtd with the following code at the start of the GenerateSalesReportData method before the using statement, making sure to just exit if the user enters malicious or incorrect data:

```
Console.WriteLine("What is the minimum amount of sales?");
var input = Console.ReadLine();
decimal filter = 0.0m;

if (!decimal.TryParse(input, out filter))
{
    Console.WriteLine("Bad input");
    return;
}
```

This code will take input and garner a variable that is a decimal called filter, with a value that is input by the user.

Next, add the following code to filter the results in the original query after the original Select and before the OrderBy statement:

```
.Where(srdata => srdata.SalesYtd > filter)
```

For clarity, the query at this point should be

```
var salesReportData = db.SalesPeople.Select(sp => new
{
    beid = sp.BusinessEntityId,
    sp.BusinessEntity.BusinessEntity.FirstName,
    sp.BusinessEntity.BusinessEntity.LastName,
    sp.SalesYtd,
    Territories = sp.SalesTerritoryHistories
                    .Select(y => y.Territory.Name),
    OrderCount = sp.SalesOrderHeaders.Count(),
    TotalProductsSold = sp.SalesOrderHeaders
        .SelectMany(y => y.SalesOrderDetails)
        .Sum(z => z.OrderQty)
}).Where(srdata => srdata.SalesYtd > filter)
    .OrderBy(srds => srds.LastName)
    .ThenBy(srds => srds.FirstName)
    .ThenByDescending(srds => srds.SalesYtd)
    .ToList();
```

The call will allow the results to only return data where the YTD sales is greater than the input filter.

Run the program to see results, using a large filter, such as 20,000,000. You should see no results. Run the program again and put in a smaller number, such as 3,000,000. This time you should see a few results (see Figure 9-17).

```
What is the minimum amount of sales?
3,000,000
275|  Blythe, Michael  |YTD Sales: 3763178.1787  |Northeast,Central  |Order Count: 450 |Products Sold: 23058
277|  Carson, Jillian  |YTD Sales: 3189418.3662  |Central,Northeast  |Order Count: 473 |Products Sold: 27051
276|  Mitchell, Linda  |YTD Sales: 4251368.5497  |Southwest |Order Count: 418 |Products Sold: 27229
289|  Pak, Jae |YTD Sales: 4116871.2277 |Canada |Order Count: 348 |Products Sold: 26231
290|  Varkey Chudukatil, Ranjit |YTD Sales: 3121616.3202 |France |Order Count: 175 |Products Sold: 14085

C:\APressEntityFramework\Code\EFCore_Activity0901\EFCore_Activity0901\bin\Debug\net6.0\EFCore_Activity0901.
```

Figure 9-17. *The query with a filter allows the manager to get details about all of the salespeople that have sold greater than 3 million dollars as reported in their YTD Sales column*

The report is looking pretty good based on our original request. You could be content at this point, but there is one more thing to consider, which is using projections to a DTO object rather than an anonymous class.

Step 3: Project the data to a DTO

To end this activity, you'll create a DTO to be mapped from the results of your query. This will allow you to see one last point – that you can project results into a pre-defined object, not just into anonymous classes. This is highly useful in larger systems, as the ability to communicate with a pre-defined object makes it much easier to transfer data between layers. This will also position you for the final two activities where you'll get to learn about using AutoMapper to help with the data type of these projections.

Ordinarily, I'd recommend putting DTOs into a separate project. For brevity, however, in this activity, you'll just add your DTOs to a folder in the EFCore_DbLibrary project.

Begin by creating a call to a new method named GenerateSalesReportDataToDTO in the main method. Comment out the original call to GenerateSalesReportData to limit results to the new method only.

For now, just make an exact copy of the GenerateSaleReportData method and call it GenerateSalesreportDataToDTO.

In the EFCore_DBLibrary project, add a new folder called DTOs and then add a new class file to that folder called SalesReportListingDto.cs. In that file, add the following code:

```
public class SalesReportListingDto
{
    [Required]
    public int BusinessEntityId { get; set; }
    public string FirstName { get; set; }
    public string LastName { get; set; }
    public decimal? SalesYtd { get; set; }
    public IEnumerable<string> Territories { get; set; }
    public int TotalProductsSold { get; set; }
    public int TotalOrders { get; set; }
    public string DisplayName => $"{LastName}, {FirstName}";
    public string DisplayTerritories => string.Join(",", Territories);
    public override string ToString()
    {
        return $"BID: {BusinessEntityId} |{DisplayName,25}|
        {DisplayTerritories,25}|" +
```

```
            $"{SalesYtd} | Orders: {TotalOrders} |" +
            $"Products Sold: {TotalProductsSold}";
    }
}
```

You will also need to bring in the using statement using `System.ComponentModel.DataAnnotations;`.

Next, replace the query in the `GenerateSalesReportDataToDTO` method with the following:

```
var salesReportData = db.SalesPeople.Select(sp => new SalesReportListingDto
{
    BusinessEntityId = sp.BusinessEntityId,
    FirstName = sp.BusinessEntity.BusinessEntity.FirstName,
    LastName = sp.BusinessEntity.BusinessEntity.LastName,
    SalesYtd = sp.SalesYtd,
    Territories = sp.SalesTerritoryHistories
                    .Select(y => y.Territory.Name),
    TotalOrders = sp.SalesOrderHeaders.Count(),
    TotalProductsSold = sp.SalesOrderHeaders
                          .SelectMany(y => y.SalesOrderDetails)
                          .Sum(z => z.OrderQty)
}).Where(srdata => srdata.SalesYtd > filter)
    .OrderBy(srds => srds.LastName)
    .ThenBy(srds => srds.FirstName)
    .ThenByDescending(srds => srds.SalesYtd)
    .ToList();
```

You will also need to bring in the using statement using `EFCore_DbLibrary.DTOs;` in order to correctly reference the new DTO object.

Then update the foreach loop to simply leverage the `ToString` method from the `SalesReportListingDto`:

```
foreach (var srd in salesReportData)
{
    Console.WriteLine(srd.ToString());
}
```

For clarity, the code for the GenerateSalesReportDataToDTO method code is shown in Figure 9-18.

```
private static void GenerateSalesReportDataToDTO()
{
    Console.WriteLine("What is the minimum amount of sales?");
    var input = Console.ReadLine();
    decimal filter = 0.0m;

    if (!decimal.TryParse(input, out filter))
    {
        Console.WriteLine("Bad input");
        return;
    }

    using (var db = new AdventureWorksContext(_optionsBuilder.Options))
    {
        var salesReportData = db.SalesPeople.Select(sp => new SalesReportListingDto
        {
            BusinessEntityId = sp.BusinessEntityId,
            FirstName = sp.BusinessEntity.BusinessEntity.FirstName,
            LastName = sp.BusinessEntity.BusinessEntity.LastName,
            SalesYtd = sp.SalesYtd,
            Territories = sp.SalesTerritoryHistories
            .Select(y => y.Territory.Name),
            TotalOrders = sp.SalesOrderHeaders.Count(),
            TotalProductsSold = sp.SalesOrderHeaders
                    .SelectMany(y => y.SalesOrderDetails)
                    .Sum(z => z.OrderQty)
        }).Where(srdata => srdata.SalesYtd > filter)
            .OrderBy(srds => srds.LastName)
            .ThenBy(srds => srds.FirstName)
            .ThenByDescending(srds => srds.SalesYtd)
            .ToList();

        foreach (var srd in salesReportData)
        {
            Console.WriteLine(srd.ToString());
        }
    }
}
```

Figure 9-18. *The new method leverages the new DTO object and appears a bit cleaner than the original select into an anonymous class*

Run the program to see the expected results.

Note that there is one last thing to clean up. In the original query, the final call is making a call `ToList`. When you make this call, you force the system to evaluate the results. In the future, you might want to do more things with the query before you actually force the execution. For this reason, it would be better to defer the execution to the point where it is needed, which, in this case, is the foreach loop.

Remove the final `ToList` call from the query and just end the query after the `ThenByDescending(srcs => srds.SalesYtd)`. Run the program. You will still see the expected results, but the difference is that the database call is not made until after you try to iterate the query, not as the query was built. Figure 9-19 shows the final result of this activity when an input of 3,000,000 is used for the sales YTD filter.

```
What is the minimum amount of sales?
3,000,000
BID: 275 |              Blythe, Michael|  Northeast,Central|3763178.1787 | Orders: 450 |Products Sold: 23058
BID: 277 |              Carson, Jillian|  Central,Northeast|3189418.3662 | Orders: 473 |Products Sold: 27051
BID: 276 |              Mitchell, Linda|          Southwest|4251368.5497 | Orders: 418 |Products Sold: 27229
BID: 289 |                     Pak, Jae|             Canada|4116871.2277 | Orders: 348 |Products Sold: 26231
BID: 290 |Varkey Chudukatil, Ranjit|              France|3121616.3202 | Orders: 175 |Products Sold: 14085

C:\APressEntityFramework\Code\EFCore_Activity0901\EFCore_Activity0901\bin\Debug\net6.0\EFCore_Activity0901.exe (
```

Figure 9-19. *The final results work as expected, and the data is projected into a DTO object rather than an anonymous class*

Activity 9-1 summary

In this activity, you used the more densely populated AdventureWorks database to learn about working with LINQ using projections. You started by getting the data using an n + 1 query and evaluated the efficiency in your SQL Server Profiler.

After learning about the pain of this query and how it is a common error, you learned how to use navigation properties on the entities to get the data populated by EF using LINQ.

You then learned that although this is more efficient than the first approach, an even better approach existed with the use of projections. By projecting your data, you found that you didn't need to explicitly define the include statements for the navigation properties, and you learned that EF with projections is an extremely efficient way to get your data when joining data across tables.

After looking at LINQ with EF using projections, you solidified the activity by also seeing how you can easily map projections to any custom DTO object that you created.

Putting this all together, you are now in position to leverage EF with LINQ and projections to create efficient solutions, and you are now ready to start utilizing AutoMapper to make your solutions easier to work with.

Activity 9-2: Setting up AutoMapper

In this second activity for Chapter 9, you're going to set up *AutoMapper* in your custom Inventory project. After you get set up, you'll do a quick check to see that things are in place correctly for using AutoMapper for the rest of the activities in this book. Activity 9-3 will then heavily leverage AutoMapper to show how to work with your efficient objects in robust solutions.

Task 0: Getting started

This activity will switch back to the code for the `InventoryDbManager` project that you've been working on throughout the book. The last time you used this project was for Activity 7-3, if you are working through each of the projects in order through the book. If you have a working `InventoryDbManager` solution and you've completed the activities in order, feel free to keep using those files for this activity. If you are unsure or just want a clean start, it may be easier to just grab the `EFCore_Activity09-2_StarterFiles` project. As always, refer to Appendix A for more information on working with starter files.

Task 1: Get AutoMapper packages and configure the solution

In this first task, you will get the AutoMapper packages for the solution.

Step 1: Get the NuGet packages

You can get the AutoMapper projects by setting your PMC to the main activity project and running the command `Install-Package AutoMapper`. If you prefer, however, you can also just use the Manage NuGet Packages for your solution tool, browse and find AutoMapper, and then install it. Either way, ensure you are using AutoMapper on your main activity project – not the DBLibrary project.

Figure 9-20 shows the installation of the AutoMapper NuGet package from the Manage Packages for Solution dialog.

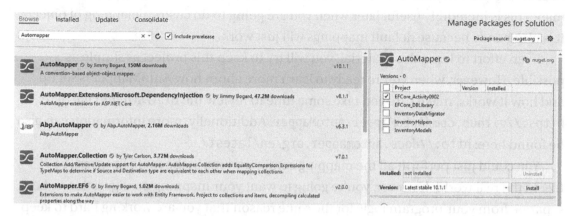

Figure 9-20. *Installing AutoMapper is easily accomplished from the Manage NuGet Packages for Solution dialog*

In addition to the base project, for your projects in this book, you will also need the `AutoMapper.Extensions.Microsoft.DependencyInjection` library. Use either the PMC or the dialog as earlier to install this package into your main activity project (see Figure 9-21).

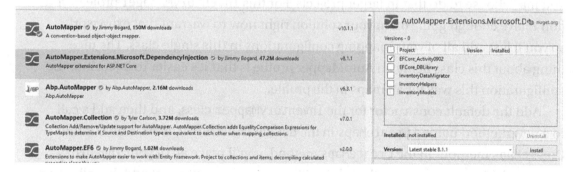

Figure 9-21. *Both AutoMapper packages are currently installed on the main activity project*

Once these packages are installed, we're done! Just kidding, there are a few more things to do.

Step 2: Create the InventoryMapper profile

In order for AutoMapper to work correctly, you have to let it know what types you want to map. This is incredibly useful later when you are going to do custom mapping of objects. It is also handy because default mappings will just work.

In an effort to learn this material, you will try to keep this project as simple as possible. However, when you're ready to learn more about how AutoMapper is set up and how it works, make sure you take some time to review the README.md file here: https://github.com/AutoMapper/AutoMapper. Additionally, more information can also be found here: http://docs.automapper.org/en/latest/.

You could just perform all the mapping configurations in the main Program.cs file. In the real world, however, you're going to want your mapping configuration to be separate from your program logic for the same reason that you are working hard to keep each piece of this entire book separate, mainly that a well-organized project will save you a number of headaches in the future.

Begin this step by adding a new class to handle your mapping declarations. Add a new class to the main activity project in a file called InventoryMapper.cs. This InventoryMapper class needs to inherit from a base class called Profile, which requires the using statement using Automapper; since it is part of the AutoMapper library. In theory, you can separate your various business unit mapping logic into separate classes. You may choose to do that in larger projects. For this InventoryManager project, you don't have enough going on in your solution right now to warrant that extra work, so you'll just add all of your mapping configurations in this single class. The nice thing about this class being an AutoMapper profile is that it's easier to inject into the configuration this way for all maps in the profile.

Add the default constructor for the InventoryMapper class, and then add a call to a new method named CreateMaps in the default constructor. Next, stub out the CreateMaps method. In the CreateMaps method, you'll place all of your Inventory mapping logic. For now, even though it will not work correctly, just add the following two lines of code (ItemDto and CategoryDto are not yet created):

```
CreateMap<Item, ItemDto>();
CreateMap<Category, CategoryDto>();
```

When that is all set up, your code should look like this:

```
public class InventoryMapper :   Profile
{
    public InventoryMapper()
    {
        CreateMaps();
    }

    private void CreateMaps()
    {
        CreateMap<Item, ItemDto>();
        CreateMap<Category, CategoryDto>();
    }
}
```

As of right now, the code will not compile, so you first need to create the two DTO classes that don't currently exist to prevent build errors. You'll also bring in missing using statements once all the code is created, but you could bring in the InventoryModels using statement now if you want to resolve issues with Item and Category.

Task 2: Create the DTO objects

The last step mapped two DTO Objects, ItemDto and CategoryDto. In this task, you will create these DTO objects for use in your solution.

Step 1: Create the Item DTO

In the InventoryModels project, under the DTOs folder, add a new class file ItemDTO.cs. In this file, add two string properties for Name and Description and two int properties for Id and CategoryId. Also, you'll have a simple ToString method to print details. The code for this new DTO should be as follows:

```
public class ItemDto
{
    public int Id { get; set; }
    public string Name { get; set; }
    public string Description { get; set; }
    public int CategoryId { get; set; }
```

```
    public override string ToString()
    {
        return $"{Name,-25} | {Description}";
    }
}
```

For clarity, review Figure 9-22 to see the position and expected code for the ItemDto class in the DTOs folder of the InventoryModels project.

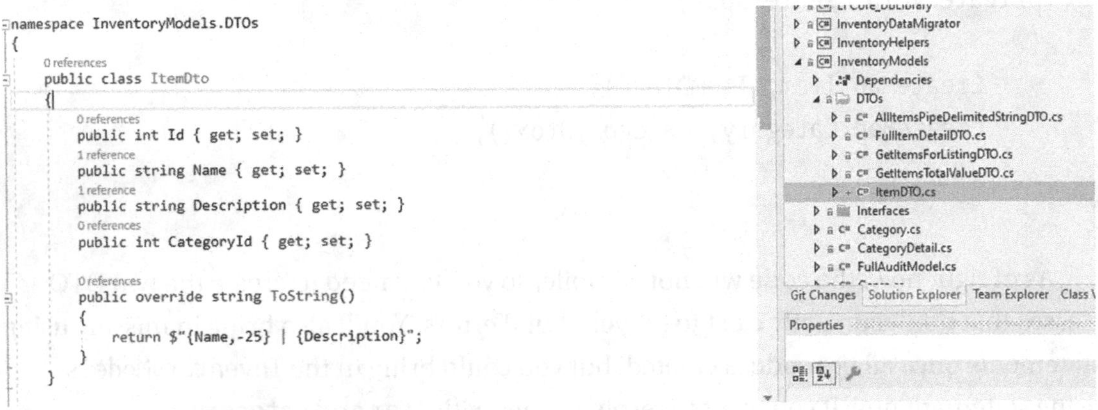

Figure 9-22. *The ItemDto class is created and placed in the InventoryModels project in the DTOs folder as expected*

Step 2: Create the Category DTO

In the InventoryModels project, under the DTOs folder, add a new class file CategoryDTO.cs. Add the following code to create the CategoryDto class with a single property for an int Id (this will be enhanced in future activities):

```
public class CategoryDto
{
    public int Id { get; set; }
}
```

Save your changes, then go back to the InventoryMapper file in the main project, and add the missing using statements using InventoryModels and using InventoryModels. Dtos to the top of the file. This fixes the issue for the two DTO types in the mapping profile.

Ensure that your project will build without error before proceeding to the next task.

Task 3: Set up the program to use AutoMapper and configure mappings

Back in the main method in the Program.cs file, in the space between the class declaration and the Main method, following the _optionsBuilder or _loggedInUserId variable, whichever is your last variable before the Main method, add three static variables using the following code:

```
private static MapperConfiguration _mapperConfig;
private static IMapper _mapper;
private static IServiceProvider _serviceProvider;
```

Make sure to also add the using statement using AutoMapper; to resolve build issues.

Next, add a call to a new method named BuildMapper right after the call to the BuildOptions method before making any calls to List or Get methods in the main method of the Program class. Add the method with a blank body for now. Remember that in this console project, methods must be static to be called from the program's main method (this is not because of AutoMapper).

Next, we need to set the configuration for AutoMapper, and we need to inject it using a service collection and a service provider. This will set up our ability to use AutoMapper.

In the BuildMapper method, add the following code, and then add the using statement using Microsoft.Extensions.DependencyInjection; to the top of the file:

```
var services = new ServiceCollection();
services.AddAutoMapper(typeof(InventoryMapper));
_serviceProvider = services.BuildServiceProvider();
```

The preceding statement sets up a service collection to allow you to use dependency injection where AutoMapper is concerned. The service collection then gets AutoMapper, and you inject the service profile assembly. If you had other assemblies, you could just add them in the same call by using commas to separate the different assemblies.

After adding the service, you need to set up the mapping configuration. Add the following lines in the BuildMapper method after the three you just added earlier:

```
_mapperConfig = new MapperConfiguration(cfg => {
    cfg.AddProfile<InventoryMapper>();
});
_mapperConfig.AssertConfigurationIsValid();
_mapper = _mapperConfig.CreateMapper();
```

These lines of code set up the configuration and tell AutoMapper to use the InventoryMapper profile (which currently has two type mappings and will eventually have more). Using the profile keeps this section much cleaner than manually adding all of the object maps directly to the configuration as inline code.

Next, you make sure that your configuration is valid, which ensures your types are correctly mapped, and then you conclude by instantiating your mapper object using the CreateMapper call.

At this point, AutoMapper is set up correctly. If you run the program, you should not get any errors, even though you aren't implementing any concrete uses of AutoMapper yet. For clarity, the finished BuildMapper method is shown in Figure 9-23.

```
1 reference
private static void BuildMapper()
{
    var services = new ServiceCollection();
    services.AddAutoMapper(typeof(InventoryMapper));
    _serviceProvider = services.BuildServiceProvider();

    _mapperConfig = new MapperConfiguration(cfg => {
        cfg.AddProfile<InventoryMapper>();
    });
    _mapperConfig.AssertConfigurationIsValid();
    _mapper = _mapperConfig.CreateMapper();
}
```

Figure 9-23. *The BuildMapper method is implemented and shown for clarity using the code from earlier*

Save and run your program to ensure there are no errors before proceeding to the final task.

Task 4: Leverage AutoMapper in your solution

In this final task for the activity, you will leverage AutoMapper to automatically map Item objects to ItemDto objects without you having to do a lot of extra work. This is the power that AutoMapper will give us.

Return to the Program class and locate the ListInventory method. In that method, add the following line of code between the database call and the printout of the results:

```
var result = _mapper.Map<List<Item>, List<ItemDto>>(items);
```

Then change the output line to

```
result.ForEach(x => Console.WriteLine($"New Item: {x}"));
```

When completed, the ListInventory code should be

```
private static void ListInventory()
{
    using (var db = new InventoryDbContext(_optionsBuilder.Options))
    {
        var items = db.Items.OrderBy(x => x.Name).ToList();
        var result = _mapper.Map<List<Item>, List<ItemDto>>(items);

        result.ForEach(x => Console.WriteLine($"New Item: {x}"));
    }
}
```

Run the program to see AutoMapper in action. If you want, put a breakpoint on the output statement to see how the result object was correctly mapped from the items list (review Figure 9-24).

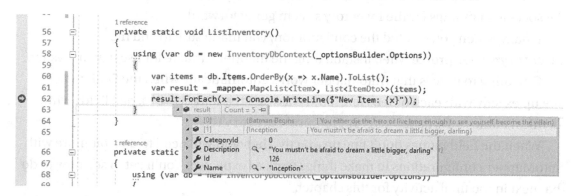

Figure 9-24. *AutoMapper has allowed for the correct translation of an Item to an ItemDto without you having to do any extra work, now that AutoMapper is in your solution and you have set the configuration and mappings*

Running the program shows the overall output of the new items correctly utilized in code, and their ToString methods are leveraged for output (see Figure 9-25).

```
New Item: Batman Begins               | You either die the hero or live long enough to see yourself become the villain
New Item: Inception                    | You mustn't be afraid to dream a little bigger, darling
New Item: Remember the Titans          | Left Side, Strong Side
New Item: Star Wars: The Empire Strikes Back | He will join us or die, master
New Item: Top Gun                      | I feel the need, the need for speed!
ITEM Batman Begins] You either die the hero or live long enough to see yourself become the villain
ITEM Inception] You mustn't be afraid to dream a little bigger, darling
ITEM Remember the Titans] Left Side, Strong Side
ITEM Star Wars: The Empire Strikes Back] He will join us or die, master
ITEM Top Gun] I feel the need, the need for speed!
All active Items: Batman Begins|Inception|Remember the Titans|Star Wars: The Empire Strikes Back|Top Gun
New Item] 125      |Batman Begins                          |1000|23990.00
New Item] 126      |Inception                              |1000|4990.00
New Item] 127      |Remember the Titans                    |1000|7990.00
New Item] 128      |Star Wars: The Empire Strikes Back     |1000|35990.00
New Item] 129      |Top Gun                                |1000|8990.00
New Item] 125      |Batman Begins                          |You either die the hero or live long enough to see yourself
New Item] 126      |Inception                              |You mustn't be afraid to dream a little bigger, darling|Leon
New Item] 127      |Remember the Titans                    |Left Side, Strong Side|Denzel Washington|          |
New Item] 128      |Star Wars: The Empire Strikes Back     |He will join us or die, master|Mark Hamill|    |
New Item] 129      |Top Gun                                |I feel the need, the need for speed!|Tom Cruise|     |
C:\APressEntityFramework\Code\EFCore_Activity0902\EFCore_Activity0902\bin\Debug\net6.0\EFCore_Activity0902.exe (process 14144) exite
To automatically close the console when debugging stops, enable Tools->Options->Debugging->Automatically close the console when debu
Press any key to close this window . . .
```

Figure 9-25. *The program is running, and the new ItemDto objects are easily leveraged as they are mapped from Item objects via AutoMapper*

Activity 9-2 summary

In this activity, you were able to successfully set up AutoMapper to map one object type to another. You created the mapping configuration by setting up the services in your project to hold a single instance of AutoMapper.

You also set up an InventoryMapper profile where you can easily add and work with the specific mappings for the Inventory system going forward.

Finally, when you created the configuration, you made sure to add the InventoryMapper profile when instantiating the mapper variable for use in your system.

One thing to note is that AutoMapper works automatically when the field names line up exactly with each other. Here, both classes, Item and ItemDto, had fields with identical names – Id, Name, Description, and CategoryId.

When the field names don't line up exactly, then you will need to do a bit more with AutoMapper configurations to make things work as expected. You'll get to see how to do that next in the final activity for this chapter.

Activity 9-3: Working with AutoMapper

In the final activity for Chapter 9, you're going to continue working with AutoMapper and LINQ so that you can solidify your knowledge of how to both work with LINQ in some more advanced queries and also so that you can be in a good place to fully leverage the power of AutoMapper in the future in all of your projects.

Task 0: Getting started

Before running through this activity, there are a couple of things that you need to do, including getting the right files (yours or the starter files) and then adding more data.

Step 1: Get the files

For this activity, you can either continue where you left off on the last project or you can get a copy of the starter files EFCore_Activity09-3_StarterFiles.zip. If you choose the starter pack, as always, make sure that your database connection string is configured correctly, then save and build the project, and run the update-database command to make sure you don't have any missing migrations. Finally, run the program to ensure that it works correctly before proceeding.

Step 2: Seed more data

In order to really leverage the power of projections and EF and AutoMapper, you'll need a bit more data. Particularly, you will want to have a couple of items in each category.

Open the InventoryDataMigrator project and add a few more Items to the mix to span a couple of Categories using the following code after the existing seeded items in the BuildItems.cs file:

```
new Item() { Name = "Practical Entity Framework", CurrentOrFinalPrice =
27.99m, Description = "The book you are reading on Entity Framework",
    IsOnSale = false, Notes = "", PurchasePrice = 28.99m, PurchasedDate =
    null, Quantity = 1, SoldDate = null, CreatedByUserId = SEED_USER_ID,
    CreatedDate = DateTime.Now,
    IsDeleted = false, IsActive = true, Players = new List<Player>() {
                new Player() { CreatedDate = DateTime.Now,IsActive =
                true,IsDeleted = false,CreatedByUserId = SEED_USER_ID,
                        Description = "https://www.linkedin/in/
                        brianlgorman",Name = "Brian L. Gorman"}
        }
},
```

```
new Item() { Name = "The Sword of Shannara", CurrentOrFinalPrice = 9.99m,
Description = "The definitive fantasy book",
    IsOnSale = false, Notes = "", PurchasePrice = 13.99m, PurchasedDate =
    null, Quantity = 900, SoldDate = null, CreatedByUserId = SEED_USER_ID,
    CreatedDate = DateTime.Now,
    IsDeleted = false, IsActive = true, Players = new List<Player>() {
                new Player() { CreatedDate = DateTime.Now,IsActive =
                true,IsDeleted = false,CreatedByUserId = SEED_USER_ID,
                        Description = "https://www.amazon.
                        com/Sword-Shannara-Terry-Brooks/
                        dp/0345314255",Name = "Terry Brooks"}
            }
},
new Item() { Name = "World of Tanks", CurrentOrFinalPrice = 0.00m,
Description = "WWII First person tank shooter",
   IsOnSale = false, Notes = "", PurchasePrice = 0.00m, PurchasedDate =
    null, Quantity = 1, SoldDate = null, CreatedByUserId = SEED_USER_ID,
    CreatedDate = DateTime.Now,
    IsDeleted = false, IsActive = true, Players = new List<Player>() {
                new Player() { CreatedDate = DateTime.Now,IsActive =
                true,IsDeleted = false,CreatedByUserId = SEED_USER_ID,
                        Description = "https://worldoftanks.
                        com/",Name = "Wargaming"}
            }
},
new Item() { Name = "Battlefield 2142", CurrentOrFinalPrice = 0.00m,
Description = "WWII First person tank shooter",
    IsOnSale = false, Notes = "Game is no longer active", PurchasePrice
    = 50.00m, PurchasedDate = null, Quantity = 1, SoldDate = null,
    CreatedByUserId = SEED_USER_ID, CreatedDate = DateTime.Now,
    IsDeleted = false, IsActive = true, Players = new List<Player>() {
                new Player() { CreatedDate = DateTime.Now,IsActive =
                true,IsDeleted = false,CreatedByUserId = SEED_USER_ID,
```

```
                                   Description = "https://en.wikipedia.org/
                                   wiki/Battlefield_2142",Name = "Electronic
                                   Arts"}
             }
}
```

As it currently stands, the seed will not run unless you delete all of the items. Things are a bit more complex now, so the easiest thing to do is just open SSMS and run the following statements:

```
DELETE FROM Player
DELETE FROM Items
```

You can leave all the Categories and Genres as is. After deleting items and players, right-click the migration project and use the Debug ➤ Start New Instance menu to kick off the seed.

The program will have no output. When it is completed, close it, and then run the statements

```
SELECT * FROM Items
SELECT * FROM Player
```

Ensure that you have both Items and Player objects (you should have nine of each).

Because there are currently no categories associated, you need to add each of the nine entries to a specific category. You could do this in a migration if you wanted; however, for brevity, just run the following query:

```
DECLARE @MoviesID INT
DECLARE @BooksID INT
DECLARE @GamesID INT
SET @MoviesID = (SELECT Id FROM Categories WHERE Name = 'Movies')
SET @BooksID = (SELECT Id FROM Categories WHERE Name = 'Books')
SET @GamesID = (SELECT Id FROM Categories WHERE Name = 'Games')

UPDATE ITEMS SET CategoryId = @MoviesID WHERE Name = 'Batman Begins'
UPDATE ITEMS SET CategoryId = @GamesID WHERE Name = 'World of Tanks'
UPDATE ITEMS SET CategoryId = @BooksID WHERE Name = 'The Sword of Shannara'
UPDATE ITEMS SET CategoryId = @BooksID WHERE Name = 'Practical Entity
Framework'
```

```
UPDATE ITEMS SET CategoryId = @GamesID WHERE Name = 'Battlefield 2142'
UPDATE ITEMS SET CategoryId = @MoviesID WHERE Name = 'Star Wars: The Empire
Strikes Back'
UPDATE ITEMS SET CategoryId = @MoviesID WHERE Name = 'Top Gun'
UPDATE ITEMS SET CategoryId = @MoviesID WHERE Name = 'Remember the Titans'
UPDATE ITEMS SET CategoryId = @MoviesID WHERE Name = 'Inception'

SELECT i.*, c.Name
FROM Items i
LEFT JOIN Categories c on i.CategoryId = c.Id
```

This query will associate your seeded items with categories appropriately. If you wanted, you could also do some genre and genre items, but you will not need them for this chapter. For convenience, this script is also included in the `InventoryDataMigrator` project in the starter and final files for this activity.

Step 3: Run the program to validate output

Now that data is in place, run the program to validate the output from the program. The output with the new data is shown in Figure 9-26.

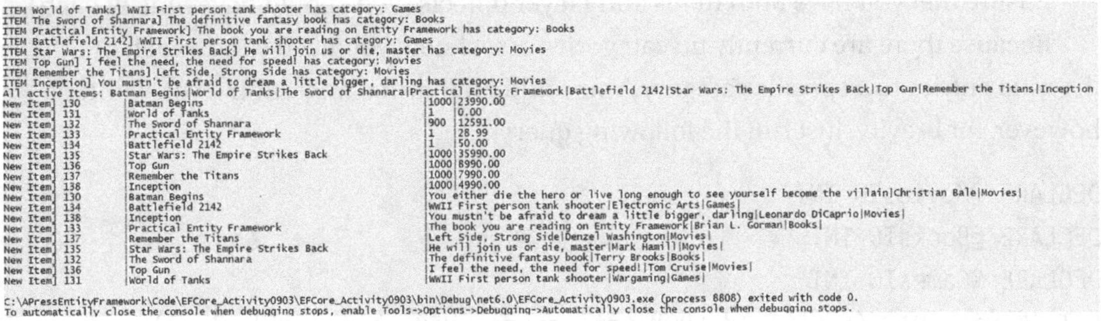

Figure 9-26. *The newly seeded data with associated categories is shown*

Task 1: Perform a more advanced query

In this task, you will use the skills you've learned with projections to perform a more advanced query similar to a query you've already run in a stored procedure or that you might have previously considered only running in a stored procedure.

Step 1: Build a new GetItemsForListing query

In a previous activity, you created a stored procedure to get items for listing. Using what you've learned in this chapter, add a new call that will recreate the procedure results using LINQ and projections.

Go to the Main method in the `Program` class for the main activity project. Comment out all method calls except `BuildOptions`, `BuildMapper`, and `GetItemsForListing`. Next, add a call to a new method named `GetItemsForListingLinq`. In the `GetItemsForListingLinq` method, add the code as follows:

```
var minDateValue = new DateTime(2021, 1, 1);
var maxDateValue = new DateTime(2024, 1, 1);
using (var db = new InventoryDbContext(_optionsBuilder.Options))
{
    var results = db.Items.Select(x => new
    {
        x.CreatedDate,
        CategoryName = x.Category.Name,
        x.Description,
        x.IsActive,
        x.IsDeleted,
        x.Name,
        x.Notes
    }).Where(x => x.CreatedDate >= minDateValue && x.CreatedDate <=
    maxDateValue)
    .OrderBy(y => y.CategoryName).ThenBy(z => z.Name)
    .ToList();

    foreach (var item in results)
    {
        Console.WriteLine($"ITEM {item.CategoryName}| {item.Name} - {item.
        Description}");
    }
}
```

Run this code to see the output in action (review Figure 9-27).

```
Select Microsoft Visual Studio Debug Console                                    —   □   ×
ITEM Batman Begins] You either die the hero or live long enough to see yourself become the villain has category: Movies
ITEM World of Tanks] WWII First person tank shooter has category: Games
ITEM The Sword of Shannara] The definitive fantasy book has category: Books
ITEM Practical Entity Framework] The book you are reading on Entity Framework has category: Books
ITEM Battlefield 2142] WWII First person tank shooter has category: Games
ITEM Star Wars: The Empire Strikes Back] He will join us or die, master has category: Movies
ITEM Top Gun] I feel the need, the need for speed! has category: Movies
ITEM Remember the Titans] Left Side, Strong Side has category: Movies
ITEM Inception] You mustn't be afraid to dream a little bigger, darling has category: Movies
ITEM Books| Practical Entity Framework - The book you are reading on Entity Framework
ITEM Books| The Sword of Shannara - The definitive fantasy book
ITEM Games| Battlefield 2142 - WWII First person tank shooter
ITEM Games| World of Tanks - WWII First person tank shooter
ITEM Movies| Batman Begins - You either die the hero or live long enough to see yourself become the villain
ITEM Movies| Inception - You mustn't be afraid to dream a little bigger, darling
ITEM Movies| Remember the Titans - Left Side, Strong Side
ITEM Movies| Star Wars: The Empire Strikes Back - He will join us or die, master
ITEM Movies| Top Gun - I feel the need, the need for speed!

C:\APressEntityFramework\Code\EFCore_Activity0903\EFCore_Activity0903\bin\Debug\net6.0\EFCore_Activity0903.exe (process
8324) exited with code 0.
To automatically close the console when debugging stops, enable Tools->Options->Debugging->Automatically close the conso
le when debugging stops.
Press any key to close this window . . .
```

Figure 9-27. *The new query is nearly as efficient as the stored procedure and easily projects the results as expected in the output as shown*

One thing to note is that you can't currently project into the DTO as you did in the stored procedure because of the need to leverage the `CreatedDate` field from the `Item`, as well as the `CategoryName` that is not currently in the `ItemDto`.

Both the original stored procedure and the new projected LINQ query were able to get the same result. Furthermore, I turned on SQL Server Profiler and for most runs was able to get similar results for the LINQ query with the projection to the actual stored procedure call (see Figure 9-28).

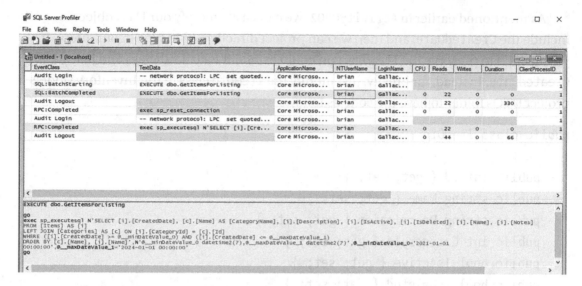

Figure 9-28. *The query from LINQ with a projection is nearly as performant as a SQL Server stored procedure when it comes to getting the data*

If your output doesn't match mine exactly, that may be due to you having set different gGenres and/or different iItems and cCategories associations than what I have in my database. It's always a good idea to validate that your results match what is to be expected based on your data.

Imagine that in the original stored procedure, there exists a small error due to including the join to the Genres and ItemGenres tables that could have been left behind when you removed the Genre data from the stored procedure. With LINQ, we avoid making the same type of mistake. This is where LINQ can really be a powerful ally, mainly because it is generally more flexible than a stored procedure.

To fix an issue with the original procedure, you would generally have to go through governance procedures to update a stored procedure on the database server. With LINQ, you can usually just fix your mistake in the code and then deploy a patch.

Step 2: Update the DTO so that it maps to the query result

In the previous run, you ended up with an anonymous type that was used for your output due to the fact that the CreatedDate is a required field and the CreatedDate is not part of your DTO. You also need to map the CategoryName field to a property.

As mentioned earlier in `Activity0902`, we can easily modify our DTO object to include the `CreatedDate`, and then we can project directly to that type in our query. If you needed to preserve the `ItemDto`, you could extend it with a subclass and just add the `CreatedDate`. Instead, for brevity, just modify the `ItemDto` class in the InventoryModels project DTOs folder to have the code as follows:

```
public class ItemDto
{
    public int Id { get; set; }
    public string Name { get; set; }
    public string Description { get; set; }
    public int CategoryId { get; set; }
    public bool IsActive { get; set; }
    public bool IsDeleted { get; set; }
    public string Notes { get; set; }
    public string CategoryName { get; set; }
    public DateTime CreatedDate { get; set; }

    public override string ToString()
    {
        return $"ITEM {Name,-25}] {Description,-50} has category:
        {CategoryName}";
    }
}
```

Once you have the DTO, go back and change the `GetItemsForListingLinq` to leverage the `ItemDto` as follows:

```
private static void GetItemsForListingLinq()
{
    var minDateValue = new DateTime(2021, 1, 1);
    var maxDateValue = new DateTime(2024, 1, 1);

    using (var db = new InventoryDbContext(_optionsBuilder.Options))
    {
        var results = db.Items.Select(x => new ItemDto
        {
            CreatedDate = x.CreatedDate,
```

```
            CategoryName = x.Category.Name,
            Description = x.Description,
            IsActive = x.IsActive,
            IsDeleted = x.IsDeleted,
            Name = x.Name,
            Notes = x.Notes,
            CategoryId = x.Category.Id,
            Id = x.Id
        }).Where(x => x.CreatedDate >= minDateValue && x.CreatedDate <=
        maxDateValue)
        .OrderBy(y => y.CategoryName).ThenBy(z => z.Name)
        .ToList();

        foreach (var itemDto in results)
        {
            Console.WriteLine(itemDto);
        }
    }
}
```

Run the program to see the expected output (see Figure 9-29).

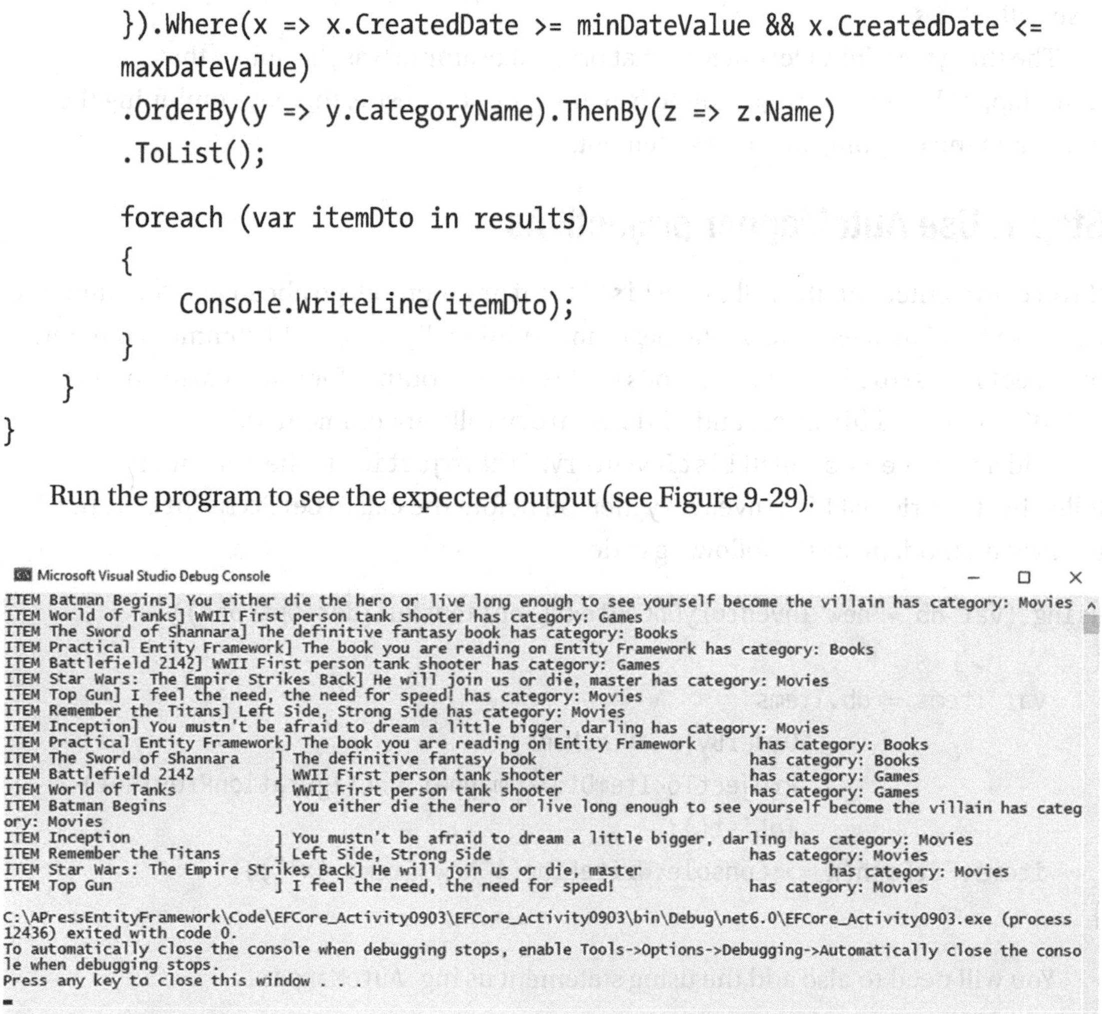

Figure 9-29. *The projection to a DTO works as expected*

Task 2: Using AutoMapper and DTO projections

In this task, you will project results directly from a query into a DTO object using AutoMapper with projections.

One of the more powerful features of AutoMapper is the ability to project directly to a type, even if the query is returning another type. When you originally set up AutoMapper in the previous activity, you saw that we were able to map an Item to an ItemDto. The ItemDto was originally a much pared-down version of the Item, which will often be the case with *DTOs*.

The thing you didn't leverage in that original example was the ability that AutoMapper has to just project directly to the type you desire, thereby combining the query and the mapping into one statement.

Step 1: Use AutoMapper projections

If you commented out the call to the ListInventory method, go ahead and uncomment it now so that it will execute on the next run. Additionally, you could comment out both of the GetItemsForListing... methods to clear up the output for now, leaving only the BuildOptions, BuildMapper, and ListInventory calls uncommented.

Add a new method called ListInventoryWithProjection to the Main method following the original ListInventory method before the call to GetItemsForListing. In the new method, place the following code:

```
using (var db = new InventoryDbContext(_optionsBuilder.Options))
{
    var items = db.Items
                    .OrderBy(x => x.Name)
                    .ProjectTo<ItemDto>(_mapper.ConfigurationProvider)
                    .ToList();
    items.ForEach(x => Console.WriteLine($"New Item: {x}"));
}
```

You will need to also add the using statement using AutoMapper. QueryableExtensions.

Run the program to see the results. You should see that both methods create the same results, where the first method has to do a manual mapping and the second method just projects the results into the DTO object (see Figure 9-30).

```
Microsoft Visual Studio Debug Console
New Item: ITEM Batman Begins             ] You either die the hero or live long enough to see yourself become the villain has category: Movies
New Item: ITEM Battlefield 2142          ] WWII First person tank shooter             has category: Games
New Item: ITEM Inception                  ] You mustn't be afraid to dream a little bigger, darling has category: Movies
New Item: ITEM Practical Entity Framework] The book you are reading on Entity Framework         has category: Books
New Item: ITEM Remember the Titans       ] Left Side, Strong Side                      has category: Movies
New Item: ITEM Star Wars: The Empire Strikes Back] He will join us or die, master             has category: Movies
New Item: ITEM The Sword of Shannara     ] The definitive fantasy book                 has category: Books
New Item: ITEM Top Gun                    ] I feel the need, the need for speed!        has category: Movies
New Item: ITEM World of Tanks            ] WWII First person tank shooter             has category: Games
ITEM Batman Begins] You either die the hero or live long enough to see yourself become the villain has category: Movies
ITEM World of Tanks] WWII First person tank shooter has category: Games
ITEM The Sword of Shannara] The definitive fantasy book has category: Books
ITEM Practical Entity Framework] The book you are reading on Entity Framework has category: Books
ITEM Battlefield 2142] WWII First person tank shooter has category: Games
ITEM Star Wars: The Empire Strikes Back] He will join us or die, master has category: Movies
ITEM Top Gun] I feel the need, the need for speed! has category: Movies
ITEM Remember the Titans] Left Side, Strong Side has category: Movies
ITEM Inception] You mustn't be afraid to dream a little bigger, darling has category: Movies
ITEM Practical Entity Framework] The book you are reading on Entity Framework         has category: Books
ITEM The Sword of Shannara     ] The definitive fantasy book                 has category: Books
ITEM Battlefield 2142          ] WWII First person tank shooter             has category: Games
ITEM World of Tanks            ] WWII First person tank shooter             has category: Games
ITEM Batman Begins             ] You either die the hero or live long enough to see yourself become the villain has category: Movies
ITEM Inception                  ] You mustn't be afraid to dream a little bigger, darling has category: Movies
ITEM Remember the Titans       ] Left Side, Strong Side                      has category: Movies
ITEM Star Wars: The Empire Strikes Back] He will join us or die, master               has category: Movies
ITEM Top Gun                    ] I feel the need, the need for speed!        has category: Movies

C:\APressEntityFramework\Code\EFCore_Activity0903\EFCore_Activity0903\bin\Debug\net6.0\EFCore_Activity0903.exe (process 15164) exited with code 0.
To automatically close the console when debugging stops, enable Tools->Options->Debugging->Automatically close the console when debugging stops.
Press any key to close this window . . .
```

Figure 9-30. *The results are the same, but the projections let you map results directly during the query execution*

Step 2: Use AutoMapper when the fields don't line up one to one

To complete your first look at AutoMapper and using projections with LINQ in your codebase, you need to learn one more concept. There are going to be times in the real world where your database object and your DTO do not map property to property. Perhaps your DTO is a combination of a couple of objects, or perhaps your DTO needs to transform some of the data from the object and use that in its lifecycle. Either way, a one-to-one mapping of fields in DTOs to objects is an unreasonable expectation in robust solutions.

The great news is that AutoMapper allows for you to map the fields as you see fit. Sometimes, you can even tell AutoMapper to ignore a field altogether. Other times, you need to map the relationship in both directions and sometimes just in one direction.

To show how this works, you'll use a bit of a contrived example. Reviewing your data in the Inventory system, you have categories, and each category has a color. Additionally, you have items that belong to one category, thereby having a color via the category.

Suppose you want to get an output of your categories and their associated colors, but instead of using the table field `Name`, you'll use a more descriptive string `Category`, and the string field `ColorValue` will just be leveraged with a string called `Color`. You can set all this up with a friendly DTO and a couple of tweaks in the mapping configuration.

Begin by creating a new class called CategoryDetailDTO.cs in the InventoryModels project in the DTOs folder. This DTO will map to the CategoryDetail. In the new DTO, add a string field for Color and a string field for Value.

```
public class CategoryDetailDto
{
    public string Color { get; set; }
    public string Value { get; set; }
}
```

In the CategoryDto class that you created earlier in the activity, add two properties as follows:

```
public string Category { get; set; }
public CategoryDetailDto CategoryDetail { get; set; }
```

Next, go into the InventoryMapper file in the main activity project to create and modify the mappings.

For the first map, when mapping Category to CategoryDto, change the code to the following:

```
CreateMap<Category, CategoryDto>()
    .ForMember(x => x.Category, opt => opt.MapFrom(y => y.Name))
    .ReverseMap()
    .ForMember(y => y.Name, opt => opt.MapFrom(x => x.Category));
```

And then add a new map for CategoryDetail to CategoryDetailDto as follows (if you currently have a mapping for Category to CategoryDto, replace it with this code):

```
CreateMap<CategoryDetail, CategoryDetailDto>()
    .ForMember(x => x.Color, opt => opt.MapFrom(y => y.ColorName))
    .ForMember(x => x.Value, opt => opt.MapFrom(y => y.ColorValue))
    .ReverseMap()
    .ForMember(y => y.ColorValue, opt => opt.MapFrom(x => x.Value))
    .ForMember(y => y.ColorName, opt => opt.MapFrom(x => x.Color));
```

By reversing the map with the ReverseMap call and going in the other direction, it is now possible to map one of the database objects to the corresponding *DTO* and also to go from the DTO back to the corresponding database object.

If one of the classes had an extra field that didn't map to anything, you could make a statement like

```
.ForMember(x => x.AFieldNotMappable, opt => opt.Ignore())
```

Note that the use of the Ignore method tells AutoMapper to skip trying to match the particular field to any field in the target object.

To complete the work, do a quick query in the main program to see all of this in action.

Figure 9-31 is shown for clarity to ensure that the CreateMaps method code is clear (make sure you don't have duplicate Category to CategoryDTO mappings).

```
1 reference
private void CreateMaps()
{
    CreateMap<Item, ItemDto>();
    CreateMap<Category, CategoryDto>()
        .ForMember(x => x.Category, opt => opt.MapFrom(y => y.Name))
        .ReverseMap()
        .ForMember(y => y.Name, opt => opt.MapFrom(x => x.Category));
    CreateMap<CategoryDetail, CategoryDetailDto>()
        .ForMember(x => x.Color, opt => opt.MapFrom(y => y.ColorName))
        .ForMember(x => x.Value, opt => opt.MapFrom(y => y.ColorValue))
        .ReverseMap()
        .ForMember(y => y.ColorValue, opt => opt.MapFrom(x => x.Value))
        .ForMember(y => y.ColorName, opt => opt.MapFrom(x => x.Color));
}
```

Figure 9-31. *The CreateMaps method is shown to ensure that it is clear what the code should be for this method*

Add a new method in the Main method of the program class called ListCategories AndColors. In the ListCategoriesAndColors method, add the following code:

```
using (var db = new InventoryDbContext(_optionsBuilder.Options))
{
    var results = db.Categories
                    .Include(x => x.CategoryDetail)
                    .ProjectTo<CategoryDto>(_mapper.ConfigurationProvider).
                    ToList();
```

```
foreach (var c in results)
{
    Console.WriteLine($"Category [{c.Category}] is {c.CategoryDetail.
    Color}");
}
}
```

Run the program to see the results with the new projections mapping as expected (see Figure 9-32).

```
ory: Movies
ITEM Inception                    ] You mustn't be afraid to dream a little bigger, darling has category: Movies
ITEM Remember the Titans          ] Left Side, Strong Side                      has category: Movies
ITEM Star Wars: The Empire Strikes Back] He will join us or die, master              has category: Movies
ITEM Top Gun                      ] I feel the need, the need for speed!          has category: Movies
Category [Movies] is Blue
Category [Books] is Red
Category [Games] is Green

C:\APressEntityFramework\Code\EFCore_Activity0903\EFCore_Activity0903\bin\Debug\net6.0\EFCore_Activity0903.exe (proces:
9720) exited with code 0.
To automatically close the console when debugging stops, enable Tools->Options->Debugging->Automatically close the con:
le when debugging stops.
Press anv kev to close this window . . .
```

Figure 9-32. The CategoryDto is correctly leveraged with mappings to translate fields that don't map one to one and also contains the relational CategoryDetailDto which is also now correctly mapped for each of the fields

Note that in this method you did use the Include syntax as the original code is grabbing categories and their details. If you select the CategoryDetail, AutoMapper will not be able to make the projection correctly from the internal CategoryDetailDto from a CategoryDetail, and you cannot use an anonymous type with ProjectTo with AutoMapper. Using Include allows the selection of the data, and then mapping is completed successfully.

If you want to see the error, change the .Include(x => x. CategoryDetail) to .Select(x => x.CategoryDetail) and run the program. Figure 9-33 shows the error that happens when trying to select and project in this manner.

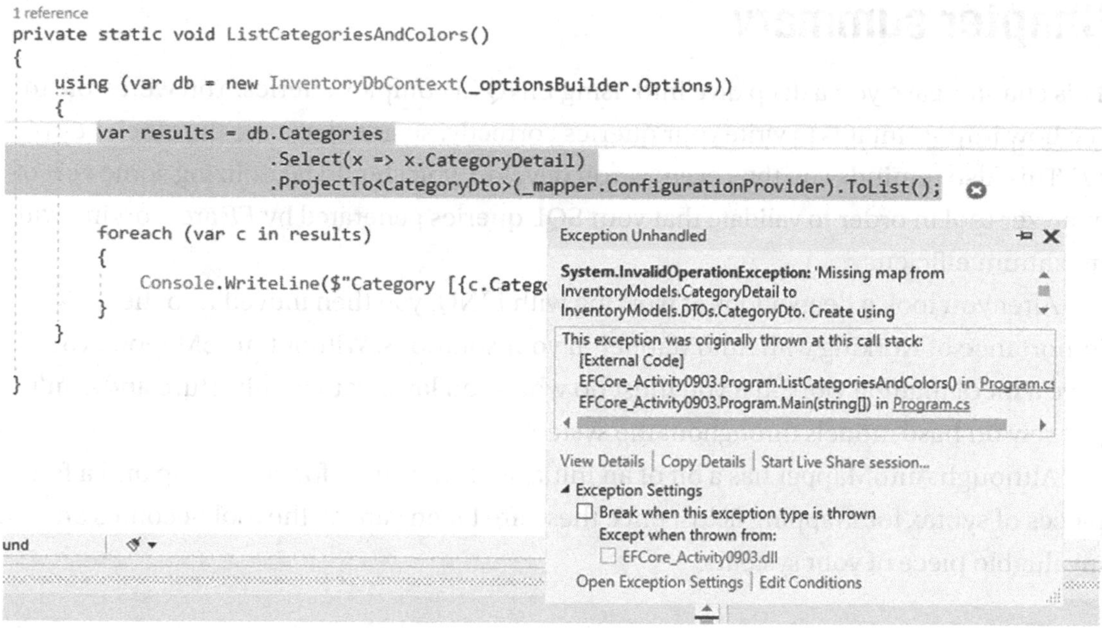

```
1 reference
private static void ListCategoriesAndColors()
{
    using (var db = new InventoryDbContext(_optionsBuilder.Options))
    {
        var results = db.Categories
                        .Select(x => x.CategoryDetail)
                        .ProjectTo<CategoryDto>(_mapper.ConfigurationProvider).ToList();

        foreach (var c in results)
        {
            Console.WriteLine($"Category [{c.Categ
        }
    }
}
```

Exception Unhandled   X

System.InvalidOperationException: 'Missing map from
InventoryModels.CategoryDetail to
InventoryModels.DTOs.CategoryDto. Create using

This exception was originally thrown at this call stack:
    [External Code]
    EFCore_Activity0903.Program.ListCategoriesAndColors() in Program.cs
    EFCore_Activity0903.Program.Main(string[]) in Program.cs

View Details | Copy Details | Start Live Share session...
▲ Exception Settings
    ☐ Break when this exception type is thrown
        Except when thrown from:
        ☐ EFCore_Activity0903.dll
Open Exception Settings | Edit Conditions

Figure 9-33. *Using Select instead of Include breaks the projections when leveraging AutoMapper and projections with navigation properties*

If you did this last step, make sure to set your code back to `.Include` so that there are no errors during execution.

Activity 9-3 summary

In this final activity, you were able to see the real power of working with AutoMapper in your EF with LINQ queries. Once you have AutoMapper configured and you learn the syntax that is necessary to create mappings, you can really start leveraging AutoMapper as a great tool to make your queries more succinct and generally just as performant as if you had written them without AutoMapper.

The added benefits of using AutoMapper include the fact that you can utilize the `.ProjectTo<T>` call to automatically map your results from one type to another. By doing this, you don't have to make manual calls to the mapper for object conversion.

Finally, using AutoMapper allows you to easily create configurations that set your conversions in place throughout your system. This means you don't have to spend any time writing manual conversions of objects, field by field. Not having to do the manual conversion also eliminates issues where you might simply forget to map a field or where you might incorrectly map data to the wrong field.

Chapter summary

This chapter gave you a deep dive into using LINQ in complex queries. You were able to see how important it is to write your queries correctly, so as to leverage the efficiency of *EF*. This also reminds you that, even as you develop, you should be utilizing some sort of analyzer tool in order to validate that your SQL queries generated by *EF* are working with maximum efficiency.

After you took a deeper look at working with LINQ, you then moved into the importance of working with AutoMapper in your solutions. Without AutoMapper, you have a lot of manual work that you must do when you layer your architecture and don't just rely on base models throughout the system.

Although AutoMapper has a bit of an initial learning curve for both setup and a few pieces of syntax for mapping fields, once these are taken care of, the tool becomes an invaluable piece of your systems.

Important takeaways

After working through this chapter, the things you should be in command of are

- Working with LINQ
- Working with projections
- Understanding AutoMapper and why it is a useful tool
- Leveraging DTO objects
- Creating DTO objects and mapping fields with AutoMapper
- Using AutoMapper with `ProjectTo<T>`

Closing thoughts

As this chapter closes, you are now in a really great place with your knowledge of EF and working with LINQ in your systems. Additionally, you now have seen how to use AutoMapper to help make your solutions more robust.

With most of the deep knowledge of working with the data complete, it's time to start working to make your real-world solutions more organized and protected. In the next chapter, you'll begin this effort by learning about how to encrypt your data.

CHAPTER 10

Encryption of Data

Keeping your system's data secure

You've implemented a system, and you've created the best database structure you can architect. Your system is taking off, and you have hundreds or thousands of clients and many gigabytes of customer data on your server. Things couldn't be better, right? Then you get a notification that something has gone wrong with your database. Somehow, a malicious entity has gained information about all of your customers because you were storing that information in your database in plain text. This nightmare scenario could be you if you don't take at least some minimal measures to prevent it.

Data at rest

In today's world, it is essentially unacceptable to keep any personal customer data at rest in your system in an unencrypted fashion. By having this data in plain text, you are putting yourself and your company at risk for major lawsuits when a breech occurs. Even storing your data off premises at a *CSP* (Cloud Service Provider) like *Microsoft Azure* or *Amazon AWS* or *Google GCP* is not going to be enough to protect you and your data.

Encryption in the past vs. encryption today

In this chapter, you are going to dive into some of the tenets of encryption using *Microsoft SQL Server*. Additionally, you'll see how encryption of data at rest can be accomplished in two different approaches by looking into a *Transparent Data Encryption (TDE)* solution and an *Always Encrypted* solution.

© Brian L. Gorman 2022
B. L. Gorman, *Practical Entity Framework Core 6*, https://doi.org/10.1007/978-1-4842-7301-2_10

Likely, when you think of encryption, the first thing you think of are passwords, so you'll start by taking a look at how you can correctly protect user passwords, and then you'll move into looking at the other fields in your database tables.

Passwords

Password mismanagement is probably the most egregious error a system developer can commit. Today, you have a number of options that can help with this issue. The simplest option available is to use a single sign-on solution via a third-party provider.

SSO via social logins

Today, you have many platforms available that provide tools to use their platform as a means to identify users and allow for you to easily build a single sign-on solution (SSO). If you don't like managing users, and you are building a non-corporate business solution, there is very little reason to not just use the SSO capabilities of one or more of these platforms.

Facebook, Google, Microsoft, LinkedIn, and others all provide solutions that are easy to wire up into your applications. When doing this, you are able to let those providers do the heavy work of managing the user's passwords, and all you need to do is associate the user in your system with the authentication information that comes back from the provider, such as the validated email of a user as returned from the third-party provider.

In general, to set up these third-party solutions, you would just go to the provider of choice and create an application at their developer tools portal, which will give you the app id and token secrets that you need in order to authenticate against the third-party provider. Once the user has authenticated, the appropriate user information (such as email or other identifier) is handed back to you for your use in your system.

ASP.Net built-in authentication

Another option you have that helps with preventing user password mismanagement comes in the form of the `IdentityDbContext`, which is part of the `AspNetCore.Identity.EntityFramework` namespace.

When using the `IdentityDbContext`, you are able to easily create a new solution that handles user authentication for you. At inception, the system creates all the tables necessary for users and roles, as well as identity claims. With all of this in place, you simply needed to perform a few actions to register and/or authenticate users, which is also baked in for a .Net 6 solution.

When registering users with built-in identity management, the user password is automatically hashed and salted. This makes it impossible for us to get the user password back to plain text. In this scenario, if a user loses their password, they need to go through a validation process to reset the password to a new password.

Salting and hashing

If you must create your own custom database user solution, you should follow a hashing and salting pattern to make sure you hash and salt your user passwords. In case you are not familiar with why this is important, consider a couple of scenarios.

Even before starting this chapter, you would likely have agreed that you wouldn't even consider using a plain text password storage solution for anything past a simple demo MVP solution (and even then, using plain text should be avoided if possible).

Now that we agree that storing passwords as plain text is a terrible idea, are you thinking encryption alone is good enough? The answer, of course, is no. Encryption is a two-way process. Anything that is encrypted can be decrypted if the common encryption algorithm and key(s) are known. So, turning on `Always Encrypted` on your fields only scrambles them from being plain text but does not make it impossible to reverse the encryption (if it did, we couldn't store user information like names, social security numbers, and such in an always encrypted column).

With hashing, you use a unique algorithm to set the length of your data to a fixed length. By combining the unique password with the hash and applying the hashing algorithm during encryption, you get a value that is mathematically improbable to reverse-engineer. Storing this hash in the database table allows the password to be decrypted by applying that hash to the password as entered by the user and using the same algorithm to decrypt for authentication. Therefore, you are no longer storing the password but are storing a hash that when combined with user input can be encrypted with the hash and compared to determine that the hashed results match.

What happens, though, when two users have the same password? Without anything else, the hash value would be identical, and this could lead to a security issue. Although it would still be tough to figure it out, a malicious user who has access to your data might be able to run common passwords and determine them from the identical hash values. Additionally, if they know the hashed value of a particular password and have proper access, they could update the stored hash for all users to the known hash value and then log in and impersonate anyone in the system, including your admin users.

In this contrived example, consider three users that have the same password. Figure 10-1 shows what it would look like if the exact same hash was used for each of them when the password hash was generated.

PasswordHash

AQAAAAEAACcQAAAAEHDZvGSClj9w7lfjdRnRVpQ4D4GS/NQOBS+NU/dDd+5hbFx0fkMvQSDPTPBB2fvW2A==

AQAAAAEAACcQAAAAEHDZvGSClj9w7lfjdRnRVpQ4D4GS/NQOBS+NU/dDd+5hbFx0fkMvQSDPTPBB2fvW2A==

AQAAAAEAACcQAAAAEHDZvGSClj9w7lfjdRnRVpQ4D4GS/NQOBS+NU/dDd+5hbFx0fkMvQSDPTPBB2fvW2A==

Figure 10-1. *A database with three users that have the same password generated with the same hash*

Using a salt in addition to the hash allows you to create a unique hash for each user that still maps correctly to a regenerated hash with salt and user input. The reason this works is because the salt is going to be unique for the user based on some other generation tactic, like a timestamp or a computer serial number or something else that is unique. The password is then combined with the salt and then hashed, and therefore, every user generates a unique hashed password value, even when the passwords are identical. Figure 10-2 shows users that are registered with the same password, but the hash is generated with a salt so that the password hash is unique to all users.

PasswordHash

AQAAAAEAACcQAAAAEBeame7+uQcv/XaCN3tYEOQi6KkCKS2qzOKc9mNdWDKW8txP5v8wQugXGmXU7B0T9A==

AQAAAAEAACcQAAAAEE91PQdiX1vioUzaXCKFYYsdqmfaT/CW8a64ITDMm8Fg1L/15Df92ubcWOYnpuDxJA==

AQAAAAEAACcQAAAAEGFZUyH5yCiqZYjneadf6/PYQKc8vBfl8pG+br8XpI46MXHsjYR+z28bC3d4fPKHIw==

Figure 10-2. *Three users with the same password have unique PasswordHash values when a salt is used*

Protecting sensitive user information

There are a couple of ways to implement encryption on data at rest using *SQL Server*. If your SQL Server version is version 2016 or greater, the easiest way to implement encryption is to use the Always Encrypted functionality of SQL Server. If you are on a previous version of SQL Server, encryption is still straightforward but involves a more manual interaction with the data.

Encryption basics

In order to encrypt columns in the database, you need to have two keys. The first key is the master key that protects the keys in the system. The second key is the individual key to encrypt columns.

With Always Encrypted, creation of the encryption keys is very easily accomplished using SSMS to encrypt columns. If no master key exists, one is created. When a column is encrypted, a column encryption key can be generated or, if one already exists, can be reused.

When encrypting with the Always Encrypted approach, two types of encryption can be used. The first is *Deterministic*, and the second is *Randomized*. The main difference here is that if you are going to be joining to the column or if you are going to use it as a condition in a query, you will want to use the Deterministic type. If you are just encrypting the data and it isn't going to be critical in a join or other query, you can just use the Randomized type.

In SQL Server versions prior to 2016 or in current versions where you don't want to use Always Encrypted, you can leverage the *Transparent Data Encryption (TDE)* method.

To work with TDE in any SQL Server instance, you need to generate a certificate for the server and then generate one or more keys to use when encrypting columns. To read columns, you'll need to use the encryption key as part of your transaction. Additionally, you'll use scripts for encryption of columns.

Since TDE requires more interaction, a general approach that works well is to leverage stored procedures any time data from an encrypted column is queried or transformed.

Which type should you use

Each type of encryption has advantages and disadvantages. Consider a couple of things that are important for anyone who is developing a secure system.

TDE encryption is server-side encryption, so data is well encrypted on the server, but the decryption also happens at the server, and then the raw data is sent over the pipe to the UI. There are ways to enforce encryption on the pipe as well, but that requires additional configuration. Additionally, the keys for the encryption must be managed at the database level so they are based on the database and server where they are generated.

The nice thing about TDE is that it can be more performant since the encryption and decryption do happen at the server. TDE also works on any version of SQL Server since 2008.

One last thing about TDE is that since it is handled on the server, any database admin with execution rights can decrypt the data and see the actual sensitive data as stored in the table, and a compromised database likely means compromised keys.

Always Encrypted is limited to being used from SQL Server 2016 and newer, so older systems or any system with a SQL Server back end that is less than the 2016 version cannot leverage Always Encrypted. Always Encrypted functionality is not database specific, however. The encryption takes place on the client side of the operation, and the encrypted data is passed on the pipe and directly stored in the database table. This means that transmission of the data over the pipe is done with the data already encrypted with no extra configuration needed.

This client-side encryption also means that any SQL Server admin cannot just decrypt the information using server certificates without a client library. Of course, SSMS can be easily configured to be the client library with a few tweaks on the connection, so your data is still not secure from a malicious database administrator who has the right server credentials.

As you'll see in the upcoming activities, encrypting specific columns with Always Encrypted functionality is as easy as a few clicks, and this goes for tables with or without data. In contrast, encrypting the data using TDE requires you to go through an entire migration process (if you are doing specific columns). Always Encrypted leverages client-side decryption while TDE sends the data plain text to and from the server. TDE makes up for its longer setup time by generally having better performance than Always Encrypted.

One final thought, which you can find more information on if you read more into the topic of encryption, is that you are going to need to implement a good key management strategy. Consider your risk for a compromised key and how you might have a plan in place to migrate to a new key in case such an event does happen. Also consider and test what happens with keys on backup and restore in the various scenarios, as well as moving to a new database server.

Ultimately, it will be up to you to make sure that you mitigate the risk by managing your keys well, and it's also up to you to implement a risk management strategy to handle scenarios where the keys are compromised or the server fails.

Chapter 10 activities: Using Always Encrypted and Transparent Data Encryption

In the activities for this chapter, you are going to cover two different ways to encrypt your data at rest. You'll start by implementing Always Encrypted, and you'll conclude with an activity that implements TDE. You'll do both solutions in *EFCore6*, but you can be certain that previous versions of EF would be just as able to be used for these activities. In fact, it is probably more likely you would see TDE in an *EF6* (or older) implementation, mostly due to the fact that TDE has been around a lot longer, and Always Encrypted wasn't available until a few years ago.

Activity 10-1: Using Always Encrypted

In this first activity, you'll learn how to add Always Encrypted in your InventoryManager database solution and then work with it in your codebase. The great news about always encrypted is that you can use it in a greenfield solution, in a legacy solution when creating new tables, or in tables that already exist, even if the encrypted columns have data.

Just keep in mind that once you do this, if you go back to other activities in the book, the system will still expect you to have Always Encrypted enabled, so you'll have to adjust for that if you rework a previous example.

Task 0: Getting started

To begin this activity, you can either continue working with your files that you've been using after completing Activities 2 and 3 from Chapter 9. If you would like a clean start, you can just grab the EFCore_Activity10-1_StarterFiles project and use those files. As always, make sure to check Appendix A for more information on using the starter files.

Note that if you're using the starter files, you'll want to ensure to run the extra script to seed the relationships for Items and Categories.

For reference, at the start of this activity, my project has commented out all the GetXXXX method calls and is only starting with the two build methods and then ListInventory, ListInventoryWithProjection, and ListCategoriesAndColors being called from the main method (see the starter files for more clarity).

Task 1: Enable Always Encrypted on the InventoryManagerDb

In this task, you will enable Always Encrypted on the InventoryManagerDb. You will then see how to work with the encrypted columns via a couple of simple modifications in your connection string.

Step 1: Create a backup [optional]

If you are worried about your data, you might take a minute to create a backup. In the InventoryManagerDb, there really isn't any new data that you couldn't just seed and run from scratch, so the need to take a backup is really not there. However, in the real world, you should take a backup of any database you are going to be relying upon in case something goes wrong with your encryption efforts.

To take a backup, open SSMS, and then right-click the database you wish to back up (see Figure 10-3).

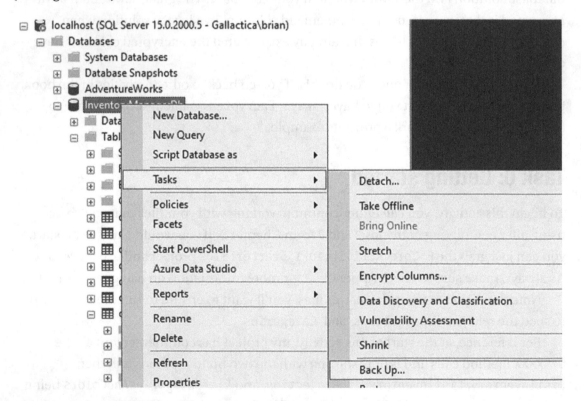

Figure 10-3. *Creating a backup of the database using the context menu Tasks ➤ Back Up... in SSMS*

Next, select the entire database for Copy-only backup. Leave the defaults for everything else and back up the database (see Figure 10-4).

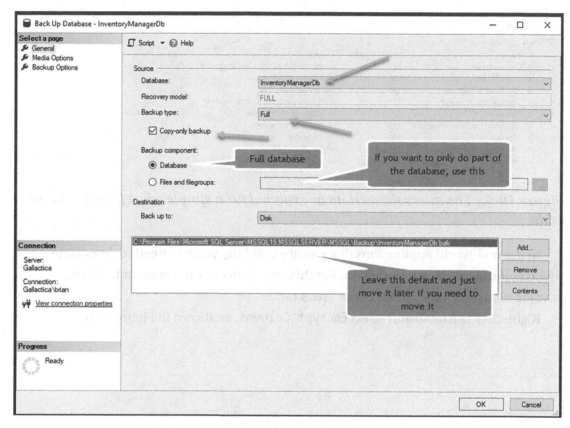

Figure 10-4. *The defaults and Copy-only backup are selected to create the backup*

Hit OK, and you will see a message that lets you know when the database is backed up.

Step 1: Prepare fields for encryption

Open the inventory database in SSMS to view the tables. Expand the Items table to see the columns, and run a query like SELECT TOP 1000 * FROM [InventoryManager]. [dbo].[Items]. The results of this query are shown in Figure 10-5.

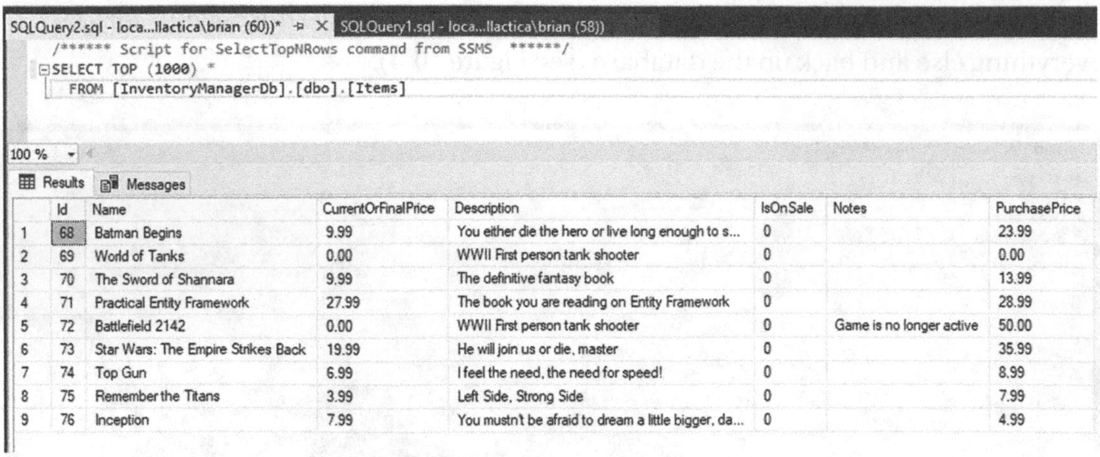

Figure 10-5. *The query shows data as expected for a simple select from the Items table*

In the real-world applications that you are building, you will need to determine which columns you want to encrypt. For this application, you'll encrypt the Name, Description, and Notes fields of the Items table.

Right-click the table and select Encrypt Columns, as shown in Figure 10-6.

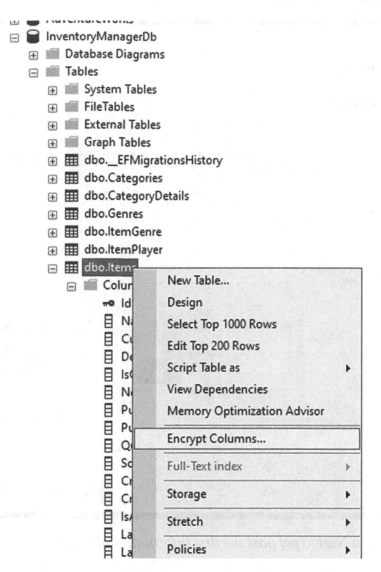

Figure 10-6. *Use Always Encrypted by starting with the context menu option to encrypt columns*

When the Always Encrypted wizard starts, select Next (review Figure 10-7).

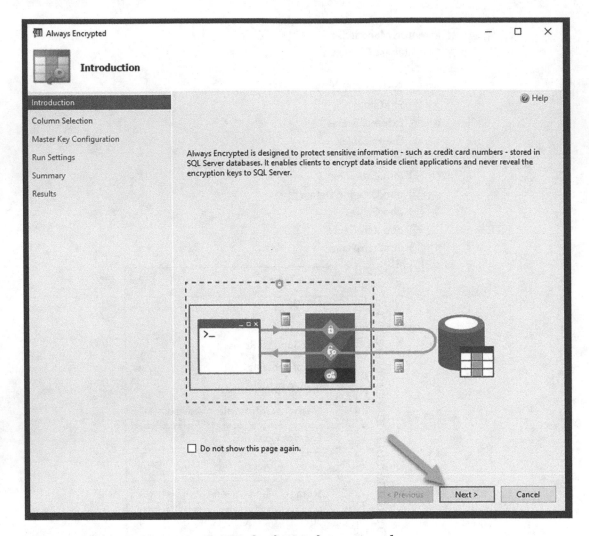

Figure 10-7. *Hit Next to get past the first informational screen*

In the Column Selection window, select the three columns you are going to encrypt. For this encryption, assume we might limit or search on Name and Description, but not on Notes. Therefore, select the *Deterministic* option for Name and Description, and select the *Randomized* option for Notes.

Unfortunately, the first thing you'll discover is that you cannot currently encrypt the Name field. This is due to the default constraint that has been put on it since the column type is NVARCHAR and it is required (see Figure 10-8).

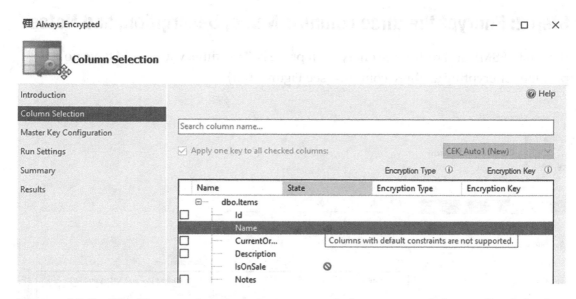

Figure 10-8. *The Name column cannot currently be encrypted due to the default constraint for a required nvarchar column*

In order to make this field encryptable, you'll need to modify the field type on the name and use a migration to update it. First, cancel the encryption operation.

Return to the InventoryModels project, and then modify the Item class to have the Name column default to a VARCHAR instead of an NVARCHAR. To do this, add the following data annotation over the field:

```
[Column(TypeName = "VARCHAR")]
```

Make sure to also bring in the using statement using System.ComponentModel. DataAnnotations.Schema.

Next, open the PMC, select the EFCore_DBLibrary project, and add a migration using the command add-migration update-itemname-type-to-varchar.

Note that this gives a warning: *An operation was scaffolded that may result in the loss of data. Please review the migration for accuracy.* This is because altering the column could cause data to get deleted or truncated. In this case, unless you've used special characters in your Item names, you are likely OK. If you wanted to be certain, you could easily create and add a script before and after in the same migration to back up to a temp table, then alter, then restore from temp table, and delete the temp table (this will error out if you do have special characters, so you would have to remove them first). However, like Austin Powers, it's time to live dangerously. Go ahead and run the update-database command to convert the column. A simple select from the Items table after the operation will ensure that no data was harmed in the making of this conversion.

Step 2: Encrypt the three columns Name, Description, and Notes

Return to SSMS and restart the encryption process. This time, you should have no problem encrypting all three columns (see Figure 10-9).

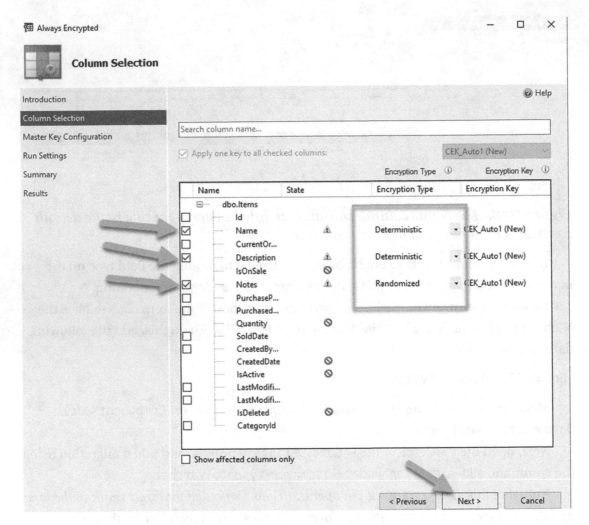

Figure 10-9. *You are now able to select all three columns, with Name and Description being the Deterministic type and Notes being Randomized*

To be clear, the main difference between Deterministic and Randomized is the ability to be able to decrypt the columns. If you want to use encrypted columns in your queries for filtering or sorting, you must make them Deterministic.

Select Next to continue to the `Master Key Configuration` step in the `Always Encrypted` wizard.

Leave the column master key set to `Auto generate column master key`, and choose your place of storage. You can store keys either in your windows certificate store or in an *Azure Key Vault*. Leave the master key source set to the `Current User` for the certificate store. Alternatively, you could log into Azure and select the key vault to store the encryption master key. For this example, you'll store in the certificate store (see Figure 10-10). In the real world for a very secure solution, it would be recommended that you store the key in the Azure Key Vault.

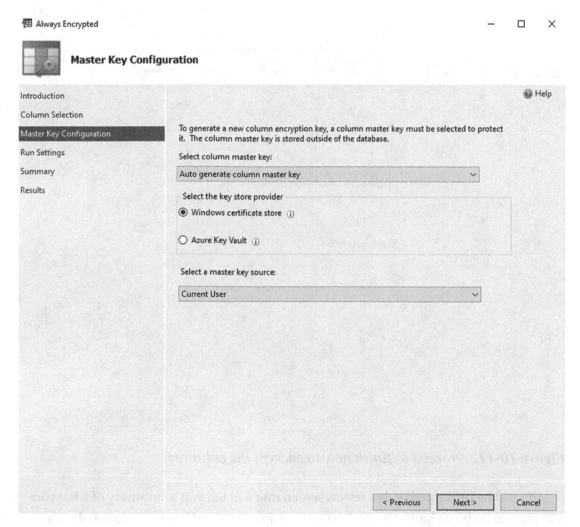

Figure 10-10. *Auto generate the column master key and store in the Windows certificate store for the Current User*

Note, if you've already created certificates in the past for the database rather than creating new keys, you would have the option here to use existing keys and might get a message such as *No further configuration is necessary*.

Hit the Next button, and on the Run Settings screen, select Proceed to finish now, and then hit Next (see Figure 10-11).

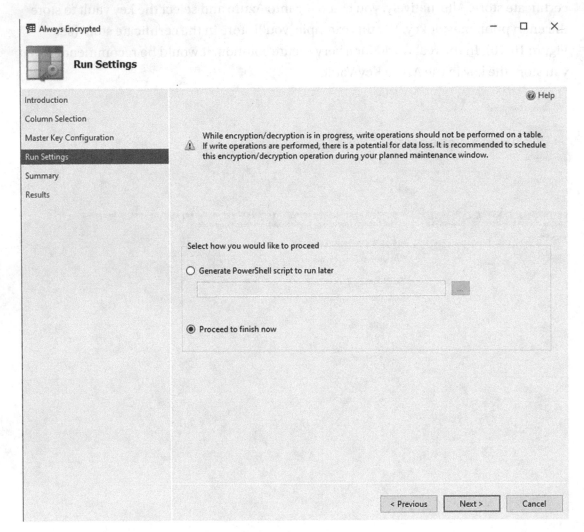

Figure 10-11. *Proceed to finish now to encrypt the columns*

You will be presented with a review screen that will tell you a summary of what you are about to do (see Figure 10-12). Review the summary, and if you are satisfied with what is about to take place, hit the Finish button.

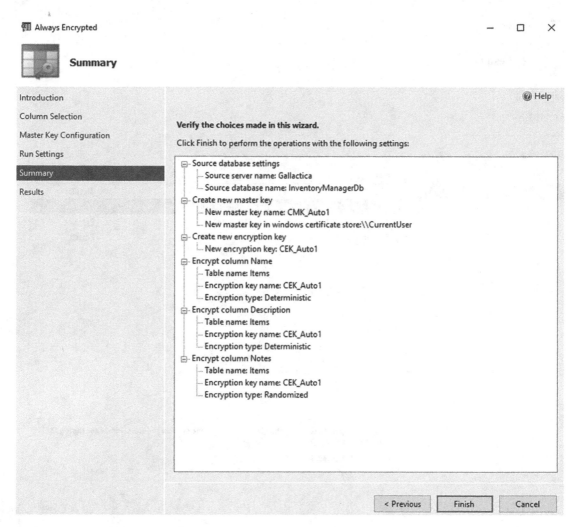

Figure 10-12. *Review the choices for the encryption wizard, and then hit Finish to run the encryption operation*

Once you hit Finish, the operation shouldn't take too long to complete (a couple of minutes). The completion of the operation is shown in Figure 10-13.

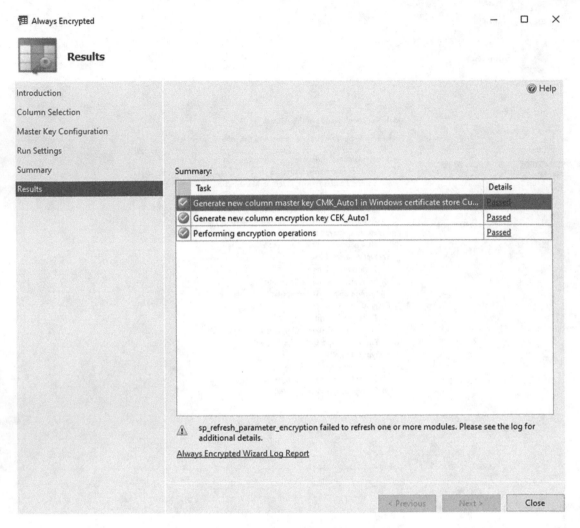

Figure 10-13. *The operation has completed as expected*

Close the wizard after the operation completes.

Step 3: Review the data

Run the same query you ran in Step 2 to see the data in the Items table. The results should now include the encrypted fields as expected (see Figure 10-14).

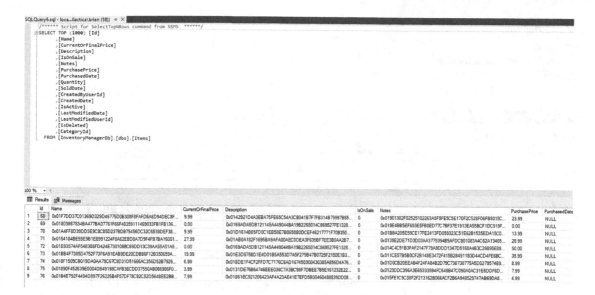

Figure 10-14. *The data is now encrypted as expected*

It is clear from this query that the Name, Description, and Notes fields that were there are now encrypted as expected. If your data is not showing as encrypted, it may be that the fields are being decrypted by SSMS based on your settings (more on this in the next step). A quick re-run of the wizard would validate the fields that are encrypted (don't re-apply the wizard if you do take a look). See Figure 10-15 for clarity.

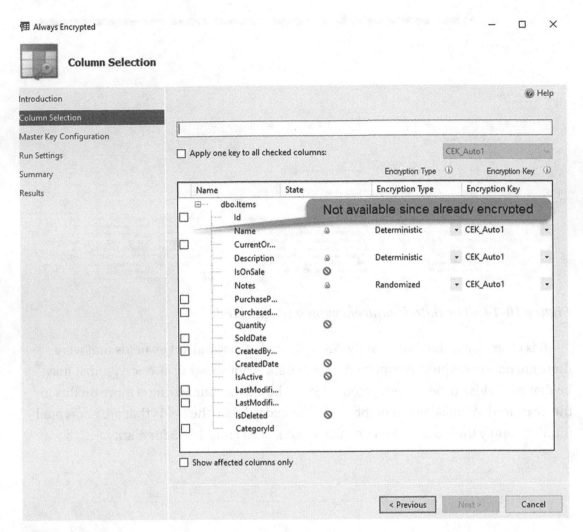

Figure 10-15. *The fields are encrypted. Reviewing the wizard shows they are not available since they are already encrypted*

Step 4: Modify SSMS to decrypt your columns automatically

If you are already seeing decrypted data, you likely already have this set. If you saw the results as earlier with encrypted columns, you'll need to make sure your results apply Always Encrypted so that you can see results in your queries.

Return to SSMS and disconnect from your database connection.

Open a new connection dialog to your SQL Server instance on SSMS, and then select the `Options` ➤ button (see Figure 10-16). On the options, move to the `Always Encrypted` tab and check the box next to `Enable Always Encrypted (column encryption)`.

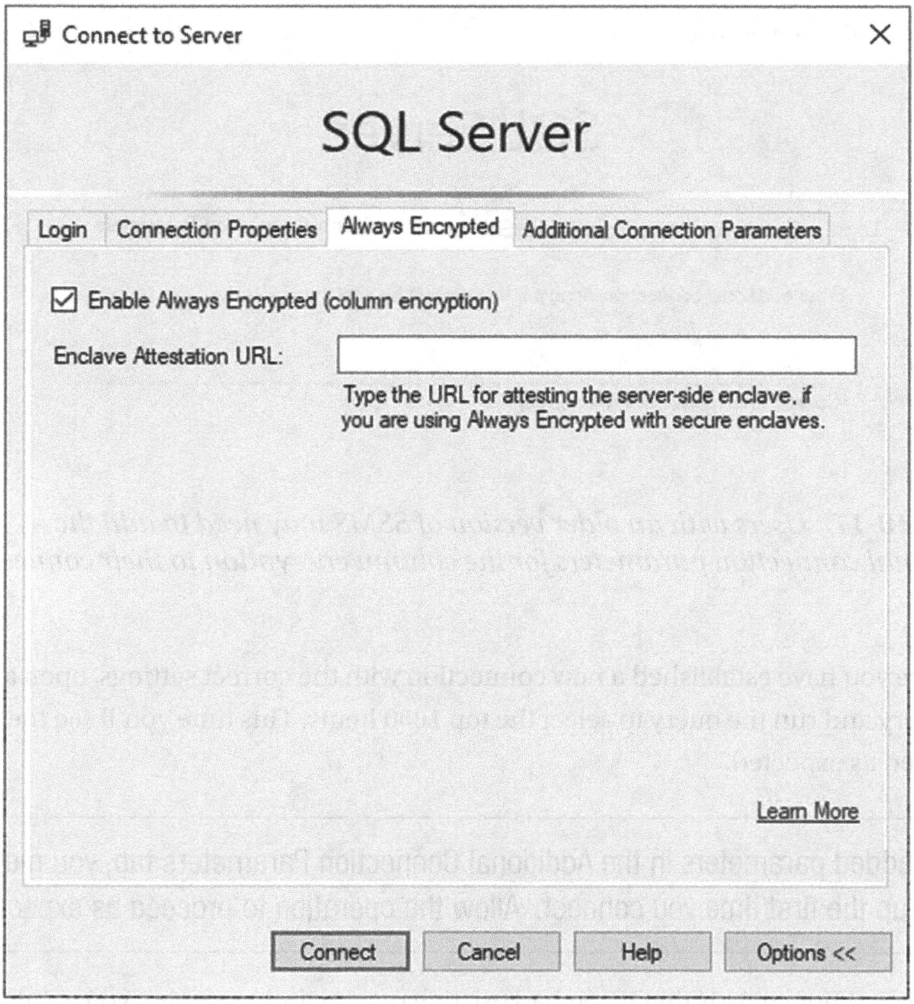

Figure 10-16. *The options allow you to turn on Always Encrypted*

You are not using Enclave Attestation in your solution, but if you were, you could set the enclave information here. Also note, if you are on an older version of SSMS, you won't have the Always Encrypted tab. If possible, you should just upgrade SSMS. If not, you can add additional settings into your `Additional Connection Parameters` tab on the `Options` dialog. Note that you do NOT need to do this if you have the Always Encrypted tab, only if you do not have that tab.

If you need to add the additional parameters, add the text "Column Encryption Setting=enabled" to the textbox (see Figure 10-17). Incidentally, this is the same setting you will add to your connection string in your .Net project soon.

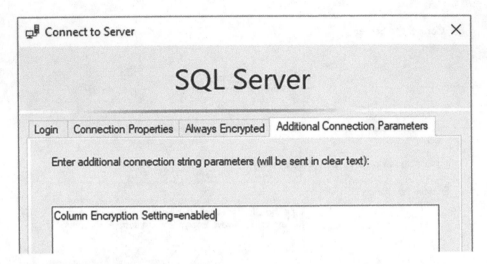

Figure 10-17. *Users with an older version of SSMS may need to add the additional connection parameters for the column encryption to their connection options*

Once you have established a new connection with the correct settings, open a new query and run the query to select the top 1000 Items. This time you'll see the data decrypted as expected.

If you added parameters in the Additional Connection Parameters tab, you may see a pop-up the first time you connect. Allow the operation to proceed as expected.

One final note here is that if you had existing query windows open, you would still not see decrypted fields. To ensure you see the decrypted fields, you may need to close query windows and create a new query for the new settings to take effect.

Now that you've set up the always encrypted database fields, let's see what happens when you work with your application.

Step 5: Run the application

Return to the Activity 10-1 project. Run the application as is. What do you think will happen?

In this case, you get an error immediately for an Encryption Scheme mismatch (see Figure 10-18).

```
1 reference
private static void ListInventory()
{
    using (var db = new InventoryDbContext(_optionsBuilder.Options))
    {
        var items = db.Items.OrderBy(x => x.Name).ToList();  ⊗
        var result = _mapper.Map<List<Item>, List<ItemDto>>(items);
        result.ForEach(x => Console.|
    }
}

1 reference
private static void ListInventoryWitl
{
    using (var db = new InventoryDbC(
    {
        var items = db.Items
                        .OrderBy(x =:
                        .ProjectTo<I
                        .ToList();
        items.ForEach(x => Console.Wi
    }
}
```

Exception Unhandled   ⊐ ✕

Microsoft.Data.SqlClient.SqlException: 'Encryption scheme mismatch for columns/variables 'Name'. The encryption scheme for the columns/variables is (encryption_type = 'DETERMINISTIC', encryption_algorithm_name = 'AEAD_AES_256_CBC_HMAC_SHA_256',

This exception was originally thrown at this call stack:
    [External Code]
    EFCore_Activity1001.Program.ListInventory() in Program.cs
    EFCore_Activity1001.Program.Main(string[]) in Program.cs

View Details | Copy Details | Start Live Share session...

▲ Exception Settings
    ☐ Break when this exception type is thrown
    Except when thrown from:
        ☐ EFCore_Activity1001.dll

Open Exception Settings | Edit Conditions

ound | ◈ ▾   ◄   ►   Ln: 64   Ch: 17   SPC

Figure 10-18. *The Application errors out due to encryption*

To begin fixing issues, add the following text to your connection string in the appsettings.json file after the *Trusted Connection=True* text (add a semicolon to separate from the previous statement):

```
Column Encryption Setting=Enabled;
```

Make sure to update all connection strings to use this new setting across all projects. Specifically, don't forget to do this in the InventoryDataMigrator project.

Now run the program again. What happens this time? Unfortunately, you still get the same error as before.

Comment out all of the calls in the main method except for GetItemsForListing. Note that this runs without any issues. Go back and comment out everything except ListInventoryWithProjection. Running the program generates the same error as before.

The reason this happens is because Always Encrypted uses client-side decryption. In this case, you're trying to work against encrypted Item fields for Name and Description before actually decrypting them.

If you had set up your Always Encrypted solution to also include enclaves, it might be possible to continue using these projections, since more operations could be handled on the server side.

This is going to be the biggest issue with using LINQ against Always Encrypted database columns when not using enclaves. You won't be able to leverage these columns without first decrypting the data. This is where using Always Encrypted can take a big performance hit.

In your current solution, you can still create a projection, but you can't do any ordering, sorting, paging, or filtering until the entire result set is decrypted on the client side.

Update the query for ListInventoryWithProjection to use the following code in the method:

```
using (var db = new InventoryDbContext(_optionsBuilder.Options))
{
    var items = db.Items
                    .ProjectTo<ItemDto>(_mapper.ConfigurationProvider)
                    .ToList();
    items.OrderBy(x => x.Name).ToList().ForEach(x => Console.
    WriteLine($"New Item: {x}"));
}
```

Run the program. This time you will see results as expected (see Figure 10-19).

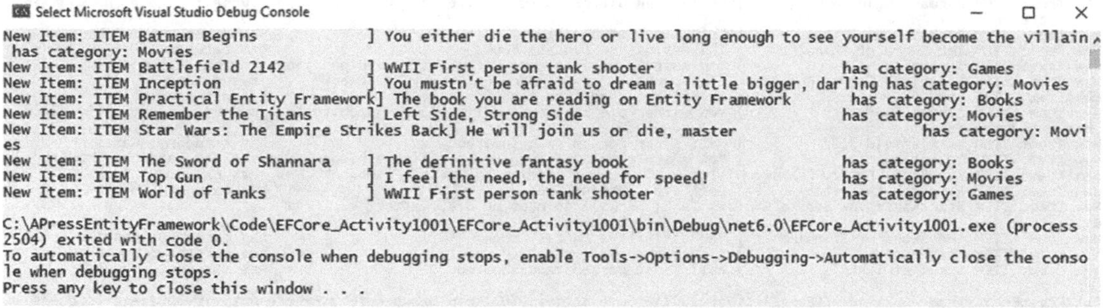

Figure 10-19. *The projection works, but ordering must happen after the query, and therefore the decryption has happened*

Additionally, update the original `ListInventory` method to use the following query to see one more issue:

```
using (var db = new InventoryDbContext(_optionsBuilder.Options))
{
    var result = db.Items.OrderBy(x => x.Name).Take(20)
                    .Select(x => new ItemDto
                    {
                        Name = x.Name,
                        Description = x.Description
                    })
                    .ToList();
    result.ForEach(x => Console.WriteLine($"New Item: {x}"));
}
```

Make sure to uncomment the call in the `Main` method so that the `ListInventory` method is called.

This time, the results will show as expected (see Figure 10-20).

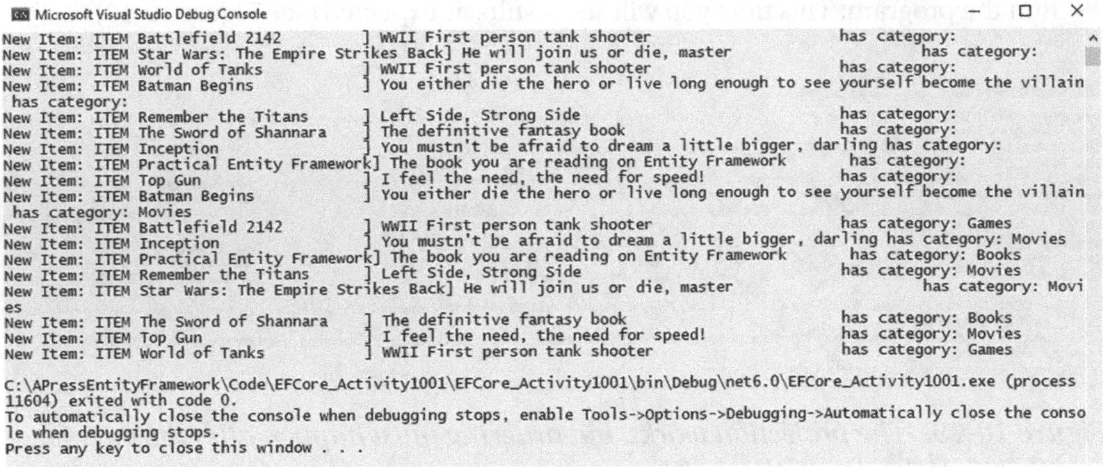

Figure 10-20. *The results for the ListInventory method are shown, and the fields are correctly decrypted as expected*

Step 6: Fix an issue with a join after Always Encrypted is on

At this point, you've seen how to encrypt and how to fix the projections. Uncomment the rest of the calls to methods in the Main method except for calls to `GetAllActiveItemsAsPipeDelimitedString` and `GetFullItemDetails` (the FromSqlRaw will no longer work, but the issue is much deeper and is explained in detail during Step 7) so that all of your Get and List operations will be run, and you should see yet another error when you run the program.

The issue to fix is the `GetItemsForListingLinq` method. Here again you have a projection with ordering, so it needs to be fixed, but also there is a join to `Categories`. To fix this, you need to do a couple of things.

First, you must get the result set to a list early so that it will be decrypted on the client side. The other issue is that the code needs to handle the join by using an include statement to get the categories. Since the code is no longer using a projection to get data, you have to go back to manually stating the join information. Modify the code in the `GetItemsForListingLinq` method as follows:

```
using (var db = new InventoryDbContext(_optionsBuilder.Options))
{
    var results = db.Items.Include(x => x.Category).ToList().Select(x =>
    new ItemDto
```

```
    {
        CreatedDate = x.CreatedDate,
        CategoryName = x.Category.Name,
        Description = x.Description,
        IsActive = x.IsActive,
        IsDeleted = x.IsDeleted,
        Name = x.Name,
        Notes = x.Notes,
        CategoryId = x.Category.Id,
        Id = x.Id
    }).Where(x => x.CreatedDate >= minDateValue && x.CreatedDate <=
    maxDateValue)
    .OrderBy(y => y.CategoryName).ThenBy(z => z.Name)
    .ToList();

    foreach (var itemDto in results)
    {
        Console.WriteLine(itemDto);
    }
}
```

This new code is similar but forces you to get all the items before you can do any sort of filtering or ordering, as you've previously seen, and again requires you to manually include the navigations in order to get the data.

The final output is shown in Figure 10-21 (your output should be similar).

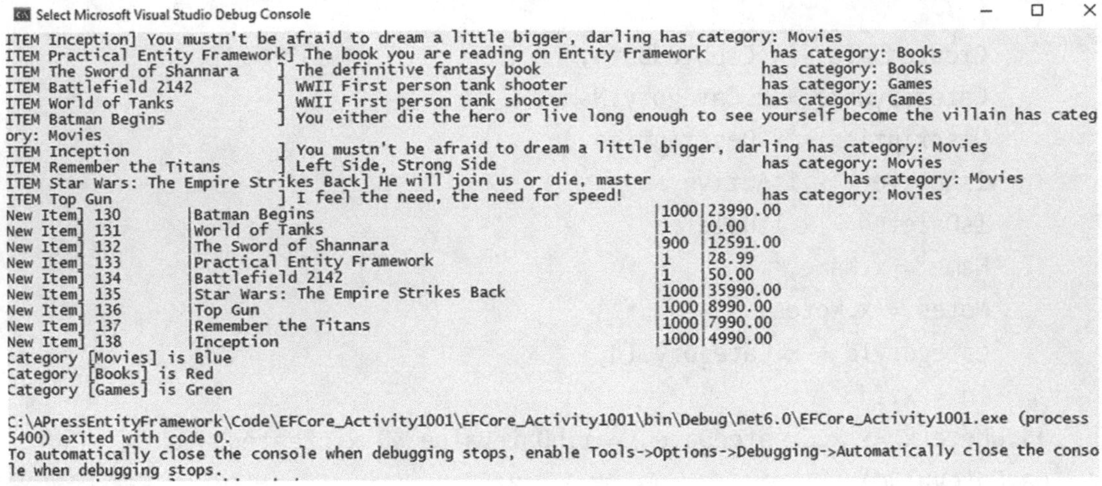

Figure 10-21. The final output for the activity is shown

Step 7: Fix the remaining issues

Fixing the two functions that remain, GetAllActiveItemsAsPipeDelimitedString and GetFullItemDetails both use the call FromSqlRaw. In this final step, you will fix both of them.

To get started, uncomment the call to the GetAllActiveItemsAsPipeDelimitedString method. Run the program so that you can see the error. You will once again see the error regarding the *Encryption scheme mismatch*.

In this case, the database is trying to perform a function that needs to have the data decrypted. Since the data is encrypted, without a secure enclave, the data cannot be parsed and joined into a comma-delimited string. For this reason, it is important to note that when you use Always Encrypted on a column, you will not be able to use the built-in aggregate functions at the database level without first establishing a secure enclave.

To fix this issue, therefore, you will just do the code to create the pipe-delimited string on the client side. Change the code in the GetAllActiveItemsAsPipeDelimitedString method to the following:

```
var result = db.Items.Where(x => x.IsActive).ToList();
var pipeDelimitedString = string.Join("|", result);

Console.WriteLine($"All active Items: {pipeDelimitedString}");
```

Run the method to see the result. This works, but you are no longer using the power of the database to create the string – it is now happening on the client side.

Uncomment the call to GetFullItemDetails, and run the code to see the error. Once again, you will see the error for the *Encryption scheme mismatch*.

This time, however, the issue is not with the view but rather with the client-side sorting that happens before decryption. Change the query for the result to the following code:

```
var result = db.FullItemDetailDtos
            .FromSqlRaw("SELECT * FROM [dbo].[vwFullItemDetails]")
            .ToList()
            .OrderBy(x => x.ItemName).ThenBy(x => x.GenreName)
                .ThenBy(x => x.Category).ThenBy(x => x.PlayerName);
```

Run the program to see the result. By changing the ordering to the client side, the method works as expected, and results are correctly returned using the view.

Activity 10-1 summary

In this activity, you were able to set up and leverage Always Encrypted on the InventoryManager database. With this encryption in place, you were able to see a couple of the pitfalls to using this approach as well as validate that the data is in fact encrypted, even during transit.

Going forward, you would be able to be confident that your data at rest is much more secure. To fully secure the data, however, you should consider storing your keys in Azure Key Vault rather than in the Windows certificate store.

Activity 10-2: Using Transparent Data Encryption

While it is more likely that you will encounter the need to use TDE in an older EF6 project, especially in projects that used versions of SQL Server prior to SQL Server 2016, it is entirely possible to implement TDE in the current version of SQL and .Net 6/EFCore6.

Therefore, to learn about TDE, you'll be using your .Net Core project that connects to the AdventureWorks database to complete this activity. Regardless of the version of EF where you are implementing this solution, the real meat of this activity will happen at the database level, with keys generated, column changes (which could/will be a code-first change), and then the heavy use of stored procedures to work with the data for read and write operations after fields are encrypted.

As mentioned earlier, it is possible to use TDE and then send the data encrypted over the pipe to be decrypted at the client; in this implementation, you will only be encrypting the data at rest. One other potential issue to this type of encryption is that it is easier for a malicious internal team member to gain access to your data at rest, and if you store your certificates with the database, a server breach could also be problematic if the bad player also gets your certificates along with the data.

Task 0: Getting started

This project will leverage the AdventureWorks database. If you are going to use your own files, the last time you used this code was at the end of Chapter 9. If you want to just get a clean start, as always, you could just leverage the provided starter files `EFCore_Activity10-2_StarterFiles`.

Since this is the AdventureWorks project, if you use the starter files, you should just ensure the connection string is set to your correct server and database name. This activity will leverage a couple of migrations, but this is the final time you'll work against the AdventureWorks database in this book so migration conflicts should not be an issue. Make sure to run the `update-database` command to ensure you have no pending migrations. You should not have made any changes to this point that would require a new migration.

One critical note here is that, in earlier activities, a class called `ImprovementPlans` was added to the library and then a `DbSet<ImprovementPlan>` was added to the `AdventureWorksContext`. It is imperative that at a minimum you do not have a `DbSet<ImprovementPlan>` in your `AdventureWorksContext` or the first migration will try to regenerate that table. It wouldn't hurt anything if you did add that table on the first migration, but it will look incorrect as compared to results in this activity.

Task 1: Plan the migration strategy

In this first task, you will plan out the migration strategy to apply TDE to a few columns in the AdventureWorks database.

Step 1: Evaluate the process to ensure data integrity

This migration strategy will work for any database that has existing data where you need to implement TDE to protect your data at rest. The AdventureWorks database solution is an existing EFCore implementation, and you have a lot of data. Your solution in the real world is likely similar, especially if it's in an older solution.

The steps you need to consider for migration of existing data to encrypted data at rest with TDE are as follows:

1. The first operation that you will likely want to do is take a backup of the entire existing database, in case something goes wrong during the encryption process.

2. The second thing to do is to add a temporary column to the table for each column that will be encrypted and back up the existing data to the temporary column to preserve the original data during encryption procedures.

3. Third, you need to create all of the keys and certificates necessary to encrypt and decrypt data with TDE.

4. Fourth, you must drop any constraints on the targeted columns.

5. Fifth, you will need to change the column type for the encrypted columns to be encrypted to `varbinary(max)`. This will destroy the existing data in those columns, which is why you backed up the data previously. Constraints will no longer be possible once the column is encrypted. Additionally, no matter the original data type, the encrypted column will be `varbinary(max)`.

6. Sixth, run a script to perform a transformation operation where the backup column data is selected, then encrypted, and finally inserted into the original column.

7. Seventh, with the data encrypted and restored to the original column(s), delete the backup column(s) from the table. Before you delete each of the temporary columns, make sure to fully document the column type and length. This will be critical during decryption, and if you don't keep a record of the column data type and length, you'll have to review backups or go through the migrations or scripts to see what the column types and lengths were before encryption. During decryption, you will explicitly use these column types and lengths to get back to the original data.

Sounds fairly straightforward, right? It's actually not too bad. In this activity, you'll walk through these steps from start to finish to ensure that it all works as planned.

There is one final note to consider, however. If you are working through the chapters of this book out of order, there are other chapters that depend on the *AdventureWorks* database to be set up and not have encrypted columns. While you could likely just restore the database at any point from the original download, you may wish to make a backup of the database before performing the remaining steps in this activity to avoid conflicts with other chapters.

If you are working on an actual database for your work or personal projects, I would recommend backing everything up before starting, on the off chance that something goes awry.

Step 2: Determine the columns you want to encrypt

Referring to the preceding steps, the first thing you want to do is perform a migration to add backup columns for every field you want to encrypt. To make this happen, you must first identify the columns to encrypt.

While a real-world scenario would likely have many tables and columns to encrypt or decrypt, you're going to home in on the HumanResources.Employee table in the *AdventureWorks* database. You should have no problem extrapolating what we learn from this activity to other tables and fields if you want to practice more or when you eventually are implementing your real-world solutions.

After an initial examination of the table for sensitive data, the columns that appear to make the most sense to encrypt are

- `NationalIDNumber`
- `JobTitle`
- `BirthDate`
- `MaritalStatus`
- `Gender`
- `HireDate`

You could do other fields and other tables, but this will be where you stop for this activity. One bummer about these fields is that there isn't a decimal field to encrypt/decrypt in this result set, but the decryption strategy would be the same as the others; just if you have a decimal field to encrypt/decrypt, don't forget to convert to the correct type and size as you decrypt.

Task 2: Create the backup columns

In this task, you will create a migration to back up the existing data from the columns that you are about to encrypt.

Step 1: Add the columns to the model

For the first part of the strategy, you need to add the backup fields to the model so that the migration will generate the columns in the database. As an alternative, you could do this by just writing a script and including it in the migration, which is similar to how it would have been done in a traditional database-first approach. The choice is yours on how you would like to proceed. If using a script, another thing you could consider is just selecting the whole table into a backup table and then encrypting from a select on that table. There are many solutions available for the migration.

In this book example, you're going to use full database migrations so that there is a small chance you could roll back the migrations without too many issues if there is a problem. Again, you could write manual rollback scripts and just use them to protect your data, as you would in a traditional database-first approach.

If you have not validated that you have no pending migrations, before continuing, you should try to add a migration and make sure it is blank. If not blank, evaluate and run it. If the migration is blank as expected, run the Remove-Migration command.

Find the Employee.cs file in the EFCore_DBLibrary project. This code translates to the HumanResources.Employee table in the database (the schema is mapped via the Fluent API in the AdventureWorksContext with the line entity.ToTable("Employee", "HumanResources"); which is in the OnModelCreating method). Add the following code to the bottom of the class file to create the backup columns for storing the temporary data during the encryption process:

```
[StringLength(15)]
public string NationalIDNumberBackup { get; set; }
[StringLength(50)]
public string JobTitleBackup { get; set; }
[Column(TypeName = "date")]
public DateTime BirthDateBackup { get; set; }
[StringLength(1)]
public string MaritalStatusBackup { get; set; }
[StringLength(1)]
public string GenderBackup { get; set; }
[Column(TypeName = "date")]
public DateTime HireDateBackup { get; set; }
```

You will also need to add using statements for the data annotations in this code as follows, so add these using statements to the top of the file:

```
using System.ComponentModel.DataAnnotations;
using System.ComponentModel.DataAnnotations.Schema;
```

Step 2: Add the migration and update the database

Open the PMC and ensure you've selected the EFCore_DBLibrary project. Add a migration to update the table using the command add-migration EncryptionMigration_Step1. After the migration runs, validate that it only contains the expected fields. When the migration generates, some of the fields may be set to nullable: false and may have a default value set on them. As long as the field you are backing up is also not nullable, this should not be an issue. If the field that is being backed up allows null values but the backup field does not, then override the definition in the migration to set the value to nullable: true and remove the default value. For clarity, review the migration shown in Figure 10-22.

```
1 reference
public partial class EncryptionMigration_Step1 : Migration
{
    0 references
    protected override void Up(MigrationBuilder migrationBuilder)
    {
        migrationBuilder.AddColumn<DateTime>(
            name: "BirthDateBackup",
            schema: "HumanResources",
            table: "Employee",
            type: "date",
            nullable: false,
            defaultValue: new DateTime(1, 1, 1, 0, 0, 0, 0, DateTimeKind.Unspecified));

        migrationBuilder.AddColumn<string>(
            name: "GenderBackup",
            schema: "HumanResources",
            table: "Employee",
            type: "nvarchar(1)",
            maxLength: 1,
            nullable: true);

        migrationBuilder.AddColumn<DateTime>(
            name: "HireDateBackup",
```

Figure 10-22. *The migration is generated to add the backup columns which will hold the data for the encrypted columns during the encryption operation*

Run the update-database command to add the backup columns to the database. If you wish, you could select from the table and/or refresh the table in SSMS to ensure they are present as expected (see Figure 10-23).

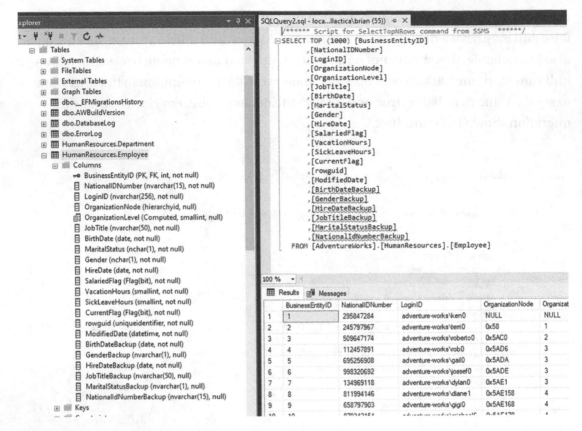

Figure 10-23. *The new columns exist as expected*

Step 3: Run a script to back up the data for the target columns

Begin by adding a new migration using the command add-migration
EncryptionMigration_Step2_BackupData.

Once the migration is created, either add some inline T-SQL to back up the table
data or you could also implement a file management solution like was covered earlier
in the text (see Chapter 7 for more information on the scripting with file management
strategy). For this activity and for purposes of brevity, you'll just do your scripting within
the migrations.

The preceding command should have generated a blank migration. In the Up method
of the new migration, add the following code to select the target column data into the
backup columns to get ready for encryption processing:

```
migrationBuilder.Sql(@"UPDATE [HumanResources].[Employee]
    SET [NationalIDNumberBackup] = [NationalIDNumber]
        ,[JobTitleBackup] = [JobTitle]
        ,[BirthDateBackup] = [BirthDate]
        ,[MaritalStatusBackup] = [MaritalStatus]
        ,[GenderBackup] = [Gender]
        ,[HireDateBackup] = [HireDate]"
);
```

For this migration, there is nothing to do in the Down method. If you need to roll back, you could reset the data in the original columns from this data. However, that is easily performed manually, and in the unlikely event that you need to do this, you will likely want to ensure you are ready to do so. For these reasons, just leave the Down method blank.

Run the update-database command to execute the script, and then select from the table in SSMS to ensure data exists as expected.

As with other activities, the end of a task is always a good place to check in changes if you are using a local GIT repository.

Task 3: Create the keys and certificates

In order to make the database keys successfully, you'll need to have three things. First, you'll need a certificate. Second, you'll need to create the symmetric keys. Finally, you need a place to back up your keys. You'll also need a strong password that can be used for the keys. An important note is that anyone that is executing the migration to create the scripts will need to make sure to have the hard-coded file path in place for storage of local backup certificates and keys. Another consideration would be to store your encryption certificates and keys in an Azure Key Vault.

When running the following scripts, make sure to validate that the physical drive contains the proper folder for storing backups of the certificates and keys generated by the migration script for creating encryption keys.

Step 1: Create the folder to store the keys

Begin by validating the folder for backup. For this activity, a suggestion could be C:\ Data\DatabaseKeys. In the real world, you'll want to do something with them to keep them secure after generation. Create the folder C:\Data\DatabaseKeys or a similar folder of your choosing for storing the physical key files.

Step 2: Create the certificate and key

Once the storage location is in place, create a new migration by running the command add-migration EncryptionMigration_Step3_CertsAndKeysGeneration.

Once again, this should generate a blank migration. After the migration is created, you need to add four statements for execution into the Up method in the exact order listed as follows (you should use a better password, but make sure you will remember the password you use):

```
migrationBuilder.Sql(@"IF NOT EXISTS (SELECT *
    FROM sys.symmetric_keys WHERE symmetric_key_id = 101)
    BEGIN
        CREATE MASTER KEY ENCRYPTION BY PASSWORD = 'Password#123'
    END");

migrationBuilder.Sql(@"CREATE CERTIFICATE AW_tdeCert
    WITH SUBJECT = 'AdventureWorks TDE Certificate'");

migrationBuilder.Sql(@"BACKUP CERTIFICATE AW_tdeCert TO
    FILE = 'C:\Data\DatabaseKeys\AW_tdeCert.crt'
    WITH PRIVATE KEY
    (
        FILE = 'C:\Data\DatabaseKeys\AW_tdeCert_PrivateKey.crt',
        ENCRYPTION BY PASSWORD = 'Password#123'
    )");

migrationBuilder.Sql(@"CREATE SYMMETRIC KEY AW_ColumnKey
        WITH ALGORITHM = AES_256
        ENCRYPTION BY CERTIFICATE AW_tdeCert;
    ");
```

Once again, you won't be doing anything in the Down method for this migration.

With all of this in place, run the `update-database` command to execute the certificate generation. Once the execution has completed, check your physical folder to see the new certificates that were generated (see Figure 10-24).

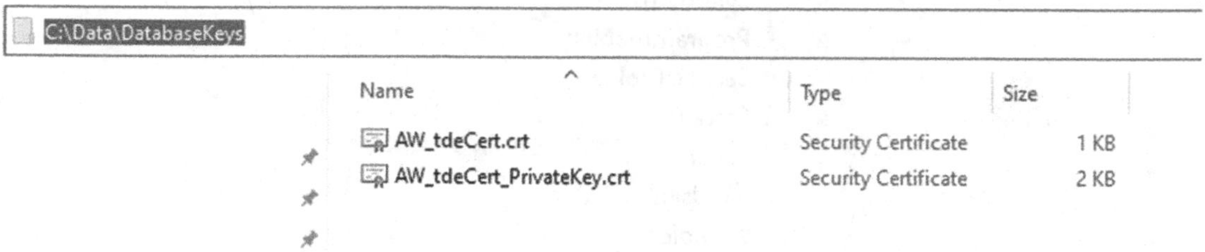

C:\Data\DatabaseKeys		
Name ^	Type	Size
AW_tdeCert.crt	Security Certificate	1 KB
AW_tdeCert_PrivateKey.crt	Security Certificate	2 KB

Figure 10-24. *Running the migration has generated the physical certificates in the folder you specified in the script*

You should see both the `AW_tdeCert.crt` and the `AW_tdeCert_PrivateKey.crt` files. If you changed the name in the script, the name should match in the physical location.

Additionally, return to SSMS and review the database to see the keys that have been added from the recent operation (review Figure 10-25).

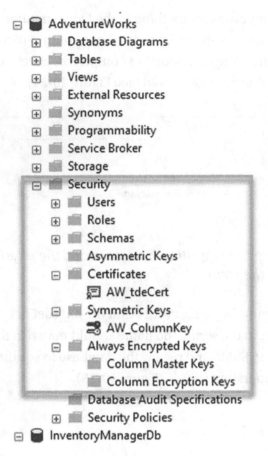

Figure 10-25. *The keys and certificates are also present in the local database under Certificates and Symmetric Keys*

When this is completed, you'll have the AW_tdeCert in the Certificates folder and the AW_ColumnKey in the Symmetric Keys folder under Security in your AdventureWorks database.

Task 4: Drop constraints on the targeted columns

Now that you're ready to encrypt data and you have your target column data backed up, you need to prepare the columns that we're using in our database to store the encrypted data.

First, you must drop all the constraints and indexes on the fields that will be changing. You can do that easily with a script within a migration.

If you miss one along the way, just update your script file, and then run the drop manually. Otherwise, make sure to change your script to be idempotent so that it could be run multiple times if necessary.

Step 1: Drop the existing constraints

Add a new migration with the command add-migration EncryptionMigration_ Step4_DropConstraints. In this migration, you will add additional scripts to drop the constraints and the index. As before, this should generate a blank migration.

To complete this step, you will have to remove a bunch of check constraints to drop from each of these columns. You may want to keep a record of what they do as you may want to enforce these constraints in the procedures that insert and/or update data in the future. Just remember that once the column is encrypted, you will not be able to add constraints back to the column.

In the migration's Up command, you need to add the drop statements to get rid of all constraints on the fields you are encrypting. For this reason, open your HumanResources. Employee table in SSMS and review the Constraints folder. Review Figure 10-26 for more information.

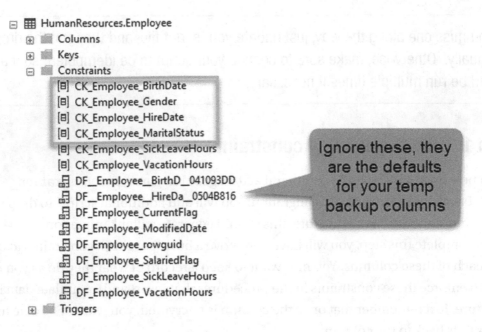

Figure 10-26. *Four of the fields have constraints that need to be dropped before the fields can be encrypted*

The four constraints to drop are the check constraints on BirthDate, Gender, HireDate, and MaritalStatus. Additionally, there is one index to drop. Review Figure 10-27 for more information.

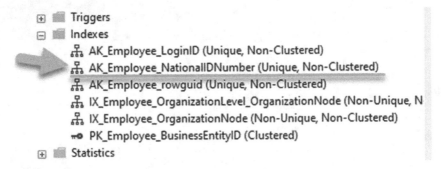

Figure 10-27. *The NationalIDNumber field has an index that needs to be dropped*

Here you can see that the NationalIDNumber field has an index that will need to be removed before the field can be encrypted.

To make the necessary changes to drop the four constraints and the index, add the following code into the Up method for the migration:

```
migrationBuilder.Sql(@"ALTER TABLE[HumanResources].[Employee]
    DROP CONSTRAINT[CK_Employee_MaritalStatus]");
migrationBuilder.Sql(@"ALTER TABLE[HumanResources].[Employee]
    DROP CONSTRAINT[CK_Employee_HireDate]");
migrationBuilder.Sql(@"ALTER TABLE[HumanResources].[Employee]
    DROP CONSTRAINT[CK_Employee_Gender]");
migrationBuilder.Sql(@"ALTER TABLE[HumanResources].[Employee]
    DROP CONSTRAINT[CK_Employee_BirthDate]");
migrationBuilder.DropIndex(
        name: "AK_Employee_NationalIDNumber",
        schema: "HumanResources",
        table: "Employee");
```

Here you should really put the revert code into the Down method to add these constraints back to the table and re-apply the index. This is not as trivial as it seems it should be as each constraint is three executable statements to re-apply the constraint. For this reason, you can skip it here.

To see the script, you could just right-click each object and script as create to a new query editor window. You could then combine the entire script and save it. I have done this and placed a copy in the final files if you would like to see what the script would look like.

If you wanted to add each statement to the Down method, remember to wrap each executable statement as `migrationBuilder.Sql(@"some_code_here...")`. You would use a new statement every time you encounter a GO statement in the normal T-SQL code.

Run the `update-database` command to drop the four constraints and the one index so that the columns will be able to be correctly altered in the next step. After execution, validate that the constraints and the index are no longer part of the database schema (see Figure 10-28).

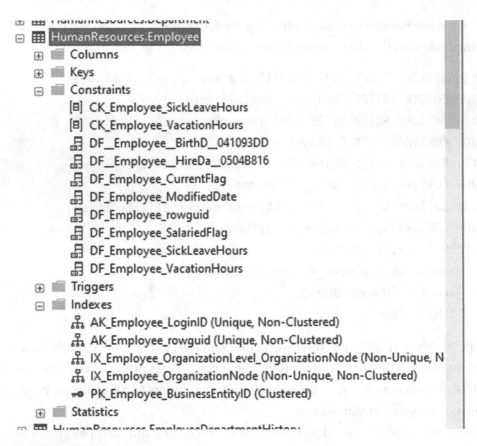

Figure 10-28. *The constraints are dropped and the index is removed*

Task 5: Drop the columns that are going to be targeted for encryption, and then recreate them

It may seem counter-intuitive. You might say, "Can't I just convert the type?" The answer is that you can if you just run a script in the database directly. Using code-first migrations, it's not so straightforward. If you try to migrate a change for any of the targeted columns, you'll get an error that says you are unable to convert from some type to varbinary(max). There is a way to do this in one migration, using a swap strategy. I used that strategy in the first edition of the text.

For this activity, in order to get the columns encrypted, you will first just drop the existing columns, and then you will recreate them with the correct type. Before you do this, ensure that you have fully backed up the data into the temp columns so that it will not be lost forever.

Step 1: Drop the existing columns

Return to the Employee.cs class, and comment out the properties for NationalIdnumber, JobTitle, BirthDate, MaritalStatus, Gender, and HireDate from the model (see Figure 10-29 for clarity).

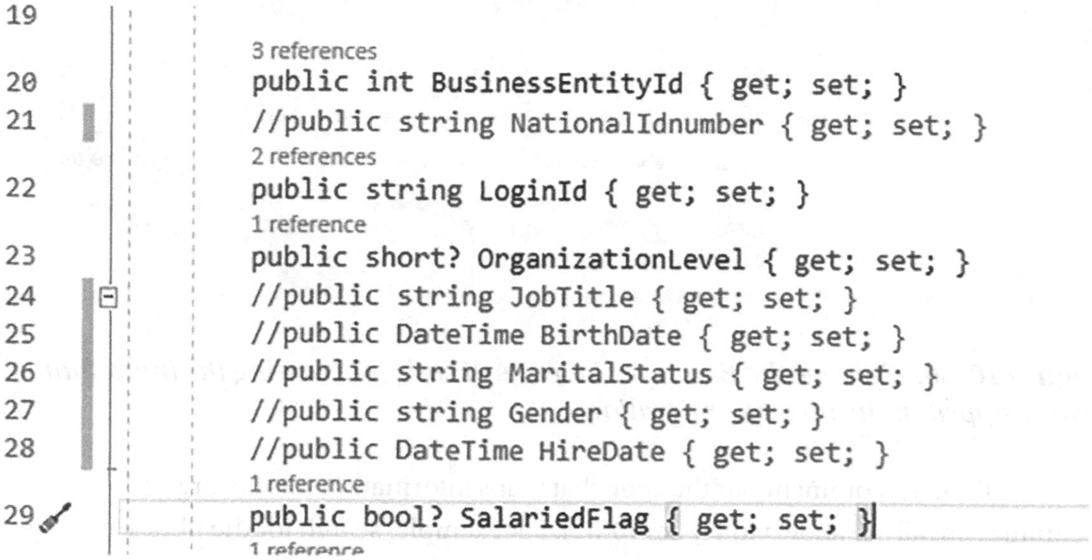

```
19
                3 references
20              public int BusinessEntityId { get; set; }
21              //public string NationalIdnumber { get; set; }
                2 references
22              public string LoginId { get; set; }
                1 reference
23              public short? OrganizationLevel { get; set; }
24              //public string JobTitle { get; set; }
25              //public DateTime BirthDate { get; set; }
26              //public string MaritalStatus { get; set; }
27              //public string Gender { get; set; }
28              //public DateTime HireDate { get; set; }
                1 reference
29              public bool? SalariedFlag { get; set; }
                1 reference
```

Figure 10-29. *The fields to drop are commented out for now*

Once you have done that, open the AdventureWorksContext and find the code in the OnModelCreating for the Fluent API representation of the Employee entity. In there, you will likely find the line of code

```
entity.HasIndex(e => e.NationalIdnumber)
                .HasName("AK_Employee_NationalIDNumber")
                .IsUnique();
```

You will need to remove this line of code (see Figure 10-30) to avoid recreating the index that was previously dropped (the correct way to drop the index would have been to remove this code in the first place, not use a script).

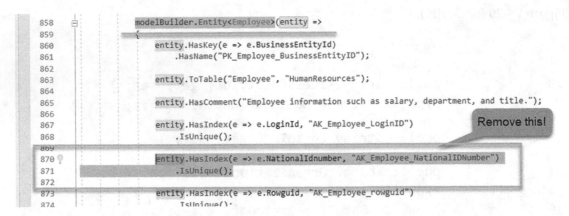

Figure 10-30. *Remove the Employee Fluent API code for creating the index that was dropped in the previous migration*

Additionally, comment out the code that maps information for the targeted columns (not all are shown in Figure 10-31). For example, search for the phrase `entity.Property(e => e.BirthDate` or any other of the targets. Comment out – do not remove – the code in the Fluent API for the six targeted columns in the `Employee` entity (see Figure 10-31).

```
876            entity.Property(e => e.BusinessEntityId)
877               .ValueGeneratedNever()
878               .HasColumnName("BusinessEntityID")
879               .HasComment("Primary key for Employee records.  Foreign key to BusinessEntity.BusinessEntityID.");
880
881        //entity.Property(e => e.BirthDate)
882        //    .HasColumnType("date")
883        //    .HasComment("Date of birth.");
884
885            entity.Property(e => e.CurrentFlag)
886               .IsRequired()
887               .HasDefaultValueSql("((1))")
888               .HasComment("0 = Inactive, 1 = Active");
889
890        //entity.Property(e => e.Gender)
891        //    .IsRequired()
892        //    .HasMaxLength(1)
893        //    .IsFixedLength(true)
894        //    .HasComment("M = Male, F = Female");
895
896        //entity.Property(e => e.HireDate)
897        //    .HasColumnType("date")
898        //    .HasComment("Employee hired on this date.");
899
900        //entity.Property(e => e.JobTitle)
901        //    .IsRequired()
902        //    .HasMaxLength(50)
903        //    .HasComment("Work title such as Buyer or Sales Representative.");
904
905            entity.Property(e => e.LoginId)
```

Figure 10-31. *The targeted fields are commented out in the Entity builder in the* *AdventureWorksContext*

Ensure the project builds. This will help to determine if you missed any code in the `OnModelCreating` method.

Run the add-migration command that follows to add a new migration to affect these first changes for Task 5: `add-migration EncryptionMigration_Step5a_` `DropTargetedFields`.

In the generated migration, the first thing will be the statement to drop the index. Just comment that statement out. The remaining statements should be drop column statements for the six targeted fields (see Figure 10-32).

```
5 references
protected override void Up(MigrationBuilder migrationBuilder)
{
    //migrationBuilder.DropIndex(
    //      name: "AK_Employee_NationalIDNumber",
    //      schema: "HumanResources",
    //      table: "Employee");

    migrationBuilder.DropColumn(
        name: "BirthDate",
        schema: "HumanResources",
        table: "Employee");

    migrationBuilder.DropColumn(
        name: "Gender",
        schema: "HumanResources",
        table: "Employee");

    migrationBuilder.DropColumn(
        name: "HireDate",
        schema: "HumanResources",
        table: "Employee");

    migrationBuilder.DropColumn(
        name: "JobTitle",
        schema: "HumanResources",
        table: "Employee");

    migrationBuilder.DropColumn(
        name: "MaritalStatus",
        schema: "HumanResources",
        table: "Employee");

    migrationBuilder.DropColumn(
        name: "NationalIDNumber",
        schema: "HumanResources",
        table: "Employee");
}
```

Figure 10-32. *The migration has the drop index statement and six drop column statements only in the Up method. The drop index statement is commented out*

Ensure this is the case and that you have commented out the drop statement, and then run the update-database command. Once the migration is completed, you are ready to recreate the columns. You may also wish to check the database to validate that the fields were removed as expected.

Step 2: Recreate the target fields

Return to the `Employee.cs` class and uncomment all of the targeted fields. Change each one to have a data type of `byte[]` (see Figure 10-33).

```
--
            3 references
20          public int BusinessEntityId { get; set; }
            0 references
21          public byte[] NationalIdnumber { get; set; }
            2 references
22          public string LoginId { get; set; }
            1 reference
23          public short? OrganizationLevel { get; set; }
            0 references
24          public byte[] JobTitle { get; set; }
            0 references
25          public byte[] BirthDate { get; set; }
            0 references
26          public byte[] MaritalStatus { get; set; }
            0 references
27          public byte[] Gender { get; set; }
            0 references
28          public byte[] HireDate { get; set; }
            1 reference
29          public bool? SalariedFlag { get; set; }
            1 reference
30          public short VacationHours { get; set; }
```

Figure 10-33. *The original properties are restored with type byte[] instead of their original types*

Next, you need to go back to the `AdventureWorksContext` and find all the code for the Fluent API that was commented out for each of these fields. Uncomment the mappings, but remove any information about type or length from any of the fields so that only things like the comment and the column name mappings remain. The code that follows is the new mapping for each of the six fields. Use caution when copying this as they are not consecutive in the context, so you will need to be careful not to delete any columns that are not affected by this operation (i.e., don't accidentally wipe out `ModifiedDate`). Additionally, do not change types on any other fields. The only Fluent API code you are changing is directly related to the fields that are targeted for migration.

```
entity.Property(e => e.BirthDate)
    .HasComment("Date of birth.");

entity.Property(e => e.Gender)
    .IsRequired()
    .HasComment("M = Male, F = Female");

entity.Property(e => e.HireDate)
    .HasComment("Employee hired on this date.");

entity.Property(e => e.JobTitle)
    .IsRequired()
    .HasComment("Work title such as Buyer or Sales Representative.");

entity.Property(e => e.MaritalStatus)
    .IsRequired()
    .HasComment("M = Married, S = Single");

entity.Property(e => e.NationalIDnumber)
    .IsRequired()
    .HasColumnName("NationalIDNumber")
    .HasComment("Unique national identification number such as a social
    security number.");
```

With the new properties restored on the Employee model and the Fluent API code in place as earlier, run the command add-migration EncryptionMigration_step5b_RestoreTargetColumnsAsVarBinaryMax.

When this migration is generated, you should see the six add column statements as expected, all of type varbinary(max). Once you have ensured this is the case, run the update-database command to apply the changes.

When the migration is run, refresh the table to ensure the columns exist as varbinary(max) columns (see Figure 10-34).

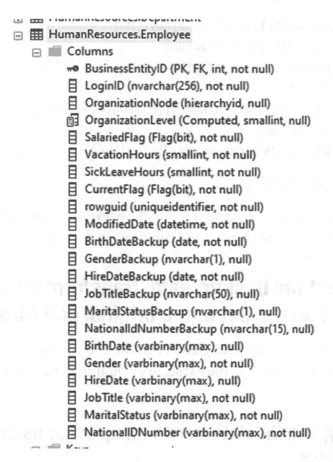

Figure 10-34. The original columns are back, and they are now of type varbinary(max)

After validating the columns are in place, run the following T-SQL query against the table in SSMS:

```
OPEN SYMMETRIC KEY AW_ColumnKey
DECRYPTION BY CERTIFICATE AW_tdeCert;

SELECT BusinessEntityID, LoginID,
ISNULL(CONVERT(nvarchar(15), decryptbykey([NationalIDNumber])), '')
[NationalIDNumber], [NationalIDNumberBackup],
ISNULL(CONVERT(nvarchar(50), decryptbykey([JobTitle])), '') [JobTitle],
[JobTitleBackup],
ISNULL(CONVERT(DateTime, decryptbykey([BirthDate])), null) [BirthDate],
[BirthDateBackup],
```

```
ISNULL(CONVERT(nvarchar(1), decryptbykey([MaritalStatus])),'')
[MaritalStatus] ,[MaritalStatusBackup],
ISNULL(CONVERT(nvarchar(1), decryptbykey([Gender])),'')
[Gender],[GenderBackup],
ISNULL(CONVERT(datetime, decryptbykey([HireDate])), null)
HireDate,[HireDateBackup]
FROM [AdventureWorks].[HumanResources].[Employee]

CLOSE ALL SYMMETRIC KEYS
```

This query shows that the original columns have no data but also gives you a glimpse at decryption of the data using the key and certificate in a query.

Task 6: Select the backup data, transform it for encryption, and store it in the original columns

For this step, you're going to run a migration that will encrypt the data that you've stored in backup columns and put it into the varbinary columns that are now holding the encrypted data.

Step 1: Encrypt all the data from backup columns into the new original columns

Create a new migration using the command add-migration EncryptionMigration_ Step6_EncryptBackupDataIntoOriginalColumns. This migration should be blank.

In the Up method of the migration, you're going to run some custom SQL to move the backup data into the destination columns. To do this, you're going to need to encrypt the data as you move it.

The important moving pieces of this process will be to first open the symmetric key to allow the encryption process to take place, as well as naming the certificate to use for encryption. In the quick check you did at the end of the last step, you used the same process. You also set the decryption to take place using a built-in function called decryptByKey. In this method, you'll do the inverse where you're encrypting the data using a function called encryptByKey.

The simple commands to open and close the keys are OPEN SYMMETRIC KEY AW_ ColumnKey

DECRYPTION BY CERTIFICATE AW_tdeCert; to open the encryption, and CLOSE ALL SYMMETRIC KEYS, to end the ability to use the keys for encryption and decryption within a query session.

To get your script in place, go to the Up method in the migration and add the following code:

```
migrationBuilder.Sql(@"OPEN SYMMETRIC KEY AW_ColumnKey
    DECRYPTION BY CERTIFICATE AW_tdeCert;

    UPDATE [HumanResources].[Employee]
        SET [NationalIDNumber] = encryptByKey(Key_GUID('AW_ColumnKey'),
        CONVERT(varbinary(max), [NationalIDNumberBackup]))
            ,[JobTitle] = encryptByKey(Key_GUID('AW_ColumnKey'),
            CONVERT(varbinary(max), [JobTitleBackup]))
            ,[BirthDate] = encryptByKey(Key_GUID('AW_ColumnKey'),
            CONVERT(varbinary(max), [BirthDateBackup]))
            ,[MaritalStatus] = encryptByKey(Key_GUID('AW_ColumnKey'),
            CONVERT(varbinary(max), [MaritalStatusBackup]))
            ,[Gender] = encryptByKey(Key_GUID('AW_ColumnKey'),
            CONVERT(varbinary(max), [GenderBackup]))
            ,[HireDate] = encryptByKey(Key_GUID('AW_ColumnKey'),
            CONVERT(varbinary(max), [HireDateBackup]))
    CLOSE ALL SYMMETRIC KEYS; ");
```

Note that the function encryptByKey(Key_GUID('keyname'), ...) allows you to use the symmetric encryption keys. Also note that the first part of the script opens the key by certificate and the last part just closes all the keys. You will have to use similar commands in SSMS and stored procedures to get data or insert/update data from these encrypted columns going forward.

Run the migration using the update-database command.

Step 2: Validate the data

Once the migration has applied, run the script that was run at the end of Task 5 to see how the data has now been transferred into the columns.

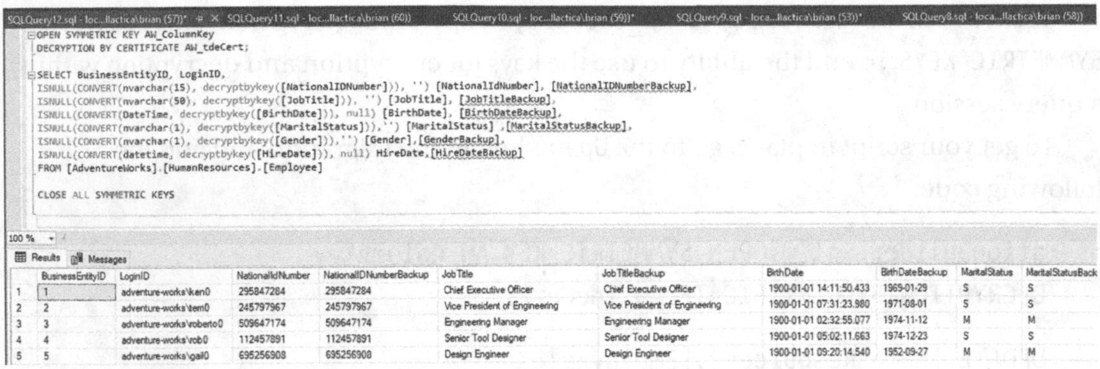

Figure 10-35. *The columns have now had their data restored*

To further validate that the encryption is working, just run a select top 1000 from the table in a new query window without the use of the keys. You should see results similar to what is shown in Figure 10-36.

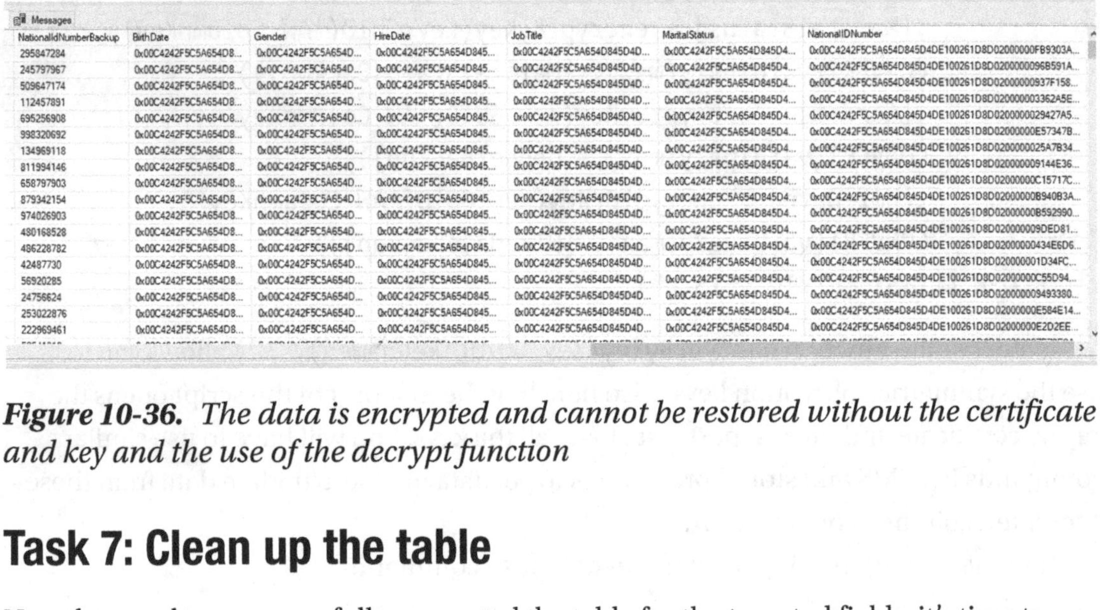

Figure 10-36. *The data is encrypted and cannot be restored without the certificate and key and the use of the decrypt function*

Task 7: Clean up the table

Now that you have successfully encrypted the table for the targeted fields, it's time to delete the backup columns.

Step 1: Remove the properties from the Employee model

Return to the Employee.cs model and remove the properties that represent the backup fields that were added in Task 2.

Step 2: Create the migration and update the database

After removing the temporary storage columns from the Employee model, run the command `add-migration EncryptionMigration_Step7_DeleteBackupColumns`. This should generate a migration that contains six statements to drop the backup columns and nothing else.

Once you are sure the migration is correct to just delete the backup columns, run the `update-database` command.

Activity 10-2 summary

In this activity, you learned how to build out TDE around six sensitive columns in the AdventureWorks database.

You followed a migration strategy to ensure that your data was preserved and you were able to successfully encrypt the data and work with the data in queries after you had encrypted it.

Chapter summary

In this chapter, you learned about two very important and different ways to encrypt your data in your database tables. The first way to encrypt is using Always Encrypted and the second is using TDE.

When you applied encryption in both approaches, you saw how Always Encrypted was easy to apply but perhaps falls short in performance in a couple of areas. You also saw that TDE is a bit more complicated to set up but once it is in place is a very powerful and efficient way to encrypt and decrypt data at rest.

Important takeaways

After working through this chapter, the things you should be in command of are

- Always Encrypted databases

- Working with migrations around data transformation

- Using the Fluent API to further define indexes and column constraints

- How to leverage EncryptByKey and DecryptByKey for TDE encryption

- Creation of certificate and keys for encryption

Closing thoughts

As you've learned about building out your robust data solutions and now you have learned to encrypt the data, the next step for you to learn is to build a more robust data solution with two critical patterns – the repository pattern and the unit of work pattern. You will learn about these in the next chapter.

Repository and Unit of Work Patterns

In this chapter, you are going to learn about two critical patterns that exist which should be on the radar of every database developer, whether you are using Entity Framework or not. The good news is that EF actually handles a lot of the *unit of work (UoW)* and *repository (Repo)* work for you. The bad news is that EF is sometimes not everything that you need when implementing your solutions.

To learn more about these patterns and how you can work with them, you'll start this chapter by discussing each pattern and why they are important, and then you'll finish the chapter by reworking your Inventory system so that it is layered with your own simple repository for working with Items. After you layer the solution, you'll have the ability to implement a simple UoW pattern on top of working with Entity Framework.

The repository (Repo) pattern

The repository pattern is one of the more popular patterns when working with databases. If you aren't using a full repository pattern, you are likely using something that is very close to the repository pattern. If not, you're likely writing a lot of redundant code around the operations to interact with your data and creating a large problem for maintenance and upgrades to your system for yourself and future developers.

Sources of information about the repository pattern

There are many resources that discuss the repository pattern, but almost all of them point back to Martin Fowler's definition as defined in the book *Patterns of Enterprise Architecture*.

B. L. Gorman, *Practical Entity Framework Core 6*, https://doi.org/10.1007/978-1-4842-7301-2_11

Microsoft itself has a great write-up on the repository pattern, which can be found here: https://docs.microsoft.com/en-us/dotnet/architecture/microservices/microservice-ddd-cqrs-patterns/infrastructure-persistence-layer-design.

If you want all the official definitions and more in-depth discussions of the pattern, I recommend you take some time to review both of those resources.

The repository pattern abstracts the database plumbing code from the implementation

The main reason you want to work with the Repo pattern is to make your life a lot easier when it comes to working with your databases in your solutions.

The way the pattern works is that the repository puts a layer in place which allows you to write common code operations and rely on the repository to handle the plumbing that is necessary to connect and perform operations against the database.

Ever since *generics* and *expressions* were added to *.Net*, it has been possible to write custom repository patterns. Writing a custom implementation of the repository pattern would even be possible without these tools, albeit not as convenient.

However, before Entity Framework, it was commonplace to use ADO.Net to write code that created a connection and then added a command to the connection. After adding the command, you would then set the command type and then the command text – either the name of the stored procedure or the actual inline SQL command. Finally, you would add parameters as needed to complete the query.

After getting that all set up, you'd then use the command with an open connection associated with a `DataReader` or a `DataSet` to retrieve the data results, and then you'd further have to work with that dataset line by line and/or field by field in order to hydrate your objects in order to display the information back to the user.

This process just described was for just one of your data operations. Press "repeat" on this process for each entity and for each specific call to the database regarding that entity.

Entity Framework's built-in repository

Entity Framework, with its implemented repository, abstracted all of that coding by implementing a default repository pattern. Instead of creating a new connection and setting up the command for every call you need to make, you wire up EF – and then just ask for one of the repositories to the DBSet<T> objects – and, with ease, can Add, Update, Remove, and perform many other actions against that entity.

In the end, this ability to generically work against any entity is the essence of the repository pattern. You are no longer writing the plumbing that is needed to build and execute commands. You can generally get a result and map it or push it directly into your matching type object, without having to loop row by row and field by field to get the data from your call into your business layer object.

Additionally, using the EF repository gives you the change tracking that you need in order to easily just push changes back into the database. As you've seen in previous chapters, there are good and bad ways to go about working with these calls, but EF has implemented the repository to make those basic database operations obscure, thus saving you hundreds of lines of code and many hours of work.

The unit of work pattern

In addition to the repository pattern, EF also implements a unit of work (UoW) pattern. As with the Repo pattern, the roots of the UoW pattern can also be traced back to Martin Fowler's book on *Patterns of Enterprise Architecture*.

Using a unit of work

Inserting data, updating data, and deleting data operations are common to working with the database. Every time you make a call, however, there is some overhead. Additionally, sometimes you don't want one of the calls to be committed if subsequent calls fail, so you utilize a transaction to *roll back* the changes.

The UoW pattern gives the ability to easily group data operations. Everything that needs to be done when the operations are ready is tracked and/or managed by the unit of work. When the unit is completed, all of the tracked operations are applied to get the database to match the current state of the objects in memory. Generally, if one part of the unit fails during a unit of work operation, the entire unit is rolled back.

Combining the repository and the unit of work

Now that you're somewhat aware of what both of these patterns are, it's time to see why putting them together as EF does is such a powerful tool.

The one-two punch

As you've seen, the repository pattern abstracts the lower-level operations for interacting with the database from the business code. With EF, you don't have to create connections and commands directly. You design the system by putting DBSet<T> into the context. Then you can just call against those DBSet<T> objects to add, remove, update, and otherwise manipulate the data.

While the repository portion of EF is working, the unit of work portion of EF is also in play. You encounter this in the fact that every time you start doing work with the DBSet<T> entities, you ultimately need to make a call to SaveChanges to get the changes to be applied and committed to the database.

Ultimately, what is going on with the SaveChanges operation is that EF serves up objects in memory to mimic the state of the database and keeps track of their previous state. When you tell EF it is time to save changes, EF can use the modified state of the object to determine what calls need to be made to persist the changes. The calls are then run just as if you had written the code to connect and execute commands yourself. Further, if any of the calls fail, the entire transaction is rolled back, so that you don't get a situation where your changes are only partially applied.

A couple of drawbacks

Using EF is a great tool for almost all scenarios you will encounter; however, the nature of how both the Repo and UoW patterns are applied can lead to a few issues and drawbacks in complex systems.

One major concern that a lot of developers share is the general overhead associated with these operations. As you've already seen in previous chapters and as you've learned more about the UoW earlier, tracking the state of every entity in memory can potentially lead to some performance issues. For this reason, EF has exposed the ability to avoid tracking the object against the database with the AsNoTracking statement. As of EFCore5, there is an additional operation called ChangeTracker.Clear, which stops tracking all currently tracked entities. In this case, you don't have to intentionally specify AsNoTracking on every query. Instead, you can simply disconnect with one call to the Clear method.

Another concern that you'll encounter as a developer will be related to concurrency. What happens to changes that are currently tracked by one user through the application if another user applies their changes first?

With EF, generally, if an error like this happens, the operation will have to be retried, sometimes even at the expense of refreshing data. This can get a bit expensive and can severely hinder the user experience in a system where lots of transactions are taking place.

A third concern is that it can be tricky to apply partial changes, or, in some cases, partial changes may be applied even when the transaction fails due to the changes not being able to be rolled back.

For example, if you're solely working with EF and you need to perform a number of operations, perhaps you only want to save some changes but not all of them. Calling save changes on the context will save all of the changes as performed in memory by the UoW, not just some of the changes.

In the opposite direction, if some of the operations make mutating change calls to stored procedures and those procedures are executed, it may be impossible to rely on EF to roll those changes back, as the procedure may have already run against the database, and EF won't have an ability to run a revert procedure on failure, at least not by default.

In cases such as these, you often have to make sure that *EF* is not applying transactions on the procedure calls or determine some way to ensure that your database is restored to the proper state even if untracked changes are applied.

Finally, not only is there risk when multiple operations may have taken place to make it so your change can't be applied, there are risks that exist when using transactions. Two such risks are that either you can get a dirty read or you might encounter deadlocks.

A dirty read happens when you pull data from the database but that data is in the process of being changed by another user. A deadlock might be a situation where you start a transaction and perform a read of data from any table. As you are using a transaction, that table becomes locked for read/write operations to other users until you commit your changes. If your operation takes a long time to complete or for some reason you keep the transaction in session for a long duration, during that time, other users will likely be experiencing a poor user experience waiting for your operation to complete before their operation can get the requested data.

In general, rely on EF

With everything that EF does provide, it is generally a good idea to rely on what EF is doing around these two patterns (Repo and UoW). Implementing our own solutions can sometimes look like the correct solution but may introduce a lot of risk for future support, unnecessary complexity to your applications, and may also compound development time, thereby increasing the time it takes to deliver new features in your solutions.

Always remember that EF is going to apply changes as a unit of work for you, so you can generally rely on it rolling back changes correctly on failure, as well as trust that applying changes will only be allowed when the data is clean and in the proper state to be committed.

Separation of concerns

A final topic for this chapter to go along with these two patterns for building robust systems is the idea of separation of concerns.

Separation of concerns (SoC) is a well-known principle in computer science. The overall idea is that you want to keep minimal functionality in its own layer and area of concern rather than tightly coupling everything together.

You have already used a lot of programming with SoC implicitly through this book as you have created separate classes for modeling your objects. While they may be relational, you don't often (if ever) make a single class that contains multiple objects in it.

For example, when you programmed your solution, you didn't put the properties for Genre in the Item class. Instead, you used a many-to-many relationship so that Genres could be their own concern and so that Items could have the ability to be separate from Genres and Categories. This is the basic idea around SoC.

Logical separation of concerns

To make your solution robust, it would be ideal to not only separate the concerns across objects but also to separate concerns across layers. In this manner, you can make functional units or components that can more easily be interchanged with new components or logic as the needs arise. While it may add complexity, this logical separation makes your overall solution easier to maintain or adapt in the future.

Another benefit of separation of concerns into layers is that you can then start correctly using dependency injection to inject the dependent components into other layers. By doing this, as long as the components are coded to a common interface, the business layer doesn't care what the database layer is doing nor how; the business layer only cares that the data is returned as expected.

Final benefits of separation of concerns

The final benefit of separating your layers into individual components that are not tightly coupled will be evident when it comes time to write unit tests around your data operations.

As the system stands as of the end of Chapter 10, it would be very difficult to unit test your solution. You could likely put some integration testing into place in the solution, but there wouldn't be a good way to just test the service layer without connecting to an actual database.

Chapter 11 activities

To complete this chapter, you will work through two activities. In the first activity, you will rework the solution to layer the solution. This will be more of an architecture exercise than a database exercise, but it will position the solution well for setting up your own repository and unit of work pattern implementations in your solution. Additionally, this first activity will position the solution to be ready for unit testing, which is covered in the next chapter.

In the second activity, you will quickly create your own unit of work around a custom business process to further enhance how your solution works with data. Specifically, you'll create unit of work implementations for batching insert, update, and delete operations. This will also give you a look at using custom transactions with EF.

Activity 11-1: Layering your solution

As the InventoryManager project stands right now, the solution is very tightly coupled, in that there is database code in the *UI* layer (your console project). Ideally, you want to separate the layers out for a number of reasons, mostly involving *SOLID* architecture, robustness, maintenance, and testing.

Additionally, separating this solution into layers is going to give you a great ability to rework different pieces of the application in the future without having to rewrite the entire application. Operations like switching or implementing a new user interface will be easily possible, as will changing out the database as needed.

By the end of this activity, you are going to have a much more robust solution with a layered architecture that is decoupled at each layer via interfaces and segregation of work.

Task 0: Getting started

To get started with this activity, you should use the files that you've been using through the text having completed Activity 10-1. If you would prefer to get a fresh start, feel free to use the starter files EFCore_Activity11-1_StarterFiles. Please remember that in Chapter 10 the database was encrypted, so the files are expecting an encrypted Items table using Always Encrypted. While it should not matter if you have columns encrypted or not, the connection string is configured for always encrypted, and the coding decisions from this point forward are based on the underlying assumption that certain columns are encrypted.

As always, refer to Appendix A for more information on using starter files.

Task 1: Creating the database layer

In this first task, you will create a new project that will work to be the database layer for your solutions going forward.

In general, I like to work from the bottom up, so for this activity, you'll start with the database and work back to the UI layer. If you are more comfortable, you can work in the other direction or piece it together from various steps in this activity. It's ultimately up to you how you want to implement your own solutions.

Step 1: Create the new project for the database layer

To begin, create a new project for the database layer by right-clicking the solution and selecting Add New Project. When the Add a new project dialog comes up, select a new Class Library as the project type, and then hit the Next button (see Figure 11-1).

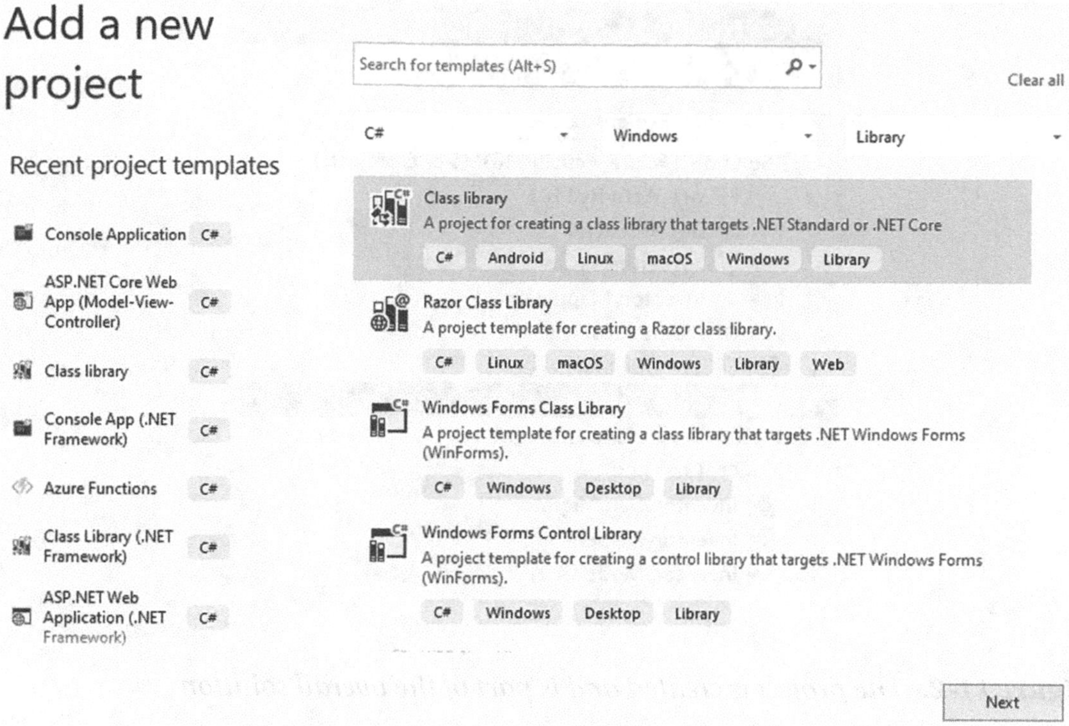

Add a new project

Search for templates (Alt+S)

Clear all

C#   ▼   Windows   ▼   Library   ▼

- Console Application   C#

- ASP.NET Core Web App (Model-View-Controller)   C#

- Class library   C#

- Console App (.NET Framework)   C#

- Azure Functions   C#

- Class Library (.NET Framework)   C#

- ASP.NET Web Application (.NET Framework)   C#

Class library
A project for creating a class library that targets .NET Standard or .NET Core

C#   Android   Linux   macOS   Windows   Library

Razor Class Library
A project template for creating a Razor class library.

C#   Linux   macOS   Windows   Library   Web

Windows Forms Class Library
A project template for creating a class library that targets .NET Windows Forms (WinForms).

C#   Windows   Desktop   Library

Windows Forms Control Library
A project template for creating a control library that targets .NET Windows Forms (WinForms).

C#   Windows   Desktop   Library

Next

Figure 11-1.   Creating a new class library to house the code for the database layer

Name the project InventoryDatabaseLayer when prompted, select .NET 6.0 as the Target Framework, and make sure to save the project in the same folder as the solution file for the project so that this project will have a folder nested in the directory like all the other included projects (the default location should be the correct folder, but it is always good to double-check this setting).

Once you've ensured the location and name of the project, hit the Create button to generate the new project in your solution. The end result will be a new project that is included in your solution named InventoryDatabaseLayer (review Figure 11-2).

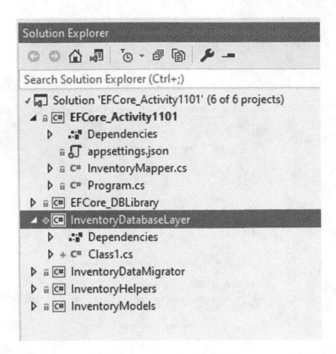

Figure 11-2. *The project is created and is part of the overall solution*

Step 2: Rename the Class1.cs file

Right-click the Class1.cs file and select Rename. When able, rename the file to ItemsRepo.cs, and select Yes when prompted to *perform a rename in this project of all references to the code element "Class1"* (see Figure 11-3).

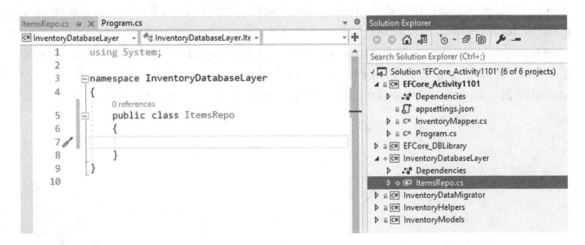

Figure 11-3. *The renaming of the file is completed to create the ItemsRepo class*

Step 3: Add an interface to define the ItemsRepo operations

To start this step, right-click the InventoryDatabaseLayer project and select Add ➤ New Item, then choose Interface, and name the interface IItemsRepo.cs (the extra "I" is intentional for the convention of naming Interfaces). Figure 11-4 shows this operation in process.

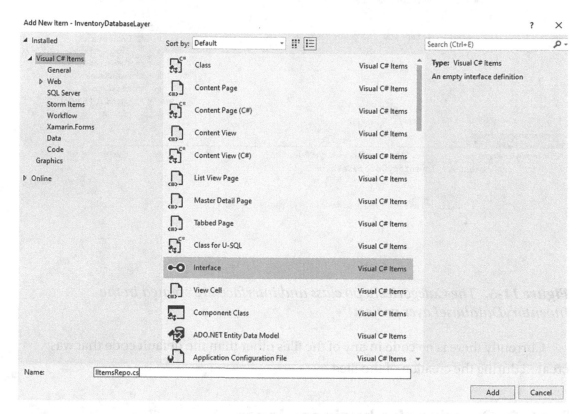

Figure 11-4. *The interface IItemsRepo.cs file is being created and added to the InventoryDatabaseLayer project*

Step 4: Add a Categories Repo and interface

To complete this first task, add a new class CategoriesRepo in a file named CategoriesRepo.cs and add a new interface named ICategoriesRepo in a file named ICategoriesRepo.cs. Ensure that the CategoriesRepo implements the ICategoriesRepo interface. Additionally, ensure that the ItemsRepo implements the IItemsRepo interface. For clarity, review Figure 11-5.

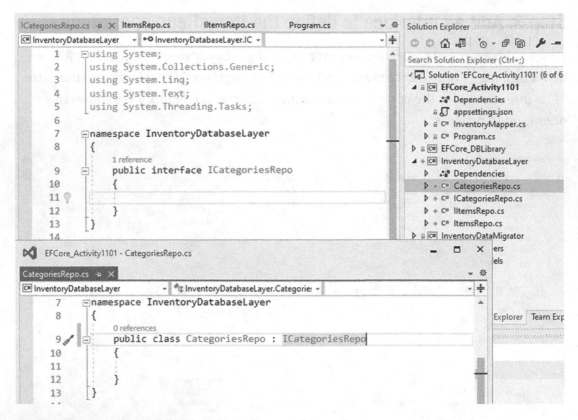

Figure 11-5. *The CategoriesRepo class and interface are created in the*
InventoryDatabaseLayer project

Currently there is no code in any of the files other than the default code that was
created during the creation of the files.

Task 2: Creating the business layer

In this task, you will complete a similar process to what you just did for the database
layer, this time adding a service layer or business layer project.

Step 1: Create the business layer class and interface

Repeat the preceding steps, but create a project named InventoryBusinessLayer. As
with the database project, start by including two files, one as an interface and one as
a class that implements the interface. Name the new interface IItemsService in a file

named IItemsService.cs. Create the class to implement called ItemsService in a file named ItemsService.cs. This will be the direct service that will be called to interact with the ItemsRepo.

Additionally, add another class named CategoriesService in a file named Categories.cs and another interface named ICategoriesService in a file named ICategoriesService.cs. For clarity, the current project structure is shown in Figure 11-6.

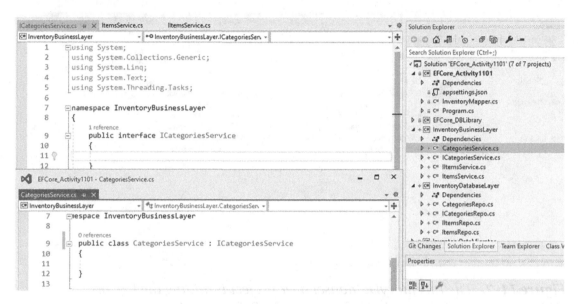

Figure 11-6. *The new business layer class ItemsService implements the new interface IItemsService, and both files are located in the new project InventoryBusinessLayer. Additionally, an interface ICategoriesService and a matching implementation CategoriesService are included in the project*

Task 3: Create and implement database operations in the database layer

In this task, you will create the database layer operations to work against the database going forward with the project. This abstraction will make it easier to test and will also consolidate calls to the database into one project, making the project easier to update and maintain in the future.

Step 1: Reference existing projects

To begin, you need to reference the EFCore_DbLibrary project. Do this by right-clicking the InventoryDatabaseLayer project and selecting Add ➤ Project Reference. When the dialog is shown for the Reference Manager, select the EFCore_DbLibrary project (see Figure 11-7).

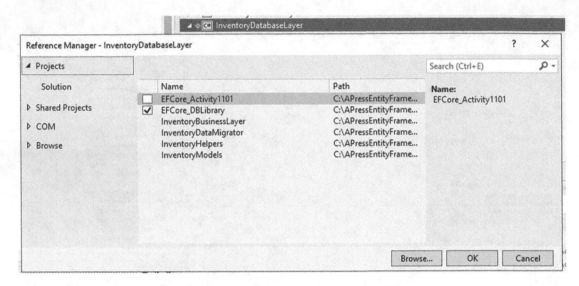

Figure 11-7. *The InventoryDatabaseLayer project is adding the EFCore_DbLibrary project as a project reference in the Reference Manager dialog*

After adding the reference, note that the InventoryModels project is referenced through the EFCore_DbLibrary project (see Figure 11-8 for clarity).

Figure 11-8. *Projects are associated and leveraged as expected in the hierarchy when a dependency is added via a project reference*

Step 2: Add the inventory database Repo interface method signatures, and implement them

With the project ready to utilize the database library, add the following code to the IItemsRepo.cs class:

```
List<ItemDto> GetItems();
List<ItemDto> GetItemsByDateRange(DateTime minDateValue, DateTime
maxDateValue);
List<GetItemsForListingDto> GetItemsForListingFromProcedure();
List<GetItemsTotalValueDto> GetItemsTotalValues(bool isActive);
List<FullItemDetailDto> GetItemsWithGenresAndCategories();
```

After adding these methods (and any necessary using statements), go to the ItemsRepo class and implement the interface as highlighted in Figure 11-9.

Figure 11-9. *The IItemsRepo interface needs to be implemented in the ItemsRepo class. This is easily done by using the helper to implement the interface*

After the interface is implemented, replace the `throw new`
`NotImplementedException();` code in the `GetItems` method with the following code:

```
var items = _context.Items
                .ProjectTo<ItemDto>(_mapper.ConfigurationProvider)
                .ToList();
return items;
```

Note that this code will not currently compile. You first need to inject a context, and you also will need to add the NuGet packages and inject your mapper file for AutoMapper.

Add a constructor to the class along with two private variables to inject the context with the following code:

```
private readonly IMapper _mapper;
private readonly InventoryDbContext _context;

public ItemsRepo(InventoryDbContext context, IMapper mapper)
{
    _context = context;
    _mapper = mapper;
}
```

Add the AutoMapper NuGet packages using the `Tools ➤ Manage NuGet Packages for Solution` to the project. Use the `Installed` tab to quickly find the packages that have already been installed on the main project (see Figure 11-10).

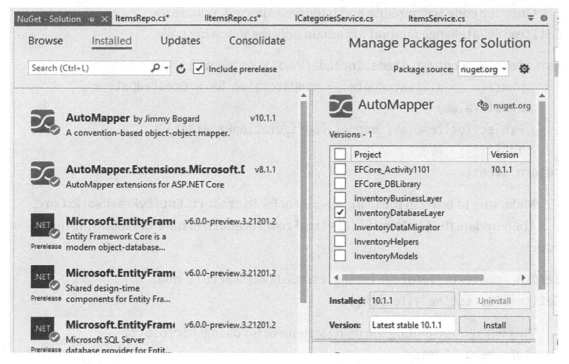

Figure 11-10. *The AutoMapper packages need to be installed on the InventoryDatabaseLayer project. This is easily accomplished from the Manage NuGet Packages for Solution dialog using the Installed tab*

Next, add the using statements for AutoMapper and the EFCore_DbLibrary to the ItemsRepo class file so that it will compile. Build the project to ensure there are no errors. For clarity, current using statements should be at minimum:

```
using AutoMapper;
using AutoMapper.QueryableExtensions;
using EFCore_DBLibrary;
using InventoryModels.DTOs;
using System;
using System.Collections.Generic;
using System.Linq;
using InventoryModels.DTOs;
using System;
using System.Collections.Generic;
```

You will likely have more, and that is fine.

Once the code is compiling and builds as expected, update the GetItemsByDateRange method to contain only the following code:

```
var items = _context.Items.Include(x => x.Category)
    .Where(x => x.CreatedDate >= minDateValue && x.CreatedDate <=
    maxDateValue)
    .ProjectTo<ItemDto>(_mapper.ConfigurationProvider)
    .ToList();
return items;
```

Make sure to bring in the using statement for Microsoft.EntityFramework.Core.

Then update the GetItemsForListingFromProcedure to have the following line of code:

```
return _context.ItemsForListing.FromSqlRaw("EXECUTE dbo.
GetItemsForListing").ToList();
```

This will require adding the using statement for using Microsoft. EntityFrameworkCore;.

Next, update the GetItemsTotalValues method to have the following code:

```
var isActiveParm = new SqlParameter("IsActive", 1);

return _context.GetItemsTotalValues
    .FromSqlRaw("SELECT * from [dbo].[GetItemsTotalValue] (@IsActive)",
isActiveParm)
    .ToList();
```

This code will require adding the using statement using Microsoft.Data. SqlClient.

Finally, add the following code to complete the initial implementation for the IItemsRepo and the ItemsRepo:

```
public List<FullItemDetailDto> GetItemsWithGenresAndCategories()
{
    return _context.FullItemDetailDtos
                  .FromSqlRaw("SELECT * FROM [dbo].[vwFullItemDetails]")
                  .AsEnumerable()
```

```
                .OrderBy(x => x.ItemName).ThenBy(x => x.GenreName)
                .ThenBy(x => x.Category).ThenBy(x => x.PlayerName)
                .ToList();
}
```

Step 3: Complete the `CategoriesRepo` and `ICategoriesRepo` code

To complete this task, working from the top down, first add the following method declaration to the ICategoriesRepo interface (and bring in any missing using statements):

```
List<CategoryDto> ListCategoriesAndDetails();
```

Next, add the following using statements to the CategoriesRepo.cs file:

```
using AutoMapper;
using AutoMapper.QueryableExtensions;
using EFCore_DBLibrary;
using InventoryModels.DTOs;
using Microsoft.EntityFrameworkCore;
using System.Collections.Generic;
using System.Linq;
```

Continue by adding the following private variables and constructor to the CategoriesRepo class:

```
private readonly IMapper _mapper;
private readonly InventoryDbContext _context;
public CategoriesRepo(InventoryDbContext context, IMapper mapper)
{
    _context = context;
    _mapper = mapper;
}
```

Finally, add the implementation in the CategoriesRepo as follows:

```
public List<CategoryDto> ListCategoriesAndDetails()
{
    return _context.Categories.Include(x => x.CategoryDetail)
        .ProjectTo<CategoryDto>(_mapper.ConfigurationProvider)
        .ToList();
}
```

You have now completed the first implementation of the database layer. In a real-world scenario, you would likely also want to do some of the remaining CRUD operations like Insert, Update, and Delete in this layer. In a very robust implementation, you might consider doing the default methods in a generic class so that all entities could easily implement basic CRUD operations through inheritance.

Task 4: Create and implement business operations in the service layer

In this task, you will create and implement the business (service) operations against which to leverage the database.

Step 1: Add a project reference for the InventoryDatabaseLayer to the InventoryBusinessLayer

Right-click the InventoryBusinessLayer project and select Add ➤ Project Reference. When the dialog comes up, add a reference to the InventoryDatabaseLayer project.

Step 2: Add method declarations for IItemsService and the code for the ItemsService

For learning purposes, all but one of the service layer methods are going to be simple pass-through methods. The overall idea is that the service exposes operations and could further manipulate the data that is returned from the data layer.

Add the following code to the IItemsService interface:

```
List<ItemDto> GetItems();
List<ItemDto> GetItemsByDateRange(DateTime minDateValue, DateTime
maxDateValue);
List<GetItemsForListingDto> GetItemsForListingFromProcedure();
List<GetItemsTotalValueDto> GetItemsTotalValues(bool isActive);
string GetAllItemsPipeDelimitedString();
List<FullItemDetailDto> GetItemsWithGenresAndCategories();
```

Then add the following code to the ItemsService to implement the methods:

```
private readonly IItemsRepo _dbRepo;

public ItemsService(InventoryDbContext dbContext, IMapper mapper)
{
    _dbRepo = new ItemsRepo(dbContext, mapper);
}

public List<ItemDto> GetItems()
{
    return _dbRepo.GetItems();
}

public List<ItemDto> GetItemsByDateRange(DateTime minDateValue, DateTime
maxDateValue)
{
    return _dbRepo.GetItemsByDateRange(minDateValue, maxDateValue);
}

public List<GetItemsForListingDto> GetItemsForListingFromProcedure()
{
    return _dbRepo.GetItemsForListingFromProcedure();
}

public List<GetItemsTotalValueDto> GetItemsTotalValues(bool isActive)
{
    return _dbRepo.GetItemsTotalValues(isActive);
}
```

```
public string GetAllItemsPipeDelimitedString()
{
    var items = GetItems();
    return string.Join('|', items);
}

public List<FullItemDetailDto> GetItemsWithGenresAndCategories()
{
    return _dbRepo.GetItemsWithGenresAndCategories();
}
```

Note that the last implemented method is the GetAllItemsPipeDelimitedString, and this method will implement the code to work with the encrypted Item names as leveraged in the previous chapter. Make sure to add the missing using statements so the code will compile.

Step 3: Add method declarations for ICategoriesService and the code for the CategoriesService

To complete the business layer, add the following code to the ICategoriesService interface:

```
List<CategoryDto> ListCategoriesAndDetails();
```

Then add the following code to the CategoriesService class:

```
private readonly ICategoriesRepo _dbRepo;

public CategoriesService(InventoryDbContext dbContext, IMapper mapper)
{
    _dbRepo = new CategoriesRepo(dbContext, mapper);
}

public List<CategoryDto> ListCategoriesAndDetails()
{
    return _dbRepo.ListCategoriesAndDetails();
}
```

Task 5: Refactor the console program

Now that the service and business layer projects are completed, you need to refactor the program class to leverage these projects. By doing this, you will see the power and flexibility that this will bring to your solution.

Step 1: Add a reference to the business layer project in the main activity project

To start, you will want to add a project reference to the `EFCore_Activity1101` project (or whatever project name you started with) that references the `InventoryBusinessLayer`. By doing this, you'll then have access to the service and be able to leverage the service to make all the necessary calls to the database.

The way this project is architected, the UI layer project will still be responsible for setting up the database connection and the AutoMapper configurations, and the UI layer project will inject these objects into the service layer, which will leverage the objects and also pass them through to the underlying `DatabaseLayer` project.

Right-click the `EFCore_Activity1101` project and select Add ➤ `Project Reference`. When the dialog appears, select the `InventoryBusinessLayer` project.

Step 2: Clean up the Program.cs file

At this point, there is likely a bunch of commented out code and code a few sections of code that need to be cleaned up. Remove any commented out code that is currently in the system (do not remove commented method calls from the `Main` method). Additionally, ensure that both methods for `BuildOptions` and `BuildMapper` are present and are set to private access level.

Another note here is that if you have been working through the book and any packages were updated, you might have to update packages in your main activity project to avoid downgrades. You can always update to the latest packages in the `NuGet Package Manager` ➤ `Manage NuGet Packages for Solution`.

Additionally, note that the methods `ListInventory` and `ListInventoryWithProjection` produce the same result. Delete the `ListInventoryWithProjection` method, and also remove the call to `ListInventoryWithProjection` from the `Main` method.

Step 3: Update the Program.cs file constructor and methods

Begin this step by updating the Program class to contain new private variables for the two service layer services as follows:

```
private static IItemsService _itemsService;
private static ICategoriesService _categoriesService;
```

Make sure to also bring in the using statement for the InventoryBusinessLayer.

Next, replace the Main method code with the code that follows:

```
public static void Main(string[] args)
{
    BuildOptions();
    BuildMapper();
    using (var db = new InventoryDbContext(_optionsBuilder.Options))
    {
        _itemsService = new ItemsService(db, _mapper);
        _categoriesService = new CategoriesService(db, _mapper);
        ListInventory();
        GetItemsForListing();
        GetAllActiveItemsAsPipeDelimitedString();
        GetItemsTotalValues();
        GetFullItemDetails();
        GetItemsForListingLinq();
        ListCategoriesAndColors();
    }
}
```

Step 4: Update the methods to leverage the service

The next step is to leverage the service layer in each of the method calls. Completing this refactoring will substantially reduce the amount of code needed in each method and will further decouple the UI layer from the database (other than during startup construction of the database).

Update the `ListInventory` method to the following code:

```
private static void ListInventory()
{
    var result = _itemsService.GetItems();
    result.ForEach(x => Console.WriteLine($"New Item: {x}"));
}
```

Update the `GetItemsForListing` method to the following code:

```
private static void GetItemsForListing()
{
    var results = _itemsService.GetItemsForListingFromProcedure();
    foreach (var item in results)
    {
        var output = $"ITEM {item.Name}] {item.Description}";
        if (!string.IsNullOrWhiteSpace(item.CategoryName))
        {
            output = $"{output} has category: {item.CategoryName}";
        }
        Console.WriteLine(output);
    }
}
```

Re-implement the `GetAllActiveItemsAsPipeDelimitedString` with the following code:

```
private static void GetAllActiveItemsAsPipeDelimitedString()
{
    Console.WriteLine($"All active Items: {_itemsService.
    GetAllItemsPipeDelimitedString()}");
}
```

Then update `GetItemsTotalValues` to the following code to leverage the new layers:

```
private static void GetItemsTotalValues()
{
    var results = _itemsService.GetItemsTotalValues(true);
    foreach (var item in results)
```

```
    {
        Console.WriteLine($"New Item] {item.Id,-10}" +
                          $"|{item.Name,-50}" +
                          $"|{item.Quantity,-4}" +
                          $"|{item.TotalValue,-5}");
    }
}
```

Replace the GetFullItemDetails method with the following code:

```
private static void GetFullItemDetails()
{
    var result = _itemsService.GetItemsWithGenresAndCategories();

    foreach (var item in result)
    {
        Console.WriteLine($"New Item] {item.Id,-10}" +
                          $"|{item.ItemName,-50}" +
                          $"|{item.ItemDescription,-4}" +
                          $"|{item.PlayerName,-5}" +
                          $"|{item.Category,-5}" +
                          $"|{item.GenreName,-5}");
    }
}
```

Update the GetItemsForListingLinq to the following code:

```
private static void GetItemsForListingLinq()
{
    var minDateValue = new DateTime(2021, 1, 1);
    var maxDateValue = new DateTime(2024, 1, 1);

    var results = _itemsService.GetItemsByDateRange(minDateValue, maxDateValue)
                    .OrderBy(y => y.CategoryName).ThenBy(z => z.Name);
    foreach (var itemDto in results)
    {
        Console.WriteLine(itemDto);
    }
}
```

Note that the ordering here is still performed by the UI, and only the selection and projection are done in the service layer.

Implement the `ListCategoriesAndColors` method as follows:

```
private static void ListCategoriesAndColors()
{
    var results = _categoriesService.ListCategoriesAndDetails();
    foreach (var c in results)
    {
        Console.WriteLine($"Category [{c.Category}] is {c.CategoryDetail.
        Color}");
    }
}
```

Step 5: Run the program to see results

Now that all the methods are updated to leverage the services, run the program. Everything should work as expected, and you should now see how reorganizing the solution into layers has provided a much more robust solution.

When running the final project, ensure that all of your methods are working and that you are getting full output now that you've refactored the UI layer to use the service layer with an underlying database layer. The output at the end of this activity should be similar to what is shown in Figure 11-11.

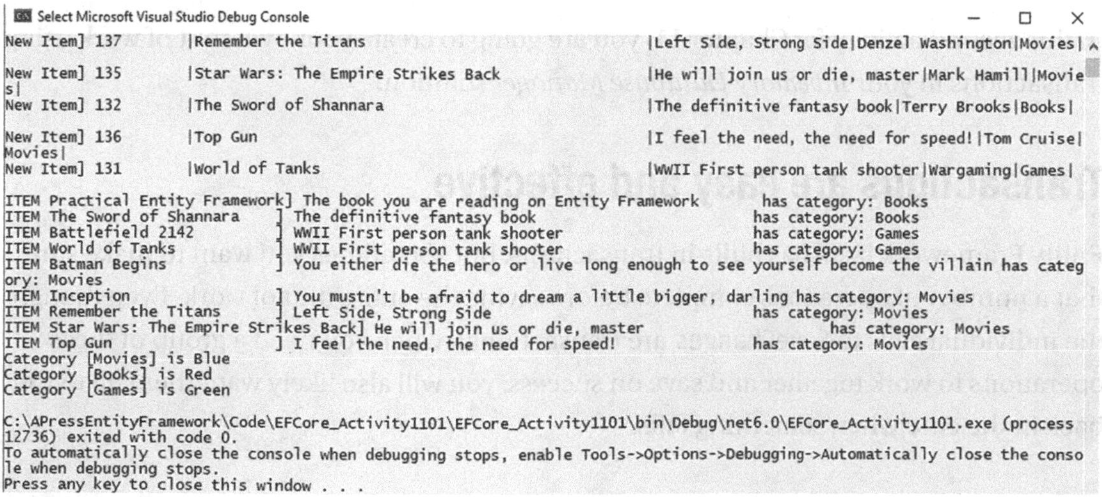

Figure 11-11. *The code is refactored and output is working as expected*

Activity 11-1 summary

In this first activity for Chapter 11, you completely refactored the system to make it more robust for future enhancements. In this solution, you've created a baseline database layer that allows you to consolidate your database code into one repository for each type of entity. While this repository is not complete without some more CRUD operations (you will add some in the next activity), you are in position to add the CRUD operations, and you should be in command of the concept of separating your database calls into their own base layer.

You then added a service layer on top of the database layer. The service layer acts as a controller. The service layer takes calls from the UI layer and makes calls to the database layer. By decoupling your UI from your database via this service, you've created a much more robust solution. Should you desire to change out your database implementation, all you would need to do is change the underlying database layer and code it to the interface so that the service could still work as expected. As an added bonus, additional operations can be added in the service layer to further customize your solution logic without having to be directly tied to database operations.

To finish up the activity, you saw the fruits of your labor. By being able to utilize the service layer, the UI layer no longer has to do anything but create the database at startup and then leverage all of the operations that it needs via the service layer.

Activity 11-2: Rolling your own UoW

In this second activity for Chapter 11, you are going to create your own unit of work using transactions in your *Inventory Database Manager* solution.

Transactions are easy and effective

Entity Framework itself has built-in transactions, but sometimes you want to make sure that a number of operations complete before saving the entire unit of work. Even though the individual calls to SaveChanges are transactional, when you need a group of these operations to work together and save on success, you will also likely want them all to roll back in the case when something fails.

As you work to further create your custom repository, you can create methods that leverage their own unit of work by wrapping the operations for each unit of work in transactions.

As a last and final statement on this matter, I will again urge you to use caution when using transactions in a highly volatile environment with high traffic volumes. Working with transactions on your own could lead to many scenarios that end in deadlock, resulting in users having long load times on different pages in the solution. Therefore, if you must use transactions, I remind you to look into the different transaction isolation levels, as well as fully test your system under the load of multiple concurrent users to ensure you have not created a deadlock in your solution.

Use the using statement for transaction lifecycles

When it comes to working with transactions, just like when you connect and work with the database context, you can rely on the fact that the transaction implements the IDisposable interface. With that knowledge, you know that you can wrap the transaction code in a using statement, making it very easy to handle the overall unit of work.

For this task, you are going to use our database layer like a full database Repo as provided by Entity Framework to do a couple of simple CRUD operations, ultimately relying on EF's underlying unit of work. You are going to then use your service layer to manage calls to that database layer.

Additionally, you're going to create a somewhat contrived example where you want to make sure that you can insert, update, or delete an entire group of Items. If any of the mutation operations fail during execution, then you will roll back the entire transaction. This will be your custom unit of work implementation.

Task 0: Getting started

As usual, to get started, you can either continue with files from the previous activity or just work with the new code. However, if you want a clean slate or you skipped to this activity, you can start with the EFCore_Activity11-2_StarterFiles. No matter how you start the activity, ensure that your database is up to date and that you do not have any pending migrations.

Task 1: Modify the InventoryDatabaseLayer

In this activity, just like the previous activity, you are going to work from the database up to the *UI* program layer. To make your solution work as expected, first you need to fix a couple of things that we would likely have caught if we had good unit and integration tests (see Chapter 12).

Step 1: Update the GetItems method to return objects of type Item

To get started, you'll change the GetItems method in the ItemsRepo.cs file in the InventoryDatabaseLayer project. For this method, you will want to return a full Item class instead of the ItemDto (you will then let the service layer do the mapping). Additionally, you should also include the Category with the Item, and finally, you should finish the method by making sure to only return non-deleted entities.

Change the GetItems method to use the following code:

```
public List<Item> GetItems()
{
    return _context.Items.Include(x => x.Category)
            .AsEnumerable()
            .Where(x => !x.IsDeleted)
            .OrderBy(x => x.Name).ToList();
}
```

You will also need to change the method signature in the IItemsRepo interface to return type Item instead of ItemDto. Make sure to bring in any missing using statements as needed (such as using InventoryModels;).

At this point, the solution will no longer build. This is expected since you've modified the interface signature and have not responded to this change elsewhere in the code. You will get this fixed later in the activity.

Step 2: Add the new method signatures to the interface and implement them

Next, you need to add four new method signatures for create, update, and delete operations to the IItemsRepo interface as follows:

```
int UpsertItem(Item item);
void UpsertItems(List<Item> items);
void DeleteItem(int id);
void DeleteItems(List<int> itemIds);
```

After defining the methods in the interface, you need to implement them in the ItemsRepo class.

In the ItemsRepo.cs file for the ItemsRepo class, stub out the four methods by using the auto-generated method implementations. Optionally, move them to the bottom of the class and break the alphabetical listing so they are easy to find. The code can be generated, but it should be similar to the following:

```
public int UpsertItem(Item item)
{
    throw new NotImplementedException();
}

public void UpsertItems(List<Item> items)
{
    throw new NotImplementedException();
}

public void DeleteItem(int id)
{
    throw new NotImplementedException();
}

public void DeleteItems(List<int> itemIds)
{
    throw new NotImplementedException();
}
```

In the `UpsertItem(Item item)` method, add code to call to update if the item id is greater than zero or to insert a new Item if the id is not greater than zero.

```
public int UpsertItem(Item item)
{
    if (item.Id > 0)
    {
        return UpdateItem(item);
    }
    return CreateItem(item);
}
```

Next, at the end of the `ItemsRepo` class, create the two new private methods called by the `UpsertItem` code you just added, one method for `CreateItem` and one method for `UpdateItem` as private methods using the following code:

```
private int CreateItem(Item item)
{
    _context.Items.Add(item);
    _context.SaveChanges();
    var newItem = _context.Items.ToList()
                    .FirstOrDefault(x => x.Name.ToLower()
                    .Equals(item.Name.ToLower()));

    if (newItem == null) throw new Exception("Could not Create the item as
    expected");

    return newItem.Id;
}

private int UpdateItem(Item item)
{
    var dbItem = _context.Items
                    .Include(x => x.Category)
                    .Include(x => x.ItemGenres)
                    .Include(x => x.Players)
                    .FirstOrDefault(x => x.Id == item.Id);
```

```
    if (dbItem == null) throw new Exception("Item not found");

    dbItem.CategoryId = item.CategoryId;
    dbItem.CurrentOrFinalPrice = item.CurrentOrFinalPrice;
    dbItem.Description = item.Description;
    dbItem.IsActive = item.IsActive;
    dbItem.IsDeleted = item.IsDeleted;
    dbItem.IsOnSale = item.IsOnSale;
    if (item.ItemGenres != null)
    {
        dbItem.ItemGenres = item.ItemGenres;
    }
    dbItem.Name = item.Name;
    dbItem.Notes = item.Notes;
    if (item.Players != null)
    {
        dbItem.Players = item.Players;
    }
    dbItem.PurchasedDate = item.PurchasedDate;
    dbItem.PurchasePrice = item.PurchasePrice;
    dbItem.Quantity = item.Quantity;
    dbItem.SoldDate = item.SoldDate;
    _context.SaveChanges();
    return item.Id;
}
```

For the UpsertItems(List<Item> items) method, you're going to use a transaction to batch your custom unit of work around all items for create or update. In this manner, if one of the operations in the batch fails, the whole transaction will be rolled back.

Implement the method with code as follows:

```
public void UpsertItems(List<Item> items)
{
    using (var transaction = _context.Database.BeginTransaction())
    {
```

```
    try
    {
        foreach (var item in items)
        {
            var success = UpsertItem(item) > 0;
            if (!success) throw new Exception($"Error saving the item
            {item.Name}");
        }

        transaction.Commit();
    }
    catch (Exception ex)
    {
        //log it:
        Debug.WriteLine(ex.ToString());
        transaction.Rollback();
        throw;
    }
  }
}
```

Make sure to add the `using System.Diagnostics;` statement to the top of the class if you keep the `Debug.WriteLine` statement.

Notice that this method uses the `using` statement to wrap the batch execution into a transaction. When all operations complete successfully, the transaction is committed. If any of the iterations fail to save correctly, then the exception is thrown and logged, and the entire transaction is rolled back.

The really nice thing to note is that even though you are calling to the context to save changes on each iteration, you are still able to roll the entire transaction back. This can also be useful in an insert and then update scenario, where you need to get an item inserted and then get the id of that item and use it to update some other piece of the system.

Also notice that this code leverages the code that was previously built for the `UpsertItem` method.

Finally, let's follow this same pattern to implement the two Delete methods:

```
public void DeleteItem(int id)
{
    var item = _context.Items.FirstOrDefault(x => x.Id == id);
    if (item == null) return;
    item.IsDeleted = true;
    _context.SaveChanges();
}

public void DeleteItems(List<int> itemIds)
{
    using (var transaction = _context.Database.BeginTransaction())
    {
        try
        {
            foreach (var itemId in itemIds)
            {
                DeleteItem(itemId);
            }

            transaction.Commit();
        }
        catch (Exception ex)
        {
            //log it:
            Debug.WriteLine(ex.ToString());
            transaction.Rollback();
            throw ex;   //make sure it is known that the transaction failed
        }
    }
}
```

This will complete your database layer for now. Next, you'll move up to the service layer. Keep in mind that as of right now the solution is still not able to be built, but the InventoryDatabaseLayer project can be built individually if you would like to check your code for accuracy and/or errors.

Task 2: Modify the InventoryBusinessLayer

In this task, you will modify the InventoryBusinessLayer project to work with the new functionality exposed by the InventoryDatabaseLayer project.

Step 1: Modify the IItemsService interface and add a new DTO

The service layer (InventoryBusinessLayer.ItemsService) will now need to respond to the new methods in the database layer, as well as do some mapping for Item to ItemDto to get your code back to a buildable and working state.

Begin by adding four new methods to the service layer interface as follows:

```
int UpsertItem(CreateOrUpdateItemDto item);
void UpsertItems(List<CreateOrUpdateItemDto> item);
void DeleteItem(int id);
void DeleteItems(List<int> itemIds);
```

You'll also need to add the CreateOrUpdateItemDto class to be able to compile this code and get it to a working state. In the InventoryModels project, under the *DTOs* folder, create a new file called CreateOrUpdateItemDTO.cs, and add the following code to the file:

```
public class CreateOrUpdateItemDto
{
    public int Id { get; set; }
    public string Name { get; set; }
    public string Description { get; set; }
    public string Notes { get; set; }
    public int CategoryId { get; set; }
    public bool IsActive { get; set; }
    public bool IsDeleted { get; set; }

    public List<Player> Players { get; set; }
    public List<ItemGenre> ItemGenres { get; set; }
}
```

Note that in this DTO the lists for Players and Genres are left null by default. In this manner, they can be ignored by the solution as to whether or not to update the relationships. If the user wanted to delete relationships, they could create a new List. If the user wanted to update the list, they could pass the new list in and fully update the relationships.

Implement the four methods as defined in the IItemsService interface and optionally move them to the bottom of the ItemsService code file to make it easy to find them all.

Step 2: Modify the ItemsService to implement the new methods

In this step, you will implement the new functionality in the ItemsService class.

Implement the four methods as defined in the IItemsService interface and optionally move them to the bottom of the ItemsService code file to make it easy to find them all.

The first thing you need to do is to be able to list the inventory and return it as an ItemDto. This will require the mapper implementation to reside in the ServiceLayer.

At the top of the ItemsService class, add the line of code private readonly IMapper _mapper; after the line for creating the readonly dbRepo. Then add the instantiation _mapper = mapper; into the constructor method (the parameter should already be present and had just not been used until now).

In the GetItems method, change the return statement to

```
return _mapper.Map<List<ItemDto>>(_dbRepo.GetItems());
```

This change should resolve any issues that existed with the GetItems method.

Next, implement the code to get the data from the database layer. Don't forget to bring in the missing using statement for InventoryModels. You are going to again be just doing mostly a pass-through at this service layer.

```
public int UpsertItem(CreateOrUpdateItemDto item)
{
    if (item.CategoryId <= 0)
    {
        throw new ArgumentException("Please set the category id before
        insert or update");
    }
    return _dbRepo.UpsertItem(_mapper.Map<Item>(item));
}

public void UpsertItems(List<CreateOrUpdateItemDto> items)
{
    try
    {
```

```
        _dbRepo.UpsertItems(_mapper.Map<List<Item>>(items));
    }
    catch (Exception ex)
    {
        //TODO: better logging/not squelching
        Console.WriteLine($"The transaction has failed: {ex.Message}");
    }
}

public void DeleteItem(int id)
{
    if (id <= 0)
    {
        throw new ArgumentException("Please set a valid item id before
        deleting");
    }
    _dbRepo.DeleteItem(id);
}

public void DeleteItems(List<int> itemIds)
{
    try
    {
        _dbRepo.DeleteItems(itemIds);
    }
    catch (Exception ex)
    {
        //TODO: better logging/not squelching
        Console.WriteLine($"The transaction has failed: {ex.Message}");
    }
}
```

The interesting things to note here are that you will make sure to have a couple of guard clauses in place to prevent issues as well as handle the cases when the transactions don't succeed. In the real world, you would also want to implement better logging to avoid just squelching issues.

Another interesting point is that our mapper now needs to go in both directions between `Item` and `ItemDto`. You will also need a mapping for the new `CreateOrUpdateDto` in the AutoMapper configuration.

In the main activity project, in the `InventoryMapper.cs` file, add the command `.ReverseMap()` to the map item for the mapping of `Item` to `ItemDto` to make the map go in both directions as follows:

```
CreateMap<Item, ItemDto>().ReverseMap();
```

Then add a new mapping for `Item` to `CreateOrUpdateItemDto` as follows to the `CreateMaps` method, making sure to ignore the `Category` after reversing the mapping:

```
CreateMap<Item, CreateOrUpdateItemDto>()
   .ReverseMap()
   .ForMember(x => x.Category, opt => opt.Ignore());
```

For clarity regarding the `InventoryMapper` changes, please review Figure 11-12.

```
1 reference
private void CreateMaps()
{
    CreateMap<Item, ItemDto>().ReverseMap();
    CreateMap<Category, CategoryDto>()
        .ForMember(x => x.Category, opt => opt.MapFrom(y => y.Name))
        .ReverseMap()
        .ForMember(y => y.Name, opt => opt.MapFrom(x => x.Category));
    CreateMap<CategoryDetail, CategoryDetailDto>()
        .ForMember(x => x.Color, opt => opt.MapFrom(y => y.ColorName))
        .ForMember(x => x.Value, opt => opt.MapFrom(y => y.ColorValue))
        .ReverseMap()
        .ForMember(y => y.ColorValue, opt => opt.MapFrom(x => x.Value))
        .ForMember(y => y.ColorName, opt => opt.MapFrom(x => x.Color));
    CreateMap<Item, CreateOrUpdateItemDto>()
        .ReverseMap()
        .ForMember(x => x.Category, opt => opt.Ignore());
}
```

Figure 11-12. *The InventoryMapper class is updated to handle mapping Item to ItemDto in both directions and the Item maps to the CreateOrUpdateItemDto as well*

Now that your database and service layers are done, you need to add some code to run the program. At this point, the solution should build successfully. Go ahead and build the solution to verify your code is in place and ensure there are no compiler errors before proceeding.

Additionally, run your project to ensure that that there are no errors with any of the mapping configurations or other changes that were implemented in the previous two tasks. If you have any errors, ensure that you have mapped names in the DTOs to the exact field names that exist in the base class (i.e., Item to CreateOrUpdateItemDto fields for Players and ItemGenres).

Task 3: Build the insert logic

In this task, you will handle the new insert logic from the main program.

Step 1: Add the code to add insert functionality

Start implementing the user layer by updating the Main method in the Program.cs file to allow for inserting new items.

After the call to list out the categories and colors, add the following code:

```
Console.WriteLine("Would you like to create items?");
var createItems = Console.ReadLine().StartsWith("y", StringComparison.
OrdinalIgnoreCase);
if (createItems)
{
    Console.WriteLine("Adding new Item(s)");
    CreateMultipleItems();
    Console.WriteLine("Items added");

    var inventory = _itemsService.GetItems();
    inventory.ForEach(x => Console.WriteLine($"Item: {x}"));
}
```

Next, add the CreateMultipleItems code as a private static method.

```csharp
private static void CreateMultipleItems()
{
    Console.WriteLine("Would you like to create items as a batch?");
    bool batchCreate = Console.ReadLine().StartsWith("y", StringComparison.
    OrdinalIgnoreCase);
    var allItems = new List<CreateOrUpdateItemDto>();

    bool createAnother = true;
    while (createAnother == true)
    {
        var newItem = new CreateOrUpdateItemDto();
        Console.WriteLine("Creating a new item.");
        Console.WriteLine("Please enter the name");
        newItem.Name = Console.ReadLine();
        Console.WriteLine("Please enter the description");
        newItem.Description = Console.ReadLine();
        Console.WriteLine("Please enter the notes");
        newItem.Notes = Console.ReadLine();
        Console.WriteLine("Please enter the Category [B]ooks, [M]ovies,
        [G]ames");
        newItem.CategoryId = GetCategoryId(Console.ReadLine().Substring(0,
        1).ToUpper());

        if (!batchCreate)
        {
            _itemsService.UpsertItem(newItem);
        }
        else
        {
            allItems.Add(newItem);
        }

        Console.WriteLine("Would you like to create another item?");
        createAnother = Console.ReadLine().StartsWith("y",
        StringComparison.OrdinalIgnoreCase);
```

```
        if (batchCreate && !createAnother)
        {
            _itemsService.UpsertItems(allItems);
        }
    }
}
```

Note that for simplicity and brevity, you are not adding any Players or Genres at this time. Feel free to add that code if you want to go to that level.

Make sure to add any missing using statements if you have previously cleaned up your using statements and are getting some errors.

There are a couple of interesting things happening in this method. First, you are taking user input to validate if they want to do a one-off insert or use a batched approach on the insert. You then gather the details from the user until they are done, and each time through you either add the new item to the database and save changes or you add the new item to a list of items to add later in a batch.

Either way, when the user has completed their operations, they have either entered multiple items and saved each item entry, or they have added multiple items and then saved them all in a batch of operations within a transaction.

Also notice that in this method is a call to a common method called GetCategoryId to get the Category so that you can assign the correct category id to the item as we add it.

Next, add that common GetCategoryId method next as another private static method that returns an integer.

```
private static int GetCategoryId(string input)
{
    switch (input)
    {
        case "B":
            return _categories.FirstOrDefault(x => x.Category.ToLower().
            Equals("books"))?.Id ?? -1;
        case "M":
            return _categories.FirstOrDefault(x => x.Category.ToLower().
            Equals("movies"))?.Id ?? -1;
        case "G":
            return _categories.FirstOrDefault(x => x.Category.ToLower().
            Equals("games"))?.Id ?? -1;
```

```
    default:
        return -1;
    }
}
```

As you may have noticed, you now have to have a reference for all of the categories in the system. At the top of the method, with the other class-level variable declarations, add this line:

```
private static List<CategoryDto> _categories;
```

Then set the categories in the `ListCategoriesAndColors` method for use in your insert and update logic. Right before you return from the `ListCategoriesAndColors` method, add the following line of code:

```
_categories = results;
```

This will set the list of categories for use in the system.

Step 2: Run the program and insert some items

Test the current insert logic by adding an item while you run the program. For an example, see Figure 11-13.

```
Creating a new item.
Please enter the name
The Wishsong of Shannara
Please enter the description
The final book in the first Shannara series
Please enter the notes
This was also featured in the Chronicles of Shannara season 2
Please enter the Category [B]ooks, [M]ovies, [G]ames
B
Would you like to create another item?

Items added
Item: ITEM Batman Begins            ] You either die the hero or live long enough to see yourself become the villain has
 category: Movies
Item: ITEM Battlefield 2142         ] WWII First person tank shooter            has category: Games
Item: ITEM Inception               ] You mustn't be afraid to dream a little bigger, darling has category: Movies
Item: ITEM Practical Entity Framework] The book you are reading on Entity Framework    has category: Books
Item: ITEM Remember the Titans     ] Left Side, Strong Side                has category: Movies
Item: ITEM Star Wars: The Empire Strikes Back] He will join us or die, master         has category: Movies
Item: ITEM The Sword of Shannara   ] The definitive fantasy book            has category: Books
Item: ITEM The Wishsong of Shannara ] The final book in the first Shannara series    has category: Books
Item: ITEM Top Gun                 ] I feel the need, the need for speed!        has category: Movies
Item: ITEM World of Tanks          ] WWII First person tank shooter            has category: Games

C:\APressEntityFramework\Code\EFCore_Activity1102\EFCore_Activity1102\bin\Debug\net6.0\EFCore_Activity1102.exe (process
11528) exited with code 0.
To automatically close the console when debugging stops, enable Tools->Options->Debugging->Automatically close the conso
le when debugging stops.
Press any key to close this window . . .
```

Figure 11-13. *A new item is added using the recently built logic*

After the first item is added, run the program again and add items as a batch. Feel free to put a debugger breakpoint in the database layer to see the operations in action as you are running them.

By the end of the exercise, try to have three or four volatile items to play with for the remaining parts of this activity (see Figure 11-14 for sample output after the operation is completed).

```
n
Items added
Item: ITEM Batman Begins           ] You either die the hero or live long enough to see yourself become the villain has
 category: Movies
Item: ITEM Battlefield 2142         ] WWII First person tank shooter               has category: Games
Item: ITEM Brian 1                  ] First Item                                   has category: Movies
Item: ITEM Brian 2                  ] Second Item                                  has category: Books
Item: ITEM Brian 3                  ] A third volatile item                        has category: Games
Item: ITEM Inception                ] You mustn't be afraid to dream a little bigger, darling has category: Movies
Item: ITEM Practical Entity Framework] The book you are reading on Entity Framework   has category: Books
Item: ITEM Remember the Titans      ] Left Side, Strong Side                       has category: Movies
Item: ITEM Star Wars: The Empire Strikes Back] He will join us or die, master         has category: Movies
Item: ITEM The Sword of Shannara    ] The definitive fantasy book                  has category: Books
Item: ITEM The Wishsong of Shannara ] The final book in the first Shannara series  has category: Books
Item: ITEM Top Gun                  ] I feel the need, the need for speed!         has category: Movies
Item: ITEM World of Tanks           ] WWII First person tank shooter               has category: Games
```

Figure 11-14. *A few more items are added as a batch*

Task 4: Build the update logic

In this task, you will perform a similar set of steps as in the previous task, this time allowing for update of existing items.

To do this, you need to add the logic to prompt the user for input as we did in the Insert method.

Step 1: Add the code to add update functionality

Add the following code in the Main program after the insert logic calls (following the end of the if (createItems) block):

```
Console.WriteLine("Would you like to update items?");
var updateItems = Console.ReadLine().StartsWith("y", StringComparison.
OrdinalIgnoreCase);
if (updateItems)
{
    Console.WriteLine("Updating Item(s)");
    UpdateMultipleItems();
    Console.WriteLine("Items updated");
```

```
    var inventory2 = _itemsService.GetItems();
    inventory2.ForEach(x => Console.WriteLine($"Item: {x}"));
}
```

Then add the UpdateMultipleItems method after the GetCategoryId method using the following code:

```
private static void UpdateMultipleItems()
{
    Console.WriteLine("Would you like to update items as a batch?");
    bool batchUpdate = Console.ReadLine().StartsWith("y", StringComparison.
    OrdinalIgnoreCase);
    var allItems = new List<CreateOrUpdateItemDto>();

    bool updateAnother = true;
    while (updateAnother == true)
    {
        Console.WriteLine("Items");
        Console.WriteLine("Enter the ID number to update");
        Console.WriteLine("******************************");
        var items = _itemsService.GetItems();
        items.ForEach(x => Console.WriteLine($"ID: {x.Id} | {x.Name}"));
        Console.WriteLine("******************************");
        int id = 0;
        if (int.TryParse(Console.ReadLine(), out id))
        {
            var itemMatch = items.FirstOrDefault(x => x.Id == id);
            if (itemMatch != null)
            {
                var updItem = _mapper.Map<CreateOrUpdateItemDto>(_mapper.
                Map<Item>(itemMatch));
                Console.WriteLine("Enter the new name [leave blank to keep
                existing]");
                var newName = Console.ReadLine();
                updItem.Name = !string.IsNullOrWhiteSpace(newName) ?
                newName : updItem.Name;
                Console.WriteLine("Enter the new desc [leave blank to keep
                existing]");
```

```
                var newDesc = Console.ReadLine();
                updItem.Description = !string.IsNullOrWhiteSpace(newDesc) ?
                newDesc : updItem.Description;
                Console.WriteLine("Enter the new notes [leave blank to keep
                existing]");
                var newNotes = Console.ReadLine();
                updItem.Notes = !string.IsNullOrWhiteSpace(newNotes) ?
                newNotes : updItem.Notes;
                Console.WriteLine("Toggle Item Active Status? [y/n]");
                var toggleActive = Console.ReadLine().Substring(0,
                1).Equals("y", StringComparison.OrdinalIgnoreCase);
                if (toggleActive)
                {
                    updItem.IsActive = !updItem.IsActive;
                }

                Console.WriteLine("Enter the category - [B]ooks, [M]ovies,
                [G]ames, or [N]o Change");
                var userChoice = Console.ReadLine().Substring(0, 1).ToUpper();
                updItem.CategoryId = userChoice.Equals("N",
                StringComparison.OrdinalIgnoreCase) ? itemMatch.CategoryId
                                    : GetCategoryId(userChoice);

                if (!batchUpdate)
                {
                    _itemsService.UpsertItem(updItem);
                }
                else
                {
                    allItems.Add(updItem);
                }
            }
        }

        Console.WriteLine("Would you like to update another?");
        updateAnother = Console.ReadLine().StartsWith("y",
        StringComparison.OrdinalIgnoreCase);
```

```
if (batchUpdate && !updateAnother)
{
    _itemsService.UpsertItems(allItems);
}
    }
}
```

Note that this method gives the user a chance to perform a single update and save or to batch the updates into one transaction.

Step 2: Run the program and update some items

Run the program and update with the single update and then run again and update as a batch. Feel free to put a breakpoint in the business or database layer to see the code in action. An example of the output is shown in Figure 11-15.

```
Would you like to update items?
y
Updating Item(s)
Would you like to update items as a batch?
n
Items
Enter the ID number to update
********************************
ID: 130 | Batman Begins
ID: 134 | Battlefield 2142
ID: 140 | Brian 1
ID: 141 | Brian 2
ID: 142 | Brian 3
ID: 138 | Inception
ID: 133 | Practical Entity Framework
ID: 137 | Remember the Titans
ID: 135 | Star Wars: The Empire Strikes Back
ID: 132 | The Sword of Shannara
ID: 139 | The Wishsong of Shannara
ID: 136 | Top Gun
ID: 131 | World of Tanks
********************************
141
Enter the new name [leave blank to keep existing]
Brian 2 Updated
Enter the new desc [leave blank to keep existing]
This has been updated
Enter the new notes [leave blank to keep existing]
Updated notes for Brian 2
Toggle Item Active Status? [y/n]
n
Enter the category - [B]ooks, [M]ovies, [G]ames, or [N]o Change
B
Would you like to update another?
n
Items updated
Item: ITEM Batman Begins           ] You either die the hero or live long enough to see yourself become the villain has
 category: Movies
Item: ITEM Battlefield 2142        ] WWII First person tank shooter         has category: Games
Item: ITEM Brian 1                 ] First Item                            has category: Movies
Item: ITEM Brian 2 Updated         ] This has been updated                 has category: Books
Item: ITEM Brian 3                 ] A third volatile item                 has category: Games
Item: ITEM Inception               ] You mustn't be afraid to dream a little bigger, darling has category: Movies
Item: ITEM Practical Entity Framework] The book you are reading on Entity Framework    has category: Books
Item: ITEM Remember the Titans     ] Left Side, Strong Side                has category: Movies
Item: ITEM Star Wars: The Empire Strikes Back] He will join us or die, master         has category: Movies
Item: ITEM The Sword of Shannara   ] The definitive fantasy book           has category: Books
Item: ITEM The Wishsong of Shannara ] The final book in the first Shannara series has category: Books
Item: ITEM Top Gun                 ] I feel the need, the need for speed!   has category: Movies
Item: ITEM World of Tanks          ] WWII First person tank shooter        has category: Games
```

Figure 11-15. *The single item update works as expected*

Make sure to also test the batching of updates.

Task 5: Build the delete logic

For this final part of the program, you will follow the same logic you have followed earlier to delete either one item at a time or a batch of items.

Step 1: Add the code to add delete functionality

Update the Main method to include logic for deleting Items. Also add a statement that lets the user know the program is done executing. Following the if (updateItems) block of code you just added in the previous step, add the following code to complete the Main method:

```
Console.WriteLine("Would you like to delete items?");
var deleteItems = Console.ReadLine().StartsWith("y", StringComparison.
OrdinalIgnoreCase);
if (deleteItems)
{
    Console.WriteLine("Deleting Item(s)");
    DeleteMultipleItems();
    Console.WriteLine("Items Deleted");

    var inventory3 = _itemsService.GetItems();
    inventory3.ForEach(x => Console.WriteLine($"Item: {x}"));
}
```

Then add the following line of code after the end of the using statement:

```
Console.WriteLine("Program Complete");
```

After implementing this logic in the Main method, add the code to delete multiple items in a method called DeleteMultipleItems.

```
private static void DeleteMultipleItems()
{
    Console.WriteLine("Would you like to delete items as a batch?");
    bool batchDelete = Console.ReadLine().StartsWith("y", StringComparison.
    OrdinalIgnoreCase);
    var allItems = new List<int>();
```

```
bool deleteAnother = true;
while (deleteAnother == true)
{
    Console.WriteLine("Items");
    Console.WriteLine("Enter the ID number to delete");
    Console.WriteLine("*****************************");
    var items = _itemsService.GetItems();
    items.ForEach(x => Console.WriteLine($"ID: {x.Id} | {x.Name}"));
    Console.WriteLine("*****************************");
    if (batchDelete && allItems.Any())
    {
        Console.WriteLine("Items scheduled for delete");
        allItems.ForEach(x => Console.Write($"{x},"));
        Console.WriteLine();
        Console.WriteLine("*****************************");
    }
    int id = 0;

    if (int.TryParse(Console.ReadLine(), out id))
    {
        var itemMatch = items.FirstOrDefault(x => x.Id == id);
        if (itemMatch != null)
        {
            if (batchDelete)
            {
                if (!allItems.Contains(itemMatch.Id))
                {
                    allItems.Add(itemMatch.Id);
                }
            }
            else
            {
                Console.WriteLine($"Are you sure you want to delete the
                item {itemMatch.Id}-{itemMatch.Name}");
```

```
            if (Console.ReadLine().StartsWith("y",
            StringComparison.OrdinalIgnoreCase))
            {
                _itemsService.DeleteItem(itemMatch.Id);
                Console.WriteLine("Item Deleted");
            }
        }
    }
}

Console.WriteLine("Would you like to delete another item?");
deleteAnother = Console.ReadLine().StartsWith("y",
StringComparison.OrdinalIgnoreCase);

if (batchDelete && !deleteAnother)
{
    Console.WriteLine("Are you sure you want to delete the
    following items: ");
    allItems.ForEach(x => Console.Write($"{x},"));
    Console.WriteLine();
    if (Console.ReadLine().StartsWith("y", StringComparison.
    OrdinalIgnoreCase))
    {
        _itemsService.DeleteItems(allItems);
        Console.WriteLine("Items Deleted");
    }
}
    }
}
}
```

Step 2: Run the program and delete some items

Run the program to see it all in action. Make sure to test the ability to delete a single item and also test deleting a batch of items. Figure 11-16 shows a sample run where I deleted one entry.

```
Would you like to delete another item?
y
Items
Enter the ID number to delete
******************************
ID: 130 | Batman Begins
ID: 134 | Battlefield 2142
ID: 140 | Brian 1
ID: 141 | Brian 2 Updated
ID: 142 | Brian 3
ID: 138 | Inception
ID: 133 | Practical Entity Framework
ID: 137 | Remember the Titans
ID: 135 | Star Wars: The Empire Strikes Back
ID: 132 | The Sword of Shannara
ID: 139 | The Wishsong of Shannara
ID: 136 | Top Gun
ID: 131 | World of Tanks
******************************
142
Are you sure you want to delete the item 142-Brian 3
y
Item Deleted
would you like to delete another item?
n
Items Deleted
Item: ITEM Batman Begins          ] You either die the hero or live long enough to see yourself become the villain has
  category: Movies
Item: ITEM Battlefield 2142       ] WWII First person tank shooter         has category: Games
Item: ITEM Brian 1                ] First Item                            has category: Movies
Item: ITEM Brian 2 Updated        ] This has been updated                 has category: Books
Item: ITEM Inception             ] You mustn't be afraid to dream a little bigger, darling has category: Movies
Item: ITEM Practical Entity Framework] The book you are reading on Entity Framework    has category: Books
Item: ITEM Remember the Titans    ] Left Side, Strong Side                has category: Movies
Item: ITEM Star Wars: The Empire Strikes Back] He will join us or die, master    has category: Movies
Item: ITEM The Sword of Shannara  ] The definitive fantasy book          has category: Books
Item: ITEM The Wishsong of Shannara ] The final book in the first Shannara series  has category: Books
Item: ITEM Top Gun                ] I feel the need, the need for speed!   has category: Movies
Item: ITEM World of Tanks         ] WWII First person tank shooter        has category: Games
Program Complete
```

Figure 11-16. *One item is deleted using the new delete functionality*

Task 6: Update the transaction scope

In this final task, you will learn about the transaction scope and how you can use it in your code.

Step 1: Learning about the transaction scope

The program is complete, but you need to be aware of one last detail. That detail is transaction scope.

Right now, you have a couple of batch methods that just use transactions in a using statement. When working with transactions, you will need to make sure to put your code into scope instead of just running a plain transaction. By doing this, you can ensure control over the transaction's isolation level.

If you don't set the isolation level, in a busy application, you will likely run into issues with deadlocks and/or concurrency conflicts.

Step 2: Update the transaction scope for UpsertItems

To see how to work with the transaction scope, return to the InventoryDatabaseLayer project and find the method for UpsertItems in the ItemsRepo.cs file. Change the UpsertItems method to use a scope instead of a raw transaction by replacing the existing method with the following code:

```
public void UpsertItems(List<Item> items)
    {
        using (var scope = new TransactionScope(TransactionScopeOption.
        Required
                , new TransactionOptions
                { IsolationLevel = IsolationLevel.ReadUncommitted }))
        {
        try
        {
            foreach (var item in items)
            {
                var success = UpsertItem(item) > 0;
                if (!success) throw new Exception($"Error saving
                the item {item.Name}");
            }

            scope.Complete();
        }
        catch (Exception ex)
        {
            //log it:
            Debug.WriteLine(ex.ToString());
            throw;
        }
        }
    }
```

For clarity, review Figure 11-17.

```
2 references
public void UpsertItems(List<Item> items)
{
    using (var scope = new TransactionScope(TransactionScopeOption.Required
                , new TransactionOptions
                { IsolationLevel = IsolationLevel.ReadUncommitted }))
    {
        try
        {

            foreach (var item in items)
            {
                var success = UpsertItem(item) > 0;
                if (!success) throw new Exception($"Error saving the item {item.Name}");
            }

            scope.Complete();
        }
        catch (Exception ex)
        {
            //log it:
            Debug.WriteLine(ex.ToString());
            throw;
        }
    }
}
```

Figure 11-17. *The transaction scope is utilized in the UpsertItems method*

You will likely also need to add the using statement using System.Transactions;.

Step 3: Update the transaction scope for delete items

To finish up, also change the delete method's transaction to use a similar transaction scope with the following code:

```
public void DeleteItems(List<int> itemIds)
{
    using (var scope = new TransactionScope(TransactionScopeOption.Required
                , new TransactionOptions
                { IsolationLevel = IsolationLevel.ReadUncommitted }))
    {
        try
        {
```

```
        foreach (var itemId in itemIds)
        {
            DeleteItem(itemId);
        }

        scope.Complete();
    }
    catch (Exception ex)
    {
        //log it:
        Debug.WriteLine(ex.ToString());
        throw;  //make sure it is known that the transaction failed
    }
  }
}
```

Step 4: Run the program to ensure it still works

Make sure to run the program, add items, update items, and delete items and ensure that the code changes just implemented have not broken any functionality.

Activity 11-2 summary

In this activity, you were able to build out your own repository and then implement a couple of units of work in the solution. As you've already read about in previous discussions, EF itself has built-in repository and unit of work patterns, and, in most cases, you should just leverage the built-in features of EF.

However, even with the abilities of EF, there are times when you want to take more control of the logic and, along with that, how, what, and when changes are applied to the database. In these cases, using your own versions of the repository and unit of work patterns on top of what EF offers can generally work to meet your needs.

Chapter summary

Chapter 11 gave you a chance to really build out your solution to make it very robust. Additionally, you had a chance in this chapter to discuss the two major patterns in any database *object-relational mapper (ORM)*.

The first pattern – the *repository pattern* – allows you to work with any entity using the same default signatures for each operation. EF has a great repository pattern built in, where we can generally leverage the context and start adding, deleting, updating, and listing data with just a few simple calls and not a lot of work on our part.

The second pattern you learned about was the *unit of work pattern*. In the *UoW* pattern, you want to make sure that your solution is robust across an entire business process. While *EF* has a built-in unit of work, waiting to save changes may not always be the most performant solution and/or may lead to a lot of frustration if operations are consistently rejected or don't work as expected due to small or unforeseen errors.

To overcome any limitations you may encounter, you saw how to easily create your own repositories for managing the business and data relationship. You also learned how to use transactions to allow the completion of your own custom units of work to save changes or roll back the changes if any part of the transaction fails.

Now that your solution is layered for separation of concerns and is fairly robust with database operations that you've built out, you could consider releasing this code to production. However, shipping the code as is right now would be extremely risky, because you haven't set up unit and integration tests.

In the next chapter, you'll add unit and integration tests so that you can modify your code in the future without fear of creating issues and with confidence that the system is ready to ship.

Important takeaways

After working through this chapter, the things you should be in command of are

- The repository pattern
- The unit of work pattern
- Working with transactions

- Transaction scope

- Layering your solution/making robust production-ready
  architectures

Closing thoughts

In the next chapter, you will take this solution to completion by adding the appropriate
unit and integration tests to ensure that modifications, adaptations, and feature
implementations can be done with confidence in your solutions.

CHAPTER 12

Unit Testing, Integration Testing, and Mocking

Testing your code is a must-have, not a nice-to-have

Your system has thousands of lines of code. There is at least one user interface (UI) that connects to your business layer, and your system has multiple user interfaces, from the Web to device to desktop to scanners to monitors and more. And now, it's time to change some code. Perhaps that code has been around for a while. Chances are you didn't write the code. The system certainly has some extremely risky scenarios where broken code can mean loss of revenue (even millions), or, in an even more high-risk scenario, lives might hang in the balance.

The code needs to be changed

The directive to make some modifications to the code has been passed to you. As a result, you will be changing code deep in the core components of one of the pillars of the system, and you need to ensure that all the other pieces of the system remain functional after these changes.

Also, as if this task wasn't already sufficiently risky, there aren't any resources available to help you perform a full regression test on the other business layer components or the UI interfaces for each of the supported devices. Like it or not, this is bound to happen to you and perhaps already has happened to you at some point in your career.

© Brian L. Gorman 2022
B. L. Gorman, *Practical Entity Framework Core 6*, https://doi.org/10.1007/978-1-4842-7301-2_12

The database is the lifeblood of the application

Even though the UI often defines how the users see and interact with the data, the database is the place where the roots of the system live. Without the database, without the business layer transformations, and without the robustness of your overall domain design, the UI would just be a form on a page that pretends to do something for the user.

Testing saves your sanity and protects the system

In the preceding scenario, having a full suite of automated tests that can be run would be the ideal place to be. This book will not go into automated UI testing solutions like Selenium or Cypress.IO, but as the back-end developer or full-stack developer responsible for the business and database layers of the application, you do need some solutions that you can easily implement and rely upon.

There are many different layers of testing that could be used, however, so you need to determine how much testing is enough testing and how each type of testing works to further your mission and protect you from issues in the future. Furthermore, you need to understand what it means to mock data for testing and how and when you will use each type of testing.

Two different approaches leading to the ability to test changes

In this chapter, you are going to take some time to examine two ways in which you can test the database portion of your code. While taking these various approaches to testing, you'll see what the differences are between unit tests and integration tests.

Unit testing

The first approach to testing your code is likely one you've heard of before – *unit testing*. Unit testing is the ability to run tests against the codebase that are simple and repeatable and are not dependent on other portions of the system – that is, single units under test. Furthermore, unit tests do not require a connection to any database or other data storage mechanism. In some instances, files might be used in unit tests, but only as an aid in testing the system under test.

There are many different approaches to writing unit tests. Most developers agree on two basic patterns for writing tests, which really come down to one overall testing strategy. You will use both approaches in conjunction with each other in your unit tests.

The first approach is a simple Red-Green-Refactor approach, where you write the test and ensure the test fails if the code is bad, then you write the code to pass the test, and then you refactor your tests to eliminate any duplicated code.

The second approach is using the Arrange-Act-Assert approach. In this approach, for each unit test you write, start by arranging the data for the test, then perform the single act that needs to be tested, and finish the test with assertions to validate the data is in place as expected.

For more information on unit testing, including the AAA pattern and how to write unit tests in Visual Studio, please review this link from Microsoft: `https://docs.microsoft.com/en-us/visualstudio/test/unit-test-basics?view=vs-2019`.

Libraries utilized

While performing your unit tests, you'll also need to mock data. To accomplish mocking, you'll be using one of the more popular mocking libraries: *Moq*. Additionally, for your unit testing, you'll also use the *Shouldly* library to provide an extremely user-friendly approach to asserting that things are as they should be.

Integration testing

The second form of testing you'll be looking at is integration testing. For integration testing, you will be leveraging the .Net in memory database instance to generate an in-memory version of your database, and then you'll write your integration tests against that database.

The nice thing about this implementation will be that it will be lightweight and portable to any development environment. Additionally, the use of the in-memory database means that you never have to be concerned with data being out of sync in your integration tests based on other users or some test database state. With integration testing, you also have no fear that you might screw up a shared test database or even a local development database, since you'll not be connecting to the actual databases.

One drawback to using in-memory database solutions might be that they are not fully functioning, or they might just not be robust enough. Therefore, if your solution has a lot of stored procedures integrated into the solution or a number of database-heavy operations using functions, you should consider just pointing your integration tests at a database hosted in a local test database specifically for testing on your development machine.

Of course, the other solution to not having access to functions and procedures is just to mock the results of your stored procedures, but that sort of defeats the purpose of an integration test.

Activities for Chapter 12

For the Chapter 12 activities, you're going to cover two different types of unit tests in two different activities and apply them to your homegrown Inventory system solution.

Each activity will cover aspects of unit testing as you build your solutions. While this simple work will not make you a testing expert, it should provide you with the foundation to become a testing expert through trial and error in the future.

The first activity you'll do is going to implement some simple unit tests against the business layer in the InventoryManager system. While you will keep these activities simple, this unit testing solution will show you how you can mock some data and work with it in your unit tests to ensure the system is functioning correctly at the business layer without being coupled to the database layer or connected to an actual database.

The second activity you will do will show you what it takes to set up your integration testing and will also show you how to ensure that your database is working as expected with the code you are writing.

By implementing fully functioning data integration tests, you can see the operation of your system from start to finish with real data, not just fabricated expected data.

With each of these solutions completed, you'll see the differences in the two approaches to testing your systems. You'll also learn why both types of testing have their place in your system. Additionally, you will see how having both types of testing implemented will set you up to have the peace of mind that you desire in the future when it's time to modify the system.

Activity 12-1: Unit testing with mocking

In this first activity, you'll set up your solution and then set the unit tests in place that will help you to determine that your code is functioning correctly at the business layer level as expected.

Mocking for your tests

As you set up these unit tests, you'll see how the data can be mocked and used in the unit tests to show the solution working as expected in both good and bad data scenarios.

Task 0: Getting started

This activity will resume with the files as they were at the end of Activity 11-2, where both the refactoring into layers and the custom unit of work have been implemented. If you've been following along in order, feel free to continue using your files. If you are joining out of order or need a fresh set of files, grab the EFCore_Activity12-1_StarterFiles and use them for this activity. Either way, as always, refer to Appendix A for more information on using the starter files. Additionally, ensure that the program runs as expected. Output should be similar to what is shown in Figure 12-1.

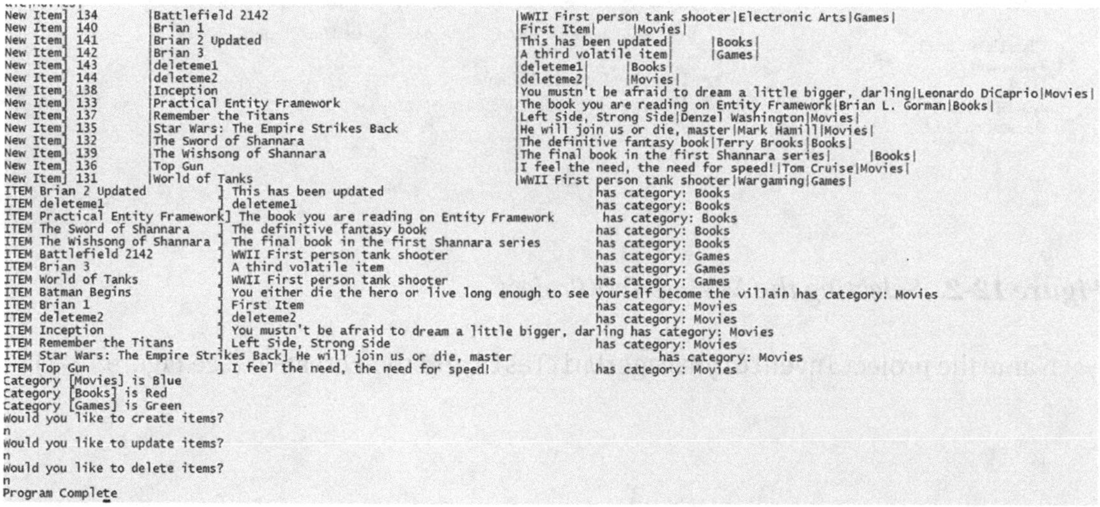

Figure 12-1. *The initial output should have most functionality as expected*

Task 1: Add the unit testing project to the solution

In this first task, you will add a new project to the solution for running unit tests.

Step 1: Add the testing project

Right-click the solution and select Add ➤ New Project.

Use the filter to select a Test project, and then select the MSTest Test Project (review Figure 12-2).

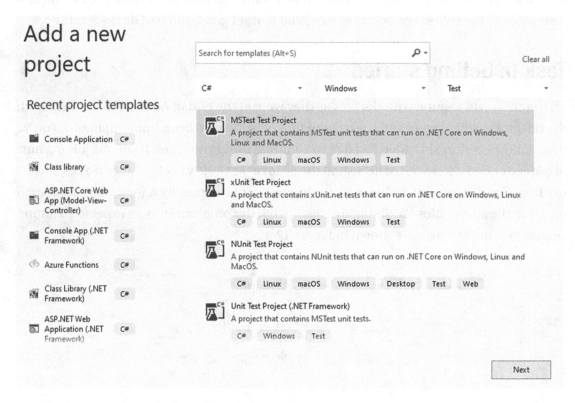

Figure 12-2. *Selecting the MSTest Test Project*

Name the project InventoryManagerUnitTests and then create it (see Figure 12-3).

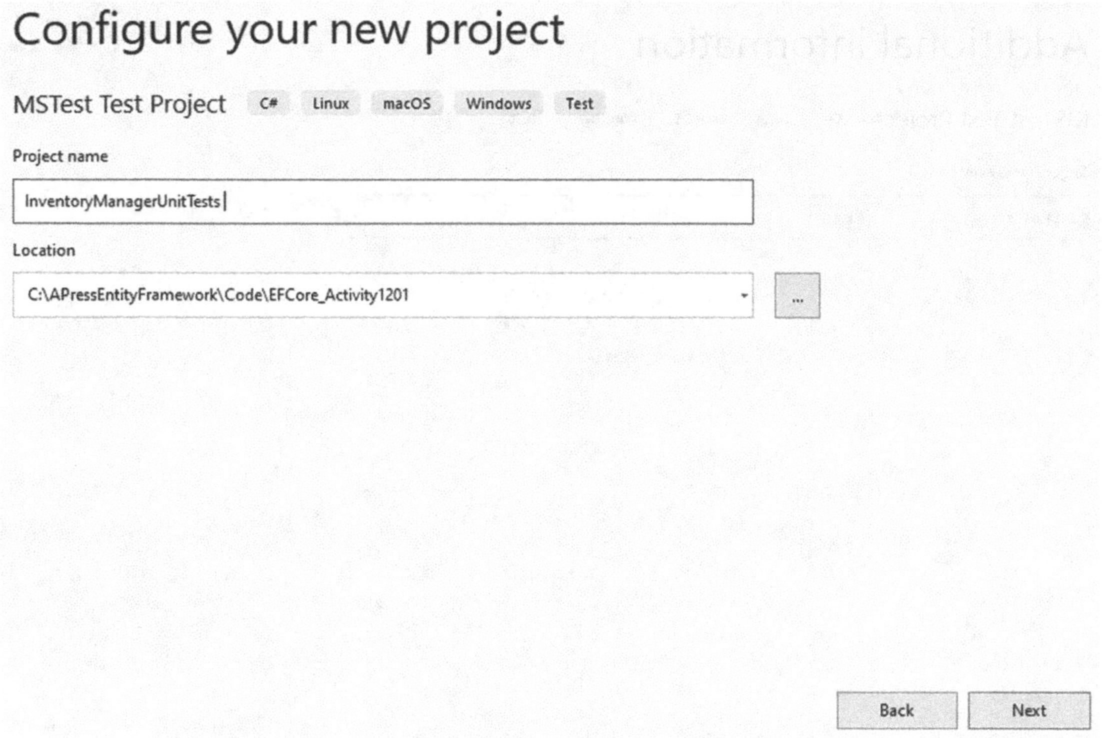

Configure your new project

MSTest Test Project   C#   Linux   macOS   Windows   Test

Project name

InventoryManagerUnitTests|

Location

C:\APressEntityFramework\Code\EFCore_Activity1201   ▼   ...

Back   Next

Figure 12-3. *Naming and creating the MSTest Test Project*

Make sure to select the correct Target Framework for the testing project (review Figure 12-4).

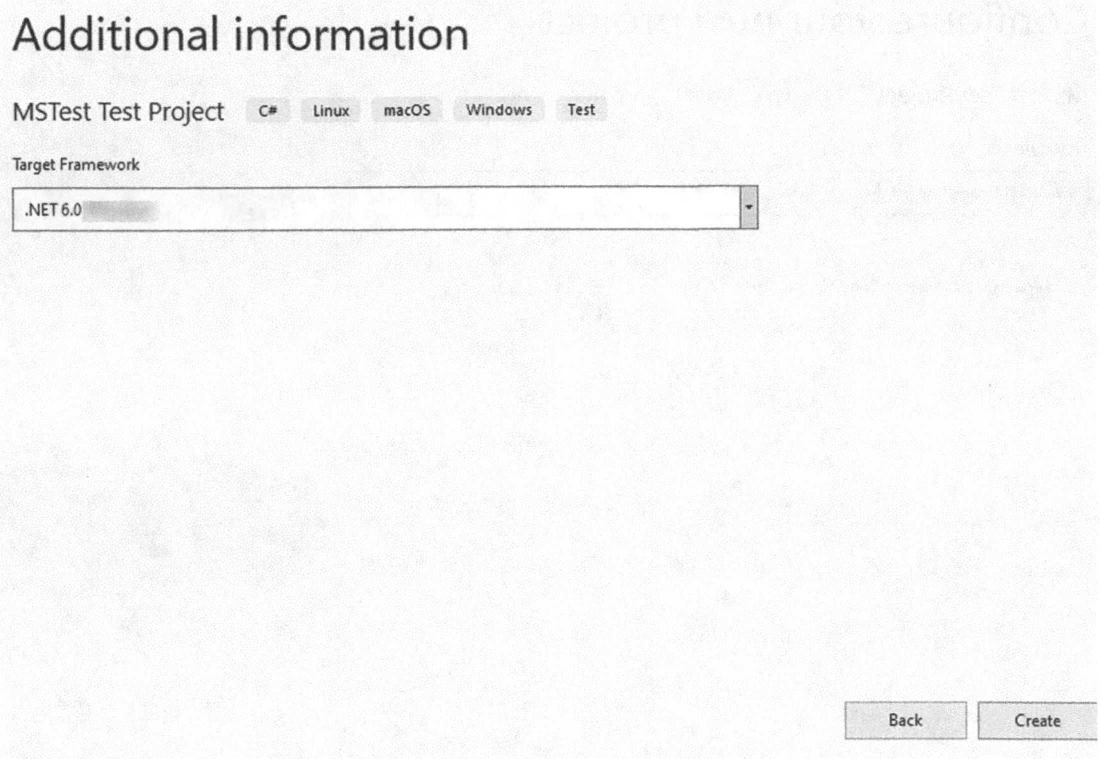

Additional information

MSTest Test Project   C#   Linux   macOS   Windows   Test

Target Framework

.NET 6.0 ████████

Back   Create

Figure 12-4. *Selecting the correct Target Framework is critical to ensure project compatibility*

Next, update the NuGet packages for the testing framework. Open the NuGet Package Manager and select the Updates tab. There will likely be four package updates that you should get for the testing project, three for testing and the coverlet.collector test (you may also have EFCore updates if you started with the starter files and a more recent version of EFCore has been released – feel free to update those as well, just remember to also update all projects to match versions). At minimum, check the box next to the three test projects, or just check all if you want to update everything, and then hit the Update button to get everything up to date. Figure 12-5 shows an overview of taking care of these updates for clarity.

Figure 12-5. *Updating the newly added test packages to the latest version*

As mentioned, feel free to also update the EFCore packages to bring everything up to the latest version.

Step 2: Rename the UnitTest1.cs file and class

To complete this first task, right-click the UnitTest1.cs file and rename it to InventoryManagerUnitTests.cs. When prompted, select Yes to update the references in the project. Figure 12-6 is shown for clarity on the current state of the solution.

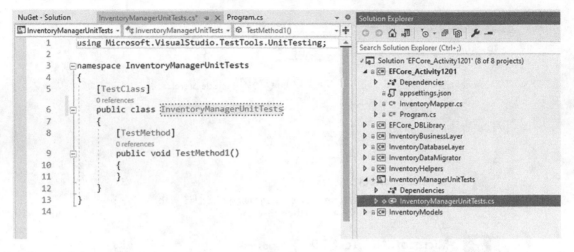

Figure 12-6. *The InventoryManagerUnitTests are ready to be written*

Task 2: Write your first unit test

In this task, you will start writing unit tests for the solution.

Step 1: Add a reference to the service layer and ensure the Target Framework

In the Solution Explorer, right-click the unit testing project you created in the last task and select Add ➤ Project Reference. Then choose the service layer project (InventoryBusinessLayer) as a reference (as shown in Figure 12-7).

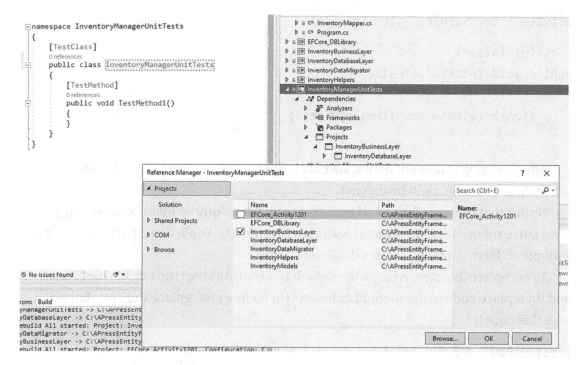

Figure 12-7. *Adding a project reference to the InventoryBusinessLayer project in the InventoryManagerUnitTests project*

Remember that the ultimate goal for these unit tests is just to test the service layer and not to test the actual database code. You'll get to the database code with integration testing in the final activity for this chapter.

Also, please remember that this solution is simple, so the mocking may seem redundant and somewhat tedious without a lot of gain. It is my hope that you will see the value and then take what you learn here and apply it to your more advanced real-world scenarios.

Step 2: Write the first unit test

Using the code that follows, add a private instance variable of type `IItemsService` to the `InventoryManagerUnitTests` class and then follow that variable with a method that will run before every test using the `[TestInitialize]` attribute:

```
private IItemsService _itemsService;

[TestInitialize]
public void InitializeTests()
{
    _itemsService = new ItemsService();
}
```

Add the using statement for the InventoryBusinessLayer project so that the IItemsService object will be defined.

Notice that the code for new ItemsService will currently be identified as having an error since there isn't a constructor with zero parameters. You'll come back to fix that in a moment. First, you need to get a database context.

To complete this step, rename the default test from TestMethod1 to TestGetItems, and then place code in the method as follows (or simply just replace the TestMethod1 with this code):

```
[TestMethod]
public void TestGetItems()
{
    var result = _itemsService.GetItems();
    Assert.IsNotNull(result);
    Assert.IsTrue(result.Count > 0);
}
```

Task 3: Get and implement Moq

In this next task, you will get the *Moq* framework and implement code to mock the InventoryManager database.

Step 1: Use the NuGet Package Manager to get Moq

Temporarily comment out the broken line of code in the InitializeTests method so that the projects will build as expected. Then use the NuGet Package Manager to Manage NuGet Packages for Solution.

Browse for *Moq*, and then add it to the InventoryManagerUnitTests project using the Install button (see Figure 12-8 for clarity).

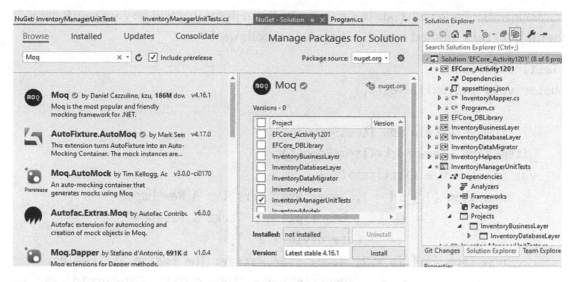

Figure 12-8. *Adding Moq to the InventoryManagerUnitTests project*

Step 2: Implement a mock database layer using the Moq library

After adding Moq, the next thing we need to do is create a mock of our database layer so that we can understand how this works.

The first step when authoring any unit tests is identifying what exactly is your system under test. The system under test for this unit test project will be the items service from the `InventoryBusinessLayer` project. This means you want to be able to call the methods in the `InventoryBusinessLayer.ItemsService` and get results that you can test. To do this without a database, you need to provide mock data for the database context.

Start by adding a new mock for the `InventoryBusinessLayer` project with the following code, added in the `InventoryManagerUnitTests` under the line of code for the `private IItemsService`:

```
private Mock<IItemsRepo> _itemsRepo;
```

Adding this code requires using statements for Moq and the `InventoryDatabaseLayer` (which is automatically referenced through the `InventoryBusinessLayer` project).

Next, add the initializer for the project in the `InitializeTests` method under the commented out line of code that creates a new `ItemsService`:

```
_itemsRepo = new Mock<IItemsRepo>();
```

587

Follow that code with code to create a new list of items that will be your mock data for the GetItems method from the ItemsRepo as follows:

```
[TestInitialize]
public void InitializeTests()
{
    //_itemsService = new ItemsService();
    _itemsRepo = new Mock<IItemsRepo>();
    var items = new List<Item>() {
        new Item () { Id = 1, Name="Star Wars IV: A New Hope"
                            , Description = "Luke's Friends",
                        CategoryId = 2  },
        new Item () { Id = 2, Name="Star Wars V: The Empire Strikes Back"
                            , Description = "Luke's Dad", CategoryId = 2  },
        new Item () { Id = 3, Name="Star Wars VI: The Return of the Jedi"
                            , Description = "Luke's Sister", CategoryId = 2}
    };
}
```

This will require the using statements for InventoryModels and System. Collections.Generic to be added to your code.

Next, add a call to tell the ItemsRepo what to return (mock) when the GetItems method is called throughout the unit tests as follows:

```
_itemsRepo.Setup(m => m.GetItems()).Returns(items);
```

For clarity, review the current state of the code as shown in Figure 12-9.

```
[TestClass]
0 references
public class InventoryManagerUnitTests
{
    private IItemsService _itemsService;
    private Mock<IItemsRepo> _itemsRepo;

    [TestInitialize]
    0 references
    public void InitializeTests()
    {
        //_itemsService = new ItemsService();
        _itemsRepo = new Mock<IItemsRepo>();

        var items = new List<Item>() {
            new Item() { Id = 1, Name="Star Wars IV: A New Hope"
                                , Description = "Luke's Friends", CategoryId = 2  },
            new Item() { Id = 2, Name="Star Wars V: The Empire Strikes Back"
                                , Description = "Luke's Dad", CategoryId = 2  },
            new Item() { Id = 3, Name="Star Wars VI: The Return of the Jedi"
                                , Description = "Luke's Sister", CategoryId = 2}
        };

        _itemsRepo.Setup(m => m.GetItems()).Returns(items);
    }

    [TestMethod]
    0 references
    public void TestGetItems()
    {
        var result = _itemsService.GetItems();
        Assert.IsNotNull(result);
        Assert.IsTrue(result.Count > 0);
    }

}
```

Figure 12-9. *The current code is shown to ensure that no mistakes have been made to this point*

Note that currently the solution still will not run or work as written; however, building the project should produce no errors, and this might be a good time to create a commit as a checkpoint that can easily be restored.

As a brief aside, note that what you have done so far shows you how Moq works:

- First, you create an instance of the thing you don't really want to instantiate that you need (i.e., the database layer).

- Then you tell the thing what to return when its methods are called (the mock data for GetItems).

- Finally, you can use that to enhance your unit testing for your system under test without coupling to other dependencies (this is what you'll do next to test the ItemsService.GetItems method).

Now you are armed with the knowledge to make sure you actually do some good testing.

Step 3: Bring in AutoMapper and the AutoMapper mappings file

In order to leverage the service layer, you will need to be able to inject a context and the AutoMapper information in a similar manner to how you've done this from the Program class in the main activity project in the past activities.

To get started, import the AutoMapper NuGet packages. An easy way to do this is to use the currently installed packages in the Manage NuGet Packages for Solution and select each AutoMapper and add them to the unit testing project (see Figure 12-10).

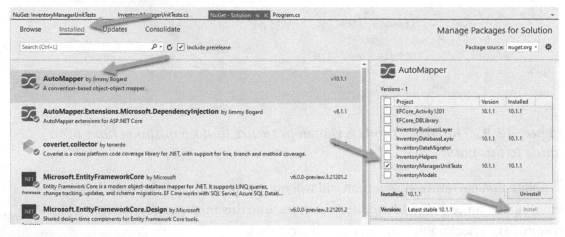

Figure 12-10. *Bring both AutoMapper libraries into the unit testing project*

After bringing in the AutoMapper libraries, use the File Explorer on your machine to copy the InventoryMapper.cs file from the main activity project and place it in the InventoryManagerUnitTests project folder on your local hard drive. It should then automatically show up in your Solution Explorer (see Figure 12-11). Optionally, change the namespace to InventoryManagerUnitTests on the InventoryMapper class for the unit test project.

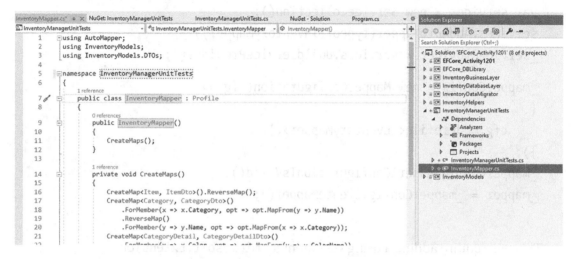

Figure 12-11. *The InventoryMapper file is copied and used in the InventoryManagerUnitTests project*

Step 4: Initialize the mapper

Next, we'll use the ClassInitialize *attribute* to make sure the mapper is set up when the test harness is instantiated. The ClassInitialize method needs a TestContext.

Add class-level variables following the declaration of the _itemsRepo so that the mapper will work as expected:

```
private static MapperConfiguration _mapperConfig;
private static IMapper _mapper;
private static IServiceProvider _serviceProvider;
public TestContext TestContext { get; set; }
```

You will need to add using statements for System and for AutoMapper for these variables to be correctly referenced.

591

Add the code from the main activity `Program` class `BuildMapper` method and add a new *Initializer* method in the `InventoryManagerUnitTests` file as follows (this contains the code you need):

```
[ClassInitialize]
public static void InitializeTestEnvironment(TestContext testContext)
{
    var services = new ServiceCollection();
    services.AddAutoMapper(typeof(InventoryMapper));
    _serviceProvider = services.BuildServiceProvider();

    _mapperConfig = new MapperConfiguration(cfg =>
    {
        cfg.AddProfile<InventoryMapper>();
    });
    _mapperConfig.AssertConfigurationIsValid();
    _mapper = _mapperConfig.CreateMapper();
}
```

This will require adding a using statement for `Microsoft.Extensions.DependencyInjection`. Note that it leverages the public property for the `TestContext`.

Task 4: Refactor the InventoryBusinessLayer to be context independent

By writing this unit test and realizing that you can't create the business layer without a specific database context, you've discovered that the business/service layer is too tightly coupled to the database.

Step 1: Add a new constructor to the InventoryBusinessLayer ItemsService class

In the `ItemsService.cs` file in the `InventoryBusinessLayer` project, add the following constructor, which will allow you to construct the business/service layer without specifying a database context:

```
public ItemsService(IItemsRepo dbRepo, IMapper mapper)
{
    _dbRepo = dbRepo;
    _mapper = mapper;
}
```

Your ItemsService should now have two explicit constructors (see Figure 12-12).

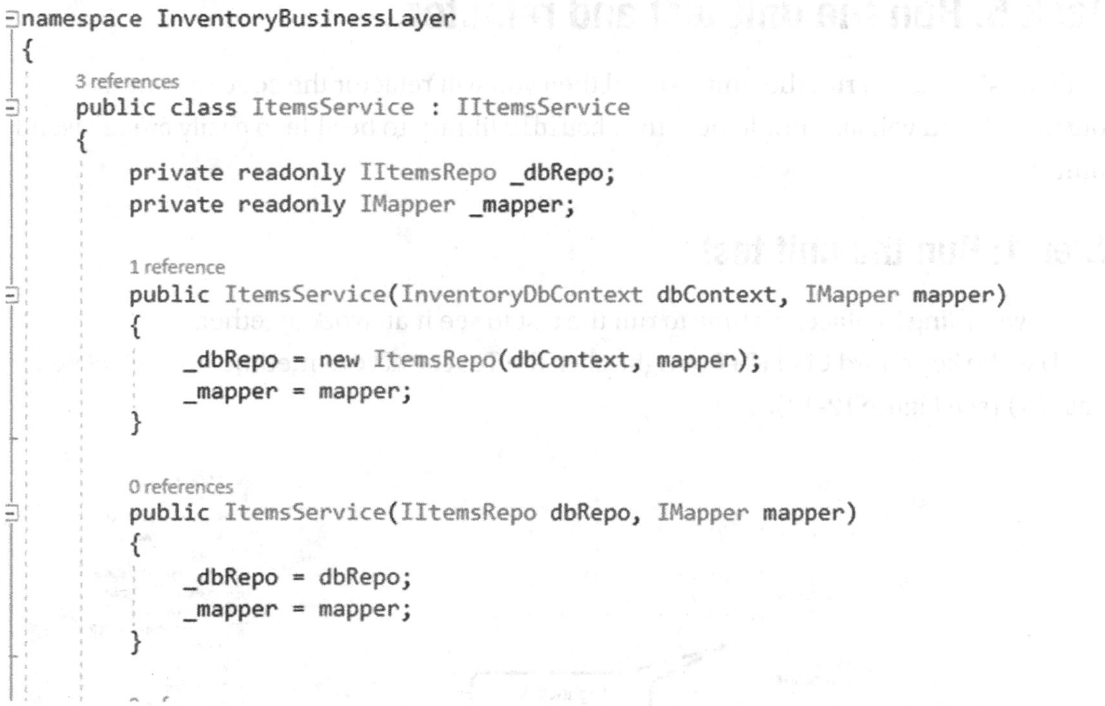

```
namespace InventoryBusinessLayer
{
    3 references
    public class ItemsService : IItemsService
    {
        private readonly IItemsRepo _dbRepo;
        private readonly IMapper _mapper;

        1 reference
        public ItemsService(InventoryDbContext dbContext, IMapper mapper)
        {
            _dbRepo = new ItemsRepo(dbContext, mapper);
            _mapper = mapper;
        }

        0 references
        public ItemsService(IItemsRepo dbRepo, IMapper mapper)
        {
            _dbRepo = dbRepo;
            _mapper = mapper;
        }
```

Figure 12-12.   *The ItemsService can now be constructed with a pre-fabricated dbRepo, making it less coupled to the database implementation*

Because this unit test has shown that the database coupling was too tight, you should eventually remove the original constructor and refactor any code that is affected by the removal of that constructor. For brevity, that step has been omitted from this activity.

Step 2: Fix the unit test to create the items service

Now that you have a mocked database and you have made it possible to instantiate the ItemsService without a database context, return to the InventoryManagerUnitTests class and uncomment the call to create a new ItemsService.

Move the call to the end of the InitializeTests method, and then change the code to the following line of code:

```
_itemsService = new ItemsService(_itemsRepo.Object, _mapper);
```

This will allow you to test the items service with the injected mock for the database layer.

Task 5: Run the unit test and refactor

In this task, you will run the unit test and then you will refactor the code to be well organized. You will also implement the Shouldly library to be able to easily create useful unit tests.

Step 1: Run the unit test

With everything in place, it's time to run the test to see it all work together.

Use the key chord Ctrl+R+T or right-click the TestGetItems method and select Run Test(s) (see Figure 12-13).

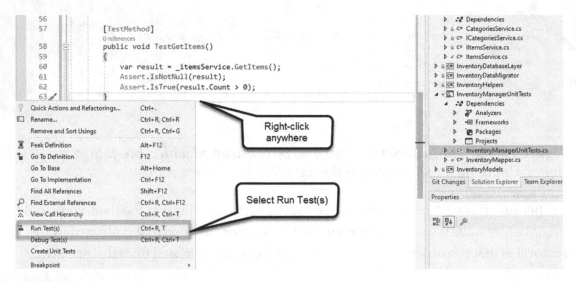

Figure 12-13. *Running the unit tests manually*

The test should pass as shown in Figure 12-14.

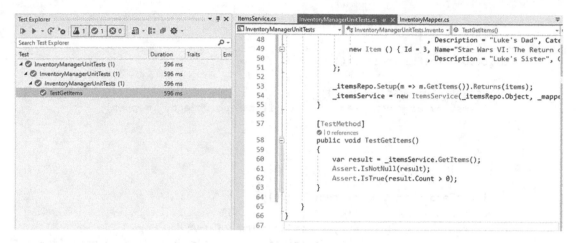

Figure 12-14. *The test passes as expected at this point*

So, if you would like to see the actual data and values, feel free to debug the test to see how it all executes from start to finish. As you can see, however, this test is too basic to simply call it "good" at this point.

Step 2: Refactor the code in the InventoryMapperUnitTest class

Next, note that at this point the unit test is very basic, and you know that to fully test this system, it is going to require much more work with the database layer, as well as eventually requiring work with the CategoriesRepo. At that point, you will not want all of your code to be piled up in the InitializeTests method.

Step 3: Refactor the database mocking

To start, right-click the code that creates the new Mock<IItemsRepo> through the line of code that includes the Setup, and then use the context menus to refactor to a new method. Name the new refactored method InstantiateItemsRepoMock (review Figure 12-15 for more clarity).

```
[TestInitialize]
0 references
public void InitializeTests()
{
    InstantiateItemsRepoMock();
    _itemsService = new ItemsService(_itemsRepo.Object, _mapper);
}

1 reference
private void InstantiateItemsRepoMock()
{
    _itemsRepo = new Mock<IItemsRepo>();
    var items = new List<Item>() {
        new Item () { Id = 1, Name="Star Wars IV: A New Hope"
                            , Description = "Luke's Friends", CategoryId =
        new Item () { Id = 2, Name="Star Wars V: The Empire Strikes Back"
                            , Description = "Luke's Dad", CategoryId = 2  }
        new Item () { Id = 3, Name="Star Wars VI: The Return of the Jedi"
                            , Description = "Luke's Sister", CategoryId = 2
    };

    _itemsRepo.Setup(m => m.GetItems()).Returns(items);
}

[TestMethod]
```

Figure 12-15. *The code to build the ItemsRepo mock is refactored to a new method*

Next, create constant values for the strings that are the titles and descriptions of the items, placing this code near the top of the class:

```
private const string TITLE_NEWHOPE = "Star Wars IV: A New Hope";
private const string TITLE_EMPIRE = "Star Wars V: The Empire Strikes Back";
private const string TITLE_RETURN = "Star Wars VI: The Return of the Jedi";
private const string DESC_NEWHOPE = "Luke's Friends";
private const string DESC_EMPIRE = "Luke's Dad";
private const string DESC_RETURN = "Luke's Sister";
```

Alternatively, in a large system, consider refactoring all constants to a separate file.

Next, refactor the original items list creation to use the constants, and move the creation of the list to its own method.

```
private void InstantiateItemsRepoMock()
{
    _itemsRepo = new Mock<IItemsRepo>();
    var items = GetItemsTestData();

    _itemsRepo.Setup(m => m.GetItems()).Returns(items);
}

private List<Item> GetItemsTestData()
{
    return new List<Item>() {
        new Item() { Id = 1, Name=TITLE_NEWHOPE
                                , Description = DESC_NEWHOPE, CategoryId = 2  },
        new Item() { Id = 2, Name=TITLE_EMPIRE
                                , Description = DESC_EMPIRE, CategoryId = 2  },
        new Item() { Id = 3, Name=TITLE_RETURN
                                , Description = DESC_RETURN, CategoryId = 2}
    };
}
```

At this point, you now have much better command over what you can do with the test data, and you will easily be able to check for values that are returned correctly from the service calls.

Step 4: Get Shouldly

While it is entirely possible to complete the unit tests at this point using the default Assert statements, you should switch to Shouldly. This will give you a much better syntax for unit testing.

Use the NuGet Package Manager to bring in the Shouldly library for the InventoryManagerUnitTests project (review Figure 12-16).

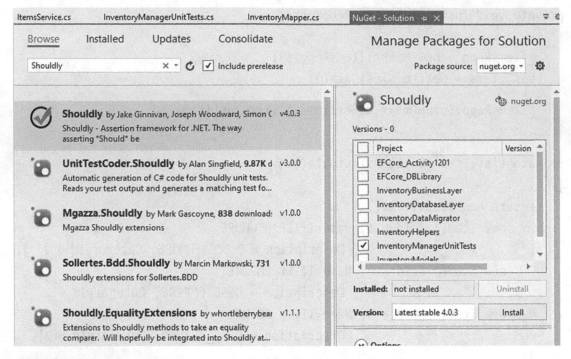

Figure 12-16.   *Using NuGet to get the Shouldly library*

Now that you have Shouldly, return to the TestGetItems method and refactor with this code:

```
public void TestGetItems()
{
    var result = _itemsService.GetItems();
    result.ShouldNotBeNull();
    result.Count.ShouldBe(3);
    var expected = GetItemsTestData();

    var item1 = result[0];
    item1.Name.ShouldBe(TITLE_NEWHOPE);
    item1.Description.ShouldBe(DESC_NEWHOPE);

    var item2 = result[1];
    item2.Name.ShouldBe(expected[1].Name);
    item2.Description.ShouldBe(expected[1].Description);
}
```

Step 5: Run the test

Run the test now that the code is refactored. Your test should still pass, and you have now set up the framework for your solution to add more complex unit tests in the future.

Activity 12-1 summary

In this activity, you learned how to start working with unit tests in your solution. A major player in the unit tests is the *Moq* library, which gives you the ability to create the underlying dependency of the database without having to actually use a database. Here you can see the value to create extremely lightweight unit tests that truly test the system under test without concern for the underlying database. The database itself will be tested as integration tests in a future project.

Keeping your unit tests and your integration tests separate is critical to ensuring that your solution is both fully tested and is easily maintained and extensible.

In this solution, you used Moq to create a mock database repository for the items service. You injected the data for a few items and were able to prove that the items service works as expected to return items from the database layer. To take this to the next level, you would need to repeat a similar process to mock the `CategoriesRepo`, leverage a `CategoriesService`, and ensure that the service layers return data as expected. Furthermore, you should write all of the unit tests that would be required. Methods that would be particularly interesting would be methods that do more than just retrieve data but also do manipulation on the data.

Activity 12-2: Integration testing with an in-memory database

In this activity, you will work through setting up integration tests in your solution. The benefit of integration tests is that you will be able to simulate working with an actual database, going one level deeper than the mocking tests you ran in the previous activity. For this activity, you will use an in-memory database to complete these tests, but if something goes wrong, there is no reason you couldn't point your integration tests at an established database instance via the connection string.

Task 0: Getting started

This activity will resume with the files as they were at the end of Activity 12-1. If you've been following along in order, feel free to continue using your files. If you are joining out of order or need a fresh set of files, grab the EFCore_Activity12-2_StarterFiles and use them for this activity. Either way, as always, ensure that your database connection strings are correct and that there are no pending migrations. Additionally, ensure that the program runs as expected.

Task 1: Create a new xUnit project

In this second activity for Chapter 12, you'll set up your solution and then set the integration tests in place that will help you to determine that your code is functioning properly at the database level as expected.

As an alternative to an MSTest project, in this activity, you'll use a different type of testing project – an xUnit test. I think you'll agree this is worth the move when you see xUnit in action.

Step 1: Create and set up the new xUnit Test Project

Begin by right-clicking the solution and selecting Add ➤ New Project as in the previous activity. This time, however, choose an xUnit Test Project (see Figure 12-17).

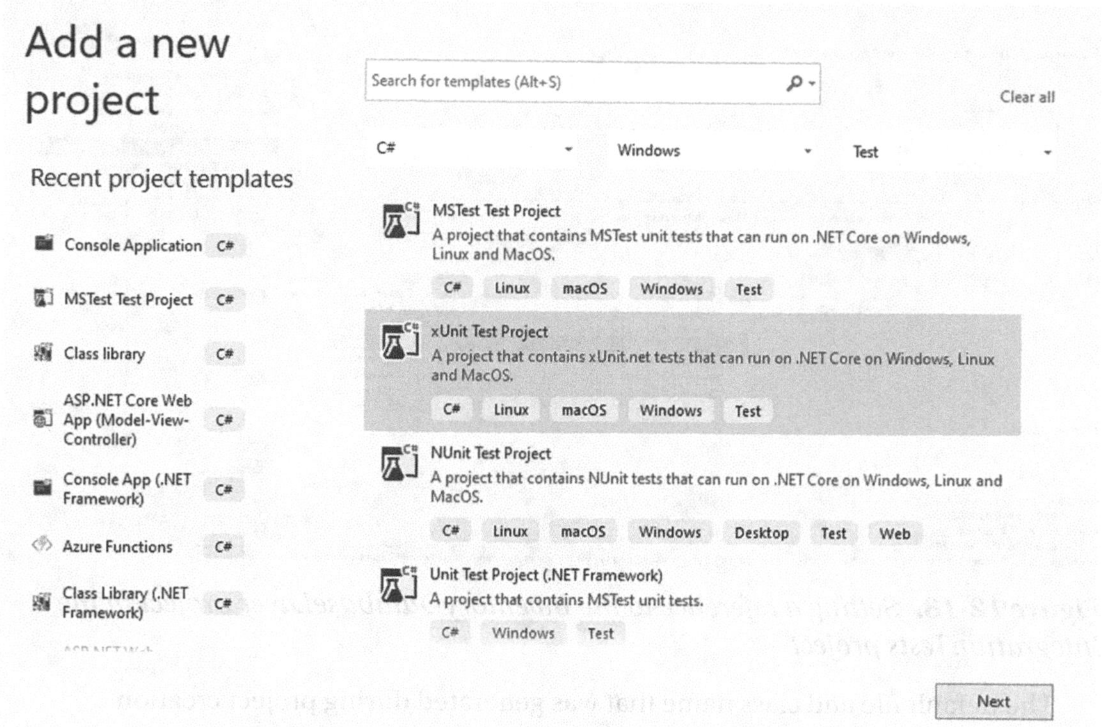

Figure 12-17. *A new xUnit project is added to the solution*

Name the new project `InventoryManagerIntegrationTests`, choose the correct Target Framework, and then create the project. This will bring up the default test that uses the `[Fact] Attribute`. A fact is a test that runs one time and takes no parameters.

xUnit also has a second type of test, the `[Theory]`. The Theory test uses inline data to set conditions and uses parameters to allow a single test to be run multiple times.

In order to perform integration tests, you're going to need to get access to the database. To do this, in the `InventoryManagerIntegrationTests` project, add a reference to the `InventoryDatabaseLayer` project using the Add ➤ `Project Reference` and then set a reference to the `InventoryDatabaseLayer` project (see Figure 12-18).

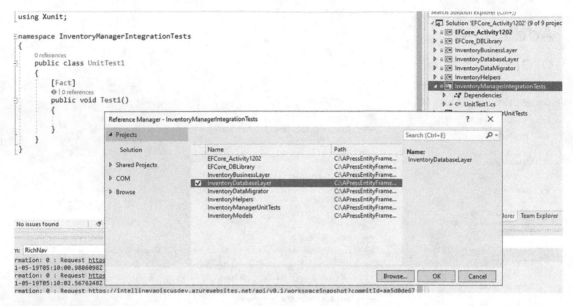

Figure 12-18. *Setting a reference to the InventoryDatabaseLayer project in the IntegrationTests project*

The default file and class name that was generated during project creation is UnitTest1. Change that file and class name to match the name of the project, InventoryManagerIntegrationTests. When prompted, select Yes for renaming the other references.

Step 2: Get NuGet packages that are needed for this solution

The integration testing project is also going to need references to *EntityFrameworkCore,* *AutoMapper,* and *Shouldly.* Ensure you have all of the following references by using the *NuGet Package Manager:*

```
Automapper
Automapper.Extensions.Microsoft.DependencyInjection
Microsoft.EntityFrameworkCore
Microsoft.EntityFrameworkCore.SqlServer
Microsoft.EntityFrameworkCore.Tools
Microsoft.Net.Test.Sdk
xunit
xunit.runner.visualstudio
coverlet.collector
Shouldly
```

Additionally, you will need a final package called `Microsoft.EntityFrameworkCore.InMemory`. Review the project file shown in Figure 12-19 to see all of the expected packages (note that your version numbers will almost certainly be different than what is shown, and that is to be expected).

```xml
<ItemGroup>
  <PackageReference Include="AutoMapper" Version="10.1.1" />
  <PackageReference Include="AutoMapper.Extensions.Microsoft.DependencyInjection" Version="8.1.1" />
  <PackageReference Include="Microsoft.EntityFrameworkCore" Version="6.      " />
  <PackageReference Include="Microsoft.EntityFrameworkCore.InMemory" Version="6.      " />
  <PackageReference Include="Microsoft.EntityFrameworkCore.SqlServer" Version="6.      " />
  <PackageReference Include="Microsoft.EntityFrameworkCore.Tools" Version="6.      ">
    <PrivateAssets>all</PrivateAssets>
    <IncludeAssets>runtime; build; native; contentfiles; analyzers; buildtransitive</IncludeAssets>
  </PackageReference>
  <PackageReference Include="Microsoft.NET.Test.Sdk" Version="16.10.0                        " />
  <PackageReference Include="xunit" Version="2.4.1" />
  <PackageReference Include="xunit.runner.visualstudio" Version="2.4.3">
    <IncludeAssets>runtime; build; native; contentfiles; analyzers; buildtransitive</IncludeAssets>
    <PrivateAssets>all</PrivateAssets>
  </PackageReference>
  <PackageReference Include="coverlet.collector" Version="3.0.3">
    <IncludeAssets>runtime; build; native; contentfiles; analyzers; buildtransitive</IncludeAssets>
    <PrivateAssets>all</PrivateAssets>
  </PackageReference>
  <PackageReference Include="Shouldly" Version="4.0.3" />
</ItemGroup>

<ItemGroup>
  <ProjectReference Include="..\InventoryDatabaseLayer\InventoryDatabaseLayer.csproj" />
</ItemGroup>
```

Figure 12-19. *The Project file for the InventoryManagerIntegrationTests shows all of the expected NuGet package references*

Task 2: Set up the expected data for seeding and integration testing

To get ready to test the database, start by setting up the data. To do this, you will need to seed some data and ensure the in-memory database is connected and working as expected.

Step 1: Configure the database, AutoMapper, and constant variables for the tests

Begin by setting the class code for the InventoryManagerIntegrationTests as follows:

```
public class InventoryManagerIntegrationTests
{
    public InventoryManagerIntegrationTests()
    {
        SetupOptions();
    }

    private void SetupOptions()
    {

    }

    [Fact]
    public void Test1()
    {

    }
}
```

To save time and avoid issues later, go ahead and put the following using statements at the top of your InventoryManagerIntegrationTests class file:

```
using AutoMapper;
using EFCore_DBLibrary;
using InventoryDatabaseLayer;
using InventoryModels;
using Microsoft.EntityFrameworkCore;
using Microsoft.Extensions.DependencyInjection;
using Shouldly;
using System;
using System.Linq;
using Xunit;
```

Add a class-level variable to store the options at the top of the class file as follows:

`DbContextOptions<InventoryDbContext> _options;`

In the SetupOptions method, you will create your database. Add the following code to instantiate the in-memory database in the setup method:

```
private void SetupOptions()
{
    _options = new DbContextOptionsBuilder<InventoryDbContext>()
                    .UseInMemoryDatabase(databaseName:
                    "InventoryManagerTest")
                    .Options;
}
```

Next, you need to set up the mapper, just as you've done in the previous activity. Create a file called InventoryMapper.cs in the project and copy the code from the InventoryMapper class from the main activity project or from the InventoryManagerUnitTests project, making sure to maintain the current namespace as InventoryManagerIntegrationTests.

Once the InventoryMapper is in place, add three class-level variables to the InventoryManagerIntegrationTests class, right after the declaration of the DbContextOptions:

```
private static MapperConfiguration _mapperConfig;
private static IMapper _mapper;
private static IServiceProvider _serviceProvider;
```

Next, set up the mapping configuration and mapper by adding the following code in the SetupOptions method following the initialization of the _options variable:

```
var services = new ServiceCollection();
services.AddAutoMapper(typeof(InventoryMapper));
_serviceProvider = services.BuildServiceProvider();

_mapperConfig = new MapperConfiguration(cfg =>
{
    cfg.AddProfile<InventoryMapper>();
});
_mapperConfig.AssertConfigurationIsValid();
_mapper = _mapperConfig.CreateMapper();
```

Make sure to add any using statements that are needed to ensure the code will compile.

Next, add a class-level variable to be used for creating a new version of the InventoryDatabaseRepo object in tests.

```
private IItemsRepo _dbRepo;
```

Finally, add the following constant variables:

```
private const string COLOR_BLUE = "Blue";
private const string COLOR_RED = "Red";
private const string COLOR_GREEN = "Green";
private const string COLOR_BLUE_VALUE = "#0000FF";
private const string COLOR_RED_VALUE = "#FF0000";
private const string COLOR_GREEN_VALUE = "#00FF00";
private const string CAT1_NAME = "CAT1 Books";
private const string CAT2_NAME = "CAT2 Movies";
private const string CAT3_NAME = "CAT3 Music";
private const string ITEM1_NAME = "Item 1 Name";
private const string ITEM2_NAME = "Item 2 Name";
private const string ITEM3_NAME = "Item 3 Name";
private const string ITEM1_DESC = "Item 1 DESC";
private const string ITEM2_DESC = "Item 2 DESC";
private const string ITEM3_DESC = "Item 3 DESC";
private const string ITEM1_NOTES = "Item 1 Notes Good";
private const string ITEM2_NOTES = "Item 2 Notes Fair";
private const string ITEM3_NOTES = "Item 3 Notes Poor";
```

Step 2: Set the data

Change the default Test1 test method name to TestGetItems. In the method, add a using statement and instantiate the context. Then use the context and the mapper to instantiate a dbRepo. Additionally, add a method call before the using statement to call to BuildDefaults. Stub out the BuildDefaults method. All of this can be accomplished with the following code:

```
[Fact]
public void TestGetItems()
{
    //arrange
    BuildDefaults();

    using (var context = new InventoryDbContext(_options))
    {
        //act
        //assert
    }
}

private void BuildDefaults()
{

}
```

In the BuildDefaults method, add code to create the three Colors, Categories, and Items. Additionally, add code to prevent creation if the database already exists with the default items.

```
private void BuildDefaults()
{
    using (var context = new InventoryDbContext(_options))
    {
        var item1Detail = context.Items.SingleOrDefault(x => x.Name.
        Equals(ITEM1_NAME));
        var item2Detail = context.Items.SingleOrDefault(x => x.Name.
        Equals(ITEM2_NAME));
        var item3Detail = context.Items.SingleOrDefault(x => x.Name.
        Equals(ITEM3_NAME));
        if (item1Detail != null && item2Detail != null && item3Detail !=
        null) return;

        var color1 = new CategoryDetail() { ColorName = COLOR_BLUE,
        ColorValue = COLOR_BLUE_VALUE };
        var color2 = new CategoryDetail() { ColorName = COLOR_RED ,
        ColorValue = COLOR_RED_VALUE };
```

```
    var color3 = new CategoryDetail() { ColorName = COLOR_GREEN ,
    ColorValue = COLOR_GREEN_VALUE };

    var cat1 = new Category()
    {
        CategoryDetail = color1,
        IsActive = true,
        IsDeleted = false,
        Name = CAT1_NAME
    };

    var cat2 = new Category()
    {
        CategoryDetail = color2,
        IsActive = true,
        IsDeleted = false,
        Name = CAT2_NAME
    };

    var cat3 = new Category()
    {
        CategoryDetail = color3,
        IsActive = true,
        IsDeleted = false,
        Name = CAT3_NAME
    };

    context.Categories.Add(cat1);
    context.Categories.Add(cat2);
    context.Categories.Add(cat3);
    context.SaveChanges();

    var category1 = context.Categories.Single(x => x.Name.Equals(CAT1_NAME));
    var category2 = context.Categories.Single(x => x.Name.Equals(CAT2_NAME));
    var category3 = context.Categories.Single(x => x.Name.Equals(CAT3_NAME));
```

```
    var item1 = new Item()
    {
        Name = ITEM1_NAME,
        Description = ITEM1_DESC,
        Notes = ITEM1_NOTES,
        IsActive = true,
        IsDeleted = false,
        CategoryId = category1.Id
    };
    context.Items.Add(item1);
    var item2 = new Item()
    {
        Name = ITEM2_NAME,
        Description = ITEM2_DESC,
        Notes = ITEM2_NOTES,
        IsActive = true,
        IsDeleted = false,
        CategoryId = category2.Id
    };
    context.Items.Add(item2);
    var item3 = new Item()
    {
        Name = ITEM3_NAME,
        Description = ITEM3_DESC,
        Notes = ITEM3_NOTES,
        IsActive = true,
        IsDeleted = false,
        CategoryId = category3.Id
    };
    context.Items.Add(item3);
    context.SaveChanges();
  }
}
```

Now you have the system set up and ready to run some integration tests.

Task 3: Write integration tests

In this final task for the activity, you will write a couple of integration tests to see how to work with both the Fact and Theory attributes.

Step 1: Test the GetItems method using an xUnit Fact test

In the TestGetItems test, inside the context using block, create a new DatabaseRepo object, and then get the inventory items. Add the following code in the "act" portion of the test:

```
_dbRepo = new ItemsRepo(context, _mapper);
var items = _dbRepo.GetItems();
```

Assert that the inventory items are as expected from the database by adding the following code in the "assert" portion of the TestGetItems method (don't forget to bring in the using statement for Shouldly):

```
items.ShouldNotBeNull();
items.Count.ShouldBe(3);
var first = items.First();
first.Name.ShouldBe(ITEM1_NAME);
first.Description.ShouldBe(ITEM1_DESC);
first.Notes.ShouldBe(ITEM1_NOTES);
first.Category.Name.ShouldBe(CAT1_NAME);
var second = items.SingleOrDefault(x => x.Name.ToLower() == ITEM2_NAME.
ToLower());
second.ShouldNotBeNull();
second.Description.ShouldBe(ITEM2_DESC);
second.Notes.ShouldBe(ITEM2_NOTES);
second.Category.Name.ShouldBe(CAT2_NAME);
```

Run the test and debug it to see the test in action. The test should pass as expected (as shown in Figure 12-20).

Figure 12-20. *The GetItems integration test is working as expected*

At this point, you have everything in place to finish writing your integration tests. In each remaining scenario, you would just need to map out the data and make sure it exists in the database as expected.

Step 2: Test the CategoryDetails with an xUnit Theory test

With *xUnit*, you can create a theory that will let you run a test multiple times with different parameters. Consider the previous test to GetItems. With a bit more code, the test could have tested all three seeded items. However, what if you could instead write the code once and test all of the items? With an xUnit Theory, you can do just that.

For this test, you will write a Theory test to test all the Categories and CategoryDetails, and you will do this with reusable code and only one test.

Add the following test method as a theory with three inline data setups, one for each category:

```
[Theory]
[InlineData(CAT1_NAME, COLOR_BLUE, COLOR_BLUE_VALUE)]
[InlineData(CAT2_NAME, COLOR_RED, COLOR_RED_VALUE)]
[InlineData(CAT3_NAME, COLOR_GREEN, COLOR_GREEN_VALUE)]
public void TestCategoryColors(string name, string color, string
colorValue)
{
```

```
    //arrange
    BuildDefaults();

    using (var context = new InventoryDbContext(_options))
    {
        //act
        var categoriesRepo = new CategoriesRepo(context, _mapper);
        var categories = categoriesRepo.ListCategoriesAndDetails();

        categories.ShouldNotBeNull();
        categories.Count.ShouldBe(3);

        var category = categories.FirstOrDefault(x => x.Category.
        Equals(name));
        category.ShouldNotBeNull();
        category.CategoryDetail.Color.ShouldBe(color);
        category.CategoryDetail.Value.ShouldBe(colorValue);
    }
}
```

Task 4: Refactor the code

To finish the activity, remove the individual calls to BuildDefaults from each test and make the call in the InventoryManagerIntegrationTests constructor.

```
public InventoryManagerIntegrationTests()
{
    SetupOptions();
    BuildDefaults();
}
```

Run the tests a final time to ensure that refactoring did not break the existing tests.

Activity 12-2 summary

In this second activity, you created the ability to run integration tests in memory using the *EFCore* built-in, in-memory database.

Running integration tests gives you the ability to test actual data from the database. After setting up the database, you were able to add Items, Categories, and CategoryDetails to the database by working directly with the context.

With data in place, you are now able to test any of the available inventory methods that are performed with *LINQ* against the DBContext.

At the end of this activity, you've only tested two of the methods. If you would like more practice, spend some time testing the insert, update, and delete methods.

One last thought is to remember that with the in-memory version of the database, you don't have access to stored procedures, so for any testing on stored procedures, you will need to test that logic outside of your integration tests to make sure they work as expected. If you needed to have a test in place that relied on the results of the stored procedure, you could potentially mock the result of the stored procedure and use that for any remaining details of the test.

Chapter summary

In this chapter, you learned about two of the ways that you can write tests against your database and solution code. The first testing strategy is to write unit tests. The second testing strategy is to use integration tests.

Unit tests

Unit tests are great for testing the layered code outside of the actual database implementation. You saw this in action when you mocked the database layer and returned simulated data from the database layer so that you could test the functionality of the service layer.

Integration tests

Integration tests are critical when you want to test the overall functionality of an actual database with your code. Integration tests provide assurance that you can rely on your database layer and DBContext to function as expected.

Shouldly and xUnit

In addition to the two types of tests, you also saw the differences between *MSTest* and *xUnit* tests. You also pulled the *Shouldly* library in so that you could easily test your code using a more user-friendly syntax.

Dependencies and injection to decouple layers

In order to test a system, dependencies must be injectable. You have spent a lot of time in the last two chapters working to decouple the system and code to an interface so that you could get to the point where your layers are easily testable.

With the system layered out and tested with both unit and integration tests, you can start to feel much more confident in the overall architecture of the system, as well as have more peace of mind during maintenance operations.

Now that you've built this robust system that is well architected and tested, you are ready to learn about some specific use case scenarios that you'll want to be aware of. The first topic will be moving to asynchronous development, which you will learn about in the next chapter.

CHAPTER 13

Asynchronous Data Operations and Multiple Database Contexts

In this chapter, you'll learn about two final critical concepts – asynchronous operations and using multiple database contexts in your solutions.

At the end of this chapter, you'll have learned how to work with asynchronous operations, which can help to leverage the full power of today's multi-core computer systems.

Additionally, you'll also have taken a look at how it is possible to use more than one database context in your solutions. Using multiple contexts can be a powerful tool to do things like building your own single sign-on solution for a suite of applications or providing connections to multiple data systems for your solutions.

Asynchronous operations

The first concept you need to learn about is working with asynchronous operations. To this point, all the code in the learning activities has done everything with all methods being synchronous. However, in most practical applications, you'll be leveraging the power of asynchronous programming, including using asynchronous database operations through EF.

© Brian L. Gorman 2022

B. L. Gorman, *Practical Entity Framework Core 6*, https://doi.org/10.1007/978-1-4842-7301-2_13

Multithreaded programming

As computer architectures changed from the dominant measure of superiority being processor-speed to the metric of superiority being processor-speed-plus-core-count, multithreaded programming became much more popular and much more important for building practical and performant solutions.

The main problem with multithreaded programming is that it is difficult. There are many issues to consider before diving into multithreaded programming. Race conditions lead to your asynchronous code executing processes or methods out of order. Thread pools run out of available threads and can still cause pieces of your program to become unresponsive. In a worst-case scenario, threads get locked in an infinite loop and your entire application becomes unresponsive.

Because of the overall difficulty of asynchronous programming, the original rate of adoption was not that high. In fact, the main use prior to the `TaskParallelLibrary` being introduced for most developers was likely just to keep desktop forms from appearing to be locked while processes ran in the background after pressing a button. I even wrote a blog post in 2009 on how to use events, delegates, and threads to avoid running into that specific problem on your desktop applications.

Because of the difficulty of multithreaded programming and the various technical problems associated with it, the .Net Framework was expanded to make multithreaded programming much easier to implement correctly.

Async, await, and the TaskParallelLibrary

In the .Net world, async and await keywords first showed up in the *.Net 3.0 Framework* but didn't become widely adopted and useable until the `TaskParallelLibrary` (*TPL*) was introduced in .Net 4.

The TPL gave all developers the ability to specify the Task operations with return types that we have come to rely on in our asynchronous code. With the TPL, we can also rely on the fact that issues with concurrency are handled correctly. For example, using the await operator or requesting to get the result of a parallel operation gives you the assurance that your code will not continue to execute until the threaded operation has completed.

Responsive solutions for the end user

To put this more into perspective, think of websites from the early 2000s through about 2010. Perhaps you've even heard the term *web 2.0*. Prior to *web 2.0* and other initiatives that happened at the end of the 2000s into the 2010s, websites were mostly one user doing one thing for themselves, or essential duties that they would perform, or were just simple, static files. *Web 2.0* really grasped the idea that there should be multiple users interacting in the same systems and that each user should see information in real time.

With *web 2.0*, it became more common to expect your changes to be immediately reflected to other users of the same system. This led to new approaches to web services and a movement into REST APIs, as well as things like the AjaxControlToolkit and SignalR, to provide an ability to abstract programmers from having to work directly with websockets. In the end, real-time dashboards as part of partial pages were able to immediately display results to the end user. Where a single-threaded approach would need to load all of the page data and then render it and also get all of the page data from the server to re-render even the smallest changes, *web 2.0* essentially moved us to having multithreaded web pages with various portions responding to different threads and no longer having to reload the whole page to see a simple change on one metric.

All of this brings you to the place where you want to land for your database as well. If you create a dashboard that requires ten different pieces of information from the database, you don't want the database calls to stop the page from working, and you don't want the page to wait to respond until all ten different calls have completed.

By placing your database calls into asynchronous operations, your web solutions can also remain asynchronous, and the overall responsiveness of the site appears to be much better, even if there are still calls that bottleneck the process.

Asynchronous database operations

With the TPL and the ability to define a return type that is based on a threaded operation, you can leverage the full power of your processor architecture. Using async and await with your operations obfuscates the need to do the heavy lifting of multithreading yourself, and you can get to a much more responsive solution with less concern about the underlying issues involved with multithreading.

Programming the database operations to also happen in an asynchronous manner thereby gives you the full power to leverage the TPL and the async and await keywords.

In other words, by using asynchronous database operations, you'll get to keep programming as if you are working with commands in a synchronous manner while leveraging the power of your multiple-core processors and the underlying multithreading that is available to you. Utilizing asynchronous database operations ultimately helps you to keep your applications responsive while querying the database in the most efficient manner possible.

Basic asynchronous syntax

Without going into a lot of detail here, setting your methods to use asynchronous operations is very straightforward. All of this will be covered in detail in the first activity later in this chapter.

To sum up what it takes to implement asynchronous operations, the main changes will require you to

- Rework all methods to be `async Task` operations
- Change all database calls to happen with the built-in async abilities of EF
- Refactor any queries that don't work as written in an asynchronous pattern
- Use the async/await pattern throughout the application
- Show how to execute an async operation from a synchronous context

Multiple database contexts

In most applications, a single database context can handle your needs. However, while it is not necessary and should ultimately be used with caution, there will be times when using multiple contexts can be beneficial.

Single sign-on (SSO)

The most common reason I can conceive of that you would want to have multiple database contexts would be in a company where you have a suite of applications and you want to provide custom sign-on capabilities to users (outside of Azure AD or an on-premises Active Directory). Another similar scenario involves users that also want to sign in via third-party providers, where perhaps your solution is open to using Azure AD, an on-premises Active Directory, and other social logins like Facebook or Google. No matter how the sign in takes place, creating an SSO solution is still the best option when you want to track the same user across multiple applications.

In an SSO solution, rather than requiring that your users register for all of your applications, you can have a single database to track a user, wherein once the user is registered with one of your applications, the same user and password combination can be used for all of your applications.

It's certainly true that you could replicate the data in the tables for user management across all of your applications with a background process. However, if all applications connect to and use the same database for identity, you can do much less work and have fewer chances to introduce errors in the process.

Business units

Another solution that might lend itself to multiple contexts would be a situation wherein you want to separate units within your corporation into their own database solutions while providing a single application to interact with the data.

For example, consider a large banking corporation that has units of work around accounting practices, customer management, financial investment operations, marketing, insurance, lending, and collections.

In this corporation, certain employees would likely need access to pieces of information in all units, such as a customer account with balance and perhaps payment and balance history in combination with mortgage and/or credit card information. Other business units might only need access to one or two of the pieces of information. For example, marketing employees might only need access to customer name and address information. Furthermore, some information might be entirely confidential, and, due to regulations, knowing the details of this information could lead to a potential violation of federal law (such as a fairness in lending act). In this scenario, it is likely critical to keep a clear separation of concerns which provide boundaries that cannot be circumvented by users, either intentionally or unintentionally.

When a case such as this exists, you'll likely need to expose certain shared data across line-of-business applications, or you may need to have directly created contexts to leverage only the parts of each system that should be accessible. Again, the choice here is which is better for your company – from background jobs to sync your data on some time interval to direct immediate access to the most valid dataset that you can provide, the choices and implementations will be your responsibility as the developer.

Multiple contexts require a bit more work

If your solution is going to use multiple contexts, there are a few things you'll need to be aware of.

The first thing to be certain to address is the injection of the context and the creation of the context at startup. Most applications will inject their context at startup, but you'll be required to also include any additional contexts in a multi-context solution. Using the additional contexts also generally requires a shared library that can leverage the shared contexts.

The second critical piece of information that is important when working with multiple contexts is the knowledge of the commands to run in the Package Manager Console. With a single context, a simple `add-migration` or `update-database` command can be run at will. Once you have introduced a second context into the solution, the PMC will need you to explicitly specify which context to use when running these commands.

A third thing to be aware of is that using multiple contexts generally requires that your entire team is on the same page as to the standards and approaches used in unit testing and interface segregation. While you could get by without some standards in these areas, having standards around processes means that any library developed around a context has been developed with a common framework and mindset and is expected to be fully unit and integration tested.

Finally, if there are security concerns when working with multiple contexts, the ability to get just a read-only version of the context without much work should be readily available. This is likely important in any scenario but becomes more critical when working across multiple databases.

Putting it into practice

You've now read about asynchronous operations and the database, as well as using multiple contexts, so it's time to implement a couple of examples so that you can see how this looks in practical examples.

The first activity for this chapter will give you a chance to rework the inventory database solution to use asynchronous operations. In the second activity, you'll take the latest version of the InventoryManager database and combine that in a web solution that has user management in a second context to simulate an SSO solution.

Activity 13-1: Asynchronous database operations

For the first activity in this chapter, you are going to rework the existing database solution to use asynchronous operations.

The main purpose of this activity is to give you the ability to implement calls that rely on the *async/await* pattern. By doing this, you should be able to free up your applications to continue processing as well as optimize the performance of your database operations, allowing you to leverage the power of multithreading without all the heavy lifting.

As mentioned earlier, there will be a few things you have to refactor, and the changes will ripple up all the way from the database layer to the main program. This also means you will have to refactor your tests. In the end, this solution will be much more like what you will encounter in any real-world application going forward.

Task 0: Getting started

This activity will resume with the files as they were at the end of Activity 12-2, where both unit and integration tests have been implemented. If you've been following along in order, feel free to continue using your files. If you are joining out of order or need a fresh set of files, grab the EFCore_Activity13-1_StarterFiles and use them for this activity. Either way, as always, refer to Appendix A for more information on using the starter files.

Task 1: Refactor the database layer

In this first task, you will start at the base database layer and work your way up through the layers. By the end of the activity, you will refactor all of the calls and methods to work as asynchronous calls to the database.

Step 1: Modify the interfaces

Begin by modifying the interface to expect each operation to work as a Task, either void or to return a value (Task or Task<T>). Do this by changing any void keywords to Task and set each return type as the return type inside a Task. For the interfaces, this means to modify the files in the InventoryDatabaseLayer project as described as follows. Note that changing to asynchronous method signatures and using Task in your code will require you to also add the using statement using System.Threading.Tasks;.

For the IItemsRepo.cs file, change the code to

```
public interface IItemsRepo
{
    Task<List<Item>> GetItems();
    Task<List<ItemDto>> GetItemsByDateRange(DateTime minDateValue,
    DateTime maxDateValue);
    Task<List<GetItemsForListingDto>> GetItemsForListingFromProcedure();
    Task<List<GetItemsTotalValueDto>> GetItemsTotalValues(bool isActive);
    Task<List<FullItemDetailDto>> GetItemsWithGenresAndCategories();

    Task<int> UpsertItem(Item item);
    Task UpsertItems(List<Item> items);
    Task DeleteItem(int id);
    Task DeleteItems(List<int> itemIds);
}
```

For the ICategoriesRepo.cs, change the code to the following:

```
public interface ICategoriesRepo
{
    Task<List<CategoryDto>> ListCategoriesAndDetails();
}
```

After modifying both files, build the project. There will be a number of errors of course, and you can reference the error list to ensure that you have all of the code updated as you go (see Figure 13-1).

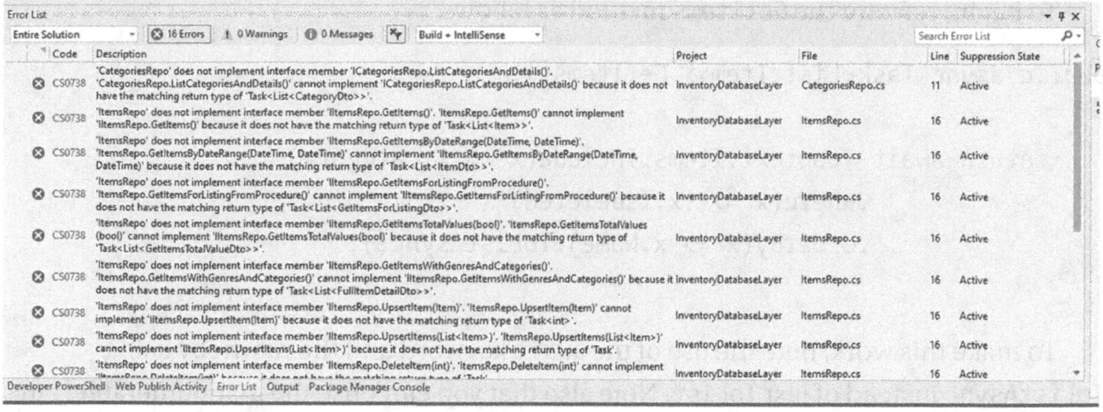

Figure 13-1. *The initial build after refactoring the interfaces has a number of expected errors. Each will need to be corrected*

You can use the errors to work out the problems going forward as a road map. You already know that you just changed the interfaces that are implemented by two implementing classes. The next step is to rework the two implementations.

Step 2: Rework the implementations

In this step, you will be refactoring the `ItemsRepo` class. Start by moving to the `ItemsRepo.cs` file.

Although you will see the red squiggly line under the `IITemsRepo` interface declaration, **do not** select *"implement interface,"* or you'll get a number of duplicated methods. Instead, you need to fix each of the existing methods and the code that executes within each method. You will not need to add any variables or modify the constructors in your implementing classes.

For each of the methods, as you did in the interface, you will wrap each return type that is not void with a `Task<T>` where `T` is the existing return type or replace any `void` methods with the `Task` declaration. Additionally, you will add the keyword `async` to each method declaration. When calling methods in an asynchronous manner, you will also preface the call with the `await` keyword. You will be given the code to refactor each method shortly.

Additionally, as with the interface, you will need to add the using statement for `System.Threading.Tasks` if it is not already present.

To begin, refactor the `GetItems` method as follows:

```
public async Task<List<Item>> GetItems()
{
    return await _context.Items.Include(x => x.Category)
                .Where(x => !x.IsDeleted)
                .OrderBy(x => x.Name).ToListAsync();
}
```

To make this work, note the use of the `await` keyword and the return by using `ToListAsync` instead of just `ToList`. Note also that you can't use the .AsEnumerable() in the call as before once this statement becomes asynchronous.

Next, refactor the `GetItemsByDateRange` to the following:

```
public async Task<List<ItemDto>> GetItemsByDateRange(DateTime minDateValue,
DateTime maxDateValue)
{
    return await _context.Items.Include(x => x.Category)
                .Where(x => x.CreatedDate >= minDateValue &&
                x.CreatedDate <= maxDateValue)
                .ProjectTo<ItemDto>(_mapper.ConfigurationProvider)
                .ToListAsync();
}
```

Note that you are cleaning up a few things as you go. Here you just returned the result since you didn't need the variable.

Refactor the `GetItemsForListingFromProcedure` method as follows:

```
public async Task<List<GetItemsForListingDto>>
GetItemsForListingFromProcedure()
{
    return await _context.ItemsForListing.FromSqlRaw("EXECUTE dbo.
    GetItemsForListing").ToListAsync();
}
```

As with previous methods, you can generally just add the `async` keyword and then change the call to use `await` and return `ToListAsync`.

Using the same technique, change `GetItemsTotalValues` to the following:

```
public async Task<List<GetItemsTotalValueDto>> GetItemsTotalValues(bool
isActive)
{
    var isActiveParm = new SqlParameter("IsActive", 1);

    return await _context.GetItemsTotalValues
        .FromSqlRaw("SELECT * from [dbo].[GetItemsTotalValue] (@IsActive)",
        isActiveParm)
        .ToListAsync();
}
```

`GetItemsWithGenresAndCategories` is refactored as

```
public async Task<List<FullItemDetailDto>>
GetItemsWithGenresAndCategories()
{
    return await _context.FullItemDetailDtos.ToListAsync();
}
```

Finish the Get/List operations with an update to the
`GetItemsWithGenresAndCategories` as follows:

```
public async Task<List<FullItemDetailDto>>
GetItemsWithGenresAndCategories()
{
    return await _context.FullItemDetailDtos
                    .FromSqlRaw("SELECT * FROM [dbo].[vwFullItemDetails]")
                        .OrderBy(x => x.ItemName).ThenBy(x => x.GenreName)
                        .ThenBy(x => x.Category).ThenBy(x => x.PlayerName)
                        .ToListAsync();
}
```

For the `UpsertItem` method, you will need to refactor this method and the
two private methods that are leveraged within the `UpsertItem` method. Change
`UpsertItem` to

```
public async Task<int> UpsertItem(Item item)
{
    if (item.Id > 0)
    {
        return await UpdateItem(item);
    }
    return await CreateItem(item);
}
```

And then update the private UpdateItem and CreateItem as follows:

```
private async Task<int> CreateItem(Item item)
{
    await _context.Items.AddAsync(item);
    await _context.SaveChangesAsync();
    var newItem = await _context.Items
                            .FirstOrDefaultAsync(x => x.Name.ToLower().
                            Equals(item.Name.ToLower())));

    if (newItem == null) throw new Exception("Could not Create the item as
    expected");

    return newItem.Id;
}

private async Task<int> UpdateItem(Item item)
{
    var dbItem = await _context.Items
                    .Include(x => x.Category)
                    .Include(x => x.ItemGenres)
                    .Include(x => x.Players)
                    .FirstOrDefaultAsync(x => x.Id == item.Id);

    if (dbItem == null) throw new Exception("Item not found");

    dbItem.CategoryId = item.CategoryId;
    dbItem.CurrentOrFinalPrice = item.CurrentOrFinalPrice;
    dbItem.Description = item.Description;
    dbItem.IsActive = item.IsActive;
```

```
    dbItem.IsDeleted = item.IsDeleted;
    dbItem.IsOnSale = item.IsOnSale;
    if (item.ItemGenres != null)
    {
        dbItem.ItemGenres = item.ItemGenres;
    }
    dbItem.Name = item.Name;
    dbItem.Notes = item.Notes;
    if (item.Players != null)
    {
        dbItem.Players = item.Players;
    }
    dbItem.PurchasedDate = item.PurchasedDate;
    dbItem.PurchasePrice = item.PurchasePrice;
    dbItem.Quantity = item.Quantity;
    dbItem.SoldDate = item.SoldDate;
    await _context.SaveChangesAsync();
    return item.Id;
}
```

To modify UpsertItems, just add the async keyword and return type Task to the
method signature, and then use the await keyword in the call to UpsertItem:

```
public async Task UpsertItems(List<Item> items)
{
    using (var scope = new TransactionScope(TransactionScopeOption.Required
            , new TransactionOptions
                { IsolationLevel = IsolationLevel.ReadUncommitted }))
    {
        try
        {
            foreach (var item in items)
            {
                var success = await UpsertItem(item) > 0;
                if (!success) throw new Exception($"Error saving the item
                {item.Name}");
            }
```

627

```
            scope.Complete();
        }
        catch (Exception ex)
        {
            //log it:
            Debug.WriteLine(ex.ToString());
            //transaction.Rollback();
            throw;
        }
    }
}
```

Finally, change DeleteItem and DeleteItems to the following code:

```
public async Task DeleteItem(int id)
{
    var item = await _context.Items.FirstOrDefaultAsync(x => x.Id == id);
    if (item == null) throw new Exception("Item Not found");
    item.IsDeleted = true;
    await _context.SaveChangesAsync();
}

public async Task DeleteItems(List<int> itemIds)
{
    using (var scope = new TransactionScope(TransactionScopeOption.Required
            , new TransactionOptions
            { IsolationLevel = IsolationLevel.ReadUncommitted }))
    {
        try
        {
            foreach (var itemId in itemIds)
            {
                await DeleteItem(itemId);
            }
```

```
        scope.Complete();
    }
    catch (Exception ex)
    {
        Debug.WriteLine(ex.ToString());
        throw;  //make sure it is known that the transaction failed
    }
    }
}
```

To complete the async operations at the database layer, refactor the `CategoriesRepo` method `ListCategoriesAndDetails` to the following (don't forget to add the using statement for `System.Threading.Tasks`):

```
public async Task<List<CategoryDto>> ListCategoriesAndDetails()
{
    return await _context.Categories
            .Include(x => x.CategoryDetail)
            .ProjectTo<CategoryDto>(_mapper.ConfigurationProvider).
            ToListAsync();
}
```

Task 2: Refactor the integration tests

Now that the base database layer is refactored for asynchronous operations, you need to refactor the unit tests to correctly call the methods. Additionally, refactoring the tests will allow you to test the code and ensure that you haven't broken anything in the process, even before the rest of the system is completely refactored.

Step 1: Refactor the integration tests

Unfortunately, the system is not fully tested, and there are only a couple of tests to refactor. In the real world, you would need to test every method and every path in each method, of course.

For this task, begin by modifying the `TestGetItems` in the `InventoryManagerIntegrationTests` project to be an asynchronous test method, and then leverage the database in an asynchronous manner to refactor the test as follows:

```
[Fact]
public async Task TestGetItems()
{
    using (var context = new InventoryDbContext(_options))
    {
        //act
        _dbRepo = new ItemsRepo(context, _mapper);
        var items = await _dbRepo.GetItems();
        //...remaining code is unchanged.
```

Next, update the `TestCategoryColors` method as follows:

```
[Theory]
[InlineData(CAT1_NAME, COLOR_BLUE, COLOR_BLUE_VALUE)]
[InlineData(CAT2_NAME, COLOR_RED, COLOR_RED_VALUE)]
[InlineData(CAT3_NAME, COLOR_GREEN, COLOR_GREEN_VALUE)]
public async Task TestCategoryColors(string name, string color, string
colorValue)
{
    //arrange

    using (var context = new InventoryDbContext(_options))
    {
        //act
        var categoriesRepo = new CategoriesRepo(context, _mapper);
        var categories = await categoriesRepo.ListCategoriesAndDetails();

        //remaining code is unchanged
```

As you can see, the bulk of the work was in the database layer itself, and leveraging the results in an asynchronous manner doesn't require a terrible amount of rework.

Step 2: Run the integration tests

Currently, the solution still will not build. However, if you build the solution, you will see that now the errors are pushed up to the higher levels, in the unit tests and business layer projects (see Figure 13-2).

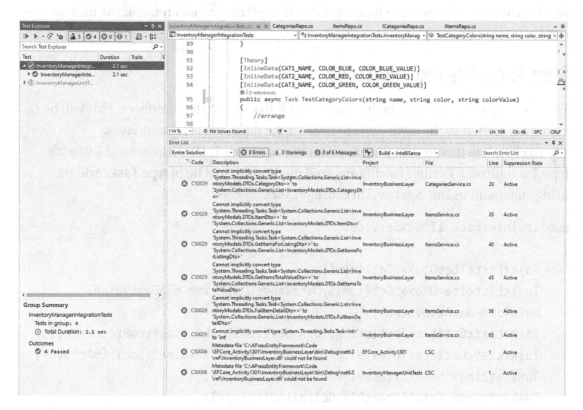

Figure 13-2. *With the database layer and integration tests reworked, errors are now pushed higher in the call stack to the business layer and the unit tests. The integration tests pass as expected after refactoring*

Because the errors do not exist at the base database layer and in the integration tests, even though the solution doesn't build, you can run the integration tests. Do so now to ensure the tests that are written still pass as expected (shown in Figure 13-2).

Task 3: Refactor the business layer

With some assurance that the base database layer and integration tests are working as expected, it's time for you to move into reworking the business layer to also be asynchronous. While doing this, you will also need to leverage the database layer calls in an asynchronous manner. Once all of that is in place, you can refactor the unit tests to run in an asynchronous manner as well.

Step 1: Modify the interfaces

The first step in refactoring the business layer is to refactor the interfaces. This will be extremely similar to the work done to refactor the database layer interfaces.

To complete this step, modify the interface to return Task<T> instead of T when a type T is returned. Further modify any void methods to just be of type Task. Add the using statement using System.Threading.Tasks.

```
public interface IItemsService
{
    Task<List<ItemDto>> GetItems();
    Task<List<ItemDto>> GetItemsByDateRange(DateTime minDateValue,
    DateTime maxDateValue);
    Task<List<GetItemsForListingDto>> GetItemsForListingFromProcedure();
    Task<List<GetItemsTotalValueDto>> GetItemsTotalValues(bool isActive);
    Task<string> GetAllItemsPipeDelimitedString();
    Task<string> GetAllItemsPipeDelimitedString();
    Task<List<FullItemDetailDto>> GetItemsWithGenresAndCategories();
    Task<int> UpsertItem(CreateOrUpdateItemDto item);
    Task UpsertItems(List<CreateOrUpdateItemDto> item);
    Task DeleteItem(int id);
    Task DeleteItems(List<int> itemIds);
}
```

Next, modify the ICategoriesService interface in the same way:

```
public interface ICategoriesService
{
    Task<List<CategoryDto>> ListCategoriesAndDetails();
}
```

632

Step 2: Rework the implementations

As with the rework for the database layer, to make the two business layer services work as expected, just modify each method to be asynchronous, add the using statement, return the type as Task<T> instead of T and Task instead of void, and then make any appropriate database layer calls asynchronous with the use of the await keyword.

The final code for the ItemsService should look as follows:

```
public class ItemsService : IItemsService
{
    private readonly IItemsRepo _dbRepo;
    private readonly IMapper _mapper;

    public ItemsService(InventoryDbContext dbContext, IMapper mapper)
    {
        _dbRepo = new ItemsRepo(dbContext, mapper);
        _mapper = mapper;
    }

    public ItemsService(IItemsRepo dbRepo, IMapper mapper)
    {
        _dbRepo = dbRepo;
        _mapper = mapper;
    }

    public async Task<List<ItemDto>> GetItems()
    {
        return _mapper.Map<List<ItemDto>>(await _dbRepo.GetItems());
    }

    public async Task<List<ItemDto>> GetItemsByDateRange(DateTime
    minDateValue, DateTime maxDateValue)
    {
        return await _dbRepo.GetItemsByDateRange(minDateValue,
        maxDateValue);
    }
```

```csharp
public async Task<List<GetItemsForListingDto>>
GetItemsForListingFromProcedure()
{
    return await _dbRepo.GetItemsForListingFromProcedure();
}
public async Task<List<GetItemsTotalValueDto>> GetItemsTotalValues(bool
isActive)
{
    return await _dbRepo.GetItemsTotalValues(isActive);
}

public async Task<string> GetAllItemsPipeDelimitedString()
{
    var items = await GetItems();
    return string.Join('|', items);
}

public async Task<List<FullItemDetailDto>>
GetItemsWithGenresAndCategories()
{
    return await _dbRepo.GetItemsWithGenresAndCategories();
}

public async Task<int> UpsertItem(CreateOrUpdateItemDto item)
{
    if (item.CategoryId <= 0)
    {
        throw new ArgumentException("Please set the category id before
        insert or update");
    }
    return await _dbRepo.UpsertItem(_mapper.Map<Item>(item));
}
```

```
public async Task UpsertItems(List<CreateOrUpdateItemDto> items)
{
    try
    {
        await _dbRepo.UpsertItems(_mapper.Map<List<Item>>(items));
    }
    catch (Exception ex)
    {
        //TODO: better logging/not squelching
        Console.WriteLine($"The transaction has failed: {ex.Message}");
    }
}

public async Task DeleteItem(int id)
{
    if (id <= 0)
    {
        throw new ArgumentException("Please set a valid item id before
        deleting");
    }
    await _dbRepo.DeleteItem(id);
}

public async Task DeleteItems(List<int> itemIds)
{
    try
    {
        await _dbRepo.DeleteItems(itemIds);
    }
    catch (Exception ex)
    {
        //TODO: better logging/not squelching
        Console.WriteLine($"The transaction has failed: {ex.Message}");
    }
}
}
```

The final code for the `CategoriesService.ListCategoriesAndDetails` method should be

```
public async Task<List<CategoryDto>> ListCategoriesAndDetails()
{
    return await _dbRepo.ListCategoriesAndDetails();
}
```

Task 4: Refactor the unit tests

Now that the business layer project is set to operate in an asynchronous manner, it's time to refactor the unit tests to leverage the service asynchronously.

Step 1: Refactor the unit tests

To refactor the unit tests, only a few lines of code need to be modified. Once again, any tests would need to be set to be asynchronous, and they would need to leverage the business layer with an await keyword. Since there is only one test, the only thing to modify is the signature and the call to GetItems from the business layer.

```
[TestMethod]
public async Task TestGetItems()
{
    var result = await _itemsService.GetItems();
    //the rest of the code is the same
```

Of course, in the real world, you would have more tests to refactor, but you would mostly find a similar ease in doing so and save a few complex methods that might be more involved.

The only other thing that needs to be changed is the mock data. Because the list of items is now returned asynchronously, you need to use a `Task.FromResult` call on the synchronous items. Modify the code in the `InstantiateItemsRepoMock` to set up the data with the following changed line of code (the rest of the method remains the same and does not need to be set to an asynchronous method):

```
_itemsRepo.Setup(m => m.GetItems()).Returns(Task.FromResult(items));
```

Those are the only changes needed to refactor the unit tests as the tests are currently written.

Step 2: Run the unit tests

Now that the unit tests are in place, build the project again to see that the errors are once again pushed farther up the stack, this time to the Program layer (see Figure 13-3).

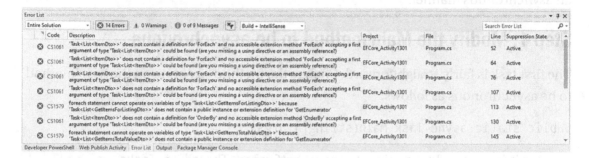

Figure 13-3. *The errors are now all the way at the top layer in the Program class, and both the service and the data layer projects and tests are error-free*

Run the unit tests to ensure that any tests you have written still pass as expected (review Figure 13-4).

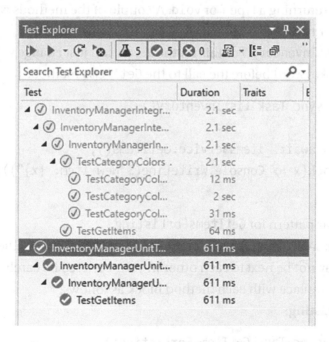

Figure 13-4. *The unit tests pass as expected after refactoring*

Task 5: Refactor the main program

The final task for this activity will require that you refactor the main program to run in an asynchronous context. After doing that, you will leverage the calls to the service layer in an asynchronous manner.

Step 1: Modify the Main method to be asynchronous

The first task is fairly straightforward. Change the method signature on the `Main` method to be asynchronous as follows:

```
public static async Task Main(string[] args)
```

Don't forget to add the using statement for `System.Threading.Tasks`.

Step 2: Modify the helper methods to be asynchronous

With the program set to run in an asynchronous context, now modify all of the methods that contain calls to the service layer to either return `Task<T>` or `Task` depending on if they are currently returning a type `T` or `void`. A couple of the methods will require an extra adjustment or two.

Begin with `ListInventory`. For this method, you can just change void to async Task and add the await keyword before the call to the `GetItems` method:

```
private static async Task ListInventory()
{
    var result = await _itemsService.GetItems();
    result.ForEach(x => Console.WriteLine($"New Item: {x}"));
}
```

Follow a similar pattern for `GetItemsForListing`, `GetAllActiveItemsAsPipeDelimitedString`, and `GetItemsTotalValues`. Note that these methods may not be next to each other in your code, so be careful to find the correct method to replace with each method block as follows:

GetItemsForListing:

```
private static async Task GetItemsForListing()
{
    var results = await _itemsService.GetItemsForListingFromProcedure();
```

```
foreach (var item in results)
{
    var output = $"ITEM {item.Name}] {item.Description}";
    if (!string.IsNullOrWhiteSpace(item.CategoryName))
    {
        output = $"{output} has category: {item.CategoryName}";
    }
    Console.WriteLine(output);
}
}
```

GetAllActiveItemsAsPipeDelimitedString:

```
private static async Task GetAllActiveItemsAsPipeDelimitedString()
{
    Console.WriteLine($"All active Items: {await _itemsService.
    GetAllItemsPipeDelimitedString()}");
}
```

GetItemsTotalValues:

```
private static async Task GetItemsTotalValues()
{
    var results = await _itemsService.GetItemsTotalValues(true);
    foreach (var item in results)
    {
        Console.WriteLine($"New Item] {item.Id,-10}" +
                          $"|{item.Name,-50}" +
                          $"|{item.Quantity,-4}" +
                          $"|{item.TotalValue,-5}");
    }
}
```

For the GetItemsForListingLinq method, you'll need to move the OrderBy statement into the ForEach loop. The asynchronous call will work to get the data, and then you do the ordering at the client side in this case.

```
private static async Task GetItemsForListingLinq()
{
    var minDateValue = new DateTime(2021, 1, 1);
    var maxDateValue = new DateTime(2024, 1, 1);

    var results = await _itemsService.GetItemsByDateRange(minDateValue,
    maxDateValue);

    foreach (var itemDto in results.OrderBy(y => y.CategoryName).ThenBy
    (z => z.Name))
    {
        Console.WriteLine(itemDto);
    }
}
```

For the remaining methods, you just follow the same pattern of using `async Task` instead of `void` in the method signature and then adding the `await` keyword. For the `Create`, `Update`, and `Delete` methods, there are a couple of places to enter the `await` keyword, since there are a couple of paths to follow for either batching or not batching requests. Make sure to leave the `GetCategoryId` method unchanged (and do not delete it).

Because the code is extensive, it has been omitted from the text here. Note that you can always find the solutions in the final version of the files, but you should be able to perform this action without help at this point.

Step 3: Make the calls in the Main method asynchronous

When you have completed the refactoring of the methods, the only thing that remains is fixing the `Main` method.

To complete this activity, use the `await` keyword wherever you see a green squiggly line. For example, add the `await` keyword before the call to `ListInventory`, `GetItemsForListing`, and the rest of the calls that are making a call to an asynchronous method without the await keyword so that all of them will be leveraged as expected with the await keyword, including the calls in the if statements to `CreateMultipleItems`, `UpdateMultipleItems`, and `DeleteMultipleItems`. Some of the changes should look like this code:

```
await ListInventory();
await GetItemsForListing();
await GetAllActiveItemsAsPipeDelimitedString();
await GetItemsTotalValues();
await GetFullItemDetails();
await GetItemsForListingLinq();
await ListCategoriesAndColors();
```

Finally, note that there are three remaining calls to the _itemsService.GetItems method. Add the await keyword before each call to fix the error on the ForEach statements. For example,

```
var inventory = _itemsService.GetItems();
```

becomes

```
var inventory = await _itemsService.GetItems();
```

At this point, you should be able to build the code with no errors. If you have remaining errors, examine them and fix them. If you need help with any of the code, don't forget to check the final files that contain the full solution.

Step 4: Run the program

With everything in place, run the program to see the program in action. If you are not using an encrypted database, then your solution will likely work right now as is.

However, if you've followed through the book, the solution will likely have a runtime error (see Figure 13-5). What happened that caused this?

Figure 13-5. *There is an error deep in the database for an encryption issue*

If you trace this through, the error happens all the way at the database layer where the call to GetItems is made. However, you might wonder why this is happening, since the testing clearly showed that it works as expected. The issue, if you haven't guessed, is because the real database is encrypted (if yours isn't, you won't see this error). However, the unit tests are using an unencrypted version of the in-memory database.

So, what do you do now? Does this mean that testing is pointless?

While it may be possible to get the in-memory database to use an always encrypted schema, the refactoring might be massive, as you may need to explicitly create every table with a T-SQL query or modify the in-memory database with T-SQL commands during the testing instantiation.

Even though testing didn't expose this error, it is still not a pointless effort, but it is incredibly important to note that even with testing, using a database that is not the same as the database you are deploying to can create a small disconnect. This is part of your job as a developer – to ensure that you have accounted for all of these possible issues.

In the end, always remember that just because you've run your test suites it does not always mean that you have safely tested the solution. You should always run through as a user as well, to ensure that you have no functionality that is not correctly tested or covered by your tests or, in this case, too much extra effort to effectively test.

Step 5: Fix issues with encryption and asynchronous operations

In the end, you will need to fix a few issues that are now in the program based on the use of asynchronous code and having an underlying database that uses Always Encrypted columns.

Return all the way to the database layer, and change the GetItems method to the following:

```
public async Task<List<Item>> GetItems()
{
    var items = await _context.Items.Include(x => x.Category)
                        .Where(x => !x.IsDeleted).ToListAsync();
    return items;
}
```

An additional fix for a similar issue is needed in the GetItemsWithGenresAndCategories method. Here, instead of just returning the results unordered, you can refactor the method to get results and then return the result in the same ordering as originally coded:

```
public async Task<List<FullItemDetailDto>>
GetItemsWithGenresAndCategories()
{
    var result = await _context.FullItemDetailDtos
                        .FromSqlRaw("SELECT * FROM [dbo].
                        [vwFullItemDetails]")
                        .ToListAsync();

    return result.OrderBy(x => x.ItemName).ThenBy(x => x.GenreName)
                    .ThenBy(x => x.Category).ThenBy(x => x.PlayerName).
                    ToList();
}
```

Running the program now will work until you try to create an item.

The code in the `CreateItem` method is also going to be broken by the combination of asynchronous calls and the underlying encryption. As it currently stands, if you run the program and try to create a new Item (do not use batching yet, just create a single item), you will get another encryption error (see Figure 13-6).

```
0 references
public static async Task Main(string[] ar...
{
    BuildOptions();
    BuildMapper();
    using (var db = new InventoryDbContex
    {
        _itemsService = new ItemsService(
        _categoriesService = new Categori
        await ListInventory();
        await GetItemsForListing();
        await GetAllActiveItemsAsPipeDeli
        await GetItemsTotalValues();
        await GetFullItemDetails();
        await GetItemsForListingLinq();
        await ListCategoriesAndColors();

        Console.WriteLine("Would you like
        var createItems = Console.ReadLin
        if (createItems)
        {
            Console.WriteLine("Adding new Item(s)");
            await CreateMultipleItems();  ⊗
            Console.WriteLine("Items added");

            var inventory = await _itemsService.GetItems();
            inventory.ForEach(x => Console.WriteLine($"Item: {x}"));
        }
    }
```

Exception User-Unhandled   🗖 ✕

Microsoft.Data.SqlClient.SqlException: 'Operand type clash: varchar(100) encrypted with (encryption_type = 'DETERMINISTIC', encryption_algorithm_name = 'AEAD_AES_256_CBC_HMAC_SHA_256', column_encryption_key_name = 'CEK_Auto1',

This exception was originally thrown at this call stack:
  [External Code]
  InventoryDatabaseLayer.ItemsRepo.CreateItem(InventoryModels.It
  [External Code]
  InventoryDatabaseLayer.ItemsRepo.UpsertItem(InventoryModels.It

View Details | Copy Details | Start Live Share session...

▲ Exception Settings
  ☑ Break when this exception type is user-unhandled
     Except when thrown from:
       ☐ EFCore_Activity1301.dll
  Open Exception Settings | Edit Conditions

Figure 13-6. *The encryption and asynchronous call causes further errors for the*
CreateItem method

To fix the issue, it comes down to getting results first and then doing things like sorting and filtering. In this case, get the results and then match the data. This is the same issue you've run into before – where the filtering and sorting cannot happen on an encrypted column before the results have been decrypted by the client.

In the `InventoryDatabaseLayer` project `ItemsRepo` class, change the code

```
var newItem = await _context.Items
                        .FirstOrDefaultAsync(x => x.Name.
                        ToLower().Equals(item.Name.ToLower()));
```

in the CreateItem method to the following:

```
var items = await _context.Items.ToListAsync();
var newItem = items.FirstOrDefault(x => x.Name.ToLower().Equals(item.Name.
ToLower()));
```

which will run as expected, and the program will now complete successfully to add items.

Put a breakpoint on the line return newItem.Id, as there is something important to see in this code. Run the program now and add an item to ensure it works as expected. Create an item (see Figure 13-7).

```
Category [Games] is green
Would you like to create items?
y
Adding new Item(s)
Would you like to create items as a batch?
n
Creating a new item.
Please enter the name
Your Best Year Ever
Please enter the description
A 5-step plan for achieving your most important goals
Please enter the notes
A fantastic book for getting on task for your dreams
Please enter the Category [B]ooks, [M]ovies, [G]ames
B
```

```
        if (newItem == null) throw new Exception("Could not Create the item as expected");

        return newItem.Id;
}
```

Figure 13-7. *Creating an item with the fixed code is working so far*

When you get to the breakpoint, put a watch on the newItem and then compare the original passed in item to the newItem.Id that you are about to return (review Figure 13-8).

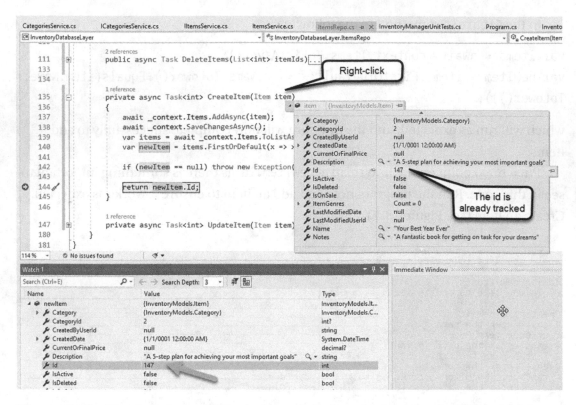

Figure 13-8. *Tracing through the code reveals that the item is already tracked, and the call to get items and find by name to get the Id is not necessary*

This latest finding validates that you don't even need the entire code to go get items, as EF has already updated your tracked item id to the new id of the inserted item, and you can just return that value.

As a result of this finding, change the CreateItem method to the following code:

```
private async Task<int> CreateItem(Item item)
{
    await _context.Items.AddAsync(item);
    await _context.SaveChangesAsync();

    if (item.Id <= 0) throw new Exception("Could not Create the item as
    expected");

    return item.Id;
}
```

The update method works as expected, but you should test it just to make sure. The same goes for the delete method. Both the update and delete methods utilize the id for filtering, which is not encrypted.

Run the program again, ensuring that you can do the single operations for Create, Update, and Delete. Once that is all working, run the create with a batch. This will lead to the final issue that needs to be resolved.

Step 6: Fix the batching operations with asynchronous calls

Another issue still exists in the code as written. If you currently try to update (or create or delete) the items in a batch, you will likely get the following error: "This connection was used with an ambient transaction. The original ambient transaction needs to be completed before this connection can be used outside of it" (see Figure 13-9).

```
var updateItems = Console.ReadLine().StartsWith("y", StringComparison.OrdinalIgnoreCase);
if (updateItems)
{
    Console.WriteLine("Updating Item(s)");
    await UpdateMultipleItems();
    Console.WriteLine("Items updated");

    var inventory2 = await _itemsService.GetItems();  ⊗
    inventory2.ForEach(x => Console.WriteLine($"Item: { }"));
}

Console.WriteLine("Would you like to delete items?");
var deleteItems = Console.ReadLine().StartsWith("y",
if (deleteItems)
{
    Console.WriteLine("Deleting Item(s)");
    await DeleteMultipleItems();
    Console.WriteLine("Items Deleted");

    var inventory3 = await _itemsService.GetItems();
    inventory3.ForEach(x => Console.WriteLine($"Item:
}

Console.WriteLine("Program Complete");
}
}
```

Exception User-Unhandled

System.InvalidOperationException: 'This connection was used with an ambient transaction. The original ambient transaction needs to be completed before this connection can be used outside of it.'

This exception was originally thrown at this call stack:
  [External Code]
  InventoryDatabaseLayer.ItemsRepo.GetItems() in ItemsRepo.cs
  [External Code]
  InventoryBusinessLayer.ItemsService.GetItems() in ItemsService.cs

View Details | Copy Details | Start Live Share session...

▲ Exception Settings
  ☑ Break when this exception type is user-unhandled
    Except when thrown from:
    ☐ EFCore_Activity1301.dll
  Open Exception Settings | Edit Conditions

1 reference

Figure 13-9. *The transaction scope doesn't work with the asynchronous calls*

Note that all of the code is the same as before, so the only potential code difference that could be causing an issue is that in the call using the batch, multiple calls are made to UpsertItem within a transaction scope, and in the single call to the UpsertItem method, there is no transaction scope being used.

Therefore, the issue seems to be with the use of a transaction and the asynchronous calls. Whenever asynchronous calls are executed and there is an error, the first thought/ question you ask yourself should be *"Is this a timing/callback error?"*

To prove this out, in the current code, put a breakpoint on the call to get the items (where the error happens), and you will see that the multiple calls to the database work for the creation, updating, or deletion of items. If you then take the time to run a query and wait on the breakpoint before making a call to get items from code, everything works as expected, including the call to the database (see Figure 13-10).

Figure 13-10. *The calls work and complete as long as you pause before calling back to GetItems (and don't wait too long and let your transaction timeout)*

This is therefore apparently a timing issue for the completion and disposal of the transaction scope before opening a new connection to run the `GetItems` call.

Updating items in a batch will have the same issue, as will deleting items in a batch. All three of them leverage a transaction scope.

So how can you prevent it?

Since this is a timing issue and is caused by using the transaction within an asynchronous call that you know works in a synchronous call, you could just reset everything and use a synchronous operation for your transactions.

Fortunately, the fix for this issue is simple and likely doesn't need you to fall back to the old ways. Instead, just go into the ItemsRepo.cs file and find the UpsertItems method. Change the using statement that creates the transaction to include a statement for TransactionScopeAsyncFlowOption.Enabled, so that the using statement is as follows:

```
using (var scope = new TransactionScope(TransactionScopeOption.Required
                    , new TransactionOptions { IsolationLevel =
                    IsolationLevel.ReadUncommitted }
                    , TransactionScopeAsyncFlowOption.Enabled))
{
                    // no other changes
```

Additionally, you will need to modify the transaction in the DeleteItems method to also allow for the TransactionScopeAsyncFlowOption.Enabled configuration:

```
public async Task DeleteItems(List<int> itemIds)
{
    using (var scope = new TransactionScope(TransactionScopeOption.Required
            , new TransactionOptions { IsolationLevel =
            IsolationLevel.ReadUncommitted }
            , TransactionScopeAsyncFlowOption.Enabled))
    {
            // no other changes
```

With both of the transactions now effectively able to complete during their asynchronous operation, you have set the database to run in an asynchronous mode and completed the updates to the Program class methods, including Main.

As before, run the program a few times and make sure that everything works.

Task 6: Fix a broken integration test

It's always a good idea to run the unit tests before closing off the activity as completed.

Step 1: Run the unit and integration tests

Open the Test Explorer and run the tests one more time. You will see that there is a small failure due to the ordering that was broken in the GetItems method (see Figure 13-11).

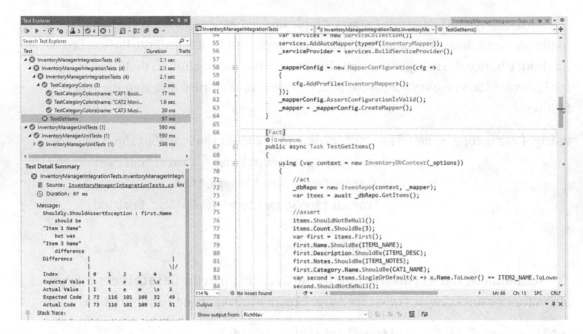

Figure 13-11. *The integration test is expecting ordering that was broken during the refactoring*

Although you didn't have a lot of testing, this one revealed that systems might be relying on the order that was expected from the GetItems method.

To make this test pass, return to the ItemsRepo class in the InventoryDatabaseLayer project, and modify the GetItems method to use a similar approach as was done in the GetItemsWithGenresAndCategories method:

```
public async Task<List<Item>> GetItems()
{
    var result = await _context.Items.Include(x => x.Category)
                .Where(x => !x.IsDeleted)
                .ToListAsync();

    return result.OrderBy(x => x.Name).ToList();
}
```

Run the tests again. They should now be passing as expected.

Activity 13-1 summary

In this activity, you learned how to refactor your entire project to use asynchronous operations. By doing this, you've leveraged the power of multithreading in today's modern architectures and have given your solution the best chance to operate as efficiently as possible.

By switching to async/await and using asynchronous database calls, you also learned about a few other issues along the way. One thing you saw was that there were a couple of places where the client had to first decrypt data before it could be filtered. This is generally the case for all calls to an encrypted database but became very evident when working with asynchronous calls.

Additionally, you learned that using a transaction with asynchronous calls can be a tricky operation but generally is available to be solved by using the TransactionScopeAsyncFlowOption.Enabled option in the transaction.

A final thing that you learned is that while using unit and integration tests is good practice, and tests correctly expose a number of issues, using a target database for your integration testing that is not as robust or the same as the actual deployment environment may lead to a false sense of assurance that things are working as expected. Therefore, it is always a good idea to ensure that you have fully tested the solution, even in addition to good unit and integration testing.

Activity 13-2: Multiple database contexts

In the second activity for this chapter, you are going to leverage a shared database context for a potential single sign-on (SSO) solution, which will manage user identities. To simplify this operation, you'll create a new web solution and integrate the inventory context into the solution after first establishing the identity database.

Task 0: Getting started

This activity will leverage the database solution from the end of the previous activity, EFCore_Activity13-1_FinalFiles, and use that database solution within a new web project that has been set to include a separate database connection to manage identity. For reasons of brevity, this book is not going to walk through the steps to set this up again. Instead, a brief description of what you would need to build follows.

To begin, you need an ASP.Net MVC web solution targeting the .Net 65 Framework, and you need to ensure that during creation, you enable using an identity that is managed from within the application. Rather than take the time to do this, two versions of the starter files are provided (additionally, a similar project was created in Chapter 6, so you could review that for more information). If you would like to add your own database library that you've been building along with each activity, grab the `EFCore_Activity13-2_WebOnly_StarterFiles`. If you would like to just use the default version of the files with the database solution already included, then grab the `EFCore_Activity-13-2_AllFiles_StarterFiles`. If you choose the Web only, you will then need to manually import your database library hierarchy into the solution.

Additionally, if building your own version, ensure that you add a project reference in the main `EFCore_Activity1302` project to the `InventoryBusinessLayer`. Finally, change the name of the default database to something like `CorporateSSOIdentityDb`.

No matter how you get started, **do not** run any migrations before proceeding into the activity. Ensure the project runs before proceeding (but don't try to register a user yet).

Task 1: Inject both contexts into the solution, and learn about working with multiple contexts

At this point, you either have the full version of the starter files (the solution as created by the end of the last activity within a new web solution) or you have imported your solution into a default web project. Now you are ready to work with multiple database contexts.

Step 1: Inject the InventoryDbContext into the web solution

To get started with multiple contexts, first you must have both contexts available. Open the `EFCore_Activity1302` web project and then find the `Startup.cs` file and the `ConfigureServices` method within this file. Note that currently there is an `ApplicationDbContext` that is being leveraged. This is the identity context. If you look into the `appsettings.json` file, you'll see that it will be configured to the `DefaultConnection` as listed in the `ConfigureServices` method and that it will be set to point to a database named `CorporateSSOIdentityDb`.

In addition to this context, you need to inject the `InventoryDbContext`. Do this by adding the following lines of code to the `ConfigureServices` method in the `Startup.cs` file before the call to `services.AddDatabaseDeveloperPageExceptionFilter();:`

```
services.AddDbContext<InventoryDbContext>(options =>
    options.UseSqlServer(
        Configuration.GetConnectionString("InventoryManagerConnection")));
```

This will require you add the using statement using EFCore_DbLibrary; to the top of the file.

In addition to the code in the Startup class ConfigureServices method, you will need to add the connection string to the configuration file with the key InventoryManagerConnection as just defined in code.

Open the appsettings.json file found in the EFCore_Activity1302 project. In that file, add a second connection by copying the DefaultConnection JSON, adding a comma to follow the DefaultConnection JSON, and then pasting the copy and replacing the name with "InventoryManagerConnection". Then set the Database to be InventoryManagerDb or whatever you have called your local database used to this point in the book (this connection string should map to whatever you are using as the database in the InventoryDataMigrator application). Assuming that you also have encryption enabled, don't forget to set the Column Encryption Setting=Enabled in the connection string. In the end, your ConnectionStrings section should be similar to this code:

```
"ConnectionStrings": {
  "DefaultConnection": "Server=localhost;Database=CorporateSSOIdentityDb;
  Trusted_Connection=True;MultipleActiveResultSets=true",
  "InventoryManagerConnection": "Server=localhost;Database=Inventory
  ManagerDb;Trusted_Connection=True;MultipleActiveResultSets=true;Column
  Encryption Setting=Enabled"
},
```

Pay close attention to the database name here for the InventoryManagerConnection. In the AllFiles starter files, the DB will be appended with the activity number 1302. If you are using a separate DB for each activity, you'll want to modify the preceding connection to use Database=InventorymanagerDb1302 to ensure the connection maps to the same DB as the InventoryDataMigrator project from the starter files. If you are using your own single DB throughout each of the activities, then you may want to modify the InventoryDataMigrator project to point to your single DB if you used the starter files for this activity.

Step 2: Run the initial migration for identity and ensure no pending migrations exist

At this point, if you have not put your code into a local Git repository, I recommend you do so, in case something gets messed up in the next part. Also, it's much easier to reset and clean up if you have some lingering files created that you don't want after completing the next couple of steps.

Because the identity context has never been migrated, you will need to do that. If you run the website and try to register, it will tell you that you need to run migrations. If there was only one context, you could likely just press that button. However, don't do that now if you happen to be on that page.

If you open SSMS on your machine, currently you will not even have a database for the CorporateSSOIdentityDb (see Figure 13-12).

Figure 13-12. *Currently there is no database for the CorporateSSOIdentityDb locally on the machine*

Open the PMC and select the default project to be the website solution EFCore_ Activity1302. In the PMC, run the command update-database. What happens? You get an error because the solution can't decide which database context to use, so it tells you exactly that with the message *More than one DbContext was found. Specify which one to use...* (see Figure 13-13). So how do you fix it?

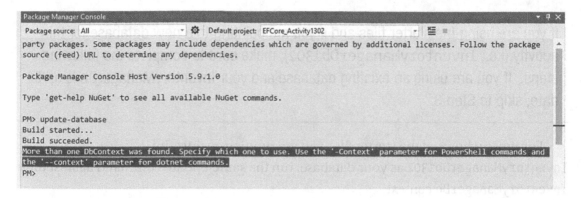

Figure 13-13. *When more than one database context is present, you must specify the context to use when running commands in the PMC*

The error says to use the -Context parameter for PowerShell and --context parameter for dotnet commands. The best solution for the PMC is to use the PowerShell update-database -Context command as follows, pointing to the identity context by name:

```
update-database -Context ApplicationDbContext
```

Run that command to migrate the context for the identity into its local database on your machine. This should work, and you should get a new database that has all of the ASPNet identity tables in it (review Figure 13-14).

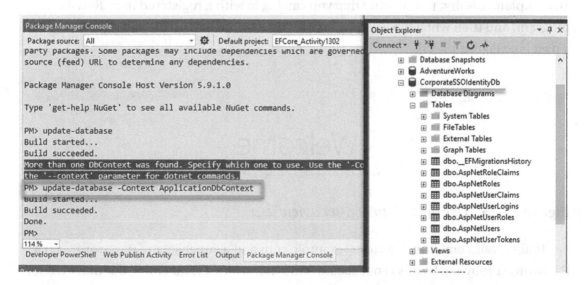

Figure 13-14. *The database is generated when the context is specified, and the migrations are applied to set the identity tables as expected*

If you are using the starter files and if you are pointing to a new database for this activity (i.e., InventoryManagerDb1302), make sure to complete the following steps. If you are using an existing database and your InventoryManagerDb is up to date, skip to Step 3.

For those who used the starter files and are running against the InventoryManagerDb1302 as your database, run the same update command against the InventoryManagerDb context:

```
update-database -Context InventoryDbContext
```

After updating the database, right-click the InventoryDataMigrator project and select Debug ➤ Start New Instance. This will work because it doesn't reference more than one database in that project.

When that operation has completed, use SSMS to map your Items to Categories with the custom script MapCategories.sql found in the InventoryDataMigrator project.

Step 3: Run the program and ensure you can register a user and log in as the user

To complete this first task, ensure that you can log in with a registered user. Run the program, and then when the web page comes up, use the link on the top right to register a user (see Figure 13-15).

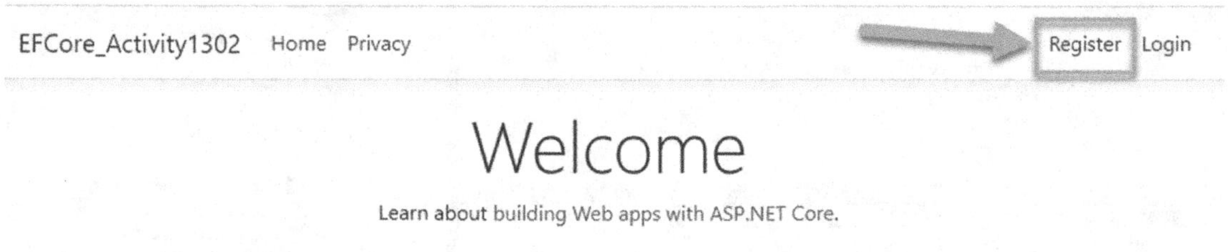

EFCore_Activity1302   Home   Privacy   Register   Login

Welcome

Learn about building Web apps with ASP.NET Core.

Figure 13-15.   *Use the link to register a new user*

Enter a valid email such as test@example.com and a super secure password such as Password#1 (obviously, this is not secure and is not using a valid email, but that's OK for this activity). When the registration completes, it is incredibly important that you click the link that says Validate Email. In the real world, you would send an email and the user would click a link to validate the email is valid, of course. Here, you need to just click the link in order to be able to log in (review Figure 13-16).

Figure 13-16. *Make sure to confirm your email for registration by clicking the link*

You will be presented with a blank page that says *Confirm email* and a green information message that states *Thank you for confirming your email* which, in this case, means you actually have confirmed your email.

Next, click Login as you will now need to log your user in, even though you just registered and validated your email.

Enter your login credentials. When successful, you will see a welcome message at the top right of the screen as shown in Figure 13-17.

Figure 13-17. *The user is logged in, and a welcome message is shown in the top right of the browser*

Finally, review the database to ensure the user was created by running the query

```
SELECT * FROM AspNetUsers
```

Incidentally, if you can't log in, run this same query and ensure you have a user, and also ensure that EmailConfirmed field is set to 1. If you didn't click the link as instructed, EmailConfirmed may be 0, and the user won't be able to log in. Figure 13-18 shows the expected result.

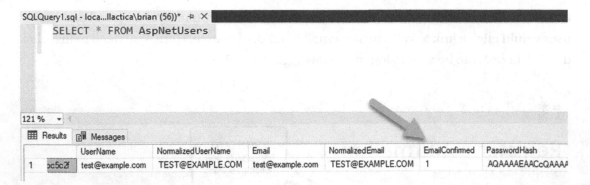

Figure 13-18. *The query reveals all the registered users in the Identity database*

Task 2: Scaffold Category pages

As this is not a book on web development, the activity will conclude with the ability to manage the Category information. This will require being able to manage Category objects via the website.

Step 1: Scaffold Category Details

Right-click the Controllers folder in the EFCore_Activity1302 project, and then select Add ➤ Controller (review Figure 13-19 for clarity).

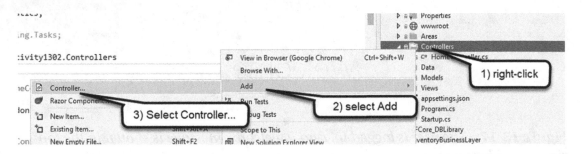

Figure 13-19. *Adding a new controller to the project that will be scaffolded*

If the option to create a controller is grayed out, ensure that you are not currently running the project. You cannot create new controllers while the project is running.

When the dialog appears, select MVC Controller with views, using Entity Framework, and then hit the Add button (see Figure 13-20).

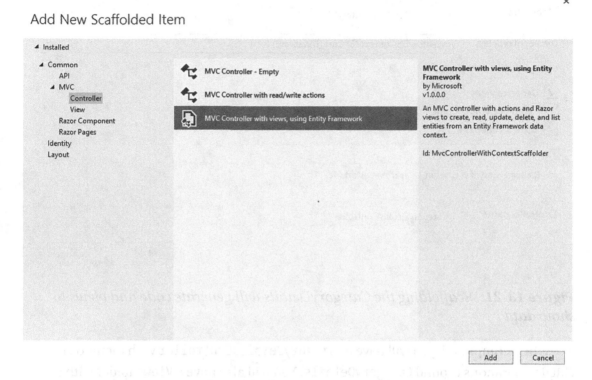

Add New Scaffolded Item

Figure 13-20. *Continuing the Add of an MVC Controller using EF*

In the next dialog, select the `CategoryDetail` object as the model class, and use the `InventoryDbContext` as the data context class. Leave everything else as is, and ensure the `Controller` name is `CategoryDetailsController` (review Figure 13-21). Use the `Add` button to scaffold the solution. This will take a minute or two to complete but should not encounter an error.

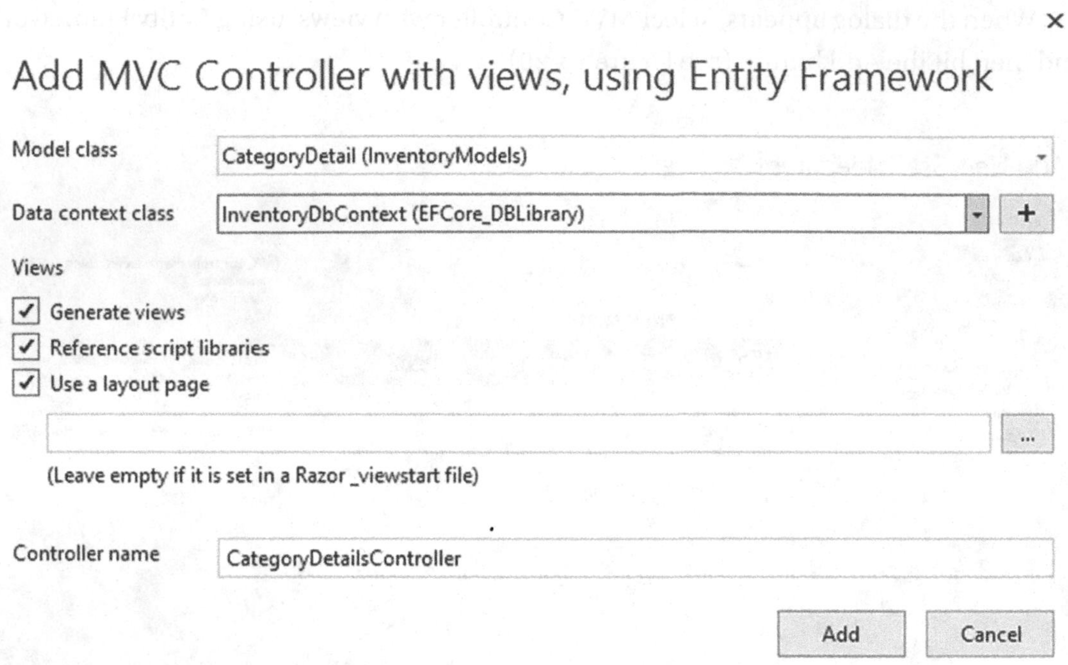

×

Add MVC Controller with views, using Entity Framework

Model class   CategoryDetail (InventoryModels)   ▾

Data context class   InventoryDbContext (EFCore_DBLibrary)   ▾ +

Views

☑ Generate views
☑ Reference script libraries
☑ Use a layout page

[   ] [...]

(Leave empty if it is set in a Razor _viewstart file)

Controller name   CategoryDetailsController

[Add]   [Cancel]

Figure 13-21. *Scaffolding the CategoryDetails will generate code and views to show data*

When completed, you will have a `CategoryDetailsController` with methods for CRUD operations around `CategoryDetails`. You will also have a `Views` folder with a subfolder for `CategoryDetails`, and the views will match the names of the methods in the controller.

You might also notice, however, that the project is directly referencing the context. While you can do this, you likely want to use the service layer that you've previously built, and, instead of `CategoryDetail` objects, you would want to use `CategoryDetailDto` objects (as a view model). Using the service layer would add a bit of complexity to the project, but this would be a much better solution in a real-world business project. Wiring up the service layer is outside of the scope of the book, but if you wanted to go to that level, almost everything you need is available in the project.

Step 2: Run the solution and review the output

Now that the scaffolding is completed, run the solution. Navigate to the `CategoryDetails` controller's Index view by entering "`CategoryDetails`" in the browser path. If you have data seeded, you should see category details in a listed view (see Figure 13-22).

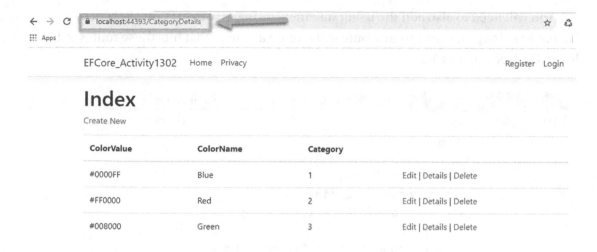

Figure 13-22.   *The Category Details are shown as expected*

You can try to create new or edit, but you will likely get an error since the user id is not mapped.

Another issue here is that this category detail is tightly coupled to a category in a one-to-one relationship, and you aren't allowed to also create a new category, so there is much work to be done.

Step 3: Delete the CategoryDetails and add Categories

Stop the program, and then you can optionally delete the CategoryDetails controller and the views that were generated (this code will never work exactly right in the scope of this book). For completeness, the code will remain in the final solution files, but note that the ability to create/edit/modify a category detail will not be working.

Repeat the preceding step to add a new Controller, but this time add the Category object. The name should stay as defaulted to CategoriesController.

When done, you should have a CategoriesController and views to map to all of the category controller's methods.

Although authorization is out of scope for this book, authentication is easy enough, and doing this will ensure that only logged in users can modify data (you will want to also learn about roles and use authorization to ensure only the right logged in users can modify data, not just any logged in user).

At the top of the CategoriesController, add the following attribute:

```
[Authorized]
```

You will need to also add the using statement using Microsoft.AspNetCore. Authorization;. Adding this attribute will require any user that hits these routes to be logged in (see Figure 13-23).

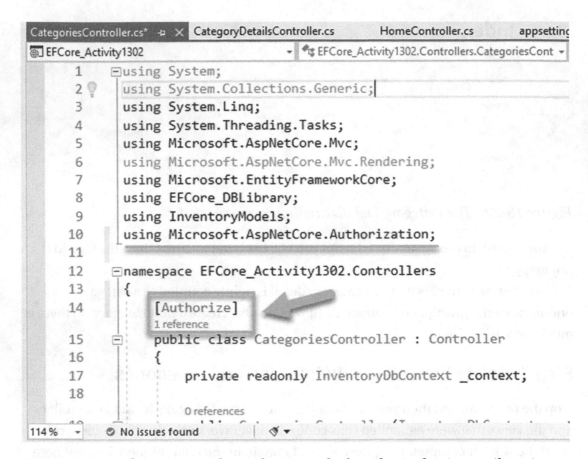

Figure 13-23. *The user must be authenticated when the Authorize attribute is added to a controller*

With an authorized user, it is easy to get the user id in a .Net web application.

Change the private variables and constructor for the CategoriesController to the following:

```
private readonly InventoryDbContext _context;
private readonly UserManager<IdentityUser> _userManager;
public CategoriesController(InventoryDbContext context,
UserManager<IdentityUser> userManager)
```

```
{
    _context = context;
    _userManager = userManager;
}
```

Add the using statement using Microsoft.AspNetCore.Identity; to the top of your class.

In the POST method for Create, add the following code:

```
if (ModelState.IsValid)
{
    var userId = _userManager.GetUserId(HttpContext.User);
    category.CreatedByUserId = userId;

    _context.Add(category);
```

Figure 13-24 shows this new code for clarity.

```
// POST: Categories/Create
// To protect from overposting attacks, enable the specific properties you want to bin
// For more details, see http://go.microsoft.com/fwlink/?LinkId=317598.
[HttpPost]
[ValidateAntiForgeryToken]
0 references
public async Task<IActionResult> Create([Bind("Name,Id,CreatedByUserId,CreatedDate,Las
{
    if (ModelState.IsValid)
    {
        var userId = _userManager.GetUserId(HttpContext.User);
        category.CreatedByUserId = userId;

        _context.Add(category);
        await _context.SaveChangesAsync();
        return RedirectToAction(nameof(Index));
    }
    return View(category);
}
```

Figure 13-24. *The code to get the user id is used in the POST method for creating a new category*

Run the application, and ensure you are logged out of any signed in user. Try to navigate to the /Categories page. You should be directed to log in, proving that you must be authorized. Figure 13-25 shows the expected page. Note also that the route in the URL has the redirect information back to the Categories page.

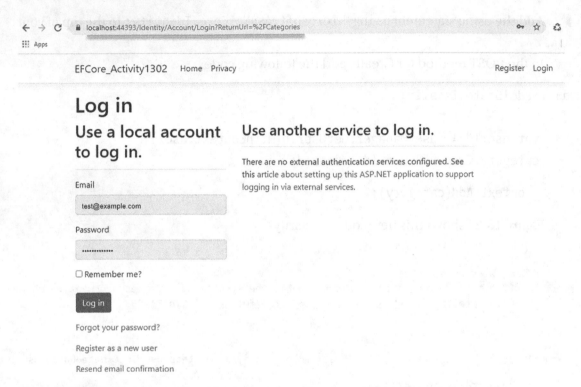

Figure 13-25. *An unauthenticated user cannot modify categories*

When you log in successfully, you will get redirected to the categories as shown in Figure 13-26.

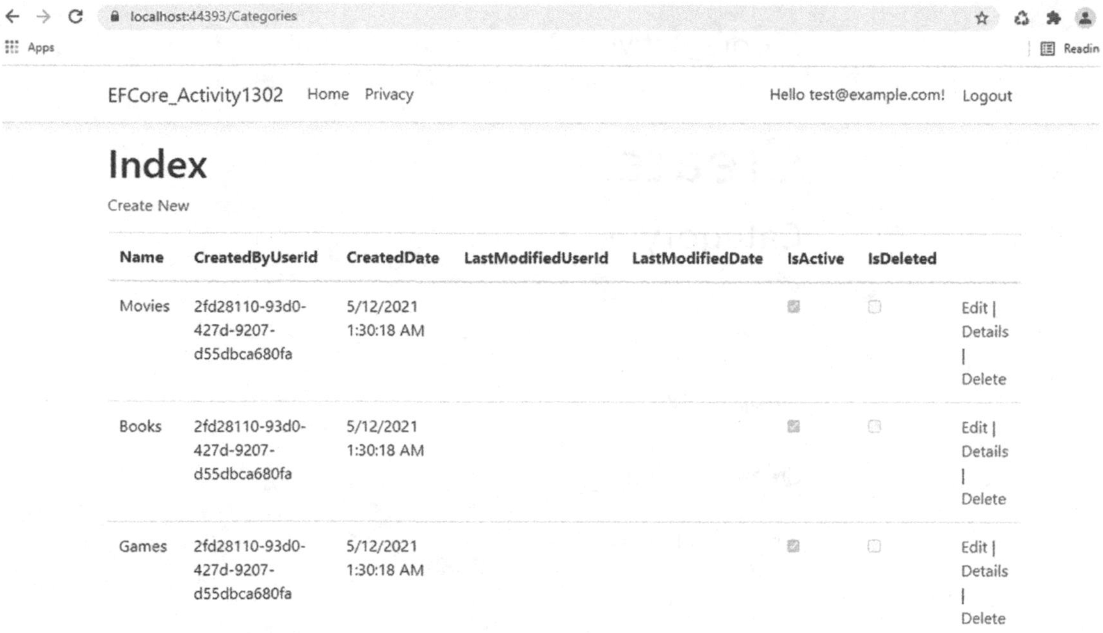

← → C   🔒 localhost:44393/Categories   ☆ △ ✦ ☺

▦ Apps | ▤ Readin

EFCore_Activity1302   Home   Privacy   Hello test@example.com!   Logout

Index

Create New

Name	CreatedByUserId	CreatedDate	LastModifiedUserId	LastModifiedDate	IsActive	IsDeleted	
Movies	2fd28110-93d0-427d-9207-d55dbca680fa	5/12/2021 1:30:18 AM			☑	☐	Edit | Details | Delete
Books	2fd28110-93d0-427d-9207-d55dbca680fa	5/12/2021 1:30:18 AM			☑	☐	Edit | Details | Delete
Games	2fd28110-93d0-427d-9207-d55dbca680fa	5/12/2021 1:30:18 AM			☑	☐	Edit | Details | Delete

Figure 13-26. *The categories index is shown as expected once you are logged in*

Add a new category such as `Appliances`. Because the model will first validate on the user id, add any string into the field. Figure 13-27 shows an attempt to create a new category.

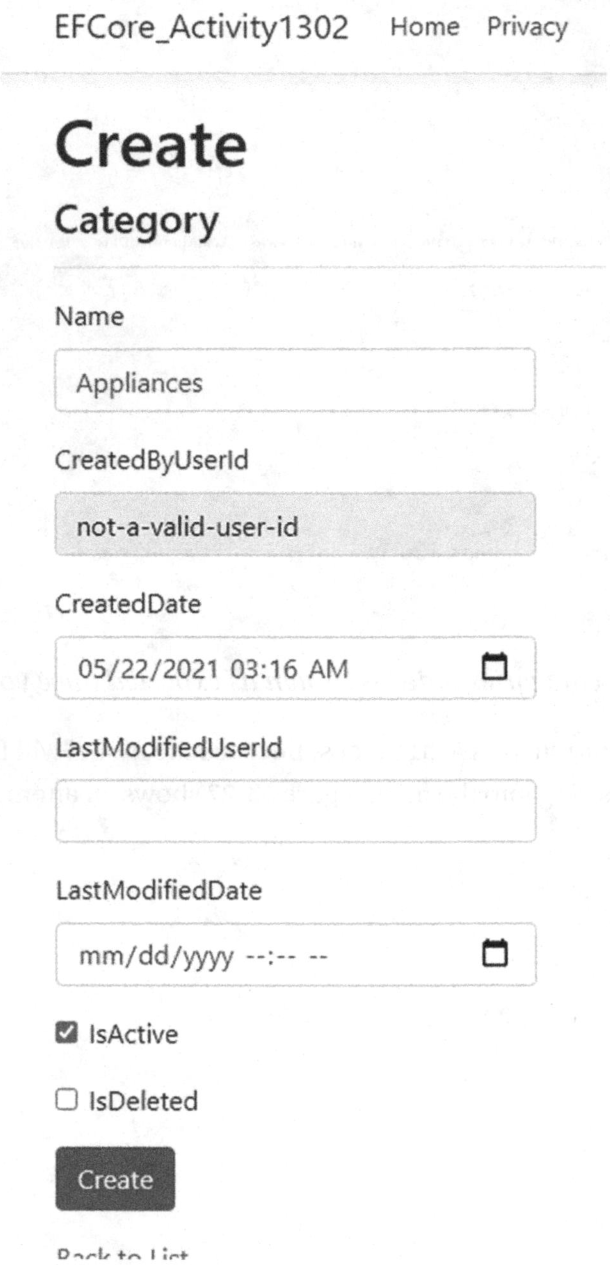

EFCore_Activity1302   Home   Privacy

Create

Category

Name

Appliances

CreatedByUserId

not-a-valid-user-id

CreatedDate

05/22/2021 03:16 AM

LastModifiedUserId

LastModifiedDate

mm/dd/yyyy --:-- --

☑ IsActive

☐ IsDeleted

Create

Back to List

Figure 13-27. *Adding a new Category works with the correct user authentication in place*

Make sure to create the category – you should be able to do this without error – and then your `UserId` should be stored in the database as the creator.

Review the `Categories` database table to see the new category (see Figure 13-28). Use the query from earlier to validate your user id in the corporate sign-on database, and then use the following query to validate your new Category:

```
SELECT * FROM Categories
```

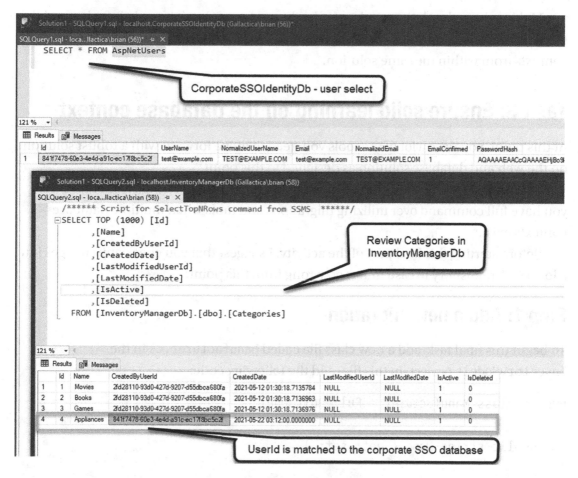

Figure 13-28. *The Category is in the database as expected*

As stated, this solution is nowhere near production ready. It is not wired up fully on anything other than `Categories` and does not have good authorization in place with roles. Additionally, all full models should be exchanged with view models that are the DTOs. All database calls should happen through the service layer, not directly against the context.

Making the web solution work completely and be production ready is far beyond the scope of this book, but you have now proven you can work against multiple database contexts from within the same solution.

Task 3: Ensure solid learning on the database context

At this point, you have a lot of the tools you need to move forward with a robust solution on the web and database solution as designed to this point.

For this last task, you are going to just make a quick model change and ensure that you have full command over utilizing migrations and tools when multiple database contexts exist.

Before starting this final part of the activity, I suggest that you check any changes into a local GIT repository in case things go wrong from this point.

Step 1: Add a new migration

To begin this final task, add a new class file called `Manufacturer.cs` in the `InventoryModels` project. In this file, add the following code:

```
public class Manufacturer : FullAuditModel
{
    public string Name { get; set; }
}
```

In order to create a migration that is not blank, you will also need to add the following to the `InventoryDbContext.cs` file in the `EFCore_DbLibrary` project:

```
public DbSet<Manufacturer> Manufacturers { get; set; }
```

With this in place, you are ready to add a new migration. Even though this is in the inventory database library, you are still working with multiple contexts. Therefore, go back into the PMC and ensure that you have the EFCore_DbLibrary project selected, and then run the following command:

```
add-migration add-manufacturer-entity -Context InventoryDbContext
```

You may see some warnings about a type being specified for decimal properties. For purposes of this activity, just ignore the warnings.

Note that the migration is generated where you would want it to be and you also get the migration code you would expect (review Figure 13-29).

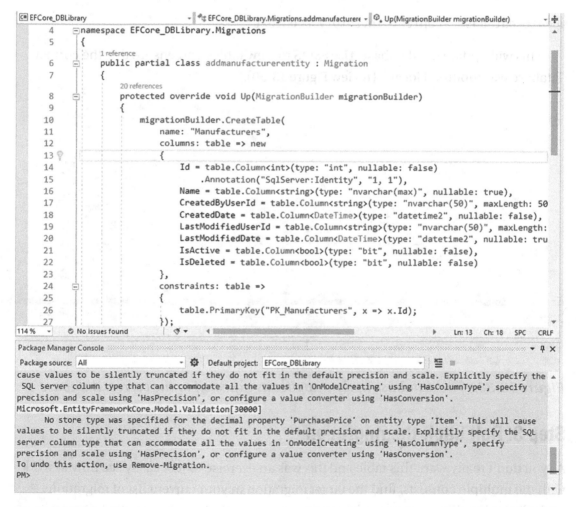

Figure 13-29. *The migration generates as expected*

You may see some warnings for the precision on decimal properties in the database. This is not ideal but will not cause any issues for our project. To make these errors go away, you could put an explicit column type with a defined precision using the FluentAPI in the OnModelCreating method.

Step 2: Update the database

With the migration in place from the previous exercise and the PMC still targeting the DbLibrary project, run the following command:

```
update-database -Context InventoryDbContext
```

This will update the database. Use SSMS to view tables and ensure that the correct database was modified locally (review Figure 13-30).

Figure 13-30.   *The database update applies as expected to the correct database*

Step 3: Roll back the migration

As you don't really want this table and this was an exercise to just easily see how to work with the multiple contexts, find the target migration in your current list of migrations as the last migration you want to keep prior to the one that was just applied. Once you have that specific migration, run a command similar to this, but make sure to replace the actual migration name with your exact migration name:

```
update-database -Context InventoryDbContext -Migration 20210515165148_
update-itemname-type-to-varchar.
```

Once the migration has been applied, ensure the table was dropped from your inventory database, and then go ahead and remove the model and reference in the InventoryDbContext so future migrations won't require this migration to take place (final files will just comment out this code).

Step 4: Remove the migration

With the migration rolled back, run the command to remove the migration as follows:

```
remove-migration -Context InventoryDbContext
```

This will remove the changes and the migration. Once again, you will want to ensure that you at minimum comment out or remove the addition of the type in the InventoryDbContext list of DbSets so that you don't have a lingering required migration in the future.

Activity 13-2 summary

In this activity, you learned how to work with multiple database contexts. You did this by generating a simulated corporate single sign-on database that used built-in ASP. Net identity management to manage users. You then brought your inventory database solution into the project in order to leverage the existing code you had already written and simulate one possible way to integrate multiple databases in the same project.

Through this activity, you also learned about the commands needed to successfully run and work with code-first migrations when using multiple databases.

Chapter summary

In this chapter, you learned how to create asynchronous database operations, and you learned how to work with multiple database contexts.

Important takeaways

After working through this chapter, the things you should be in command of are

- Async/await.

- Asynchronous database operations.

- Further understanding of the need for the client to decrypt data before filtering on encrypted columns.

- Using the `TransactionScopeAsyncFlowOption.Enabled` option to aid transactions in an asynchronous database call.

- Use the -Context flag in the PMC when dealing with multiple contexts.

- Contexts do not need to be in the same project to be utilized in a project.

Closing thoughts

As you've moved through this book, you have learned a great deal about how to work with entity framework, specifically with EFCore5.

You've learned the major moving pieces and have now also seen a couple of recipes for robust development.

In the next chapter, you will learn about some of the things that are new to working with EFCore as of the EFCore5 release (the final chapter will dive deeper into EFCore6).

PART IV

Recipes for Success

CHAPTER 14

.Net 5 and EFCore5

In this chapter, we're going to have a brief discussion about the November 2020 version of the .Net ecosystem: .Net 5. This book has used EFCore6 throughout the samples, but there are a few features that were released with EFCore5 that were not possible until it was released. As such, I wanted you to spend a little time just exploring a couple of the new things you can do as of the EFCore5 release.

One framework to rule them all, with more coming

One thing of note is that with the .Net 5 release that happened in November of 2020, there is no longer a .Net Framework by name, and there is no more .Net Core by name (with the exception of EFCore, due to the versioning confusion that would likely happen until we get to version 7 in 2022, at which time I expect EFCore will also just become EF7 – but I'm just speculating on that).

EF6, EFCore, and .Net 5/6/7/…

With the direction of .Net 5/6/7/… being the wave of the future, we need to know what that will do to our current legacy EF6 and EFCore applications. The good news for us is that, for the most part, we should be able to keep working with our solutions.

With .Net going forward, everything will be housed in the same place, and all of the moving pieces should work together from this point on, and even a legacy application written in the .Net Framework can be upgraded into the new .Net 5/6/7/… framework.

Additionally, EF6 still works in the .Net 5 Framework, as of the last release 6.4.4 (EF6 version 6.3 was actually ported to work in EFCore3, so this is not entirely new). Of course, EFCore works in the .Net 5/6/7/… framework, as even EFCore5 was working in .Net Core 3.1, and all of that was recombined into .Net 5. With the release road map of a yearly release, EFCore6 will likely be packaged with .Net 6 and will likely be limited to .Net 6 or greater solutions.

© Brian L. Gorman 2022
B. L. Gorman, *Practical Entity Framework Core 6*, https://doi.org/10.1007/978-1-4842-7301-2_14

As a .Net developer, therefore, you should be able to have a similar development experience from this point on, no matter which version of the framework you are using.

.Net 6/7 and EFCore6/7

Do not fear, almost everything that you have learned (if not everything) in this book will work in the latest flavor of .Net 6 and EFCore6 and will continue to work in .Net 7 and EFCore7 even after they are released in November 2022. However, the next chapter will deal with a forecast of expected changes for .Net 6 and EFCore6, so that you can be prepared for those changes when they happen. Currently, .Net 6 and EFCore6 are slated for official release in November of 2021, just a few weeks after this book is released.

Don't get too used to .Net 6 and EFCore6, however, because .Net 7 and EFCore7 (EF7?) are slated to be released in November of 2022. With this pace, the really good news, again, is that the concepts and tools you've learned in this book will continue to be the base you need to use the technology, regardless of the version, and you'll just want to make sure to keep up with any new features that are released as .Net 6 and 7 are released.

Changes with EFCore5

The rest of this chapter will take you through practical applications with brief descriptions of some of the critical changes that came along with EFCore5 in November of 2020. While a couple of new features were already used in the previous chapters, most were not.

For simplicity and consistency, the final version of the files from Chapter 13, Activity 1, will be used to examine some of the changes. The sample files will also apply each of these techniques in the order presented in this chapter. For example, code for the Split Queries example will contain the code generated for learning about many-to-many navigations, table-per-type inheritance, and filtered includes. Each activity will have its own starter files so you can always just grab the starter files for the activity if you don't want to do all of the activities.

This approach should allow you to have familiarity with the code and also allow you to be set up and ready to roll on any of the activities by simply using the appropriate starter files. If you do run activities out of order, consider just using a new database named in the connection string and running migrations to ensure you don't have any conflicts.

I did not come up with this list of features to learn on my own. Further information and the original documentation used to help define this list and features can be found here: `https://docs.microsoft.com/en-us/ef/core/what-is-new/ef-core-5.0/whatsnew`.

Activity 14-1: Many-to-many navigation properties

In the activities to this point previously in the text, you were able to create a couple of many-to-many relationships. To that end, the bulk of this activity will be revisiting those entities.

Task 0: Getting started

To get started, ensure you have a current version of the files, either the version at the end of Activity 13-1 or just use the starter files for this activity, `EFCore_Activity14-1_StarterFiles`. Either way, remember to review Appendix A for information about using starter files.

One thing that has changed in this code from Activity 13-1 is due to working through Activity 13-2. In that activity, you built a web page and added a new category – *Appliances*. If you did not do the activity, you will be just fine. If you did do the activity and you are using the same database as that activity, then running the code initially would create an error due to a null reference on details for that category (see Figure 14-1).

```
1 reference
private static async Task ListCategoriesAndColors()
{
    var results = await _categoriesService.ListCategoriesAndDetails();
    foreach (var c in results)
    {
        Console.WriteLine($"Category [{c.Category}] is {c.CategoryDetail.Color}");    ⊗
    }
    _categories = results;
}

1 reference
private static async Task CreateMultipleItems()
{
    Console.WriteLine("Would you like to create i
    bool batchCreate = Console.ReadLine().StartsW
    var allItems = new List<CreateOrUpdateItemDto

    bool createAnother = true;
    while (createAnother == true)
    {
        var newItem = new CreateOrUpdateItemDto():
```

Exception Thrown   ⇥ X

System.NullReferenceException: 'Object reference not set to an
instance of an object.'

InventoryModels.DTOs.CategoryDto.CategoryDetail.**get** returned null.

View Details | Copy Details | Start Live Share session...

▲ Exception Settings
  ☑ Break when this exception type is thrown
     Except when thrown from:
     ☐ EFCore_Activity1401.dll
  Open Exception Settings | Edit Conditions

Figure 14-1. *The additional category doesn't have any details, so the code as per Activity 13-1 encounters a null reference exception*

To fix this error, simply add a null-conditional operator to prevent failure on the CategoryDetail.Color as follows:

```
Console.WriteLine($"Category [{c.Category}] is {c.CategoryDetail?.Color ??
"Not associated to any detail/color"}");
```

Alternatively, you could just delete the *Appliances* category from the database, or you could both delete the category and add the code.

Once you have the fix in place, your code would work as expected. The starter files already contain this fix.

Task 1: Review the existing relationships

In this task, you'll just take a quick look at the existing many-to-many relationships in the solution. All code for this example is already completed as per Chapter 5, Activity 5-2, Task 3, Step 3 (Items and Players many-to-many relationship, along with Chapter 5, Activity 5-3, Task 2 (Items and Genres many-to-many relationship).

Step 1: Review the Item and Genre many-to-many relationship

The Item to Genre relationship was created in the traditional manner. Here, a new join entity called ItemGenre was created, and each entity – Item and Genre – referenced a list of the ItemGenre. By default, this created a many-to-many relationship, where an Item can be associated with many Genres and a Genre can be associated with many Items.

Figure 14-2 shows the two entities creating a relationship via the ItemGenre entity.

```
Item.cs  ⊣ ×
C# InventoryModels                                          ⚙ InventoryModels.Item                           ⚙ Name
     24              public decimal? PurchasePrice { get; set; }
     25              [Range(InventoryModelsConstants.MINIMUM_PRICE, InventoryModelsConstants.MAXIMUM_PRICE)]
                     11 references
     26              public decimal? CurrentOrFinalPrice { get; set; }
                     8 references
     27              public int? CategoryId { get; set; }
                     8 references | ❶ 0/1 passing
     28              public virtual Category Category { get; set; }
     29
                     14 references
     30              public virtual List<Player> Players { get; set; } = new List<Player>();
                     4 references
     31              public virtual List<ItemGenre> ItemGenres { get; set; } = new List<ItemGenre>();
     32          }
     33
     34      }
     35
114%  ▾      ⊘ No issues found      | ⌀ ▾                                                          Ln: 1   Ch: 1   SPC

Genre.cs  ⊣ ×
C# InventoryModels                                          ⚙ InventoryModels.Genre                          ⚙ Name
      7
      8      ⊟namespace InventoryModels
      9      {
                     8 references
     10      ⊟    public class Genre : FullAuditModel
     11          {
     12              [Required]
     13              [StringLength(InventoryModelsConstants.MAX_NAME_LENGTH)]
                     5 references
     14              public string Name { get; set; }
     15
                     0 references
     16              public virtual List<ItemGenre> GenreItems { get; set; } = new List<ItemGenre>();
     17          }
     18      }
     19
```

Figure 14-2. *The Item and Genre entities created a many-to-many relationship via the ItemGenre entity*

Having the ItemGenre entity also allows for additional fields that can be associated with the entity. Although none were added, should it be desired, it would be easy enough to accomplish in the join entity ItemGenre, highlighted in Figure 14-3.

```
namespace InventoryModels
{
    [Table("ItemGenres")]
    [Index(nameof(ItemId), nameof(GenreId), IsUnique = true)]
    5 references
    public class ItemGenre : IIdentityModel
    {
        21 references
        public int Id { get; set; }

        1 reference
        public virtual int ItemId { get; set; }
        0 references
        public virtual Item Item { get; set; }

        1 reference
        public virtual int GenreId { get; set; }
        0 references
        public virtual Genre Genre { get; set; }
    }

}
```

Figure 14-3. *The ItemGenre join entity is shown. It would be easy enough to add additional fields to this entity in the traditional manner*

This entity, of course, gets its own table in the database as shown in Figure 14-4. As a reminder, the data annotation [Table("ItemGenres")] was added to the class (see Figure 14-3) to ensure the name of the table was pluralized to ItemGenres.

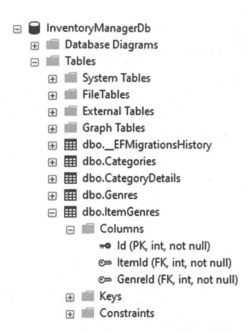

Figure 14-4. *The database contains a table ItemGenres that stores the relationships*

All of this was established in more detail in Chapter 5. The main takeaways here are the fact that you can still use the traditional approach to creating a many-to-many relationship (and you may have scenarios where you desire to do so). Taking this approach gives you full control over the join entity in a traditional code-first approach with data annotations. This approach is also accomplished without having to do anything via the Fluent API.

Step 2: Review the Item and Player many-to-many relationship

The Item to Player relationship was created with the new implicit mapping that can happen as of the release of EFCore5 (and by default in EFCore6). In this relationship, the Item and Player directly reference a list of the other entity. Rather than using a join entity such as ItemPlayer, this relationship was created directly by the associations in the individual entities (see Figure 14-5).

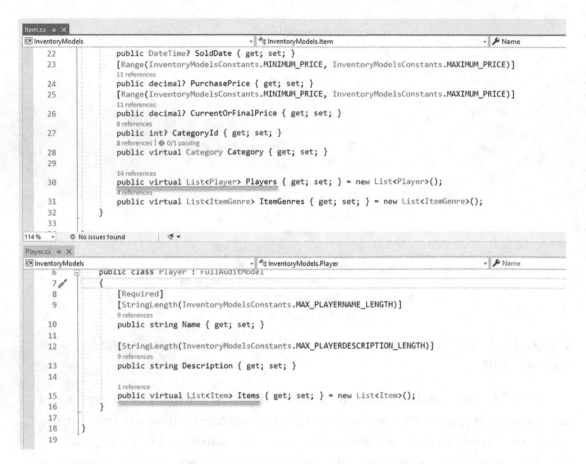

Figure 14-5. *The Item and Player many-to-many relationship is created by including a direct list of the other type in their entity definitions*

Even though there is not a direct join entity defined in the `InventoryModels` project, the table is still created (see Figure 14-6), and the many-to-many relationship is still possible. This was not possible in EFCore before EFCore5, as all join entities would have been required to be explicitly defined as in the `ItemGenre` relationship.

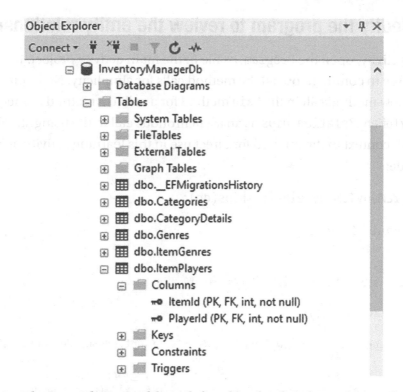

Figure 14-6. *The ItemPlayers table is defined in the database due to the direct mapping of each type to one another and the internal operations made possible in the release of EFCore5 (and therefore also possible in EFCore6)*

A couple of things to remember here as well. The names of these columns originally came in as ItemsId and PlayersId. Additionally, the table name was not pluralized. The techniques to make this happen are discussed as follows and were implemented in detail in Chapter 5.

As a final note, with the lack of a pre-defined entity, you generally don't reference the join entity in code at all, whereas you might actually reference a list of `ItemGenre` in code.

Task 2: Explore this implicit mapping

In this second task, you will take a deeper look at the entity mapping and how it works in EFCore with the many-to-many navigations with skip properties.

Step 1: Modify the program to review the entity relationships

To start this activity, open the `Program.cs` file in the main activity project. In the file, feel free to comment out all the method calls for simplicity. No matter what, add a new method call in the `Main` method for a call to a method named `ExploreManyToManyRelationships` as an asynchronous call in the using statement that passes the full context to the method for direct use in this learning activity using the following code:

```
await ExploreManyToManyRelationships(db);
```

Review Figure 14-7 for clarity.

```
0 references
public static async Task Main(string[] args)
{
    BuildOptions();
    BuildMapper();
    using (var db = new InventoryDbContext(_optionsBuilder.Options))
    {
        _itemsService = new ItemsService(db, _mapper);
        _categoriesService = new CategoriesService(db, _mapper);

        await ExploreManyToManyRelationships(db);
        /*
        await ListInventory();
        await GetItemsForListing();
        await GetAllActiveItemsAsPipeDelimite        Comment out the rest
        await GetItemsTotalValues();                 of the code, except
        await GetFullItemDetails();                  the "Program
                                                     Complete" statement
```

Figure 14-7. *The only call active in the Main method at this time is the call to a new method (yet to be implemented)*

Next, add the new method to the program as follows:

```
private static async Task ExploreManyToManyRelationships(InventoryDbContext db)
{
    var items = await db.Items.ToListAsync();
```

```
    foreach (var item in items)
    {
        Console.WriteLine($"New Item: {item.Name} found...");
        foreach (var itemGenre in item.ItemGenres)
        {
            Console.WriteLine($"Item {item.Name} has genre {itemGenre.
            Genre.Name}");
        }

        foreach (var player in item.Players)
        {
            Console.WriteLine($"Item {item.Name} has player {player.Name}");
        }
    }
}
```

Of course, this returns no genre or player information, even if you have some, due to the lack of include statements in the LINQ query.

Performing the join in the traditional way requires a statement that has multiple includes. Doing the join with the new way as of EFCore5 allows you to "skip" the include, and this is actually called a skipNavigation property.

Modify the code to get the items from the database to the following:

```
var items = await db.Items
                .Include(x => x.Players)
                .Include(x => x.ItemGenres).ThenInclude(x => x.Genre)
                .Where(x => !x.IsDeleted && x.IsActive)
                .ToListAsync();
```

Note that the Player associations are retrieved directly, but the Genre associations require the use of ThenInclude to get to them through the ItemGenre associations. Also note a clause is added to prevent pulling items that are deleted or are set to inactive.

Note that if you don't see associations for Genres or Players on this run, you likely don't have associations defined. Ensure that you have Players and Genres in your database and that you have the links set in the join tables as expected. Running the InventoryDataMigrator project will take care of the player associations.

For example, I didn't have any genres associated, so I needed to add some. If you need to add some, use the following additional code and methodology. First, add a new method call before you call to the ExploreManyToManyRelationships in the Main method:

```
await EnsureItemsHaveGenres(db);
```

Next, add the new method in the Program class as follows, and make sure to set the min and max ids to map to your genre ids (mine are 1–5):

```
private static async Task EnsureItemsHaveGenres(InventoryDbContext db)
{
    var items = await db.Items
                        .Include(x => x.ItemGenres).ThenInclude(x => x.Genre)
                        .Where(x => !x.IsDeleted && x.IsActive)
                        .ToListAsync();
    var genres = await db.Genres
                        .Where(x => x.IsActive && !x.IsDeleted)
                        .ToListAsync();

    foreach (var item in items)
    {
        await AssociateItemsAndGenres(genres, item);
    }
    await db.SaveChangesAsync();
}
```

This will also use the following helper method to associate, which you need to add as well:

```
private static async Task AssociateItemsAndGenres(List<Genre> genres, Item item)
{
    if (item.ItemGenres.Count > 0) return;

    int minId = 1;
    int maxId = 5;
    int maxGCount = 3;
```

```
Random r = new Random();
var gCount = r.Next(1, maxGCount);
var used = string.Empty;
for (int i = 0; i < gCount; i++)
{
    var ig = new ItemGenre();
    var next = r.Next(minId, maxId);
    while (used.Split("|").ToList().Contains(next.ToString()))
    {
        next = r.Next(minId, maxId);
    }
    used = string.Join(used, $"{next}|");
    ig.GenreId = next;
    ig.ItemId = item.Id;
    item.ItemGenres.Add(ig);
}
}
```

In the end, now you should see output similar to what is shown in Figure 14-8 (note that I've only made the call to the new method and cleaned up any data that existed from testing in previous runs, and due to the random nature, it is highly unlikely your output would be identical to this).

```
Microsoft Visual Studio Debug Console
New Item: Batman Begins found...
Item Batman Begins has genre Fantasy
Item Batman Begins has genre Sci/Fi
Item Batman Begins has player Christian Bale
New Item: World of Tanks found...
Item World of Tanks has genre Horror
Item World of Tanks has player Wargaming
New Item: The Sword of Shannara found...
Item The Sword of Shannara has genre Fantasy
Item The Sword of Shannara has genre Sci/Fi
Item The Sword of Shannara has player Terry Brooks
New Item: Practical Entity Framework found...
Item Practical Entity Framework has genre Sci/Fi
Item Practical Entity Framework has genre Fantasy
Item Practical Entity Framework has player Brian L. Gorman
New Item: Battlefield 2142 found...
Item Battlefield 2142 has genre Fantasy
Item Battlefield 2142 has genre Comedy
Item Battlefield 2142 has player Electronic Arts
New Item: Star Wars: The Empire Strikes Back found...
Item Star Wars: The Empire Strikes Back has genre Sci/Fi
Item Star Wars: The Empire Strikes Back has player Mark Hamill
New Item: Top Gun found...
Item Top Gun has genre Fantasy
Item Top Gun has genre Horror
Item Top Gun has player Tom Cruise
New Item: Remember the Titans found...
Item Remember the Titans has genre Horror
Item Remember the Titans has genre Fantasy
Item Remember the Titans has player Denzel Washington
New Item: Inception found...
Item Inception has genre Sci/Fi
Item Inception has genre Fantasy
Item Inception has player Leonardo DiCaprio
Program Complete

C:\APressEntityFramework\Code\EFCore_Activity1401\EFCore_Activity1401
15184) exited with code 0.
To automatically close the console when debugging stops, enable Tools
le when debugging stops.
Press any key to close this window . . .
```

Figure 14-8. *The output shows that the many-to-many relationships are working as expected and highlights the differences in the traditional vs. the EFCore5 skip navigations*

Open the BuildItems class file in the InventoryDataMigrator project. In that file, review the BuildItems method and note how the Players are directly associated with an Item.

By understanding the differences between a traditional many-to-many mapping and the new many-to-many navigation properties (skip navigations), you are now fully aware and able to work with each type.

Step 2: Review the model builder as it was used to modify the ItemPlayers table

In this step, you will review the use of the model builder to modify the ItemPlayers table. As noted earlier, with a pre-defined entity, the ItemGenre entity can be easily modified by adding new fields to the entity. However, this doesn't help if you need to do this in the ItemPlayers, and you likely don't want to go and create a new ItemPlayers entity unless you need to explicitly work with that entity.

As also noted earlier and in Chapter 5, the ItemPlayers had an undesirable syntax of ItemsId and PlayersId for the columns in the table. This is not the end of the world but would likely be a pain for your team that is querying the database, and all queries would have to make that subtle correction.

Even with the automatic skip navigations, you can explicitly define the columns using the model builder.

In the InventoryDbContext file from the InventoryDbLibrary project, in the OnModelCreating method, in Chapter 5, you added the following code:

```
modelBuilder.Entity<Item>()
        .HasMany(x => x.Players)
        .WithMany(p => p.Items)
        .UsingEntity<Dictionary<string, object>>(
            "ItemPlayers",
            ip => ip.HasOne<Player>()
                    .WithMany()
                    .HasForeignKey("PlayerId")
                    .HasConstraintName("FK_ItemPlayer_Players_PlayerId")
                    .OnDelete(DeleteBehavior.Cascade),
```

```
        ip => ip.HasOne<Item>()
                .WithMany()
                .HasForeignKey("ItemId")
                .HasConstraintName("FK_PlayerItem_Items_ItemId")
                .OnDelete(DeleteBehavior.ClientCascade)
    );
```

By adding this code, you resolved any issues with the name of the table and the fields. After adding that code, you created and ran a migration to make the appropriate updates to the database.

Activity 14-1 summary

In this activity, you took a second look at the many-to-many relationships in the Inventory system you've been building throughout the text. In this activity, you saw how the traditional relationships are modeled, which is good to know as you likely will need to support the previous relationships that are explicitly defined. Additionally, you saw how the skip navigations are used to allow you to just define the left and right sides of the relationship and not have to explicitly define the join table as an entity or in the include statement.

Finally, you finished the activity by taking a deeper look into the `OnModelCreating` method and reviewing how you can explicitly define the skip table relationships using the Fluent API.

Activity 14-2: Filtered include

This activity may be short, but this feature is one of my favorite new features that was introduced in EFCore5. In the past, whenever you used an include, you had to pull in all of the subset items, even if you didn't want all of them. When you got the results back, then you had to filter the objects to meet the needs of your system.

As of EFCore5, you can now filter on the include statements, performing the filtering at the time of the query rather than after.

There is a scenario that causes issues in these queries, however, which I ran into while building the example for this activity. As such, you'll also go down that road, so you can see the issue and be aware of it in case you encounter a similar issue in the future.

Task 0: Getting started

In order to complete this activity, you need a version of the files as per the end of Activity 14-1 or your own files that you were working on through the book. If you want a fresh start, use the EFCore_Activity14-2_StarterFiles. As always, review Appendix A for more information on using starter files.

Task 1: Create the method and set up the filtered include query

In this first task, you will create the code necessary to run the query and execute the filtered query. You will then look at the underlying T-SQL to see that the query is working as expected, even when you don't get the expected results. You will also write an alternate query that lets you see a different approach to get the data.

Step 1: Create the new method

In the Program.cs file in the Main method, replace the code that makes the two calls from Activity 14-1 with the following code:

```
await EnsureItemsHaveGenres(db);

//Activity 14-1 - ManyToMany Navigation Properties
//await ExploreManyToManyRelationships(db);

//Activity 14-2 - Filtered Includes
await QueryWithFilteredIncludes(db);
```

With the method call in place, create the new method in the Program class as follows:

```
private static async Task QueryWithFilteredIncludes(InventoryDbContext db)
{
    var nonFilteredItems = await db.Items.Include(x => x.Players).
    ToListAsync();
    var allPlayers = new List<Player>();
```

```
    foreach (var item in nonFilteredItems)
    {
        //Console.WriteLine($"Item: {item.Name}");
        foreach (var player in item.Players)
        {
            //Console.WriteLine($"Player: {player.Name}");
            allPlayers.Add(player);
        }
    }
    Console.WriteLine("Non-Filtered Items:");
    allPlayers.ForEach(x => Console.WriteLine($"{x.Name}"));
    Console.WriteLine(new string('*', 80));
    Console.WriteLine(new string('*', 80));

    //using filtered include
    var filteredItems = await db.Items
                        .Include(item => item.Players
                                    .Where(player => player.Name.
                                    Contains("ar")))
                        .ToListAsync();

    var filteredPlayers = new List<Player>();
    foreach (var fi in filteredItems)
    {
        //Console.WriteLine($"Item: {fi.Name}");
        foreach (var player in fi.Players)
        {
            //Console.WriteLine($"Player: {player.Name}");
            filteredPlayers.Add(player);
        }
    }

    Console.WriteLine("Filtered Players");
    filteredPlayers.ForEach(x => Console.WriteLine($"{x.Name}"));
}
```

Run the method to see what happens. You will likely see results similar to Figure 14-9.

```
Microsoft Visual Studio Debug Console
Non-Filtered Items:
Christian Bale
Wargaming
Terry Brooks
Brian L. Gorman
Electronic Arts
Mark Hamill
Tom Cruise
Denzel Washington
Leonardo DiCaprio
*********************************************************************************
*********************************************************************************
Filtered Players
Christian Bale
Wargaming
Terry Brooks
Brian L. Gorman
Electronic Arts
Mark Hamill
Tom Cruise
Denzel Washington
Leonardo DiCaprio
Program Complete
```

Figure 14-9. *The filtered include is set, but it's not working as shown here, with all player names being listed*

This error is very elusive, and it can take some time to figure this out if you don't know what to look for.

Step 2: Determine the T-SQL is working

The T-SQL is actually working as generated by EFCore5. This is even more perplexing. How is it possible that the T-SQL could return null but the data would still show?

To prove this out, open SSMS, connect to your local db, and then start a SQL Server Profiler session. Add a breakpoint on the code that uses the filtered include. This is the line that follows the comment `//using filtered include`.

Run the program again, and when you hit the breakpoint, clear the profiler and then execute the line of code and get the result of the T-SQL that was sent.

Once the query executes, select it and copy it to your clipboard to paste into a new query in SSMS (see Figure 14-10).

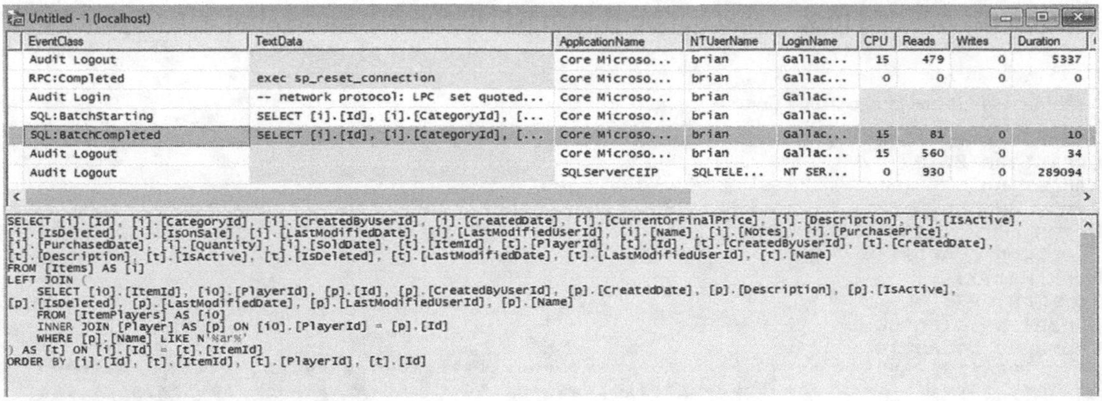

Figure 14-10. *The query is captured as executed in the SQL Server Profiler*

For clarity, the T-SQL code generated should be similar to this:

```
SELECT [i].[Id], [i].[CategoryId], [i].[CreatedByUserId], [i].
[CreatedDate], [i].[CurrentOrFinalPrice], [i].[Description], [i].
[IsActive], [i].[IsDeleted], [i].[IsOnSale], [i].[LastModifiedDate], [i].
[LastModifiedUserId], [i].[Name], [i].[Notes], [i].[PurchasePrice], [i].
[PurchasedDate], [i].[Quantity], [i].[SoldDate], [t].[ItemId], [t].
[PlayerId], [t].[Id], [t].[CreatedByUserId], [t].[CreatedDate], [t].
[Description], [t].[IsActive], [t].[IsDeleted], [t].[LastModifiedDate],
[t].[LastModifiedUserId], [t].[Name]
FROM [Items] AS [i]
LEFT JOIN (
    SELECT [iO].[ItemId], [iO].[PlayerId], [p].[Id], [p].[CreatedByUserId],
    [p].[CreatedDate], [p].[Description], [p].[IsActive], [p].[IsDeleted],
    [p].[LastModifiedDate], [p].[LastModifiedUserId], [p].[Name]
    FROM [ItemPlayers] AS [iO]
    INNER JOIN [Player] AS [p] ON [iO].[PlayerId] = [p].[Id]
    WHERE [p].[Name] LIKE N'%ar%'
) AS [t] ON [i].[Id] = [t].[ItemId]
ORDER BY [i].[Id], [t].[ItemId], [t].[PlayerId], [t].[Id]
```

With the query captured, run it against your local database to ensure that you have the correct data being generated by the query (review Figure 14-11).

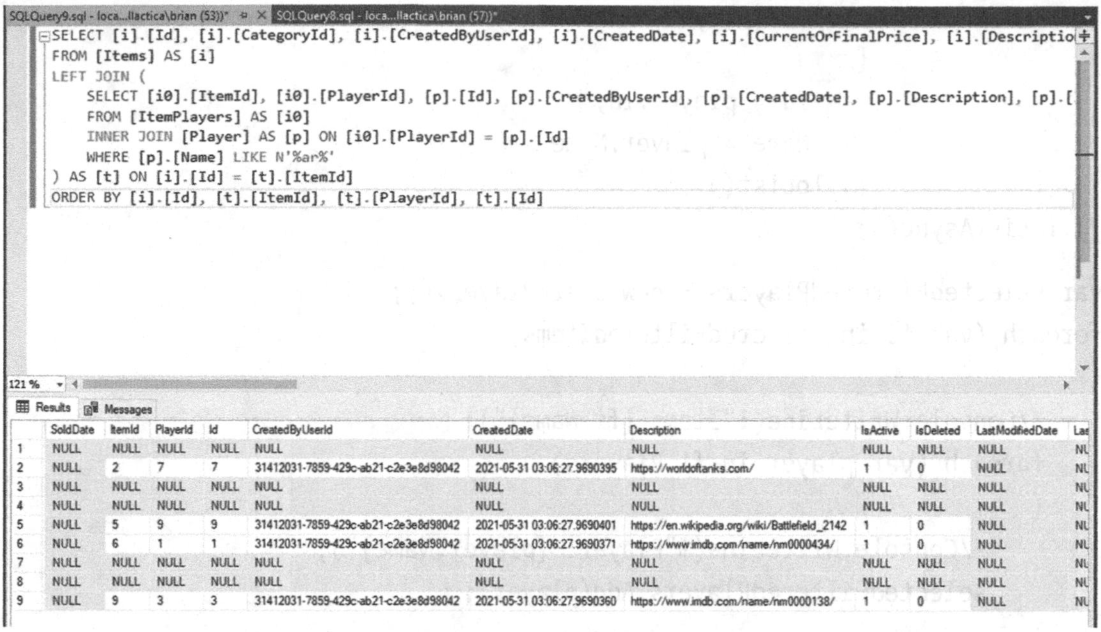

Figure 14-11. *The query as executed shows the correct data is being queried and the item players are only populated when the filter is matched*

Step 3: Write an alternate query using projections

As a bit of an aside, there is another way to get this data and to ensure that you get only what you want. An efficient and easy way to get the data is to just use a projection.

In the QueryWithFilterIncludes method, after the output of the filteredPlayers, add the following code:

```
Console.WriteLine(new string('*', 80));
Console.WriteLine(new string('*', 80));

//using projections
var selectedFilteredItems = await db.Items.AsNoTracking().Select(item =>
new
{
    Id = item.Id,
    Name = item.Name,
    Players = item.Players.Where(player => player.Name.Contains("ar"))
```

```
                .Select(player => new Player
                {
                    Id = player.Id,
                    Name = player.Name
                }).ToList()
}).ToListAsync();

var selectedFilteredPlayers = new List<Player>();
foreach (var fi in selectedFilteredItems)
{
    //Console.WriteLine($"Item: {fi.Name}");
    foreach (var player in fi.Players)
    {
        //Console.WriteLine($"Player: {player.Name}");
        selectedFilteredPlayers.Add(player);
    }
}

Console.WriteLine("Selected [Projected] Filtered Items");
selectedFilteredPlayers.ForEach(x => Console.WriteLine($"{x.Name}"));
```

With this new code in place, run the program. Additionally, you may wish to capture the T-SQL that is generated by the projection to see how it compares to what EF has generated. Your output should look like what is shown in Figure 14-12.

```
Non-Filtered Items:
Christian Bale
Wargaming
Terry Brooks
Brian L. Gorman
Electronic Arts
Mark Hamill
Tom Cruise
Denzel Washington
Leonardo DiCaprio
****************************************************************************
****************************************************************************
Filtered Players
Christian Bale
Wargaming
Terry Brooks
Brian L. Gorman
Electronic Arts
Mark Hamill
Tom Cruise
Denzel Washington
Leonardo DiCaprio
****************************************************************************
****************************************************************************
Selected [Projected] Filtered Items
Wargaming
Electronic Arts
Mark Hamill
Leonardo DiCaprio
Program Complete
```

Figure 14-12. *The output is filtered in the projection version as expected*

As you can see, the projection works very well (and may even prove to be more efficient than the filtered include, as well as more complicated to write, utilize, and understand).

Furthermore, the T-SQL generated by the projection is a bit more straightforward and should be similar to the following:

```
SELECT [i].[Id], [i].[Name], [t].[Id], [t].[Name], [t].[ItemId], [t].
[PlayerId]
FROM [Items] AS [i]
LEFT JOIN (
    SELECT [p].[Id], [p].[Name], [io].[ItemId], [io].[PlayerId]
    FROM [ItemPlayers] AS [io]
    INNER JOIN [Player] AS [p] ON [io].[PlayerId] = [p].[Id]
    WHERE [p].[Name] LIKE N'%ar%'
) AS [t] ON [i].[Id] = [t].[ItemId]
ORDER BY [i].[Id], [t].[ItemId], [t].[PlayerId], [t].[Id]
```

Furthermore, running the code produces a more concise data result (see Figure 14-13).

```
SELECT [i].[Id], [i].[Name], [t].[Id], [t].[Name], [t].[ItemId], [t].[PlayerId]
FROM [Items] AS [i]
LEFT JOIN (
    SELECT [p].[Id], [p].[Name], [i0].[ItemId], [i0].[PlayerId]
    FROM [ItemPlayers] AS [i0]
    INNER JOIN [Player] AS [p] ON [i0].[PlayerId] = [p].[Id]
    WHERE [p].[Name] LIKE N'%ar%'
) AS [t] ON [i].[Id] = [t].[ItemId]
ORDER BY [i].[Id], [t].[ItemId], [t].[PlayerId], [t].[Id]
```

121 %

Results   Messages

	Id	Name	Id	Name	ItemId	PlayerId
1	1	Batman Begins	NULL	NULL	NULL	NULL
2	2	World of Tanks	7	Wargaming	2	7
3	3	The Sword of Shannara	NULL	NULL	NULL	NULL
4	4	Practical Entity Framework	NULL	NULL	NULL	NULL
5	5	Battlefield 2142	9	Electronic Arts	5	9
6	6	Star Wars: The Empire Strikes Back	1	Mark Hamill	6	1
7	7	Top Gun	NULL	NULL	NULL	NULL
8	8	Remember the Titans	NULL	NULL	NULL	NULL
9	9	Inception	3	Leonardo DiCaprio	9	3

Figure 14-13. *The query and result for the version using the projection are shown. This is a bit more concise than the T-SQL from the filtered include. This code also works as expected without any further code modifications*

Task 2: Fix the original query

In this task, you will further examine the issue with the filtered include and will fix the filtered include so that it will work as expected.

Step 1: Examine the issue

As you start working through the issue with the filtered include, you might try a number of things. You might try updating the version of EFCore to the latest to see if that was an issue. You also have already gone through the examination of the actual queries being produced. Clearly, this is an elusive issue.

Further analysis proves that somehow the filtered query is essentially ignored in this code. This should trigger the thought that the client must have all the data and the filter is just not being used at all in this case.

Taking the time to look closely into the documentation reveals that there is a specific caution statement that deals with this exact issue.

The caution statement found at `https://docs.microsoft.com/en-us/ef/core/querying/related-data/eager#filtered-include`, says:

In case of tracking queries, results of filtered include may be unexpected due to *navigation fixup.* All relevant entities that have been queried for previously and have been stored in the change tracker will be present in the results of filtered include query, even if they don't meet the requirements of the filter. Consider using NoTracking queries or recreate the DbContext when using filtered Include in those situations.

Step 2: Use AsNoTracking in your queries

As stated in the caution from the official documentation, the issue is that the data is in fact stored once you have it within the change tracker. As the sample is first pulling all the data, it's no wonder that the filtered include didn't work.

To make the code work, add the simple code statement `.AsNoTracking` by updating the code in the first two queries.

Change the code `var nonFilteredItems = await db.Items.Include(x => x.Players).ToListAsync();` to

```
var nonFilteredItems = await db.Items.AsNoTracking().Include(x =>
x.Players).ToListAsync();
```

Then change the code

```
//using filtered include
var filteredItems = await db.Items
                .Include(item => item.Players
                            .Where(player => player.Name.Contains("ar")))
                .ToListAsync();
```

to

```
//using filtered include
var filteredItems = await db.Items.AsNoTracking()
                .Include(item => item.Players
                        .Where(player => player.Name.
                            Contains("ar")))
                .ToListAsync();
```

With this code in place, run the solution. You should now see the correct results for both the filtered include and the projection as expected (see Figure 14-14).

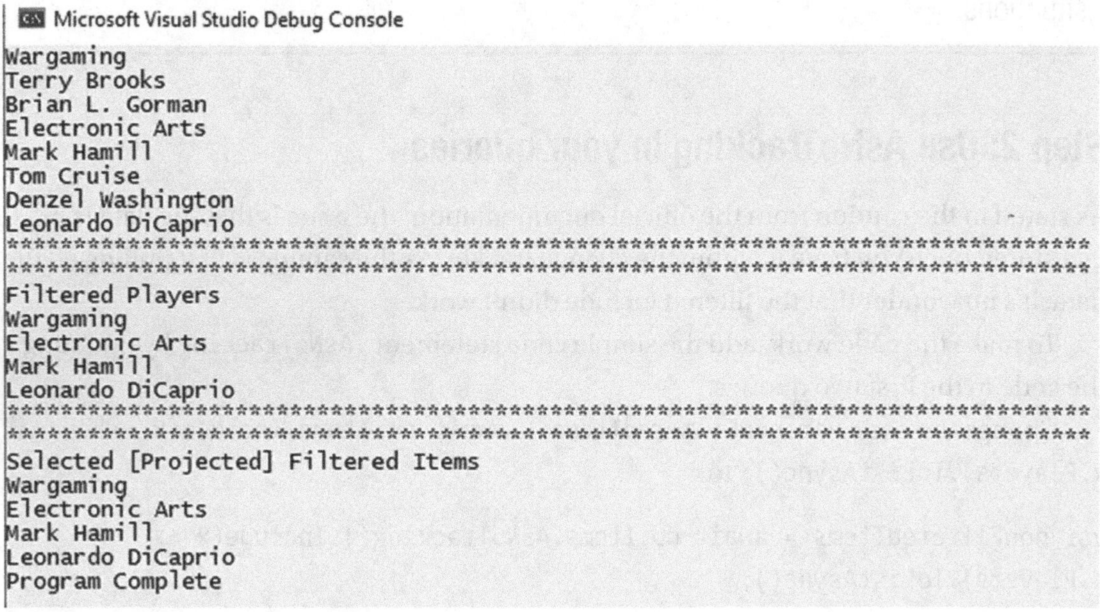

Figure 14-14. *The filtered include works as expected once changes are no longer tracked*

If you want, compare their execution time and reads to see the difference in efficiency (see Figure 14-15).

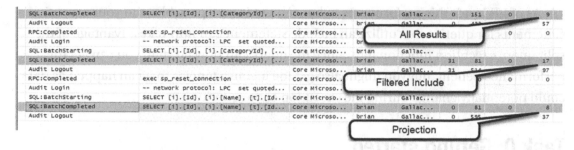

Figure 14-15. *The three queries' performance is shown in SQL Server Profiler*

One thing to note here is that even with the filtered include, the projection is still more performant – at least for this query.

Activity 14-2 summary

In this activity, you learned about using the *filtered include* statement to limit the results for your data selection based on a filter used during the include operation.

In the activity, you also had the opportunity to see how important it is to apply the AsNoTracking call to the queries in order to allow the filtered include to work.

As further practice and understanding, you also wrote another projection query to get the same results that you get from the filtered include. This allowed you to be able to optionally profile the performance for each of the three queries.

Activity 14-3: Split queries

As your database is leveraged in a system with a number of queries and users, there are times when you might have data getting modified quite regularly. As such, there are times when you want to use transactions to make sure that data doesn't get modified out of order or the data doesn't get changed during your operations by other parts of the system.

In the previous version of EFCore, all queries generated were executed as a single statement. The main purpose of this execution pattern was to ensure that consistency occurred for the entire lifecycle of the query. The problem with using only one statement during execution is that whenever a query contains an include statement, this single-query execution doesn't perform as well as the execution might have performed had the query been split into multiple queries for execution.

As of EFCore5, this performance enhancement is now possible, and your execution statements for queries that utilize an include statement can now take advantage of the split query execution functionality. Since the query can now be split, you can get the performance benefit, but you might also get the inconsistencies that can happen as data could potentially change during the execution of the queries.

Task 0: Getting started

As with previous activities, you can keep using the code from the previous activities if you are up to date, or you can just get a fresh start with the EFCore_Activity14-3_ StarterFiles. As always, follow the instructions as laid out in Appendix A for working with the starter files if you go that route.

Task 1: Create the query

In this first task, you will build a query that leverages an include statement and review the execution using the SQL Query Profiler.

Step 1: Create the query

Most of the queries you've already written have an include. You could use any of them. For purposes of demonstration, you'll create a new one for this activity.

Begin by commenting out the Activity 14-2 code await QueryWithFilteredIncludes(db) in the Main method of the Program class, and then add the code as follows for Activity 14-3 in the Main method:

```
//Activity 14-3 - Split Queries
await DemonstrateSplitQueries(db);
```

To create the new method, add the following code:

```
private static async Task DemonstrateSplitQueries(InventoryDbContext db)
{
    var fullItemDetails = await db.Items
                        .Include(x => x.Players)
                        .Include(x => x.ItemGenres).ThenInclude
                        (y => y.Genre)
```

```
                    .Include(x => x.Category)
                    .Where(x => x.IsActive && !x.IsDeleted)
                    .AsNoTracking().ToListAsync();
    var outputItems = _mapper.Map<List<ItemDto>>(fullItemDetails);
    foreach (var item in outputItems)
    {
        Console.WriteLine($"New Item: {item}");
    }
}
```

This output will not show the genre information or the player information, so if you want to add that in, feel free to make adjustments or use the FullItemDto (you'd have to add a mapping to do that). The important thing here is the creation of the query with the joins.

Run the program to see the results and ensure the query works and is called as expected (review Figure 14-16).

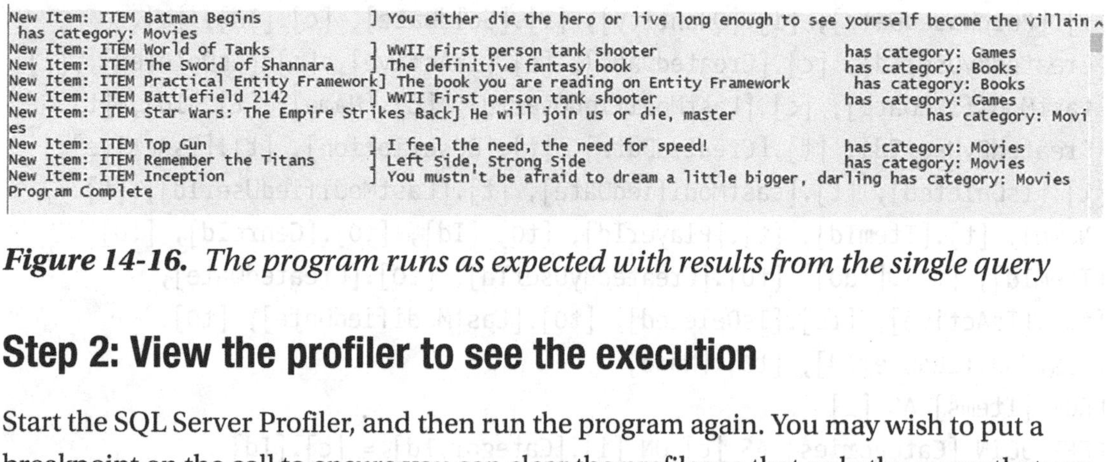

Figure 14-16. *The program runs as expected with results from the single query*

Step 2: View the profiler to see the execution

Start the SQL Server Profiler, and then run the program again. You may wish to put a breakpoint on the call to ensure you can clear the profiler so that only the query that you are focused on is run in the analyzer.

Running the program should be similar to the output shown in Figure 14-17.

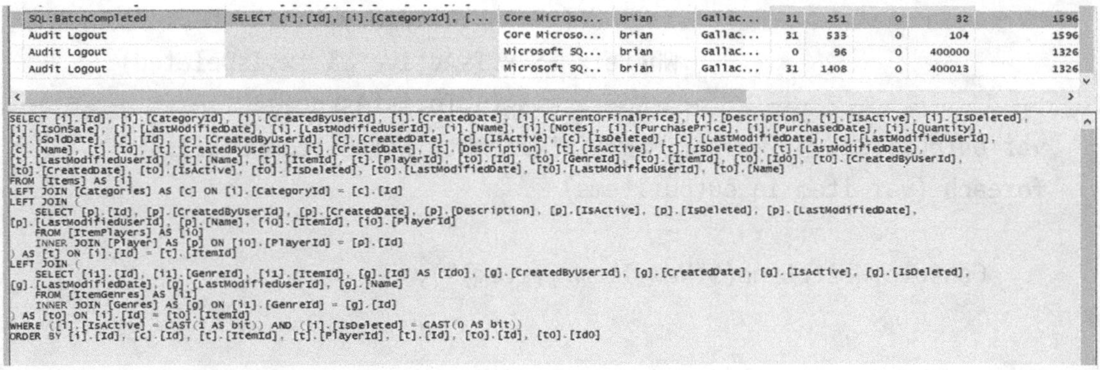

Figure 14-17. *The query is executed and revealed in the SQL Server Profiler*

Reviewing the query reveals the following query was executed:

```
SELECT [i].[Id], [i].[CategoryId], [i].[CreatedByUserId], [i].
[CreatedDate], [i].[CurrentOrFinalPrice], [i].[Description], [i].
[IsActive], [i].[IsDeleted], [i].[IsOnSale], [i].[LastModifiedDate],
[i].[LastModifiedUserId], [i].[Name], [i].[Notes], [i].[PurchasePrice],
[i].[PurchasedDate], [i].[Quantity], [i].[SoldDate], [c].[Id], [c].
[CreatedByUserId], [c].[CreatedDate], [c].[IsActive], [c].[IsDeleted], [c].
[LastModifiedDate], [c].[LastModifiedUserId], [c].[Name], [t].[Id], [t].
[CreatedByUserId], [t].[CreatedDate], [t].[Description], [t].[IsActive],
[t].[IsDeleted], [t].[LastModifiedDate], [t].[LastModifiedUserId], [t].
[Name], [t].[ItemId], [t].[PlayerId], [t0].[Id], [t0].[GenreId], [t0].
[ItemId], [t0].[Id0], [t0].[CreatedByUserId], [t0].[CreatedDate],
[t0].[IsActive], [t0].[IsDeleted], [t0].[LastModifiedDate], [t0].
[LastModifiedUserId], [t0].[Name]
FROM [Items] AS [i]
LEFT JOIN [Categories] AS [c] ON [i].[CategoryId] = [c].[Id]
LEFT JOIN (
    SELECT [p].[Id], [p].[CreatedByUserId], [p].[CreatedDate], [p].
    [Description], [p].[IsActive], [p].[IsDeleted], [p].[LastModifiedDate],
    [p].[LastModifiedUserId], [p].[Name], [i0].[ItemId], [i0].[PlayerId]
    FROM [ItemPlayers] AS [i0]
    INNER JOIN [Player] AS [p] ON [i0].[PlayerId] = [p].[Id]
) AS [t] ON [i].[Id] = [t].[ItemId]
```

```
LEFT JOIN (
    SELECT [i1].[Id], [i1].[GenreId], [i1].[ItemId], [g].[Id] AS [Id0],
    [g].[CreatedByUserId], [g].[CreatedDate], [g].[IsActive], [g].
    [IsDeleted], [g].[LastModifiedDate], [g].[LastModifiedUserId],
    [g].[Name]
    FROM [ItemGenres] AS [i1]
    INNER JOIN [Genres] AS [g] ON [i1].[GenreId] = [g].[Id]
) AS [t0] ON [i].[Id] = [t0].[ItemId]
WHERE ([i].[IsActive] = CAST(1 AS bit)) AND ([i].[IsDeleted] = CAST(0 AS bit))
ORDER BY [i].[Id], [c].[Id], [t].[ItemId], [t].[PlayerId], [t].[Id], [t0].
[Id], [t0].[Id0]
```

As you can see, that's quite an intense query. You could make the query more specific by using projections so that you wouldn't be selecting every field, but no matter how you execute it, this query runs in one statement.

Task 2: Use the new split query functionality

In this task, you will modify the query to use the split query functionality and review the output, as well as the execution via the SQL Server Profiler.

Step 1: Add AsSplitQuery to the query

Modify the query that you created in the previous task by adding the simple call to AsSplitQuery in the query syntax:

```
var fullItemDetails = await db.Items
                    .Include(x => x.Players)
                    .Include(x => x.ItemGenres).ThenInclude(y =>
                    y.Genre)
                    .Include(x => x.Category)
                    .Where(x => x.IsActive && !x.IsDeleted)
                    .AsSplitQuery()
                    .AsNoTracking().ToListAsync();
```

Run the query to validate you still get the same results. Review the output and also review the SQL Server Profiler to see how the query now splits into multiple queries (see Figure 14-18).

SQL:BatchStarting	SELECT [i].[Id], [i].[CategoryId], [i].[Cr...	Core Microso...	brian	Gallac...				
SQL:BatchCompleted	SELECT [i].[Id], [i].[CategoryId], [i].[Cr...	Core Microso...	brian	Gallac...	0	54	0	6
SQL:BatchStarting	SELECT [t].[Id], [t].[CreatedByUserId], [t...	Core Microso...	brian	Gallac...				
SQL:BatchCompleted	SELECT [t].[Id], [t].[CreatedByUserId], [t...	Core Microso...	brian	Gallac...	0	186	0	8
SQL:BatchStarting	SELECT [t].[Id], [t].[GenreId], [t].[ItemI...	Core Microso...	brian	Gallac...				
SQL:BatchCompleted	SELECT [t].[Id], [t].[GenreId], [t].[ItemI...	Core Microso...	brian	Gallac...	0	126	0	8
Audit Logout		Core Microso...	brian	Gallac...	0	648	0	150

Figure 14-18. *The AsSplitQuery command splits the query into multiple calls instead of one single call*

The queries are separated by the different joins that happen to get the includes into the result set.

The queries are first to get the Categories:

```
SELECT [i].[Id], [i].[CategoryId], [i].[CreatedByUserId], [i].
[CreatedDate], [i].[CurrentOrFinalPrice], [i].[Description], [i].
[IsActive], [i].[IsDeleted], [i].[IsOnSale], [i].[LastModifiedDate],
[i].[LastModifiedUserId], [i].[Name], [i].[Notes], [i].[PurchasePrice],
[i].[PurchasedDate], [i].[Quantity], [i].[SoldDate], [c].[Id], [c].
[CreatedByUserId], [c].[CreatedDate], [c].[IsActive], [c].[IsDeleted], [c].
[LastModifiedDate], [c].[LastModifiedUserId], [c].[Name]
FROM [Items] AS [i]
LEFT JOIN [Categories] AS [c] ON [i].[CategoryId] = [c].[Id]
WHERE ([i].[IsActive] = CAST(1 AS bit)) AND ([i].[IsDeleted] = CAST(0 AS bit))
ORDER BY [i].[Id], [c].[Id]
```

Then the Items joined to the Category result and then joined to get the Player information:

```
SELECT [t].[Id], [t].[CreatedByUserId], [t].[CreatedDate], [t].
[Description], [t].[IsActive], [t].[IsDeleted], [t].[LastModifiedDate],
[t].[LastModifiedUserId], [t].[Name], [i].[Id], [c].[Id]
FROM [Items] AS [i]
LEFT JOIN [Categories] AS [c] ON [i].[CategoryId] = [c].[Id]
INNER JOIN (
```

```
SELECT [iO].[ItemId], [p].[Id], [p].[CreatedByUserId], [p].
[CreatedDate], [p].[Description], [p].[IsActive], [p].[IsDeleted], [p].
[LastModifiedDate], [p].[LastModifiedUserId], [p].[Name]
FROM [ItemPlayers] AS [iO]
INNER JOIN [Player] AS [p] ON [iO].[PlayerId] = [p].[Id]
) AS [t] ON [i].[Id] = [t].[ItemId]
WHERE ([i].[IsActive] = CAST(1 AS bit)) AND ([i].[IsDeleted] = CAST(0 AS bit))
ORDER BY [i].[Id], [c].[Id]
```

Finally, the last query gets the Genre results:

```
SELECT [t].[Id], [t].[GenreId], [t].[ItemId], [t].[IdO], [t].
[CreatedByUserId], [t].[CreatedDate], [t].[IsActive], [t].[IsDeleted], [t].
[LastModifiedDate], [t].[LastModifiedUserId], [t].[Name], [i].[Id], [c].[Id]
FROM [Items] AS [i]
LEFT JOIN [Categories] AS [c] ON [i].[CategoryId] = [c].[Id]
INNER JOIN (
    SELECT [iO].[Id], [iO].[GenreId], [iO].[ItemId], [g].[Id] AS [IdO],
    [g].[CreatedByUserId], [g].[CreatedDate], [g].[IsActive], [g].
    [IsDeleted], [g].[LastModifiedDate], [g].[LastModifiedUserId],
    [g].[Name]
    FROM [ItemGenres] AS [iO]
    INNER JOIN [Genres] AS [g] ON [iO].[GenreId] = [g].[Id]
) AS [t] ON [i].[Id] = [t].[ItemId]
WHERE ([i].[IsActive] = CAST(1 AS bit)) AND ([i].[IsDeleted] = CAST(0 AS bit))
ORDER BY [i].[Id], [c].[Id]
```

Note that the join for the Categories happens in every query, since there is only one Category per Item and this doesn't create a lot of overhead in your queries.

Step 2: Use transactions to ensure consistency of results

Now that you've split the data queries, in a scenario where multiple users are working against your data, you could see issues where the Categories or the Genres or Players or even Items change from one query to the next. This inconsistency could pose an issue or cause undesired results.

To make the query absolutely safe, use a serializable transaction by modifying the method to be wrapped in a transaction as follows:

```
using (var scope = new TransactionScope(TransactionScopeOption.Required
                    , new TransactionOptions { IsolationLevel =
                    IsolationLevel.Serializable }
                    , TransactionScopeAsyncFlowOption.Enabled))
{
    var fullItemDetails = await db.Items
                        .Include(x => x.Players)
                        .Include(x => x.ItemGenres).ThenInclude(y =>
                        y.Genre)
                        .Include(x => x.Category)
                        .Where(x => x.IsActive && !x.IsDeleted)
                        .AsSplitQuery()
                        .AsNoTracking().ToListAsync();
    var outputItems = _mapper.Map<List<ItemDto>>(fullItemDetails);
    foreach (var item in outputItems)
    {
        Console.WriteLine($"New Item: {item}");
    }
}
```

Run the program to ensure the results are still generated. Also note that it would be incredibly difficult to test a changed data value that happened during the execution of one of the split queries, since you don't have the ability to just stop in the middle of the split queries and change something and then continue with the queries.

Step 3: A final note

A couple of final notes to keep in mind about split queries that are important.

First, using split queries may give you better efficiency, but it may also hurt your efficiency due to creating multiple calls to the database, so you will have to decide which is the best for your solution.

Second, as with `AsNoTracking`, you can enable the `AsSplitQuery` to be the default behavior. To do this, you modify the `OnConfiguring` method for the `DBContext` to `UseQuerySplittingBehavior(QuerySplittingBehavior.SplitQuery)`. If you do use this global statement, you will have to explicitly make calls with `AsSingleQuery` to get back to a single query result when desired in database queries.

A third issue is related to the consistency issue highlighted earlier. When using split queries, if others modify your data in the middle of your query results, you may end up with a dirty read that gives results that are not entirely accurate to the current state of the database, so now you also should wrap your split queries in a transaction to ensure data integrity.

Finally, when using split queries, keep in mind that making multiple calls to the database may hurt your application performance. Not only will you be making more direct calls to the database (instead of just one), but you will be storing each query in memory within the application while the remaining queries complete, which could add overhead or load on your execution environment.

Activity 14-3 summary

In this activity, you learned about using split queries to change the behavior of a query that has includes or projections to leverage the new `AsSplitQuery` call. By doing this, you were able to see how the original query only ran one database call in the SQL Server Profiler, and the split queries call added multiple calls to the database, splitting each query to only get part of the data result.

Splitting the query added multiple trips to the database and also added a need to use transactions to ensure data integrity during the multiple database calls.

Although you didn't implement it explicitly, you also read about how you could set your context to always use split queries as the default execution pattern and how doing this would require a call to `AsSingleQuery` to get back to the original functionality shown at the start of the activity.

In the end, you may choose to use this split query functionality when it makes sense for your solution.

Activity 14-4: Simple logging and tracking queries with the DBCommandInterceptor

Another new feature that is available as of EFCore5 that has received much praise is the feature of simple logging with improved diagnostic capabilities. The DBCommandInterceptor has been around since EFCore3.1. However, use of the interceptor is definitely worth mentioning here with the logging activity.

Task 0: Getting started

This activity picks up where Activity 14-3 ended. If you are working through the activities in order, feel free to use the files you have been using; otherwise, grab the files for the EFCore_Activity14-4_StarterFiles and use those files for this activity. As always, review Appendix A for information on working with the starter files if you go that route.

Task 1: Add a method to use for demonstration, and then add logging

In this task, you will create another method to demonstrate a couple of logging capabilities that have been added as of EFCore5. You will then use the new LogTo method to show how easy it is to write to your logs with EFCore.

Step 1: Create a new method

To begin this activity, comment out any previous calls to methods for previous activities in the Main method of the Program.cs file (leave the call to EnsureItemsHaveGenres uncommented). After commenting out other calls, add the following code for Activity 14-4:

```
//Activity 14-4 - Simple Logging
await DemonstrateSimpleLogging(db);
```

To create the new method, add the following code:

```
private static async Task DemonstrateSimpleLogging(InventoryDbContext db)
{
    var fullItemDetails = await db.Items
                            .Include(x => x.Players)
                            .Include(x => x.ItemGenres).ThenInclude(y =>
                            y.Genre)
                            .Include(x => x.Category)
                            .Where(x => x.IsActive && !x.IsDeleted)
                            .AsNoTracking().ToListAsync();
    var outputItems = _mapper.Map<List<ItemDto>>(fullItemDetails);
    foreach (var item in outputItems)
    {
        Console.WriteLine($"New Item: {item}");
    }
}
```

Run the code to ensure it works as expected. The output should be the same as was shown in Figure 14-16 in Activity 14-3, Task 1, Step 1.

Step 2: Add simple logging with the LogTo call

With the query implemented earlier, navigate to the OnConfiguring method that is overridden in your InventoryDbContext.cs file in the EFCore_DBLibrary project.

In the OnConfiguring method, add a simple call at the end of the method following the if(!optionsBuilder.IsConfigured) block as follows:

```
optionsBuilder.LogTo(Console.WriteLine);
```

With the new code in place, run the project again to see the logging output (review Figure 14-19).

```
        SELECT [i].[Id], [i].[CategoryId], [i].[CreatedByUserId], [i].[CreatedDate], [i].[CurrentOrFinalPrice], [i].[Descr
iption], [i].[IsActive], [i].[IsDeleted], [i].[IsOnSale], [i].[LastModifiedDate], [i].[LastModifiedUserId], [i].[Name],
[i].[Notes], [i].[PurchasePrice], [i].[PurchasedDate], [i].[Quantity], [i].[SoldDate], [c].[Id], [c].[CreatedByUserId],
[c].[CreatedDate], [c].[IsActive], [c].[IsDeleted], [c].[LastModifiedDate], [c].[LastModifiedUserId], [c].[Name], [t].[I
d], [t].[CreatedByUserId], [t].[CreatedDate], [t].[Description], [t].[IsActive], [t].[IsDeleted], [t].[LastModifiedDate]
, [t].[LastModifiedUserId], [t].[Name], [t].[ItemId], [t].[PlayerId], [t0].[Id], [t0].[GenreId], [t0].[ItemId], [t0].[Id
0], [t0].[CreatedByUserId], [t0].[CreatedDate], [t0].[IsActive], [t0].[IsDeleted], [t0].[LastModifiedDate], [t0].[LastMo
difiedUserId], [t0].[Name]
        FROM [Items] AS [i]
        LEFT JOIN [Categories] AS [c] ON [i].[CategoryId] = [c].[Id]
        LEFT JOIN (
            SELECT [p].[Id], [p].[CreatedByUserId], [p].[CreatedDate], [p].[Description], [p].[IsActive], [p].[IsDeleted],
 [p].[LastModifiedDate], [p].[LastModifiedUserId], [p].[Name], [i0].[ItemId], [i0].[PlayerId]
            FROM [ItemPlayers] AS [i0]
            INNER JOIN [Player] AS [p] ON [i0].[PlayerId] = [p].[Id]
        ) AS [t] ON [i].[Id] = [t].[ItemId]
        LEFT JOIN (
            SELECT [i1].[Id], [i1].[GenreId], [i1].[ItemId], [g].[Id] AS [Id0], [g].[CreatedByUserId], [g].[CreatedDate],
 [g].[IsActive], [g].[IsDeleted], [g].[LastModifiedDate], [g].[LastModifiedUserId], [g].[Name]
            FROM [ItemGenres] AS [i1]
            INNER JOIN [Genres] AS [g] ON [i1].[GenreId] = [g].[Id]
        ) AS [t0] ON [i].[Id] = [t0].[ItemId]
        WHERE ([i].[IsActive] = CAST(1 AS bit)) AND ([i].[IsDeleted] = CAST(0 AS bit))
        ORDER BY [i].[Id], [c].[Id], [t].[ItemId], [t].[PlayerId], [t].[Id], [t0].[Id], [t0].[Id0]
dbug: 5/31/2021 04:32:53.126 RelationalEventId.DataReaderDisposing[20300] (Microsoft.EntityFrameworkCore.Database.Comman
d)
      A data reader was disposed.
dbug: 5/31/2021 04:32:53.126 RelationalEventId.ConnectionClosing[20002] (Microsoft.EntityFrameworkCore.Database.Connecti
on)
      Closing connection to database 'InventoryManagerDb1404' on server 'localhost'.
dbug: 5/31/2021 04:32:53.127 RelationalEventId.ConnectionClosed[20003] (Microsoft.EntityFrameworkCore.Database.Connectio
n)
      Closed connection to database 'InventoryManagerDb1404' on server 'localhost'.
New Item: ITEM Batman Begins          ] You either die the hero or live long enough to see yourself become the villain
 has category: Movies
New Item: ITEM World of Tanks         ] WWII First person tank shooter                  has category: Games
New Item: ITEM The Sword of Shannara  ] The definitive fantasy book                    has category: Books
New Item: ITEM Practical Entity Framework] The book you are reading on Entity Framework  has category: Books
New Item: ITEM Battlefield 2142       ] WWII First person tank shooter                 has category: Games
New Item: ITEM Star Wars: The Empire Strikes Back] He will join us or die, master                  has category: Movi
es
New Item: ITEM Top Gun                ] I feel the need, the need for speed!           has category: Movies
New Item: ITEM Remember the Titans    ] Left Side, Strong Side                         has category: Movies
New Item: ITEM Inception              ] You mustn't be afraid to dream a little bigger, darling has category: Movies
Program Complete
dbug: 5/31/2021 04:32:53.165 CoreEventId.ContextDisposed[10407] (Microsoft.EntityFrameworkCore.Infrastructure)
      'InventoryDbContext' disposed.
```

Figure 14-19.   The LogTo method is added to the optionsBuilder in the OnConfiguring method. With that in place, running the program also now contains verbose log messages as shown in this image

Note that the logging contains not just the things that are happening with connections, datareaders, and the context but also contains full output of executed SQL commands.

Step 3: Move the logging to a file

You can do a number of different outputs with the logging. You can move it to the Debug console rather than your general output. You can also leverage the output and push it to the logger of your choice.

In this task, you will just write the output to a flat file to see how to move the logging to another location, as pushing into the console is not a very good use case.

Ensure you have a folder on your machine such as C:\Data, and, no matter what output folder you choose here, ensure you have mapped the following code to that root folder (i.e., C:\Data\).

Additionally, you could create idempotent directory checks and creations if you wanted to ensure the program would execute even if the folder didn't exist, but for simplicity, that is beyond the scope of this activity.

In the InventoryDbContext, at the top of the file, add the following private variables:

```
private string _logFilePath = $@"C:\Data\{Environment.MachineName}_
{DateTime.Now.Ticks}_efcore_logs.txt";
private readonly StreamWriter _logger;
```

With that code in place, add the following line of code to both constructors:

```
_logger = new StreamWriter(_logFilePath, append: true);
```

Note that having this in place could potentially break scaffolding in solutions like an ASP.Net MVC project, so you would want to double-check to ensure that scaffolding still worked if you were utilizing scaffolding in your solution.

Because the file has to live for the lifecycle of the context and you need to wrap up the file when the context is disposed, add the following code to the end of the InventoryDbContext file:

```
public override void Dispose()
{
    base.Dispose();
    _logger.Dispose();
}
public override async ValueTask DisposeAsync()
{
    await base.DisposeAsync();
    await _logger.DisposeAsync();
}
```

This will likely require you to bring in the using statement using System.Threading.Tasks.

Finally, with the code in place, make a simple change in the OnConfiguring method to output to the logger instead of the console:

```
optionsBuilder.LogTo(_logger.WriteLine);
```

Now run the program to see that your results are clean as expected, then browse to the root folder you chose for your logging, and view the text file that was created with the logging information for your application execution (review Figure 14-20).

Figure 14-20. *The Output is now logged to a file as expected for each execution of the application*

Task 2: Use the ToQueryString output

In this task, you will utilize the ToQueryString functionality available as of EFCore5 to see a quick and easy way for you to view the SQL Query that will be executed for a specific query.

In the previous task, you ran code that logged everything from the context to the output and then moved it into a logging file. This is an exceptionally easy way to set up verbose logging on your entire project.

However, what if you just wanted to see the queries? In the last activity (Activity 14-4), you worked through using SQL Server Profiler to view the output for split queries.

Step 1: Utilize the new ToQueryString functionality

For this task, you will just see both the single and split queries for the query in your console.

Just like the last task, you are currently starting by running a single query for the includes.

In the `DemonstrateSimpleLogging` method, add the following code to the beginning of the method, before the call to get the `var fullItemDetails`:

```
var queryToExecute = db.Items.Include(x => x.Players)
        .Include(x => x.ItemGenres).ThenInclude(y => y.Genre)
        .Include(x => x.Category)
        .Where(x => x.IsActive && !x.IsDeleted)
        .AsNoTracking().ToQueryString();Console.WriteLine("Single
        Query:");
Console.WriteLine(queryToExecute);
```

Run the program to see the output (see Figure 14-21).

```
Single Query:
SELECT [i].[Id], [i].[CategoryId], [i].[CreatedByUserId], [i].[CreatedDate], [i].[CurrentOrFinalPrice], [i].[Description
], [i].[IsActive], [i].[IsDeleted], [i].[IsOnSale], [i].[LastModifiedDate], [i].[LastModifiedUserId], [i].[Name], [i].[N
otes], [i].[PurchasePrice], [i].[PurchasedDate], [i].[Quantity], [i].[SoldDate], [c].[Id], [c].[CreatedByUserId], [c].[C
reatedDate], [c].[IsActive], [c].[IsDeleted], [c].[LastModifiedDate], [c].[LastModifiedUserId], [c].[Name], [t].[Id], [t
].[CreatedByUserId], [t].[CreatedDate], [t].[Description], [t].[IsActive], [t].[IsDeleted], [t].[LastModifiedDate], [t].
[LastModifiedUserId], [t].[Name], [t].[ItemId], [t].[PlayerId], [t0].[Id], [t0].[GenreId], [t0].[ItemId], [t0].[IdO], [t
0].[CreatedByUserId], [t0].[CreatedDate], [t0].[IsActive], [t0].[IsDeleted], [t0].[LastModifiedDate], [t0].[LastModified
UserId], [t0].[Name]
FROM [Items] AS [i]
LEFT JOIN [Categories] AS [c] ON [i].[CategoryId] = [c].[Id]
LEFT JOIN (
    SELECT [p].[Id], [p].[CreatedByUserId], [p].[CreatedDate], [p].[Description], [p].[IsActive], [p].[IsDeleted], [p].[
LastModifiedDate], [p].[LastModifiedUserId], [p].[Name], [i0].[ItemId], [i0].[PlayerId]
    FROM [ItemPlayers] AS [i0]
    INNER JOIN [Player] AS [p] ON [i0].[PlayerId] = [p].[Id]
) AS [t] ON [i].[Id] = [t].[ItemId]
LEFT JOIN (
    SELECT [i1].[Id], [i1].[GenreId], [i1].[ItemId], [g].[Id] AS [IdO], [g].[CreatedByUserId], [g].[CreatedDate], [g].[I
sActive], [g].[IsDeleted], [g].[LastModifiedDate], [g].[LastModifiedUserId], [g].[Name]
    FROM [ItemGenres] AS [i1]
    INNER JOIN [Genres] AS [g] ON [i1].[GenreId] = [g].[Id]
) AS [t0] ON [i].[Id] = [t0].[ItemId]
WHERE ([i].[IsActive] = CAST(1 AS bit)) AND ([i].[IsDeleted] = CAST(0 AS bit))
ORDER BY [i].[Id], [c].[Id], [t].[ItemId], [t].[PlayerId], [t].[Id], [t0].[Id], [t0].[IdO]
New Item: ITEM Batman Begins           ] You either die the hero or live long enough to see yourself become the villain
 has category: Movies
New Item: ITEM World of Tanks          ] WWII First person tank shooter              has category: Games
New Item: ITEM The Sword of Shannara   ] The definitive fantasy book                has category: Books
New Item: ITEM Practical Entity Framework] The book you are reading on Entity Framework   has category: Books
New Item: ITEM Battlefield 2142        ] WWII First person tank shooter              has category: Games
New Item: ITEM Star Wars: The Empire Strikes Back] He will join us or die, master              has category: Movi
es
New Item: ITEM Top Gun                 ] I feel the need, the need for speed!        has category: Movies
New Item: ITEM Remember the Titans     ] Left Side, Strong Side                      has category: Movies
New Item: ITEM Inception               ] You mustn't be afraid to dream a little bigger, darling has category: Movies
Program Complete
```

Figure 14-21. *The query is captured, and output is displayed in the console as expected*

Finally, comment everything out in the `DemonstrateSimpleLogging` method, and then add the following code to the end of the method:

```
Console.WriteLine("Split Query:");
var queriesToExecute = db.Items.Include(x => x.Players)
                    .Include(x => x.ItemGenres).ThenInclude(y => y.Genre)
                    .Include(x => x.Category)
```

```
                    .Where(x => x.IsActive && !x.IsDeleted)
                    .AsNoTracking().AsSplitQuery().ToQueryString();
Console.WriteLine(queriesToExecute);
```

Run the program one more time to see the output for the split queries directly in the console (review Figure 14-22).

```
Split Query:
SELECT [i].[Id], [i].[CategoryId], [i].[CreatedByUserId], [i].[CreatedDate], [i].[CurrentOrFinalPrice], [i].[Description
], [i].[IsActive], [i].[IsDeleted], [i].[IsOnSale], [i].[LastModifiedDate], [i].[LastModifiedUserId], [i].[Name], [i].[N
otes], [i].[PurchasePrice], [i].[PurchasedDate], [i].[Quantity], [i].[SoldDate], [c].[Id], [c].[CreatedByUserId], [c].[C
reatedDate], [c].[IsActive], [c].[IsDeleted], [c].[LastModifiedDate], [c].[LastModifiedUserId], [c].[Name]
FROM [Items] AS [i]
LEFT JOIN [Categories] AS [c] ON [i].[CategoryId] = [c].[Id]
WHERE ([i].[IsActive] = CAST(1 AS bit)) AND ([i].[IsDeleted] = CAST(0 AS bit))
ORDER BY [i].[Id], [c].[Id]

This LINQ query is being executed in split-query mode, and the SQL shown is for the first query to be executed. Addition
al queries may also be executed depending on the results of the first query.
Program Complete
```

Figure 14-22. *The split query shows only the first query in the console with a message about the fact that the other queries are not shown*

Because of the default operation of EFCore and the split queries, only the first query is shown. To review the queries, you need to use the SQL Server Profiler or a similar tool. If you check your log file created from the most recent execution, which contains the logs from your database activity for the last run, you'll see the results do not include the full queries.

Figure 14-23 contains the text of the log file to validate that all split queries were not logged with the SimpleLogging solution from the first part of the activity.

```
     Compiling query expression:
     'DbSet<Item>()
           .Include(x => x.Players)
           .Include(x => x.ItemGenres)
           .ThenInclude(y => y.Genre)
           .Include(x => x.Category)
           .Where(x => x.IsActive && !(x.IsDeleted))
           .AsNoTracking()
           .AsSplitQuery()'
dbug: 5/31/2021 04:43:33.236 CoreEventId.NavigationBaseIncluded[10112] (Microsoft.EntityFrameworkCore.Query)
      Including navigation: 'Item.Players'.
dbug: 5/31/2021 04:43:33.237 CoreEventId.NavigationBaseIncluded[10112] (Microsoft.EntityFrameworkCore.Query)
      Including navigation: 'Item.ItemGenres'.
dbug: 5/31/2021 04:43:33.239 CoreEventId.NavigationBaseIncluded[10112] (Microsoft.EntityFrameworkCore.Query)
      Including navigation: 'Item.Category'.
dbug: 5/31/2021 04:43:33.244 CoreEventId.NavigationBaseIncluded[10112] (Microsoft.EntityFrameworkCore.Query)
      Including navigation: 'ItemGenre.Genre'.
dbug: 5/31/2021 04:43:33.323 CoreEventId.QueryExecutionPlanned[10107] (Microsoft.EntityFrameworkCore.Query)
      Generated query execution expression:
      'queryContext => new SplitQueryingEnumerable<Item>(
          (RelationalQueryContext)queryContext,
          RelationalCommandCache.SelectExpression(
              Projection Mapping:
              SELECT i.Id, i.CategoryId, i.CreatedByUserId, i.CreatedDate, i.CurrentOrFinalPrice, i.Description, i.IsActive, i.IsDeleted, i.IsOnSale,
i.LastModifiedDate, i.LastModifiedUserId, i.Name, i.Notes, i.PurchasePrice, i.PurchasedDate, i.Quantity, i.SoldDate, c.Id, c.CreatedByUserId,
c.CreatedDate, c.IsActive, c.IsDeleted, c.LastModifiedDate, c.LastModifiedUserId, c.Name
              FROM Items AS i
              LEFT JOIN Categories AS c ON i.CategoryId == c.Id
              WHERE i.IsActive && Not(i.IsDeleted)
              ORDER BY i.Id ASC, c.Id ASC),
          Func<QueryContext, DbDataReader, ResultContext, SplitQueryResultCoordinator, Item>,
          Action<QueryContext, IExecutionStrategy, SplitQueryResultCoordinator>,
          null,
          EFCore_DBLibrary.InventoryDbContext,
          False,
          False,
          True
      )'
dbug: 5/31/2021 04:43:33.331 CoreEventId.ContextDisposed[10407] (Microsoft.EntityFrameworkCore.Infrastructure)
      'InventoryDbContext' disposed.
```

Figure 14-23. *The log file from the last run using AsSplitQuery is shown to validate that the logs did not capture all of the individual queries that were originally seen using the SQL Server Profiler as in the previous activity*

Task 3: Implement the DBCommandInterceptor to log slow running queries

This final task for Activity 14-4 is actually something I've just learned about myself. I would like to once again thank Dave Callan for his excellent post on this topic on LinkedIn and his permission to share it with you.

The overall implementation will need to be tweaked a bit for your implementation, but the general idea is the same as what is shown in Dave's post.

Here is a screenshot of Dave's original post (shown in Figure 14-24).

Dave Callan • 1st
.NET Contractor based in Ireland / Follow for helpful .NET posts
1w • iii

In ENTITY FRAMEWORK CORE we can log SLOW RUNNING QUERIES using the interceptor system...

- 1 -

Create an interceptor class which inherits from DbCommandInterceptor and implement the ReaderExecuted method.

- 2 -

Register the interceptor class from the ConfigureServices method in Startup.cs

```
public class LogSQLQueriesInterceptor : DbCommandInterceptor
{
    public override DbDataReader ReaderExecuted(DbCommand command,
        CommandExecutedEventData eventData, DbDataReader result)
    {
        if (eventData.Duration.TotalMilliseconds > 500)
        {
            File.AppendAllText("longQueries.txt", command.CommandText +
                " MS:" + eventData.Duration.TotalMilliseconds +
                Environment.NewLine +
                Environment.NewLine);
        }

        return base.ReaderExecuted(command, eventData, result);
    }
```

```
//This method gets called by the runtime.Use this method to add services to the
public void ConfigureServices(IServiceCollection services)
{
    services.AddControllersWithViews();

    services.AddDbContext<EFContext>(options => options.
        UseSqlServer(Configuration.GetConnectionString("AdventureWorks")).
        AddInterceptors(new LogSQLQueriesInterceptor()));
}
```

Figure 14-24. *Dave Callan's original LinkedIn post to highlight using the DBCommandInterceptor to log long running SQL Queries*

Step 1: Implement the DBCommandInterceptor inheriting class

To implement this code in your solution, start by adding a class file named LogSQLQueriesInterceptor.cs in the EFCore_DBLibrary project. Inherit from the DBCommandInterceptor as in Figure 14-24. Since your implementation is in an asynchronous call, you'll need to override the ReaderExecutedAsync method instead of the ReaderExecuted method as in Dave's original post.

718

Therefore, implement the necessary code by using the following code block to complete the class file (feel free to modify the path and threshold as desired/required):

```
public class LogSQLQueriesInterceptor : DbCommandInterceptor
{
    private int _longRunningQueryThreshold = 500;
    private string _logQueriesFilePath = $@"C:\Data\{Environment.
    MachineName}_longQueries.txt";

    public override ValueTask<DbDataReader> ReaderExecutedAsync(DbCommand
    command, CommandExecutedEventData eventData
            , DbDataReader result, CancellationToken cancellationToken =
            default(CancellationToken))
    {
        if (eventData.Duration.TotalMilliseconds >= _
        longRunningQueryThreshold)
        {
            File.AppendAllText(_logQueriesFilePath
                , $"{command.CommandText} MS: {eventData.Duration.
                TotalMilliseconds}" +
                    $"{Environment.NewLine}{Environment.NewLine}");
        }

        return base.ReaderExecutedAsync(command, eventData, result,
        cancellationToken);
    }
}
```

Step 2: Register the DBCommandInterceptor in the Program class

Return to the EFCore_Activity1404 project, and open the Program.cs file. In the Program.cs file, locate the BuildOptions method, and then add a final line under the _optionsBuilder.UseSqlServer(…) line of code as follows:

```
_optionsBuilder.AddInterceptors(new LogSQLQueriesInterceptor());
```

Step 3: Run the program to see the new interceptor logs

Run the program and then check your destination folder to see if any logs have been recorded.

Assuming that none have been recorded, uncomment the calls to the other methods in the activity to ensure some longer running queries are hit. Next, modify the threshold to be 10 milliseconds in the `LogSQLQueriesInterceptor`.

Put a breakpoint on the line that is writing the log, and then execute the program again. You should now see the code getting hit a few times. If you don't see any of the breakpoints getting hit, you may need to clean your solution and try again as some of the data may be cached (review Figure 14-25).

```
6    public class LogSQLQueriesInterceptor : DbCommandInterceptor
7    {
8        private int _longRunningQueryThreshold = 10;
9        private string _logQueriesFilePath = $@"C:\Data\{Environment.MachineName}_longQueries.txt";
10
         0 references
11       public override ValueTask<DbDataReader> ReaderExecutedAsync(DbCommand command, CommandExecutedEventData eventData
12           , DbDataReader result, CancellationToken cancellationToken = default(CancellationToken))
13       {
14           if (eventData.Duration.TotalMilliseconds >= _longRunningQueryThreshold)
15           {
16               File.AppendAllText(_logQueriesFilePath
17                   , $"{command.CommandText} MS: {eventData.Duration.TotalMilliseconds}" +
18                   $"{Environment.NewLine}{Environment.NewLine}");
19           }
20
21           return base.ReaderExecutedAsync(command, eventData, result, cancellationToken);
22       }
```

Figure 14-25. *The LogSQLQueriesInterceptor is executed and will record any queries that run longer than your specified threshold*

The final file output will look something like what is shown in Figure 14-26.

```
91.0656 MS: SELECT [i].[Id], [i].[CategoryId], [i].[CreatedByUserId], [i].[CreatedDate], [i].[Curr
[LastModifiedUserId], [i].[Name], [i].[Notes], [i].[PurchasePrice], [i].[PurchasedDate], [i].[Quan
[t].[IsActive], [t].[IsDeleted], [t].[LastModifiedDate], [t].[LastModifiedUserId], [t].[Name]
FROM [Items] AS [i]
LEFT JOIN (
    SELECT [i0].[Id], [i0].[GenreId], [i0].[ItemId], [g].[Id] AS [Id0], [g].[CreatedByUserId], [g]
    FROM [ItemGenres] AS [i0]
    INNER JOIN [Genres] AS [g] ON [i0].[GenreId] = [g].[Id]
) AS [t] ON [i].[Id] = [t].[ItemId]
WHERE ([i].[IsDeleted] = CAST(0 AS bit)) AND ([i].[IsActive] = CAST(1 AS bit))
ORDER BY [i].[Id], [t].[Id], [t].[Id0]

11.6016 MS: SELECT [g].[Id], [g].[CreatedByUserId], [g].[CreatedDate], [g].[IsActive], [g].[IsDele
FROM [Genres] AS [g]
WHERE ([g].[IsActive] = CAST(1 AS bit)) AND ([g].[IsDeleted] = CAST(0 AS bit))

14.8975 MS: SELECT [i].[Id], [i].[CategoryId], [i].[CreatedByUserId], [i].[CreatedDate], [i].[Curr
[LastModifiedUserId], [i].[Name], [i].[Notes], [i].[PurchasePrice], [i].[PurchasedDate], [i].[Quan
[Description], [t].[IsActive], [t].[IsDeleted], [t].[LastModifiedDate], [t].[LastModifiedUserId],
[IsActive], [t0].[IsDeleted], [t0].[LastModifiedDate], [t0].[LastModifiedUserId], [t0].[Name]
FROM [Items] AS [i]
LEFT JOIN (
    SELECT [i0].[ItemId], [i0].[PlayerId], [p].[Id], [p].[CreatedByUserId], [p].[CreatedDate], [p]
    FROM [ItemPlayers] AS [i0]
    INNER JOIN [Player] AS [p] ON [i0].[PlayerId] = [p].[Id]
) AS [t] ON [i].[Id] = [t].[ItemId]
LEFT JOIN (
    SELECT [i1].[Id], [i1].[GenreId], [i1].[ItemId], [g].[Id] AS [Id0], [g].[CreatedByUserId], [g]
```

Figure 14-26. *The log file is created and the long running queries are logged as expected*

Don't forget to set the threshold back to a more reasonable time, such as the original 500.

Activity 14-4 summary

In this activity, you learned how to leverage the new simple logging available as of EFCore5. You started by just outputting the log to the console, but then you made a more robust solution logging the output to a flat file. You could take that to the next level in your production solutions.

You then learned about the new ToQueryString call that allows you to get the generated SQL for any query that you are creating. This will be highly useful for your debugging purposes to validate your queries and their efficiency without having to go to the SQL Server Profiler.

You then reviewed one limitation of the ToQueryString as it exists at the time of this writing, which is that the method only shows the first query in a split query, instead of showing each of the queries that are generated.

Finally, the activity closed off with a look at using a custom class to override the DBCommandInterceptor to log long running queries in your solution.

Activity 14-5: Flexible entity mapping

This activity picks up where Activity 14-4 left off. In this activity, you are going to look at another way you can utilize the FullItemDetailDtos view in code. Using *flexible entity mapping*, you will be able to get the results you expect for a function or view or even get results directly mapped from an inline query.

Task 0: Getting started

As with all other activities, keep working with your files from the end of the previous activity or grab the EFCore_Activity14-5_StarterFiles. As always, refer to Appendix A for more information on working with starter files.

Task 1: Use flexible entity mapping to retrieve the results of a view

In this task, you will use flexible entity mapping to create a mapping to leverage the results of the vwFullItemDetails view.

Step 1: Rework the main program to call to just the GetFullItemDetails view

To get started, in the Main method of the main activity project in the Program.cs file, comment out the code await DemonstrateSimpleLogging(db); that calls the Activity 14-4 method.

Next, add the following code to start the activity. Note that there is already a call for await GetFullItemDetails, so you could just uncomment that line, but it's likely easier to just copy/paste this code, which will be removed in the next step:

```
//Activity 14-5 - Flexible Entity Mapping
await GetFullItemDetails();
```

With the changes in place, run the program. The only thing that should be called is the method for `GetFullItemDetails`, and it will have results similar to what is shown in Figure 14-27.

```
New Item] 1        Batman Begins                      You either die the hero or live long enough to see yourself become the villain|Christian Bale|Movies|Fantasy
New Item] 5        Battlefield 2142                   WWII First person tank shooter|Electronic Arts|Games|Fantasy
New Item] 5        Battlefield 2142                   WWII First person tank shooter|Electronic Arts|Games|Sci/Fi
New Item] 9        Inception                          You mustn't be afraid to dream a little bigger, darling|Leonardo DiCaprio|Movies|Comedy
New Item] 9        Inception                          You mustn't be afraid to dream a little bigger, darling|Leonardo DiCaprio|Movies|Sci/Fi
New Item] 4        Practical Entity Framework         The book you are reading on Entity Framework|Brian L. Gorman|Books|Fantasy
New Item] 8        Remember the Titans                Left Side, Strong Side|Denzel Washington|Movies|Sci/Fi
New Item] 6        Star Wars: The Empire Strikes Back He will join or die, master|Mark Hamill|Movies|Comedy
New Item] 6        Star Wars: The Empire Strikes Back He will join us or die, master|Mark Hamill|Movies|Horror
New Item] 3        The Sword of Shannara              The definitive fantasy book|Terry Brooks|Books|Comedy
New Item] 7        Top Gun                            I feel the need, the need for speed!|Tom Cruise|Movies|Comedy
New Item] 2        World of Tanks                     WWII First person tank shooter|Wargaming|Games|Horror
New Item] 2        World of Tanks                     WWII First person tank shooter|Wargaming|Games|Sci/Fi
Program Complete
```

Figure 14-27. *The current call to GetFullItemDetails works as expected*

One thing to note is that the original view is returning all of the data from the table, including deleted rows (and potentially inactive rows as well). The full view does have the fields in the result set, so they can be further filtered if desired to only display active and non-deleted rows.

With this in place, you have now successfully mapped the view and leveraged it through the service and database layers as expected. However, you haven't really done flexible entity mapping yet. While it's true you did map the entity to a view in the model builder, you still aren't doing anything new that couldn't be accomplished in previous versions of EFCore. For reference, the code in the `InventoryDbContext.cs` file that is doing the mapping is

```
modelBuilder.Entity<FullItemDetailDto>(x =>
{
    x.HasNoKey();
    x.ToView("FullItemDetailDtos");
});
```

Step 2: Add the flexible entity mapping

An example of using flexible entity mapping to get the view can be easily accomplished. For this activity, you won't go through the layers. Instead, you will just quickly leverage the data from the context using a flexible entity mapping.

For this activity, in the InventoryModels project, start by creating a copy of the FullItemDetailDTO as a new DTO named FullItemDetailEMQueryDTO in a class with the same name. The properties should be exactly the same as the original DTO in order to map directly to the view fields.

After adding the new class, return to the InventoryDbContext in the EFCore_DBLibrary project, and add a property as follows:

```
public DbSet<FullItemDetailEMQueryDto> FullItemDetailEMQueryDtos { get; set; }
```

Then add the new flexible entity mapping somewhere in the OnModelCreating method, such as right after the mapping for the FullItemDetailDtos view as follows:

```
//just map the query directly:
modelBuilder.Entity<FullItemDetailEMQueryDto>()
        .ToSqlQuery(
            @"SELECT * FROM [dbo].[vwFullItemDetails] WHERE IsActive = 1
            and IsDeleted = 0"
        ).HasNoKey().ToView("FullItemDetailEMQueryDtos");
```

Note that this mapping will just do everything the other mapping did but leverages the SQL Query directly in the mapping and limits results to just the active and non-deleted records. You could write any T-SQL query you wanted, as long as the fields map to the output DTO.

In the Main method in the Program file, add a call to a new method named GetFullItemDetailsEMQuery with the call await GetFullItemDetailsEMQuery(). Comment out (or remove if you duplicated it) the original call to GetFullItemDetails so the new call will be the only code that executes. Then implement the code for the method as follows:

```
private static async Task GetFullItemDetailsEMQuery()
{
    using (var context = new InventoryDbContext(_optionsBuilder.Options))
    {
        var results = await context.FullItemDetailEMQueryDtos.ToListAsync();

        foreach (var item in results.OrderBy(x => x.ItemName).ThenBy
        (x => x.GenreName)
                                    .ThenBy(x => x.Category).ThenBy(x
                                    => x.PlayerName))
```

```
    {
        Console.WriteLine($"New Flexible Entity Mapping Query Item]
        {item.Id,-10}" +
                          $"|{item.ItemName,-50}" +
                          $"|{item.ItemDescription,-4}" +
                          $"|{item.PlayerName,-5}" +
                          $"|{item.Category,-5}" +
                          $"|{item.GenreName,-5}");
    }
  }
}
```

This method will accomplish the same thing that you just did with the other entity using the traditional mapping.

Run the program to see that the results work as expected (review Figure 14-28).

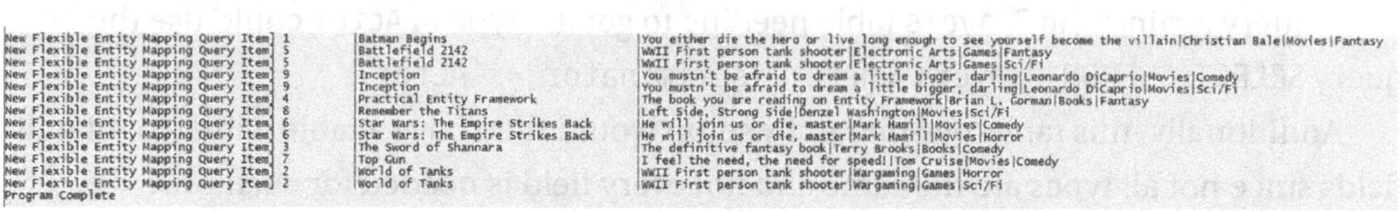

Figure 14-28. *The new query returns results using the flexible entity mapping to a direct SQL Query*

Activity 14-5 summary

In this activity, you learned about the new flexible entity mapping and how it can be used to map entities to views. A couple of things that were not covered that you can also do are the ability to map to functions and the ability to map to a view for queries and to an entity for updating data.

Activity 14-6: Table-per-type (TPT) inheritance mapping

In this final activity for Chapter 14, you will walk through the new *table-per-type* functionality that exists in EFCore5.

725

Table-per-type is exactly how it sounds, but, just in case you're not sure what this means, here is a quick overview.

As currently programmed in the InventoryDbContext, Items as a whole have Categories like Movie, Book, and Game. This is likely the correct implementation, since all of them do have basic characteristics. However, adding in Players was dicey. Is the Game Player the person playing it, or some entity who created the Game? Also, the Player of a book is an Author, not a Player, and the people in movies are generally called Actors, not Players.

In the past, you could use inheritance, having Player be the base and then having a specific type of player – that is, Author, Actor, Company, etc. Each of these types would be a class that inherits from Player and then would be stored in the Players table. One database table would be created with all the fields needed for all types.

This table-per-hierarchy operation could result in fields like FirstName and LastName for Author, maybe also for Actor, and perhaps StockSymbol and City for Company. You then also get a field called Discriminator that essentially stores the type of object for that row.

A query against the Players table needing to get the type of Actor could use the query SELECT * FROM Players where Discriminator = 'Actor'.

Additionally, this table-per-hierarchy setup would then have a table with a lot of null fields since not all types are the same and not every field is needed for each row.

In a TPT operation, each inherited type gets a new table as a one-to-one relationship with the base table. Instead of a table of Players with a bunch of null fields and a discriminator, you get the base Players table, and then you can further define player attributes in the tables created for each inheriting class, such as Person ➤ Actor, Person ➤ Author, and Publisher.

Task 0: Getting started

To get started, this activity assumes you have code as per the end of Activity 14-5. As always, you can use the files that you've been working with and continue with this activity, or you can start with the EFCore_Activity14-6_StarterFiles.

Additionally, once you've gotten the project up and running, ensure that you have commented out any method calls other than EnsureItemsHaveGenres. Running the program should have no output other than *Program Complete* statement when this is configured correctly.

For this activity, there is a script that will be used to migrate data. You will want to get a copy of that script if you are using your own version of the files. The script file is `MigratePlayers.v0.sql` and is found in the `EFCore_DbLibrary` project under `Migrations` ➤ `Scripts` ➤ `CustomScripts` in the `EFCore_Activity14-6_StarterFiles`.

Task 1: Create the inheritance hierarchy

In this task, you will add additional types to further define players as either `Person` or `Company`. Each type will have a couple of unique attributes to track.

Step 1: Add the inheritance structures

To begin, in the `InventoryModels` project, create two classes that inherit from `Player` called `Person` and `Company`.

In the `InventoryModelsConstants` file, add the following constants:

```
public const int MAX_STOCKSYMBOL_LENGTH = 10;
public const int MAX_COMPANYNAME_LENGTH = 150;
public const int MAX_CITY_LENGTH = 50;
public const int MAX_FIRSTNAME_LENGTH = 50;
public const int MAX_LASTNAME_LENGTH = 50;
```

Then, in the Person class, implement the following code:

```
[Table("People")]
public class Person : Player
{
    [StringLength(InventoryModelsConstants.MAX_FIRSTNAME_LENGTH)]
    public string FirstName { get; set; }
    [StringLength(InventoryModelsConstants.MAX_LASTNAME_LENGTH)]
    public string LastName { get; set; }

    public override string Name => $"{FirstName} {LastName}";
}
```

Note that you will get an error that you cannot override the inherited member `Player.Name`. To fix this, open the `Player` class and add the virtual keyword to the `Name` property:

```
public virtual string Name { get; set; }
```

Next, in the Company class, implement the following code:

```
[Table("Companies")]
public class Company : Player
{
    [StringLength(InventoryModelsConstants.MAX_COMPANYNAME_LENGTH)]
    public string CompanyName { get; set; }

    [StringLength(InventoryModelsConstants.MAX_STOCKSYMBOL_LENGTH)]
    public string StockSymbol { get; set; }

    [StringLength(InventoryModelsConstants.MAX_CITY_LENGTH)]
    public string City { get; set; }

    public override string Name => $"{CompanyName} - {StockSymbol}";
}
```

To make sure that the types are added to a migration, find the `InventoryDbContext` in the `EFCore_DbLibrary` project, and add the following `DbSet` properties:

```
public DbSet<Company> Companies { get; set; }
public DbSet<Person> People { get; set; }
```

Step 2: Create the migration, and update the database

With all of the new hierarchy in place, add a new migration with the command `add-migration create-tpt-hierarchy-player-person-company`. Make sure to select the EFCore_DbLibrary project in the PMC.

The most important thing to note here is that you must include the table attribute for this to work. Here it made sense to use a table attribute since `Person` pluralized becomes `People` and `Company` becomes `Companies`, but what if you had another table type called `Organization` that would easily become `Organizations` when pluralized? If you didn't explicitly name the table, EFCore wouldn't recognize that you are trying to do a TPT mapping and you'd get an error about not having a discriminator (see Figure 14-29, where I purposefully didn't map Person to a table to generate the error).

```
Both 'Person' and 'Player' are mapped to the table 'Player'. All the entity types in a hierarchy that don't have a discriminator must be mapped to different tables. See https://go.microsoft.com/fwlink/?linkid=2130430 for more information.
PM> |
```

Figure 14-29. *If you try to create a migration without the entities explicitly naming tables, you would get an error about not having a discriminator as shown in this image*

Once the migration is added, examine it to see that you are going to get the base table plus the TPT tables that have a one-to-one foreign key relationship back to the base table `Player` (review Figure 14-30).

```
protected override void Up(MigrationBuilder migrationBuilder)
{
    migrationBuilder.CreateTable(
        name: "Companies",
        columns: table => new
        {
            Id = table.Column<int>(type: "int", nullable: false),
            CompanyName = table.Column<string>(type: "nvarchar(150)", maxLength: 150, nullable: true),
            StockSymbol = table.Column<string>(type: "nvarchar(10)", maxLength: 10, nullable: true),
            City = table.Column<string>(type: "nvarchar(50)", maxLength: 50, nullable: true)
        },
        constraints: table =>
        {
            table.PrimaryKey("PK_Companies", x => x.Id);
            table.ForeignKey(
                name: "FK_Companies_Player_Id",
                column: x => x.Id,
                principalTable: "Player",
                principalColumn: "Id",
                onDelete: ReferentialAction.Restrict);
        });

    migrationBuilder.CreateTable(
        name: "People",
        columns: table => new
        {
            Id = table.Column<int>(type: "int", nullable: false),
            FirstName = table.Column<string>(type: "nvarchar(50)", maxLength: 50, nullable: true),
            LastName = table.Column<string>(type: "nvarchar(50)", maxLength: 50, nullable: true)
        },
        constraints: table =>
        {
            table.PrimaryKey("PK_People", x => x.Id);
            table.ForeignKey(
                name: "FK_People_Player_Id",
                column: x => x.Id,
                principalTable: "Player",
                principalColumn: "Id",
                onDelete: ReferentialAction.Restrict);
        });
}
```

Figure 14-30. *The migration is going to generate the tables to map with a foreign key id back to the base table, as expected. This creates the proper TPT relationships, where Person is just a more specific player as is Company*

After reviewing the migration and ensuring it looks good, run the `update-database` command to apply the changes.

If you are tracking your code in a GIT repository, this would be a great time to commit changes.

Task 2: Move data

If you have used the migration project, then you have items, and the items were generated with `Players` to provide some simple mappings. In this task, you will move data so that the more specific `Player` and `Company` types can be leveraged.

Step 1: Create a new script to migrate existing data

Currently, the `BuildItems` class in the `InventoryDataMigrator` project builds out the `Items` data and is idempotent. Because you already have data, you need to write a script to make the data work as `Person` or `Company` from the `People` or `Companies` tables, respectively, bound back to the `Players` table.

If you don't want to do this in a script, you could do this with code, but you would likely need to wipe existing data and modify the migrator project to seed data as the specific types due to Id and tracking conflicts. For this activity, the scripting option will be used.

Begin by adding a new blank migration using the command `add-migration` `migrate-players-to-people-and-companies`. This will generate a blank migration. When the migration is generated, add the following code to the Up method:

```
migrationBuilder.SqlResource("EFCore_DBLibrary.Migrations.Scripts.
CustomScripts.MigratePlayers.v0.sql");
```

Then add the following code to the Down method:

```
migrationBuilder.Sql("DELETE FROM Companies; DELETE FROM People;");
```

You will also need to add the using statement using `EFCore_DbLibrary.` `Migrations.Scripts;` to the top of the file.

Because the script is long, a copy of the script has already been placed in the correct folder for the migrations as of the starter project, and the file was set as an embedded resource. If you are using your own files, locate the starter files' project and download the project to get a copy of the script, and then place the script in the appropriate folder.

Either way, ensure that the script is set as an embedded resource in the project (see Figure 14-31).

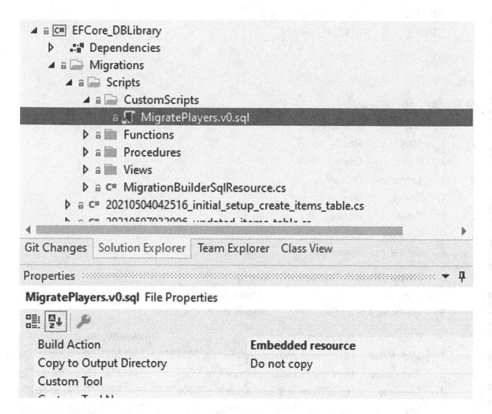

Figure 14-31. *Ensure that the script is set as an embedded resource*

Once you are sure that the data script is in place as an embedded resource and you have the migration in place, run the script by executing the update-database command in the PMC.

After the command is run, use SSMS to ensure that the People and Companies tables have data (review Figure 14-32).

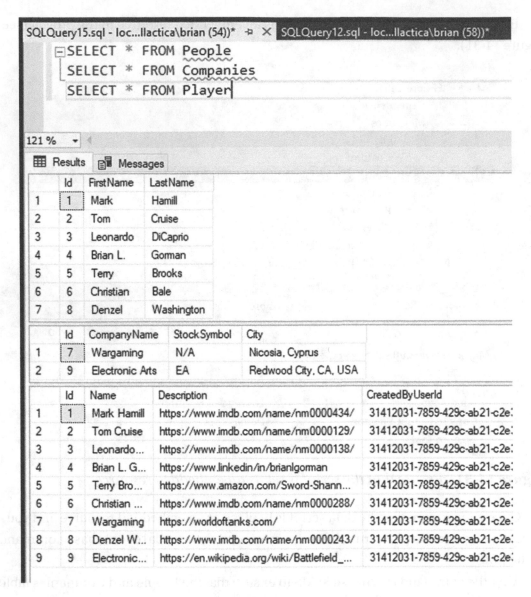

Figure 14-32. *The migration will execute the script to update the TPT tables for People and Companies*

Step 2: Use the new TPT tables in code

Now that the data has been created, you should run a couple of quick calls to ensure that the data works as expected.

Note again that the code for the Main method in the Program class of the main activity file has been set so that no other code will execute. In the Main method, add a call to a new method called ShowPlayerTPTData with the code

```
//Activity 14-6 - TPT data
await ShowPlayerTPTData(db);
```

and then add the method as follows:

```
private static async Task ShowPlayerTPTData(InventoryDbContext db)
{
    var items = await db.Items.Include(x => x.Players).ToListAsync();

    if (items != null && items.Any())
    {
        foreach (var item in items)
        {
            var players = item.Players;
            if (players == null || !players.Any()) continue;

            Console.WriteLine($"New Item with players: {item.Name}: ");

            foreach (var player in players)
            {
                if (player is Person)
                {
                    var p = player as Person;
                    Console.WriteLine($"{p.LastName}, {p.FirstName} --
                    {p.Name}");
                }
                else if (player is Company)
                {
                    var c = player as Company;
                    Console.WriteLine($"{c.CompanyName} - {c.City} --
                    {c.Name}");
                }
```

```
        else
        {
            Console.WriteLine($"Player only: {player.Name}");
        }
    }
  }
 }
}
```

Once the code is in place, run the program. You should see results similar to what is shown in Figure 14-33.

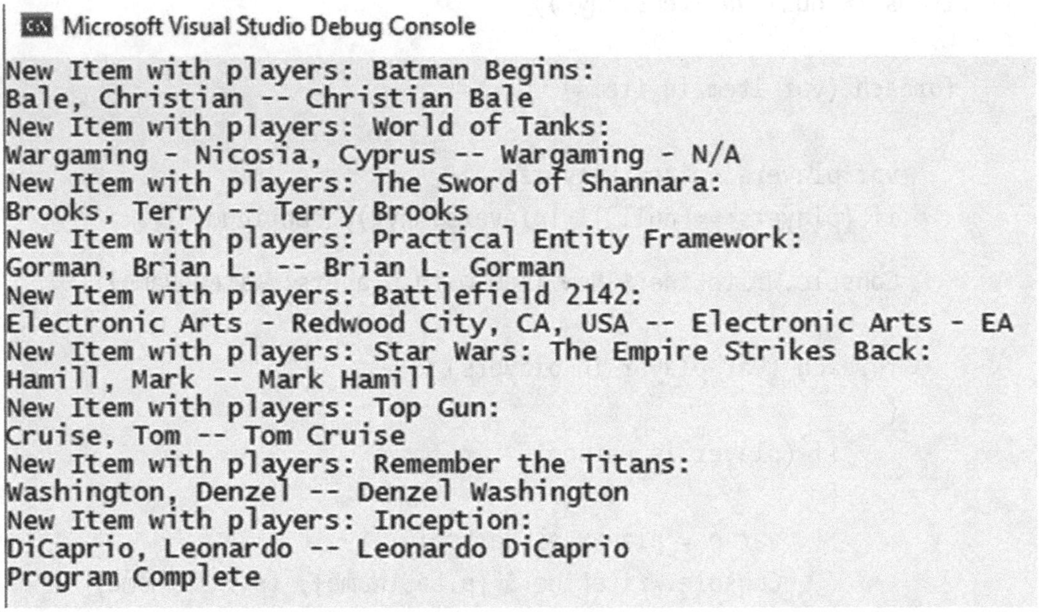

```
Microsoft Visual Studio Debug Console
New Item with players: Batman Begins:
Bale, Christian -- Christian Bale
New Item with players: World of Tanks:
Wargaming - Nicosia, Cyprus -- Wargaming - N/A
New Item with players: The Sword of Shannara:
Brooks, Terry -- Terry Brooks
New Item with players: Practical Entity Framework:
Gorman, Brian L. -- Brian L. Gorman
New Item with players: Battlefield 2142:
Electronic Arts - Redwood City, CA, USA -- Electronic Arts - EA
New Item with players: Star Wars: The Empire Strikes Back:
Hamill, Mark -- Mark Hamill
New Item with players: Top Gun:
Cruise, Tom -- Tom Cruise
New Item with players: Remember the Titans:
Washington, Denzel -- Denzel Washington
New Item with players: Inception:
DiCaprio, Leonardo -- Leonardo DiCaprio
Program Complete
```

Figure 14-33. *The TPT data works very well and allows you to get the full data by type just by including the base type*

Activity 14-6 summary

In this activity, you learned how EFCore5 now allows you to work with table-per-type hierarchies. While it can be a bit tricky to get started, you've seen that by using the inheritance built into C#, you can easily put the types in place to separate your entity data across tables instead of using the discriminator column.

By using this TPT hierarchy instead of the traditional table-per-hierarchy approach, you can see that the data is streamlined and easily associated with the correct type.

Chapter summary

In this chapter, you learned about some of the new features that exist as of EFCore5 that didn't exist prior to the release of EFCore5. While not all of the new features from EFCore5 were covered, you now have been through working with EFCore in both traditional and new approaches. By default, anything that was made available in EFCore5 is also available in EFCore6.

Taking this information forward, you will have the ability to use the best options, traditional or new, in your solutions.

Important takeaways

After working through this chapter, the things you should be in command of are

- Many-to-many navigation properties

- Filtered includes

- Split queries

- Simple logging

- DB command interceptors

- Flexible entity mapping

- Table-per-type inheritance mapping

Closing thoughts

With this chapter, you've seen EFCore in action for a robust database solution, and you've seen some of the features that were released with EFCore5 applied to the solution. The final chapter for this book will conclude the book with things that are going to be released in the next version, which is EFCore6 with .Net 6.

CHAPTER 15

.Net 6 and EFCore6

In this final chapter, you'll take a quick look at some of the new stuff coming in EFCore6 with .Net 6, which are scheduled for simultaneous release in November of 2021.

Planned highly requested features and enhancements

A number of features and enhancements that have been highly requested are planned for release in the next version of EFCore. The following features are currently or were originally planned for release. These features as well as a few additional features that are planned are listed and discussed in more detail at the following link: `https://docs.microsoft.com/en-us/ef/core/what-is-new/ef-core-6.0/plan`. Note that some of these features will be available and others will get cut or won't be fully implemented in the first release of EFCore6.

SQL Server temporal tables

In SQL Server 2016 and later, an option exists to use temporal tables. Temporal tables allow for tables to have the ability to keep history based on timestamps. The benefit of temporal tables is that you can specify a datetime and you can see what the value of the data in the table was at that point in time. Essentially, all data changes are tracked. Temporal tables are also called system-versioned temporal tables.

In order to track the changes, a second table is leveraged to keep the history of the previous versions of rows of data that have changed.

In EFCore6, work is currently underway to begin implementing the ability to work with temporal tables. The main priority for implementation at the time of this writing is the ability to use the `AS OF` operation to get information `"AS OF"` a certain timestamp. Additionally, the hope is to be able to get the ability to specify the name of the history table, along with columns for start and end time.

© Brian L. Gorman 2022
B. L. Gorman, *Practical Entity Framework Core 6*, https://doi.org/10.1007/978-1-4842-7301-2_15

If this functionality gets implemented by the final release, the idea would be that you could select queries using a join statement to get data from the history of the table. For example, you might be able to run a query similar to `context.Items.TemporalAsOf` `(YYYY/MM/DD).Select(i => i.Price)`, which would pull out the `Items` as they existed in the table as of the specified date, and leverage the value of the price from that history.

JSON columns

JSON columns are interesting because they essentially allow any developer to start using JSON to store things like settings or other volatile data that is somewhat well structured but also flexible. NoSQL databases have been leveraging JSON as the mechanism to store data since their inception. With SQL JSON columns, you can get a bit of the best of both worlds, with perhaps a bit of a performance hit.

All of that being said, using JSON columns in your database can be highly useful for creating solutions that are not so tightly bound to the database schema and thereby become more flexible for rapid implementation of new features.

In Activity 15-2, Task 1, a value type is created that stores data in an `nvarchar` column. That value is essentially JSON stored as `nvarchar`. In the activity, JSON data is serialized and deserialized by the client.

The plan for JSON columns with EFCore6 was to create a common way to handle JSON columns for multiple database implementations, including SQL Server. Unfortunately, this feature was cut from the final release.

ColumnAttribute.Order

As you've seen in this book, each migration generates new columns as you specify; however, they are alphabetical and in order based on migration. For example, if the first migration contains Id and Name, you would get those two in order. If a second migration contains Description, the fields would be in the order Id, Name, and Description.

In the new functionality, you could create the columns from each migration in any order, not just alphabetical. Note, however, that the stated plan mentions there is no plan to allow for restructuring columns of an existing table, since doing so is not trivial and requires a rebuild of the entire table. Rebuilding a table would also imply the need to back up data and restore it after the table was successfully rebuilt.

Compiled models

This feature will be used to help with performance of the overall solution. In the current solution, the migrations are based on the database model; however, the model is not precompiled, so there is a bit of overhead at the startup of a new project. Additionally, the compiled model should give an additional performance gain during operation when the model is leveraged.

Migrations bundles

In this book, you created a custom project to ensure that migrations were applied. This is highly useful and easy to implement in a real-world solution. The idea behind a migration bundle would be to give you the ability to build an executable that would allow for easily performing migrations for deployment. The real benefit for this would be in making it easier to deploy your migrations into production.

.Net integration improvements

There are a number of planned improvements for working with EFCore6 in .Net 6. Here you'll read about a couple of them, but you can find more at the link `https://docs.microsoft.com/en-us/ef/core/what-is-new/ef-core-6.0/plan#net-integration`.

System.Data

One of the main improvements planned for EFCore6 with .Net 6 will be to implement the batching API to allow for batching SQL queries. The main improvement will be to allow for the developer to write multiple queries that can be batched and will not require parsing by the client, providing a single trip to the database, rather than parsing the query and making multiple trips from the client to the database. Additional hopes would be to allow for mixed type queries to be batched, such as select and insert in the same batch.

Microsoft.Data.SqlLite

The main enhancements planned would allow for connection pooling and prepared statements.

As noted in the testing chapter of this text, one of the limitations of the in-memory database is the inability to test procedures. With prepared statements, it could potentially be possible to emulate the behavior of stored procedures for integration testing.

Additional new features

In addition to the enhancements and changes listed earlier, a number of new features are planned. A comprehensive list can be found at the following link: `https://docs.microsoft.com/en-us/ef/core/what-is-new/ef-core-6.0/whatsnew`.

A few of the features will be highlighted to close this chapter.

More flexible free text search

In the past, you would not be able to search a field that has been serialized to binary or has been mapped using a value converter. This will enhance your ability to use `Contains` or `FreeText` when looking for matches in your LINQ queries. In the past, this would only work when the column was stored as a string. In EFCore6, you'll be able to leverage this enhanced search against your types, not just against strings. For example, you can add a type for AdditionalProperties that stores JSON data to the Items table, and then you can search the column for matches within that JSON data (see Activity 15-2, Task 1).

UnicodeAttribute

In the past, you would have to use the `IsUnicode` property in the model builder in order to set the type of a field to be `Unicode`. Additionally, you would set that to false for a non-Unicode field. In EFCore6, you'll be able to directly map a field using the new `DataAnnotation` for `Unicode(true|false)` to map a property as Unicode or non-Unicode (see Activity 15-1, Task 3).

PrecisionAttribute

In EFCore6, another `DataAnnotation` that will be added is a `Precision(n,m)` attribute. This attribute will allow you to easily map the precision of a decimal field. In the past, you would have had to use the column `DataAnnotation` similar to the following: `[Column("PurchasePrice", TypeName = ("decimal(18,2)")]`. In EFCore6, you'll be able to set it more simply as `[Precision(18,2)]` (see Activity 15-1, Task 1).

EntityTypeConfigurationAttribute

Another change coming with EFCore6 will be the ability to create configurations for your entities that can be leveraged from outside of the `OnModelCreating` override without having to do any extra configuration.

This will allow for easier use of a layer of abstraction to allow you to better manage your entities and will also help to keep the `DbContext` cleaner. With the `EntityTypeConfigurationAttribute` added to your model, you just reference the model in the `DBContext` as you ordinarily would, and the configuration will be applied as expected (see Activity 15-1, Task 2).

Translate ToString on SQLLite

Translation of non-text types is already possible with EFCore5 for SQL Server, but with EFCore6, you will be able to do this for SQLLite as well. With this feature, non-text fields will be automatically cast to text so that you can search the value for a match (see Activity 15-3).

EF.Functions.Random

Another feature coming with EFCore6 will be the random number function. This function will generate a number between 0 and 1. The underlying SQL will translate to the RAND function (see Activity 15-2, Task 3).

Support for SQL Server sparse columns

When you have data where the column values across the dataset are going to be mostly null, with just a few instances containing data, using sparse columns is a great choice. In the last chapter, you saw how to use the table-per-type mapping. In a table-per-hierarchy mapping, there are going to be many fields that might benefit from being optimized for null values.

In EFCore6, you will be able to use the `IsSparse` mapping in the `OnModelCreating` method via the Fluent API to map a field as a sparse column (see Activity 15-2, Task 5).

Command timeout in the connection string for SQLLite

Another feature for EFCore6 will be the ability to set the command timeout in the connection string for SQLLite databases. To set the command timeout, you can add the command directly to the connection string with the statement `Command Timeout=30` or `Default Timeout=120`.

In-memory database – Validate required parameters

One of the updates to the in-memory database is a new exception being thrown when a required field is null.

Savepoints API – Use partial transactions to roll back to a previous savepoint

Another update to the SQLite database is the ability to use savepoints. When using savepoints, you can save the transaction that is in process. Once you've done that, you can then continue working, and if something goes wrong, you can roll the transaction back to the created savepoint. In this manner, you can commit the changes to the point where the savepoint was created.

Reverse-engineering preserves database comments in code

Another update to EFCore6 is that any comments that exist in a database that is being reverse-engineered will also be translated into comments in the classes generated during the reverse-engineering process.

Chapter 15 activities

In order to keep this simplistic, all activities for Chapter 15 use a prebuilt minimal implementation. For the easiest possible solution, just grab the starter files for each activity, then validate the connection string will connect to your database, open the *Package Manager Console (PMC)* and select the EFCore_DbLibrary project, and then run an update-database command. Always remember a solution is included in the final files for the activity, in case you need to review something or just want to see the solution. For brevity, a few of the enhancements have been combined where it makes sense to limit the number of activities.

As a final note here, remember that I'm working against a preview version of EFCore6, so certain features may change slightly and/or features may be available to you that are not available as I am writing these activities. I will continue to support the codebase at GitHub to make sure any issues are quickly resolved, should any arise.

Activity 15-1: New attributes

One of the easiest ways to get started with new features is to look at the new attributes for Unicode and Precision and then dive a bit into the EntityTypeConfiguration attribute. In this activity, you will take a quick look at all three of these new attributes.

Task 0: Getting started

To get started, grab the EFCore_Activity15-1_StarterFiles and then run the steps mentioned earlier to get the project ready for the activity.

Task 1: Use the Precision attribute

In this task, you will look at two different ways to set the precision and scale on a database column using EFCore6.

Step 1: Note the update-database warning

When you first get the starter files and run the update-database command, you'll note that there is a warning that is happening on two of the fields as follows: *No store type was specified for the decimal property 'CurrentOrFinalPrice' on entity type 'Item'.*

743

This will cause values to be silently truncated if they do not fit in the default precision and scale. Explicitly specify the SQL server column type that can accommodate all the values in 'OnModelCreating' using 'HasColumnType,' specify precision and scale using 'HasPrecision,' or configure a value converter using 'HasConversion.'

The same thing is repeated for the `PurchasePrice` field.

Note that the warning tells you directly to *specify precision and scale using* `HasPrecision` *or configure a value converter using* `HasConversion` (see Figure 15-1).

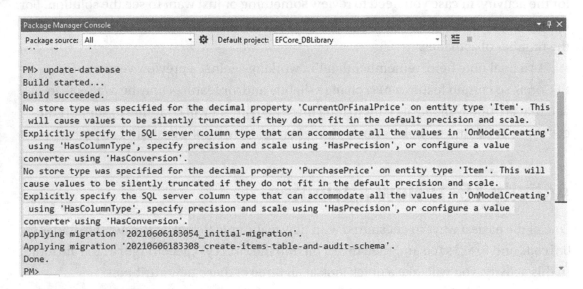

Figure 15-1. The initial run of update-database contains a warning for the lack of using precision and a potential side effect of truncation

There are a couple of ways to get rid of this error. Before you can fix this issue, however, you will want to roll back the migration that creates the Item entity and the schema for auditing. To do this, run the command

```
update-database -migration 20210606183054_initial-migration
```

Once the command is run, you'll be able to apply changes that will fix the problem and re-apply the migration.

Step 2: Fix the precision and scale using the Fluent API

Prior to EFCore6, one way to fix this issue would be to use the Fluent API to set the precision. For this step, you'll use the Fluent API to set the precision and scale on the `CurrentOrFinalPrice` column.

This is easily accomplished by going to the `InventoryDbContext` in the `EFCore_DBLibrary` project. Add the following code to the context after the `OnConfiguring` method and before the `SaveChanges` method:

```
protected override void OnModelCreating(ModelBuilder modelBuilder)
{
    modelBuilder.Entity<Item>()
                .Property(x => x.CurrentOrFinalPrice)
                .HasPrecision(18, 2);
}
```

This will set the precision and scale to 18, 2, which is a familiar setting for decimals if you've used SQL database for a long time. Feel free to use a smaller number for the precision if you so desire.

Do not run the migrations yet. Also note that if you are reviewing the final solution files, this code will be commented out in the final files due to changes coming in Task 2 of this activity. At this point, of course, you would not want to comment out that code.

Step 3: Fix the precision and scale using the new Precision attribute

A second way to fix the precision and scale is to use the new `Precision` attribute available in EFCore6. For this step, you will use this new attribute to fix the `PurchasePrice` column precision warning.

Navigate to the `Item.cs` class file in the `InventoryModels` project. Locate the line of code `public decimal? PurchasePrice { get; set; }` and replace that code with the following two lines of code above that line to decorate the property with the new `Precision` attribute:

```
[Precision(18, 2)]
public decimal? PurchasePrice { get; set; }
```

Unfortunately, the code won't work just yet. If you try to use the suggested fixes, the solution would be to install the package MathNet.Numerics, which is not the correct package (as shown in Figure 15-2).

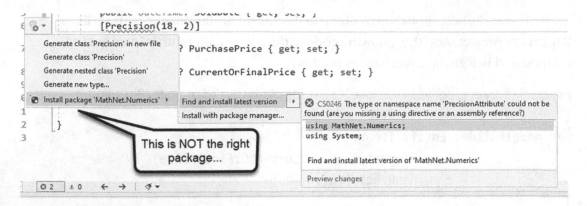

Figure 15-2. *The current suggestions do not contain the correct way to get this new attribute to work*

To fix this, you need to add a reference to `Microsoft.EntityFrameworkCore` into your solution. You can do this using the `Manage NuGet Packages for Solution` dialog, or an easy way to get it is to just add the following lines of code to your `InventoryModels.csproj` project file:

```
<ItemGroup>
  <PackageReference Include="Microsoft.EntityFrameworkCore"
Version="6.0.0-*" />
</ItemGroup>
```

Note that I'm using schema 6.0.0-* since I'm working against preview versions and want to get the latest version of the code. Your version number might be different and shouldn't matter as long as the first number is 6.

You could also just add this code and then use the Manage NuGet Package Manager for the solution to see if any updates are available.

Save the project file, and then you will be able to add a using statement for `Microsoft.EntityFramework` to your `Item.cs` class file as shown in Figure 15-3.

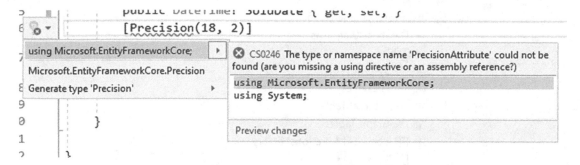

Figure 15-3. *Once the NuGet package for EntityFrameworkCore is loaded into the project, you can add the correct using statement to leverage the Precision attribute*

Step 4: Build the project and run the `update-database` command

With the two fixes for precision issues, ensure that you've rolled the current migration back to the `initial-migration` so the create items table migration will be re-applied, and then run the `update-database` command in the PMC to run the `create-items-table-and-audit-schema` migration. Note that as the `update-database` command executes this time, there are no longer any warnings generated about precision and scale for the two fields (see Figure 15-4).

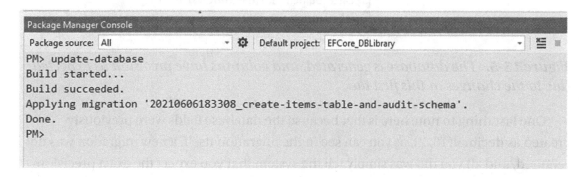

Figure 15-4. *The project is updated, and there are no longer warnings for precision and scale as the migrations are applied*

Note that running these migrations has generated the appropriate database and columns with precision as expected (review Figure 15-5 for clarity).

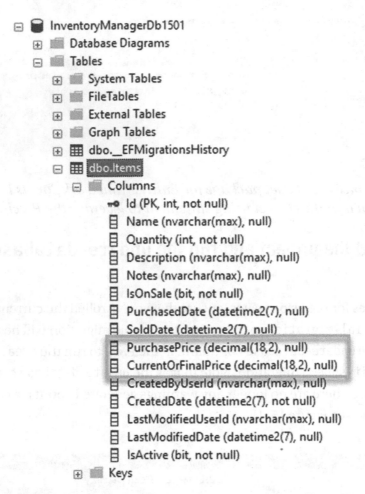

Figure 15-5. *The database is generated, and columns have precision as expected due to the changes in this first task*

One last thing to note here is that because the database fields were previously created as decimal(18, 2), as you can see in the migration itself, a new migration was not required, and all you did was simply tell the system that you expect the exact precision and scale as defined. Had you changed the precision or scale, you would likely need to create a new migration to also affect the data structure changes in the database.

Task 2: Leverage the EntityTypeConfigurationAttribute

In this second task for Activity 15-1, you will leverage the EntityTypeConfigurationAttribute to see how you can move entity configuration using the Fluent API into its own class, instead of the DbContext or OnModelCreating.

Step 1: Revert the database again

To get a fresh start for the migrations, once again roll your database back to the initial migration using the command

```
update-database -migration 20210606183054_initial-migration
```

You can likely get this command back by simply using the up arrow in the PMC if you haven't closed out the project.

Step 2: Move the Fluent API declaration for precision out of the DbContext using the new EntityTypeConfigurationAttribute

In this step, you will rework the precision and scale fix that uses the Fluent API to use the new EntityTypeConfigurationAttribute by implementing a new class to contain the information. I think that once you've seen this, you'll understand how useful this approach would be in the real world due to the ability to keep your context file cleaner while also keeping entity code and configuration details together in the same project.

Begin by navigating to the InventoryDbContext file in the EFCore_DBLibrary project. In this file, locate the code for the OnModelCreating method that you implemented in the last task. Remove the code that sets the precision for the Item entity (note that I am just going to comment this code out for clarity in the final files, but you will not need it so you can remove it).

Step 3: Add a new class file called ItemConfiguration to the InventoryModels project, and implement IEntityTypeConfiguration<Item> in the new class

To complete this step, navigate to the InventoryModels project and add a new class file named ItemConfiguration.cs to create the new configuration class. Set the code for the class to the following block of code:

```
public class ItemConfiguration : IEntityTypeConfiguration<Item>
{
    public void Configure(EntityTypeBuilder<Item> builder)
    {
        //configuration code here...
    }
}
```

Note that this code is creating the class and implementing the interface for IEntityTypeConfiguration on type Item. You will need to add the using statements using Microsoft.EntityFrameworkCore and using Microsoft.EntityFrameworkCore. Metadata.Builders to the file.

Once you have that code in place, replace the Configure method code with the following to set the precision for the CurrentOrFinalPrice column on the Item entity:

```
public void Configure(EntityTypeBuilder<Item> builder)
{
    builder
        .Property(x => x.CurrentOrFinalPrice)
        .HasPrecision(18, 2);
}
```

To complete the operation, you also need to tell the Item class to leverage this configuration. Open the Item.cs file and add the following declaration to the top of the Item class:

```
[EntityTypeConfiguration(typeof(ItemConfiguration))]
```

Another way you could have done this previously would be to register it in the OnModelCreating, but this still kept the implementation tightly coupled to the DbContext. With this new approach, you can use your model with its appropriate configuration in any DbContext without having to register it in the OnModelCreating method. Figure 15-6 shows the implementation in the Item class for clarity.

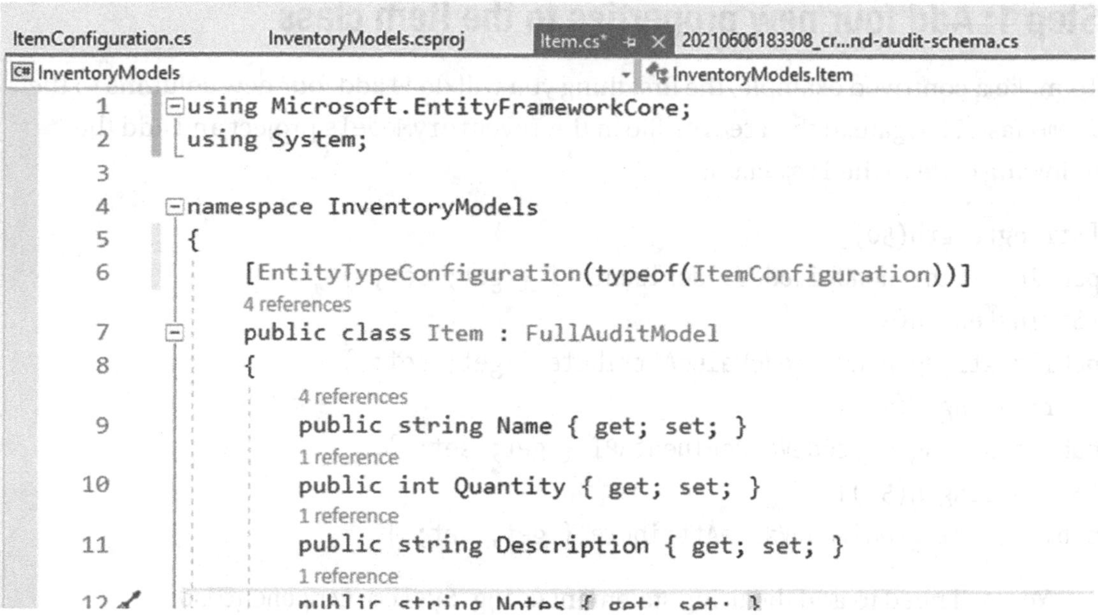

Figure 15-6. *The EntityTypeConfiguration attribute is used on the Item class to register the ItemConfiguration implementation*

Step 4: Run the update-database command to see the final result

With the new EntityTypeConfiguration in place, ensure you have deleted the InventoryManagerDb1501 database and then run the update-database command again.

Once again, the operation will complete as expected, with no warnings for precision or scale. With this, you've successfully moved the configuration from the DbContext into the ItemConfiguration class.

Task 3: Use the new Unicode attribute

For this final task of Activity 15-1, you will see how to leverage the new Unicode attribute for a property in your entity. Once again, there are two ways to do this. The traditional way is using the Fluent API, and the new way is to use the Unicode attribute.

Step 1: Add four new properties to the Item class

To make a contrived example, the first thing you will do is add four new columns to the Item class. Navigate to the `Item.cs` file in the `InventoryModels` project and add the following code to the Item class:

```
[StringLength(50)]
public string nonUnicodeValueFluentAPI { get; set; }
[StringLength(50)]
public string nonUnicodeValueAttribute { get; set; }
[StringLength(50)]
public string UnicodeValueFluentAPI { get; set; }
[StringLength(50)]
public string UnicodeValueAttribute { get; set; }
```

You will need to add the using statement using `System.ComponentModel.DataAnnotations` due to the `StringLength` attribute on the new properties.

Step 2: Create the FluentAPI Unicode mapping implementations

In this step, you will set two of the properties to be either a Unicode or a non-Unicode field by setting them correctly in the configuration (you will leverage the `ItemConfiguration` you built in the last task to do this).

Navigate to the `ItemConfiguration` class and add the following code to build out the properties to be Unicode or non-Unicode as expected:

```
builder
    .Property(x => x.nonUnicodeValueFluentAPI)
    .IsUnicode(false);
builder
    .Property(x => x.UnicodeValueFluentAPI)
    .IsUnicode(true);
```

Hopefully, the code is clear enough here that you can see how this should work, setting one property to be Unicode and the other property to be non-Unicode.

Do not run any migration commands yet.

Step 3: Use the new Unicode attribute to map the other two properties

Return to the Item class and update the nonUnicodeValueAttribute property with the following attribute: [Unicode(false)].

Above the UnicodeValueAttribute property, use the attribute [Unicode(true)].

For clarity, the four new fields should now be declared with the following code:

```
[StringLength(50)]
public string nonUnicodeValueFluentAPI { get; set; }
[StringLength(50)]
[Unicode(false)]
public string nonUnicodeValueAttribute { get; set; }
[StringLength(50)]
public string UnicodeValueFluentAPI { get; set; }
[StringLength(50)]
[Unicode(true)]
public string UnicodeValueAttribute { get; set; }
```

Step 4: Add a new migration and update the database

To see how both the Fluent API and the new attribute for Unicode can be used in your code, run the command add-migration adding-properties-unicode-attribute.

Review the generated migration to ensure that both approaches to creating Unicode and non-Unicode fields work as expected (Figure 15-7 shows the expected migration Up method).

```
0 references
protected override void Up(MigrationBuilder migrationBuilder)
{
    migrationBuilder.AddColumn<string>(
        name: "UnicodeValueAttribute",
        table: "Items",
        type: "nvarchar(50)",
        maxLength: 50,
        nullable: true);

    migrationBuilder.AddColumn<string>(
        name: "UnicodeValueFluentAPI",
        table: "Items",
        type: "nvarchar(50)",
        maxLength: 50,
        nullable: true);

    migrationBuilder.AddColumn<string>(
        name: "nonUnicodeValueAttribute",
        table: "Items",
        type: "varchar(50)",
        unicode: false,
        maxLength: 50,
        nullable: true);

    migrationBuilder.AddColumn<string>(
        name: "nonUnicodeValueFluentAPI",
        table: "Items",
        type: "varchar(50)",
        unicode: false,
        maxLength: 50,
        nullable: true);
}
```

Figure 15-7. *The migration is generated and both approaches work, either via the Fluent API declaration or via the new Unicode attribute*

Run the update-database command, and review the database in SSMS to ensure fields are generated as expected (see Figure 15-8).

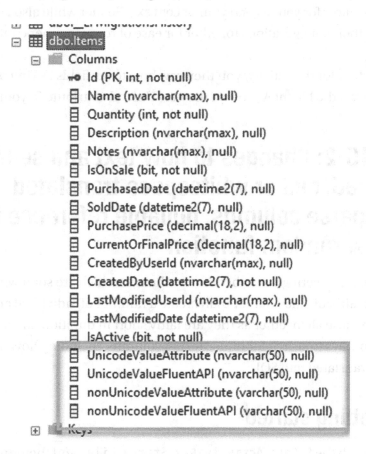

Figure 15-8. *The columns are generated in the database as expected with two Unicode and two non-Unicode columns*

Activity 15-1 summary

In this first activity for the chapter, you were able to implement a number of the new features regarding attributes and the ability to move Fluent API code to a new configuration file.

First you saw the use of the `Precision` attribute and how that allows you to define the precision and scale as a data annotation as of EFCore6. For comparison, you also saw a traditional way to accomplish this same task in the Fluent API, which you would have done prior to EFCore6 (and still works in EFCore6).

You then took a look at the implementation of the IEntityTypeAttribute interface in a class that you can use to build out the properties for a specific entity. This is a great feature as it will allow for you to keep your DbContext cleaner while also keeping your properties and their configurations together for ease of reuse in other contexts and projects.

In the final task for the activity, you then saw how to set fields as Unicode or non-Unicode, either via the Fluent API or via the new Unicode attribute in your model class.

Activity 15-2: Changes to how text and searching are handled, null or whitespace translated to SQL, sparse columns, nullable reference types, and a new random function

This activity will be covering a number of new changes which are somewhat closely related, but yet fairly distinct. Rather than create a number of individual activities, I've chosen to wrap these all together as they are fairly short in duration and are mostly concerned with ways to search for or use text in columns, including how null or whitespace is translated into SQL.

Task 0: Getting started

To get started, grab the EFCore_Activity15-2_StarterFiles and then run the steps mentioned earlier to get the project ready for the activity.

A couple of quick notes is that in order to make this activity a bit more robust and create the ability to use some of the new functionality, this project has everything from the first activity plus a new Category entity. Items have one Category associated, and Categories can have many Items. All of this relationship information is defined using regular virtual properties and Fluent API configurations in the individual EntityTypeConfigurations for Item and Category.

Task 1: Improved free text search

In this first task, you will explore how EFCore6 has enhanced your ability to search for text using Contains.

Step 1: Ensure you have full-text search installed

This first task will not work unless you currently have installed full-text search capability on your database. If you are not sure, right-click the Items table. If Full-Text index is grayed out, it's likely you didn't install it. To install it, re-run SQL Server installer with a custom installation, and then when the prompt is available, select update an existing installation. Select your installation, and then make sure to select the Full-Text and Semantic Extractions for Search under Database Engine Services (see Figure 15-9).

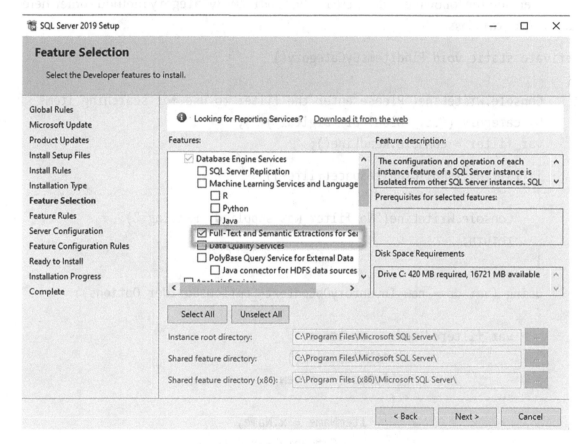

Figure 15-9. *You will need to have the Full-Text and Semantic Extractions for Search enabled to complete Task 1 of this activity*

Note that turning this feature on can take some time. Additionally, you will need to reconnect to your database or potentially even restart SSMS if you already have it open at the time of installation of this feature.

Step 1: Search for Items by Category Name with a traditional approach

To begin this activity, the first thing to do is examine a traditional search for Items by using one of the properties of a Category.

Navigate to the Program.cs file in the EFCore_Activity1502 project, and add a method call to a new method named FindItemsByCategory following the call to ListInventory in the Main method.

Then add the following code to create the FindItemsByCategory method somewhere in the Program class:

```
private static void FindItemsByCategory()
{
    Console.WriteLine("Please enter the filter to use for searching items
    by category (i.e. 'Blue' or 'Digital'):");
    var filter = Console.ReadLine();

    if (string.IsNullOrWhiteSpace(filter))
    {
        Console.WriteLine("No filter was supplied. Exiting.");
        return;
    }

    using (var db = new InventoryDbContext(_optionsBuilder.Options))
    {
        var filteredItems = db.Items
                    .AsNoTracking()
                    .Select(x => new
                    {
                        ItemName = x.Name,
                            Category = x.Category,
                        CategoryName = x.Category.Name,
                        CategoryColor = x.Category.Color,
                        CategoryColorValue = x.Category.ColorValue
                    })
```

```
            .Where(x => x.CategoryName.Contains(filter)
                || x.CategoryColor.Contains(filter)
                || x.CategoryColorValue.Contains(filter))
            .OrderBy(x => x.ItemName).ToList();

    filteredItems.ForEach(x => Console.WriteLine($"New Item:
    {x.ItemName} " +

                            $"has Category {x.CategoryName} " +
                            $"with color {x.CategoryColor}"));

    }
}
```

Run the program, and you should be able to get results similar to what is shown in Figure 15-10.

```
New Item: Apollo 13 has Category Digital with color Blue
New Item: Batman Begins has Category Digital with color Blue
New Item: Hitch has Category Physical with color Green
New Item: Inception has Category Physical with color Green
New Item: Liar Liar has Category Digital with color Blue
New Item: Remember the Titans has Category Pre-Release with color Red
New Item: Stand By Me has Category Physical with color Green
New Item: Star Wars: The Empire Strikes Back has Category Pre-Release with color Red
New Item: The Martian has Category Physical with color Green
New Item: The Prestige has Category Pre-Release with color Red
New Item: Top Gun has Category Pre-Release with color Red
New Item: WarGames has Category Pre-Release with color Red
Please enter the filter to use for searching items by category (i.e. 'Blue' or 'Digital'):
Red
New Item: Remember the Titans has Category Pre-Release with color Red
New Item: Star Wars: The Empire Strikes Back has Category Pre-Release with color Red
New Item: The Prestige has Category Pre-Release with color Red
New Item: Top Gun has Category Pre-Release with color Red
New Item: WarGames has Category Pre-Release with color Red
Program completed
```

Figure 15-10. *The filter works as expected using the contains method in a traditional query*

This traditional approach works as expected. However, note that you had to explicitly define all of the properties for the Category entity to search against in the Where clause of the query.

Step 2: Leverage the improved free text search in EFCore6

In order to see how this new EF.Functions.Contains operation works, you will need to create a new value type property that doesn't map to a navigation. Since the Category is a navigation on the Item, you can't use the Fluent API to map it as a property.

For that reason, in the InventoryModels project, add a new class file called AdditionalProperty.cs for a new class AdditionalProperty, which will be stored as JSON in the database, not as a full entity that is mapped to a table.

In the new AdditionalProperty class, add the following code:

```
public class AdditionalProperty
{
    public string Name { get; set; }
    public string Value { get; set; }
}
```

Then return to the Item class and map this new class with a new property as follows:

```
public List<AdditionalProperty> AdditionalProperties { get; set; }
```

Don't forget to add the using statement using System.Collections.Generic.

In order to leverage the JSON mapping for this new property, return to the ItemConfiguration class in the InventoryModels project to further define how this property is mapped in the Fluent API.

In the ItemConfiguration, add the following code:

```
builder
    .Property(i => i.AdditionalProperties)
    .HasConversion(ap => JsonSerializer.Serialize(ap, null),
                   ap => JsonSerializer.Deserialize<List<AdditionalProperty>>
                   (ap, null),
                    new ValueComparer<List<AdditionalProperty>>(
                        (c1, c2) => c1.SequenceEqual(c2),
                        c => c.Aggregate(0, (a, v) => HashCode.Combine(a,
                        v.GetHashCode())),
                        c => c.ToList()));
```

This code will require a number of using statements to be added to the class. Ensure that your ItemConfiguration class has all of the following using statements at the top of the file:

```
using Microsoft.EntityFrameworkCore;
using Microsoft.EntityFrameworkCore.ChangeTracking;
using Microsoft.EntityFrameworkCore.Metadata.Builders;
```

```
using System;
using System.Collections.Generic;
using System.Linq;
using System.Text.Json;
```

Step 3: Add a migration to affect the changes to the Items table

Now that you've created a new property for the Item class, you need to add a migration to be able to store the data.

Use the command `add-migration add-additional-properties-to-Item` to create a new migration. The migration should be simple and should look like what is shown in Figure 15-11.

```
1 reference
public partial class addadditionalpropertiestoItem : Migration
{
    0 references
    protected override void Up(MigrationBuilder migrationBuilder)
    {
        migrationBuilder.AddColumn<string>(
            name: "AdditionalProperties",
            table: "Items",
            type: "nvarchar(max)",
            nullable: true);
    }

    0 references
    protected override void Down(MigrationBuilder migrationBuilder)
    {
        migrationBuilder.DropColumn(
            name: "AdditionalProperties",
            table: "Items");
    }
}
```

Figure 15-11. *The migration contains the new column for Additional Properties, and it's stored as nvarchar(max)*

Once you've reviewed the migration, run the `update-database` command.

Step 4: Create the code to perform the search

Now that you have the data structures in place to store additional properties as JSON in your database in a single column, you need to add data and then leverage those additional properties.

Begin by returning to the `Program.cs` file in the `EFCore_Activity1502` project and then adding a new method call to `FindItemsByAdditionalProperty` in the `Main` method. Comment out the call to `FindItemsByCategory` to make the output easier to review.

Next, add the following code to define the new method somewhere in the `Program` class:

```
private static void FindItemsByAdditionalProperty()
{
    Console.WriteLine("Please enter the filter to use for searching items
    by additional properties:");
    var filter = Console.ReadLine();

    if (string.IsNullOrWhiteSpace(filter))
    {
        Console.WriteLine("No filter was supplied. Exiting.");
        return;
    }

    using (var db = new InventoryDbContext(_optionsBuilder.Options))
    {
        var filteredItems = db.Items
                        .AsNoTracking()
                        .Select(x => new
                        {
                            ItemName = x.Name,
                            AdditionalProperties = x.AdditionalProperties
                        })
                        .Where(i => EF.Functions.Contains(i.
                        AdditionalProperties, filter))
                        .OrderBy(x => x.ItemName).ToList();
```

```
    foreach (var item in filteredItems)
    {
        Console.WriteLine($"New Item: {item.ItemName}");
        item.AdditionalProperties.ForEach(ap => Console.WriteLine($"AP:
        {ap.Name} | {ap.Value}"));
    }
}
}
```

To complete the initial code changes, add the following method to generate a couple of additional property lists:

```
private static List<AdditionalProperty> GenerateAdditionalProperties(int
modifier)
{
    if (modifier % 2 == 0)
    {
        return new List<AdditionalProperty>() {
            new AdditionalProperty() { Name = "Genre", Value="Sci/Fi"},
            new AdditionalProperty() { Name = "Rating", Value="PG"},
            new AdditionalProperty() { Name = "RottenTomatoes",
            Value="68/45"},
        };
    }
    else
    {
        return new List<AdditionalProperty>() {
            new AdditionalProperty() { Name = "Genre", Value="Action"},
            new AdditionalProperty() { Name = "Rating", Value="R"},
            new AdditionalProperty() { Name = "RottenTomatoes",
            Value="92/71"},
        };
    }
}
```

Finally, add the line of code

```
AdditionalProperties = GenerateAdditionalProperties(r.Next(0, 99))
```

to the declaration of a new `Item` under the `CategoryId` in the `EnsureItem` method.

Run the program to see what happens. Do you think this will work? If you answered No, you are correct (unless you already have defined a full-text index on the Items table). Running the code currently without a full-text index generates the error as shown in Figure 15-12.

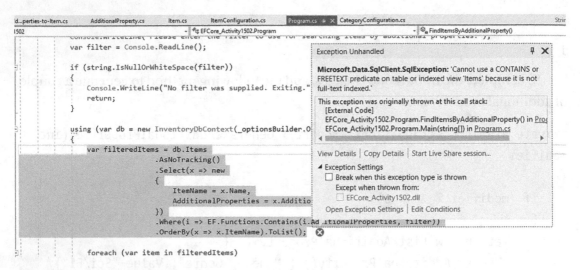

Figure 15-12. *The Items table is not yet set up with a full-text index so an error is shown during execution*

Step 5: Create a full-text index on the Items table

Open SSMS and connect to your database if you haven't already. Right-click the Items table, and then select `Full-Text index` ➤ `Define Full-Text Index`.

Use the wizard to create the full-text index for the Items table. Select the `AdditionalProperties` field when asked to select table columns, and do not select `Statistical Semantics` as using that option requires additional configuration and should not be necessary for this activity. Track changes automatically. If you have an existing catalog, select it. If not, create a new one and set it as the default. Leave the index filegroup and full-text stoplist with the default selections. Skip through the population schedules. Review settings and click Finish. For clarity, review Figure 15-13.

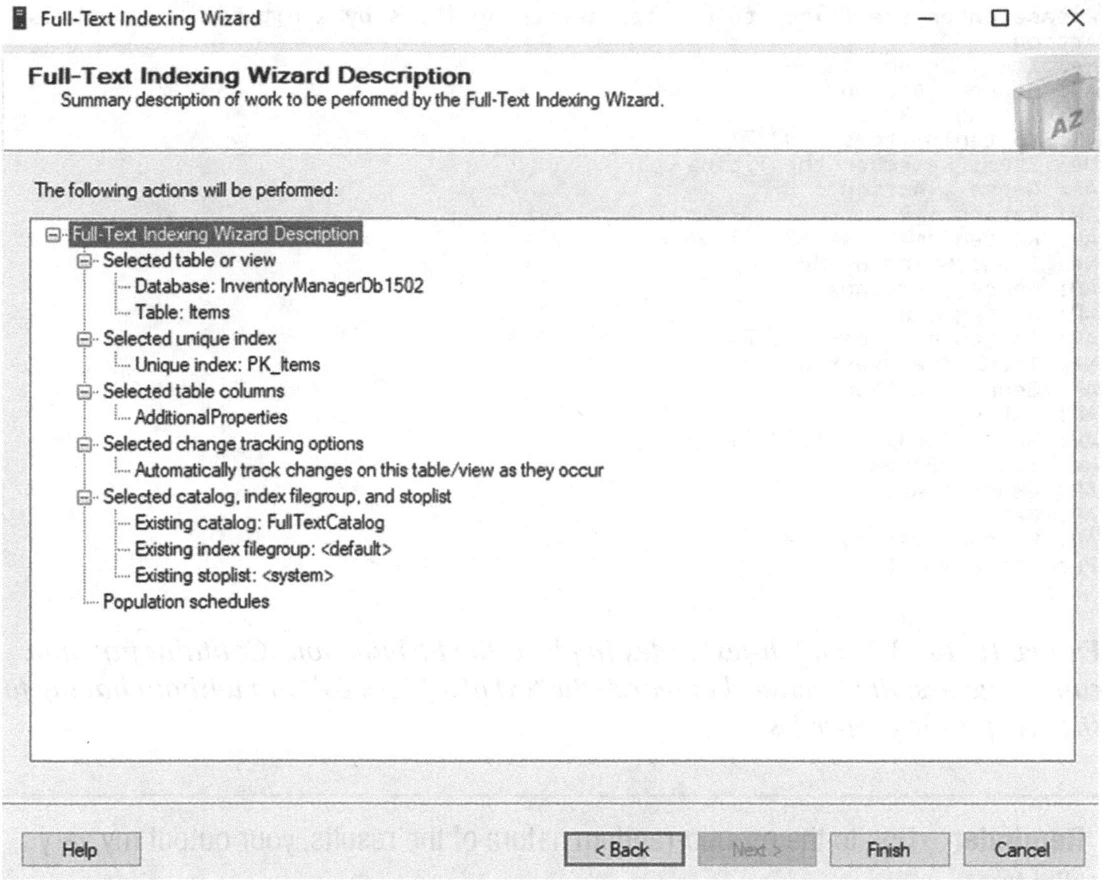

Figure 15-13. *The final page of the Full-Text Indexing Wizard is shown to help with clarity on expected configuration*

Once the wizard completes, run the program again. This time you should have no problem searching your additional properties field (see Figure 15-14 for sample results).

```
Please enter the filter to use for searching items by additional properties:
Action
New Item: Inception
AP: Genre | Action
AP: Rating | R
AP: RottenTomatoes | 92/71
New Item: Remember the Titans
AP: Genre | Action
AP: Rating | R
AP: RottenTomatoes | 92/71
New Item: Stand By Me
AP: Genre | Action
AP: Rating | R
AP: RottenTomatoes | 92/71
New Item: The Prestige
AP: Genre | Action
AP: Rating | R
AP: RottenTomatoes | 92/71
New Item: WarGames
AP: Genre | Action
AP: Rating | R
AP: RottenTomatoes | 92/71
Program completed
```

Figure 15-14. *With a full-text index in place, the EF.Functions.Contains function can be successfully leveraged to search the text of a JSON column without having to specify specific properties*

Reminder   Due to the pseudo-random nature of the results, your output my vary slightly.

Task 2: Review the upgrade to string.Concat

For this activity, you will run a simple query to show that string.Concat is no longer limited to just two arguments as it was in previous versions of EFCore.

Step 1: Add the method

For this first step, return to the Main method in the Program class for the EFCore_Activity1502 project. Add a method call for a new method named StringConcatWithMultipleArguments. As the output for this will be verbose, comment out your other calls to ListInventory, FindItemsByCategory, and FindItemsByAdditionalProperty.

Next, add the method code as follows somewhere in the Program class:

```
private static void StringConcatWithMultipleArguments()
{
    using (var db = new InventoryDbContext(_optionsBuilder.Options))
    {
        //in the past, you could only concat two
        var result = db.Items
                    .AsNoTracking()
                    .Select(x => new
                    {
                        ItemName = x.Name,
                        ItemDetail = string.Concat("Item: ", x.Name
                                        , " Description: ",
                                        x.Description
                                        , " Notes: ", x.Notes),
                        Category = x.Category,
                        CategoryDetail = string.Concat("Category: ",
                        x.Category.Name
                                        , " Color: ", x.Category.
                                        Color
                                        , " Value: ", x.Category.
                                        ColorValue)
                    })
                    .OrderBy(x => x.ItemName).ToList();

        result.ForEach(x => Console.WriteLine($"{x.ItemDetail} |
        {x.CategoryDetail}"));
    }
}
```

Step 2: Run the program to see the results

With the code in place, run the program to see the results of the use of string.Concat in EFCore6 with more than two parameters allowed (review Figure 15-15).

```
Item: Apollo 13 Description: Houston, we have a problem Notes: Tom Hanks, Gary Sinise, Kevin Bacon, Ed Harris | Category: Pre-Release Color: Red Value: #FF000
0
Item: Batman Begins Description: You either die the hero or live long enough to see yourself become the villain Notes: Christian Bale, Katie Holmes | Category
: Pre-Release Color: Red Value: #FF0000
Item: Hitch Description: Never lie, steal, cheat, or drink. But if you must lie, lie in the arms of the one you love. If you must steal, steal away from bad c
ompany. If you must cheat, cheat death Notes: Wil Smith, Eva Mendes, Kevin James | Category: Pre-Release Color: Red Value: #FF0000
Item: Inception Description: You mustn't be afraid to dream a little bigger, darling Notes: Leonardo DiCaprio, Tom Hardy, Joseph Gordon-Levitt | Category: Phy
sical Color: Green Value: #00FF00
Item: Liar Liar Description: The pen is blue. The pen is blue. The #$#^°|(# pen is blue Notes: Jim Carrey | Category: Pre-Release Color: Red Value: #FF0000
Item: Remember the Titans Description: Left Side, Strong Side Notes: Denzell Washington, Will Patton | Category: Digital Color: Blue Value: #0000FF
Item: Stand By Me Description: I never had any friends later on like the ones I had when I was 12 Notes: Wil Wheaton, Jerry O'Connell, Corey Feldman, River Ph
oenix | Category: Physical Color: Green Value: #00FF00
Item: Star Wars: The Empire Strikes Back Description: He will join us or die, master Notes: Harrison Ford, Carrie Fisher, Mark Hamill | Category: Pre-Release
Color: Red Value: #FF0000
Item: The Martian Description: So Mars is international waters. Now, NASA is an American non-military organization, it owns the Hab. But the second I walk out
side I'm in international waters. So Here's the cool part. I'm about to leave for the Schiaparelli Crater where I'm going to commandeer the Ares IV lander. No
body explicitly gave me permission to do this, and they can't until I'm on board the Ares IV. So I'm going to be taking a craft over in international waters w
ithout permission, which by definition... makes me a pirate. Mark Watney: Space Pirate. Notes: Matt Damon | Category: Pre-Release Color: Red Value: #FF0000
Item: The Prestige Description: Now you're looking for the secret. But you won't find it because of course, you're not really looking. You don't really want t
o work it out. You want to be fooled. Notes: Michael Caine, Christian Bale, Hugh Jackman | Category: Physical Color: Green Value: #00FF00
Item: Top Gun Description: I feel the need, the need for speed! Notes: Tom Cruise, Anthony Edwards, Val Kilmer | Category: Digital Color: Blue Value: #0000FF
Item: WarGames Description: Intersting game. The only way to win is not to play. Notes: Matthew Broderick | Category: Physical Color: Green Value: #00FF00
Program completed
```

Figure 15-15. *The string.Concat method can now leverage more than just two arguments in EFCore6*

Task 3: Review the use of EF.Functions.Random

In this task, you will check out the EF.Functions.Random to return a pseudo-random number between 0 and 1.

Step 1: Add a new method to review EF.Functions.Random

Return to the Main method in the Program class. Comment out the call to the StringConcatWithMultipleArguments method, and add a new method called EFFunctionsRandom.

Add the code for the method somewhere in the Program class as follows:

```
private static void EFFunctionsRandom()
{
    using (var db = new InventoryDbContext(_optionsBuilder.Options))
    {
        var items = db.Items.AsNoTracking()
                    .Where(i => i.PurchasePrice >= (decimal)(EF.
                    Functions.Random() * 33) + 1)
                    .ToList();
        items.ForEach(x => Console.WriteLine($"{x.Name} | {x.PurchasePrice}"));
    }
}
```

Next, add the following line of code to the Item declaration in the EnsureItem method after the AdditionalProperties:

```
PurchasePrice = r.Next(4, 33)
```

Step 2: Run the program a couple of times to see results

With the code in place, run the program a few times to see various results. They should be similar to what is shown in Figure 15-16.

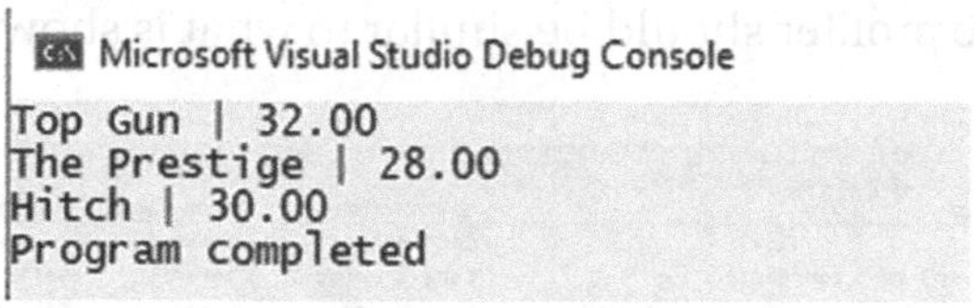

```
Microsoft Visual Studio Debug Console
Top Gun | 32.00
The Prestige | 28.00
Hitch | 30.00
Program completed
```

Figure 15-16. *The EF.Functions.Random can be used to get results based on the returned value of a pseudo-random number*

Task 4: Reviewing improved SQL Server translation for IsNullorWhiteSpace

This task shows how EFCore6 now handles IsNullorWhiteSpace to optimize query execution.

Step 1: Create the new method

For this first task, return to the Main method of the Program class. Comment out the call to EFFunctionsRandom, and add a new method call for a method named IsNullOrWhiteSpaceReview.

Add the code for the IsNullOrWhiteSpaceReview method somewhere in the Program class as follows:

```
private static void IsNullOrWhiteSpaceReview()
{
    using (var db = new InventoryDbContext(_optionsBuilder.Options))
    {
        var items = db.Items.AsNoTracking()
                    .Where(i => string.IsNullOrWhiteSpace(i.Description)
                                || string.IsNullOrWhiteSpace(i.
                                Notes))
                    .ToList();
```

```
    items.ForEach(x => Console.WriteLine($"{x.Name} | has null or
    whitespace in description or notes"));
  }
}
```

The output from the profiler should be similar to what is shown in Figure 15-17.

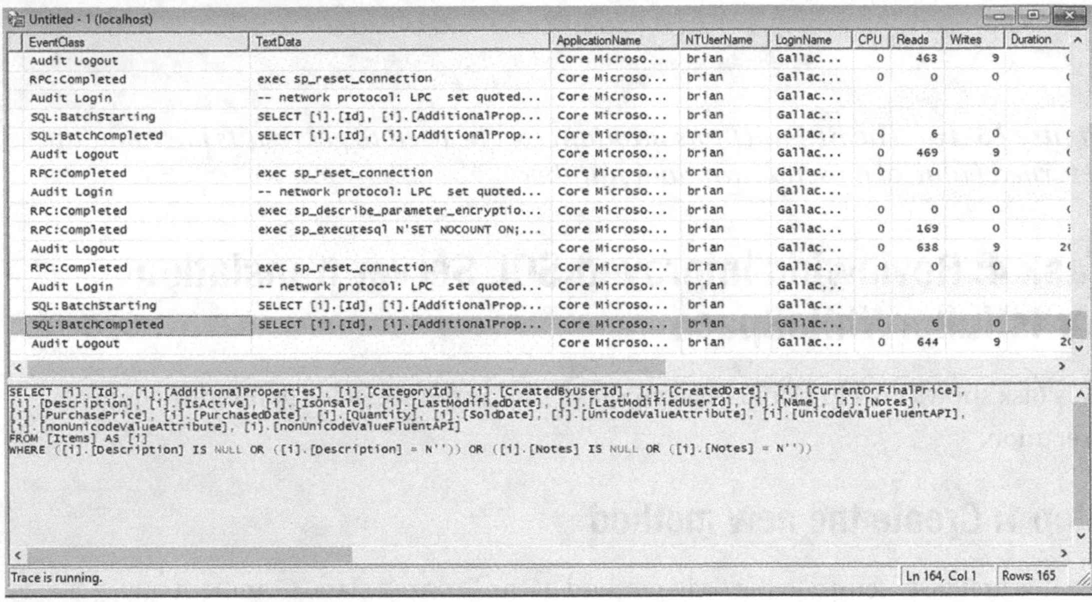

Figure 15-17. *The SQL Server Profiler reveals the output from the query that has optimized the IsNullOrWhiteSpace query*

In the past, the Where clause would have run operations like `LTRIM(RTRIM([i].`
`[Description]))` = N" instead of the simple `[i].[Description]` = N".

Step 2: Review the SQL output in SQL Server Profiler

Use SSMS to turn on a new session for the SQL Server Profiler. Once the profiler session is running, run the program and review the query output.

Task 5: Support for sparse columns

If you worked through the book prior to reading this chapter, you've already seen the changes related to the *table-per-type (TPT)* vs. *table-per-hierarchy (TPH)* (review Activity 14-6 for more information).

In this task, you will see how EFCore6 has optimized the database for sparse columns in a TPH implementation.

Briefly, the difference is that a TPT implementation creates a table for each of the classes that inherit from the base type. In a TPH implementation, only one table is used, and a column is added to differentiate the specific type. In TPT, columns can map exactly to the type that is being stored. In TPH, you end up with a number of columns that do not get data due to the general nature of the table spanning multiple types.

Step 1: Implement the TPH model classes

Begin this first step for this final task by creating a new class file named Player.cs in the InventoryModels project. Then add two implementing classes Person.cs and Company.cs.

Define the Player.cs class with the following code:

```
public class Player : FullAuditModel
{
    [Required]
    [StringLength(50)]
    public virtual string Name { get; set; }

    [StringLength(500)]
    public string Description { get; set; }

    public virtual List<Item> Items { get; set; } = new List<Item>();
}
```

Define the Person.cs class as follows:

```
public class Person : Player
{
    [StringLength(50)]
    public string FirstName { get; set; }
    [StringLength(250)]
    public string LastName { get; set; }

    public override string Name => $"{FirstName} {LastName}";
}
```

Implement the Company.cs file as follows:

```
public class Company : Player
{
    [StringLength(150)]
    public string CompanyName { get; set; }

    [StringLength(10)]
    public string StockSymbol { get; set; }

    [StringLength(50)]
    public string City { get; set; }

    public override string Name => $"{CompanyName} - {StockSymbol}";
}
```

In order to create a many-to-many relationship between Players and Items, also add the following to the Item class:

```
public virtual List<Player> Players { get; set; }
```

Step 2: Add the new entities to the DbContext

There are a number of ways to register the entities. Using the DbSet<T> approach is the easiest, but you could also register each entity in the OnModelCreating if you prefer to use the Fluent API.

In the InventoryDbContext, add the following three lines following the line that declares the DbSet<Category>:

```
public DbSet<Player> Players { get; set; }
public DbSet<Person> People { get; set; }
public DbSet<Company> Companies { get; set; }
```

With the declarations in place, run the command add-migration create-tph-players-person-company. The migration that is generated should create the Players table and also creates a join table between Items and Players. The main thing to note is the additional column Discriminator that is added to the Players table and columns like StockSymbol and FirstName and LastName, which are specific to sub-types, but all included in the table.

Also note, however, that no columns are currently marked as sparse. Run the command `remove-migration` to remove the generated migration.

Step 3: Mark StockSymbol as sparse

To show how the sparse column supports, you will just tell the system to mark the stock symbol as a sparse column. This is a bit contrived, but good enough to get the point across.

Navigate to the `InventoryDbContext` in the `EFCore_DBLibrary` project. Add the following line of code to the `OnModelCreating` method:

```
modelBuilder.Entity<Company>().Property(x => x.StockSymbol).IsSparse();
```

Note that as of the time of this writing, you cannot use `IsSparse` in the `EntityTypeConfiguration`, which is why it is being done in the `OnModelCreating` method here.

Step 4: Regenerate the migration

Return to the PMC and run the add-migration command again:

```
add-migration create-tph-players-person-company
```

You should be able to easily get this back with your up arrow.

Note that this time the migration is created and the column `StockSymbol` is created with a special annotation `SqlServer:Sparse` (see Figure 15-18).

```
0 references
protected override void Up(MigrationBuilder migrationBuilder)
{
    migrationBuilder.CreateTable(
        name: "Players",
        columns: table => new
        {
            Id = table.Column<int>(type: "int", nullable: false)
                .Annotation("SqlServer:Identity", "1, 1"),
            Name = table.Column<string>(type: "nvarchar(50)", maxLength: 50, nullable: false),
            Description = table.Column<string>(type: "nvarchar(500)", maxLength: 500, nullable: true),
            Discriminator = table.Column<string>(type: "nvarchar(max)", nullable: false),
            CompanyName = table.Column<string>(type: "nvarchar(150)", maxLength: 150, nullable: true),
            StockSymbol = table.Column<string>(type: "nvarchar(10)", maxLength: 10, nullable: true)
                .Annotation("SqlServer:Sparse", true),
            City = table.Column<string>(type: "nvarchar(50)", maxLength: 50, nullable: true),
            FirstName = table.Column<string>(type: "nvarchar(50)", maxLength: 50, nullable: true),
            LastName = table.Column<string>(type: "nvarchar(250)", maxLength: 250, nullable: true),
            CreatedByUserId = table.Column<string>(type: "nvarchar(max)", nullable: true),
            CreatedDate = table.Column<DateTime>(type: "datetime2", nullable: false),
            LastModifiedUserId = table.Column<string>(type: "nvarchar(max)", nullable: true),
            LastModifiedDate = table.Column<DateTime>(type: "datetime2", nullable: true),
            IsActive = table.Column<bool>(type: "bit", nullable: false)
        },
        constraints: table =>
```

Figure 15-18. *The SqlServer:Sparse annotation is added to the StockSymbol field as expected*

With the field marked as Sparse, run the update-database command.

By making this field known to the database as a field that will not be leveraged often, the database can further optimize this table since the column will be expected to be null for most of the rows.

Activity 15-2 summary

This activity was pretty intense, but a number of great features were discovered that are new as of EFCore6.The first thing you learned about was the improvements that have been made for free text searching. This did require you to potentially update your server installation to include the ability to create a full-text index. Once all of that was in place, you were able to see how you can easily search a column that is loaded with JSON data by both defining the column and then also using the Fluent API to tell the system how to serialize and deserialize the column text.

You then learned about a few simple features like the upgraded ability to send more than two arguments to the string.Concat function, the ability to use a pseudo-random number generator in EF.Functions.Random, and the improved efficiency of the translation of `string.IsNullOrWhiteSpace` into SQL. The activity finished up by looking at the added support for sparse columns in tables, which is especially useful in a TPH implementation where one or more fields may be expected to be null for most rows.

Chapter summary

In this chapter, you learned about some of the new features that are coming with EFCore6. This list of features and enhancements presented is not intended to be all inclusive. Additionally, as the framework is a work in progress, it's entirely possible that a mentioned feature won't be implemented in the first release of the new framework and may get pushed into the next version of EFCore.

Hopefully through this book, you've enhanced your overall skills with Entity Framework and you will be looking forward to the next version, and hopefully you'll be able to leverage some or all of the features mentioned in this chapter as makes sense for your solutions.

Important takeaways

Now that you've seen some of the features that are coming with EFCore6, you should be positioned to use the skills you've learned and implement solid solutions in EFCore5, 6, and beyond.

Closing thoughts

I hope you have enjoyed reading and working through this book as much as I've enjoyed creating it for you. Alas, the end is nigh.

Our time together doesn't have to be over, however. Please don't hesitate to connect with me on LinkedIn or Twitter. I would love to hear your story and get your thoughts on how this book has helped you in your day-to-day work.

I wish you all the best in your development endeavors. May you have peace, joy, and abundance in your life.

CHAPTER 16

Appendix A: Troubleshooting

There are a number of activities in this book, and, while I've tried to keep them consistent, I am certain there may be times where things could be a bit difficult. Therefore, I wanted to put together a quick reference to help in case something goes wrong during your application of the activities from the book.

Migrations

As you are likely aware, troubleshooting migrations can be very painful if things don't work as expected. From cryptic error messages to things that really should work not working, a lot of figurative hair can get pulled out.

If you started by working with your own solution, but then switch to one of the starter packs, you would likely run into some issues with database conflicts, simply because my dates are clearly going to be different than yours. For this reason, all of the starter packs that could conflict if used against a common database are currently pointed to their own database via the connection string.

Note that if you want to do this entire book in a single database, that is entirely possible as well. You can always switch a connection string to point to any database of your choice. Just remember that your migrations and my migrations will never line up exactly.

The overall goal/expectation for the book would be that you would work on your own files the entire way through the book and only reference mine as needed and then implement the solution in your own projects. However, you may wish to skip around, or you may just desire a fresh start at some point with files that are set up and ready to run the activity you are wanting to work through, so it is more than likely you will need or want to leverage one of the pre-fabricated project files at some point in your journey. In a couple of the solutions, such as the web projects, using the starter files will be the easiest choice.

© Brian L. Gorman 2022
B. L. Gorman, *Practical Entity Framework Core 6*, https://doi.org/10.1007/978-1-4842-7301-2_16

Objects exist/objects don't exist

Another major issue you may run into as you work through the book is that the initial migrations are not idempotent. Therefore, if your database already has an Items table, and you pick up my starter pack and point at your database, you would likely get an error that the `update-database` command cannot be applied because the Items table already exists.

Again, for this reason, the starter packs have been reworked to contain a reference to a new database. Because of this, using the starter packs does require a few steps to get started. Table A-1 expounds upon this.

Along the way, if you try to run a migration and an object is missing, you might be able to simply add the object and try again. Another thought here could be to find the activity where the object was created and use that to build out the object and then come back to where you were in your current project.

One final thought here is that if you are working with scripts, ensure that you have included all scripts as embedded resources in your DBLibrary project where you are creating the migrations.

Comment out code

One solution that we might use in this text is to create a migration and then just comment out the code. This is not a recommended solution, but it works in a jam. For example, if you already created the `Items` table, then I have a migration that also wants to do the same thing, and you pick up my files and get a conflict due to pointing to the same database, and then just comment my migration code out and let it execute with no effect on the schema or data in your database. Use this approach sparingly, but know that it can be done in a jam (you wouldn't really want to do it this way in a real-world project).

The one exception to this where it is entirely useful is when you are reverse-engineering an existing database. In that scenario, there is likely never a time that you will want to recreate any of the original schema, so that migration code should be removed or commented out on the initial migration from an existing database into a code-first approach.

Manual insert to the database

If an object is missing, you could insert it manually with a script using SSMS. This might be handy for a missing function or view or procedure. Again, this is likely not the correct approach as you should be able to get everything you need through migrations.

Another thing to note here is that you can attempt to make EF think that a migration has executed by simply performing an insert into the __EFMigrationsHistory table. Simply insert the migration id and product version, and the next time you run update-database, EF should skip your conflicting migration.

Additionally, if something goes horribly wrong and a migration is idempotent, you could potentially force a reset by deleting a MigrationId from the table to make EF think it still needs to run that migration.

Change DB connection

Probably one of the easiest things you could do if things are off kilter is just to change the name of the database in the connection string or point to a different server where the database doesn't exist. In this way, no conflicts could possibly exist.

When starting a new database, you'll also have to reset your data. Since all the starter projects are set to do this, instructions on how to work with the files are in Table A-1. For the same reason, if you build your own solutions, you should follow a similar approach to reseed your data as you progress through the exercises.

In the event you are in the latter part of the book and you need to just point to a new database, you could just set the database connection to the new database and then run the migrator project by right-clicking and selecting Debug ➤ Start New Instance. This action will ensure that the database exits and then apply the migrations, as well as run a quick seed as seen in the text. Note also that from Activity 10-1 on, there is a simple script being used to reset the relationships between Items and Categories.

Feel free to use multiple databases, as well as multiple database servers to suit your needs. Just remember that your connection string holds all the power when you work through the activities.

Starter packs

Every activity except the first has an accompanying starter pack. If something isn't working or you just want to jump around, leverage the starter packs to get the code in the state it needs to be at the start of the activity.

General starter pack creation

Rather than keep working with the same files, I chose to do a unique project for each activity. As you might imagine, this added a bit of work. In general, if you want to roll your own starter packs, you could follow a similar process. Here are the steps I took on generally every new project:

1. Create a new .Net Core console application for .Net 6.

2. Copy and paste the existing project folders for all of the class libraries that are needed for the activity.

3. Add each class library to the solution, and build the project to restore NuGet packages.

4. Get the list of NuGet packages from the previous solution (the last completed activity) from the project file, and copy/paste that into the new activity's *.csproj file. This is much faster than doing them one by one in NuGet Package Manager.

5. Copy/paste the appsettings.json file into the new activity project, add it as Content, Copy if newer. Do the same for the InventoryMapper file once the project is leveraging AutoMapper (also update the namespace to the new project's namespace when doing this).

6. Set project references on the new activity to appropriate class libraries.

7. Build and run.

8. Copy/paste the code from the Program file of the previous activity into the Program file of the new activity (be careful – just get the methods, not the class or the namespace). Then add all the missing using statements and run the project.

9. In some instances, you may choose to do an `update-database` command to make sure there are no pending migrations.

10. Finally, if in doubt, add a new migration called `test` to ensure that there are no pending changes. This is very important if the activity is going to be adding new migrations, because you don't want to start with something in your way.

What you should do every time

When you get a starter pack for an `InventoryManagerDb` activity, make sure that you do the same thing at the start, every time.

First, build the project. Once it builds, check the connection string to make sure it points to the correct database server. Use Table A-1 to see specific information about each starter project.

When you have completed the initial build, run an `update-database` command to apply the pending migrations. If the activity you are about to start has migrations in it, then you should run an `add-migration` command to make sure that you don't have any untracked pending changes that could get in the way. Although you should not have any, if you do have pending changes in the new migration just created, examine the migration and consider just updating the database if the changes are not going to hurt anything. If no pending operations exist and you get a blank migration (this should generally be the case), just run the `remove-migration` command so that you don't have unnecessary blank migration.

If the project contains the `InventoryDataMigrator` project, you should also run that by right-clicking the project and selecting Debug ➤ `Start New Instance`. If the activity is Activity 10-1 or greater, you should also run the script to remap the relationships for Items and Categories. If the activity is Activity 11-1 or greater, the original database would be encrypted; however, new databases won't be. The connection string is ready to work against an encrypted database, but you do not need to redo the encryption on every new database, unless you would like the practice. The code should work either way, regardless of if the data is encrypted or not.

Finally, after all of that, make sure that the main activity project is set as the startup project and then run the project to ensure that it is working as expected.

Simple instructions

The information in Table A-1 will help you get started with each of the starter packs as a quick reference.

Table A-1. *Instructions on how to work with each starter file pack*

Activity	Instructions
EFCore_Activity02-1_StarterFiles	Just use the provided files in your new project.
EFCore_Activity03-1_StarterFiles	These are AdventureWorks-based files, so just use the provided files. There are no migrations at the start of this activity so there should be no conflicts.
EFCore_Activity03-2_StarterFiles	These are InventoryManagerDb-based files, and there are no migrations at the start, so you can just use these files against your initial database.
EFCore_Activity04-1_ StarterFilesEFCore_Activity04-2_ StarterFiles EFCore_Activity05-1_StarterFiles EFCore_Activity05-2_StarterFiles EFCore_Activity05-3_StarterFiles EFCore_Activity07-1_StarterFiles EFCore_Activity07-2_StarterFiles	These starter files are pointed to their own database based on the connection string due to the potential for conflicts with migrations. Open the starter files, and check the connection string to make sure it points to a valid server. Each activity will point to a new InventoryManagerDbXXXX version of the database. This will add more databases to your local server but avoids migration conflicts due to the timestamp on each migration.Build the project, and then run an update-database command in the PMC. Once that update has completed, run the project to ensure it works. Potentially run an add-migration test command to ensure a blank migration, and then run the command remove-migration to remove the test migration once you've validated there are no pending migration-causing changes.

(continued)

Table A-1. (*continued*)

Activity	Instructions
EFCore_Activity-06-1_StarterFiles	This is a new project for a web-based implementation to help show simple CRUD operations with minimal work. Because this is a new project, you can use this without any extra steps on your part.
EFCore_Activity07-3_StarterFiles EFCore_Activity09-2_StarterFiles EFCore_Activity09-3_StarterFiles EFCore_Activity10-1_StarterFiles EFCore_Activity11-1_StarterFiles EFCore_Activity11-2_StarterFiles EFCore_Activity12-1_StarterFiles EFCore_Activity12-2_StarterFiles EFCore_Activity13-1_StarterFiles EFCore_Activity14-1_StarterFiles EFCore_Activity14-2_StarterFiles EFCore_Activity14-3_StarterFiles EFCore_Activity14-4_StarterFiles EFCore_Activity14-5_StarterFiles EFCore_Activity14-6_StarterFiles	As with other InventoryManagerDb projects, these projects all have their own database connection set in the starter files, so ensure the server is correct. When you get these projects, you should run the update-database command. You should then use the Debug ➤ Start New Instance on the InventoryDataMigrator project to seed additional data. Then run the project to ensure it is working as expected. As earlier, you could also run the add-migration test command and then remove-migration when you've validated there are no pending migration changes. For Activity 10-1 and greater (Activities 11-1, 11-2, 12-1, etc.), remember to also run the script MapCategories.sql against your new database after seeding data. Additionally, Activity 11-1 and greater are set to work against encrypted data on their own database via the connection string. This should not be an issue, and you don't have to encrypt the new database. However, if you want to encrypt the database, it will not hurt anything.

(continued)

Table A-1. (*continued*)

Activity	Instructions
EFCore_Activity08-1_StarterFiles EFCore_Activity09-1_StarterFiles	Runs against the AdventureWorks database. There is an initial migration that was created, but the migration is commented out so that it will not make any changes as per Activity 3-1. Therefore, you should be able to pick up this project and run with it.
	There is no need to do so, but you could still run an update-database and ensure there are no pending changes with an add-migration test command and a remove-migration when you've validated there are no pending migration changes.
	*Note: If you have run the encryption in Chapter 10 before doing the Chapter 9 activity, you will get an error for byte[]. In that case, restore a new copy of AdventureWorks and name it something different than the first, and point your connection string to the new version of the database to avoid the error with encryption.
EFCore_Activity10-2_StarterFiles	This is another AdventureWorks activity. This will be the final AdventureWorks project for the book, so it's OK that this has a number of migrations. If you do this before the others, however, you will likely need to restore another version of AdventureWorks for the other activities as this will break one or more of them. If you're doing them in order, there is nothing to worry about.
	You should be able to use these starter files against the default AdventureWorks instance on your local machine with no issues.

(*continued*)

Table A-1. (*continued*)

Activity	Instructions
EFCore_Activity13-2_WebOnly_ StarterFiles	For this activity, get the project and ensure it works, and then follow the instructions at the start of the activity to build the rest of your solution. Essentially, you will bring in the libraries to work against the `InventoryManagerDb` in addition to the `CorporateSSOIdentityDb`.
EFCore_Activity13-2_AllFiles_ StarterFiles	This is essentially the same as all the others, except you will build out the project as you go in the activity. Therefore, get these files and return to the activity for further instructions. Do not try to update the database. Do not run the migrator project. **Do not run a new migration.** You will be directed to get everything completed during the activity.

Final packs

Final packs are exactly what they sound like. This is the finished version of the code as it was on my machine after the activity was completed. You can use these to see the code as it should exist at the end of the activity. This is highly useful if something from the text is unclear or if there is anything that you want to double-check to be certain that what you've done was as intended.

As with the preceding activities, I did go back and point all of the `InventoryManagerDb` projects at their own database solutions (i.e., `InventoryManagerDb0902` or `InventoryManagerDb0701`). If you are using the final pack, and you want to get the database to the final state, you could run the update-database command to get all the migrations applied.

When there is a seed project (Activity 7-3 on), you should not need to run the `InventoryDataMigrator` project unless you did not run it for the starter files.

Review your solution

In general, the final pack should be used as a "check your answer" solution only. If something is unclear from the text, the final pack will likely have the answer. Things like "Where does this code go?" or "How did he do that?" or "I'm completely lost" can often be quickly resolved just by comparing what you have to what is in the final pack.

Use a diff tool like GitHub, VSCode, or WinMerge

A neat trick you can do (as long as your files are named the same as mine) is that you could just use a tool to do a diff on files. For example, I'll often use the built-in capability to compare files in VSCode. In rare instances when things are really off track, I might check in my code and push to GitHub, then create a branch and drop the final pack code in, and push to GitHub and create a pull request. This gives me a great tool to easily see the differences in files. Finally, other tools like *WinMerge* or *Perforce* or even *GitKraken* might be enough to help you see the differences in your code from the final pack.

Index

A

AdditionalProperty class, 760, 762, 763
add-migration command, 102, 773, 781
add-migration createFunction_
    GetItemsTotalValue, 341
ADO.Net, 5, 26
AdventureWorksContext, 74, 92
AdventureWorks database, 33, 34, 60, 90
AlwaysEncrypted, 467, 468
    enable AlwaysEncrypted on
        InventoryManagerDb
        backup creation, 470, 471
        columns Name, Description, and
          Notes, 476–480
        data review, 480–482
        fix issue, 488–491
        modify SSMS, 482–484
        prepare fields for encryption,
          471, 473–475
        run application, 485–488
ApplicationDbContext, 20, 21, 278
appsettings.json file
    add code to leverage connection
        string, 71, 73, 74
    NuGet packages, 70, 71
    store connection details, 68, 69
AsNoTracking, 522, 699–701
ASP.Net built-in authentication, 464
AsSingleQuery, 709
AsSplitQuery, 705, 707
async and await keywords, 616, 617
Asynchronous database operations

async/await pattern, 621
async/await/TaskParallelLibrary, 616
broken integration test, 649, 650
business layer, refactor, 632–636
database, 617, 618
database layer, refactor, 621–629
integration tests, refactor, 629–631
multithreaded programming, 616
refactor main program
    batching operations with
        asynchronous calls, 647–649
    fix issues with encryption, 643–647
    helper methods, 638–640
    Main method, 638
    run program, 641, 643
responsive solutions, end user, 617
syntax, 618
unit tests, refactor, 636, 637
Auto generate column master key, 477
AutoMapper, 412
    CategoryDto class, 458
    CreatedDate, 453
    DTO objects
        BuildMapper method, 444
        Category DTO, creation, 442
        Item DTO creation, 441, 442
        mapping configuration, 443, 444
        solution, 444, 445
    GetItemsForListing query, 451–454
    Ignore method, 459
    InventoryMapper profile, creation,
        440, 441

787

© Brian L. Gorman 2022
B. L. Gorman, *Practical Entity Framework Core 6*, https://doi.org/10.1007/978-1-4842-7301-2

Printed in the United States
by Baker & Taylor Publisher Services